LAUNCH THE INTRUDERS

LAUNCH
THE INTRUDERS
A Naval Attack Squadron in the
Vietnam War, 1972

Carol Reardon

 University Press of Kansas

Published by the University Press of Kansas (Lawrence, Kansas 66049), which was organized by the Kansas Board of Regents and is operated and funded by Emporia State University, Fort Hays State University, Kansas State University, Pittsburg State University, the University of Kansas, and Wichita State University

Library of Congress Cataloging-in-Publication Data

Reardon, Carol.

  Launch the intruders : a naval attack squadron in the Vietnam War, 1972 / Carol Reardon.

    p.   cm. — (Modern war studies)

  Includes bibliographical references and index.

  ISBN 0-7006-1389-7 (cloth : alk. paper)

  1. Vietnamese Conflict, 1961–1975—Regimental histories— United States. 2. United States. Navy. Attack Squadron 75— History. 3. Vietnamese Conflict, 1961–1975—Aerial operations, American. I. Title. II. Series.

  DS558.4.R43 2005

  959.704'348—dc22   2005000780

British Library Cataloguing in Publication Data is available.

Printed in the United States of America

10 9 8 7 6 5 4 3 2 1

The paper used in this publication meets the minimum requirements of the American National Standard for Permanence of Paper for Printed Library Materials Z39.48–1984.

To the 1972–1973 Sunday Punchers of VA-75
 those who flew
 those who kept them flying
 those who did not come home

And to the memory of 2nd Lt. C. W. Higginbotham, USAAF,
KIA in the skies over Germany, March 1945

Contents

Illustrations

Abbreviations

Naval Ranks

ADM	admiral
CAG	commander, air group
CAPT	captain
CDR	commander
LCDR	lieutenant commander
LT	lieutenant
LTJG	lieutenant, junior grade
RADM	rear admiral
VADM	vice admiral

Other Abbreviations

AAA	antiaircraft artillery
AOM	All Officers Meeting
AOCS	Aviation Officers Candidate School
ARVIN	Army of the Republic of Vietnam
AVROC	Aviation Reserve Officer Candidate
BOQ	bachelor officer quarters
BARCAP	barrier combat air patrol
B/N	bombardier/navigator
BDA	bomb damage assessment
CNO	Chief of Naval Operations
CO	commanding officer
COM	Concerned Officers Movement
CTF	Carrier Task Force
DASC	Defense Air Support Center
DMZ	Demilitarized Zone
DIANE	Digital Integrated Attack Navigation Equipment
DFC	Distinguished Flying Cross
ECM	electronic countermeasures
XO	executive officer
FRAMP	Fleet Replacement Aviation Maintenance Program
FOD	foreign object damage
FAC	forward air controller
GQ	general quarters

IFF	identification friend or foe
INS	inertial navigation system
IOIC	Integrated Operational Intelligence Center
JCS	Joint Chiefs of Staff
JEST	Jungle Evasion and Survival Training
JOs	junior officers
LSO	Landing Signals Officer
LDO	Limited Duty Officer
LORAN	Long Range Navigation
MATWING ONE	Medium Attack Wing One
MiGCAP	MiG combat air patrol
MACV	Military Assistance Command–Vietnam
MERs	multiple ejector racks
NAVAIRLANT	Naval Air Forces Atlantic
NATOPS	Naval Aviation Training and Operations Procedures Standardization
NESEP	Naval Enlisted Scientific Education Program
NFO	Naval Flight Officer
NROTC	Naval Reserve Officer Training Corps
ORE	Operational Readiness Exercise
ORI	Operational Readiness Inspection
PAR	Periodic Aircraft Rework
PLAT	pilot landing-aid television
PHD	pilot's horizontal display
PIRAZ	Positive Identification Radar Advisory Zone
RIO	radar intercept officers
RAG	Replacement Air Group
RESCAP	rescue combat air patrol
RNO	"results not observed"
SAR	search and rescue
SIOP	Single Integrated Operational Plan
SDO	Squadron Duty Officer
STARM	Standard Anti-Radiation Missile
"Strike Ops"	Strike Operations center
SURCAP	surface combat air patrols
SAM	surface-to-air missile
SERE	survive, escape, resist, and evade
TARCAP	target combat air patrol
TRIM	trails, roads, interdiction multi-sensor
VA	Attack Squadron
VAW	Airborne Early Warning Squadron
VDI	vertical display indicator
VF	Fighter Squadron
VSI	vertical situation indicator
VFR	Visual Flight Rules
VT	Training Squadron
WBLC	water-borne logistical craft

Preface

The "Sunday Punchers" did not expect to go to war in the spring of 1972. The pilots and bombardier/navigators—the B/Ns—who launched in their A-6 Intruders from the flight deck of USS *Saratoga* (CVA-60) and the chiefs and enlisted men who kept them flying had just completed an Operational Readiness Exercise and had begun final preparations to deploy to the Mediterranean in early May. At the end of March 1972, however, North Vietnam's Nguyen Hue Offensive, quickly dubbed the "Easter Offensive" by the American media, changed their futures forever. *Saratoga* and the Sunday Punchers became part of President Richard M. Nixon's air and naval buildup to stop the invasion and support the South Vietnamese government of President Nguyen Van Thieu.

The voluminous historical literature concerning air operations in Vietnam tells little of their experiences, however. The history of the air war in Southeast Asia largely reflects the institutional perspectives, doctrinal biases, and operations of the U.S. Air Force. Thus, this study of the 1972–73 combat cruise of the Sunday Punchers, officially Medium Attack Squadron 75—or VA-75—sheds light on one small portion of naval aviation's contributions to the air war during the final year of American military involvement in Southeast Asia. Four interrelated themes compel attention.

First, this study presents a comprehensive operational history of VA-75's 1972 combat deployment in Southeast Asia, from its emergency recall in April 1972, through its month-long transit to the theater of war, and through each of its seven line periods from mid-May 1972 through the first week of January 1973. The A-6 Intruder's sophisticated navigation and weapons system made it an outstanding aircraft for low-level strikes, day and night, and in all weather. It could deliver a larger bomb load than any other carrier-based aircraft at the time, and it could drop a wide range of ordnance—from general-purpose iron bombs to mines to anti-radiation missiles to first-generation smart bombs to nuclear weapons. VA-75 only used the first three types during the LINEBACKER I interdiction campaign of May–October 1972 and LINEBACKER II, the "Christmas Bombings" of December 1972, but the crews dropped ten million pounds of that ordnance in executing a wide range of missions—from participation in large-scale alpha strikes to one- and two-plane missions designed to suppress the surface-to-air missile threat, to mine harbors and river crossings, and to strike bridges, power plants, storage areas, truck convoys, ferry slips, dockyards, and other targets. This study attempts to reconstruct a detailed squadron-level operational history of the day-to-day efforts to answer the call: "Launch the Intruders!"

Second, the squadron is the basic building block of naval aviation. As in any such unit, the Sunday Punchers' personnel—approximately thirty-five officers and three hundred twenty chiefs and enlisted men—represent its brain, brawn, and heart. While this study unapologetically focuses most immediately on the men who climbed into the cockpits on a daily basis, they would be the first to salute the men who kept those planes flying. The men who flew these A-6s off *Saratoga*'s flight deck and those who worked in the maintenance shops all volunteered for this duty, and their world also included wives, children, parents, and friends at home, some of whose hatred for the war almost matched their love for their warriors. Proud of their skill and confident in their ability, the men of VA-75 took professional satisfaction in doing a difficult job well, at a time when the nation that sent them to war also seemed to revile them for going. This examination into the day-to-day life of men in combat—too often reduced to either entertaining or unimaginably tragic vignettes that single out one or two individuals only—reveals what made the Sunday Punchers a particularly effective military organization.

Third, the A-6 is a tactical attack aircraft. Its mission is to drop ordnance on target. The crews did not chase MiGs through North Vietnamese skies or challenge enemy pilots to dogfights. They dropped bombs. Their story—to some—lacks the flash and dash of 1972's best-known naval aviators, the F-4 Phantom crew of LT Randall Cunningham and LTJG William Driscoll, who became the Navy's only aces during the Vietnam War in May. Those who flew the A-6 in combat understand the "Top Gun" spirit that draws many naval aviators and naval historians to the work of the fighter community. But the attack community's contributions—equally as dramatic and dangerous—merit study, too. Its members, including the Sunday Punchers of 1972, believed in its mission. They boasted: "If you're not attack, you must be support."[1] In time, they came to agree that "fighter guys make movies, attack guys make history."[2] Except for popular works such as Stephen Coonts's novel *Flight of the Intruder* and the movie it inspired, the attack community has languished too long in the shadow of the fighters. This study expands coverage of the naval air war to give the attack community its due.

Finally, this study will illuminate elements of naval aviation's specific contributions to the controversial late-war air campaigns, LINEBACKER I and II. Like the general history of the air war in Vietnam, the most influential studies of these important campaigns—James R. McCarthy and George B. Allison's *View from the Rock* (1979) and Marshall L. Michel's *The Eleven Days of Christmas* (2002)—emphasized almost exclusively the employment of U.S. Air Force strategic bombers, the B-52s. Karl Eschmann's *Linebacker Raids: The Untold Story of the Air Raids over North Vietnam* (1989) promised to accord due credit to the contributions of tactical aircraft to the total effort, but his narrative and statistical tables included only Air Force sorties. They ignored naval tactical aircraft, and especially the A-6 squadrons flying from Yankee Station, which carried a significant sortie load in 1972. At night and in bad weather, the Navy's A-6s filled the skies for months before the Air Force's heralded F-111s returned to air operations in late September 1972. This is an effort to explore, through one squadron's experiences, the contribution of the A-6 to LINEBACKER I and II.

This is also a book about historical memory. Early on, while recalling long-ago events, several Sunday Punchers clarified for me the distinction between a fairy tale and a sea story. The former, they advised, begins "once upon a time." The latter starts with "no shit, this really happened." The warning proved useful many times over. Historians of memory have discovered its applicability to the study of military history. From work as diverse as my own *Pickett's Charge in History and Memory* (1997) to Emily S. Rosenburg's *A Date That Will Live: Pearl Harbor in American Memory* (2003), military historians have learned to treat eyewitness recollections of combat with a critical eye. A combatant locked in mortal strife—whether jousting with an armored knight or with a SAM site—departs from what one military historian has called an individual's "great gray level plane" of everyday existence and, for a while, becomes so focused on mission accomplishment and survival that he often becomes unaware of all that happens around him. When the adrenaline rush ebbs, historian Richard Holmes asserted, he may remember snippets of the experience he has just survived, but his memory tends to "record clips of experience, often in erratic sequences."[3] Combatants believe they remember what happened, but on occasion, their memories fool them. A World War II aviator who penned his memoirs described the trick: "My memory, it's accurate and false at the same time. It's complex and simple. It changes constantly, often just to fit the circumstances. And yet, all this time I know I'm telling the truth because I'm relying on my memory."[4]

Over time, without intent to deceive, as the 1972 Sunday Punchers tried to make sense of what they witnessed, endured, and believed they remembered, it did not prove difficult for some to attribute to themselves the similar experiences of others in the group. On occasion, they perfectly demonstrated military historian John Keegan's "Bullfrog Effect"—when "*old* warriors, particularly if surrounded by Old Comrades who will endorse his yarn while waiting the chance to spin their own on a reciprocal basis," start retelling favorite stories—and they "are notoriously prone to do so."[5]

The historical method provides the most effective antidote for the Bullfrog Effect. During the Vietnam era, the Department of the Navy required each command—including naval air squadrons—to submit a history report on 1 March annually. The command historian who compiled it did so as an additional duty, and thus, the historical record of the Vietnam years is incomplete and irregular. While an official form existed through 1966, the reports took tabular and narrative form after that year, with no apparent guidance as to information to include. Thus, the command history—much like individual memory—often records only those peaks and troughs of experience that dip below or spike above the great gray level plane of experience. Filling in the spaces between the peaks and troughs requires luck, patience, and persistence to fill the gaps in record keeping. As a case in point, VA-75's master logbook that registered every mission, crew, ordnance load, target, bomb damage assessment, opposition—in short, the operational backbone to a study such as this—has rested for the past thirty years in an unlikely place: not in the National Archives, and not in the Naval Historical Center, but in the basement of one of the squadron's junior officers, who rescued it from a pile of papers about to be discarded at the end of the combat cruise. Its recovery made it possible to check—but not always resolve—the accuracy of the Sunday Punchers' testimony. Some of the most interesting moments in the process of reconstructing their history came when long-held memories confronted incontrovertible contemporary 1972 sources. More than one conversation ended with a puzzled shake of the head and the tongue-in-cheek comment, "I guess I'll have to read the book to find out what I did."

The history of the Sunday Punchers' 1972 combat cruise never can be reconstructed fully, of course. In September 1972, as VA-75's pilots and B/Ns launched into the hostile skies of North Vietnam, journalist and World War II veteran Arthur T. Hadley considered the problem of trying to recapture the combat experience of American military personnel in Southeast Asia. He concluded, despite all his knowledge of military history and institutions, that "the ultimate explanation of Vietnam must come from those involved there. An observer, even when blood splatters his clothes, remains outside." All a chronicler can hope to do is "report." Perhaps, "with compassion and sympathy," one can understand a great deal; "but the final truth remains with those who must exist . . . in the combat of their war."[6] The thinness of the 1972 base of official and operational materials, the inherent interpretive problems of eyewitness accounts, and the frailty and malleability of human memory make this only the "recoverable past" of the Sunday Punchers of VA-75 in 1972.[7] But it is a past worthy of remembrance.

Acknowledgments

Just before I left for my first year of graduate school in history, military historian Jay Luvaas, then of Allegheny College, offered one bit of parting advice—given with the authority of a command: "Don't become a one-war wonder." With this history of the 1972–73 combat cruise of the Sunday Punchers of VA-75 aboard USS *Saratoga*, I finally obeyed orders. As an old navy man himself, Jay would approve.

First and foremost, I thank Michael Briggs and all the professional staff at the University Press of Kansas. Mike saw merit in this project and provided support and encouragement well beyond the requirements of his position. I will always appreciate his outstanding efforts. Many good people at Pennsylvania State University provided essential assistance along the way. Professor A. G. Roeber—head of the Department of History from 1996 until 2004—provided encouragement and the essential element of uncommitted time to devote to preparing the final manuscript. Financial support from the College of Liberal Arts and the George and Ann Richards Civil War Era Center funded several important research efforts. History professor Gary S. Cross and Gregory J. Johnson of Penn State's Applied Research Laboratory answered important questions. Penn State undergraduate history majors Michelle Boyer and Elizabeth Delafield and graduate student Leah Vincent assisted with source transcriptions. Major Scott Ward, USMC, fielded a key question and prevented a major error from slipping into the text.

Dr. Timothy K. Nenninger at the College Park branch of the National Archives took the time to shepherd the 1972 *Saratoga* deck log through internal review processes to make it available to me. Patrick Yack, editor of the Jacksonville, Florida, *Times-Union*, the major newspaper of *Saratoga*'s home port in 1972, took an early interest in this project and supplied copies of relevant local news coverage published during the combat cruise.

For each of the past seven years, it has been my distinct pleasure to spend one weekend annually on a staff ride to a Civil War battlefield with the members of the U.S. Naval Reserve's Combat Documentation Unit 206. They have taken a deep interest in this project, and they actively supported my research efforts at the Naval Historical Center at the Washington Navy Yard. LCDR Jim Rossi, a naval aviator who flew off *Saratoga* when he served on active duty, deserves special thanks many times over for his outstanding efforts.

Various other elements of the U.S. Navy actively contributed to my naval history education. The personnel of two VAQ squadrons based at Whidbey Island Naval Air Station contributed to my introduction to mission briefing, manning up, and cockpit and flight-deck launch procedures. At Headquarters COMNAV-AIRLANT at Norfolk, Mike Maus handled arrangements to fly me and two Vietnam-era A-6 bombardier/navigators to USS *Theodore Roosevelt* to allow me to learn about carrier life and air operations in the best classroom in the world. I especially thank then-Captain David Bryant for his superb hospitality, and I commend Senior Chief Legalman Christine DeZwaan for making me climb every ladder on the entire carrier. My special thanks go to VADM Joseph S. Mobley, once an A-6 B/N himself, for taking an interest in this project, understanding why I needed to see a carrier in action, and granting permission for me to visit one of "his" ships. My "honorary tailhooker" certificate from that experience hangs on my office wall, still my most effective tool for starting—or stopping—conversations. I also thank the Bulls of VA-37, the A-7 squadron whose ready room shared a common wall with that of VA-75 aboard *Saratoga,* for their interest and input. From start to finish, Ted Been of the Intruder Association willingly answered a host of big and little questions.

Most of all, I owe incalculable gratitude to the 1972–73 Sunday Punchers, who opened their homes and lives to me, made me feel like part of their families, and dug into long-closed boxes (some marked simply "Navy stuff"), scrapbooks, and memories to help me attempt to reconstruct the events of 1972. Not all of them found it an easy or pleasant journey; some past events cannot be revisited without an element of emotional duress. Thus, I thank them most of all for their honesty and frankness. To the families of the 1972–73 Punchers who have supported this effort so generously, I give a special salute; they very quickly convinced me that the Sunday Puncher story would not be complete without considering the most personal home-front ties that bound the sailors to the nation they defended. Thanks to all these good folks over the past several years, my conversation is now salted with such phrases as "check six" and "no risk, no air medal," much to the bemusement or consternation of many of my academic colleagues. The Sunday Punchers' interest and involvement saved me from many missteps along the way. They improved both the content and tone of the final product. Any errors are all mine.

Finally, I always will feel deeply the loss of two very special Sunday Punchers—Harold W. King and Roger G. Lerseth—who believed in this project and contributed heavily to it but passed away before its completion.

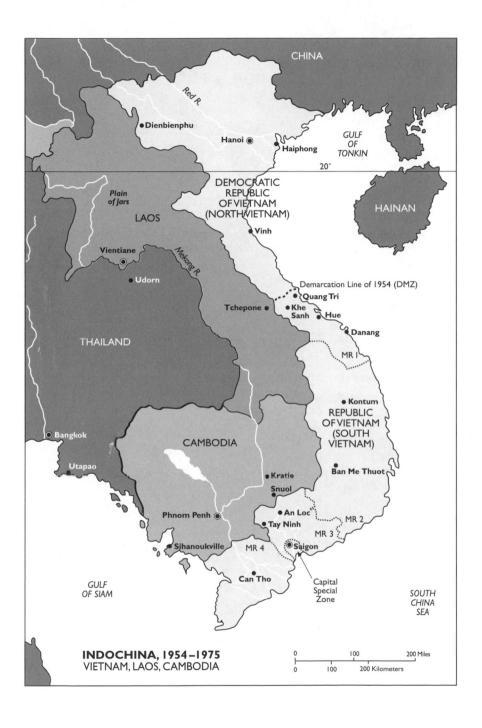

CHINA

Red R.

•Dienbienphu

Hanoi ◎

•Haiphong

GULF
OF
TONKIN

20°

Plain
of Jars

LAOS

DEMOCRATIC
REPUBLIC
OF VIETNAM
(NORTH VIETNAM)

HAINAN

•Vinh

Vientiane ◎

Mekong R

•Udorn

Demarcation Line of 1954 (DMZ)

Quang Tri

Tchepone •

•Khe
Sanh

•Hue

THAILAND

•Danang

MR 1

•Kontum

REPUBLIC
OF VIETNAM
(SOUTH
VIETNAM)

◎ Bangkok

CAMBODIA

•Ban Me Thuot

•Utapao

•Kratie

Snuol

•An Loc

MR 2

Phnom Penh•

•Tay Ninh

MR 3

•Sihanoukville

MR 4

◎ Saigon

GULF
OF SIAM

•Can Tho

Capital
Special
Zone

SOUTH
CHINA
SEA

INDOCHINA, 1954–1975
VIETNAM, LAOS, CAMBODIA

0   100   200 Miles

0   100   200 Kilometers

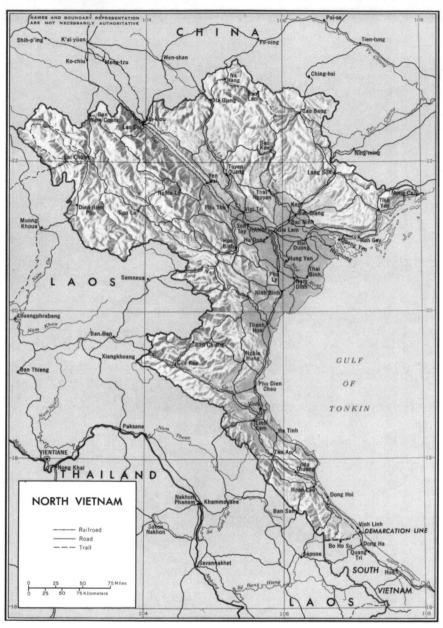

In 1965, North Vietnam was divided into seven route packages (RPs) to facilitate U.S. mission planning. VA-75 flew only a few missions in RP I (extending from the DMZ to a point halfway between Dong Hoi and Vinh) but many strikes in RPs II (north to just south of Vinh) and III (northward toward Thanh Hoa). In RP IV, they faced the AAA batteries and SAM sites around Thanh Hoa, the Bai Thuong airfield, and the Hourglass. The Navy generally did not plan missions in RP V in northwestern Vietnam or in RP VI-A on the western and northern approaches to Hanoi; the Air Force launched against targets there from Thailand. Missions into RP VI-B (from the coast south of Haiphong westward through the area near Nam Dinh to just southwest of Hanoi, then angling around the capital and up the northeast railway toward the China border) proved most costly to the Sunday Punchers.

CHAPTER ONE

"F Troop"

They loved to fly. In late February 1972, the "world-famous Sunday Punchers" looked forward to spending their summer in the cockpits of their A-6 Intruders, sweeping through the skies over the blue waters of the Mediterranean Sea. Port calls in Greece, Italy, France, and Spain awaited all hands, too, but most of all the pilots and bombardier/navigators—the B/Ns—looked forward with eager anticipation to the opportunity to test themselves almost daily doing one of the toughest jobs the military world can offer: launching off the deck of a carrier at sea, delivering ordnance on target, and recovering aboard safely. The darkness of the night, the pouring of the rain, or the swelling of the seas that created a pitching deck added an extra jolt of adrenaline, but the fundamental sequence remained the same: launch, fly the mission, arrest aboard safely. Indeed, the U.S. Navy had declared 1972 as "the year of the carrier," and the Sunday Punchers pushed hard in February and March to prepare for departure to "the Med" in early May.[1]

The men of the Sunday Punchers composed a squadron, naval aviation's basic operational and administrative building block. In the U.S. Navy, each such unit represents a team made up of commissioned officers who man the cockpits of its aircraft, intelligence officers and maintenance specialists—both military and civilian technical representatives—and, most numerous of all, the chiefs and enlisted personnel who keep its planes flying. Faces changed frequently, sailors came and went, but the Sunday Punchers always represented more than the sum of the talents of its individual members. Indeed, the unit exemplified the astute description of an anonymous chronicler of naval aviation: "A squadron is a swirling multicolored pool of experience from which is painted the freewheeling sweep of life in the air in individual brush strokes."[2]

Officially, the U.S. Navy designated the Sunday Punchers as VA-75. The "V" stood for heavier-than-air craft, a designator used since the 1920s when the Navy still used zeppelins and other lighter-than-air machines classified as "Z." The "A" stood for "attack," reflecting its primary mission: delivering ordnance on target. Fighter pilots could keep their dreams of dogfights in the skies. The men of the attack community took pride in taking the battle to an enemy's doorstep—and then blowing open the door.

The Sunday Punchers of 1972 traced the history of their squadron to World War II, when the U.S. Navy established Bombing Squadron 18 (VB-18) at the Alameda Naval Air Station on 20 July 1943. That squadron flew SB-2Cs and F-4Us off USS *Intrepid* (CVA-11) in the Pacific theater, participating in operations at Palau and Cape Engano and serving with special distinction at Leyte Gulf, where it took part in the sinking of the Japanese battleship *Musashi*. Although its origins remain hazy, the squadron's nickname and its distinctive logo—an encircled boxing glove with wings—extended back to that conflict, too.

Postwar reorganizations changed VB-18 first to Attack Squadron 7A (VA-7A), then in 1948 to Attack Squadron 74 (VA-74), and finally to Attack Squadron 75 (VA-75) on 15 February 1950. The Sunday Punchers flew their first combat missions as VA-75 on 23 June 1950, just a few days into the Korean War, launching AD-4 Skyraiders from USS *Bon Homme Richard* (CVA-31). In the mid-1950s, the squadron transitioned to the improved A-1H version of the Skyraider.[3]

In October 1957, VA-75 opened a new chapter in its history when it was reassigned to the Oceana Naval Air Station, near Virginia Beach, Virginia. Before World War II, the Navy had shown little interest in the expanse of marshy ground, once writing it off as "too far from Norfolk for commercial use and too far from the Atlantic Ocean for the Navy." Still, the U.S. government purchased it in November 1940 for development as an auxiliary airfield to support naval activity in the Norfolk area. A bit more than a decade later, its runways became so busy that they had to be lengthened for jet aircraft. VA-75 arrived in the middle of yet another major construction project designed to improve its hangar and support facilities. From their home at the East Coast's premier naval air station, the Sunday Punchers served aboard USS *Independence* (CVA-62) on extended deployments to the Caribbean, North Atlantic, and the Mediterranean. In 1961, the squadron stood ready to launch from that same carrier as it steamed south of Guantanamo Bay during the Bay of Pigs crisis.

VA-75's future changed dramatically in the early 1960s when the Navy began its "base-loading program" to concentrate specific types of aircraft at selected individual naval air stations for improved training and maintenance. In February 1963, Oceana Naval Air Station won the designation as the East Coast home of a new aircraft just about to enter the Navy's inventory: the A-6 Intruder.[4] The Sunday Punchers learned that they would give up their Skyraiders and transition to the new aircraft. Thus, VA-75 started down a path that would make it the U.S. Navy's first operational A-6 fleet squadron.

The development of the new aircraft stemmed from a need identified by the Navy and Marine Corps during the Korean War for a carrier-based subsonic attack aircraft that could provide close air support for troops on the ground and expand the range of options for delivering conventional or nuclear ordnance.

Aircraft design for the unforgiving and restrictive environment of an aircraft carrier always challenged engineers, but seldom to the degree the type specifications for this new plane did. The requirements called for a small, two-crew airframe suitable in size for carrier operations that could fly at a minimum of 500 knots and had a mission range of 300 nautical miles for close support missions and 1,000 nautical miles for long-range bombing missions. Most important, the new aircraft also had to possess a sophisticated integrated navigation and weapons system that would permit crews to find and destroy targets in all kinds of weather, in all kinds of terrain, both day and night.

Aeronautical engineers from Boeing, Douglas, Vought, Martin Bell, Lockheed, Grumman, and North American all submitted designs. Some companies even offered two models—one with a turboprop propulsion system and the other with turbojet engines. Lawrence M. Mead, Jr., the project engineer for the A-6, explained the key decisions that finally led to Grumman's selection to design and build the new aircraft. Beginning in 1957, its design engineers interviewed crews in operational attack squadrons to ask how they might help the aviators do their jobs more effectively. As Mead explained, "A key decision, which drove the design, was whether the two crewmen should be tandem or side-by-side." Their discussions led them to design an unusual side-by-side arrangement. The pilot sat on the left, slightly higher and forward of the operator of the navigation and weapons system, the bombardier/navigator. This key decision to seat the crew side-by-side instead of one behind the other inspired the development of the "crew concept" at the very core of the successful operation of the A-6.

Grumman's engineers also decided early on that two Pratt & Whitney J52 turbojet engines—not one jet engine, and certainly not turboprops—would give the new aircraft the high level of reliability and performance they desired. The introduction of two types of radar—search and track—created an airframe design with a bulbous radome at the plane's nose. "The radars, with the inertial platform, the crew, and the engines, wanted to be forward to get good, efficient, short inlets and help to get the center of gravity (CG) forward for a long tail arm," Mead explained. As a consequence, he continued, when they designed the rest of the plane to meet length restrictions—it could not be longer than 56 feet and still fit onto elevators on the carriers—"you automatically get the tadpole shape which characterizes the fuselage of the A-6."[5] "Tadpole" became only one nickname accorded the unlovely aircraft over time. Others dubbed it a "flying drumstick." A veteran A-6 B/N described its nose as "a regular W. C. Fields affair" and deemed the overall shape of the aircraft as something "seemingly in violation of one of those laws of aerodynamics named for some Italian physicist."[6] Some even borrowed the U.S. Air Force acronym often applied to the B-52: "Buff," which—in polite company—stood for "big ugly fat fellow."

An airplane often described as a "flying tadpole" or a "flying drumstick," or by even more colorful nicknames, the A-6 excelled as a day-night, high-low, all-weather attack aircraft. This Sunday Puncher A-6A is delivering an ordnance load of Mark 82 500-pound general-purpose bombs. The bulbous radome at the aircraft's nose houses much of the inner workings of its radars and sophisticated, computerized navigation and weapons system. Its angled refueling probe is also distinctive. (David F. Warren Collection)

At the heart of the ungainly aircraft rested the innovative navigation and weapons delivery system called the DIANE system. DIANE stood for Digital Integrated Attack Navigation Equipment. The engineers considered as an integrated whole and not as independent components three key elements: sensors, analog computer, and cockpit display. The resulting design, Mead suggested, made a real breakthrough because "the computer calculated the automatic weapon release point during the pull up for a successful hit for any dive angle, pull up G, wind, airspeed, target range and velocity." Depending on circumstances, the crew in the cockpit could choose to drop their weapons while flying level, with a low-angle dive, or with a high-angle release. Just as important, the DIANE system worked with the full range of ordnance the aircraft might be called upon to carry. In addition to conventional iron bombs weighing from 25 to 2,000 pounds, the A-6 could lay mines and meet specifications for a suitable platform for the delivery of nuclear weapons. Most important of all, with this system the crew could do all these things "under nonvisual conditions on radar significant stationary or moving targets."[7]

After much testing and tweaking, the first two A-6As—the first model accepted by the Navy—arrived at Oceana in February 1963. The B/N's side of the plane consisted of only a blank panel because the weapons system had not yet been installed. These first two aircraft went to VA-42, designated as the emerging East Coast A-6 community's training unit, or Replacement Air Group (RAG). Full-system A-6As arrived in June, and the instructor pilots and B/Ns—many just selected from the A-4 and A-3 attack communities—began their own training program. As their future instructors mastered their new plane and designed a training curriculum during the first six months of 1963, the Sunday Punchers gave up their Skyraiders and began the process of reconfiguring flight crews and maintenance personnel to fit the requirements of their new aircraft. When LT Donald V. Boecker joined VA-75 in the summer of 1963, he found a total strength of only 110 men, one-third of a typical squadron's strength.

On 3 September 1963, a full complement of prospective pilots and B/Ns assigned to VA-75 reported to their RAG instructors to learn to fly and operate the systems in the A-6. In November, the Sunday Punchers received their own A-6s, and by February 1964, that first contingent of pilots and B/Ns who would fly them—including Boecker—completed the RAG curriculum. The Sunday Punchers became the first squadron fully qualified to take the new aircraft on deployment.[8]

Eight years later, in February 1972, Boecker—now a lieutenant commander and a combat veteran—once again served with the Sunday Punchers. During ejection-seat refresher training one day, one of LT Thomas E. Wharton's squadronmates asked the Florida-born pilot if he knew about Boecker's long connection to VA-75. When Wharton admitted that he did not, Boecker presented a brief history lesson.

In 1965, as American involvement in Vietnam intensified, a shortage of carriers in the Pacific Fleet forced the Navy to commit Atlantic Fleet assets to Southeast Asia. *Independence* left Norfolk on 10 May 1965 for the Western Pacific theater—"Westpac" to most sailors—taking the Sunday Punchers with it. VA-75 launched its first missions on 2 July 1965, the very first fleet squadron in the U.S. Navy to fly the new A-6A in combat.[9] On 14 July, LT Boecker and his B/N, LT Donald R. Eaton, prepared to crater a road in northern Laos. As they rolled in on their target and released their bombs, the plane shook from the effects of an explosion under the right wing. At least one of their Mark 82 (Mk82) 500-pound general-purpose bombs had detonated prematurely, immediately after release. The starboard fire warning light glowed red. Boecker shut off that engine, put 100 percent power on the other, and tried to pull out of his dive. Then, another A-6 crew reported flames coming from the stricken aircraft. Boecker and Eaton ejected—and watched their plane crash into a hillside. After a harrowing time on the ground, a rescue helicopter recovered the two Sunday Punchers.[10] Wharton viewed Boecker with new respect.[11]

Tales of Boecker's exploits composed only one part of VA-75's Westpac saga in 1965. Four days later, on 18 July, Secretary of Defense Robert S. McNamara came aboard *Independence,* observed the briefing for an alpha strike on the Thanh Hoa power plant in North Vietnam, and then watched the launch of a Sunday Puncher A-6A carrying CDR Jeremiah A. Denton and LT William M. Tschudy, the strike leaders. Denton looked forward to the upcoming change of command ceremonies on 20 July that would make him skipper of VA-75, but now, as they rolled in on a warehouse, a jolt rocked his A-6A. Denton, too, got the impression "that a bomb had gone off upon release." The aircraft lost hydraulics, speed brakes, and radios, forcing Denton and Tschudy to eject. They became VA-75's first POWs.[12] On 24 July, VA-75 lost a third A-6A, again from the premature detonation of one of its own Mk82s. This time, a helicopter rescued the pilot and B/N, LCDR Richard P. Bordone and LTJG Peter F. Moffett. On 17 September 1965, North Vietnamese automatic weapon fire brought down the Sunday Puncher skipper, CDR Leonard F. Vogt, and his B/N, LT R. F. Barber, killing both men near Bach Long Vi Island. Despite its losses, VA-75 personnel won 91 Air Medals, 15 Navy Commendation Medals, and 6 Distinguished Flying Crosses, while flying 588 combat sorties and dropping 1.5 million pounds of ordnance—one-quarter of the airwing's total delivery—in 66 days on the line.[13] They also resolved their ordnance-release problem, changing the fusing on the bombs and replacing the mechanical bomb racks on the aircrafts' five weapons pylons with more reliable Multiple Ejector Racks (MERs) that released bombs sequentially to provide greater separation from the aircraft and other falling rounds before detonation.[14]

As the war in Vietnam continued, more A-6 squadrons followed VA-75 to Westpac. Even in 1972, however, Boecker—and other senior officers with long service in A-6s—still lived with the legacy of the Intruder's earliest combat experiences. Two major issues emerged in 1965–1966 that still generated heated debates in the naval aviation community. First, the A-6 initially developed a poor reputation for durability and reliability in the carrier environment. Heat, humidity, salt air, and the force of catapult launches all compromised the aircraft's complex avionics package that controlled the aircraft's navigation and weapons system. The frequency of serious malfunctions—called "downing gripes" when they took planes off the flight schedule—created headaches for both mission planners and flight schedulers. Over the course of VA-75's first cruise, it reported full availability of its navigation and weapons systems at rates as low as 26 percent and radar availability at only 40 percent.[15] In looking back over his command of USS *Enterprise* (CVAN-65) in 1967, VADM Kent L. Lee recalled frequent trips to the hangar deck to check the status of his RA-5Cs, a reconnaissance plane he considered "a hopeless cause," and his A-6s. "Almost without exception, an A-6 would make one flight and have to go to the hangar deck for maintenance," he complained.[16] He exaggerated, but even in 1972, nagging questions about the durability of the A-6's systems persisted.

Concerns about the reliability of its new technology spawned a second debate, a doctrinal discussion about how best to use the Intruder in combat. Some carrier skippers and CAGs—commanding officers of carrier airwings, who still used the acronym for the obsolete title, "commander, air group"—preferred to assign A-6s to large-scale alpha strikes of twenty or more bombers launched against specific targets. This allowed them to take advantage of the aircraft's substantial ordnance load. Others devoted their A-6s primarily to one- and two-plane strike missions that utilized the aircraft's night and all-weather navigation capabilities.[17] The aircraft could perform either role, but the question remained: Should it be called upon to do so?

In 1966, as CDR Robert C. Mandeville of VA-65 asserted, "We had to prove the plane." But after one deployment, he boasted, "We don't need to blow our own horn—the results will show." That year, *Time* dubbed it "a plane for all seasons."[18] In 1966, RADM Martin D. Carmody, commanding officer of Carrier Task Force 77 (CTF-77)—all carriers operating in Westpac—wished he could create an airwing solely made up of F-4s and A-6s.[19] The Intruder community enjoyed touting the effectiveness of the one- and two-plane strike, citing the extensive damage inflicted on the Uong Bi power plant in North Vietnam by just two A-6As from VA-85. Radio Hanoi announced that the plant had been hit by B-52 strategic bombers.[20] As time passed, the A-6 drew more praise. In 1968, the *Washington Post* heralded the Intruder as "the shape of planes to come, inside as well as out," as American airpower focused on interdiction targets in the narrow southern panhandle of North Vietnam.[21] Still, the Intruder won friends in part from its perceived versatility, which allowed it to perform a dual mission as an outstanding ordnance platform for alpha strikes and as a day-or-night, low-level, all-weather attack aircraft. During VA-75's second combat cruise from December 1967 through June 1968 aboard USS *Kitty Hawk* (CVA-63), the Sunday Punchers performed both missions, dropping a substantial thirteen million pounds of ordnance in six months of heavy alpha strike commitments. But the squadron took its losses only on single-plane missions that relied more heavily on the A-6's systems capability. A surface-to-air missile (SAM) took down LCDR John D. Peace and LT Gordon S. Perisho's A-6A on 31 December 1967, as it conducted a daylight single-plane strike west of Vinh. On 6 March 1968, LT R. C. Nelson and LT G. L. Mitchell failed to return from a low-level night strike on a railroad yard near Haiphong.[22]

By February 1972, unfortunately, except for stories handed down to them by Boecker and other veterans of Westpac cruises, most Sunday Punchers knew little about their squadron's combat history and the operational and doctrinal debates it had spawned. Since June 1968, the squadron had not served in Southeast Asia's hostile skies. As part of CVW-3—the airwing that launched from the flight deck of USS *Saratoga* (CVA-60)—VA-75 made extended annual cruises in 1969 and 1970, either as part of Sixth Fleet activities in the Mediterranean or attached to the Third Fleet in the North Atlantic in support of NATO obligations. On the most recent cruise to the Mediterranean in the summer and fall of 1971, the Sunday Punchers participated in the testing of the "CV concept" for carriers, designed to create a multipurpose warship able to carry out a full range of missions, combining attack, air defense, and antisubmarine warfare capabilities.[23] In addition, VA-75's pilots and B/Ns trained for nuclear weapons delivery, their role in the Single Integrated Operational Plan (SIOP), designed as part of the response to potential communist aggression against NATO allies in western Europe.[24] With the war in Vietnam apparently winding down, they had no reason to anticipate a return to Westpac or to train in skills required for combat deployments there.

During that 1971 Mediterranean cruise and still in February 1972, CDR Everett W. Foote commanded VA-75. As commanding officer—the skipper or the CO—he bore primary responsibility for the morale, safety, discipline, and operational readiness of his squadron. Born in December 1930, the son of an Ohio judge, Foote knew from childhood that he wanted to fly, inspired in part by an uncle who wore naval aviator wings during World War II. After one year at Kent State University, he enlisted in the Navy in June 1951 and gained admission to the Naval Academy Preparatory School at Bainbridge, Maryland. Foote then won an appointment to the United States Naval Academy and graduated with the class of 1956.

Foote's path to command of the Sunday Punchers was typical for a naval officer during the Cold War, blending operational postings with advanced schooling and administrative billets. Designated a naval aviator after basic flight training at Pensacola in 1957, Foote joined VAH-5 as a bombardier/navigator and then pilot of the A-3D Skywarrior, a carrier-borne heavy attack aircraft designed to deliver nuclear weapons. He completed three Mediterranean cruises on USS *Forrestal* (CVA-59) with that squadron. After midcareer advanced schooling and shore assignments, in August 1965, he transitioned—somewhat unwillingly, he admitted—from the A-3D community into the A-6 community; he preferred a different aircraft, but he allowed himself to be convinced to change his mind. In November 1966, he deployed to Southeast Asia with VA-35 and flew sixty-two combat missions in A-6As, then went to Whidbey Island Naval Air Station,

CDR Everett W. Foote, a 1956 graduate of the U.S. Naval Academy who already had completed two combat tours in Southeast Asia, commanded VA-75 from June 1971 until June 1972. (U.S. Navy photograph, Everett W. Foote Collection)

Washington, where he helped to organize VA-128, the West Coast A-6 RAG. In September 1968, he deployed once again to Southeast Asia as operations officer of VA-52, accumulating many more combat hours in A-6s. After his second combat cruise, he served at the Pentagon in the Office of Aviation Plans and Policies until August 1970, when he joined VA-75 as executive officer. He won early promotions to the ranks of lieutenant commander and commander, and he succeeded CDR Charles E. Cellar as the commanding officer of the Sunday Punchers in June 1971.

In many ways, Foote represented a traditionalist element in the Vietnam-era U.S. Navy. A product of the peacetime force of the late 1950s and early 1960s, he began his career in a professional culture in which leadership rested on unquestioned obedience to superiors. Now, he commanded as he had followed. But Foote took over his squadron at a time of great discontent and change within the service. The growing unpopularity of the Vietnam conflict in itself had forced the Navy to rethink many of its ways, and Foote found himself caught uncomfortably in the changes.

Since 1 July 1970, when ADM Elmo R. Zumwalt, Jr., became Chief of Naval Operations (CNO), sweeping reforms in personnel policy altered traditional relationships between commanders and their subordinates. Recruiting and retaining talented personnel ranked high among Zumwalt's top priorities. As the war in Vietnam wound down amid talk of an all-volunteer force, the CNO listened to the findings of focus groups sent to talk to enlisted men and officers. He had begun with the naval aviation community and identified four problem areas: 1) restrictions on personal behavior, including grooming and uniform standards; 2) dissatisfaction with operational scheduling that required long absences from family; 3) lack of job satisfaction among Navy men and women seeking opportunities to advance; and 4) discrimination based on race, ethnicity, and gender. Based on what he learned, he issued a number of "Z-Grams," directives to eliminate "the Mickey Mouse" and to cultivate respect up and down the chain of command.[25]

Foote's command style—decidedly Old Navy—often clashed with the different expectations of his junior officers, or JOs—the squadron's lieutenants and lieutenants junior grade. Although they did not concur with the liberal and leveling nature of some of Zumwalt's changes, they perceived too much "Mickey Mouse" in the operation of Foote's squadron.

Soon after he took command of the Sunday Punchers, Foote nicknamed the squadron "F Troop," after the first initial of his last name—but, unfortunately, also the name of a 1960s television show about an inept U.S. cavalry unit. CDR Paul T. Gillcrist, the CAG of *Saratoga*'s airwing, recalled during the 1971 Mediterranean cruise that Foote "had a squadron flag and flagstaff designed like a cavalry guidon; the triangular flag contained the words 'VA-75 F Troop.' Anytime the squadron was required to fall into formation on the flight deck, the F Troop guidon was proudly paraded."[26] But the junior officers viewed such antics as exactly the kind of "Mickey Mouse" they found unprofessional and somewhat demeaning. Indeed, as LT John M. Miller, one of the junior pilots, recalled, "We hated that!"[27]

Miller nursed a second grievance, related to the first. Most naval aviators, sooner or later, obtained a squadron nickname. Often, it played on a man's own name. For instance, LTJG Roger G. Lerseth, a South Dakota–born B/N, simply went by "Rog." Another B/N, LTJG Paul C. Hvidding, usually answered to "Hvids." If a man received a nickname for a character trait or some interesting adventure (or misadventure), he at least hoped it would enhance his image. Most of all, no one wanted a name that caused personal or professional embarrassment. Foote tagged Miller with his nickname during a Dependents' Day cruise. The young pilot had a remarkably boyish face, and when a guest aboard *Saratoga* commented to Foote on Miller's apparent extreme youth, the CO immediately dubbed him "John-John." Foote loved it, but Miller hated it. In time, with effort, he convinced his squadronmates to shorten it to "JJ."[28] Similarly, LTJG Lamar Don Petersen, a B/N from Utah, grew up answering to his middle name, Don. Foote preferred "Lamar," however, and he used it often and loudly despite the B/N's respectful request that he not do so. Indeed, following Foote's

CDR Foote, "F Troop" flag in hand, on the flight deck of USS Saratoga, *during the fall 1971 Mediterranean cruise. (Everett W. Foote Collection)*

lead, most of Petersen's fellow JOs called him "Lamar," too. He did not want to contradict the skipper, but, one-by-one, he finally asked his squadronmates to call him "Don" instead.[29] These incidents seem trivial—except to those directly involved—but they illustrate one kind of "Mickey Mouse" for which junior Sunday Puncher pilots and B/Ns had little patience.

They remained equally unimpressed by open displays of authority for its own sake. Foote reminded them constantly that he signed off on their fitness reports. Failure to be a team player—on either his team or the Navy team—ranked high on Foote's list of grave offenses he would not tolerate. LTJG William F. Wardlaw, the Sunday Punchers' junior air intelligence officer, learned his lesson the hard way. During the 1971 Med cruise, his wife went through a religious conversion, and, in time, he did the same. Before then, he had drunk and partied with his squadronmates on liberty, participating fully in all activities. Now he pulled back. Finally, he informed the skipper that he did not want to remain in the Navy, even expressing interest in an "early out," if that option presented itself. His very next fitness report dropped him from top ratings to the lowest possible evaluations.[30] Foote's extroverted personality lent itself to bluster, but Wardlaw's case suggested that the CO would go beyond threats and make subordinates pay for mistakes in action or judgment that might reflect negatively on him.

Still, even if they did not like his way of running the squadron, few doubted their skipper's love for the Navy. Some even took away positive lessons from it. Coming back aboard *Saratoga* after a party in Athens during the 1971 Med cruise, LTJG Hvidding realized that the officer standing next to him in the liberty boat was his considerably inebriated skipper. As the junior B/N watched, Foote looked up at the carrier and, using one of its nicknames, murmured, "I love you, Sara Maru." Hvidding did not doubt his skipper's sincerity.[31]

Foote already knew that in June he would turn over command of the Sunday Punchers to his executive officer—the XO—CDR Charles "M" Earnest. Born in Opelika, Alabama, in 1934, Earnest graduated with a bachelor of science degree in physics from Auburn University in June 1955. He had entered the Naval Reserve Officer Training Corps (NROTC) program, however, so he remained for a year of graduate work while completing commissioning requirements; he became an ensign in August 1956. Like Foote, Earnest's naval aviation career began before the introduction of the A-6. Designated a naval aviator in May 1958, his first squadron assignment took him to VHAW-33 where he flew the Douglas AD-5N Skyraider. After a shore billet with Training Command, he attended the U.S. Naval Postgraduate School at Monterey, California, obtaining a master's degree in operations research. He then transitioned to the A-4 Skyhawk, a single-seat light attack aircraft. In November 1966, he joined VA-153, and over the course of two combat tours, he accumulated 221 combat missions in the A-4. Foote met Earnest on the latter's second cruise, when each man served as operations officer of his respective squadron. A shore assignment in the Office of the Secretary of Defense, serving as an analyst for the Air Force, Navy, and Army Tactical Air Programs, followed. When the Navy began to replace the underpowered A-4, Earnest transitioned to the A-6 Intruder, went through the RAG with VA-42, and reported to VA-75 as prospective executive officer in May 1971.

At least at the beginning, the JOs observed in CDR Earnest some of the same traits they saw in their skipper. The responsibilities of the XO covered a wide range of day-to-day operations, and Earnest kept after the junior pilots and B/Ns to complete their paperwork and to take on additional duties to increase the squadron's efficiency. According to LT Alan G. Fischer, a New Jersey–born pilot, the XO never seemed to sleep and expected everyone else to keep that same schedule.[32] Worse, if Earnest decided upon a squadron project, he wanted it completed immediately and without question. Late on a Friday afternoon just before Christmas 1971, he called in LT Wharton, laid out his plan for a new set of mailboxes for the squadron ready room, and then told the junior pilot to build it before he left on holiday leave. Wharton already had plans to leave for Florida, but more to the point, as a bachelor residing in a small room in the Oceana Bachelor Officer Quarters (BOQ), he lacked the tools, materials, and paint to complete the assignment to the XO's specifications. Thus, he requested a delay so he could obtain assistance from the squadron's various shops. For reasons he did not explain, Earnest refused. LTJG Petersen, who had plenty of tools at home, stepped in and completed the project. But neither JO could fathom why the XO made such a big deal over such an insignificant item as a new mailbox.[33]

Next in VA-75's chain of command, reporting directly to CDRs Foote and Earnest, came the department heads who supervised specific core functions. Every naval aviator who achieved the rank of lieutenant commander knew that a successful tour as a department head mattered greatly to selection boards if he hoped to screen for command of his own squadron someday. Thus, a significant degree of competition with peers and pressure came with these assignments. How each of these officers combined the performance of squadron duties with personal career ambitions underwent constant scrutiny from both superiors and subordinates. Squadron JOs referred to the CO, the XO, and the department heads as the Sunday Punchers' "heavies."

Foote considered his appointments as department heads carefully. During the 1971 Med cruise, LCDR Donald F. Lindland held the position of Operations Department head. As the "ops officer," he handled such mission-related matters as the flight schedule, training, tactics, intelligence, weapons, and communications.[34] Lindland, a graduate of the University of Oregon, never flew in an airplane until the day he traveled to Pensacola to begin flight training. A man of many interests—from jazz to higher mathematics—he possessed a keen sense of humor often hidden by a quiet demeanor. He started out in multi-engine propeller-driven planes but transitioned to jet aircraft and the A-6 just as it entered the Navy inventory. He already had completed an A-6 combat tour in 1968 with VA-35. A member of VA-75 since December 1970, he led by example, and the JOs admired the calm and insight that marked his professional dealings.[35]

The Maintenance Department worked hand in hand with Operations to keep squadron aircraft ready to meet mission schedules. The Maintenance Department head handled issues related to corrosion control, airframes, power plants, avionics, electronics, material control, and quality control, among others.[36] When Saratoga returned from the 1971 Med cruise, CDR Foote reassigned LCDR Lindland from Operations to Maintenance. LCDR Boecker had held the assignment during the recent cruise, but he now prepared to leave VA-75. With the approach of workups during February and March 1972, Foote needed a proven performer to take over.

To replace the head of the Administrative Department who left the squadron after the 1971 Med cruise, CDR Foote appointed LCDR Robert S. Graustein. The responsibilities of that department centered on the maintaining of squadron personnel records, legal services, educational opportunities, public affairs, and control of classified materials.[37] Graustein joined VA-75 in the late fall of 1971. A 1961 graduate of the United States Naval Academy, he began his naval aviation career in S-2s, an antisubmarine warfare aircraft, and his experience in this plane brought useful insight to VA-75 as *Saratoga* continued its testing of the CV concept. He also had served as a test pilot at Patuxent River Naval Air Station. Graustein had only recently transitioned into the A-6 community by completing the RAG curriculum with VA-42. Compared with most of the other squadron heavies, he had relatively little experience in attack aircraft. But he acknowledged it and worked that much harder to overcome it.

LCDR Richard L. Engel joined the Sunday Punchers early in 1972, and CDR Foote had not yet assigned him to a specific duty. Given his seniority—he was the squadron's second most senior officer of his rank—when active operations started, he would be in line for the billet of either Operations or Maintenance head, depending on where Foote decided to place Lindland. The youngest of three brothers to attend the United States Naval Academy—he graduated with the class of 1959—Engel understood too well both the euphoria of flight and the dangers it hid. His older brother, Gordon, USNA class of 1948B, had been killed in a flight-deck crash just after Engel left for his own first deployment as a naval aviator. He began his aviation career flying EA-1Fs, a four-man version of the A-1 propeller-driven attack plane. Later transitioning to jets, he served as an instructor in advanced student jet training at Beeville, Texas, and then requested assignment to A-6s. After completing the RAG curriculum, he went to the Med with VA-176 and returned to the RAG as safety officer.[38] Despite all his flight hours in A-6s, however, he had flown none of them in combat.

At the CO's discretion, a department might be divided further into divisions headed by junior lieutenant commanders being groomed for greater responsibilities. Other specific functions not accorded department status but considered central to the squadron's core mission also could be assigned to the more junior lieutenant commanders. The Sunday Puncher JOs considered these officers, too, to be squadron heavies. In February 1972, VA-75 counted four such officers in their ranks, LCDRs James J. Kennedy, Grady L. Jackson, John A. Pieno, Jr., and Richard W. Schram.

LCDR Jim Kennedy, a native New Yorker, joined the U.S. Navy in November 1951. He spent over ten years as an enlisted man, much of it as an aviation electronics technician. Accepted into the Navy's Limited Duty Officer (LDO) program that gave technical specialists sufficient rank and authority to make the best use of their experience and free up unrestricted line officers for other assignments, he pinned on the gold bar of an ensign in March 1962. He already had deployed to Southeast Asia in the early years of the American involvement, serving with VA-76, an A-4 squadron launching from the decks of USS *Enterprise*. He later transitioned to A-6s, and now his greatest challenge centered on keeping VA-75's planes in the air, supervising the men who repaired them, and overseeing the burdensome logistical apparatus that supplied—or failed to supply—the necessary parts and testing equipment that allowed his men to do their job. The squadron's Maintenance LDO, Kennedy expected to rotate out of VA-75 during the summer of 1972.[39]

LCDR Grady Jackson entered Aviation Officer Candidate School at Pensacola, Florida, in 1961 after graduating from Newberry College in South Carolina, influenced by several older friends from his basketball team who had gone into naval aviation. He entered the Naval Aviation Observer pipeline—which later became the Naval Flight Officer (NFO) program—in large part because early on he discovered his career-long special interest in electronic warfare. He first flew in EA-1Fs, a propeller-driven electronic warfare aircraft, and served in several instructional and staff billets in his specialty, including a stint in Southeast Asia. By 1970, he realized that he had not been part of an operational squadron for nearly six years and he had flown no combat tours. The aircraft he most wanted to fly—the EA-6B Prowler, an electronic countermeasures aircraft—had not yet come into the inventory, so he opted to enter the A-6 community. After completing the curriculum at VA-42, he joined VA-75 for the 1971 Med cruise.[40] He served as the Avionics Division Officer within the Maintenance Department.

LCDR John Pieno always knew he would join the Navy and fly. He had grown up fishing with his father on Lake Ponchartrain, just beyond the end of the runway of the naval air station at New Orleans. Pilots used to wave to them, hold dogfights over the field, and fly off in large formations. "It was the greatest free show in the area," he recalled; "how could you not be inspired?" After enlisting in 1961 and entering the aviation program, he, too, began in propeller aircraft, but requested a transfer to jets and the attack community as soon he could, entering the NFO pipeline to become a B/N and completing the A-6 RAG curriculum. Like LCDR Jackson, he had served a staff tour but no combat tour in Westpac. He, too, accompanied the Sunday Punchers on the 1971 Med cruise.[41] In February 1972, he served as VA-75's Training Officer.

CDR Foote appointed LCDR Richard W. Schram to serve as squadron Safety Officer. The son of a famous stunt pilot best known as "the Flying Professor," Schram grew up around airplanes. During an air show, as he explained the aerobatics his father planned to demonstrate, he watched "the Flying Professor's" plane crash in flames. But this did not dissuade him from pursuing a career in naval aviation. He graduated from Purdue University in 1963, obtained his commission as an ensign in the U.S. Navy the next year, and ultimately became an A-6 B/N. Like Lindland, Schram had logged an earlier combat tour in Vietnam, accumulating over 100 missions with VA-65. He came to VA-75 directly from a stint as the Public Affairs Officer with the Blue Angels, the Navy's demonstration flying team. Now he made sure the pilots and B/Ns remained qualified under Naval Aviation Training and Operations Procedures Standardization (NATOPS) guidelines.[42]

In VA-75's table of organization, each department and division was subdivided further into functional branches, each headed by a lieutenant or lieutenant junior grade. In short, each officer had a chance to lead, plan, administer, and evaluate at levels appropriate to his rank and experience. Each branch officer reported directly to his department head. For instance, the Sunday Punchers' two air intelligence officers—LT William C. Martin, who had just come from the intelligence school at Lowry Air Force Base, and LTJG Wardlaw—"worked for" the Operations Department head. Except for specialists like Martin and Wardlaw, however, few Sunday Puncher JOs identified themselves by their branch assignment. They perceived themselves first and foremost as pilots or B/Ns who flew Intruders for the U.S. Navy.

No single personal or intellectual profile embraces all the JOs assigned to VA-75 in February 1972. Most began their naval service as ensigns in 1967, 1968, or 1969. They followed different paths to obtain that first gold bar. Five JOs with the squadron—LTs Kenneth L. Pyle, Thomas C. "Kit" Ruland, and Paul H. Wagner, along with LTJGs Alden F. Mullins, Jr., and Robert A. Tolhurst, Jr.—had graduated from the United States Naval Academy in 1968 and 1969. Several others earned commissions through various university-based NROTC programs— LT Ronny D. Lankford at Auburn University, LTJG Robert F. Miller at Rensselaer Polytechnical Institute, LTJG Hvidding at the University of Virginia, and LTJG Lerseth at the University of Washington. LTJG David F. Warren, a new B/N who had just joined VA-75, had joined the Navy right out of high school to get electronics training, and, after over eight years of enlisted service, had won acceptance into the Naval Enlisted Scientific Education Program (NESEP), and had received both his commission and a degree in mathematics upon graduation from the University of Washington. LT Kenneth K. Knapp, a geology major at Northern Iowa University, obtained his commission through the Aviation Reserve Officer Candidate (AVROC) program, devoting a period of weeks during the summers after his junior and senior years to military training at the naval air station at Pensacola. LTJG Ronald D. McFarland followed the same course as a student at Texas Tech University. The squadron's two warrant officers—Chief Warrant Officer 2 Howard P. Smith in maintenance and Warrant Officer 1 Jerry

Walden, an ordnance specialist—had put in many long years as enlisted men before rising to their current ranks in their fields of expertise.

Other junior officers among the 1972 Sunday Punchers had made no decision about military service until after they had graduated from college. Some, including LTJG John R. Fuller, a history major who attended Williams College, and LT Terry L. Anderson, who played basketball at Wittenberg College in Ohio, graduated from small liberal arts institutions. Others came from small state-supported colleges; and LTJG Wardlaw graduated from North Texas State. Still others had attended the nation's private, religiously affiliated schools, including LT Fischer, who attended Villanova, and LTJG Douglas W. Ahrens, who attended Pacific Lutheran College. The squadron's most junior B/N, LTJG John J. Swigart, Jr., graduated from Princeton University. These men first donned military uniforms on their first day in Aviation Officers Candidate School (AOCS) at Pensacola and became ensigns upon graduation. LT Martin won his commission through the Navy's officer candidate school at Newport, Rhode Island, after graduating from Roanoke College.

Regardless of the sources of their commissions, each of these men had volunteered for military service. Their reasons for serving their country in uniform during wartime varied widely. For some, such as for LT Fischer, "patriotism" provided the only inspiration needed. LTJG Tolhurst, son of a career Air Force officer, believed that everyone had an obligation to serve their country, stating, "I could not imagine not wanting to do one's share for the greatest, and most freedom loving, nation in the world."[43]

Family history shaped the decision for some. For LT Pyle, hearing stories about his uncle who died in the crash of his naval aircraft during World War II, watching a 1950s television show called *Men of Annapolis*, and even following the Navy football team in the days of Joe Bellino and Roger Staubach all combined to lead him to the Naval Academy.[44] The father of LTJG Leslie M. Sanford, Jr., had commanded a naval air squadron earlier in the Vietnam War. LT Anderson's older brother graduated with the United States Military Academy's class of 1964, and he did not want his older sibling to claim "all the glory," since military service "was a very positive character attribute to the home town folks."[45]

Some would not have considered military service as part of their life plan at all, were it not for the pressure imposed by Selective Service. Indeed, LTJG McFarland admitted, "I don't believe I would have finished college if I had not wanted to stay out of the draft."[46] LTJG Swigart admitted that he joined because he was about to graduate, felt no desire to pursue an advanced degree—especially given the likelihood that he could not continue his student deferment by doing so—and decided that rather than wait for the draft to find him, he would "do something that sounded interesting, like flying jets."[47] In other cases, the prospect of the draft simply helped some, like LT Anderson, to choose "a self selected program" of military service, a course he deemed much smarter than leaving his fate to the arbitrariness of the Selective Service system.[48]

Some seriously contemplated joining one of the other armed services before they committed to the U.S. Navy. LT Pyle considered going after a Marine Corps commission when he graduated from the Naval Academy.[49] LTJG Sanford began his military career as an Army ROTC cadet in the Virginia Tech Corps of Cadets.[50] LTJG Ahrens declined an opportunity to enter the Coast Guard Reserve in an enlisted billet and instead entered AOCS, convinced in part by his brother-in-law's stories of flying A-4s earlier in the war.[51] When his local draft board terminated his student deferment, LTJG Fuller approached his decision with an open mind. The Army had its allure if he could get into the armor branch, but he realized that a tank fight in triple canopy jungles differed greatly from the World War II campaigns in Europe or North Africa about which he enjoyed reading. He heard rumors that the Air Force only gave wings to graduates of the Air Force Academy. He seriously considered Marine Corps aviation, but his father expressed grave doubts about their maintenance procedures and talked him out of it. Given Fuller's longtime interest in military aviation, however, AOCS ultimately made the best sense to him. As he explained, "One cannot read about the Coral Sea and Midway and the challenges inherent in flying off a boat, finding a target and then finding the boat again . . . and not want to do it."[52]

A few of those who had an easier time reaching a decision to join the Navy nearly committed to other specialty fields before deciding in favor of aviation. LTJG Bob Miller first considered going into submarines, until he realized that the required nuclear power school carried with it an extended service obligation. Only then did he turn to aviation as an option, since his father had also been a military pilot.[53] While a midshipman at the Naval Academy, LTJG Mullins thought he would go into destroyers, until his experiences during his first-class cruise changed his mind. "I was on a good destroyer forward deployed in the Med, and I couldn't stand it. Everything happened too slowly," and the captain always seemed to be looking over his subordinates' shoulders, giving them no latitude for error or, often enough, no opportunity for learning. When the Navy changed regulations to make it possible for Naval Flight Officers to command squadrons, a posting previously reserved for pilots only, Mullins finally decided upon aviation.[54] LTJG Warren let his wife make the final decision between submarines and aviation. The sinkings of the USS *Thresher* and USS *Scorpion* had filled the newspapers and airwaves in dramatic fashion, but since Warren did not tell his wife that the Navy also lost aircraft on a fairly regular basis, she chose aviation as her husband's career track.[55]

A few even found themselves headed for naval aviation almost by accident. LT Anderson gave in to a recruiter's pitch on a Saturday morning after a fraternity party. While walking with some friends through the student union, he watched a Navy recruiter set up his booth. "The white uniform and the pictures of jets" played to his hidden desire to become a pilot. The recruiter's call sign was "Lucky," and he convinced Anderson and his friends to sit down and take the Navy's aptitude tests. Anderson passed, with "very high scores despite my physical state." As a result, he noted, "I had sealed my fate . . . and I hadn't ever been in an airplane."[56] By contrast, LT Wharton had grown up around them and planned to follow in his father's footsteps to fly for Eastern Airlines. He wanted to start flight training through his local community college, not realizing that the courses did not qualify him for a student deferment. The draft and that "dinky war" in Vietnam did not concern Wharton deeply in 1965 when a "Fly Navy" recruiter came to Brevard Community College. He and a friend took the aptitude test, passed, and learned that the scores would be good for three years. His friend went into the Army's helicopter pilot program (and subsequently died in Vietnam), but Wharton transferred to the University of Florida to continue his studies. When he graduated in 1968 and realized both that his scores were still good and that naval aviation excited him, he joined the Navy.[57]

Unlike the squadron heavies who transitioned to A-6s well into their careers, each Sunday Puncher JO assigned to the squadron in February 1972 made a conscious choice at some early point in his aviation training to aim for the A-6 community. Competition for each seat in an A-6 fleet squadron proved to be stiff, and each man reached his individual decision to try for one of those slots for his own reasons and in his own time. Regardless of how or when he reached his decision, however, the path to an A-6 cockpit began on the first day of pilot or Naval Flight Officer training.

Those who became pilots most often began with preflight ground school at Pensacola and then, usually, moved up to Saufley Field, just north of the naval air station, for primary flight training as part of VT-1. There, each man accumulated approximately twenty-six hours of flight time in the T-34, to include soloing. Instructors evaluated students during each of these training exercises, and final grades determined each man's future course. Depending on his performance, a prospective pilot could choose from three training pipelines: jets, maritime patrol, or helicopters. The needs of the Navy dictated the number of slots in each pipeline at the next level of flight training, but any man who wanted to fly an A-6 had to graduate near the top of his primary flight training to "get jets."

Those who made the cut usually went on to Naval Air Station Meridian in Mississippi to join VT-7 or VT-9 for basic jet training. For nearly five months, the students flew T-2s, learning both instrument flying and formation work.

Those who completed the curriculum then returned to Pensacola as part of VT-4 for two to four months to learn air-to-air gunnery and to complete their first carrier qualifications, often aboard USS *Lexington* (CVT-16), the Training Command's designated carrier. There they experienced what one chronicler of naval history has called "one of the most eagerly awaited and emotionally testing times in a young naval aviator's life": his first carrier qualification landing. As one veteran wrote, "Nothing in civilian life comes close to the demanding physical and nerve-edged life of a carrier pilot. Few nonmilitary tasks require the quickness of mind and the steadiness of hand necessary to bring an aircraft aboard a pitching four-acre plot. From that day forward, he knows only one standard. That is all a pitching deck allows."[58]

Those who made it that far reported to one of two naval air stations in Texas—Beeville or Kingsville—for advanced jet training. For the next six months, the prospective pilots trained in either the F-9 Cougar or the TA-4J Skyhawk, mastering still more instrument training, learning air-to-air and air-to-ground tactics and formation flying, and completing preparation for a second round of carrier qualifications. Since the pilot pipeline offered more than one path into jets, not all students at Beeville or Kingsville arrived there after training at Saufley and Meridian. Because he entered a Navy-sponsored graduate program at the University of West Florida, LT Ruland began his primary flight training flying propeller-driven T-28s at Whiting Field near Pensacola. He transitioned to jets when he arrived at Kingsville.[59] By now, though, they all knew that their instructors evaluated each performance. At the end of the curriculum, each man filled out his "dream sheet," ranking in order his aircraft preferences. Once again, the needs of the Navy and class rank controlled the selection process. Those nearest the top of the class got the chance to pick from the A-6 Intruder, A-7 Corsair, F-4 Phantom, and the RA-5C Vigilante reconnaissance aircraft.

This important decision demanded serious consideration. At first, LTJG Tolhurst considered both the F-4 and the A-6, but quickly chose the Intruder because he believed that the chances for air-to-air combat were declining while "the Intruder would always be tasked to support almost any conceivable mission." He also preferred the side-by-side seating of the A-6. For him, it "fostered the 'crew' concept for which the Intruder community was almost legendary." By contrast, he explained, "the fighter community treated RIOs [radar intercept officers] like second class citizens," and that did not satisfy his sense of fair play.[60]

LT Ruland also decided early on to aim for a slot in the attack community. "I didn't view myself as a fighter pilot," he explained, adding, "I guess that I had the football lineman's mentality—not much flash, just go out and do the job." The teamwork required for the A-6 mission sealed the deal for him.[61] LT Anderson also found himself drawn to the Intruder's mission. "I really liked the challenge

. . . and I knew that if I ever had the chance to go into conflict, I would be doing a mission that could make a difference. The A-6 was a relatively new platform when I received my wings, and it was touted as 'state of the art' even for 1970."[62] LT Pyle held similar views. "Fighters did not interest me," he noted, adding that "it seemed like they spent most of the mission just 'hanging on the blades' waiting for the last 10–15 minutes when they could do some 'burning and turning' air combat maneuvering." Many of his instructors had flown single-seat A-4s or A-7s, and he found himself turned off by their egotistical attitudes "all about 'doing it themselves.'" Pyle found himself attracted to the A-6 mission, first and foremost. "All the intricate planning, weapons delivery, target area study, ground and air threat assessment" convinced him that attack pilots "did the real work of air warfare in projecting power to where the enemy lived." But he also appreciated the Intruder's two-man crew and its two engines. A married father with a new son, he had decided that "Intruders fit where I was comfortable serving, both personally and professionally."[63]

At the end of training at Beeville or Kingsville, graduation culminated with a winging ceremony. Class rank determined the order in which graduates chose not merely their airplane but also their first station—East Coast or West Coast. In LT Anderson's class, fourteen graduates submitted A-6s as their first choice for the four Intruder slots available, two in East Coast squadrons and two on the West Coast. Anderson earned high honors at every step of his pilot training and earned the East Coast A-6 slot he cherished, as well as a commission in the Regular U.S. Navy, instead of the Naval Reserves.[64] Likewise, LT Ruland sought an A-6 East Coast slot and got it.[65] LT Pyle graduated second in his class in November 1970, high enough to select the one A-6 slot available. His initial set of orders sent him to Whidbey Island, where West Coast Intruder squadrons trained, but for family and professional reasons, he preferred the East Coast. Since there were no immediate openings, he accepted a roundabout course of action, taking an assignment to Legal Officer School at Newport until an East Coast A-6 slot opened.[66] All who won A-6 East Coast slots knew they headed next to VA-42 at Oceana, the East Coast A-6 RAG.

At Oceana, they met for the first time the future B/Ns who would enter the fleet squadrons with them after completing the RAG curriculum together. For those who entered the NFO pipeline, becoming an A-6 B/N demanded the same consistent high performance in the classroom the pilots had demonstrated. Many future B/Ns, but not all, had wanted to be pilots, but less-than-perfect eyesight made the NFO program their only path into a cockpit. LTJG Bob Miller flunked his eye exam when he first arrived at Pensacola for pilot training and quickly found himself reassigned to the NFO pipeline.[67] LTJG McFarland decided quickly that, with his 20/40 vision, "being an NFO in an Intruder was as close as I could get to being a pilot."[68] LTJG Lerseth could identify with McFarland's sentiments. When his eyesight kept him out of the pilot program, he entered the NFO program and immediately penned onto the first page of his notebook: "THINK A-6!!!"[69]

Those who sought to sit in the right-hand seat of an A-6 cockpit began their flight training at VT-10, the NFO basic training squadron at Pensacola. Based on class rank at graduation and the needs of the Navy, they too had a chance to choose further training in either the jet or maritime patrol pipeline. Competition remained intense for slots in jets. In LTJG Mullins's VT-10 class, too, the six top students all selected as their next assignment the Basic Jet Navigation School at the Naval Air Station at Glyncoe, in Georgia.[70] LTJG Hvidding first thought he might want to fly the propeller-driven P-3 Orion, chiefly because his college roommate flew them. But when his class rank proved to be sufficiently high to pick jets, he jumped at the chance.

High class rank at Glyncoe provided yet another opportunity for a future NFO to make a choice. Graduates faced three possible options: A-6 B/N, F-4 RIO, or RA-5C navigator. LTJG Hvidding found himself marveling at the sleekness of the RA-5C Vigilante and its "mysterious" reconnaissance missions, but he did so largely because he had been told that getting selected for the A-6 program was nearly impossible.[71] LTJG Ahrens finished high enough in his class to investigate all the opportunities for carrier-based NFOs to pick the jet community in which he wanted to fly. He investigated the F-4, but he quickly became disenchanted with what seemed to him to be the limited and secondary role of the Phantom RIO. By contrast, he explained, an "A-6 B/N sits in front, has great visibility and has gadgets galore."[72] For LTJG Swigart, "sitting side by side, as opposed to in the back like in an F-4, also gave a sense of parity with the pilots."[73]

The fact that combat-experienced A-6 B/Ns served in instructor billets shaped the decisions of many of the future VA-75 NFOs. The enthusiasm and persuasiveness of an A-6 B/N who served as one of his instructors at VT-10 contributed to LTJG Ahrens's decision to aim for Intruders. LTJG Fuller also found the testimony of tested A-6 B/Ns convincing. He ultimately cited four reasons to explain why he went A-6: First, "if you're going to fly in the Navy you have to fly off boats—or want to"; second, "the B/N was essential to the primary mission of the aircraft, since, except for visual dive bombing that pilots could handle by themselves, everything else relies on teamwork"; third, the low-level single-plane night strikes reminded him of "Mosquito missions in Europe and the B-25 low level attack missions in the Pacific"; finally, the A-6 was a tactical aircraft, "which meant blowing things up—like the SBDs [dive bombers] at Midway—and blowing things up is neat."[74]

Graduates of the Basic Jet Navigation Course at Glyncoe who won the coveted A-6 East Coast slots all knew that their next posting would take them to VA-42. The top six graduates in LTJG Mullins's class at Glyncoe all chose the A-6 community, and five of them—Mullins, along with LTJGs Bob Miller, Hvidding, Lerseth, and Fuller—went through East Coast RAG training together before receiving assignment to VA-75.[75]

By the time these JOs—pilots and B/Ns—reached the RAG in 1969, 1970, and 1971, the initial iteration of the curriculum LT Boecker had completed in early 1964 had become a standardized program of instruction. About one hundred students completed the 27-week curriculum each year. The CO of VA-42 in 1970 explained the RAG's mission succinctly: "We take a student who has never flown in the A-6 and in approximately 120 flight hours we teach him how to fly the airplane or operate the system."[76] The pilots went through instructional phases devoted to learning flight characteristics and visual weapons delivery before deploying to Marine Corps Air Station at Yuma, Arizona, for ten days on nonsystem bombing techniques and instruction in formation flying. Upon their return to Oceana, pilots took up instruction in navigation and weapons drops using the A-6's unique systems.

The B/N curriculum paralleled the pilot's instructional phases. The B/Ns spent fewer hours in the air initially, as they mastered the operation of the weapons system. Then they, too, took to the air to master the radars, computers, and inertial and Doppler navigations systems. They flew many of these training hops not in A-6s but in specially outfitted TC-4C trainers with cockpits simulating that of an Intruder. The practice hops that B/Ns flew in real A-6s took them across Virginia's countryside, the instructor making sure they could acquire targets and other radar significant points. In one case, LTJG Sanford—who grew up in Virginia east of Fredericksburg and just northwest of Oceana—realized that he was quite familiar with the next point he had to find on his test flight: his own grandmother's house.[77] Instructors stressed the need for detailed planning; for every two-and-one-half-hour training flight, they spent between twelve and twenty hours in preparation. All prospective A-6 pilots and B/Ns completed over five hundred hours of classroom work and attended the Navy's SERE (survive, escape, resist, and evade) school in Maine.

Finally, after completion of the coursework, instructors paired the members of a pilot class and a B/N class for field carrier landing practice at an airstrip and then carrier qualifications aboard *Lexington*. During this phase of RAG training, the most important lessons stressed the importance of the "crew concept" at the core of the successful completion of the A-6 mission. Pilots and B/Ns had to learn to trust each other's skills. Repeatedly, instructors reminded them that the A-6 required two minds functioning in synch with each other. In a more practical vein, they pointed out that individuals did not enjoy success or failure—crews did. Both members of an A-6 crew got the same award for the same mission. Both suffered the consequences of an error. The A-6 community could afford no loners.[78]

As early as 1966, combat-tested A-6 squadrons returning from Westpac deployments recommended that Intruder pilots and B/Ns meet the very highest standards of technical proficiency and airmanship. "The large variety of missions coupled with the night and weather conditions at low altitudes and an unparalleled defensive environment, has placed unprecedented demands on the knowledge, skills and adaptability of flight crews," VA-85's 1966 annual command history noted. To get the best pilots and B/Ns, the report stressed the imperative for "only the highest quality inputs, particularly from the training command," who could "be highly motivated to participate in the demanding operations routine to an A-6 squadron" operating in Westpac.[79] Each of the JOs in VA-75 in the spring of 1972 had achieved this record of performance excellence. As LTJG Warren reflected back, "Almost without exception, everyone in the A-6 community got there through a lot of hard work and dedication. They had to fight to get there, and were the cream of the Naval Aviation crop. . . . I was top of my class at VT-10, so I got to BJN [basic jet naviation]. I was top of my class at BJN, so I got A6s. . . . everyone in the A-6 community had to do something similar in order to get there."[80]

The Sunday Punchers of 1972 who worked so hard to win their assignment to the A-6 community now continued to press their efforts to prepare for workups in late February and March 1972, culminating in the Operational Readiness Exercise (ORE) before their scheduled departure for the Med in May. But one essential element of Sunday Puncher life could not be found in any formal Department of the Navy table of organization, hangar, or classroom. Mirroring in structure the squadron's own roster, a VA-75 Officers' Wives club met at least monthly for a host of activities ranging from formal teas to potluck suppers to movie nights to yard sales to "support the troops" rallies. Laura Foote, the CO's wife, served as president, of course, with Minna Earnest, the XO's wife, as vice president. A similar group for enlisted wives, headed by the spouses of the chief petty officers, also supported squadron family activities.

The two wives' groups represented another Old Navy tradition. Spouses of commanders and lieutenant commanders and chief petty officers, to a greater or lesser degree, generally considered their lives an extension of their husbands' careers. They used the pronoun "we" frequently, in acknowledgment that the family—not merely the officer—went and did whatever the Navy told them to do.[81] Most married early, started families, and knew little beyond Navy life. In time, Sue Engel, Linda Jackson, Judy Pieno, and Duddie Graustein came to enjoy much of it, just as Laura Foote had done, even with its frequent moves and uprooting of lives. While their husbands flew, they kept the home fires burning, raised the children, and tried hard not to send domestic problems into the cockpits. When their husbands returned, they provided a welcoming home. They accepted, with a few qualms, the fundamental truth of a well-known aphorism about their husbands' first true love: "He is married to naval aviation. It is true that whenever he cannot fly he thinks I am the greatest thing since peanut butter. But when he can go flying, then I become just another ray of sunshine for a man who owns the world."[82] They learned, too, that as their husbands won promotions, the Navy expected more leadership from their spouses. Some participated in family support activities for the squadron, airwing, or base, while others volunteered with the Red Cross or Navy Relief, to help the families of enlisted personnel with financial problems, health issues, and family emergencies.[83]

Duddie Graustein received a very typical welcome to military life, beginning even before her future husband graduated from the Naval Academy. During Midshipman Graustein's first class year in 1960–61, she obtained a copy of Florence Ridgely Johnson's *Welcome Aboard: A Service Manual for the Naval Officer's Wife.* "It became my bible," she admitted, and she leaned on it heavily to learn about naval customs and traditions and looked to it for advice on "a wife's place in the Navy." After their move to Virginia Beach when her husband joined VA-75, she became a substitute teacher, but she took no assignment that interfered with squadron events.[84] She admitted that she held nothing against wives who worked outside the home, but she did not understand why the spouses of some of the squadron's JOs did not attend evening meetings after work. The most visible trappings of the days of calling cards and the wearing of gloves of a length suiting one's husband's rank had faded, but tradition had not died entirely.

But much had changed by 1972. Just the previous year, the local newspaper triggered heated debate with its special feature, "Just How Liberated Are Navy Wives?" The writer suggested that while few service wives would call themselves "women's liberationists," they "are often more liberated than their civilian counterparts," in large part because "they've had to be. . . . They've had to go out and do things when their husbands are gone." Interviews revealed a wide range of gendered complaints about the way the service treated them, including the disrespectful nature of the word "dependent," the inconvenience to working wives of daytime-only commissary and medical clinic hours, their inability to obtain information about abortion and family planning at military medical facilities, the cliquishness of the wives' clubs, and even a lingering sense that "Navy wives are viewed as property."[85]

The wives of some of the Sunday Punchers' heavies already had begun to break with tradition. At squadron parties, CDR Foote baited Bobbe Lindland, who worked outside the home, with comments like "I control you," a very unsubtle reminder that her behavior might influence his evaluations, which could help or hurt her husband's career. Such a comment from a CO a decade earlier might have convinced a dutiful spouse to accept a more traditional role, but Bobbe retorted to Foote's jests with the challenge that she would like to see him try to make her bend to his will.[86] Flight attendant Sharon Schram still continued to meet her full schedule of hops.

If such changes had just begun to infiltrate the ranks of the wives of the squadron heavies, the spouses of the JOs—especially those whose husbands did not plan on naval careers—far more clearly worked from a different set of priorities. While many proved quite willing to participate in squadron activities when they made their own decision to join in, they did not respond well when pressured to do so. The phrase "my husband joined the Navy—I didn't" became common among wives who pursued their own careers and accorded them top priority in the allocation of their time and effort. Others simply did not like the politics or "lack of democracy" of the wives' group. Stephanie Knapp, wife of LT Ken Knapp, considered it "hilarious" that the CO's wife automatically served as president and the XO's wife became vice president. To young wives still new to Navy ways this simply was not intuitively obvious.[87] Some adjusted easily to their husbands' love of flying, while others reached a level of acceptance in time. Others never accepted a secondary role as a "ray of sunshine." Regardless, even if they did not choose to become actively involved in the officers' wives' club, none cut their ties completely. During deployments especially, important news often arrived most quickly through the wives' club telephone tree, providing a modicum of security otherwise absent.[88] On 22 February 1972, those information channels activated as the Sunday Punchers departed Oceana for training aboard *Saratoga*, all part of the ongoing preparations for their May departure to the Med.

The squadron's deployment automatically changed the way it conducted its daily business. As long as it remained in Virginia Beach, VA-75—and all East Coast A-6 squadrons—reported to a larger administrative unit, Medium Attack Wing One (MATWING ONE), established in the fall of 1971. If the Sunday Punchers lost a plane, they requested a new one through MATWING ONE. When the squadron faced personnel issues—a need for additional aircrews or replacements to fill gaps in its enlisted ranks—MATWING ONE would attempt to supply the need. Since the CO of MATWING ONE served also as the CO of VA-42, the East Coast RAG, he had a direct link to the personnel pipeline. If an accident resulted in the death or injury of a squadron member in stateside training or while deployed, officers from MATWING ONE handled the notification of the family and, in the case of training accidents, investigated the incident.

MATWING ONE also facilitated supply and maintenance efforts. In addition to its service as instructors to future A-6 pilots and B/Ns, VA-42 operated the A-6

Fleet Replacement Aviation Maintenance Program (FRAMP). All enlisted personnel in aviation ratings slated to join an East Coast A-6 fleet squadron reported to Oceana first for FRAMP training, and by 1972, the program was producing approximately 800 graduates annually. One A-6 veteran who worked with the program's graduates in the early 1970s offered especially high praise: "I was amazed at how well these people performed under the most adverse conditions. When they leave VA-42, they are *really* ready for the fleet."[89] Such news gladdened VA-75's senior leadership. In late winter 1972, VA-75 suffered from a lack of skilled mechanics and technicians. Many experienced sailors had left the squadron since the 1971 Med cruise, and nearly 50 percent of the sailors assigned to VA-75's maintenance billets in mid-February 1972 were "new to the Navy." Just before deploying on workups, LCDR Lindland had to forge new maintenance teams at a time when he also had five aircraft due for Periodic Aircraft Rework (PAR) modifications, and maintenance control had scheduled six more planes for stripping and repainting. All squadron aircraft still required extensive additional work on their electronic countermeasures (ECM) gear, as well. MATWING ONE provided the Sunday Punchers with needed skilled manpower.[90]

MATWING ONE's assistance proved essential now for another reason, too. Over the past few years, Grumman had developed several additional versions of the A-6 on the same general airframe. Beginning in 1967, the A-6B came on line, and VA-75 now had two of these "missile birds" designed to suppress surface-to-air missile tracking and guidance radars. With an ordnance load of air-to-ground missiles, most notably the AGM-78 (usually called the Standard Anti-Radiation Missile or simply STARM) and the shorter-ranged AGM-45 called the Shrike, they could not only shut down SAM sites—with a good hit, they could destroy the vans holding the missiles' radars. The Sunday Punchers also flew the KA-6D tanker version of the A-6. Grumman introduced an A-6C variant with Trails, Roads, Interdiction Multi-Sensor (TRIM) technology, but VA-75 possessed none of these aircraft.[91] Still, with the original A-6A strike aircraft and the newer A-6B and KA-6D to keep flying, LCDR Lindland's maintenance challenge had grown more complex than ever.

Once VA-75's aircraft flew off Oceana's runways, however, VA-75 maintained only an administrative link to MATWING ONE as it rejoined its operational command: Attack Carrier Airwing Three (CVW-3). On 22 February 1972, the Sunday Punchers trapped aboard *Saratoga* and met the airwing's new CAG, a man already familiar to many in the A-6 community. CDR Richard P. "Deke" Bordone, whose call sign was "Guinea One," had just replaced CDR Gillcrist earlier in the month. A native of Pittsburgh and a 1954 graduate of the U.S. Naval Academy, he knew VA-75's history quite well. After surviving the downing of his A-6A in July 1965, Bordone had returned to the squadron in 1968 to serve as the

The USS Saratoga *(CVA-60), from whose flight deck the Sunday Punchers launched into the hostile skies over Vietnam. This photo shows approximately half the number of aircraft assigned to Airwing Three (CVW-3) during the 1972–1973 combat cruise spotted on the flight deck. The spiral-topped E-2B Hawkeyes stand out. The A-7 Corsairs of VA-37 and VA-105 line the port side at the stern of the ship. The long and slender RA-5C reconnaissance aircraft are the largest planes in the picture. The pointed noses of the F-4s of the VF-31 and VF-103 can be picked out along the port side amidship, mixing in with some of VA-75's A-6s, the rounded bulbous radome that shapes each Intruder's nose clearly visible. (John R. Fuller Collection)*

Sunday Punchers' XO and then, from 25 July 1969 until 3 July 1970, as its skipper. Since his earliest connection to VA-75, his reputation—as colorful as it was genuine—included stories that attested to his achievements as a golfer, a drinker, and a prankster, but most of all as a warrior.[92] In addition to the A-6s of VA-75, Bordone's airwing included two squadrons of A-7A Corsairs, two squadrons of F-4J Phantoms, the RA-5C Vigilante reconnaissance aircraft of RVAH-1, the E-2B Hawkeyes of VAW-123, the S-2E Trackers of VS-28, and the SH-3D Sea King helicopters of HS-7.[93] He had to forge these squadrons into an integrated team to execute the multiple missions of a CV-concept carrier. That included an ongoing effort to resolve each aircraft's unique supply and maintenance issues to maximize mission readiness.

Aboard *Saratoga,* CDR Bordone reported to CAPT James R. Sanderson, the carrier's skipper since 7 August 1971. Sanderson, himself a veteran aviator, had commanded CVW-3 earlier in his career and came to *Saratoga* after a successful tenure as CO of USS *Rainier.* His new command, a fixture in the Atlantic Fleet since its christening in October 1956, belonged to the *Forrestal* class of carriers. It stretched for 990 feet at the waterline, and the flight deck—which towered 67 feet above the water line—was 252 feet wide. Four Westinghouse turbine engines powered by eight Babcock & Whitney boilers could generate 280,000 horsepower, and *Saratoga* could steam at "30-plus knots." It contained a 64-bed medical facility, 2,300 telephones, and over 10,000 miles of electrical wiring. Typical ship's company numbered 2,800 officers and men, but when CVW-3 came aboard, the carrier's population jumped to over 5,000.[94]

The carrier's recent performance had not been impressive. Maintenance problems plagued the carrier, and during the 1971 Med cruise, it nearly sank in the port at Athens. It took a month to fix the carrier then, and her crew began calling her the "Sorry Sara." The squadrons launched from the ship at anchor—no mean feat—and VA-75 had tried to make up training time at the American naval air station at Rota, Spain. Sufficient repairs done on-site permitted the completion of the 1971 cruise, but the workups in February and March 1972 leading to the ORE (operational readiness exercise) late that month would provide the first conclusive evidence of the carrier's seaworthiness before its departure for the Med.[95]

Saratoga and CVW-3 performed its workups off the coast of Florida, not far from Jacksonville and Mayport, the carrier's home port. The exercises took place in three phases. During the first phase, 22 February until 2 March, VA-75's pilots and B/Ns updated their carrier qualifications. At one point *Saratoga* steamed into a fog bank and several crews diverted to Cecil Field in Florida and returned the next day. After the completion of the carrier qualifications, three Sunday Puncher JOs who took part in the 1971 Med cruise—LTs Fischer and Anderson and LTJG Mullins—qualified as *Saratoga* "centurions," validating that they each had made 100 arrested landings on that carrier.[96] CVW-3 also provided air support for the evaluation of new equipment tested by USS *Biddle* before *Saratoga* steamed for Norfolk to host the change-of-command ceremony to install VADM Frederick H. Michaelis as the new commanding officer of Naval Air Forces Atlantic (NAVAIRLANT).

The second element of the spring training period, 7 through 16 March, concentrated on mastering antishipping strike tactics, part of *Saratoga*'s new mission as a CV. Over the course of these few days, ten more Sunday Puncher JOs became centurions. Appropriate ceremonies followed, with CDR Bordone and CAPT Sanderson in attendance, and—as the squadron familygram reported— the accomplishment became "the excuse for the procuring of a large cake to celebrate the event in the ready room."

The familygram's editor also reported, "The large size of this group indicates the high level of experience of the aircrews VA-75 is preparing to deploy with."[97] He emphasized an important point. VA-75 included many cruise-experienced pilots and B/Ns who already had functioned as part of an A-6 crew. The heavies already had begun to team each newly arrived "nugget" pilot and B/N with a veteran of at least one extended period at sea. At the conclusion of this week's effort, evaluations demonstrated the benefits of experience. As the airwing's 1972 command history noted, "The Wing Intelligence Team in concert with RVAH-1 and VA-75 completed . . . competitive exercises with overall grades of outstanding."[98]

On the surface of things, the Sunday Punchers had continued to meet high standards of performance. But a look behind the scenes revealed some disquieting contradictions. LT Fischer wondered about the validity of the evaluation when, to recover from a night tanker hop safely, he had to use a piece of gum for a marker on his vertical display indicator (VDI). "A million dollar plane?!?" he questioned in his diary.[99] On 17 March, LTJG Warren delivered an emergency telegram to LTJG Lerseth, bearing the sad and unexpected news of the death of the latter's father in Spokane. Lerseth's quick departure for home created a problem for CDR Foote. In January, the JO had attended a short course at mining school, and the CO expected him to apply his new expertise to one specific element in the last phase of their training: a mining exercise near the mouth of the harbor at Charleston, South Carolina. Foote now stormed up to LTJG Petersen and ordered him to take over. Petersen promised to do his best, but Foote came down hard on him, once again reminding a squadron JO that his fitness report hung in the balance. If VA-75—and Foote—got low marks for their performance, Petersen would pay the price. Several other JOs witnessed the exchange, and it did little to inspire confidence.[100]

Even worse, as *Saratoga* entered the third phase of the workups, as Fischer's recent experience suggested, the Sunday Punchers' aircraft just did not seem to

Sunday Puncher junior officers celebrate their new status as Saratoga *"centurions" in their ready room, after making their one-hundredth arrested landing aboard the carrier in March 1972. From left to right: LT Thomas E. Wharton, LT Ronny D. Lankford, LT Thomas C. "Kit" Ruland, LT John M. Miller, LTJG Roger G. Lerseth, LTJG John R. Fuller, LTJG Robert F. Miller, LT Kenneth K. Knapp. (U.S. Navy photograph, Everett W. Foote Collection)*

be performing at all well. "I'd just like to go somewhere where things aren't so Mickey Mouse," LTJG Fuller complained. After nearly seventeen hops over the past few weeks, he had not flown one in which his navigation and weapons systems had worked properly. Worse, he worried, "nobody with any authority gives a damn. As long as the skipper can launch a tanker and make CAG happy he could [not] care [less] about systems." Appealing to CDR Earnest would make no difference because "the XO doesn't believe in the A-6 anyway so he's no help." Fuller's frustration boiled over to the point where he gave in to hyperbole: "I almost wish I'd gone F-4s."[101]

Fuller touched on a key concern that troubled many JOs in VA-75. Those who had belonged only to the A-6 community knew their aircraft and its capabilities well. They appreciated what an A-6A with a "full-up system" could do. If hitting targets at low level, day or night, in any kind of weather lay at the core of the A-6 mission, then they questioned the squadron's readiness and professionalism if the upkeep and maintenance of those systems did not claim a top priority. In the minds of many JOs, the squadron's more senior A-6 pilots and B/Ns—whether from the frustration borne of experience in attempting to keep systems functioning properly, or from previous tours with less technically sophisticated aircraft—did not seem to place the same importance on systems readiness they did, and they could not understand why. Reflecting back on the occasion, LCDR Pieno admitted that the heavies flew many less-than-perfect planes to meet the Sunday Punchers' sortie obligations, in large part because they did not care to admit to CAG Bordone that VA-75 lacked sufficient mission-ready aircraft to pull their weight.[102] Few JOs, however, comprehended why the heavies considered the squadron's performance in workups to be more important than maintaining full-system aircraft capable of accomplishing the A-6's core mission. "We must look good, although the thought of being good remains in the background," LT Fischer complained.[103]

Through the period extending from 21 until 30 March, *Saratoga* and CVW-3 yet again practiced antisubmarine tactics. VA-75, along with the airwing's two A-7 squadrons and its two F-4 squadrons, participated in an exercise to sink the ex-USS *Gansevoort*. The final three days of the exercise concluded with the ORE. On 29 March, LT Fischer worried, "The squadron is trying but I don't believe we are doing well."[104] Still, when the evaluations were announced, *Saratoga* and CVW-3 received an overall grade of "outstanding."[105] Even more astounding, despite the JOs' concerns about their systems, the Sunday Punchers flew all their scheduled sorties, and, in the end, won recognition as the top squadron in CVW-3 with a grade of "High Excellent."[106]

At the end of March, after much hard work, the Sunday Punchers turned their thoughts to their families and friends. The spring days promised good times ahead before the start of their six-month deployment in May. "Soon, we will return to Oceana for a short period before another Summer Cruise to the Mediterranean Sea," wrote CDR Foote to those at home who read the Sunday Punchers' spring familygram. He congratulated everyone and thanked them all for their contributions to the squadron's good showing in the ORE. He ended his missive with a promise: "We will make every effort to spend this time with our families and to enjoy a well deserved rest."[107]

CHAPTER TWO

"Temporary Additional Duty"

"Don't pick up that phone!" LT Alan G. Fischer warned his friend. But he spoke too late. She had picked up the receiver. That telephone call changed Fischer's life forever, and that scene—or one much like it—replayed itself in the homes and quarters of Sunday Punchers several hundred times more during the weekend of 8–9 April 1972. Those telephone calls summoned VA-75 to war.[1]

On 30 March 1972, the North Vietnamese Army, supported by heavy artillery and armored columns, flooded southward over the DMZ in great numbers, cutting into South Vietnam's northernmost provinces and heading for cities and towns long familiar to Americans, places such as Quang Tri, Hue, and Danang. A week later, from Cambodian and Laotian bases, more North Vietnamese columns knifed through the Annamese mountains into the Central Highlands, heading for the key towns of Pleiku and Kontum. Farther south, yet another force left Cambodian sanctuaries to advance toward Tay Ninh and An Loc, threatening Saigon. In time, a fourth North Vietnamese offensive launched into the fertile Mekong Delta.

Only the exact jump-off time of the Nguyen Hue operation—quickly dubbed by the American media as the "Easter Offensive"—caused a bit of surprise. Intelligence activities already had revealed many signs of the North Vietnamese buildup. In late 1971, sensors emplaced along the Ho Chi Minh Trail picked up dramatically increased activity. Reconnaissance flights uncovered substantial truck and tank parks in southern North Vietnam and close to the trail, including some located farther south than ever before. North Vietnamese troops were moving southward in greater numbers, and intelligence reports identified units not previously deployed to the South. Captured political documents suggested strongly that the North Vietnamese leadership had decided that the time had come to set aside their commitment to prolonged small-unit conflict for conventional large-scale offensives conducted by heavily armed divisions. General Creighton Abrams, commanding the Military Assistance Command–Vietnam (MACV), reported to his superiors at the Pentagon in January 1972 that all the signs pointed to "a major military action by the North in South

Vietnam during the weeks ahead," one with the potential to become "the maximum military effort the North is capable of making."[2]

President Richard M. Nixon needed no convincing. Already, on 26–30 December 1971, he had approved a limited resumption of bombing against North Vietnamese targets extending up to the 20th parallel, just seventy-five miles south of Hanoi. Air assets from Air Force bases in Thailand and from carriers in the Gulf of Tonkin had executed a limited series of strike missions, dubbed Operation PROUD DEEP, to hit supply depots, surface-to-air missile (SAM) sites, and other targets that might disrupt or delay the offensive. A series of controversial "protective reactions strikes" ordered by Seventh Air Force commander General John D. Lavelle—until his relief in March—hit North Vietnamese airfields and air defenses in late 1971 and early 1972. Despite Lavelle's removal, however, the number of authorized monthly B-52 sorties rose by 20 percent in early 1972, and additional strategic bombers arrived at Andersen Air Force Base on Guam. The Air Force made plans to increase its tactical air assets in Southeast Asia as well. Dubbed COMMANDO FLASH, during the first three months of 1972, additional squadrons of F-4s arrived at air bases in South Vietnam and Thailand. Naval air and sea assets in the Pacific Fleet went on alert, USS *Kitty Hawk* deployed to Westpac three weeks earlier than scheduled, and in Washington, the armed services began to design a range of possible responses if the North Vietnamese launched their threatened invasion of the South. For them, the question centered not on *whether* they would respond to North Vietnam's actions, but *how*.[3]

Military planners had kept in mind political realities, however. Already thinking ahead to the November elections, President Nixon in January declared his Vietnamization policy such a grand success that he expressed confidence that he could meet his 1 May goal for reducing the number of American ground troops in Vietnam to 69,000. Still pursuing a diplomatic settlement as well—even though nothing had come from Henry Kissinger's private peace negotiations with Le Duc Tho and Xuan Thuy in Paris—Nixon now revealed the secret exchanges, noting, "Nothing is served by silence when the other side exploits our good faith to divide America and to avoid the conference table. Nothing is served by silence when it misleads some Americans into accusing their own government of failing to do what it has already done."[4] The Pentagon understood that any military response to the expected offensive had to protect the president's commitment to continue the withdrawal of American ground troops, hit with sufficient power to support ARVN defenders and the government of President Nguyen Van Thieu, and punish the North Vietnamese for their aggression. Airpower played the central role in that planning.[5]

During the first few days of the Nguyen Hue Offensive, largely due to bad weather, the Air Force and naval air assets already in place in Southeast Asia did little to slow the North Vietnamese attacks. On 3 April, in a meeting with the Joint Chiefs of Staff, Nixon "really banged [Chairman of the JSC, ADM Thomas] Moorer around . . . on the Air Force's inability to get moving," presidential adviser H. R. Haldeman recorded. Thus, Nixon decided to start amassing an even greater concentration of air and sea power in the Gulf of Tonkin and at air bases in Thailand and Guam. He also planned to expand the use of B-52s deep into North Vietnam's heartland as soon as the weather permitted.[6]

Nixon's renewed interest in wielding "the air weapon" came at a time of significant public debate about its efficacy. In March 1972, in the introduction to a newly published and highly praised study on the use of airpower in Southeast Asia, produced by the Air War Study Group of the Cornell University Program on Peace Studies, journalist Neil Sheehan had noted that in each of the past few months American military aircraft had dropped an average of 55,000 tons of bombs. Few Americans protested, however, because "the public has appeared to sense the existence of the Indochina war in proportion to the number of American ground combat troops in South Vietnam and to the casualties they suffer in the ground fighting there." As the withdrawal of American ground forces continued and casualty rates continued to fall, "the war has seemed to be going away."[7]

Even before the start of the Nguyen Hue Offensive, however, the Cornell study warned that the president could reinvigorate the entire war effort by turning to air power. "One of the tactical advantages of air power, in fact, is that it can be turned on and off, up or down, with a simple order from the White House," Sheehan asserted. If he proved to be correct, this administration had a free hand to act with little risk of negative political repercussions. "The air war seems to be perceived by the American public only intermittently, when the Administration varies the pattern of raids over South Vietnam, Cambodia, and Laos with a series of heavy strikes against North Vietnam itself for military or psychological purposes," Sheehan wrote, adding cynically, "Even then, once the initial brouhaha subsides, those pilots who survive the downing of their planes by anti-aircraft fire and are captured become objects of pity and patriotic outrage which the Administration has been able to exploit to its advantage with the public."[8] The great folly of it all, of course, followed from the study's findings that bombing probably would not produce the desired result of ending the war on terms acceptable to the United States.

The Sunday Punchers paid close attention to military developments in Southeast Asia, especially as rumors spread throughout the squadron that *Saratoga* and its airwing might be added to the buildup. At a February barbecue, LCDR

Ted Been—operations officer of VA-42, the East Coast A-6 RAG—talked at length with LCDR Don Lindland about recent developments in Southeast Asia and the possibilities that VA-75 might soon head for Westpac.[9] The discussion grew animated, but it remained in the realm of "what ifs."

By Thursday, 6 April, the Sunday Punchers mostly had returned to their hangar at Oceana, fresh from *Saratoga*'s successful ORE. Squadron personnel turned their efforts to preparations for an Administrative Material Inspection scheduled for mid-April.[10] The squadron's most junior pilot, LTJG Bob Tolhurst, a 1969 graduate of the Naval Academy and record-setting pole vaulter on its plebe track team, served as Squadron Duty Officer (SDO) that day. When CAG Bordone called for CDR Foote, Tolhurst could not locate his skipper right away. But within the hour, Foote returned the call. Bordone posed some hard questions, the most pointed one asking how quickly VA-75 could be ready to leave on an emergency deployment. That discussion left Foote uneasy. His corrosion control teams already had begun to strip down the aircraft for the freshwater wash-down required after extended operations in a saltwater environment. His check crew and other maintenance teams also had broken down several more planes scheduled for calendar inspection or for some phase of PAR (Periodic Aircraft Rework) modification. Airplane parts lay scattered on the hangar floor.[11]

All that Thursday, rumors of an impending emergency deployment continued to spread. CDR Foote called a special All Officers Meeting (AOM) early on Friday, 7 April, to address the speculation. Those who read that morning's Norfolk newspaper noted that, while the Pentagon refused to make any official statements, "it was understood that still more planes will be sent into Vietnam." As ADM Moorer vowed, "We are not going to permit them [North Vietnam] to have a free ride in providing resources to the battlefield. So long as the battle currently going on is supported, we will attack the support for this operation."[12] LTJG Paul Hvidding recalled that the skipper characterized the credibility of the various rumors sending VA-75 to war as "extremely thin."[13] Still, since the possibility could not be dismissed out of hand, the squadron's four combat veterans—CDRs Foote and Earnest and LCDRs Lindland and Schram—talked about their previous experiences. Everyone listened intently to each lesson they imparted, and some left with a heightened sense of concern when CDR Foote warned them to keep the subject of the meeting to themselves.

Later on that Friday afternoon, however, the mood seemed far more positive. LT Terry Anderson recalled Foote walking through the hangar to assure everyone that all his contacts in Washington told him "on the ding-a-ling"—one of the CO's frequently used phrases, accompanied by his "talking" into an imaginary telephone receiver—that there was "no chance" that VA-75 would be sent to Vietnam.[14] Foote told LT Ken Pyle and other officers still present at midafternoon to go home and enjoy the weekend. Pyle, a high-ranking graduate of the U.S. Naval Academy's class of 1968 who had just joined VA-75 after graduate school and pilot training, intended to do just that. But he left the hangar with a sense of foreboding that he could not dismiss. He and his wife, Sandy, went to see *The Godfather* that night as planned, but he could not concentrate on the movie. Sandy noticed "an underlying tension that just wasn't right," but, following his skipper's admonition, Pyle did not explain to his wife the reasons for his distraction.[15]

Foote's optimism lasted only until he arrived home on Friday afternoon. CAPT Sanderson, *Saratoga*'s skipper, already had phoned once, and even as Foote reached for the receiver to dial, he called back. He apparently knew nothing of the earlier conversation between Bordone and Foote, and he too mentioned nothing specific about Vietnam, but he asked the same question: How soon can your squadron be ready to deploy? Foote replied that it depended on how much help he could get to rebuild his aircraft. Sanderson assured him that, if needed, he would get all he required.

That short and relatively cryptic chat soon ended, but the implications seemed clear enough to Foote. He immediately called CDR Charlie Earnest, his XO. "There was nothing I kept from him," Foote later explained. He also tried to find LCDR Jim Kennedy, the squadron's experienced Maintenance Limited Duty Officer (LDO), but could not locate him. In the last few weeks before the scheduled deployment to the Med, family time remained a precious commodity to most of Foote's officers and men. The Kennedy family had endured many long separations since he had enlisted in 1951, and they already had departed for a long-anticipated camping trip to North Carolina. Hedging their bets, Foote and Earnest decided to act without Kennedy and ordered some of the squadron's maintenance chiefs and technicians to return to the hangar on Saturday to start rebuilding the dismantled aircraft. Foote also alerted his department heads to prepare for the possibility of an emergency deployment.

If Foote talked to his XO and senior subordinates immediately, he told his wife, Laura, nothing at all, at least for the time. He saw no point in distressing her unless he received orders. If his suspicion played out, Foote knew he might be heading to Vietnam for the third time, and he knew that Laura "had had it with losses and combat."[16]

On Saturday, 8 April, at 1700, *Saratoga*'s Emergency Recall Bill was activated.[17] LTJG Bob Miller served as squadron duty officer, expecting a long, dull day since "being the SDO on a weekend after shakedown and before deployment is never a favorite task." When CAG Bordone called the ready room this time, he gave Miller very precise instructions: Call CDR Foote, tell him to get as many aircraft as possible ready for immediate departure, transport your enlisted men and equipment to Mayport to board *Saratoga*, and plan to fly aboard the carrier at sea after its scheduled departure at 0800 on Tuesday morning, 11 April. "It had been a pleasantly boring day before the CAG called," Miller recalled, "and a real mess after."[18]

VA-75—aircraft, personnel, and their families—now had a maximum of sixty hours to prepare for departure. Many had much less time than that. The emergency recall order brought several days of chaos to all the Sunday Punchers and their loved ones. They all had much to do and little time to think. At first glance, the task seemed nearly impossible. *Saratoga* itself had just returned to its base at Mayport earlier that day. Within hours of its arrival, CAPT Sanderson received positive orders to prepare for immediate redeployment westward, its final destination still kept officially secret. The recall instructions issued to the ship's company included vague wording to report "for temporary additional duty in connection with an operational deployment for an indefinite period."[19] Since *Saratoga*'s size prevented its transit through the Panama Canal, Sanderson told his navigator to chart a 13,000-mile course across the Atlantic, around the Cape of Good Hope, and through the Indian Ocean to the Philippines. "A carrier is normally given up to a month to make the necessary preparations for deployment," wrote a navy journalist who observed the quickening pace of activity in Mayport.[20] Sanderson did not have a month.

Back at Oceana, CDR Foote's hunches had paid off. Several department heads had arrived at the hangar before the recall order arrived. They immediately called in some of the pilots and B/Ns who lived close to the base for help in rounding up squadron personnel and with other preparations. Some of the chief petty officers already had arrived at the hangar to do the same thing. Chief Aviation Mechanic Wright Cade, Jr., of the Power Plants Branch got the word from a friend serving in the airwing's E-2B squadron. He and other VA-75 chiefs began calling in their sailors, telling those who could not return to Oceana by 10 April for the airlift to Florida to go straight to Mayport.[21]

One by one, the Puncher officers checked in at the squadron's hangar at Oceana. Most came in response to a call that stirred their curiosity as much as it heightened their concerns. The exchange between LCDR Lindland and LTJG John Fuller represented the typical notification. When the operations officer informed Fuller of the emergency recall for "training," the Michigan-born B/N asked him where they were going. Lindland replied that he could not say. When Fuller pressed him, asking specifically if they might be headed to Vietnam, Lindland once again repeated that he could not say.[22] Most Punchers received similarly vague summonses.

When he received orders to come in, LTJG Hvidding resisted the temptation to confide to his wife his concerns about the various rumors discussed at the Friday meeting. Even now, he explained his return to the base by citing the official account given in the recall order read to him over the phone—that *Saratoga* would head out for "training." Then he cancelled their babysitter and drove into the base.[23] LTJG Doug Ahrens, the squadron's Material Control Branch officer, also answered an early call to the center hangar to assist with packing the initial shipment of VA-75's supplies and equipment in preparation for a Sunday airlift to Mayport. The flurry of activity that greeted him spoke volumes.[24] He did not tell his wife, Linda, the reason for his unusual weekend trip to base, either. He waited until he returned home that evening, and finding her in the kitchen making spaghetti sauce, he broke the news there. They ate dinner in silence, Linda's tears falling into the sauce she had just made.[25]

LT Tom Wharton had just returned from a movie and a pizza with LT Paul H. Wagner, when the "in-house" phone in his BOQ room rang. He kept two phone lines: a personal one for friends, which he always answered, and the standard line connected to the main desk of the BOQ, which he usually ignored. This time, however, he answered it. LCDR Don Boecker told Wharton, the squadron's Communications Branch officer, to return to the hangar to deal with incoming messages. Wharton could not fathom the reason for so much message traffic on a weekend. Then Boecker enlightened him: "Haven't you heard? We're going to war."[26]

For one man at a time, one family at a time, the phone calls disrupted plans and changed some lives forever. LCDR Grady Jackson, the Sunday Punchers' senior B/N, had gone with his wife, Linda, to a coffee hosted by the Community United Methodist Church in Virginia Beach that Saturday morning. During that gathering, many of those present shared deeply personal stories about family or health problems that had led them to a closer relationship with Jesus Christ. When it came Linda's turn to speak, she reaffirmed her strong belief in God, but said, "I really haven't had any personal tragedies." A few hours later, a phone call sent LCDR Jackson off to war.[27]

LTJG Jay Swigart and his wife, Penny, dined with civilian friends that Saturday evening. As they enjoyed their coffee, their host's phone rang, and he beckoned the squadron's junior B/N to take the call. Before they left the Friday meeting, CDR Foote had reminded all officers to remember to leave emergency contact numbers for the weekend, not because he expected orders but simply to follow standard administrative procedure. Although the Princeton graduate did not pick up the receiver with undue concern, when he hung up, Penny recalled later, "he just had a look on his face." He told her he had to pack to leave in a few days, but she simply refused to believe him.[28]

LTJG Roger Lerseth got the call just as he and his wife, Jean—better known as Nini—greeted their guests for a long-planned backyard barbeque. When he hung up, he told Nini only that plans had changed and that he had to pack and report to the squadron's hangar on Sunday morning. Their guests, a veteran chief and his wife, apparently understood the implications of such an order, and they quickly made their excuses and left.[29]

LTJG Dave Warren and his wife, Carol, attended an art auction that Saturday at the Oceana Officers' Club, one of their first social functions since joining the squadron a few months previously. Although Warren had served over ten years in the Navy, mostly as an enlisted man, VA-75 was the B/N's first assignment to a fleet squadron. The two enjoyed the auction immensely until Warren, too, got called to the phone. When he hung up, he simply told Carol that he had to go home and pack.[30]

"I thought it was a big joke," Pixie Tolhurst remembered when she thought back on the day LTJG Tolhurst got the call.[31] Many of the Sunday Punchers' wives had looked forward to a formal squadron dance scheduled just before *Saratoga* deployed in May. Harkening back to their high school days, they invariably called it "the prom." When the phones began to ring in several VA-75 homes in one block of a Virginia Beach neighborhood, LT John Miller's wife, Diane, sounded one of the day's few lighter notes when she hollered over to LT Ron Lankford's wife, Loretta, to ask, "Does this mean the prom's cancelled?"[32]

Delivering the recall order to squadron personnel who left the Virginia Beach area on weekend liberty proved far more challenging. LTJG Don Petersen dialed the phone number in New York City that one of the enlisted men had left as his point of contact. When no one on the receiving end spoke English, he had to call the local police station to find an officer who could speak Spanish to deliver the recall order.[33] In North Carolina, a park ranger located the campsite of the VA-75 maintenance LDO and growled, "You Kennedy?" Within minutes after the gruff ranger delivered his message, the family had repacked their gear and headed north.[34]

LT Kit Ruland, a former lineman who had played football for the Naval Academy, had taken his wife, Brigid, to her sister's home in northern Virginia. As they headed out the door for a nice Saturday evening dinner, the phone rang. The message varied little from that delivered to other officers: Pack your cruise box and return to base for an AOM at 0900 on Sunday. Brigid's father, an admiral, made a few calls and confirmed *Saratoga*'s imminent departure. The Rulands returned to Virginia Beach that night.[35]

LTJG Bill Wardlaw, the squadron's junior air intelligence officer, had taken his wife, June, to Washington to see the cherry blossoms in bloom and to visit Marie and LTJG Richard DuChateau, a fellow air intelligence officer who had just detached from VA-75 after the 1971 Med cruise. The phone rang at almost midnight on Saturday, and DuChateau awoke the Texan to take the call. Wardlaw later recalled, "Probably I've never in my life had a worse feeling in the pit

LCDR Jim Kennedy, VA-75's Maintenance LDO, learned about the emergency recall during a family camping trip when a North Carolina park ranger tracked him down to deliver the message. (Everett W. Foote Collection)

of my stomach than after I got the phone call that night." Nonetheless, he and his wife, four months pregnant with their second child, also left immediately for Virginia Beach.[36]

Two pilots, LTs Anderson and Bruce Cook—one of the Sunday Punchers' so-called "golden boys"—proved to be especially difficult to contact. They had departed on Friday for a weekend cross-country flight to watch a Blue Angels air show at Williams Air Force Base in Arizona. Cook dreamed of flying with them one day soon, and although it was unusual for two pilots to man an A-6, CDR Foote had authorized their flight. Late on Saturday, an airman at the base operations center delivered orders to Anderson to return to Oceana immediately. Their aircraft had developed mechanical trouble during the trip, and they could fly only under Visual Flight Rules (VFR). Nonetheless, and despite breaking numerous regulations in the process, Anderson and Cook arrived early on Sunday, bringing back yet another plane that required the close attention of maintenance crews to ready it for a Tuesday departure.[37]

Saratoga's recall notice also reached out to New Mexico, where LT Fischer and LTJG Jerry Mullins had taken a cross-country flight. CDR Foote had encouraged such treks because they contributed to the squadron's flight-hour goals and kept

The activation of the emergency recall bill on 8 April required all officers to return to Oceana Naval Air Station immediately. The next morning, LT Alan G. Fischer, LT Terry L. Anderson, and LTJG Alden F. "Jerry" Mullins, Jr.—shown here at their Saratoga *centurion ceremony in March 1972—flew Sunday Puncher aircraft back to Virginia from Arizona and New Mexico to prepare for deployment on 11 April. (U.S. Navy photograph, Everett W. Foote Collection)*

costs down, since jets are most fuel-efficient on long flights at high altitude.[38] The two men had flown to Albuquerque to spend the weekend with two sisters, friends of Fischer's family in New Jersey. After an exciting Saturday exploring the mountains, ghost towns, and an Indian village, they were preparing to leave for dinner when the phone rang. The call from Kirkland Air Force Base transmitted an order to return to Oceana on Sunday.[39]

Like the aircraft Anderson and Cook flew cross-country, the plane Fischer and Mullins took also experienced mechanical trouble. On Friday, after refueling at Tinker Air Force Base, the engines had refused to restart until Mullins whacked "something" with a screwdriver. Now, as they prepared to return, small drops of reddish fluid on the ground also alerted them to a small hydraulics leak. Mullins lay on his back underneath the airplane, engine bay door open and screwdriver once more in hand. Despite his best efforts, he could not repeat on Sunday his successful tinkering of Friday. Mullins looked at Fischer, who just shrugged, stared at the instruments, and then watched the engine finally start "for no particular reason at all." Their radio gave out on the way back, but they arrived safely at Oceana early on Sunday afternoon with yet another malfunctioning aircraft that had to be readied to fly aboard *Saratoga* within thirty-six hours.[40]

For years, many of the officers and their wives remembered where they were and what they were doing that Saturday, 8 April, when the deployment order shattered the promise of spring. Even the lack of specificity in the recall turned routine issues into gnawing questions. A problem as fundamental as which uniforms to pack in cruise boxes required serious consideration. Uniform requirements varied by location. "It would still be spring in the Med," LT John Miller had pondered, "but tropical in SEA [South East Asia]."[41] LT Pyle had a more pressing problem. A new arrival into the squadron, he had never been to sea on an extended cruise before. He did not even own a cruise box. He got his first one that day.[42]

In any case, there was much to do and little time to do it. Part of the weekend was devoted to informing their extended families about the change in plans. Some cases required special delicacy. Since his father had just died on 17 March, LTJG Lerseth worried about how to tell his mother in Spokane that now her only son was going off to war. After breaking the news as carefully as he could, he and Nini agreed that if anything happened to him, she would return to Spokane to look after his mother and two younger sisters.[43] Carol Warren worried about how her own mother and father would take the news of LTJG Warren's departure, since her younger brother had been killed in Vietnam in 1968. As she recalled, "More than anything Dave wanted to go and get some revenge. I kept thinking how my parents would feel when they heard he'd gone because they were terrified that if he went he would die" too. As it turned out, LT Fischer did not have to break the news to his parents; when he called home, his father asked him point-blank, "You're going to Vietnam, aren't you?" Fischer tried to pass it all off as rumor to calm his father's fears, but he knew he could not sustain the charade later that day when, while watching the news, he heard Walter Cronkite's deep voice inform the nation that *Saratoga* had begun to prepare for deployment to Southeast Asia.[44]

The parents of two of the officers had chosen that weekend to visit their sons, and they were present when the calls came. LCDR Jackson's parents had been through this before. Since Jackson's father had served in the U.S. Army for thirty-two and one-half years and had participated in the Salerno and Anzio landings in World War II, his mother tried to explain to Linda that all service wives had to learn to accept leave-taking as a part of military life. She reminded Linda that her husband had trained for this eventuality and he had to answer the call to duty. Linda remained unconsoled. As her husband recalled, she seemed absolutely convinced "that she was never going to see me alive again and that she was going to have to raise two children by herself."[45]

The parents of LTJG Ronald D. McFarland, a Texas-born B/N who had made the 1971 Med cruise, also had come to visit that weekend. They had not seen their son and his wife, Shari, since May 1969, and for the first time they met their eighteen-month-old granddaughter, Kelly. After they arrived early on 7 April, McFarland had enjoyed taking his father—who had worked on B-24s as an enlisted man in World War II—on a tour around the base. Watching his father's reaction when he returned the salutes of enlisted men, he remembered, "For one of the first times in my life I saw pride in my dad's eyes." Then he received the phone call to report to the squadron's hangar at 0900 on Sunday with his cruise box packed. Stunned, he sat down to a newscast about Nixon's plan to intensify the bombing of North Vietnam. McFarland's mother and father shared glances that seemed to him to say, "Is this the last time we are going to see our son?" He, too, wondered if God had sent them to Virginia Beach that weekend to say good-bye.[46]

Just as the squadron members found it difficult to tell their parents, those who were themselves parents had to tell children about their impending departures. The prospect never seemed easy. The children of career navy men, already used to the long absences of their fathers, seemed better able to handle it. LCDR Bob Graustein and his wife, Duddie, felt fortunate that their three sons, aged 6, 7, and 10, took the unexpected change in schedule in stride. After all, this would be Graustein's third tour to Southeast Asia. Still, they both knew that, for the first time, he would go directly into harm's way on a regular basis. He spent as much time as he could that weekend playing basketball and talking to his sons, but they did not seem to understand the gravity of the situation. Six-year-old Kent's most vivid memory of those hectic days centered on the fun he had jumping off the bar stools onto his father's packed duffel bag.[47] The squadron's new fathers took the orders especially hard. LTJG Hvidding, who had become a father for the first time in January 1972, confided to his diary during those last few April evenings at home, "I found myself peeking in on Jennifer more often than ever, realizing how different she would be when I saw her again."[48] LTJG Tolhurst reflected on the potential impact of his quick departure on his one-year-old daughter, Kim. In one of his first letters home, he admitted to Pixie just how difficult it had been for him to leave his daughter. "I really feel sorry for Kim because she just can't understand what is going on," he wrote.[49]

Myrna Smith, wife of Chief Warrant Officer Howard P. Smith, had left town on Friday for a kindergarten teacher workshop. When she got home on Sunday afternoon, she saw her husband's half-filled cruise box in the foyer. She asked Gary, the oldest of their three sons, where his father had gone. Gary replied that he only knew that CDR Earnest had called and that "dad didn't even put on his uniform and said he had to go to the squadron." Myrna had not read a newspaper in several days, but a quick scan of the Sunday headlines suggested that Smitty, who had followed family tradition and joined the Navy in 1956 immediately after graduation from Taylor-Allderdice High School in Pittsburgh, soon would leave for his third Westpac tour. If young Gary did not seem too disturbed by the prospect, Myrna's thoughts centered immediately on three things: the safety of her husband and other friends in the squadron, the difficulty of raising three sons alone for an unspecified period of time, and the prospect of handling alone the family's impending move into a new house they had just built.[50] LCDR John Pieno's family, including four children, also looked forward to moving into a new house when contractors finished it in July. He and Judy immediately began to line up help to handle the move.[51]

The sudden change in plans particularly unnerved those families facing their first extended separation. Carol Warren wondered how their three young children would react to the news that their father's first cruise would take him to war, but she chose to believe that children imitate their parents. She determined to hide her fears. They already had tried to prepare the children for Warren's departure on the Med cruise long scheduled for May, so Carol determined to tell them only that their father had to leave earlier than planned and that he was not going to the Med. Then, she hoped, they would just make the best of it.[52]

In the homes of several pilots and B/Ns, differing views on the war spawned intense discussions between husbands leaving to fight in it and wives who strongly opposed it. Shari McFarland started to cry. "Surely he couldn't be going to Vietnam," she recalled, remembering that they chose the East Coast so that "he would not be going to Vietnam." She freely acknowledged, "I don't want him to go—period," repeating again, "This is not real."[53] LTJG Bob Miller also had chosen an East Coast squadron at least partly because he did not want to go to Vietnam, but, as he noted, "no one asked how you felt about it. It was part of the job."[54] His wife, Barbara, had concurred entirely on his choice of posting for the same reason. LT Kenneth K. Knapp and his wife, Stephanie, newly married in January, also discussed the matter at length. Stephanie, a flight attendant with Pan Am just back from an international hop, learned that her pilot husband had to leave on Tuesday, most likely for Vietnam. A political science and history major in college, Stephanie opposed the war strongly. She did not want her husband to go. They discussed all their options, including her entirely sincere suggestion that they leave immediately for Canada.[55]

The rearrangement of lives in the stress of an immediate and unexpected departure and an uncertain future forced many families to change long-set plans quickly. Some couples already had decided that the wives would stay with family during the Med cruise, so they simply moved up the timetable. Shari McFarland made plans to return to her parents' home in Waco, Texas.[56] Jeane Petersen, six months pregnant and with a two-and-one-half-year-old son named Danny, put on hold the family's plan to build a house in Virginia Beach, stepped down from teaching at their local Sunday school, and prepared to return home to Salt Lake City. During that weekend as she helped LTJG Don Petersen pack, she desperately wanted to hear her late father-in-law—who had died just the previous December—repeat his comforting words, "Now, Jeanie, everything will be okay."[57] Linda Ahrens and her husband had only leased their townhouse through June because she had planned go to Europe to "follow the boat" during the Med cruise; she now prepared to move back home to Minnesota.[58]

As some wives prepared to leave, others decided to stay in Virginia Beach. They could not bear to go through this without a connection to the larger Navy community. "I wasn't about to go to family in New Jersey," wrote Susan Hvidding, because "I would feel out of touch there."[59] The senior officers' wives, most of whom had jobs or children in school or both, simply could not consider moving. By Saturday evening, many of the wives had begun calling each other for mutual support and to share the latest rumors. The officers' wives club quickly planned a coffee for Wednesday, 12 April, the day after the squadron's flyoff, and many of the spouses of the junior officers hoped that they might learn coping strategies from those who had been through this before.

Even CDR Foote, who had left on cruise many times before, faced a particularly weighty matter on Saturday. He already had orders to a new posting in June, after he turned over command of VA-75 to CDR Earnest. Since the timing of his new assignment would coincide closely with the start of the squadron's active operations in the Gulf of Tonkin, his detailer phoned him during that hectic weekend to ask if he wanted to move up the date of his change of command. Now he faced a tough decision. If he chose not to deploy with VA-75, the formal change of command would have to take place in the next two days. Foote considered the possibility. He had flown over two hundred combat missions already and no one could say that he had not done his part. He also knew his wife's feelings about the war. But he did not consult her. She and the children had just returned from shopping, and, when she interrupted his musing, she saw the look on his face and simply said, "You're going again." Indeed, he had decided to retain command of VA-75. As he later explained, "Since everyone in the squadron knew that I was scheduled to leave in June," he believed that "it would be bad for morale if I bailed out early."[60]

Every squadron member about to deploy, regardless of their individual family situations, faced a myriad of financial, legal, and personal matters that required attention before they left. Since many learned of their imminent departure late on Saturday, and businesses, professional offices, government agencies, many parts of the naval bases at Norfolk, and Virginia Beach did not open on

Sunday, the challenge proved daunting. LTJG Lerseth spent part of Sunday morning attempting to get power of attorney for Nini so that she could sell their mobile home.[61] LCDR Pieno had to do the same thing for his wife so that she could handle the closing on their new home.[62] Even more complicated, the Lankfords had ordered a Volkswagen in Germany while on their recent honeymoon, so Loretta could travel around Europe and meet her husband wherever *Saratoga* made a port call during the upcoming Med cruise. After a flurry of international phone calls, they cancelled the purchase.[63]

Important possessions required special care. With a young son at home, LTJG Petersen and his wife took a shotgun and a rifle over to CDR Earnest's house for secure storage. As the younger couple left, Earnest tried hard to calm Jeane's worst fears, reassuring her, "Don't worry, I'll take good care of him and bring him back."[64] LTJG Mullins, a bachelor, called his parents to tell them he was leaving and arranged for them and his sister to come down to Virginia Beach the next weekend to drive his MGB, loaded with his possessions, back to their home in Pennsylvania.[65] Even something as fundamental as storing furniture and cars became a problem. LT Wharton, also a bachelor, stored some of his belongings in the BOQ storeroom and piled the rest of his belongings into his car. Since the base's compound for car storage did not operate on weekends and he did not have time to locate a friend to move his vehicle there, Wharton simply left it in the parking lot when he departed. The only exceptional step he took concerned his prized color television, which he left with LTJG Fuller's wife.[66] The garages and basements of Sunday Punchers who had bought homes in Virginia Beach now became storage areas for the property of bachelor pilots and B/Ns or those whose wives now planned to go home until the squadron returned.

The squadron's enlisted men faced the same kinds of challenges. When some became overwhelmed by all the chaos and confusion, they turned to the only people they knew to trust: their chiefs and their branch officers. LT Pyle received a panicked phone call from one of his sailors begging for help to a common problem that weekend: "What do I do? My wife's crying." Pyle had no solution for the young sailor. He could only say, "If you figure it out, let me know."[67] When some of his men could not retrieve their uniforms from the base dry cleaner, LTJG Fuller arranged for his wife to pick them up.[68] The weekend departure made it impossible for some very young Navy families to complete paperwork for allotment checks, and since banks did not open on Sunday, some enlisted men left behind unsatisfied financial obligations that led to ruined credit ratings and repossessed furniture and cars. The enlisted men's wives' group also planned an emergency meeting for Tuesday morning, its leaders asking Laura Foote to help them field the many questions they knew they would face.

Early on Sunday morning, CDR Foote arrived in the parking lot outside the VA-75 hangar at Oceana. Also arriving early that morning was Warrant Officer Jerry "Gunner" Walden, who showed up for scheduled duty at 0715 and saw LCDR Jackson unloading his cruise box from his car. A Kentuckian and proud of it, Walden and his wife, Joan, had been visiting family in Baltimore and had received no recall message. He stood there utterly stunned to learn that he had orders to deploy immediately. Running into the ready room, he discovered his name on the passenger manifest for the squadron's first airlift to Mayport, scheduled to leave at 0900, with two pallets of equipment, one officer, and sixty enlisted men. Nonplussed—this would be his fourth tour to Westpac—he asked Joan to go home and pack all his uniforms. She pulled in at 0845, taking literally his request that she pack everything. As he recalled, "I am sure to this day I was the best prepared for any Navy function imaginable as I had in my cruise box everything I owned including my bridgecoat, my choker whites, winter greens, khakis and whites."[69]

The officer assigned to take that first detachment to Florida, LTJG Sandy Sanford, desperately wanted to be part of the squadron flyoff from Oceana. The Virginia Tech graduate deeply resented his designation as an on-load officer. As the son of a naval aviator, the junior B/N understood that he had joined the squadron too recently—only a bit more than one month earlier—to merit assignment to a flight crew. Still, he did not want to miss one of the most stirring moments in any squadron's experience: flying off to war.[70] The flight carrying the first detachment of VA-75's personnel—including Sanford and Walden—departed on time that Sunday morning, only sixteen hours after receiving the official recall order.

As his first detachment departed, CDR Foote convened the Sunday AOM at 0900. He still had received no official information on their destination, although few lingering doubts remained. Instead, he focused attention on the long list of tasks the squadron had to complete in a very short time. Foote now knew that eleven of the squadron's planes—seven A-6As and four KA-6Ds—would depart Oceana midmorning on Tuesday to rendezvous with *Saratoga*, set to depart from Mayport early that morning. He also announced the names of the pilots and B/Ns who would fly those aircraft aboard the carrier. Then they reviewed the departure schedules for the rest of Sunday and Monday that would deliver the rest of the officers, all enlisted personnel, and squadron equipment to Florida. CDR Earnest planned to leave for Mayport on Monday morning to handle squadron affairs, and VA-75's air intelligence officers, maintenance officers, and all pilots and B/Ns not scheduled to fly aboard now learned for certain that they would leave with the XO in about twenty-four hours. Between the end of the meeting and their individual departures, each lieutenant and lieutenant junior grade serving as a branch officer had to make certain that his troops packed up all mission-essential supplies and equipment, prepared them for shipment to Mayport, and secured the squadron's spaces at Oceana. There did not seem to be nearly enough time to complete all that had to be done.

For most of the officers, the meeting went by in a blur. Only a single frequently remembered point stood out in their memories. CDR Foote ordered his married officers to kiss their wives good-bye outside the hangar's gate. He would permit no wives in the hangar or ready room. As he later explained, "I didn't want the Ready Room filled with crying women." He had learned this lesson from personal experience. When he had deployed with VA-35 in November 1966, he had said good-bye to Laura in the car, but they both had watched LCDR Eugene B. "Red" McDaniel and his wife, Dot, go aboard the carrier together. Laura always remembered the look on Dot's face that day. As Foote put it, "Wives seem to sense things." McDaniel was shot down in May 1967, and in April 1972 he still fought on from a POW cell in North Vietnam. Foote wanted no such fatalism in his ready room on the day of departure.[71]

Even before the Sunday AOM broke up, the VA-75 hangar had become a beehive of activity. After Chief Warrant Officer Smith learned that he would leave the next day, he went into Maintenance Control to check on the status of the squadron's aircraft to judge for himself whether or not VA-75 could launch eleven working planes by Tuesday morning. He had reason for skepticism. That Sunday morning, as he looked out on the hangar floor, "all I could see were planes with engines out, others on jacks."[72] To get the aircraft up and running, VA-75 now enjoyed outstanding support from MATWING ONE. CDR Michael Andrassy, dual-hatted as commanding officer of MATWING ONE and VA-42, approved all assistance requested, and LCDR William Westerman, his readiness officer, oversaw the effort. CDR Foote had harbored some initial concerns that personnel from other A-6 squadrons might strip off hard-to-get parts from VA-75's aircraft, hoping to get away with it in the chaos surrounding the hasty departure. Fortunately, Foote noted, the spirit of true cooperation held fast and "that did not happen." Mechanics from VA-42 and other A-6 commands pitched in, and parts came from everywhere. Crews from other A-6 squadrons came over to help test fly aircraft. "It was a miracle that it all came together," Foote recalled.[73] Indeed, from the perspective of those at Oceana not facing Foote's challenge, the effort to prepare VA-75 for departure progressed so smoothly that MATWING ONE's senior leaders recalled little that was exceptional about the process.[74] As LT Fischer later recalled, "It was the best I ever saw the Navy operate." He watched a VA-75 maintenance officer tell a counterpart from another A-6 squadron that he needed a specific piece of equipment, and, Fischer marveled, "He would get it."[75]

Most JOs did meet CDR Foote's expectation that they look after their branch obligations before returning home to their families. As the squadron legal officer, LTJG Warren had it easy; he only had to pack up a few file folders.[76] LTJG Mullins, about to step down as squadron first lieutenant, confronted the challenge of accounting for all of VA-75's gear in all its spaces not involving aircraft maintenance. His biggest task centered on clearing the barracks of the squadron's enlisted personnel and accounting for linens, janitorial equipment, typewriters, and such. In the rush to move out, Mullins quickly realized that he simply could not check on every little thing. He also refused to let it bother him, explaining later that "there was nothing more they could do to me than they already were," and that knowledge "kept me on an even keel."[77] The squadron's chiefs also earned their pay over this April weekend. In retrospect, LTJG Lerseth admitted freely that he probably slighted his enlisted men. Even though "I technically 'owned' about 40 of them," he recalled, "I was probably too wrapped up in dealing with all those personal issues and trying to do my bit to get airplanes up and ready to care for their welfare. AQC [Chief Aviation Firecontrolman] Mooney covered my ass on that one."[78]

The pace of activity in VA-75's hangar caught the attention of pilots and B/Ns from other A-6 squadrons based at Oceana. Indeed, as LTJG Mullins recalled, "several junior officers stopped by the squadron spaces that weekend to inquire if there were any vacant billets they might fill, but we had no holes and I pitied them."[79] Some willing volunteers took a more direct approach. LTJG Thomas C. Vance, a B/N with VA-65, introduced himself to CDR Earnest and requested immediate reassignment to VA-75. "He looked at me as if I was some kind of whacko," Vance later recalled, but Earnest did not brush him off. Even though VA-75's destination remained officially unknown, the XO knew that a squadron headed for combat likely would pick up a few additional aircraft to complement its original numbers. Then the Sunday Punchers would need augmentation crews to meet its operational obligations. After two combat tours, he also understood the possible need for replacements for downed crews. Any personnel request from an East Coast A-6 squadron such as VA-75 went to the commanding officer of MATWING ONE at Oceana. Earnest suggested that if Vance were serious, he should inform the MATWING ONE operations officer of his interest. Vance did so immediately.[80]

As CDR Foote continued to worry about getting all eleven of his planes in the air, he also wondered if, when Tuesday morning arrived, he would find eleven fully manned cockpits. He did not know much about the political views of his pilots and B/Ns. Nor did he understand the strength of the antiwar views held by some of their wives. But he did realize that more and more Navy men had begun to refuse orders to Southeast Asia. In 1971, antiwar groups had tried to prevent USS *Constellation* from departing San Diego and USS *Coral Sea* from leaving San Francisco. In February 1972, 150 sailors from the USS *Kitty Hawk* attended an antiwar rally featuring Joan Baez, who planned to try to stop the carrier's departure. When it sailed a few days later, seven enlisted sailors chose to miss the movement by taking sanctuary in local churches.[81]

Discontent with the war effort had begun to manifest itself among officers, too. In 1969, the Concerned Officers Movement (COM), an antiwar organization that included a significant number of junior naval officers, had become active in the Washington, DC, area. In 1971, the Norfolk/Virginia Beach COM chapter had rented a billboard along Taussig Boulevard, a major thoroughfare onto the Norfolk Navy Base and Air Station, and posted a large sign emblazoned with the words "PEACE NOW."[82] In a celebrated challenge to military authority, LTJG John Kent, a naval aviator and Naval Academy graduate, spoke out in support of COM's agenda and incurred the wrath of his superiors for doing so. "They've taken my wings away from me and I'm no longer allowed to fly. My job is that of an assistant janitor," he told the press, but he was willing to endure this if his case alerted the American people that they needed to "force the military to change its policy" on continued military action.[83] Although Foote knew of no aviator in his command who openly sympathized with those views, he wondered if the change of orders from the Med to Vietnam, family pressures, or their sentiments about the war might give some of his officers pause. A news item that hectic weekend noting that twenty-seven sailors missed the movement when *Constellation* hurriedly left Japan for Westpac had not escaped his notice.[84]

He could do nothing about his officers' individual decisions, so he centered his concerns on the mechanical readiness of his planes. As he later wrote, "We used to have an old saying. . . . If you really wanted to check out an aircraft[,] send a young pilot out on a night cat shot and he would find everything wrong with the plane." He wondered how many of his young crews might conduct major checks and "find a hundred reasons NOT TO GO."[85] Several planes just coming out of maintenance went through test flights as close to departure as early in the morning of 11 April, when LCDRs Boecker and Jackson tested Foote's own aircraft.[86] Others had not been flight-tested at all.

At Mayport on Sunday, the first detachment of VA-75 enlisted personnel began to settle into *Saratoga*'s compartments and shops. As soon as Gunner Walden arrived, he made his way to a construction battalion (Seabee) compound, found the chief petty officer there, and began some serious bargaining. Walden told the Seabee chief that he needed a two-ton truck for eight hours and a pickup truck for the next forty-eight hours. The Seabee responded, "Yes, Gunner, you and everyone else on the Saratoga." Walden then offered two leather flight jackets and four pairs of aviator flight glasses in trade for the necessary transport. The Seabee said, "Gunner, I like the way you do business!" Experience and ingenuity sealed the deal.

With their newfound fleet of two vehicles, the first detachment transported from the airstrip to the docks the two pallets of gear and personal belongings. To get the squadron equipment aboard *Saratoga,* Walden "hustled" the ship's company operating the conveyor belt from the dock to the hanger deck the same way he had worked the Seabee chief. During that day, he repeated the process three times. Reflecting on it later, Gunner Walden noted that it was "truly amazing what a little com-shaw can accomplish when applied in the proper situation and to the right people. Com-shaw can be a court martial offense, yet good commanders will turn a blind eye toward it if it's not abused. The following day we paid off our part of the bargain to the 'Seabees' and everyone was happy with the outcome."[87]

Aboard *Saratoga,* LTJG Sanford inspected the compartments assigned to VA-75, directed his men to the squadron's work spaces, and set them to work stowing personal gear and shop equipment. As he checked out the areas for which he and his men had become responsible, he discovered that he now "owned" the only escalator on the entire carrier. To Sanford, that was like "owning the crown jewel of the *Saratoga.*"[88]

For those Punchers and their families still remaining in Virginia, Sunday night passed in a blur. Most couples chose to spend the time alone. Those who cared to tune in to the Oscar presentations that night would have watched the award for Best Actress go to the star of *Klute,* Jane Fonda.[89] But LT Fischer, who shared an apartment with a B/N from another A-6 squadron, joined his roommate for the biggest entertainment event to hit the Norfolk–Virginia Beach area in ages: the first Elvis Presley concert there since the mid-1950s. His roommate had planned to take his girlfriend, but, at the last minute, he decided to invite Fischer instead.[90]

On Monday, 10 April, several individual detachments of VA-75 personnel left by air for Mayport. LT Wharton and Chief Warrant Officer Smith took charge of one group of about forty men. As Myrna Smith recalled, she and Smitty followed CDR Foote's injunction to the letter; when she dropped him off at Oceana, "we said our goodbyes in the parking lot."[91] Despite his relative seniority among the squadron's pilots, this assignment denied Wharton the opportunity to participate in the Tuesday morning flyoff. Like LTJG Sanford, Wharton regretted that he had to miss the event.[92]

CDR Earnest, along with some of the squadron's more junior pilots and B/Ns, air intelligence officers Martin and Wardlaw, and the remaining enlisted personnel, also mustered on Monday for the airlift to Mayport. When they arrived, they marveled at the activity on the pier. CDR Earnest went to check on the squadron's progress in settling into its spaces, seeking out Gunner Walden for an update. Walden reported that all the gear and personnel that had arrived so far was aboard. They had stowed the equipment in its proper work spaces, and the men had found their berthing compartments. He had to return the two-ton truck soon, but the pickup was CDR Earnest's to use until they left port. The amazed XO asked, "Gunner, what is this going to cost me?" Walden assured him that he did not want to know.[93]

Not all elements of *Saratoga*'s airwing that had just completed the recent ORE took part in the hectic activity on the Mayport docks that April weekend. CAPT Sanderson and CAG Bordone had altered the force package they planned to take with them. Since they had little need for their antisubmarine warfare assets on this combat cruise, the S-2 squadron detached from the airwing. On 8 April, HS-7—the helicopter squadron—first received orders to send all eight of its aircraft aboard *Saratoga* for immediate departure on an extended combat deployment; two days later, half the unit received orders to return to the naval air station at Quonset Point, Rhode Island, while only four of the unit's helicopters deployed.[94] *Saratoga* also had to prepare to recover and chain down the aircraft from two F-4 squadrons (VF-31 and VF-103) from Oceana, two A-7 squadrons (VA-37 and VA-105) from nearby Cecil Field, the RA-5Cs of RVAH-1 from Albany Naval Air Station in Georgia, and the E-2Bs of VAW-123 from Norfolk. These units—with the Sunday Punchers—would make up CVW-3's table of organization for the upcoming deployment.

Spaces had to be prepared for their personnel, too, and the ship's company and other volunteers helped to deliver over 2.5 million pounds of food and other supplies into *Saratoga*'s refrigeration and cargo storage areas. Over 2 million pounds of distillate fuel poured into the carrier's fuel tanks. Portable floodlights, backed up by truck and tractor headlights, lit the pier at night to allow the work to continue after dark. The entire area "became a maze of cranes, crates, and cargo trucks," a Navy journalist reported. The men and supplies from forty separate transports had to be unloaded at the airstrip, transferred to the pier, and gotten aboard the carrier. The effort required the total cooperation of all support activities at the Mayport Naval Station.[95]

LTJG Ahrens took time to stand in line at a pay phone near the pier on Monday evening to call his wife once more. It was a sad call, neither knowing what might happen or when they might see each other again. All in all, he noted, it was "probably like three or four thousand other phone conversations that evening."[96] Ironically, during a Pentagon briefing that same day, a journalist asked about the impending deployment of *Saratoga* to Southeast Asia. The briefer "refused to confirm that the *Saratoga* will sail," conceding only that a number of ships had begun to move toward the Pacific.[97]

Late on Monday, ADM Elmo R. Zumwalt, Jr., Chief of Naval Operations (CNO), and VADM Frederick H. Michaelis both visited the carrier and expressed their entire satisfaction with the zeal and professionalism the crew had demonstrated over the past few days. Zumwalt praised the teamwork that facilitated the rapid deployment and thanked both the crew and their families for their support. The CNO had become a familiar sight to many Sunday Punchers, but his presence reinforced LTJG Warren's suspicions that they must be headed to Vietnam. The admiral "didn't normally do that for departing carriers" heading for the Med, he noted.[98]

Saratoga departed Mayport about 0800 on Tuesday, 11 April 1972, to start the carrier's very first combat deployment since its commissioning in 1956. The carrier left so quickly that many of its crew left their cars parked haphazardly all around the pier until family members could retrieve them.[99] A Jacksonville reporter noted a dramatic change in the sendoff. "When Mayport-based carriers leave on assignments in the Mediterranean," he noted, "bands play on the docks and wives and children wave, many of them looking forward to flying to Europe for reunions during the six-month tour abroad." He concluded, "There was none of this as the *Saratoga* departed on what could be a battle mission."[100]

There was also "none of this" when the eleven aircraft of VA-75 left Oceana on Tuesday morning, 11 April, to rendezvous with *Saratoga*. As ordered, wives and children stayed outside the gate. Jeane Petersen and Danny followed LTJG Petersen as far as they were allowed to go, and then, she recalled, "I wanted to hang on forever." But, in the end, she simply watched him go, and then left to get ready for the trip home to Utah.[101] LCDR Graustein's wife dropped him off at the gate outside the hangar and returned home immediately.[102] LCDR Jackson had his father—not his wife—take him to the hangar.[103] LT Fischer's roommate not only brought him to the hangar but also strapped him into his plane.[104] LTJG Bob Miller recalled that during these final emotional moments in Oceana, mixed feelings prevailed. He heard one of his squadronmates say that they were about to embark on "our chance to be heroes," but Miller admitted, "I didn't feel very heroic just then."[105]

CDR Foote's concern that he might not be able to man all his planes proved to be unfounded. Every pilot and B/N on the flight schedule reported on time. They held a final brief, and they said good-bye to LCDR Boecker, who had been preparing to detach from VA-75 to become XO of VA-85 when news of the deployment broke. The young squadron with few combat veterans surely could have taken advantage of his experience and his advice even for the short time Boecker still belonged to the Sunday Punchers. Nonetheless, CDR Foote—against the advice of his own XO—allowed Boecker to stay behind.[106]

As CDR Foote climbed into the cockpit of his A-6A with LCDR Jackson in the B/N seat, he started his engines and watched all his crews do the same. LT Lankford noted that strangers from other squadrons handled the launch; VA-75's own enlisted men had long departed for Florida and now awaited them aboard *Saratoga*.[107] They remained on squadron common frequency so CDR Foote could be apprised of any problems that might prevent a plane from taking off. Fully expecting mechanical problems to down at least one aircraft, Foote recalled that "you could have knocked me over with a feather" when all pilots signaled they were ready for takeoff. He switched over to ground control frequency and called for his crews to taxi to the end of the designated runway. Once there, he signaled he was ready to go. All his other pilots continued to verify their readiness to launch as well. LT Ruland and LTJG McFarland actually found something wrong with their plane, and, as McFarland noted, "under normal condition we would not have flown" it. "But," he added, "we were not going to be left behind or leave an airplane in Virginia."[108] Then, in the ultimate irony, when CDR Foote switched to channel 2 to call the tower for takeoff, his own radio malfunctioned. A broken radio could down a plane, but CDR Foote simply signaled his situation to his wingman—the crew of LT Cook and LTJG Fuller—who took over and called for takeoff.

Once in the air, the squadron divided into three elements for the flight to the carrier, one two-plane advance party and, flying just behind them, the main body in two larger groups. LCDR Dick Engel, just designated the new Maintenance Department head, flew one of the first two planes, with LTJG Mullins as his B/N. The young bachelor specifically had requested to be assigned to the first aircraft to man up, since he "didn't want to be around when the married guys said goodbye to their families."[109] LTs Fischer and Wagner joined on their wing. With CDR Foote's radio down, LCDR Lindland and LTJG Lerseth took the lead for the main elements.[110] From the delivery of the official recall order until the eleven Sunday Puncher crews took off from Oceana, approximately sixty hours had passed.

Among those watching VA-75 take off was Sally Fuller. She had no doubts about the ultimate destination of her husband's squadron. On her planning calendar for 11 April, she wrote only two words: "John—West."[111] Shari McFarland and young Kelly also found a place to park so they could see the planes leave. "We stayed for a while and saw some leave. I don't know if it was Ron or not, but because we couldn't stay long, I pretended it was Ron and I said good-bye with lots and lots of prayers."[112]

Laura Foote did not have time to dwell on her husband's departure just then. She went to meet with the enlisted men's wives who had said their own good-byes on Sunday or Monday. As soon as she arrived, she faced a barrage of questions from confused and frightened young wives about allotment checks, mail delivery, automobile repairs, rides to doctor's appointments, possible return dates, and more. Usually a model of propriety, Laura suddenly snapped. As she recalled, she silenced the women completely by blurting out, "I don't give a damn if you get a check. I don't give a damn if you get mail. If your husband is not being shot at, you don't have troubles." Then they all broke down in tears.

When Laura got home, a bad day quickly got worse. The bathroom toilet overflowed the first time she flushed it. On Tuesdays, the maid came to help with the housework, and both of them watched the water flood over the bathroom floor. Laura sat down on the floor, motioning the maid to join her. After a few minutes in tears, she decided that the toilet broke just then to keep her mind off her husband's departure. She said to herself, "You're going to sit in water today and you're going to get over this." Then Laura and the maid stood up and both mopped up the mess.[113]

Of course, the local Virginia Beach and Norfolk newspapers covered the departure of VA-75 and the two Oceana-based F-4 squadrons deploying aboard *Saratoga*. Even though the Sunday Punchers and their families still remained officially uninformed about their destination, a local journalist, citing "reliable sources," confirmed that "the aircraft carrier *Saratoga*, a detachment of escort ships, and at least three squadrons of Norfolk-based fighter planes are scheduled to leave Mayport, Fla., early today for Vietnam." The report also noted that the emergency deployment would last eight months, longer than the typical Med cruise. In addition to providing apparent confirmation of unwelcome news, the journalist also made a seemingly small but glaring error, asserting that "sources said that Fighter Squadrons 31, 75, and 103 from Oceana Naval [Air] Station will deploy to Vietnam aboard the *Saratoga*. Squadrons 31 and 103 fly the F-4 Phantom and Fighter Squadron 75 is equipped with A-6 Intruders."[114] The reporter apparently did not know the difference between fighter squadrons and an attack squadron such as VA-75. An editor who watched the flyoff struck an equally discordant note by suggesting that these squadrons likely faced a future that included great risk for insignificant results. "Airplanes are antiseptic and bombing is clean killing, somehow," the editorial writer opined, adding, "The best hope for now seems to be a stalemate through airpower, pending a peaceful settlement at some future time."[115]

Ironically, the most precise information about the massive April 1972 naval and air deployment to Southeast Asia came not from the Pentagon or the various armed services but from an antiwar coalition called the Ad Hoc Military

Buildup Committee. Based in Cambridge, Massachusetts, the group gathered information on troop movements from disaffected servicemen and disseminated it to the public. In the absence of official word from Washington, journalists relied heavily upon the committee's reports. On the day VA-75's eleven aircraft left Oceana for *Saratoga,* the group announced that "at least 21,600 men, 411 planes and 11 ships had left the United States or will leave soon for Indochina due to the North Vietnamese invasion of South Vietnam."[116] That same day, Representative Bella Abzug (D-NY) took the floor of the House and told her colleagues: "I almost feel as if today could be April 11, 1968, instead of April 11, 1972. Four years ago, candidate Richard Nixon told us that he had a plan to end our involvement in Vietnam, but today U.S. planes and ships are pounding the soil of that beleaguered nation as never before and other U.S. forces are being mobilized for its future and perhaps final devastation."[117]

The Ad Hoc Committee's final report on the naval buildup, issued on 15 April, noted that—in addition to *Saratoga*—the carriers USS *Midway* (CVA-41) and USS *Oriskany* (CVA-43) also had left their homeports in recent days, and *Kitty Hawk* and *Constellation* had already arrived in Southeast Asian waters. Eight carriers now rotated in and out of the Gulf of Tonkin, where, before the North Vietnamese invasion of the South, the Navy had typically stationed only three. In addition, three cruisers, fourteen destroyers, thirteen destroyer escorts, and one oiler had deployed to Westpac in the past two weeks. The Navy's strength off the Vietnamese coast had increased by 390 additional aircraft and 32,500 men. The Sunday Punchers would find plenty of company.[118]

For the men of VA-75 and their families, the passing of time did not dull the memories of the waves of wildly swirling and conflicting emotions that swept over them during those sixty hectic hours in April 1972. The departure gave pause to those who held moral, ethical, or practical qualms about the conduct of the war in which they were about to become active participants. LT Wharton admitted that, in April 1972, he felt "very confused as to why the US continued conducting the war the way it was." Everything he read or heard suggested that "it all seemed to be a futile effort. I heard stories of missions blowing up trees in Laos and rules of engagement that seemed like something out of a bizarre satirical novel; and this thing had been going on for such a long time! I grew up with a strong sense of patriotism but I couldn't figure out what our real purpose being there was anymore. Was I an anti–Vietnam war type? Absolutely not! That's what made everything so difficult."[119] Still, despite his strong reservations about the war, he never doubted his willingness to meet his professional obligation to report for duty.

Nearly all of them considered the potential impact of their deployment on those they left behind. LT Ken Knapp contemplated, "What a dirty deal I had dealt my wife, in that if I had known that this [combat deployment] might happen, I probably would not have gotten married" in January 1972.[120] LTJG Petersen admitted he felt "torn about leaving my 2-year-old son and pregnant wife and living up to my obligations to my country." Many years later, he added, "It still bothers me."[121] In his very first letter home, written just a few hours out of Oceana, LTJG Warren asked his wife to "make the kids understand that Daddy *will* be back and that he will miss them very much. Maybe some day they will understand."[122]

A few considered the potential implications of combat on their own mortality, but they did not obsess about it. LTJG Lerseth admitted that he thought about it briefly, but he set aside his concerns, an action he considered "interesting thinking" since he had just buried his father.[123] LCDR Engel acknowledged that "we all faced the realization that the possibility existed that some of us might not return," but, like others, he felt confident in his ability and training and his aircraft. Moreover, "with our side having control of the air war I went forward expecting that the chances of any of us not coming home were relatively slim but still possible."[124]

Many of the squadron heavies shared one specific concern only with each other. LCDR Lindland wanted desperately to go back to Vietnam, desiring a measure of payback for friends lost during his 1968 combat cruise with VA-35. But he worried about the readiness level of some of the squadron's junior pilots and B/Ns.[125] LCDR Pieno later recalled frequent conversations behind the closed doors of the senior officers' staterooms centering on the squadron's inexperience. He and LCDR Jackson had come to share CDR Earnest's quiet—but real—concerns about some of their junior pilots and B/Ns preparing to go into combat for the first time. "As a vet of Yankee Station he knew we weren't ready," Pieno noted. "We did not have the luxury of the West Coast squadrons as far as experience and familiarity with the area."[126]

Even a few JOs wondered how they might stack up. LT Anderson considered his squadron—and, indeed, the entire *Saratoga*—as "ill prepared for this mission—an East Coast carrier and airgroup with zero recent combat time."[127] Still, each man accepted his professional obligation to perform to the best of his abilities. LTJG Warren felt "almost HAPPY about the prospect of getting involved over there," since the former enlisted man had spent eleven years in the Navy "getting trained and paid to do what others had been doing for quite a while."[128] LTJG Swigart figured that "most of us who had never been to Vietnam, and particularly those of us who had never even been on a cruise, spent most of the time worrying about how we would perform, wondering whether we were going to die, and being excited about the prospect of actually doing the mission for which we had been trained."[129] Even LT Anderson realized that, in the end, his apprehensions split evenly between "a fear of death and a fear that I would not perform."[130]

Despite the sadness of leaving families and personal questions of all sorts, in the end, the Sunday Puncher pilots and B/Ns acknowledged as their strongest sentiment during those hectic days a genuine excitement at the prospect of testing themselves in combat. LCDR Jackson admitted that even as he tried to console his crying wife, he "couldn't wait to get to the ship and then over to Vietnam and start flying combat hops."[131] LCDR Engel felt "exuberance that we would be given the opportunity to put into practice in a wartime environment all that we had been trained to do."[132] LT Fischer had become "very frustrated on the Med cruise knowing there was a war on and I wasn't in it. I wanted to get my two cents in before it ended."[133] LTJG Mullins recalled feeling "elated and unnerved all at once," admitting that "I'd wanted to fly combat for half my life and thought assignment to an east coast squadron had ended my chances." He viewed the emergency deployment as "a great adventure and I was very happy it happened to my squadron."[134] LTJG Swigart admitted that when he got that phone call on Saturday night, "I think I had secretly been hoping it would come."[135] But such elation mixed with yet another emotion—guilt—for wanting something that they knew caused those they loved real pain.

LTJG Hvidding nicely summed up the conflicting emotions of that April weekend. As he and his wife walked along the beach the night before he flew off to war, they talked about the challenges that lay ahead. To his diary, he later confided that "every experience in someone's life impresses something in his character that is lifelong." He understood that "going to war and meeting the demands and challenges of flying combat is an experience that will change me—my self-confidence, my relationship with other people, my approach to future situations." He did not care that much about the "why's" of the war. "The principle of this particular war is beside the point. I'm willing to *risk* my life for the defense of South Vietnam, but I'm not willing to *give* it outright. I'm committed to the oath of my commission, and the war probably has something to offer *me* in the form of raw experience, but I'm not the avid volunteer to defend SVN [South Vietnam] at all costs." Then he recalled a popular expression that summarized the professional detachment of many naval aviators—"They pay your salary, you take your chances."[136]

Few of these thoughts intruded on their minds for long during those few April days between recall and departure, however. Events had proceeded at such a breakneck pace that, as LCDR Pieno noted, "you really didn't have time to dwell on the realities. That would come later during the long transit. Then it started to hit home."[137]

CHAPTER THREE

"Would You Believe?"

Through the late morning of 11 April, eleven VA-75 aircraft—seven A-6As and four KA-6D tankers—flew south through a thick overcast. The flight to USS *Saratoga* took nearly two and one-half hours. As the planes prepared to trap aboard, the Air Boss asked each aircraft in turn to provide the pilot's name to check on qualification status. When his turn came, LTJG Roger Lerseth reported the name of his pilot: LCDR Don Lindland. The Air Boss did not understand and asked Lerseth to repeat the name. When he still could not make it out, he asked the B/N to spell it. Lerseth began using the standard military alphabet to do so—Lima, India, November—and then paused. In his excitement, he had completely forgotten the word that represented the next letter. So, he simply spelled out the rest of the letters: "D, L, A, N, D."[1] The gaffe caused only chuckles, and all squadron aircraft trapped aboard safely.

The Sunday Punchers had answered the emergency recall in fine form. Despite CDR Foote's fears that some of his troops might refuse to deploy, first reports counted all squadron personnel—all thirty-five officers and just over three hundred enlisted men—aboard and on duty. Not all squadrons or the ship's company could make that claim. Indeed, *Saratoga* departed Mayport so quickly that over one hundred men from the ship's company and airwing missed the movement. Helicopters flew from Mayport all day, returning late-arriving sailors to the carrier.[2]

Even as they departed, however, those aboard still had received no official word on their destination. "The atmosphere and information on the ship convinced me 90% that we were indeed on our way to Southeast Asia," LTJG Paul Hvidding recorded in his diary shortly after landing.[3] After filing routine flight and maintenance paperwork, the aircrews went to their ready room. There they found on a bulletin board a huge chart of Southeast Asia with a sign attached: "Would you believe?"[4]

Hunches and tantalizing tidbits of information still did not constitute official word, however. Nonetheless, the Punchers found fewer and fewer reasons to doubt the veracity of the rumors. In just the past few days, the American response to the North Vietnamese invasion of the South had increased. Even before they departed Oceana, President Nixon had approved the start of Operation FREEDOM TRAIN, a sharp increase in air strikes on approved military targets in North Vietnam south of the 20th parallel; he also approved a substantial expansion of the target list, to include many previously unhit sites. On 7 April, the U.S. Air Force initiated Operation CONSTANT GUARD, a series of deployments extending over several months that sent additional squadrons of tactical aircraft to Southeast Asia. At the same time, Operation BULLET SHOT began a similar buildup of the strategic bomber fleet. On 10 April, twelve B-52s bombed the Vinh oil tank farm and a nearby railyard. Navy A-6s and A-7s had paved the way, hitting SAM sites, followed by specially adapted Air Force F-105 "Wild Weasels" and F-4s laying a chaff (strips of aluminum foil to confuse radars) corridor.[5] The next day—the same day VA-75's planes departed Oceana—more B-52 strikes hit North Vietnamese troop concentrations near Kontum in the Central Highlands.

Saratoga steamed off Puerto Rico on 12 and 13 May to allow late-arriving ship's company and squadron personnel to catch flights out to the carrier. The RA-5Cs of RVAH-1 finally trapped aboard, too. In the meantime, the officers and warrants settled into their staterooms, unpacked uniforms, set up stereo gear, and plugged in mini-refrigerators—their "reefers." The enlisted men organized their compartments and their shops, generally enjoying fewer amenities. When the last flight back to shore launched on 13 April, the final opportunity to tie up personal and financial arrangements left with it. Like a number of others in the squadron, LT Kit Ruland now sent his wife, Brigid, a copy of his will and also reminded her about a life insurance policy he had bought, just in case.[6] Despite the continuing absence of official word of their destination, squadron aviators still offered last-minute reassurances. LTJG Bob Tolhurst reported rumors of sending *Saratoga* to a station off South Vietnam, noting, "That means missions will be lightly opposed, if we fly any there, as compared to the North."[7] After briefings about the rapidly changing military situation in North and South Vietnam, LTJG Dave Warren assured his wife that "it doesn't look bad at all, considering how it used to be. It won't be a piece of cake, but it isn't all hellfire and damnation either." He encouraged her to ask around the base at Oceana for a large map of Vietnam so she could track the action.[8]

Only now, as *Saratoga* steamed out of Puerto Rican waters, did the word become official: They were going to Westpac. The navigator plotted a course through the south Atlantic, around the southern tip of Africa, through the Indian Ocean and the Strait of Malacca, to Cubi Point Naval Air Station on the island of Luzon in the Philippines. After a quick stop to refuel and pick up supplies, the carrier then would proceed to the waters off Vietnam. CAPT Sanderson informed the crew to expect no further mail deliveries until they reached Cubi, probably about 8 May.

As *Saratoga* headed into the South Atlantic, CDR Foote received a piece of bad news. Despite the initial reports that all his men had made it aboard on time, Aviation Electronics Technician Second Class O. W. Carter of the avionics shop could not be found. During the final muster before departure, a chief reported to Master Chief Aviation Mechanic Jacob Pena—the squadron's senior enlisted man responsible for the muster—that Carter probably had gone to a work station in another part of the ship, as he often did. But no one checked to make certain. Two days after leaving Florida, when Carter failed to answer a second roll call, a more thorough check confirmed the sailor's absence. After learning of the belated discovery of the missing man, XO Earnest called in LTJG John Fuller, Carter's branch officer. The JO got "jumped on for not knowing where my people were." The oversight embarrassed Fuller, who clearly understood his official responsibility in the matter.[9] Carter became the only member of VA-75 to miss the movement.

By Friday, 14 April, CVW-3 and all its squadrons aboard *Saratoga* initiated an intensive training program for its flight crews. Realizing that his preliminary training program for operations in the Med required total revision, CAG Bordone quickly formed an airwing-level tactics board made up of commanders and lieutenant commanders with combat experience to update and promulgate CVW-3's basic procedures for successful operations, as well as to address safety issues and anticipated rules of engagement. Bordone viewed this board as a "living tool" that, throughout the transit, would continue to evaluate message traffic coming in from Westpac so that they could inform and instruct the aircrews who would fly in its hostile skies. Representatives from COMNAVAIRPAC and COMCARDIV SEVEN—the West Coast–based airwings that routinely trained for combat and the carrier element of the naval task force operating in Southeast Asia—accompanied CVW-3 during the transit, and Bordone took full advantage of their experience and advice.[10]

The standard working day for the Sunday Punchers' officers during the transit quickly fell into a routine. Each day began with a meeting at 0900 or 0930 for lectures and discussions about a wide variety of topics unique to the A-6 mission. The squadron's four combat veterans reviewed basic knowledge each aviator needed to understand, covering a wide range of topics including the nature of the threat environment, the characteristics of SAMs and antiaircraft artillery (AAA) and how to defend against them; MiG identification; specific airmanship topics that ranged from the importance of sticking with your flight lead to the need to maintain situational awareness; reviews of specific responsibilities of pilot and B/N in the operation of the A-6's various systems; specific procedures, such as switch sequences; the need for a high degree of radio discipline; the theater rules of engagement; and survival tips. CAG Bordone advised VA-75's senior leadership to emphasize the crew concept, safety instructions, and equipment procedures for the conduct of low-level air operations.

Not all lectures dealt with mission execution, nor did the senior officers do all the briefing. LT John Miller reviewed the various kinds of conventional ordnance they would use, the fuses they required, and preflight procedures.[11] Gunner Walden and Chief Aviation Ordnanceman Loyd Kaneaster, a veteran of VA-75's previous combat cruise, came to the ready room to offer a more hands-on approach to fusing and other weapons system matters.[12] LTJG Petersen lectured on AAA and summed up its essence with "don't duel with a flak site, you solve his tracking problem."[13] Briefers from VAW-123, the E-2B squadron, visited VA-75's ready room to provide the latest information about the methods and degrees of navigation assistance and flight coordination the A-6 crews could expect from them.[14] LTJG Bob Miller remembered especially clearly the discussion led by CDR Foote and other veterans of previous tours in Southeast Asia about unique points of interest in potential ports of call, the hazards to be avoided in the Philippine town of Olongapo, and the "social etiquette" of shore leave.[15]

The information came in such torrents, however, that most JOs found it increasingly difficult to separate the essential from the interesting. First alerted to the likelihood that they would work in South Vietnam or Laos under the control of U.S. Air Force forward air controllers (FACs), the squadron heavies assigned LTJG Hvidding to brief on the subject. The day he stood up to make his presentation, however, he got bumped from the schedule.[16] Instructional priorities from the airwing tactics board continued to shift as news from Westpac changed. Some Punchers responded cynically to what they heard. After reviewing the complicated sequence to call for special clearances from local political leaders before releasing ordnance on targets in Laos, for instance, LT Fischer asked if they had to clear it with Hanoi to drop bombs in North Vietnam.[17]

The lecture and discussion sessions continued daily despite a fundamental logistical problem: a genuine lack of planning maps and charts of Southeast Asia. *Saratoga*'s chart locker overflowed with maps of the Mediterranean, but the intelligence officers possessed very few for their new destination. Moreover, as long as they stayed out of range for resupply, they could not expect to get any. As they heard about the progress of mid-April's Operation FREEDOM PORCH BRAVO, a joint U.S. Navy–U.S. Air Force tactical and strategic air campaign against targets in the Hanoi and Haiphong areas, the pilots and B/Ns badgered LT Martin and LTJG Wardlaw for maps of the area. "The intel guys got real frugal with them at the same time we got real antsy to have them," LTJG Lerseth recalled.[18]

The morning session usually broke up around 1100 for an early lunch. Some officers then went to the catwalk on the flight deck to talk, while others wrote home or caught an extra hour of sleep. They reported back to the ready room at

1230 for a series of lectures given by the air intelligence staff of the Integrated Operational Intelligence Center (IOIC). The topics ranged from updated reports of current air operations over North and South Vietnam and Laos, new wrinkles in North Vietnamese air defenses, reviews of communication procedures between the various elements of the airwing and the carrier, and more.[19] *Saratoga* used IOIC's closed-circuit television system to reach into each ready room, so aviators in the entire airwing heard these briefings at the same time. The afternoon training periods usually lasted until about 1400 or 1430.

At that point in the day, many junior officers devoted time to their individual branch assignments and other collateral duties. All of the branch officers and chiefs faced mountains of paperwork. The rapid deployment did not relieve them of preparing evaluations and recommendations for the enlisted men. All squadron property had to be accounted for and stowed away. Inventories discovered that a number of VA-75's toolboxes got lost or stolen during the loading process, and the junior officers in those branches had to file official reports to explain the loss. "One can't just say because some blockhead left them out where they could be easily lifted," LTJG Fuller wrote home, noting, "It's necessary to have some better story made up."[20]

The maintenance chiefs instituted a two-shift schedule for the enlisted men, each man reporting to his assigned duty station for a daily twelve-hour shift. Now, more than they had on previous cruises, some branch officers decided to use this time to get to know the enlisted men who worked for them and kept their planes in the air. LTJG Jerry Mullins devoted hours of his time to talking with the personnel of the Power Plants shop. Among other things, he took great pains to pass on the flight surgeon's warnings about venereal diseases they might encounter in the Philippines.[21]

But others did not spend much time in the shops at all. They knew their veteran chiefs did not need their help to keep things running, and, often enough, they felt sufficiently intimidated by them that they simply stayed out of the way. As LTJG Hvidding later reflected, as the transit continued, it increasingly became "a time of self-absorption" for the pilots and B/Ns to prepare for combat.[22]

After the end of formal lectures and other duties, on bright days—and the weather for most of the transit remained clear—the sun drew many Puncher officers to the flight deck, quickly turning it into an impromptu running track. LTJG Bob Miller, for one, admitted that he "got religious on the subject of 'PT'" and enthusiastically joined in.[23] Only two JOs rarely participated: LTs Tom "Jack" Wharton and Paul Wagner. As LT Fischer explained it, "Jack never did like to work out and Paul felt that you were allotted only so many breaths in life and he didn't want to waste them by working out." He named them "members of Athletics Anonymous"—if you started to exercise, the group would "send someone over to drink with you until you return[ed] to your senses."[24]

Although the wardroom served dinner from 1700 until 1830, most of the Sunday Punchers' officers ate early and then wandered out to the catwalk again. Talk often centered on the length of their deployment. Even though initial reports pointed to an eight-month tour in Westpac, every night on the ship's loudspeaker—the 1MC—CAPT Sanderson assured the men that *Saratoga* would be home by October. He explained that the carrier had a yard date for a major overhaul then, and after its problems in Athens harbor in 1971, the Navy had given its rehabilitation a high priority.

On most nights at about 1930, many officers returned to the ready room for a movie. The Squadron Duty Officer bore the responsibility for getting the film. One April night, LT Fischer ordered *Blackbeard's Ghost* and *How Sweet It Is*. The squadron heavies quickly banned him from picking any more movies because, as he explained, they preferred "something with ordnance and skin."[25] In any case, they rarely got first-run films; indeed, on the transit, they watched movies as old as *Spartacus* and installments of *Victory at Sea*.[26]

Invariably, after the film, they drifted out of the ready room to the place where they absorbed some of their most lasting lessons: Buff Boulevard. A dead-end passageway that ran fore and aft on the 0–2 level, above and a bit forward of the hangar bay below, Buff Boulevard had become a gathering place for the squadron during the 1971 Med cruise. CDR Earnest kept a stateroom there, the first on the left as one entered the passageway. LCDRs Lindland, Graustein, Jackson, and Pieno lived there, too, as did several of the squadron's most senior lieutenants. The passageway served as a gathering place for impromptu parties and for still more movies, generally of dubious quality and colorful content, shown on a screen mounted on its blank end wall. But, far more important, the informality of Buff Boulevard allowed the squadron's few tested veterans to answer questions and impart lessons well beyond the formal training syllabus.

The spontaneous nightly meetings on Buff Boulevard quickly turned CDR Earnest into the squadron's primary teacher. Knowing that CDR Foote would be leaving them almost as soon as they went on the line, the JOs did not seek him out for advice about combat. While he participated in the formal instructional periods during the day, he rarely appeared in this more informal setting to share his experiences. Thus, Foote created the impression in the minds of some JOs that he was more than ready to rotate home. At the same time, however, LTJG Hvidding wondered if Foote purposely stayed away because it had become "a little awkward for him," especially since "even though he was still CO, we were looking to Charlie [Earnest] for leadership and reassurance."[27]

CDR Earnest embraced his role as teacher and leader with skill. Indeed, he made it clear that he planned to keep his stateroom on Buff Boulevard when he became skipper rather than move to quarters near the other squadron commanders. He kept his door open. Although this would be his first combat deployment in A-6s, he already had flown over 220 combat missions in A-4s, and the junior pilots and B/Ns respected that experience. LT Anderson, who shared a nearby stateroom with LT John Miller, frequently listened to Earnest talk about tactics. In retrospect, Anderson recalled, Earnest "brought a level of tactical expertise and innovation that made his voice credible." He also remembered warnings to "plan the hell out of a mission."[28] LTJG Swigart recalled Earnest explaining what he had done on an earlier cruise when AAA hit his A-4 and started a fire. Earnest's presence of mind to fly up to a higher altitude to reduce the oxygen and extinguish the flames impressed Swigart. "I remember thinking to myself to tuck that one away someplace so if it ever happened to me I would at least consider it as an option," the junior B/N noted.[29] LTJG Hvidding recalled several practical pieces of advice he attributed to CDR Earnest's talks on the Boulevard. The XO had told him that if a SAM headed toward him, watch it until the flame got as big as his thumbnail and only then break hard so that the missile would miss his aircraft. He paid close attention whenever Earnest talked about survival skills, even fine details about maneuvering a parachute. He counted among his most important lessons the realization "that I not only needed to learn as much as possible, but I need to THINK in every situation."[30]

LCDR Lindland inspired nearly the same degree of respect. Unlike CDR Earnest, Lindland had flown combat in A-6s before, and that experience, at times, seemed to make his advice even more applicable. LTJG Lerseth rated Lindland's comments on planning and standard procedures as "clearly number one" on his list of important lessons imparted on the transit. As an established crew pair, they talked constantly about putting "as much of our cockpit activities on automatic as we could." Lindland wanted to limit chatter only to information necessary to ensure they got to the target, dropped their bombs on it, and cleared the area safely. "All naval aviators try to do that in all environments," Lerseth noted, "but Don brought home to me how combat could mess with standard ops real fast." But Lindland encouraged questions from all JOs, not simply from his own B/N. He also encouraged them to express their own opinions. Many agreed with Lerseth that Lindland excelled at one key to good leadership: "He could both advise and listen."[31]

Many of the junior B/Ns now began to turn to LCDR Dick Schram for advice. Although he was not the senior B/N in the squadron, he was the only one with combat experience in the A-6. In time, his stateroom, too, became a popular hangout. Dubbed the "Great Bald Eagle" for his premature loss of hair, he possessed a sharp tongue and a wit to match. He soon became the source for squadron nicknames as well as tactical advice. LTJG Petersen became one of the first men Schram renamed. Aviators and car enthusiasts complimented top-notch machines as "high-speed, low drag." Schram saw a chance to match the concept to the initials of Petersen's first and middle names: Lamar Don. Very quickly, he became "Low Drag" Petersen.[32] Other new nicknames followed.

A typical evening on Buff Boulevard might not end until 0200. The talk never centered solely on tactics and technology. One evening, the conversation turned to the importance of good luck. LTJG Fuller produced a pair of Royal Canadian Air Force wings that had belonged to one of his father's friends who had worn them on his battle dress uniform when he flew Spitfires during World War II. Since he had survived unscathed, he had handed down those wings to Fuller to wish him good fortune. LTJG Bob Miller immediately trumped him by producing his own father's gold wings from his days as a Hellcat pilot in World War II.[33] LT Ron Lankford carried a poker chip from a bar at the naval air station at Fallon, Nevada, one that guaranteed him a free drink when he returned home.[34] LCDR Pieno continued to wear a St. Christopher's medal his mother had given him when he first left for college.[35]

As the transit continued, the pilots and B/Ns of all ranks bonded over talk and popcorn. "Out of the seven rooms on the boulevard, there are at least 5 popcorn poppers and I would guess probably 150 to 200 pounds of popcorn and 5 gallons of oil," LTJG Warren explained to his wife.[36] But the nightly sessions, informative as they might be, also could be fueled by beer and scotch. Although regulations prohibited alcohol aboard ship, most of the officers had smuggled their chosen libation aboard anyway. And occasionally, Buff Boulevard parties got out of control. CDR Earnest finally decided to restore a measure of decorum and called a halt to such activity. That night, quiet fell over the passageway for a while, even though the stateroom doors remained open to facilitate muted conversation. Then came the distinctive "pop" of a beer can opening. Then another. By 2300, Buff Boulevard had returned to what passed for "normal." The biggest challenge soon centered on hiding the evidence. The empties were gathered up into plastic bags that, under the cover of darkness, were to be tossed overboard. One night, the wind caught one of the bags in an updraft and carried it upward. It split open, sending dozens of empty beer cans clattering across the flight deck. They came to count upon the reliability—and the discretion—of a young Filipino steward named Jose, who added to his duties the cleaning of Buff Boulevard after the gatherings. The officers repaid him for his silence with a round-trip plane ticket home to see his family.[37]

The impromptu meetings occasionally drew guests from other squadrons. The helicopter crews from HS-7 and the A-7 pilots from VA-37, whose ready room adjoined that of VA-75, dropped in to renew old friendships first forged in AOCS or flight training, swap lies, and boast about the prowess of their own specific aircraft. The A-6 crews and the A-7 pilots argued about who had the more difficult mission and who would do more damage to the North Vietnamese. The banter generally remained good-natured, but, as LTJG Fuller recalled, at times it seemed somewhat like "whistling while walking through the graveyard."[38]

The Sunday Puncher pilots and B/Ns soon balked at the days of constant briefing and lecturing—and no flying. By mid-transit, LTJG Hvidding noted, their attention had begun to wane, especially because "people ran out of interesting useful information."[39] In retrospect, LTJG Ahrens reduced the typical day at mid-transit to four big events—the three meals, plus the movie—with the possible addition of a fifth, "if you count the ice cream after the movie."[40]

Thus, the men welcomed diversions to enliven their days and provide distraction. Events large and small captured their attention. As *Saratoga* approached the equator, a few of the pilots and B/Ns began to discuss the Coriolis effect. According to this principle, water will swirl down a drain counterclockwise when north of the equator and clockwise when south of it. By 16 April, several officers dutifully began observing the water draining out of their stateroom sinks—counterclockwise, they all agreed.[41] Early on 18 April, the carrier crossed the equator. As LT Fischer noted as the first entry in his log on that date: Upon crossing the equator, "water does in fact go straight down the drain."[42] LTJGs Lerseth and Petersen actually tried to stay awake late into the night to wait for the moment when the direction of drainage changed. Both men got bored and went to sleep, but Petersen awakened at 0300 just to check the swirling at the estimated time *Saratoga* planned to cross the equator. His observation: "It goes straight down."[43]

Most of the men of VA-75 slept restlessly that night. But neither swirling waters nor dreams of combat caused their distress. They knew that when the sun rose, as U.S. Navy tradition dictated, "King Neptune" would order an immediate initiation ceremony for *Saratoga*'s nearly 4,000 "pollywogs"—all sailors who had not crossed the equator in a naval vessel—to introduce them to "the solemn mysteries of the ancient order of the deep."[44] Only the "shellbacks"—those who had crossed the equator on a Navy ship during a previous cruise—could serve in the king's welcoming party that included his queen and princess and Davy Jones. The carrier's few hundred shellbacks planned a ceremony on a grand scale. Indeed, it had to be so, since the pollywogs included both CAPT Sanderson and *Saratoga* itself.

Anticipation of the event began well before the crossing. A few nights into the transit, one of the chiefs asked LTJG Sanford if he was worried about the future. Thinking about the prospects of flying into hostile skies, the young B/N admitted he had some qualms. The chief acknowledged that he felt the same. Indeed, he told Sanford, "this thing's got me all kinda bound up." Sanford could not figure out why a chief, busy in his shop below decks of a mighty carrier, felt so strongly, and tried to reassure him that he had nothing to fear. Then Sanford realized what really terrified the chief. "Yeah, they're worse on chiefs than anybody else on that shellback thing," he complained.[45] Sanford was not sympathetic.

The hijinks actually began a few days before the ceremony itself. Starting two nights before the event, the "Pollywog Press"—published after hours by the carrier's Public Affairs Office—encouraged mayhem directed at all shellbacks. Pollywogs trashed or toilet-papered shellback officers' staterooms or taped their doors shut. Shellbacks of all ranks caught below decks by roving bands of pollywogs became the target of eggs, fruit juices, shaving cream, even butterscotch syrup. The carrier's XO, the ranking shellback aboard, returned to his cabin to find it filled with streamers of paper, inflated weather balloons, and even a porcelain toilet plopped on his desk.[46] Some of VA-75's junior enlisted men took part in the "Pollywog Rebellion" by retaliating against Master Chief Pena's constant harping on the length of their hair. The day before *Saratoga* crossed the equator, knowing that the upcoming initiation likely meant tonsorial disasters during the required visit to the "Royal Barber," sailors assigned to the Line Division and some others in the squadron preemptively shaved their heads. Many other sailors did this as part of their preparation for the event, but these men saved their shorn locks to make a special statement. When Master Chief Pena came into his office that day, he saw—prominently displayed on his desk—a large clear trash bag full of hair. If nothing else, the ceremony gave the young sailors an original way to tell a superior to get off their backs.[47] The squadron's shellback officers did not escape harassment either. After serving them their meals and treating them like royalty, a number of JO pollywogs ambushed shellback LCDR Pieno, who offered them a target they could not resist: a clean and pressed uniform. They immediately rolled him in grease and goo.[48]

Among the Punchers, only LCDRs Kennedy, Lindland, Pieno, Jackson, and Schram and some of the senior chiefs stood unchallenged in the ranks of shellbacks. CDR Foote had crossed the equator before and claimed the same status, but at the crucial time, he could not produce the required proof: his shellback card. At least once during the chaotic weekend before departure, CDR Earnest thought about his card, too, but in his haste to pack for his early flight to Mayport, he had forgotten it. He asked his wife to mail it to him, but it did not arrive before *Saratoga* left port, and the shellbacks gave him no choice but to go through the initiation again, too.[49] Gunner Walden actually pulled his card out of his wallet, but LCDR Graustein—as head of the squadron's Administrative Department—refused to accept it; he claimed that since no appropriate notation appeared in Walden's personnel file, he too had to repeat the initiation ceremony.[50]

The next day, VA-75's pollywogs—and a few disgruntled shellbacks—assembled on the hangar deck. At least most of them did. LTs Ron Lankford and Ken Knapp overslept and had to go through the experience without the moral support of their fellow Punchers.[51] The shellback directors split up those who arrived on time, putting one group at a time on Elevator 3 up to the flight deck. There, on the rough antiskid, the initiates did the "pollywog shuffle," crawling on hands and knees through a gauntlet of shellbacks, who paddled them with three-foot lengths of canvas fire hose and heaped colorful verbal abuse on their bowed heads. Pollywogs marked with "SC" on their foreheads, denoting their status as "Special Cases," invariably drew extra attention. Both LCDR Graustein and LTJG Petersen, who taunted their tormenters, won that designation.

LCDRs Schram and Kennedy worked the fire hose line. Pollywogs were not supposed to be able to identify their initiators, but LT Bruce Cook glanced up to catch a glimpse of the man with the hose who seemed to take special pleasure in flailing him. He recognized a familiar face. "You Kennedy?" he grunted, in imitation of the North Carolina park ranger who had informed the maintenance officer about the emergency recall. Shellback Kennedy added a little extra to the next few strokes.[52]

At the end of the gauntlet, the pollywogs met the "Royal Surgeons" who squirted some foul concoction into their mouths. Described as a combination of "oyster juice, aviation gasoline, lemons, salt, sugar, and shoe polish," it had a taste "that lingered . . . and lingered . . . and lingered." Its only positive attribute came in the form of the distraction it provided as the pollywogs moved on to their next tormentors.[53]

Crawling forward, their mouths still full of the surgeon's foul mixture, each man in turn met the "Royal Barbers" who wielded large pairs of rough shears designed to cut ragged, irregular hunks of hair from pollywog heads. LTJG Wardlaw gave them little to work with; like the enlisted men, he had gotten a very close haircut a few days before the event.[54] The barbers chopped a hunk of hair right over the center of LTJG Fuller's forehead, cutting it to within a quarter inch of his scalp. "It looks great," he wrote home soon afterwards, relishing CDR Earnest's unsuccessful efforts afterward to make him cut his remaining hair to even out its length.[55] LT Wharton recognized one "Royal Barber" as a first-class petty officer from the administrative shop who disliked him. When the sailor saw Wharton in line, he immediately took a strong personal interest in initiating the officer, chopping off a substantial hunk of his hair, just above his forehead almost to the scalp. Wharton decided to cut his remaining hair very short "so I wouldn't look totally ridiculous."[56]

Easily the most memorable moment of the entire procedure came when each pollywog had to "kiss the royal baby." A big-bellied shellback chief decked

Chief Frank J. Pittman, one of VA-75's shellbacks, enjoys his duties on "the hose line" during the initiation of the Sunday Punchers' pollywogs. (Frank J. Pittman Collection)

out in diapers and baby bonnet, his paunch smeared with some unidentifiable goop, sat in a deck chair, while—one by one—the pollywogs came forward to plant a big smooch on his stomach. If a pollywog seemed too tentative in his effort, a shellback pressed his face deeply into the "baby's" belly folds. Those who did not call him "the royal baby" sometimes opted for "the Buddha" or "big Baby Huey."

Next they crawled through the "slime tube." As LTJG Swigart recalled it, the shellbacks had filled a twenty-foot-long canvas garbage trough about two feet wide with "all kinds of revolting kitchen sludge" and the vomit of those men who had preceded him "who were marginally seasick to begin with and whose stomachs couldn't take this final abuse."[57] At the end of the tunnel, the shellbacks separated the pollywogs into two groups. The SCs continued to have abuse heaped upon them. All the rest, in groups of about ten, climbed into a net attached to a crane. It lifted up off the flight deck a few feet, and fire hoses sprayed jets of water on the filthy men. Shellback LCDR Jackson observed from nearby to keep the proceedings under control. "But even standing by and watching wasn't easy," he recalled, "because it smelled so bad!"[58]

Begrudgingly, CDRs Foote and Earnest went through the initiation with their JOs. Since he could not get out of it, Foote turned it into an opportunity to protect

CDR Earnest, who could not produce on demand the card that proved his status as a "shellback," begrudgingly went through the "crossing of the Equator" initiation ceremony for a second time, joining all the Sunday Puncher "pollywogs" on Saratoga's *flight deck on 18 April 1972. (David F. Warren Collection)*

his people from the worst harassment. LTJG Fuller, for one, appreciated his efforts. "I was pleasantly surprised" by Foote's performance, he wrote, noting that "whenever one of the J.O.'s near him started to get a little extra attention he would say or do something to draw attention away from the other and to himself."[59]

This key rite of passage completed, LTJG Hvidding wrote, "I guess that contributes towards rounding out my service in the Navy. Why go half way?"[60] As they tried to get the unidentifiable slimy liquids off their faces and out of their hair, several also noticed yet again that, yes, the water now swirled clockwise, and LT John Miller discovered that Prell Shampoo cut through the most greasy glop better than any other product on the ship.[61] The crossing-of-the-equator ceremony left one unexpected legacy. Over the next few days, all the Puncher pilots and B/Ns stood for special identification pictures—full-face and profile photos to help with verification of identities during search-and-rescue operations. A few photos showed faces with irregular patches of hair missing from their heads, courtesy of the Royal Barbers.[62]

With little else to capture their imaginations by mid-transit, some Punchers became keen observers of the increasingly unfamiliar natural world around them. Captivated by the flying fish, some started a contest to look for those that could glide in the air for the greatest distance or for the longest time, with the record established at thirty-two seconds.[63] Others who stayed out on the catwalk until after sunset developed a fascination for stargazing. Many, for the first time, saw the Southern Cross. Anyone with questions about the heavens knew to turn to LT Wagner, who frequently pulled out his star chart to try to spot the various constellations.

One afternoon, the officers gathered on the fantail to qualify with their pistols. When some members of *Saratoga*'s Marine detachment heard the gunfire, they hauled out some other weapons to test, including machine guns. Some Marines threw bottles over the sides of the ship so the pilots and B/Ns could shoot at them with their pistols as they floated aft. During the target practice, someone shot off a flare gun that started a small blaze—always dangerous on a carrier—and the ship's fire crews had to extinguish it.[64]

Not all diversions from the routine provided entertainment. Because they had deployed so quickly, they now had to complete some necessary, and occasionally painful, medical preparations. Beginning on 21 April, the flight crews received the first of three sets of inoculations, the first offering protection against plague, typhus, and cholera. Two more series of shots followed, one on Sunday, 30 April, and a third on 3 May, when each man received two gamma globulin shots, one in each buttock. Of the last, LTJG Warren noted, "It wasn't really bad if you like golf balls on your butt."[65]

The unexpected diversion that highlighted 24 April could be summed up in one word: mail! Word had it that the Navy had convinced the State Department to allow USS *Detroit*, the oiler that accompanied *Saratoga* across the South Atlantic, to bring the mail out to the carrier as part of a scheduled underway replenishment. South Africa's policy of apartheid had strained its diplomatic relations with the United States, and Washington reportedly did not want any major ship such as *Saratoga* to make a port call there. But the smaller ship could do so without compromising diplomatic protocol.[66] The plan almost fell through when heavy swells temporarily prevented the planned linkup with *Detroit*. Still, the welcome delivery of mailbags came late that evening.[67] Mail call came at midnight, but nobody complained. Among the items arriving in that first mail delivery was CDR Earnest's missing shellback card. Also delivered to the carrier was Aviation Electronics Technician Carter, along with several other sailors who had missed the carrier's departure.[68]

Those welcome letters from home provided squadron members with their first clues about their families' adjustment to their sudden departure. Most of the officers' wives attended a coffee on the morning of 12 April, the day after the flyoff, hoping for reliable news about the carrier's destination or date of return. The wives of those officers going off to war for the first time especially sought reassurance or at least some guidance on what to expect. Unfortunately, they heard little to either encourage or inform them. "The only good thing that occurred was that I won the door prize," noted Sandy Pyle, wife of LT Ken Pyle.[69] Jeane Petersen also found the meeting "a great disappointment." The discussion concerned only upcoming bake sales and a bridge night. "I thought they would give us some word about what to expect or something," she wrote. Worse, she felt that the wives of the senior officers held back important information. She overheard two of them talking about what their husbands might do in Vietnam, and she asked if they would explain it to her. One of them "flatly said 'no,'" she complained. At the very least, they hoped to hear about the possibility of a special charter flight to Hong Kong or Singapore or Japan where they could meet their husbands during an in-port period. That subject never came up either.[70]

Protesters at the gates of the Navy base at Norfolk on 22 April did not attract the wives' notice, nor did their signs reading "Drop Nixon, Not Bombs."[71] But they found it far more disconcerting to learn that they could not count on moral support from other Navy spouses in the Norfolk and Virginia Beach area. Indeed, Sandy Pyle and Carol Warren discovered quite the contrary at a social gathering at the Officers' Club at Oceana, when they became the targets of angry invectives from irate wives of aviators belonging to squadrons on another carrier departing to the Mediterranean in May, five months early, to replace *Saratoga* and its airwing. The fact that VA-75 went into a combat zone seemed to matter little to those whose own families' summer plans fell apart when their husbands received orders to deploy earlier than anticipated.[72]

The mothers of small children reported on their initial efforts to create a sense of stability for the family. Jeane Petersen and little Danny made a ritual of watching the evening news together, hoping for some mention of *Saratoga*. When the carrier appeared on television just a few days after it sailed, "I told Danny that was Daddy's big boat & he watched so quietly & then he grinned a big grin when the report was over."[73] Mothers with children of similar ages forged new bonds or tightened old ones. Pixie Tolhurst and Sandy Pyle began taking their children to drive-in movies and other fun activities together.[74] When it came to caring for the children, the wives did not always let their husbands' ranks get in the way. Judy Pieno's four children and Carol Warren's three shared similar ages and interests and often played together, despite the fact that one woman's husband was a lieutenant commander and the other's was a lieutenant junior grade.[75]

Not all the mail brought good news. The quickness of the departure had forced a number of VA-75's enlisted men to leave without resolving all financial responsibilities. In that first mail delivery, the squadron legal officer received four letters of indebtedness from various Virginia Beach and Norfolk banks concerning Sunday Puncher sailors who left without paying all their bills. This happened every time a squadron deployed, even with plenty of advance warning. Given how quickly they left, however, the legal officer actually marveled that he had received so few notices.[76] Still, it took much of the deployment for some enlisted men to straighten out financial problems that, often enough, created genuine hardship and sacrifice at home.

On 25 April, *Saratoga* rounded the Cape of Good Hope. The transition from the Atlantic to the Indian Ocean brought some dramatic changes. The waters became choppier and even the carrier rolled in the waves. Traffic on the sea lanes picked up, and the watch on the carrier noted the near presence of several Soviet naval vessels and at least one submarine. The following day, *Saratoga* went on alert to guard against the possible approach of Soviet planes, and combat air patrols readied to prevent the too-close approach of unfriendly surface vessels or submarines.[77]

To fill the final two weeks until they reached the Philippines, the Punchers struggled to find interesting ways to fill the hours not taken up by training or collateral duties. Some read to pass the time, books remaining in such short supply that anyone who possessed such treasures lingered over them. Just before he shipped out, LT Knapp's wife had given him a book about French involvement in Vietnam that traced the war up to the very recent past. Of the history of the conflict he was about to enter, he admitted, "I truly knew very little about it, other than the news, which was primarily body counts." Since he deemed himself a reluctant participant in the conflict, the reading gave him pause for sober reflection.[78]

By contrast, LT Fischer—the eternal optimist—visited the ship's library and borrowed *The Power of Positive Thinking*. From this and other sources, including the Bible, he jotted down inspiring quotations in his journal, ranging from a short commentary from Philippians—"I can do all things through Christ which strengthens me"—to Stonewall Jackson's "Never take counsel of your fears."[79] As one of few Punchers who regularly attended religious services, Fischer found additional strength in the counsel of the Catholic chaplain, CDR G. R. Witt. During their frequent talks, the chaplain told Fischer that the war would end only when B-52s bombed Hanoi. A Communist only understands brute force, the priest opined, and the only way to negotiate with him is with one foot on his throat. Thus, he reinforced Fischer's own beliefs and confirmed for the pilot the rightness of his course.[80]

But interludes such as these could not dispel entirely a mix of boredom and anxiety that grew as they proceeded eastward. Little problems became major irritants. Such things as the changing of the clocks as they passed through time zones generated major complaints. When CAPT Sanderson ordered the clocks to be reset at night, some argued that the change should take place during the day while they were awake to make the transit seem a bit shorter.[81] The frequent changes led to uncomfortable disturbances in sleep patterns. By 26 April, LTJG Tolhurst groused, "We've had to set our clocks ahead three nights in a row counting tonight. It's really goofing up my sleeping; I just can't fall asleep at night & then I'm sleepy all morning."[82]

As *Saratoga* entered the eastern Indian Ocean and neared Indonesia, the squadron began the transition from training to entry into active air operations. The change revealed itself in many ways, including a tightening of discipline. On 28 April, a number of Sunday Puncher JOs participated in a surprise locker inspection in the compartments of some of the squadron's enlisted personnel. "It was an uncomfortable job and certainly one which did not endear us to the troops," wrote LTJG Fuller.[83] But the officers knew that *Saratoga* had developed a bit of a drug problem and they decided to act now, before the onset of combat operations. LTJG Warren, as squadron legal officer, dealt most directly with the aftermath of the searches. He acknowledged the confiscation of three large knives, and, additionally, the discovery of a small amount of marijuana in one sailor's locker. Still, he did not consider the results of the raid to be a portent of future trouble. "It wasn't a lot" of marijuana, he admitted. He considered it far more important, at the start of truly serious work, to "put the fear of God in some of the kids."[84] VA-75's enlisted men got off comparatively easy, as it turned out. VAW-123 required its enlisted men to undergo urinalysis.[85]

On 29 April, the day after the locker inspection, *Saratoga* officially "in-chopped"—became administratively attached—to the U.S. Navy's Seventh Fleet, becoming part of the growing American military presence in and near Southeast Asia's combat zone.[86] Recent changes in the air effort now reshaped the content and tone of the morning AOMs. During the first part of the transit, most discussion centered on operations in South Vietnam and along the Ho Chi Minh Trail, especially in Laos, where naval aviators had flown many missions over the previous few years. As late as 25 April, LTJG Petersen reassured his wife that "most of our work will be against supply routes in South Vietnam and Laos. They are very lightly defended, if at all, and very low threat. Some strikes are going north but until we get some experience we will be down south."[87] Nonetheless, from the day they left the United States, news of the deteriorating military situation in South Vietnam had held their attention. And now, when they joined the Seventh Fleet, they also received even more complete daily briefings about recent events in the skies over North Vietnam from IOIC over the closed-circuit television system. Until that practice began, "We actually had no idea that things were hot and heavy up North," LT Wharton recalled, adding, "Once or twice we got news of some action in NVN but we were not really expecting to go there ourselves."[88]

The Sunday Punchers now began to realize that they faced a much hotter military situation than that for which they had prepared on the transit. Word of the loosening of target restrictions and increased bombing farther and farther north in North Vietnam alerted them to a possible enlargement of their mission. As LTJG Hvidding admitted, when attending briefings now, "We were well informed and really interested for a change."[89] LTJG Ahrens recalled that, after multiple lectures on operations in Laos, CDRs Foote and Earnest finally told them to "forget all that Laos stuff [be]cause we would not be working there."[90] As if to underscore their message, to prepare for the loading of ordnance *Saratoga* began the routine of inspecting the carrier's magazines on 3 May, a procedure repeated daily to track internal temperature and humidity conditions and to control security of access.[91]

As they grew more serious, any good news became reason for celebration. At 0300 on 2 May, a telegram arrived for LT Ruland. The brief note from his wife announced: "Soon we will be three." The news of Ruland's impending fatherhood spread quickly among the squadron's officers, and despite the late hour, a small, but joyous, celebration ensued. The good news probably explained his smile the next day when VA-75's officers gathered on the flight deck for a photograph in their tropical white long uniforms. LTJG Warren hoped they would publish it in the very next familygram sent home to their loved ones. That way, he told his wife, "you'll get to see my new *moustache*."[92] The photo did not get printed, though, and at least one officer probably breathed a sigh of relief. The squadron had left so quickly that LCDR Schram had forgotten to pack his white uniform shoes. He appeared for the photo wearing white sneakers with black stripes on their sides, clearly visible to the sharp of eye. Always extraordinarily fastidious in the care and wearing of his uniform, Schram became the target of much teasing because of his inappropriate footwear.

Saratoga turned out of the Indian Ocean into the Strait of Sumatra on 4 May. Nearly the entire crew came out near midnight to see Krakatoa's glowing lava as they passed through the channel between Sumatra and Java and headed toward the South China Sea. After sunup, the sharks, turtles, flying fish, and the antics of the porpoises caused much amusement. Sea snakes caused an opposite reaction. LCDR Engel recalled a briefing on those reptiles that stressed their aggressive nature and venomous bite. He decided to log those deceptively safe waters as "another place not to be found swimming."[93] No doubt LTJG Swigart concurred. He

On 4 May 1972, as Saratoga *neared the Philippines, the officers of VA-75 gathered on the flight deck in front of one of the squadron's A-6As for this official photograph. Kneeling in front, from left to right, are CDR Everett W. Foote, LCDR Richard L. Engel, LCDR Donald F. Lindland, LCDR Robert S. Graustein, and CDR Charles "M" Earnest. Note the unauthorized footgear worn by LCDR Richard W. Schram, standing in the back row on the extreme right. (U.S. Navy photograph, John R. Fuller Collection)*

had heard rumors that the snakes' poison could kill in four seconds. "Not too comforting if you ever had to eject over the ocean," he concluded.[94] Still, despite the potential dangers, the ocean's overwhelming beauty inspired LTJG Lerseth to tell his mother, "It's hard to believe that they could have a war here. It's hot, humid and so serene that it would surprise you. The water is glassy and clear and, out here at least, the air is clear." He ended on a wistful note: "The sunsets the last few days have been spectacular. If only this were a pleasure cruise and you all could be here."[95]

But everyone knew that the serenity would not last much longer. Providing an outlet for pent-up energies, the nightly gatherings on Buff Boulevard continued. On the night of 4 May—and after some drinking—a group of the Punchers prevailed upon CDR Earnest to demonstrate his well-known ability to "blow flames." The XO had mastered the process of ingesting a bit of lighter fluid, then igniting it as he spewed it out of his mouth with some force. The effect suggested a dragon, and he apparently enjoyed his reputation as a human flamethrower. Earnest picked his target: a balsa wood model of an A-6 hanging from the overhead of the stateroom shared by LTJGs Swigart and Tolhurst. The JOs' room was around the corner from those on Buff Boulevard. Thus, when a group of Punchers—the XO, with LCDR Pieno, LT Lankford, and others—emerged from the Boulevard laughing and shouting, Tolhurst and Swigart awoke and guessed their intent. As the crowd pushed open their stateroom door, Tolhurst and Swigart leaned hard against it. When they did so, they slammed the door on LCDR Pieno's foot, triggering screams of pain and a cloud of profanity from the injured officer and raucous laughter from the rest of the crowd outside the stateroom. Swigart and Tolhurst opened the door just enough to let Pieno's foot go free, and—whoosh!—Earnest shot a bright flame across the length of their stateroom, singeing the fishing line suspending the aircraft and sending the model crashing to the floor.

Unfortunately, at nearly the same time Earnest lit the flame, the comic antics about him made him laugh. Some of the lighter fluid, now set afire, dribbled down his face and onto his neck and t-shirt. The XO had caught fire. LT Lankford, standing nearby with a wet towel "just in case," quickly doused the flames. But the damage had been done. The flames burned one side of Earnest's face and neck severely. The flight surgeon gave him a white ointment to put on his raw cheeks and throat. Fortunately, at least for a few more days, he would not have to worry about his flight status; the burns would have made it too painful, if not outright impossible, to don an oxygen mask in the cockpit. In the end, he merely had to stop shaving for a few days. Tolhurst and Swigart took the damaged model A-6 to a catwalk off the flight deck, filled it with lighter fluid, and, with great ceremony, ignited it and then watched as it spiraled down to its own burial at sea.[96]

Just before *Saratoga* reached the Philippines, the ship's company and all the squadrons competed in the "*Saratoga* Olympics," inspired by the upcoming 1972 Summer Games. The pursuit of the Captain's Cup began with trials on 5 May in the 100-yard dash, the 400-yard relay, the mile run, a football distance-throw, and sit-up and push-up contests. Each sailor could take part in only a single event, so anyone could participate if he chose.[97] LCDR Grady Jackson and Aviation Ordnanceman Third Class Bill Bolena tried out in the football throw, while Aviation Machinist Mate Airman Al Dunbar participated in the mile run and Aviation Electronics Technician Third Class Tim O'Sullivan ran in the 100-yard dash. The Sunday Punchers put together a crack 400-yard relay team—LT John Miller, LTJG Tolhurst, Seaman William Stokes, and Airman Apprentice Teddy

Keeby—that defeated all comers in the preliminary heats.[98] In the elimination round of the push-up contest, LT Fischer placed third, completing eighty push-ups in ninety seconds. With confidence, he boasted, "I think I can win tomorrow in [the] finals." During the medal round the next day, however, Fischer finished in fourth place. He took some consolation at placing second in the airwing, but he still believed that the winner, a Marine who did ninety-four push-ups in that same time period, cheated by not "going all the way up each time."[99] Other Punchers also won laurels for the squadron. As Tolhurst reported home, "We won the relay from all the relay teams on the whole ship. . . . We beat the second team by about three yards."[100] Unfortunately, the squadron lost the overall team title to the Tomcatters of VF-31.[101] The next day, Fischer—with LT Wagner as his active accomplice—turned his disappointment into entertainment with a new list of "Olympic events." In the "Kick Ass and Take Names Later" contest, they named LTJG Hvidding, one of the easiest-going B/Ns in the squadron, as the Punchers' entrant into the imaginary competition.[102]

Finally, *Saratoga* neared the Philippines. The carrier had run so low on fuel that CAPT Sanderson briefly contemplated an emergency stop in Singapore. Indeed, by now, the only item aboard the carrier not reported to be in short supply was paperwork. "We've got paper work up to our necks right now," complained LTJG Fuller, and, worse, it struck him—and most of the other JOs—as "pointless."[103] Veterans had told them that one great benefit of being on the line was the elimination of much of the paperwork that they considered to be part of the "Mickey Mouse" peacetime Navy. If that were true, they could not wait for that change to occur.

Their gripes about paperwork may have masked a deeper disappointment. On 4 May, ADM Zumwalt issued a message of appreciation to all the ships, crews, and families that had responded to the emergency recall. But he also warned that "decisions on levels of forces to be employed, and thus the duration of deployments, depend on the outcome of the battle. We cannot be precise at this time because the battle is not over." During this difficult time of uncertainty, the CNO encouraged all commanding officers, even those who "are busy in combat [and] have little free time," to issue familygrams to keep an information flow going to those back home.[104] To the men of VA-75 and thousands more sailors and their loved ones, this message came as unwelcome news. Not only did Zumwalt's announcement dash hopes for a brief absence from home, it also destroyed any remaining illusions about the veracity of early-transit rumors that they would fly their missions only in South Vietnam, Laos, and Cambodia.

As the carrier came within flying distance of the airfield at Cubi Point on 6 May, a senior officer from each of the airwing's squadrons flew to the naval air station for an introductory operational briefing. CDR Earnest, his lower face still unshaven and smeared with ointment, represented VA-75.[105] In the meantime, since at least nine of the squadron's aircraft required some kind of specialized work that could not be completed aboard *Saratoga*, the VA-75 operations officer prepared a flight schedule for 7 May so that nine of the more senior crews could prepare to fly those aircraft to Cubi.

Chief Warrant Officer Howard P. Smith needed to go ashore to coordinate the maintenance effort, especially the extra work required to update the electronic countermeasures (ECM) equipment. To make room for him in one of the aircraft, LCDR Lindland put him in LT Lankford's right seat. Lankford planned to put the plane through some sharp turns and complicated maneuvering, just for practice—and, if possible, to unsettle Smitty's staid demeanor. But when the nine aircraft launched, several immediately developed problems. LCDR Engel's plane suffered a badly cracked front windscreen, obscuring the pilot's vision. After his aircraft climbed to altitude, LT John Miller's oxygen system malfunctioned, and his B/N—LTJG Sanford—passed out. Lankford flew between the two stricken planes, keeping visual contact with one flying high to his left while telling Smitty to watch the other one flying low to the right. Lankford had planned to fly at a fairly high altitude to conserve fuel for a long flight, but circumstances now forced him to fly lower. Thus, he also had to watch his fuel gauge. They all reached Cubi safely, but none of them reported much fuel left when they landed.[106] What should have been an easy hop proved far more exciting than expected. When Smitty reflected back on the flight—which began with his first-ever catapult shot—he noted with remarkable restraint, "It was quite an experience."[107]

Since they arrived the day before the rest of the squadron and the ship's company, the nine Puncher crews that flew VA-75's planes to Cubi got first crack at the stereo equipment, china, electronics, and other reasonably priced goods at the base exchange. Indeed, the promise of making multiple purchases provided one way for the aviators to assuage their wives' worst fears. "I want you to think of this cruise as just another extended foreign shopping trip," LTJG Petersen had told his wife, encouraging her to "sit at home and think of things to buy. I'm sure your womanly instinct can think of a thousand places to spend my money, so go to work on it."[108] Early arrivals enjoyed a second advantage, too—a better chance of finding an available telephone to call home. When LTJG Ahrens finally located one, he learned just how much that privilege could cost; his first call to Linda in Minnesota cost ninety-three dollars.[109]

Saratoga moored at the starboard side of Leyte Wharf at Cubi Point on the early afternoon of 8 May as scheduled.[110] As the carrier docked, a Filipino band greeted the sailors with a grand selection of polka music. "Weird," admitted LTJG Warren, but, he decided, "for a Filipino polka band, they weren't bad."[111] For two of the Punchers, however, a disquieting note ruined the gaiety of the moment. CDR Earnest, returning from the previous day's operations brief, met *Saratoga* at the pier. What he had learned troubled him, and when Earnest boarded the carrier, LT Wharton and LTJG Bob Miller noticed a grim look on his face. They asked him about the briefing, and, as Wharton recalled, "All he said to us was 'It's 1965 all over again.'"[112]

If that briefing had disabused the airwing's senior officers of an easy cruise ahead, those sailors and JOs on their first deployment to Westpac focused more on the brief liberty period that introduced them to an exotic world they knew only from the sea stories of veterans. Now they were about to experience the Philippines for themselves. But they would do so on only a limited basis. Aircrews and ship's company alike all put in full training days before heading ashore in the evenings.

As they flooded the base exchange in far greater numbers now, many Punchers wanted one specific item: Mother's Day cards. They discovered quickly that the shelves at the exchange and at Filipino shops had been cleaned out of special cards for mothers and wives. LTJG Lerseth apologized to his mother for his handmade card. "You'll have to settle for a Wallmark rather than a Hallmark this time," he told her, but assured her that "the feeling is there."[113]

Nearly all the officers made a visit to the Cubi Point Officers' Club, where drinks cost ten to fifteen cents and $1.75 bought a good beef kabob dinner. Many visited the downstairs bar at the club for their first glimpse of the "slide for life." For one dollar, one could get into a mock cockpit set on rails. At the "ready" signal, the cockpit would be cut loose to hurtle down the track. The rider then had a single chance to catch the only arresting wire. Failure to do so resulted in a dousing in a pool of water at the base of the slide. Success brought rewards. As LT Fischer explained, "If you do it you get your name on the board and a bottle of champagne! Johnny Unitas has his name there."[114]

For many, Olongapo beckoned. Already the stuff of legend among American sailors, they called it Po City or simply "the Po." The Punchers who went there crossed a bridge over the Olongapo River, a sludgy, garbage-filled waterway often simply called "Shit River." Little children stood on both shores or in dugout canoes begging sailors to throw coins into the filthy water so they could retrieve them. Once across the bridge, a different world awaited. Bars and brothels lined the streets. Drivers of the numerous multicolored jeepneys honked to clear paths through the crowded streets. Vendors selling charbroiled meat—often called "monkey meat"—competed for customers' attention. LTJG Mullins witnessed for himself the effectiveness of his safety and health warnings to his enlisted men in the Power Plants Branch as he watched every one of them follow the shop's senior petty officers right over the bridge and into the bars. "One of my two first class petty officers got 'the clap' on that very first port call," he recalled, adding, "I knew it was going to be a long cruise for the docs."[115]

Some Puncher officers made the trip across the bridge, too. LCDRs Pieno and Graustein took LTJGs Warren, Lerseth, and Petersen on their first trip into Olongapo. They sipped the cold San Miguel beer at New Pauline's, a bar famous for its moat stocked with live alligators. Children stood outside the moat, offering to sell customers live baby chicks to feed the alligators for two pesos each; for two pesos more, they would bite off the bird's head before pitching it into the moat. Then Pieno and Graustein took them to the East End Club. As they walked in the door, young Filipino women greeted them as they had welcomed many American sailors before, with flirtatious talk, requests for drinks, and offers of sex. Several others who visited later, however, had to use chairs to fend off the more zealous girls. "It became a game," LTJG Hvidding later explained, adding, "The more we fended them off, the more determined they were to welcome us to the Po in the proper fashion." Still, they all left with their honor "somewhat intact."[116]

LTJG Tolhurst experienced a particularly memorable introduction to Olongapo. As junior pilot in the squadron, he drew shore patrol duty his first night there. He linked up with the two largest enlisted members of the detachment he could find. As they hulked over him, he readily conformed to their first instruction that he stay one-half step behind them and in between them at all times. At their direction, he also removed all ribbons and insignia on his uniform shirt so that if he were hit or punched in the chest, the pins would not be driven into his skin. As they completed their orientation, a fight between two American sailors broke out a few blocks away. They rushed to the scene, but the local police arrived first. Tolhurst heard gunshots. At first he just stood there, stunned, but the enlisted men with him told him "that it was not that unusual" and they returned to the base to fill out a report on the incident.[117]

As the men of VA-75 enjoyed their first evening off the ship for nearly a month, they could not guess how dramatically President Nixon's 8 May speech to the American people would change their immediate futures. On 26 April the president had told the nation that the United States so far had limited its response to the North Vietnamese invasion to increased air and naval strikes on military targets and renewed efforts to seek a negotiated settlement at the Paris peace talks. Now, Nixon reported the failure of Henry Kissinger's recent diplomatic efforts. "All we heard from the enemy was bombastic rhetoric and a replaying of their demands for surrender," he noted. The United States had offered a cease-fire, a plan to withdraw all American military forces, a proposition for elections in South Vietnam that would include Communist participation, and a favorable prisoner exchange that would release ten North Vietnamese

LTJG Don Petersen, LTJG David F. Warren, and LTJG Roger G. Lerseth enjoying their first visit to Olongapo on 8 May 1972. The photograph shows some wear and tear because Petersen tucked it into his flight helmet and carried it with him on every mission he flew after 6 September 1972. (Don Petersen Collection)

prisoners for every American turned over. But "North Vietnam has met each of these offers with insolence and insult," the president reported, and they "have flatly and arrogantly refused to negotiate an end to the war." As a consequence of their intransigence, Nixon announced that the time had come for the United States to make a "clear, hard choice" among three options: immediate withdrawal of all American troops, continued negotiation, or "decisive military action to end the war." He rejected the first option, noting, "By simply getting out, we would only worsen the bloodshed." His frustration with the North Vietnamese negotiators and his own refusal to offer any additional concessions that might jeopardize President Nguyen Van Thieu's government or South Vietnam's seventeen million people convinced Nixon that additional diplomatic efforts would remain unproductive. The only way to stop the war, especially in the face of an enemy that "abandons all restraint, throws its whole army into battle in the territory of its neighbor, [and] refuses to negotiate" now forced him to take steps to deny Hanoi "the supplies and weapons it needs to continue the aggression."

To accomplish this end, Nixon announced the mining of the entrances to all major North Vietnamese ports to stop delivery of military supplies. Even as the men of VA-75 enjoyed their first liberty in the Philippines, A-6s and A-7s from USS *Coral Sea* had begun to lay minefields near the mouth of Haiphong harbor, with the detonators set to activate seventy-two hours later to permit international vessels currently in port to leave unharmed, if they chose. Pentagon leaders had endorsed the highly controversial step since 1965, but President Johnson had not embraced the option then or later, concerned in large part about the likely reaction of the Soviet Union or mainland China to the damage, destruction, or restriction of their commercial vessels. But his recent visit to Peking and upcoming trip to Moscow made Nixon more confident that he could exercise this option now. Indeed, just a few weeks before the Intruders and Corsairs launched from *Coral Sea*'s flight deck, a national defense specialist had informed an audience at the Naval War College that "successful weapons are never outlawed by international action" and "the much maligned mine is a successful weapon" that violated no legal strictures.[118]

Additionally, the president noted, he approved the expansion of air strikes against North Vietnamese communication lines and railways—and, by extension, all internal modes of transport—to hit targets above the 20th parallel, including selected sites near Hanoi and Haiphong, to interdict the flow of military supplies. The North Vietnamese could prevent this if they chose. They only had to agree, first, to return all American POWs and, second, to respect an internationally supervised cease-fire throughout Southeast Asia, to be followed by the withdrawal of all American forces. If the North Vietnamese did not accept these terms, Nixon planned to render them unable to continue the fight.[119]

Without knowing much about their commander in-chief's announcement, the Sunday Punchers nonetheless continued the hard business of preparing themselves for Southeast Asia's combat environment. On 9 May, the flight crews went through JEST (Jungle Evasion and Survival Training), a nine-hour exercise designed to teach them how to stay alive in the tropics if they got shot down. The instructors were Negritos, small but tough Filipinos known for their effective guerrilla tactics against the Japanese during World War II. During the course, the aviators learned how to rappel from tall trees like those in the tropical highlands of North Vietnam and to vector in a rescue helicopter by radio. They learned how to hide themselves from potential captors. The Negritos taught them dozens of uses for bamboo and how to obtain quinine and water. They learned that an iodine plant had its leaves set in a 2–2–1 arrangement and that the bark would help stop bleeding, knowledge that LT Knapp applied immediately when he cut his hand on a razor-sharp palm frond. The course helped to demystify the dangerous jungle habitat. When the course ended, LCDR Jackson recalled, "we all said that what we really wanted to take into combat with us was one of the Negrito instructors!"[120]

Saratoga's airwing resumed flying from the airfield at Cubi on 10 May.[121] All of the squadrons needed this time to polish skills, some to a far greater degree than others. In the few days between the time of the emergency recall and the squadron's departure, the Tomcatters of VF-31 had welcomed into their ranks ten new pilots and three new RIOs, along with a new ordnance warrant officer and chief, a significant turnover of key operational personnel. The fighter squadron's heavies had created new crews only during the transit over to the Philippines. As a consequence, many of them would fly together for only four days before their first combat action.[122] VF-103 also included a number of new pilots and RIOs fresh from the F-4 RAG. At least most of VA-75's crews enjoyed the advantage of having flown together during the workups and the Operational Readiness Exercise in March.

Regardless of experience, they all needed time in the air. LTJG Ron McFarland took a training hop with a pilot from the airwing staff that quickly reinforced for the seasoned B/N the importance of the crew concept. McFarland had never flown with this pilot, who took off and headed toward the mountains. "Some of the mountain tops extended above the clouds," recalled McFarland, and the pilot flew into a valley between two obscured peaks. All of a sudden, McFarland could not locate the mountaintops visually or on radar. He told the pilot to climb immediately to get above the clouds. When the pilot did not comply at once, the B/N even threatened to eject. They popped out of the overcast without incident, and McFarland said nothing more about it at the time. He decided on the spot, however, that he could not fly with a pilot who seemed so casual about what McFarland considered an unsafe practice. Except for one tanker hop, he never flew with that pilot again.[123]

VA-75's B/Ns had to refresh basic skills, too. LTJG Ahrens found it particularly troubling that even though he had participated in the 1971 Med cruise, he seldom had practiced dropping bombs on targets at low level at night or in bad weather. He considered his substandard level of mastery of a necessary skill not merely the predictable aftereffect of the thirty-day layoff but also the long-term result of a difference in philosophy between the East Coast and the West Coast Navy. West Coast A-6 squadrons stationed at Whidbey Island expected to deploy to Vietnam and thus practiced all elements of the day/night all-weather attack mission. By contrast, with the war apparently winding down by 1972, the East Coast Navy had focused on experiments with the CV concept and its antisubmarine role. "The west coast A6 squadrons trained by flying night low levels in the mountain. We rarely did that," Ahrens noted. Thus, Ahrens felt a level of unpreparedness entirely unrelated to the one-month layoff.[124]

Each evening, they paid increasing attention to the war news. On 10 May, massive air strikes by both U.S. Navy and Air Force planes had hit multiple targets near Hanoi and Haiphong. In an F-4 flying off USS *Constellation*, LT Randy Cunningham and LTJG William Driscoll shot down their fifth MiG to become the first aces of the war. While the men aboard *Saratoga* could brag that the aces represented Navy—and not Air Force—aircrews, that same cause for pride reminded them of the dangers that lay ahead. They also learned that the interdiction campaign in North Vietnam now had a name: Operation LINEBACKER.

Early on 13 May, newly refueled with 1.8 million gallons of JP-5 jet fuel, *Saratoga* departed Subic Bay for the waters off South Vietnam. VA-75's planes flew off from Cubi's airstrip later that morning, leaving behind a small number of enlisted men as part of a beach detachment to service airwing aircraft requiring repairs too complex to be completed aboard the carrier. By 1300 all of VA-75's planes had trapped safely aboard, their first arrested landings in over a month. CVW-3 then launched three large-scale simulated alpha strikes, each one using at least four aircraft from VA-75 and each of the airwing's two A-7 and F-4 squadrons. Planners also scheduled each division of four aircraft to recover at a specific time and at reasonable intervals to permit all pilots to complete four touch-and-goes and one trap to update their carrier qualifications. As if they needed the reminder, that very day *Saratoga* received a flash message from Carrier Task Force 77 (CTF-77) ordering all carriers on alert to fend off a threatened MiG attack. Although meant only for the carriers already in the Gulf of Tonkin, *Saratoga* went to full combat readiness, too. "It was no joke," wrote LTJG Hvidding.[125]

Fine tuning continued. The medical department completed final precautionary regimens. The flight crews received an issue of malaria pills and a final set of gamma globulin shots on 14 May.[126] That same day, LCDR Lindland assigned LTJG Petersen the additional duty of compiling basic information from each mission debrief for the inevitable end-of-line-period reports the squadron owed to the airwing. He set up a notebook with spaces to record for each mission: the crew names; type of mission; type and amount of ordnance, ordnance expended, and ordnance hung; targeting information with coordinates and, where possible, a brief description; type of control—FAC, flight lead, or single aircraft; type of delivery; bomb damage assessment (BDA); and type of resistance (AAA, SAMs, or MiGs). For tanker hops, he left spaces to record pounds of fuel delivered. Petersen became the keeper of the operational history of the Sunday Punchers' 1972–73 combat cruise.[127]

Until 16 May, the aviators continued to hone their skills in the air over the Philippines. While F-4 crews conducted AIM7/AIM9 missile practice at the Poro Point Control Facility, the A-6 and A-7 crews completed a series of mock bombing runs by dropping 25-pound practice bombs on targets at Tabones and

Scarborough Shoals. As they practiced, several crews noticed small canoes in the target zone, the boats of local people who regularly paddled out into those dangerous waters to gather up scrap metal to sell. The drills seemed like a good idea to LTJG Ahrens, especially because his own pilot proved to be a bit rusty. As he noted, "I recall some lousy hits." Most pilots preferred to use raked targets—those with manned observation towers and measured impact areas—to raise their proficiency in visual dive-bombing, but they had not practiced that way in a long time.[128]

Training flights also gave the crews an opportunity to check out the repair work done at Cubi and to make sure the rest of the instrumentation worked as well. Multiple gripes popped up almost immediately. Even before *Saratoga* left port, LT Fischer and LTJG Sanford launched to practice low-level bombing techniques, and their radio went dead.[129] Three days later, when Fischer flew a different aircraft aboard the carrier, its radio died too.[130] On 15 May, LT Wharton's radio went out, and the one in the A-6 escorting him back to the carrier failed too.[131] Other equipment malfunctioned as well. On 15 May, when LT Pyle started his first practice run, his B/N discovered that the reselect light on the armament system would not go out to permit an auto-release. They switched to visual dive-bombing instead. The next day, as the same crew prepared to launch on another practice bombing run, the strut lock light failed to come on. The aircraft, already on the catapult, had to be downed until maintenance could solve the problem.[132] To take care of routine gripes, troubleshooters from the various squadrons remained up on the flight deck to make quick repairs or adjustments, hoping to keep a plane in the air for one or two more training cycles.

These final four days of preparation reinforced to all aboard a basic truism about carrier life. As CAPT Sanderson wrote to the crew's families in May, "The thing to remember when you read and hear of *Saratoga*'s operations is that a carrier is not made up of only pilots. Each man, be he pilot or mess cook, mechanic or Jack-of-the-Dust, has his important job to do. An aircraft carrier is a teamwork ship, especially *Saratoga*. Every task we perform in our daily routine is a contribution to the total effort; every job is vitally important. The 'can do' spirit and quiet efficiency that has become a hallmark of her name will prove *Saratoga* a major link in the U.S. Seventh Fleet force. None of it, however, would be possible without each individual doing his part. Our pilots in the air mean that every *Saratoga* man is doing his job."[133]

Final briefings continued. Late on 15 May, based on new intelligence, VA-75's crews received a brief on the SA-7, a portable, shoulder-fired, heat-seeking surface-to-air missile just appearing in the North Vietnamese arsenal. Indeed, in recent weeks, those missiles had taken down several of the low- and slow-flying aircraft piloted by FACs in the northernmost provinces of South Vietnam. The next day, each pilot and B/N in the squadron received an issue of fifty blank kneeboard cards for communication information and other data issued at mission briefs before individual combat hops.[134]

The approach of active operations was evident in other ways, too. After the last recoveries on the evening of 17 May, the fleet oiler USS *Ashtabula* came alongside to refuel *Saratoga*. This first delivery began the process of keeping the carrier supplied with food, fuel, ordnance, spare parts, and other support required for combat operations. Called an "unrep"—short for "underway replenishment"—this evolution occurred nearly every second or third day or night after the carrier ceased air operations. The carrier and the supply ship followed parallel courses only eighty to one hundred feet apart, linked for perhaps six hours by a tangle of lines and hoses. Delivery of fuel required the handling of specialists. Electrical winches made it possible to move cargoes as heavy as four tons from one ship to the other. It was dangerous work, but any enlisted man not currently on his work shift—whether he belonged to ship's company or airwing—could be called upon to help move and stow the supplies, unarmed general-purpose bombs, and other ordnance. Experienced Sunday Puncher chiefs and petty officers already knew this, but many of their young charges did not. In a short time, the chiefs taught them the basics, and with a bit more experience, even the most junior sailors learned to identify—and occasionally hijack—special deliveries, such as ice cream or steaks originally destined for the officers' mess.[135]

While they focused on the task ahead, the Punchers enjoyed the renewal of mail deliveries. Some still paid a price for their quick departures. LTJG Warren had detected an unsettling tone in letters from his wife, parents, and mother-in-law. He came to feel they considered him to be "some kind of war-monger or something and that I'd rather be over here than at home with my family where I belong." Before entering combat, he felt he had to set the record straight. "I don't *want* to be over here, risking my life every day. I'm just as scared or maybe even more scared as the next guy. But I do feel that I owe it to myself, to you, and to my country to do my part and to do the best I can." The former enlisted man pointed out that he had now served in the United States Navy for more than ten years, and he had never shouldered the burden of combat in all that time. Now he asked for his family's understanding, hoping that they would not think badly of him if he appeared "happy at the chance to do this. I'm not happy. I just feel that as long as it came up, this is my chance to catch up a little and to make me feel like I've contributed something and helped out in some little way."[136]

Others contemplated their futures, too. On that last quiet evening at sea before arriving at Cubi, LTJG Lerseth had written home to his mother and two sisters.

Still concerned about how well they were dealing with the death of his father in March, he reassured them that good things lay ahead. He also contemplated what might await him. "Thirty days ago I wouldn't have given 100:1 odds that I'd be here," he wrote. Now, he found it "amazing and a little startling that one day you can be planning a trip to the Med and the next be flying aboard a carrier bound for Vietnam." Echoing Warren's sentiments, Lerseth acknowledged that "now the Navy will get something from me for all the training they've given me. Am I bitter? Yes and no. Yes, because I'm stingy and want to have Nini and my family near me; yes, because war is a sickening thing at best—no, because there is a job Uncle Sam wants done, and I have as much an obligation to do that job as the next guy; no, because I believe in our way of life and in the lives of those KIA's, MIA's and POW's who are still there in North and South Vietnam." He believed that a "multitude of mistakes" had been made in the conduct of the war, but "the alternatives at this point are extremely limited, and most of them are unacceptable to me as a citizen of a free country. Therefore, here I am, and as distasteful the job I have is, I will do it to the best of my abilities. Yes, I'm a little scared. I think I'd have to be some kind of a nut not to be. But at the same time I'm confident enough about my own abilities that I can say I'll spend my time in this man-made mess and come back just a little bit wiser."[137]

Sometime during the evening of 17 May, an enlisted man from the squadron's operations shop slipped under the door of the stateroom of each Sunday Puncher pilot and B/N a copy of the next day's flight schedule. There on the mimeographed blue-and-white page, they saw their immediate future spelled out for them. On 18 May, VA-75 would launch into combat against targets in South Vietnam.

CHAPTER FOUR

"A Piece of Cake"

At first light on 18 May 1972, *Saratoga* prepared to commence its first day in an active combat zone. During a carrier's deployment in Westpac, it alternated between active air operations and brief periods in the Philippines or elsewhere for rest and equipment repair. The Navy called each rotation into the combat zone a line period. *Saratoga*'s initial line period began with two weeks of combat missions in South Vietnam. During this time, CVW-3 hit targets in all four Military Regions (MR I, II, III, and IV), from Quang Tri in the north in MR I, to Kontum in the Central Highlands in MR II, to the area around besieged An Loc in MR III, south through the Mekong Delta in MR IV. VA-75 concentrated its efforts in MR IV.

The Sunday Punchers' introduction to combat in the southern half of South Vietnam sent them against comparatively weak air defenses, providing a welcome opportunity to perfect section and division strike tactics. Small-arms fire from the ground presented the greatest threat, but aircraft above 3,500 feet could fly in relative safety. Just the same, VA-75's pilots and B/Ns still flew into a military situation that had deteriorated badly since they had left Oceana.

On 5 April, North Vietnamese troops advanced from Cambodia and attacked Loc Ninh in MR III, just northwest of Saigon. After two days of hard fighting, the ARVN defenders and their American advisers pulled back to An Loc. If that town fell, the road to the South Vietnamese capital would be open. President Thieu ordered his senior commanders to hold the town. In so doing, wrote historian James H. Willbanks, "Thieu all but challenged the North Vietnamese to take it," and they took the dare. Fighting around An Loc began on 9 April, continued until 15 April, re-escalated between 19 and 22 April, and ignited once again on 9 May, just as *Saratoga* arrived in the Philippines. At the start, Maj. Gen. James F. Hollingsworth, the senior U.S. Army military adviser in MR III, had urged his subordinates to encourage their ARVN counterparts to force the North Vietnamese to concentrate there. "Hold them and I'll kill them with air power," he told them, adding "give me something to bomb and I'll win."[1] *Saratoga*'s airwing contributed to that effort, with VA-75 playing a part.

The military situation in the Mekong Delta in MR IV also became increasingly bleak. Just as worrisome to U.S. military advisers and the Saigon government, but far less publicized in the shadow of the fighting at Quang Tri, Kontum, and An Loc, clashes between North Vietnamese forces and ARVN troops erupted in mid-May throughout the delta. The Saigon government worried about its most important agricultural area, a region called home by more than one half of the nation's population. Over the previous few years, the area had remained calm, seemingly offering evidence of the success of American and ARVN pacification efforts. To keep the peace, South Vietnam's Joint General Staff had deployed three ARVN divisions to the region. Nonetheless, Hanoi had set its sights on gaining control of the Mekong Delta and the Ca Mau peninsula. In 1970, the 1st Division of the People's Army of Vietnam (PAVN) had begun to concentrate in southern Cambodia, just across the border from the region, and elements of six North Vietnamese regiments infiltrated into the delta over the next two years. When the 30 March 1972 invasion first began, MR IV remained comparatively quiet, seemingly so stable that the Joint General Staff redeployed to An Loc one of the three ARVN divisions and elements of another then posted in the delta. Once these troops had moved off, the North Vietnamese began more active large-unit operations. They struck first at Kien Luong on 18 May, the day *Saratoga* arrived on the line.[2]

The fluidity of the action on the ground made it essential for all aircrews aboard *Saratoga* to understand the rules for operating in South Vietnamese airspace. On 17 May, the night before its first missions, CVW-3 issued to all flight crews a new set of kneeboard cards. Unlike the set of fifty blank forms the VA-75 pilots and B/Ns had received a few nights before, these included the specific information that outlined the standard procedures for flying combat and support missions in South Vietnam. They included key radio frequencies for Air Force flight controllers, forward air controllers (FACs), and ARVN divisions; instructions for handling hung and unexpended ordnance and low-fuel states; search-and-rescue procedures; Communist-bloc ship recognition silhouettes; squadron call signs for all carriers operating in Westpac; and much more.[3] As they tried to absorb all the information, they received the 18 May flight schedule.

The scheduling process for any given day of *Saratoga*'s air operations began the evening before with the arrival of the daily strike planning message from the operations staff of Carrier Task Force 77 (CTF-77). Since the staff usually worked regular daylight hours, that message generally arrived at *Saratoga*'s Strike Operations center ("Strike Ops") late each afternoon. The airwing staff immediately went to work to compile intelligence reports for all assigned targets. Early each evening, the airwing and squadron operations officers gathered at Strike Ops to decide which units would fly the various missions assigned to

CVW-3. To do that, VA-75's operations officer—LCDR Don Lindland—had to know the mission-ready status of the squadron's aircraft to determine how many planes he could allot to various missions. Once these issues were settled with the operations officers of the airwing and the A-7 and F-4 squadrons and with VA-75's own maintenance and ordnance branches, Lindland brought the next day's flight requirements to the VA-75 flight officer, LT John M. Miller. Following his ops officer's guidance, Miller then assigned crews to the various missions. Lindland—with active involvement of other senior officers in the squadron—reviewed the preliminary schedule and made changes in crew assignments if deemed necessary. Then CDR Foote signed off on it. Miller called each flight leader to inform him of his next day's mission, launch time, and other squadron crews assigned to the hop. A mimeographed copy of the next day's flight schedule also appeared under the stateroom door of each pilot and B/N. For these first two weeks, most aircrews knew about their next day's missions by 2000 or 2100 the night before.[4]

The Sunday Punchers began their first line period as full participants in CVW-3's scheduling and operations matrix, usually referred to as "cyclic operations." Every day for their first two weeks on the line, the airwing planned five to seven cycles—one complete multiplane launch through recovery—to send aircraft against targets in South Vietnam. When Miller's schedule reached the crews on the evening of 17 May, they learned that seven cycles would launch on 18 May. For five of them, VA-75 would contribute a two-plane element of A-6As for strike missions. In addition, they also had to man eight KA-6D hops, at least one each cycle. Thus, each pilot and B/N in VA-75 now knew how many and what kind of missions he would fly and the times of the cycle or cycles in which he would participate. Airwing planners staggered the seven launches over daylight hours, beginning about 0600 and concluding about 1900.[5]

Preparations for the first cycle began approximately two hours before the first launch with the Air Boss's call to flight quarters. The flight deck became alive with activity, appearing chaotic, yet, in reality, executing a reasonably choreographed plan. Crewmen in blue shirts and brown-shirted plane captains unchained aircraft on deck, ran the elevators to bring up other planes, and ran tractors to move aircraft scheduled for the first launch into positions where they could taxi to the catapults. Each plane captain checked and rechecked the condition of "his" plane. Near the bow and waist catapults and back along the wires of the arresting gear, green-shirted crewmen tested the machinery. The purple-shirted "grapes" prepared to fuel the aircraft. Gunner Walden, who usually rose at 0300 for an 0600 launch, supervised the red-shirted ordnancemen as they hung bombs on squadron aircraft and checked fusing. Before any engine started, all hands then on the flight deck conducted a search for debris that could cause foreign object damage (FOD)—a "FOD walkdown"—picking up any loose material that might be sucked into an engine or thrown up by the jet blast. Plane-guard helicopters prepared to launch, and *Saratoga* prepared to steam a course into the wind to put at least 30 knots of wind over the flight deck.

As these preliminaries concluded, flight crews—who began their briefings perhaps two hours before launch—came up to the flight deck and completed the inspection of their aircraft. Manning the planes began approximately forty-five minutes prior to launch. One by one, each pilot followed the directions of yellow-shirted plane directors to taxi forward and be spotted in turn on the catapult. A greenshirt attached each plane to the catapult shuttle. At the yellow-shirt's signal, the pilot released his brakes and brought the engine to full power. Using hand signals, the catapult officer checked with the pilot to make sure all systems were functioning properly, waiting for the pilot's verifying salute. After a final readiness check, the catapult officer touched the deck—the signal to press the button that operated the steam catapult. One by one, each aircraft sped down the deck, going from zero to 160 knots in three seconds. Cooperation, attention to detail, and a strong commitment to safety came together about one hundred thirty times each day to launch CVW-3's aircraft during the last two weeks of May 1972.[6]

Planners expected each cycle's strike aircraft to cross over the beach—go "feet dry," in naval aviation's unique vocabulary—complete their ordnance drop, go "feet wet" to return to the carrier, refuel when necessary, get into the landing pattern, and recover within a specific time period. *Saratoga* completed a full cycle in "1+45," one hour and forty-five minutes, a slightly longer time period than the "1+30" most other carriers used. The time extension had been a considered decision by CAPT Sanderson and CAG Bordone. To make cyclic operations work, aircraft had to be "re-spotted" on the flight deck constantly. From the start of a day's first cycle, the area forward along all four catapults—two amidship on the port side and two more on the bow of the carrier—had to remain clear of parked planes. Thus, prior to the first launch, all aircraft had to be spotted—or parked—aft of the catapults. For recovery of aircraft, the reverse held true. As each aircraft recovered, a plane director taxied it forward toward the bow to clear the landing area. Once all aircraft recovered, they had to be re-spotted aft to prepare for the next launch.

These evolutions required great care by all hands to prevent collisions, fires, explosions, and other accidents. Catastrophic and deadly fires on several carriers—especially USS *Oriskany* in 1966 and USS *Forrestal* in 1967—had dictated a fleet-wide tightening and enforcement of the rules concerning the safe handling of ordnance. CVW-3 policy prohibited maintenance work or ordnance circuit testing on any airplane already loaded with bombs, mines, or missiles.

Moreover, no aircraft could go below to the hangar bay with ordnance loaded. Strict adherence to these rules increased the time required to keep planes mission-ready for multiple launches on a single day's flight schedule. Thus, a 1+45 cycle became standard operating procedure aboard *Saratoga*.[7]

CAG Bordone, as former commanding officer of the Sunday Punchers, indulged in one privilege of his position by scheduling himself to lead the squadron's first strike mission. He wanted to drop his airwing's first bombs, and thus on the first launch of 18 May, he and LCDR Dick Schram, the squadron's only combat-tested B/N, flew against two companies of enemy troops in the Mekong Delta. On Bordone's wing, CDR Foote took LCDR Grady Jackson on his first combat hop. As it turned out, Bordone did not get his wish. He had not flown in combat or dropped live ordnance on a hostile target in a few years, and neither had his B/N. When Bordone hit the button to drop his bombs—naval aviators used the word "pickle" both as a noun to describe the button and as a verb to describe the action of pushing it—nothing happened. They failed to notice that the master arm switch remained in the "off" position. He got on the radio and thundered at Foote not to deny him the privilege of releasing his ordnance first, but the skipper simply could not resist. He dropped on target.[8]

CAG Bordone chose to mark the start of combat operations by climbing into the cockpit, but he did not order the senior officers in all of his squadrons to follow his lead. But VA-75's senior leadership already had decided to lead from the front. CDRs Foote and Earnest had not flown in combat for several years, and they needed to refresh their skills as they assessed the current threat environment. They also had an obligation to evaluate their senior subordinates in action. No one knew what fate had in store for any of them, and CDR Foote's impending departure after his scheduled change of command in early June might very soon place more command responsibility on the lieutenant commanders. Also, the heavies used these first few weeks to observe their junior crews under fire for the first time. That way, when *Saratoga* moved north into far more hostile airspace, they could assign them to missions appropriate to their demonstrated skills. Thus, at least in May 1972, senior crews flew strike hops once or sometimes twice a day, while junior crews did so only once a day or, sometimes, once every other day. Instead, the junior crews flew the largest share of the tanker missions.[9]

The wisdom of the heavies' decision became apparent immediately. Even the squadron's most experienced combat leaders discovered that, in addition to adjusting to their return to a combat zone, they also had to master procedures they had not briefed or practiced recently. On that very first day of air operations, VA-75 aircrews were assigned FAC-controlled close air support missions to assist ARVN troops in contact with North Vietnamese forces. Unfortunately for all the VA-75 crews, the RAG syllabus had not devoted much attention to the

CDR Richard P. Bordone, commanding officer—or "CAG," for the outmoded term "commander, air group"—of Saratoga's airwing, led CVW-3's first strike hop on 18 May 1972 in one of VA-75's A-6As. He had flown with the Sunday Punchers during their first combat deployment in 1965 and served as skipper of VA-75 several years later. (U.S. Navy photograph, Everett W. Foote Collection)

complexities of close air support, and the squadron heavies had not given it a high priority during training at Oceana or on the bombing ranges of Dare County, North Carolina. Additionally, the cancellation during the transit of LTJG Hvidding's brief about operating with FACs came back to haunt the squadron. Some of the pilots and B/Ns who had made the 1971 Med cruise had worked with ground FACs, but they had not worked with airborne FACs before.[10] During the winter of 1971–72 after their return to Oceana, some pilots and B/Ns had dropped practice bombs while working in concert with Army FACs at Camp Pickett, Virginia, but recent changes in squadron personnel separated many of the crews who had worked and trained together in those exercises.[11] Now they had to learn quickly the complicated check-in process that linked a Sunday Puncher flight leader with two A-6As to an individual U.S. Air Force FAC requesting air support. All airborne FACs maintained radio contact with U.S. Army advisers and sometimes ARVN commanders, who used a different kind of map from those most aircrews used. Thus, the FAC served as "translator" between the incoming aircraft and troops on the ground. Standing rules of engagement required the Sunday Punchers—and all other strike aircraft—to make and maintain visual contact with their assigned FAC before executing any ordnance drop.[12]

Sunday Puncher pilots and B/Ns learned to descend from 20,000 feet to perhaps 12,000 feet to look for their assigned FAC, who usually flew an OV-10 or an O-2B at low altitude. When they spotted him, they switched to his radio frequency to verify identities. For these first two weeks, usual practice called for the two A-6s to follow the FAC to the target area and set up an orbit over it. At the

FAC's direction, each aircraft in turn rolled in from 12,000 feet, pickled at about 6,000 feet, then pulled out of its dive at no less than 3,500 feet to avoid small-arms fire. If the FAC requested it, an aircraft might make successive runs on the target area, dropping a few bombs each time and adjusting to the observer's input.

To master the procedures quickly, CDRs Foote and Earnest each flew two strike missions on 18 May. At the same time, they guided untested B/Ns through unfamiliar procedures and evaluated their performances. CDR Foote took a different senior B/N on each of his two hops. During his first mission on CAG Bordone's wing, the CO and LCDR Jackson destroyed two bunkers and uncovered three more. Foote then gave LCDR Pieno his first taste of combat flying, when they hit enemy troops in MR IV.[13] CDR Earnest also took LCDR Jackson on a strike hop against troop concentration that first day, but for his second mission, he chose a junior B/N, LTJG Jerry Mullins.[14]

The Foote-Pieno and the Earnest-Mullins strikes demonstrated a second method the squadron's veterans used to bring along the more junior crews. Foote and Earnest really had three students on each of their hops. First, each man observed the B/N in the right seat of his own aircraft, encouraging him when he seemed to need it, or simply reminding him of standard procedures along the way. As a consequence, Mullins considered his first mission to be "thoroughly unremarkable. If I was surprised it was that it was so easy and normal," a result he credited largely to CDR Earnest's willingness to "walk me through the whole thing."[15] The evening before, the XO handed out sets of mimeographed sheets so his pilots and B/Ns could keep personal logs of all of their missions. He intended for each officer to maintain it as a backup to the official entry—in green ink, signifying combat—made in each man's black flight logbook after each mission by operations personnel. The forms included a column for "comments," and Mullins developed a "pucker factor" system to evaluate each mission. When he filled in the comment square to describe his hop on 18 May, he wrote POC—"piece of cake."[16]

The crew in the aircraft on the heavies' wing became the senior pilot's other two students. After returning from his strike with CAG Bordone, Foote took LT Bruce Cook with LTJG Jay Swigart on his wing for his second strike of the day. CDR Earnest put LCDR Dick Engel, making his first combat hop with LCDR Schram, on his wing, and then took LT Ron Lankford with LTJG Dave Warren on his second strike of the day. As the squadron's two most senior lieutenants, Lankford and Cook possessed both the experience in the cockpit and reputation for outstanding airmanship that convinced the heavies to test their readiness to take on greater responsibilities. The heavies did not believe in independent on-the-job training. As Lankford described it, he and Warren flew their first missions "'holding hands' on the wing" of senior crews.[17]

Two Sunday Puncher A-6As returning from a strike mission. During the squadron's first two weeks in combat against targets in South Vietnam's Military Regions III and IV, the Sunday Punchers flew their missions in twos or threes, usually with junior crews flying on the wing of a senior crew. (U.S. Navy photograph, John A. Pieno, Jr., Collection)

That night, Warren wrote home about his first combat mission. Encouraging his wife to use her new map of Vietnam, he explained, "If you look at your chart all the way down South Vietnam, you will see where the Mekong River empties into the ocean. But before it empties, it splits into three rivers. We hit Viet Cong troop concentrations, bunkers, and supplies just to the south of the center river, just before it empties." Warren boasted a bit: "The XO didn't do too well. He dumped his bombs in the river off target. Ron and I destroyed two bunkers and hit what looked like an oil or ammo dump. Anyway, it made a hell of a fire."[18] LTJG Swigart returned from his first mission somewhat puzzled by the experience. He had watched his bombs hit what appeared to him to be nothing more than a rice paddy. While he took satisfaction from performing the mission he had been trained to do, years later he still remained "kind of disappointed that it seemed so ineffective and meaningless to be blowing up some soggy dirt."[19]

Veteran LCDR Lindland reintroduced himself to combat flying on 18 May and gave LTJG Lerseth his first taste of action on a strike hop against a river crossing, dropping ten of their twelve Mk82 500-pound bombs but jettisoning two duds in the ocean before they returned to the ship. Their hop became the squadron's sole single-plane mission that first day; the second A-6A intended to fly on their wing aborted on deck.[20] Lerseth's strongest memory of his first mission centered on the maze of controller and FAC radio frequency changes that kept him especially busy. "I do not remember seeing the beautiful coastline, or the Mekong winding its way to the sea," he recalled of his first strike over the beach. He remembered instead "a kneeboard full of FAC frequency and call signs, and a left hand that got sore making those freq[uency] changes on our single radio."[21]

The pilots and B/Ns already knew that the mission did not end when they trapped aboard. Even after training flights, they reported on the condition of the aircraft and notified Maintenance Control of gripes. But now, the debriefing process carried operational significance. Although none of the squadron's aircraft met with any serious resistance on their first day of air operations, at least one member of each two-man crew—usually the B/N—reported directly to the airwing's intelligence officers to provide details about their mission. A standardized operational debriefing process began that first day and evolved relatively quickly, using a variety of forms that covered the operational details of a strike, from target information to preliminary bomb damage assessment. Any kind of enemy reaction required the completion of separate forms for radar homing and warning, or the firing of AAA or SAMs, or confrontation with MiGs, but no one in CVW-3 had met that level of resistance yet. In time, they learned that any damage to or loss of an aircraft had to be documented as well. As it became more familiar, the debriefing process for routine missions soon boiled down to a ten-to-fifteen-minute exercise.[22]

The debriefing process also came into play in the accumulation of "points," twenty of which led to the awarding of a Strike/Flight Air Medal. A pilot and B/N who met opposition got two points. An uncontested mission won only a single point. A combat support mission, such as a tanker flight, received 0.4 points. From the start, CVW-3 adopted the practice of awarding two points to the crew of any aircraft carrying ordnance that went feet dry, whether or not they reported enemy resistance. Many of the Sunday Puncher heavies accumulated their first four points on 18 May.

Most of the JOs who pulled a tanker hop, however, ended the day with only 0.4 points for their efforts. After flying one of those KA-6D sorties, LTJG Hvidding wrote in his diary, "My first day at war. Ho!Hum!"[23] LTs Fischer and Wagner came closer to going "feet dry" that day than most tankers, moving nearer the beach to refuel two F-4s that were "super low on gas." Fischer claimed they had flown so close to the action that they could hear "gibberish Vietnamese saying 'Yankee, Saratoga, etc.' as our boys crossed over the beach!" But they stayed over water, Fischer desperately wishing they could go "feet dry."[24]

The schedule for 19 May, Day 2 of the Punchers' war, resembled that of Day 1. Senior officers once more led all of the strike missions, this time against a wider range of targets extending into both MR III and IV. CAG Bordone once again launched early with LCDR Jackson, to strike enemy troops in contact with ARVN forces about forty-five miles southwest of Saigon, taking LT Lankford and LTJG Warren on his wing.[25] CDR Foote once again flew two strike missions. During his first hop, he put LTJG Fuller in his right seat for a strike against a transshipment point, and took LT Cook and LTJG Petersen on his wing. Like LTJG Mullins the day before, Petersen, too, considered his first mission to be "a piece of cake." Indeed, he explained to his wife, "the bombing was unopposed and that was it."[26] Foote made his second run of the day against a suspected regimental headquarters with LT John Miller and LTJG Sandy Sanford making their first strike on his wing. CDR Earnest's schedule that day followed a similar path.[27]

On 19 May, LCDR Lindland and LTJG Lerseth made VA-75's first strike into MR III, an area of some of the most intense action in all of South Vietnam. They reported to a FAC with a target approximately two nautical miles south of An Loc. ARVN forces holding that key city on the road to Saigon had struggled there since mid-April, awaiting the arrival of reinforcements. Over the past few days, B-52s had inflicted heavy losses on the temporarily static North Vietnamese units around the city. Hard fighting began anew on 15 May, when ARVN commanders attempted to open a new fire-support base at the small hamlet of Tan Khai, south of An Loc, to serve as a jump-off point for reinforcements and as an obstacle to North Vietnamese units trying to surround the beleaguered town. ARVN commanders called for air support to cover the placement of 105-mm and 155-mm howitzers by Chinook and Sky Crane helicopters, and Lindland and Lerseth followed a FAC's direction to hit bunkers south of An Loc and north of Tan Khai. "There were more airplanes than you could shake a stick at up there," Lerseth wrote his mother, "and the ground fire was heavy—(most of it being directed to other places on the ground, thank God)." LCDRs Graustein and Pieno flew a similar single-plane mission against a troop concentration not far away, with positive results.[28]

The practices adhered to by the squadron heavies in those first two days of combat did not change dramatically as May continued, and some junior crews became impatient. After flying a tanker hop on 18 May, LTJG Hvidding had voiced their collective disappointment when they did not receive assignments to strike missions: "All the JO's are anxious to get in on the gaggle."[29] After two days of tanker hops, LT Fischer itched to see his name on the flight schedule for his first strike mission, openly admitting that he had "no qualms or hang ups about bombing the V.C.—I'll stop if they surrender." By 20 May, he declared himself to be "super frustrated" by the realization that the junior pilots in the airwing's two A-7 squadrons had "been over the beach 4–5 times" already, while he had yet to make his first strike hop.[30]

This difference in initial mission assignments especially bothered those junior pilots and B/Ns who had made the 1971 Med cruise. They knew they had accumulated at least as many—if not more—hours in A6s as some of the squadron heavies who had transitioned into Intruders from another community. They believed that they understood both the plane and its mission better than did some of their superiors, and they felt confidence in their abilities to do their jobs. Some felt so strongly about this point that they expressed dissatisfaction with the airmanship of several of the squadron's senior officers. LT Fischer, for one, confided to his diary his concerns about what he deemed as the heavies' favoritism toward their peers. He resented the fact that some senior officers flew daily in combat "when no one will fly with them in peacetime," while capable JOs "only fly tankers for now."[31]

In reality, every Puncher in the cockpit, regardless of rank or experience in A-6s, had much to learn. During their first two weeks in combat, their work with the FACs instilled a deeper understanding of many important factors. No two missions unfolded in quite the same way. Even in a low threat environment, they learned to plan missions carefully. Close air support strikes demanded exacting precision. Thus, missions that produced positive results brought professional satisfaction. On 20 May, a three-plane flight led by CDR Earnest with LCDR Jackson, taking along LTJG Tolhurst with LTJG Ahrens, and, at last, LT Fischer with LT Wagner, followed FAC guidance to bomb enemy positions along both sides of a canal near an ARVN outpost. The FAC had radioed to the commander on the ground to send up some white smoke. The three Sunday Puncher crews quickly identified the ARVN position, a triangular fortification built of logs that reminded Fischer of a scene from *Drums along the Mohawk*. Once they had separated friendly positions from those of the enemy, the three planes rolled in on their targets and dropped 100 percent of their bombs where the FAC wanted them.[32]

But cooperation between Sunday Puncher aircraft and FACs could break down at any time, and every crew had to be prepared to react to the unexpected at any point in the strike. The communication network itself created all manner of problems. Sometimes two-plane flights of A-6s found themselves waiting for twenty or thirty minutes until someone—airborne or on the ground—directed them to a FAC with a target. Occasionally, South Vietnamese FACs took to the airwaves, and LT Anderson recalled rumors that "they may have been on the take from local land barons" and directed air strikes to affect local power struggles rather than to repulse a communist foe.[33] The process could become so confusing and time-consuming that at times VAW-123's E-2Bs stepped in and, as their command historian explained it, "provided much-needed assistance in eliminating the confusing communications tangle with 7th AF and vectored strike aircraft directly to and from the Forward Air Controllers where they were most needed."[34]

But even after getting a mission, something as simple as failure to make visual contact with the assigned FAC could stop the strike. If the flight lead could not locate his FAC for any reason—whether due to miscommunication, bad weather, or some other cause—the mission had to be aborted. This occurred at least three times to VA-75, once each day on 20, 21, and 22 May, resulting in the jettisoning of a total of eighty-four 500-pound Mark 82s.[35] Even a simple delay in linking up with the FAC might cause a mission to end in failure. On 22 May, when LT Ken Knapp flew a strike hop with LTJG Hvidding, they initially had difficulty finding their FAC. They finally connected, but, by then, their aircraft had run so low on fuel that they had no choice but to roll in quickly, drop the ordnance, and depart. They released their bombs in a nice string, but—as Hvidding noted in his diary—"none of them [landed] where the FAC wanted them." They exploded "in a line of fireballs," leading him to suspect that they only "broke a lot of trees." The experience inspired him to conclude: "It's a very inefficient war."[36]

When A-6As successfully linked up with a FAC, however, the crews grew to enjoy the enthusiastic greeting they usually received. For most of these first missions over MR III and IV, each VA-75 A-6A strike aircraft carried twelve to fourteen Mk82s, far from their maximum load but more than other attack planes carried. After confirming identities, a VA-75 flight lead—denoted as "Flying Ace" (the squadron's call sign) followed by the 500-series aircraft number on the plane's nose—began a typical exchange this way: "Flying Ace 501, checking in with a flight of three Alpha 6s with fourteen Mk82s." A FAC unfamiliar with A-6As often answered back, "Roger Ace, fourteen 82s for the flight," indicating that he understood that the three A-6s carried a combined total of fourteen 500-pound bombs. The A-6 flight leader invariably enjoyed correcting the FAC's misperception, clarifying that *each* A-6 carried fourteen Mk82s, for a total of forty-two 500-pound bombs. Since FACs more typically worked with aircraft that carried smaller ordnance loads, they gladly accepted the correction. As one FAC exulted, "Jesus Christ, I'm in heaven. I've got my own B52 raid."[37] Also used to dealing with aircraft in low-fuel states that had to drop their bombs quickly and then leave, FACs quickly learned to make good use of the loiter time (or "playtime") of A-6As, which could stay for forty-five minutes to an hour.

At times, even after Puncher aircrews located their FACs, a low cloud deck or some other obstacle interfered with the execution of a bombing run. This occurred on 23 May 1972, when a two-plane strike in MR IV led by CDR Foote and

LCDR Jackson tried to cover the extraction of some ARVN troops under intense pressure from enemy forces. By the time they found the FAC who directed them to the target, the clouds had descended to 3,000 to 4,000 feet, too low for safe visual dive-bombing. "The FAC was literally pleading with us," recalled LTJG Ahrens, flying with LTJG Tolhurst on Foote's wing that day. To hit only the North Vietnamese troops while avoiding the ARVN soldiers under these weather conditions, the A-6As had to utilize a shallower-than-usual dive angle at an altitude that greatly exposed them to ground fire. CDR Foote ordered Tolhurst and Ahrens to stay above the cloud deck while he made a test run. The low clouds and the smoke from the action below obscured the target area, and he did not pickle off his bombs. When Foote determined that the two aircraft could not complete the mission, Ahrens found it "pretty demoralizing." But he also admitted that "in a way" CDR Foote "was right. . . ," his unfinished thought representing a wish that the result could have been otherwise.[38] LCDR Jackson had concurred with Foote's decision to abort, but he, too, gave voice to his frustration at their inability to help, describing in his personal log the unfortunate situation as "disgusting as hell!"[39]

It did not take long for the squadron's aircraft to show the effects of daily launches and recoveries. On 20 May, LT Lankford and LTJG Warren got their first chance to serve as the flight lead on a two-plane strike mission. Scheduled to take LT Anderson and LTJG Bob Miller on their wing, one of their engines refused to start. As troubleshooters tried to resolve the problem, Anderson and Miller launched and waited overhead. The balky engine finally started, and Lankford taxied forward, only to find the catapult temporarily inoperative. Finally they launched at 1225, fully forty minutes later than scheduled. They linked up with Anderson and Miller and made visual contact with their assigned FAC at 1255, a full ten minutes after the time they had planned to head back to the carrier for recovery. Lankford told his FAC that they had twenty-eight Mk82s, but absolutely no playtime. When the FAC could not assign him a target immediately, Lankford had to lead the two A-6As feet wet, still carrying their full ordnance loads. *Saratoga* steamed about 250 miles away, and now the aircraft did not have enough fuel to get back to the ship unless they jettisoned their bombs. They asked the carrier to designate a clear area over water to drop them, but they were told simply to "find an area where we were sure there were no boats and drop them on safe." When their scheduled recovery window began, they still had to fly 120 miles to reach the carrier. Lankford's bad day turned even worse when he failed on his first attempt to catch a wire—naval aviators called that a "bolter"—and had to make a second pass. "Fifty traps with VA-75 and that's the first bolter I personally have been involved in," Warren complained, lamenting, "nothing goes well forever, I guess."[40]

As May continued, ordnance malfunctions also began to hamper the squadron's efforts. A few incidents early on suggested a growing problem. On 19 May, CDR Earnest tried to drop twelve Mk82s on a machine gun site and not one exploded. The last five Mk82s that LT Pyle and LTJG Hvidding dropped during a 20 May strike against a suspected supply storage area one hundred miles south of Saigon turned out to be duds.[41] On 26, 27, and 28 May, at least one Puncher crew each day dropped ordnance that did not explode. On 29 May, both CDR Foote and CDR Earnest dropped duds, too.[42] After he landed, LCDR Pieno, who had flown as CDR Earnest's B/N, bypassed the squadron's senior maintenance personnel to seek out Gunner Walden to demand that he check out the ordnance, fix the problem, and report back to him.

Walden and his redshirts examined everything. He suspected that the Mark-1 arming solenoids used in the squadron's multiple ejector racks (MERs) most likely caused the problem. But he could not be certain. He had required his ordnancemen to count the arming wires on each returning aircraft and report their findings to him. If they had loaded fourteen Mk82s and found fourteen arming wires hanging from the MERs, then all the bombs had armed. He had gotten no reports over the past few days to alert him to a developing problem. Worse, they could not reproduce it. After a close check of the equipment on one of the problem aircraft, CDR Earnest took it up and discovered that it worked flawlessly. Whatever caused the malfunction had been a temporary glitch that disappeared as suddenly as it had started.[43]

If the combat hops always brought their share of excitement for many reasons—good and bad—as May progressed, time spent flying tanker hops really began to drag. By then, LTs Fischer and Wagner had developed unorthodox ways to make them pass more quickly. Sometimes, when F-4s linked up with them, they flashed a *Playboy* centerfold at the crew. Other times, Wagner would remove his boots and socks and prop his bare feet up on the instrument panel, unzip his flight suit, under which he wore a flashy shirt, and plop a baseball cap with upturned brim on his head—the total effect looking for all the world like a rather casual gas station attendant. When the F-4s showed up, their crews might watch him eat a sandwich or sip from what appeared to be a can of beer. Still other times, he would simply duck down in his seat so he could not be seen. When the F-4 pilots invariably asked, "Where's your B/N?" Fischer would look up with surprise on his face and reply, "Gosh, I knew I forgot something!"[44] When LT Lankford and LTJG Warren flew a tanker, they used the squares that created a grid for the fuel graph on the back of their briefing cards as an impromptu game board to play "Battleship."[45]

Since all the combat sorties during these first few weeks took place during daylight hours, the first night flights these crews experienced since March came on tanker hops, too. A tanker that started or closed each day's air operations launched or landed in darkness. This proved to be one skill in which the squadron clearly needed a refresher. When LCDR Graustein tried to land a tanker after dark, one of the junior officers described his recovery as "colorful." Indeed, he boltered the first time he attempted to land before succeeding on his second try.[46]

Incidents such as this night landing provided yet another reminder—if they really needed it—that naval aviators enjoy only limited forgiveness for their errors. Any mistake, even those that merely embarrassed, triggered contemplation about potentially fatal consequences of similar missteps in a more heated combat zone. At least, many of their early errors provoked more laughter than recrimination. On their first combat hop on 20 May, LT Pyle and LTJG Hvidding went about ten miles off course when they "mistook an F-4 for our A-6 lead" and took off after it.[47] A few days later, during a daylight dive-bombing run, LTJG Lerseth—as did most B/Ns—became his pilot's "audio altimeter," calling out the altitude to keep LCDR Lindland from developing target fixation and flying into the ground. The B/N usually made his calls on the plane's intercom so only his own pilot heard him, but Lerseth keyed the radio instead and broadcast the altitude readings "to all of the immediate world," confusing other pilots making their own bombing runs. LTJG Petersen caught it all on tape and rather enjoyed embarrassing his roommate by replaying it for all interested parties.[48] In an episode that soon became part of squadron lore, after LT Fischer pulled out of a bombing run on gun emplacements near the coast, his flight lead—LT Cook—could not locate him. All A-6 pilots and B/Ns flying as wingmen knew to keep their lead in sight, but Fischer also lost visual contact with Cook. When Cook asked his location, Fischer found himself out over the ocean with no distinct landmarks. Then, he noticed a thunderhead nearby and replied, "I'm by the cloud." Noticing lots of puffy white masses, he quickly altered his commentary: "I'm by the BIG cloud."[49] When Fischer next entered the ready room for a brief, CDR Earnest threw his flight helmet at him, as much for his answer as for losing his flight lead.

Still, many of the Punchers' most lasting memories from their first two weeks on the line—coming into clearer relief with the passage of years—centered on matters other than their professional performance in the cockpit, their efforts to complete their missions, their occasional failures to respect airwing procedures, or their attempts to deal with in-flight malfunctions. They learned from these experiences, and they seldom if ever repeated the first two weeks' errors again. Thus, many pilots and B/Ns found their most vivid recollections in their personal reactions to their initiation into combat.

Some, for instance, had anticipated that the first shot fired at them in anger might become a supremely memorable event, if they survived it. LTJG Ron

McFarland remembered flying at 3,000 or 4,000 feet over seemingly serene and beautiful country in MR IV with his pilot LT Ruland when he saw some flashes on the ground. "Look," he commented to Ruland, "fireworks!" The next thing McFarland remembered, "we were going straight up and my face was buried in the radar scope because of the G forces." Ruland understood what McFarland saw: someone on the ground was shooting at them. "Well, I had just had my first real combat experience," McFarland explained. "They were trying to kill me and I had just bumbled my way into their war. That's when I knew this was for keeps. NO more fun and games. This was REAL."[50] But unless something entirely unanticipated happened, most Punchers in time came to recall their baptisms of fire as unexceptional. The details of their first combat experiences in the comparatively benign environment of the skies over MR III and IV faded in time and generally did not sear into their memories.

Some, however, made uncomfortable personal discoveries during those first two weeks. Even though he had performed decently well on bombing ranges back in the United States, LT Wharton realized that during his first hops in MR IV he just could not hit his targets. The harder he tried, the worse the results. Finally, he sought LCDR Lindland's advice. The squadron operations officer listened to the junior pilot's concerns, questioned him about cockpit procedures during his first week's missions, and then suggested that Wharton might have tensed up enough on his bombing runs that, without realizing it, his foot pressed on his rudder pedal during his dive just enough to throw off the alignment of his aircraft and the placement of his ordnance. He simply had to be aware of his reactions in the cockpit and relax a bit. Wharton took the advice to heart, and once he understood his problem, he found a way to remedy it. By the end of the second week, he had resolved it. Now alerted to the junior pilot's concerns, Lindland watched for signs of improvement. When Wharton flew on his wing on 24 May against a troop concentration and a .51 calibre machine gun site, he made some good hits. LTJG Petersen, Wharton's B/N, kept a tape recorder in the cockpit during some of these early missions, and after one particularly effective run, he captured LCDR Lindland's praise for the junior pilot's efforts, noting, "Tom's really putting them in there!"[51]

A particular concern that produced a wide variety of personal reactions among the Punchers concerned a fundamental problem that crews flying FAC-controlled missions frequently faced: they dropped on targets that seldom were clearly defined. As LTJG Ahrens explained, "When you dive from 11,000 or 12,000 and start to pull out at 5500 feet or so, you really can't see much on the ground if you are bombing troops in the jungle or bushes." If he followed the FAC's directions on the first run, and then received different instructions for a second run, "you don't know if that is because you killed the guys in the first spot or you missed the first spot by 70 meters or the spotter on the ground is making a correction or what."[52] Worse, to LTJG Swigart, "when a guy tells you drop a bomb a 'half a click [northeast] of my smoke,' there's a lot of room for error."[53]

Since they could not measure their effectiveness themselves, the aviators quickly developed a great interest in bomb damage assessment (BDA) reports. A crew's first measure of the accuracy of their ordnance drop invariably came from the FAC as the aircraft pulled off the target, and the B/N reported it to the air intelligence officers during the debrief. The U.S. Air Force FACs with whom the Punchers worked during these last two weeks of May 1972 proved to be fairly responsible in confirming the initial report, often sending more complete follow-on BDA out to *Saratoga* in a day or two, sometimes after guiding troops on the ground into the target area for a close-up examination of the results of the bombing runs.

Most of these initial BDA reports described the number of fires started or the destruction or uncovering of a specific quantity of supply caches, bunkers, or other military structures. But metrics alone did not provide the greatest satisfaction. Most aircrews quickly grew to appreciate a more subjective measure of success: enthusiastic feedback from their FAC. "It was like having a cheerleader right there for you, and it was fun," recalled LT John Miller.[54] They also learned that a FAC who merely rattled off some numbers with no emotion probably just made something up to cover an ineffective drop. After a strike on 26 May that caused no explosions or other major visible damage on an easy target, LTJG Hvidding admitted that he found it "sort of disappointing when the FAC doesn't get all excited about your bombing," but, given his own observations, the unenthusiastic response had not surprised him.[55] By the end of the first line period, the Punchers learned the utility, the frustration, and even the simple inevitability of BDA reports ending with "RNO," an abbreviation meaning "results not observed," for reasons ranging from dust to smoke to trees to darkness.

In one specific case, the Punchers' usual appreciation for enthusiastic FACs could just as quickly turn to a strong sense of resentment. Invariably, that situation centered on BDA that included commentary on human casualties. LTJG Warren wrote home after one May mission about how disquieting it could be when "the FAC will come up with something like 'Jesus Christ, did you see that body come flying out of there?'"[56] LTJG Swigart recalled flying a mission in late May near the coast with LT Cook when an excited FAC reported that "he had 'arms and legs flying over the canopy,' there were 17 KIA and that the river was turning red from the blood." It continued to bother Swigart for years that the "hyperbole and exaggeration that we were reporting from the FACs back to the boat ultimately found its way onto the 10 o'clock news" back home.[57]

Initial BDA, often followed by notations of "KBA [killed by air] to be provided later" forced many Punchers to confront for the first time the strong possibility that their bombs had killed other human beings. LTJGs Mullins and
Hvidding, who shared a stateroom, spent some time after these early missions
discussing whether or not it felt "different" to be bombing real people. Mullins,
for one, "thought no big moral thoughts about it. Delivering ordnance in a war
had been on my list of things I had always wanted to do, the Viet Cong were
counted as bad guys to me, and so I had no problem with it."[58] While Hvidding
felt deep dismay when a FAC lacked enthusiasm in his BDA report on structures
or bunkers, he nonetheless came to dislike one particular observer who
screamed, "in an almost bloodthirsty way," about human casualties. "*That* bothered me," Hvidding remembered. It was "not just the fact that we may have actually killed human beings and there was eyewitness evidence" that bothered him,
but the additional realization that "that FAC was not one of the good guys, yet
he was on *our* side."[59] LT Ruland expressed surprise at "how detached" he felt
during bombing runs. "The action was far below, and appeared to be taking
place in miniature. There was no sound of bombs exploding, and no fog of
war," he explained, adding, "I wasn't surprised that I was able to go out and drop
bombs with the intent of killing people. Everyone had defense mechanisms to
cope with this, and I always view what I did as doing what I had been trained to
do—drop bombs on target."[60] Such sentiments did not emerge after the passage
of time. After just his first few missions, LTJG Petersen confessed in a letter
home, "It's difficult to think that those flashes on the ground are really killing
people but I try not to dwell on that. I guess I try to think that the bomb really
killed that guy, I didn't. It's a rather comfortable way of getting around it, I
guess."[61] LTJG Warren shared a similar sentiment: "It's not really like looking at
a guy and shooting him or having to watch the agony and blood. I mean, I know
I'm killing people but I don't have to look at them while I'm killing them. And it
makes a great difference. At least I think it does."[62]

Still, not all Punchers addressed the issue in personal terms, at least not in any
public forum. Even years after the fact, some Punchers continued to view BDA,
even that which included human casualties, as simply a part of the professional
evaluation of how well they did their jobs. LCDR Engel found it "discouraging to
know that we would have had better success if our electronic system was fully
functional and reliable as it was designed, but it wasn't[,] so the BDA information
confirmed our proficiency and accuracy" while working in less than perfect conditions.[63] For LTJG Tolhurst, BDA simply offered "proof of a job well done."[64]

This range of personal and professional reactions to the probability that their
actions had led to the deaths of other human beings fits that described by
psychologists who study aggression in its many forms and who conclude that

military personnel who drop bombs can limit the psychologically traumatic impact of their actions. "Bombing deaths are buffered by the all-important factor of distance," wrote psychologist Dave Grossman, who added that dropping ordnance in this manner represents "an impersonal act of war in which specific deaths are unintended and almost accidental in nature."[65] Thus, a lethal act can become simply part of one's job. And, after two weeks at it, the Punchers believed they performed that job well.

A key reason for their initial success, the junior officers especially believed, rested on their complete acceptance of the crew concept unique to the A-6 community. When he flew with LT Knapp on 22 May as a replacement for the pilot's regular B/N, LTJG Hvidding admitted that they had not done well, in part because they were not used to working with each other; they had paired up only because Knapp's usual B/N had suffered a sinus blockage that grounded him for a few days. Later, when LT Pyle, Hvidding's regular pilot, came down with a viral infection, the B/N found himself on a tanker hop with LCDR Graustein. Already, all A-6 air crews understood that tanker hops provided the one exception to crew-pair integrity; depending on availability and collateral duty requirements, any pilot and any B/N might be crewed up for a KA-6D mission. Still, what impressed Hvidding, even in this entirely typical situation, was "the feeling I had that I was less comfortable flying" with Graustein, "even though Bob is a LCDR and a test pilot."[66] He felt much the same a few days later when he took a tanker with LCDR Dick Engel. The experience "wasn't too scarey," he wrote in his diary that night, but to his way of thinking, Engel did "irritating things in the cockpit."[67] Pyle's recovery restored his confidence. "Ken is a good, capable pilot who keeps his head on his shoulders under all conditions," Hvidding wrote, adding, "I think we work together well, and I feel more comfortable flying with him than with most other pilots in the squadron. I'm fortunate in that respect."[68]

LTJG Tolhurst related to his wife very few details of the missions that he and LTJG Doug Ahrens flew, but he assured her that one reason why no A-6s had been hit yet had much to do with the crew concept. Although they mostly flew above the range of ground fire, he argued that "very few A-6s have been shot because they have good power, two engines, two men, etc. We're basically as safe as anyone who goes over the beach and safer than many."[69] A week later, he reiterated that while none of *Saratoga*'s aircraft had been hit yet, most of the damaged planes over South Vietnam were single-seat A-4s and A-7s. He had become convinced that "one guy just can't do everything by himself."[70]

Increasingly, as their commitment to the crew concept grew, the JOs did not take lightly perceived violations of the practice. This proved especially true if they believed that the lapse hurt operational readiness or cut into experience-building flight time they felt belonged to them. When CDR Foote permitted a few officers who did not belong to the Sunday Punchers to sit in the B/N seat during tanker hops, LTJG Warren groused, "It's still flight time, and it's my flight time." He added, "A lot of the B/Ns aren't very happy about it."[71]

In yet another way, the value and importance of the crew concept so central to the A-6 experience also became more clearly understood. In most circumstances, the pilot and B/N made up the key pairing. But the entire A-6 team— operations, maintenance, ordnance, every element of the squadron—had to work together. When LCDR Pieno confronted Gunner Walden about the hung bombs, the ordnance warrant officer had argued loudly with him in return. Others had witnessed the confrontation, and CDR Earnest heard about it. Afterwards, the XO pulled Walden aside and said, "Gunner, even if you're right, you're wrong." Even if Walden did not agree with LCDR Pieno's assessment, he had violated professional courtesy in his own response. Worse, he had done so in front of young sailors who might take away the wrong lesson from that occurrence. To reinforce the need for the kind of teamwork that made an A-6 squadron work, Earnest admonished Walden not for any lapse in the performance of his duties, but for telling off LCDR Pieno in front of the troops "in the manner you did." Even though he and his redshirts could find no technical reasons for the recent poor performance of squadron ordnance, Walden apologized to LCDR Pieno for his lapse in professional decorum.[72]

The emphasis on teamwork stemmed from a realization that greater effort would be required from all the men soon, and they knew it. Perhaps this is why the senior officers kept a close eye on the JOs' reactions to each day's new experiences. CDRs Foote and Earnest and other squadron veterans frequently asked crews as they returned from missions a simple, open-ended question: "How'd it go?" The neat thing, LTJG Hvidding noted, was that "they let us talk, probably overly excited. They always affirmed what we described and never put us down for our enthusiastic naivete." As he later admitted, "They accepted us into the brotherhood of combat veterans even before we deserved it."[73]

To keep the junior pilots and B/Ns focused on their jobs, the senior leaders also kept alert for personal distractions that might play out disastrously in the cockpit. Just as LT Ruland had learned of his impending fatherhood while on transit to Westpac, in mid-May LTJG Sanford received the same news in a letter from his wife, Brenda. As soon as he could arrange it, CDR Earnest sent Sanford into Danang so that he could call home. When the telephone operator could not get a clear connection to Virginia Beach, however, Sanford turned to other business. Before returning to *Saratoga,* he made a deal for some short-sleeved fatigues, CDR Earnest's preferred—if unorthodox—uniform in the cockpit and lost all his cash gambling with LT Thomas B. Latendresse, an A-4 pilot from VA-55 on USS *Hancock.* (Latendresse may have lost it all a few days later when he got shot down and the North Vietnamese captured him.) A few days later, Earnest sent Sanford with LCDR Engel to ferry a damaged aircraft to the naval air station at Cubi Point. There, he finally learned the details of his impending fatherhood. When he returned, the B/N found himself scheduled to fly the next day with CDR Earnest. He had never flown with the XO before, but he quickly realized from Earnest's questions that the senior officer simply wanted to see if the news from home shook his concentration in the cockpit. He assumed his answers reassured the XO; a malfunction forced them to abort, and he never flew with Earnest again.[74]

The heavies looked for consistent improvement each day. During the last five days of their break-in period in MR III and IV, CVW-3 took on missions with a higher degree of difficulty. On 26 May, CAG Bordone and LCDR Pieno took LTs Fischer and Wagner on their wing to hit enemy troops in contact with ARVN forces in the Mekong Delta. To make sure they did not hit friendly troops, they made their drops at the end of fifty- to sixty-degree dives, much steeper than the forty-degree dives they generally used. As a consequence, the pullout after dropping the ordnance proved much more stressful as well. "Paul blacked out on the first pull out and was sorta out of it the rest of the hop," Fischer noted that night.[75]

Also upping the level of challenge toward the end of their break-in period, VA-75 aircraft began to receive more FAC assignments to hit targets around two of the most famous battlegrounds of spring 1972: An Loc in MR III and Kontum in MR II. Although two of VA-75's A-6As had hit targets in the An Loc area on 19 May, the squadron made no more strikes there until 25 May. When LTJG Hvidding first flew against a target in the An Loc area that day, the town seemed "devastated" and the terrain "pock-marked." The air assets now devoted to lifting the North Vietnamese pressure amazed him. As the three-plane strike in which Hvidding took part did its job, a flight of A-7s worked nearby simultaneously and a flight of Marine F-4s followed on. CAG Bordone and LCDR Jackson led the strike against a water tower outside the town itself that the enemy used as its water supply. Each of the three A-6As carried eight Mark 83 (Mk83) 1,000-pound bombs, the first time during the combat cruise that the Punchers carried something other than Mk82 500-pound bombs.[76] LT Pyle got two good hits, but the strike got credit for only 25 percent destruction of the target. To Hvidding, "it all seemed rather silly, expending 24 Mk83's against such a target, but I only work here." He mused, "The cost of bombs has been said to be $1 per pound, so that means $24,000 was spent against a water tower in a town we're trying to save for our allies."[77]

The schedule for 27 May called for a continued pounding of North Vietnamese positions around An Loc. A two-plane strike—CDR Foote with LTJG

Loaded with ordnance, an A-6A from VA-75 launched from USS Saratoga *heads toward its target. The unique tail markings indicate that this is the "CAG bird," by tradition flown by the squadron's skipper or by CAG Bordone when he flew a strike mission with the Sunday Punchers. (John R. Fuller Collection)*

Hvidding, and LT Anderson with LTJG Bob Miller—followed a FAC's directions to a stalled truck on the side of the road. On their second run against the target, LT Anderson hit it with two Mk82s; since the vehicle started smoking and then burned for a long time, the FAC determined that it carried military supplies. Following that success, the FAC led the two planes against a supply depot just outside a group of houses near An Loc. This time, their very first bombs started fires immediately, and the FAC guessed that they had hit a hidden petroleum storage area.[78] LTJG Petersen felt equally good when they received a call from a FAC the next day to drop their bombs ten feet from a wall the North Vietnamese were preparing to storm. They made their run, and the FAC asked the flight to stand by for preliminary BDA. A few minutes later, he reported excitedly, "Shit hot, you blew one of the bad guys over the wall and he's still alive and they are interrogating him!"[79]

On 28 May, LT Lankford and LTJG Warren led LT Ruland and LTJG McFarland on a hop into Cambodia, the first such assignment for any VA-75 crew. Their target, a 105-mm gun in an emplacement protecting a supply area, lay in the region of the "Parrot's Beak" northwest of Saigon. When they arrived in the area, however, the FAC told them that the ARVN ground commander below needed some air support to stop a force of about 100 Vietcong troops out in the open in the middle of a field. The two aircrews saw their new target and began to roll in. Suddenly, the FAC came back on the air and told them to break off the attack immediately. The ground commander realized in time he had made a mistake. The soldiers in the target area belonged to his own unit. The two A-6s adjusted to the changing circumstances with no problem and went on to knock out the gun and destroy or damage five bunkers.[80]

The same day as this Cambodian adventure, CAG Bordone and LCDR Jackson flew one of VA-75's A-6As over to USS *Midway* to join VA-115 on an alpha strike against a heavily defended transshipment point at Dan Hai near Vinh, the first aircraft in CVW-3 to hit a target in North Vietnam. Since *Saratoga's* squadrons soon would start flying these complex multiple-plane strikes when the carrier moved farther north, Bordone needed to know more about the current threat environment in North Vietnam. Although they dropped their fourteen Mk82s as planned, they did not learn much about North Vietnamese air defenses because they met no opposition—no AAA, no SAMs, no MiGs.[81] The weather had deteriorated over the original target, and they had diverted to secondary targets. As he listened to their report, LTJG Hvidding thought that Jackson "sounded disappointed" about that.[82]

Bordone and Jackson had another important reason for participating in the strike, however. They needed to try out the brand-new ALR-45/ALR-50 combination radar homing and warning receivers, just installed in some of *Saratoga's* aircraft. Bordone did not want to launch his squadrons into the skies over North Vietnam until he had tested it in a combat environment himself. His concerns paid off. As soon as they had launched from *Midway* to rendezvous for the attack, Jackson explained that "our ALR-45/50 went berserk." They received multiple false indications and false warnings, including alarms that suggested a SAM had been fired at them. "It was a bit disconcerting," Jackson noted. Indeed, they turned off the equipment when the noise became too distracting.

The combat test clearly revealed that a key piece of equipment necessary for flying in North Vietnam did not meet mission requirements. After they returned to *Saratoga*, Bordone reported the interference problem to his superiors and made it clear that until it was fixed, he considered his airwing not properly equipped for combat north of the Demilitarized Zone (DMZ). This was a gutsy call on Bordone's part, with potential negative career consequences. Nonetheless, his message triggered a quick response. In just a few days, the Pacific Fleet's electronic warfare officer and a team of engineers and technical representatives from Applied Technology and Magnavox came aboard to check the equipment. Their examination revealed that many of the units had been installed improperly. Routine test flights ordinarily would expose such glitches, but technicians had just begun to put the new equipment in the aircraft when the airwing received its emergency recall order in April, and there had been no time to complete the evaluation process. In addition, engineers also tweaked the signals processor to filter out friendly radars. In a short time, all the original ALR-45/50s were removed and replaced with the improved version. Bordone's prudence paid off for CVW-3 and VA-75.[83]

Even as airwing and squadron heavies considered the difficult combat missions ahead, a touchy nonoperational issue arose. Soon after *Saratoga*'s quick departure, the wives of some of the JOs had begun to consider moving to the Philippines to spend time with their husbands when they came off the line. Some of them had "followed the ship" from port to port during the 1971 Med cruise, and they had intended to do it again when the carrier returned there in May 1972. The change in destination to Southeast Asia did not alter their basic plan. To Penny Swigart, for one, the change in direction from east to west simply did not hit them as "a big deal."[84]

CDRs Foote and Earnest both felt strongly that the theater of war was no place for wives. First, it defied a tradition adopted during earlier tours as members of West Coast squadrons. A combat cruise carried its own hazards. What if someone got shot down? What kinds of extra stress would it place on the squadron's readiness for flight operations if officers had to be detached to escort the wives back to the United States? Moreover, political and social unrest made the Philippines a dangerous place for all Americans, and the heavies worried about the potential for distraction if any of the wives got into trouble. And, more pointedly, when the aviators came off the line, some men who remained dutiful and loyal spouses while at home with their families might choose to decompress in ways unacceptable to their wives. The veterans extended the old chestnut, "what happens on the ship stays on the ship," to include liberty during in-port periods. For all these reasons, they officially discouraged the extended stay of any of the squadron wives in the theater of operations.

Some of the JOs concurred with their senior officers' views. LTJG Warren noted that "the CO and XO are torqued" because they did not want wives in the war zone. "I think I kind of agree with them," he explained to Carol, "because we're fighting a war, and war isn't a place for wives."[85] LTJG Hvidding also had made it clear to his wife, Susan, that, as much as he missed her, he did not want her to come over except as part of a short-term dependents' charter flight. "Paul told me it was stupid for a wife to go over there and live," Susan wrote to Jeane Petersen, now at home in Salt Lake City, awaiting the birth of her second child. "It's not so safe like the Med," Susan had continued, and "a husband has one more worry thinking about his wife being safe" over there. In fact, she added,

"Paul says none of the husbands really want their wives living over there. I think it's mostly the wives insisting on going."[86]

A number of the JOs' wives exchanged letters with their husbands to explore mutually the possibilities of extended stays in the Philippines. LT John Miller did not want Diane to come over, but she finally insisted on doing so and he relented.[87] LTJG Lerseth and Nini discussed it, too, including potential repercussions from the squadron heavies. They ultimately agreed that while she should explore travel arrangements, if her presence in the Philippines caused him any serious trouble with his superiors, she would return to the United States.[88] Both LTJGs Fuller and Ahrens raised questions with their wives about lodging plans and personal safety issues. Still, both women pressed forward with plans to make the trip, with Sally Fuller checking into taking an extended leave-of-absence from her nursing position.[89]

As they reached their joint decisions, just as some JOs ignored the advice of the heavies, few of their wives sought the support or approval of Laura Foote, Minna Earnest, or the other senior officers' spouses. Still, they knew unequivocally how the senior wives felt, and they knew as well that others in Virginia Beach's naval community did not accept their decision either. Indeed, several who intended to go to the Philippines received calls or visits from various members of the RAG at Oceana to try to convince them of the ill-advised nature of their plan.[90] Nonetheless, they emptied their bank accounts, checked into the legal requirements for extended overseas stays, and—like their husbands—received inoculations against cholera and yellow fever and the uncomfortable gamma globulin shots. When they discovered that they needed affidavits of support from their husbands to verify that they would not become burdens on the countries they planned to visit, they convinced their spouses to procure the necessary documents. With some misgivings, LCDR Lindland signed them.[91]

Even as VA-75 flew its first missions in mid-May, Loretta Lankford obtained a visa, got her shots, bought airline tickets, and departed for the Philippines with another Navy wife, whose husband flew with a different squadron. They arrived at the Manila airport right after a bombing by local insurgents. Since they did not have return tickets, customs officials took their passports. They decided to walk into the city, because every cab driver they saw carried a gun. Tired, unnerved, and still far from downtown Manila, they met a Good Samaritan—a retired American congressman—who drove them into the city, found them a hotel, and, the next day, helped them retrieve their passports. Finally, on 31 May, Loretta sent a very surprised LT Lankford a message that she had arrived safely in Manila, leaving out all details of her misadventures.[92]

Her message arrived as VA-75 completed its last two days of operations in South Vietnam. On 30 May, CDR Foote led a two-plane strike against enemy troops in MR II. Since mid-May, when the North Vietnamese had launched a major assault in the Central Highlands, aiming to take Kontum, fighting had grown fierce. American B-52s had inflicted heavy casualties on the attackers, and by month's end ARVN ground forces had launched limited counterattacks that ultimately stopped the North Vietnamese offensive. The Sunday Punchers played only a bit part in the effort. Bad weather prevented them from hitting their original target in the most heated part of the combat zone at Kontum. Instead, they followed the directions of a FAC to targets about ten miles outside the nearby airfield at Phu Cat. As Foote's B/N, LCDR Jackson, noted, all their ordnance hit within twenty-five meters of the FAC's designated target, and they made six direct hits. The ARVN infantry on the ground pressed on and won the battle. This strike and a second two-plane strike later that day led by CDR Earnest with LTJG Mullins, with LTJG Tolhurst and LTJG Ahrens on their wing, became the northernmost missions conducted by VA-75 during its break-in period.[93]

After a final day of pounding targets in MR IV on 31 May, *Saratoga* prepared to steam north toward Yankee Station and flight operations over North Vietnam. During those hops on their last day in South Vietnam, VA-75 dropped its one-millionth pound of ordnance.[94] A postwar study of the air war in the delta over the period from 31 March until 31 May 1972 determined that, of an average sixty-one sorties launched daily on targets in MR IV from all sources (U.S. Navy, U.S. Marine Corps, U.S. Air Force tactical strikes, U.S. Air Force B-52 strikes, gunships, and South Vietnamese Air Force strikes), naval and Marine Corps air assets accounted for an average of thirteen of them. During its first two weeks on the line, VA-75 alone had carried at least 80 percent of the Navy/Marine Corps sorties in South Vietnam's southernmost military region. An analysis by the U.S. Air Force noted that "air power proved as important here as it was elsewhere in halting the Easter Offensive."[95]

On 1 June, *Saratoga* enjoyed its first stand-down day. The cooks made grills out of 55-gallon drums cut in half and barbecued steaks and hamburgers up on the flight deck. VA-75's Aviation Storekeeper First Class, G. T. Vandersloot, probably did not find much to enjoy during the break, however. He ended up in sick bay, undergoing an emergency appendectomy.[96]

CDR Foote used the stand-down to prepare two documents. First, he wrote a letter of commendation for inclusion in each squadron member's official record. He thanked them for their professionalism in the March ORE and especially throughout the hectic weekend of the emergency deployment. He also wrote a note to the families of the Sunday Punchers for inclusion in the next squadron familygram. He reiterated his praise for the way in which the squadron answered the recall, but he also acknowledged to the families at home that "this year has been extremely demanding on you."[97]

The officers contemplated the consequences of the upcoming change of leadership. Most of the junior officers, at least, had come to prefer CDR Earnest's leadership style over that of CDR Foote. Nonetheless, some still harbored lingering concerns about the new command team of CDR Earnest and the new XO, CDR William H. Greene. Both men came from a single-seat attack community, and that especially concerned the B/Ns. "At least the Hooter [Foote] has flown A-6s for years and knows that the system is invaluable," wrote LTJG Warren. He knew that "the A-4 drivers aren't used to that much sophistication in an airplane and it takes them a while to get used to it." Even though CDR Earnest had flown the A-6 for two years now, Warren, for one, remained unconvinced that his new skipper appreciated all that its systems could do. "Oh, well," he wrote, "I guess I'll have to teach him and our new XO."[98]

The officers of VA-75 used the stand-down on 1 June to throw CDR Foote a going-away party. Although the formal change of command would not take place until 7 June, the squadron expected to be back in action by then. The party included a skit lampooning the squadron's senior leaders and showcasing some of the junior officers' eccentricities as well. LT Paul Wagner had set the scene in a ready room, with the "C.O." as lead briefer wearing a white silk scarf, sunglasses, a hat with an oversized silver leaf—the insignia denoting the rank of commander—and carrying three ducks. The "C.O." entered the room and placed the ducks on the front table, carefully aligning them, one behind the other. He had put his ducks in a row, as CDR Foote had often advised.

Everyone howled when LTJG Bob Miller entered, playing a second briefer, the "X.O." Miller had tousled his short hair and stuffed a pillow in the front of his flight suit to give the appearance of a slight paunch. He also put shaving cream on the lower part of his face and neck, and then let it dry. On that night, he reminded everyone of the ointment-slathered CDR Earnest in the aftermath of the unsuccessful flame-throwing effort on the transit. When the "X.O." could not find a match to light his pipe, he demanded a staff study to determine why there were no matches, yelling, "Where's Graustein?" As he transitioned to squadron command, CDR Earnest had named LCDR Graustein as his special assistant to pick up many of his routine duties as XO. The new special assistant had poked so thoroughly into the minutiae of so much of the squadron's day-to-day business that he had picked up a new nickname: the "XO's ass." Thus, assigning Graustein to do a staff study of the match supply seemed just right. Similarly, when the "C.O." spotted a briefee using a green felt-tip pen, which only CDR Foote used, he bellowed, "Put yourself on report for insubordination." But the "X.O." chimed in with, "Let's have a staff study of green felt-tip pens."

LT Wagner then inserted a partial roll call of junior officers. A reluctant attendee at AOMs—he skipped them when he could—Wagner did not answer to his name this time either. The "C.O." apologized for even asking if Wagner was present. LTJG Petersen—playing the Squadron Duty Officer—let loose with one of his well-known Tarzan yells when the "C.O." called his name. The "C.O." shook his head and said only, "Will you put your shirt back on and swing back down to your desk? The phone is ringing."

The mission brief continued into a discussion of contingencies. "In case we have to divert, our primary divert field is Rota, Spain," the "C.O." intoned. When a briefee pointed out, "Wait a minute. We're in the Gulf of Tonkin. Rota is over 12,000 miles away," the "C.O." retorted, "That's just between you, me and CAG. I don't want that information to get outside these four walls." A briefee got in the last word, injecting, "The VC got Rota at 0900 this morning."

Trying to regain control over his briefees, the "C.O." reminded them that they had a mission to fly. He wanted no more distractions. Suddenly, a "little girl" ran up to the "C.O." to announce, "Daddy, Daddy, my group had fewer cavities," triggering a chorus of praise for the father of such a dental marvel. The brief ended abruptly when the "orders" called for a night mission. The briefer simply picked up his ducks-in-a-row and left. Even after more than two hundred of them, CDR Foote never liked night landings.[99]

On a more traditional note, the officers enjoyed the usual cake and "bug juice" (Kool-Aid) that marked such occasions. "It struck me as kind of funny that we sit around eating cake and ice cream when between the 36 officers in the squadron, we've probably got 20 gallons of booze on board," wrote LTJG Warren.[100] The squadron presented CDR Foote with a mug, a plaque, and a handsome scrapbook featuring the highlights of the past year.

As public relations officer, LTJG McFarland had compiled the book, bound in leather and hand-tooled with CDR Foote's name and "VA-75." Inside, he had mounted photos from the 1971 Med cruise and the squadron's arrival back in Oceana the previous fall, unit parties, formal ceremonies, and a few shots from their first missions in South Vietnam. McFarland also included a photograph of every VA-75 officer who had started the Southeast Asia deployment in April, plus LCDR Boecker, who had stayed behind. Each pilot sat in the left seat of his airplane; each B/N sat in the right seat. Chief Warrant Officer Smith, Gunner Walden, and LCDR Kennedy stood on the flight deck. McFarland had frozen a single moment in the life of a squadron. CDR Foote's departure denoted the first of many changes in the ranks of the squadron's officers; it would not be the last. Back home in Virginia Beach, the officers' wives also marked the change of command. In a far more dignified event—a luncheon at the Ocean Hearth Restaurant—they feted Laura Foote and presented her with a silver chafing dish.[101] The traditions of the Old Navy still had their place.

Just a few days before, in the widely read *Stars and Stripes,* a correspondent had compared the military situation in the late spring of 1972 to the annual Army-Navy football game. "It was the Army's game for a long time," he wrote, adding, "but now the Navy has the ball. You can feel it." Since early April, carrier-based planes had begun to hit targets in North Vietnam previously considered off-limits. The mining of North Vietnam's key harbors in early May seemed to be working. VADM William P. Mack of the Seventh Fleet asserted that his review of reconnaissance photos convinced him that "no ship is going in or out to our knowledge, and certainly the ones claimed by the North Vietnamese to have gone in or out, have not." Salvoes from three cruisers and two destroyers hit land targets just south of Haiphong in "the first multi-cruiser gunfire action since World War II."[102]

CDR Foote's farewell party ended on an attention-getting note. The flight schedule for 2 June had just come out. As the flight crews of VA-75 went to sleep that night, many did so knowing that tomorrow they, too, would join in the game. Back home, Jeane Petersen had just mailed LTJG Petersen her "Lecture #521." "I want to say something about this 'piece of cake' business," she wrote. She hoped their efforts so far did not "lull you into a false sense of security, so that when you go into where there is hostile fire that it won't take you by surprise." She pleaded, "Don't you & Tom get too sure of yourself."[103] But her warnings did not arrive until after VA-75 completed their initiation as full participants in LINEBACKER's interdiction effort in the skies over North Vietnam.

CHAPTER FIVE

"Into the Badlands"

Despite the stand-down day, a cookout on the flight deck, and the farewell party for CDR Foote on 1 June, most Punchers looked beyond those activities to the next day's air operations. "We were finally going into the badlands," LTJG Lerseth recalled of his anticipation of his first day in North Vietnam, and "the threat was not just small arms and light AAA, but all that plus heavy AAA, SAMs and MiGs."[1] Even that understated the changes.

In briefings over the past few days, the Sunday Puncher pilots and B/Ns had begun to consider the differences between their recent experience and the challenges that lay ahead. Some tactics they had used in South Vietnam could not be used safely in the North. They no longer could make multiple runs over targets. Nor could they loiter over them. Nor would they follow FACs to their targets; now they had to sharpen their own navigation skills and master target acquisition.

The move northward also made them full partners in the LINEBACKER interdiction campaign, rotating *Saratoga* into the mix of three or four carriers posted at any given time on Yankee Station. They reviewed procedures for dropping mines, for flying low-level strikes and armed reconnaissance missions during the day and at night, and for alpha strikes of twenty aircraft or more. They familiarized themselves with types of ordnance they had not delivered yet, including the Mark 20 (Mk20) "Rockeye" cluster bomb and various types of mines. Search-and-rescue procedures now commanded closer attention. In short, they faced a whole new game, and they knew it.

As the Sunday Punchers launched into North Vietnamese airspace, the squadron heavies once again flew the first combat sorties. But, as evidence of the maturation of the unit, they continued to let the two senior JOs—LTs Cook and Lankford—head up two-plane strikes. Still, other JOs cried foul. Lankford and LTJG Fuller had flown together on the 1971 Med cruise and had wanted to continue to do so. The heavies, however, had separated them earlier in the year to let a newly arrived junior B/N learn from Lankford's experience. Now with Lankford slated to fly strike missions at the start of operations in the North, Fuller complained to LCDR Lindland that a green B/N was getting "his" hops. Lindland understood the apparent unfairness of the situation but simply replied, "That's the way it is."[2] LTJG Hvidding—also a veteran of the 1971 Med cruise but recently paired with LT Ken Pyle, a first-cruise pilot—understood the heavies' reasoning, too, but he still resented the fact that more junior B/Ns got to fly strike missions, while he took tanker hops. They were not "more ready than I," he noted. They just flew with senior pilots.[3]

On 2 June, *Saratoga* joined USS *Coral Sea*, USS *Hancock*, and USS *Kitty Hawk* on Yankee Station. Often described as a set of coordinates in the Gulf of Tonkin, Yankee Station was more—and less—than that. The Seventh Fleet designated a single point in the gulf as ZZ, or "Yankee Station." Carriers assigned to the gulf launched from one of two operating areas that used ZZ as its point of reference. The more northern area reached out in a circle extending 35 nautical miles off Point ZZ. The northern half of this circle became known as "blue," and the carrier assigned to that area became the "blue carrier." The southern semicircle took the second of the U.S. Navy's traditional colors and became known as "gold." The second operating area lay to the southeast of ZZ. It, too, had been subdivided into two semicircles. Its northern semicircle became designated as "red" and the southern one as "gray." If the number of carriers in Yankee Station permitted it, one operated in each sector. Regardless of assignment, however, each carrier moved to the best position to support the strikes on its schedule. Thus, CTF-77 assigned each carrier a different altitude for ingress and egress to help avoid collisions in the air. A ship designated as "Red Crown" served as an "aircraft control center" for all airwings operating in the Gulf of Tonkin. Red Crown also established a Positive Identification Radar Advisory Zone (PIRAZ) through which all aircraft heading to or returning from strikes had to pass, controlled MiG intercepts, and sent out warnings to American aircraft approaching the Chinese border.[4] Coordination of effort in this crowded airspace presented *Saratoga* with an issue it had not faced even a week previously.

In 1965 at the start of Operation ROLLING THUNDER, North Vietnam had been divided into seven sectors, called "route packages"—or simply "route packs"—to facilitate the planning of air operations and eliminate interservice friction between the U.S. Air Force and the U.S. Navy. Control of air operations against targets in Route Package I (RP I), the region just north of the DMZ, remained with MACV headquarters in Saigon, and all air assets in Westpac might be called upon to operate there. Progressing northward, air operations in Route Packages II, III, and IV (RP II, RP III, and RP IV), all possessing a lengthy coastline and a segment of Route 1A—a major north-to-south transportation route for North Vietnamese military supplies—became the primary responsibility of the Navy. The Air Force, flying from bases in Thailand, took primary responsibility for landlocked Route Package V (RP V), the mountainous area around Dien

Bien Phu and the western approaches to Hanoi. Route Package VI included the key North Vietnamese cities of Hanoi and Haiphong, including most of the nation's industrial capacity. Planners split this target-rich, heavily defended area into two halves. The area around Hanoi, military sites to its west, north, and northwest, and the northwest railway to China became familiar to U.S. Air Force pilots as Route Package VI-A (RP VI-A). Other military targets south, east, and northeast of Hanoi, along the important northeast railway to China, and around the key port city of Haiphong became the U.S. Navy's responsibility. CVW-3 and the Sunday Punchers soon became very familiar with the road network, rivers, air defenses, and targets in this area, designated Route Package VI-B (RP VI-B). Under the standing rules of engagement, American aircrews could not fly into the thirty-mile buffer zone along the Communist Chinese border or overfly the Chinese Hainan Island. Until 1972, Hanoi also had enjoyed a measure of protection. A ten-nautical-mile restricted zone surrounded it, and approval to hit targets inside that boundary came only from Washington. A similar four-nautical-mile ring encircled Haiphong. Since April, greater flexibility had been introduced into those rules, as the Punchers soon learned.[5]

From 2 June through 5 June, VA-75 eased into action against North Vietnamese targets in Route Packs II and III, far south of the more intense air defenses around Hanoi and Haiphong. Most of these first hops faced little opposition, but new kinds of missions quickly broadened the young squadron's experience base.

Those lessons began on its first full day of operations in North Vietnam. On 2 June, for the first time working without a FAC, CDR Earnest and LCDR Jackson, with LCDR Graustein and LTJG Mullins on their wing, took off on a strike mission into RP II. CDR Earnest, now providing "flight lead control," led the two aircraft to a highway bridge south of Vinh. They found their target, but, not wanting to make more than a single pass over it, both Earnest and Graustein dropped their entire ordnance loads on their first run. All the bombs fell wide of target and landed in the paddies below. LCDR Jackson assessed the effectiveness of his initial mission in North Vietnam as "lots of puffed rice." The master log recorded simply "RNO/smoke."[6] That same day, LCDR Lindland and LTJG Lerseth took LT Cook and LTJG Swigart against a highway bridge in RP III. They missed, too.[7]

Also on 2 June, some Puncher crews dropped their first mines. Ever since Nixon had announced the mining of Haiphong harbor and other coastal waters in early May, the North Vietnamese and their Communist-bloc trading partners had tried to circumvent the minefields. They began to offload cargoes from large freighters onto shallow-draft barges or boats and then ran them into nearby rivers or inlets to deposit the supplies on protected beaches. Since they could not bomb third-nation shipping, naval aviators over the past few years had developed several tactics to stop the delivery of military goods. Most commonly, a section of A-6s or A-7s simply attacked the smaller North Vietnamese boats— usually called "water-borne logistical craft" or WBLCs (pronounced "wiblicks")—carrying the cargo to shore. Alternatively, A-6s or A-7s sowed minefields with 500-pound Mark 36 Destructors (Mk36 DSTs) or the larger 1,000-pound Mark 52s (Mk52s) in preapproved locations near potential offloading sites. They also dropped mines at river crossings, ferry landings, or other elements of the transportation infrastructure to prevent their use.

To stop the offloading of Chinese ships off the coast near Vinh, CDR Foote led a four-plane mission into RP II to mine a river mouth. During the mission brief, the four crews learned that they had to use a 30-degree dive to drop their fourteen Mk36 DSTs, a shallower approach than the 40-degree dive they had used almost exclusively on their strikes in South Vietnam. The dive slope provided one way to control the distance between mines and thus established a minefield of the specific dimensions CTF-77 planners considered most effective. As CDR Foote made his run to lay the first string, LCDR Pieno spotted some light AAA fire. Still, they dropped their mines on target. LT Ruland, with LTJG McFarland, began his roll-in on a precise south-to-north line to drop his mines when he, too, saw red tracers coming at his plane. He hyperventilated at first but then repeated a phrase CDR Earnest frequently used: "Once you roll in, your ass belongs to Uncle Sam." He, too, dropped on target. After years of experience and perspective, Ruland ultimately looked back on his first mission in the North as "very low risk." Low risk, perhaps, but not absent of risk. LT Lankford and LTJG Warren flew the last of the four A-6As that mined the river mouth and, for the first time, experienced the eerie sensation of being painted by a Fan Song radar from a nearby SAM site. They scanned the skies, but saw no missile.[8] The Sunday Punchers' first mining mission succeeded nicely.

Still, that first day on Yankee Station, flying in closer proximity to other carriers, also caused some minor embarrassments. The squadron's KA-6Ds now supported a variety of new missions they had not flown while in the skies off South Vietnam. The squadron now refueled CVW-3's barrier combat air patrol (BARCAP), usually two F-4s that took up positions near the coast to intercept any MiG threat to the carrier. The F-4s required refueling while on station, and the KA-6D assigned as BARCAP tanker kept them supplied with sufficient JP-5 to last them through a fight, if a threat appeared. LT Pyle and LTJG Hvidding flew a BARCAP tanker on 2 June. When an F-4 drew up for refueling, they extended the drogue, just as they had done in the South. When the plane departed, however, the two men realized they did not recognize the aircraft as one belonging to VF-31 or VF-103. They soon discovered that they had played unwitting gas station to an F-4 from *Kitty Hawk*. They also learned that their generosity complicated fuel accounting figures back aboard *Saratoga*.[9] And they never did it again.

The first day of missions over North Vietnam did not seem to live up to the hype. As LTJG Hvidding confided to his diary, "No one came back with stories of AAA and missiles, but everyone went in and out as quickly as possible, dropping their ordnance on the most likely target after taking an initial look." As he summed up the Sunday Punchers' first day north of the DMZ, "No one claims to have done a great deal of damage to NVN today."[10]

The next day brought more opportunities for familiarization flights against little stiff opposition. CDR Earnest with LCDR Jackson led LT Cook and LTJG Swigart on a strike mission against a suspected North Vietnamese truck park in RP II. Swigart half expected the sky to fill with AAA and SAMs, and he suspected Cook felt the same way, since "we were jinking pretty good." No one fired at them, and years later Swigart reflected on their evasive maneuvering and concluded that "we had definitely overdone the jinking bit."[11] LCDR Lindland, with LTJG Fuller, led a two-plane mining mission to a river mouth in RP II, experimenting with an unusual mixed-ordnance load of seven Mk82s, four Mk36 DSTs, and three Mk82s with long-delay fuses. After dropping on target, Lindland took time on the return trip to fly along the coast to give Fuller a chance to get his first look at key geographical features as they appeared on his radar.[12]

Now that they had entered North Vietnamese skies, the Sunday Punchers also began to utilize the special SAM-suppressing capabilities of the A-6B. When VA-75 departed Oceana in April, its two "missile birds" stayed behind, stripped down for required maintenance. In May, two Oceana-based crews flew the aircraft across the Pacific to catch up with the squadron. Both planes came aboard while *Saratoga* worked against targets in South Vietnam, but the squadron had not needed to use them there. Now, however, they stood ready for action. Both members of a crew pair had to master the sophisticated systems of the A-6B. At this point in the cruise, only a few pilots and B/Ns had qualified.

LTJG Petersen had served as electronic warfare branch officer during the 1971 Med cruise and understood the systems, but his pilot, LT Wharton, still needed to accumulate more hours in the A-6B cockpit. On 4 June, the two prepared to fly an A-6B up and down the coast of southern North Vietnam in RPs II and III, essentially as a training hop. While on the flight deck taxiing toward the catapult, all the ambient noise distracted Wharton, who cut off his electronic countermeasures (ECM) master audio switch for some quiet in the cockpit. After they launched, they ranged up and down the coast in RPs II and III, "trolling" for SAM radars. All of a sudden, not far from Vinh, Wharton saw a flashing red light on his instrument panel. At first he thought he was seeing a fire warning light. Then he realized he was looking at a rapidly flashing missile launch warning light. He had no prior warning of any kind. In that moment, he realized that he had forgotten to turn his ECM master audio switch back on.

The rapid blinking meant not only that a missile had launched but also that it had received guidance signals toward a target. A quick look at his APR-25 told him that the missile had been fired from his right rear, about the four o'clock position, so he rolled right to turn into the missile, went into a split-S maneuver, and then reversed his turn and pulled up left, dumping chaff—strips of aluminum foil to confuse radars—as he went. Wharton and Petersen looked behind them and off to the left. They saw the SAM detonate about one-half mile behind them, very near the point from which Wharton had started his evasive maneuvers. "It was the ugliest dirty orange, brown, black sight I had ever seen. Also the scariest!" Wharton later explained.[13]

Only after the explosion did he and Petersen hear an Air Force electronic warfare plane broadcast, "SAM, SAM, vicinity of Vinh." And only much later did they learn that even if Wharton had turned his equipment back on, they still might not have had much advance notice of the approaching missile. During the summer of 1972, the North Vietnamese experimented with new tactics, including firing a SAM optically with no radar warning at all, and airwing intelligence officers suggested that this might explain what happened.[14]

They knew they had been lucky. But, as the first crew in the squadron and CVW-3 to survive a SAM, they also became temporary celebrities. A journalist from *Saratoga*'s daily newspaper interviewed them, and the two won new nicknames: Wharton became "SAM" and his B/N became "Magnet" Petersen.[15]

The squadron's good luck held on 5 June, when its crews flew several mining missions in RPs I and II. After two launches of A-7s seeded an inlet in RP I, LT Lankford and LTJG Warren led a third element to the same target to continue the effort. About five miles from their target, and about 45 seconds from their roll-in point, the two saw a huge explosion. A WBLC came too close to an Mk36, triggered it, and flew through the air about 100 feet. When they returned from dropping their own ordnance, they found LCDR Graustein preparing to lead a fourth strike against that same target. He asked if they had met any opposition. Assured that they had not, Graustein launched. As Lankford and Warren headed down to the ready room, however, one of the A-7 pilots on their run told them that at least two AAA guns had fired at them during their entire dive. His own aircraft had returned with several holes in it. The two Punchers had seen none of it. Later, when Graustein returned to the ship, he collared Warren and told him that North Vietnamese AAA had "hosed him pretty well." He saw the tracers in the dark. He never let Warren forget that he had described a flak trap as "a cake target," and the B/N learned a lesson about maintaining situational awareness.[16]

Despite the A-6B's near miss and Graustein's heavy flak, VA-75 had it easy so far. They knew alpha strikes into RP VI-B lay ahead, but CDR Foote told them that *Saratoga* would remain in the southern part of the Gulf of Tonkin for several weeks to continue flying against targets in the lower route packs before heading into the heavily defended skies over Hanoi and Haiphong.[17] Thus, it came as a surprise when Flight Ops received the daily strike planning message for 6 June to learn that the familiar cyclic operations they had flown since 18 May had been switched to an alpha strike schedule. Indeed, CVW-3 received targeting information for three separate alpha strikes on 6 June against military sites near Haiphong. In addition, preliminary schedules for 7 and 8 June both called for three alpha strikes on each of those two days.

When CVW-3 received the daily strike planning message for the 6 June alpha strikes, CAG Bordone already had decided upon a planning process for multiplane missions drawing upon the assets of his entire airwing. Over the course of the next two weeks, that process evolved as planners grew in experience and developed a specific sequence of actions. When CTF-77 sent down the daily strike planning message for the next day—with specific alpha-strike targets originating within the Joint Chiefs of Staff's planning cells or at CINCPAC headquarters in Honolulu—CAG Bordone and the CVW-3 operations officer began by assigning each individual mission to a "strike lead," usually the CO or XO from one of the A-6, A-7, or F-4 squadrons.

Planning one alpha strike required the lead to consider many factors; organizing three major efforts simultaneously complicated matters exponentially. Thus, while Bordone assigned strike leads, IOIC began preparation of a "target folder" for each alpha strike that included target information, reconnaissance photographs, and appropriate charts and maps. The intelligence officers from the airwing staff and all the various squadrons worked together in IOIC to update all information, noting positions of combat air patrols and search-and-rescue (SAR) support, and they did the same for the charts noting known operational SAM sites and heavy concentrations of AAA. Each officer took charge of one portion of this information, and LTJG Wardlaw from VA-75 routinely briefed alpha strike leaders on the SAM threats on the route and in their target areas. The daily strike planning order that designated the targets for alpha strikes invariably included alternate targets, and even weather alternates, if low clouds or heavy rains were to force a diversion, and intelligence officers supplied complete information for these secondary sites, as well.

Armed with all this information, each strike leader began planning the night before the mission. He determined aircraft requirements, usually thinking in terms of between twenty and thirty aircraft, sometimes more. He could draw upon F-4s in two-plane sections or four-plane divisions to serve multiple roles

as bombers—CAG Bordone had insisted upon using the F-4s in this manner—
and as target combat air patrol (TARCAP) to provide close-in protection to the
strike group or MiG combat air patrol (MiGCAP) to intercept airborne opposition.[18] He could use A-7s in dual roles as well, utilizing them as attack aircraft
with full bomb loads or as missile-bearing "Iron Hands" to accompany the strike
force over the beach to provide close-in protection from the SAM threat. A-6As
carried bombs, of course, but a strike lead also could call upon VA-75's A-6Bs for
standoff SAM suppression. From among the F-4s, A-7s, and A-6As, the strike
lead chose a "navigation lead"—usually a lieutenant commander, but possibly
an experienced senior lieutenant—to take the strike group to the target area. The
strike lead also had to consider tanker support, E-2B requirements, ECM support from Marine Corps EA-6As from Danang, and the need for RA-5C coverage. Finally, after each of the three alpha strike leaders determined his force requirements, the airwing and squadron operations officers deconflicted the plans
so that each mission received a reasonable measure of the support requested.
Each strike leader then prepared a strike coordination message, worked with the
airwing staff to determine ordnance loads and fusing, and drafted a kneeboard
card for all crews on the mission that included key information on the target, the
composition and call signs of the strike force, radio frequencies, rendezvous altitudes, navigation points, and more.[19] So much had to happen to bring all these
pieces together smoothly that CVW-3 very quickly developed alpha strike planning teams of three commanders and/or lieutenant commanders who worked
together to expedite the process.

Finally, after all the preliminary planning had been completed, LT John Miller
prepared the flight schedule for VA-75's first day of alpha strikes. As always, the
squadron heavies examined carefully the schedule for 6 June. Now that they had
had a chance to evaluate the combat performance of individual crews, they decided who could be assigned to alpha strikes in Route Pack VI-B and who
needed more seasoning before receiving these assignments. LT Miller, best
placed to see the results of the scrubbing senior officers gave to each day's schedule, noticed from the start that, once again, "junior crews were slowly worked in
to the different types of missions that we did."[20]

Approximately two to two-and-one-half hours before launch, the strike lead
briefed all his element leaders representing the various participating squadrons.
He learned to follow CVW-3 guidelines to make certain that he covered all essential information. These element leaders, mostly lieutenant commanders at
this point in the cruise, then returned to their individual squadron ready rooms
to brief their own crews, often using the well-kept charts tacked to their walls
that recorded the most recent information on SAM sites, AAA sites, MiG air-
strips, and other threats. The final planning and briefing could take as long as

four hours at this early point in the airwing's experience. Thus, the leader of an alpha scheduled to launch at 0700 might begin his day at 0300.[21]

Until 5 June, the airwing's senior officers had considered the process of planning alpha strikes only as a training exercise. They had yet to do it for real. The next sixteen days revealed both strengths and weaknesses.

The target for the first of CVW-3's three alpha strikes into RP VI-B on 6 June was a highway bridge near Haiphong. VA-75 provided two A-6As for the strike, both carrying eight Mk83s. Senior crews took the mission. CDR Earnest and LCDR Jackson, in one A-6A, became the navigation lead for the entire strike force, with LCDRs Engel and Schram on their wing. Briefing, manning up, and launch went as expected, but then CDR Earnest's nose gear hung up. He had to jettison his ordnance on safe at sea and return to the carrier. Still, Engel and Schram stayed the course, linking up with a section of A-7s, flying into heavy AAA, and seeing at least one possible SAM. Clouds of dust and smoke from exploding bombs obscured the target, however, so they did not know how much damage they caused.[22]

The airwing's second alpha strike into RP VI-B on 6 June targeted Tieu Gao Petroleum Products Storage Area near Haiphong. CAG Bordone with LCDR Pieno took one of VA-75's A-6As on that strike, with LCDR Graustein and LTJG Mullins on their wing, both planes carrying fourteen Mk82s. Mullins admitted to being apprehensive, comparing the sensation to one he had experienced during intercollegiate fencing matches at the Naval Academy: "I was always nervous before a bout, so much so that I could barely squeak out 'ready sir' to the judge before he started us; but once under way all that adrenalin converted itself into something useful, and I did OK." Soon after the strike group went feet dry, the SAM warning alarm went off in Mullins's helmet. It was the first time he had ever seen the red light on his aircraft's ECM panel flash steadily to warn of a SAM launch. "I didn't see a SAM," Mullins recalled, "but I got a little squeaky in the voice."[23] He set the pucker factor for his first alpha strike at 40 percent.[24]

LCDR Lindland and LTJG Lerseth took LT Cook and LTJG Swigart on 6 June's third alpha strike, this one against the Yen Lap railroad bridge. Swigart looked up and down the deck before the catapult shot, impressed by the variety and number of planes manned and loaded with ordnance, "all with one target." Used to watching planes rendezvous and fly off in twos or fours on various missions, he marveled that "for the first time we were all now part of one huge mission."[25] To the strike lead, however, the marshaling process provided more than aesthetic interest—he updated the number of aircraft in his strike force, eliminating those that had aborted on deck and assuring that all mission tasks remained covered.

The great number of aircraft in the skies over the carrier and the flight to the target area that Swigart so admired represented both the strength and the vulnerability of the strike force. LTJG Lerseth recalled that it took him little time to realize that he hated alpha strikes "not so much because I was afraid of the enemy as I was of running into one of the other 30+ airplanes milling about in the strike group."[26] Lerseth did not see any SAMs or take heavy AAA that day, although debriefers recorded both types of enemy opposition from other participants. But Swigart, like Mullins, heard SAM launch warnings. As he wrote his wife, Penny, that night, his alpha strike against the railroad bridge "was a fairly tame one, but my asshole was tight enough to pick pins off a floor."[27] They carried Mk83s bombs—1,000-pounders—rather than the usual Mk82s they used on most missions, but Swigart did not believe they hit much with them. After returning from these first day's strikes, the crews went through the debriefing process as usual. They had become accustomed to filling out simple forms with spaces to list target information, crews involved, enemy reactions, and any additional useful information. Now they had to complete the special forms to register heavy AAA, SAM launches, and MiG sightings.[28]

After the drain of adrenaline and the burden of paperwork, no wonder the formal change of command that evening made so little an impression on the squadron. In very understated formalities, CDR Foote handed over command to CDR Earnest and left the ship for his new assignment back in Norfolk. Foote flew his last mission on 2 June in RP II, and the junior officers' single most frequently expressed resentment—one lingering even after the passage of many years—rested on his failure to man up on 6 June, the day of the squadron's first alpha strikes. Because of this, one junior pilot noted, "I was glad to see him go, because I felt he was not setting an example as a C.O. always should."[29] Nonetheless, Foote had returned to Westpac when he had the option to stay behind, he flew combat for the first two weeks of their initial line period, and he handed over to CDR Earnest a solid command that would improve with experience. Foote went on to become a CAG and to command a deep-draft vessel.

As CDR Earnest took over command he also welcomed aboard CDR William H. Greene, Jr., the Sunday Punchers' new XO. Now on his fourth tour of duty in Southeast Asia, the Arkansas-born Greene already had flown more than three hundred combat missions in A-4s. Indeed, when he served in VA-212 in 1967, he had worked on the development and initial utilization of the Walleye, one of the U.S. Navy's first "smart bombs." One of the so-called "Succulent Seven," the first men trained to deliver this new ordnance, he took part in a strike on the Hanoi thermal power plant, using the new weaponry to good effect. His A-4 took numerous hits, but he still somehow nursed his crippled aircraft—on fire and with

CDR Charles "M" Earnest succeeded CDR Foote as commanding officer of the Sunday Punchers on 7 June 1972. (Everett W. Foote Collection)

broken landing gear—back to his carrier. When the Navy began to phase out the A-4, he wanted to stay in the attack community. The A-7 may have been better suited to his years of single-seat experience, but with no explanation he found himself reassigned to the A-6 community instead. He screened for command and won assignment as prospective commanding officer of VA-75 as he went through the A-6 RAG at Oceana to complete his transition to his new aircraft.

Despite their common roots in the A-4 community, Greene did not know Earnest before they first met in VA-75's hangar at Oceana. Even while going through the RAG—and well before the start of this combat deployment— Greene visited the squadron's spaces several times a week and talked with Earnest to establish the foundation of their professional relationship. Through a long series of informal conversations, Greene came to understand what Earnest expected from him, and they developed the kind of rapport that permitted a free exchange of opinions. "He allowed me to act . . . almost as a direct peer," Greene later explained, even as he acknowledged Earnest's clear seniority. When they had disagreements, they talked them out. And they became friends. The relationship began—and remained—strong.[30]

But Earnest and Greene had forged that bond as they prepared to deploy to the Mediterranean. Now Greene prepared to leave behind once again his wife, Lilliane, and his three children for yet another combat tour. The ritual of leave-taking had become a familiar rite in the Greene home, but this time it seemed different. With the air war heating up again, and after so many close calls, Lilliane did not believe her husband had much of a chance of coming through unscathed again. When it came time for them to part at the airport, they said what she feared would be their final good-byes. "I thought he had run out of his cat-lives," she recalled later, believing that "this was his fourth time over there, we will not see him again."[31]

Greene's arrival again triggered concerns among some JOs, who continued to wonder what would happen to the squadron under the leadership of a one-two tandem of A-4 veterans. Greene made a positive first impression, though. "I think the new XO will be okay," LTJG Warren wrote his wife shortly after his first extended chat with Greene. He felt certain that Greene would learn the benefits of flying with a second man in the cockpit "the first time the B/N saves his ass for him." As Warren figured, "It won't take long."[32]

The pilots and B/Ns did not have much time to greet their new XO. After their three alpha strikes on 6 June, CVW-3 planned three more such missions for 7 June. The strike message revealed only one major difference: 7 June's targets rested in three different areas of North Vietnam, only one lying in RP VI-B.

LT Lankford and LTJG Warren became the navigation lead for a so-called "mini-alpha" of fifteen aircraft in RP II against coastal defense guns on the islands of Hon Mat and Hon Nieu that had obstructed the work of American naval vessels operating off the North Vietnamese coast. "We had it coordinated with a destroyer," LTJG Warren wrote, explaining that "he was going to run in fairly close to the islands, hoping that they would bring the guns out." But after the mission had been planned and briefed, their aircraft went down on deck.[33] Thus, LT Pyle and LTJG Hvidding, the only other A-6A assigned to the strike, took over the navigation lead. When Pyle pickled off his bombs, only four of his eight Mk83s landed on the island. "Ken was kinda disappointed, but he admitted he rolled in a little early because he was getting nervous sitting up at 12,000 in the SAM envelope," Hvidding wrote.[34] They had not forgotten what had nearly happened to Wharton and Petersen just a few days earlier in that same area.

In RP IV, LCDR Graustein with LTJG Mullins led two additional A-6As as part of an alpha strike against the Tra Ly barracks. After they dropped their bombs, Mullins looked out the windscreen and noticed, about one hundred feet below his plane, dozens of little white AAA bursts. The first thought that struck him unnerved him just a bit: If the gunner had shot just a little higher, he would have hit Mullins's plane. After two alpha strikes in two days, he decided, "OK, I've checked the block—we can sail for home now."[35]

In RP VI-B, CAG Bordone and LCDR Pieno led the airwing's third alpha on 7 June, taking LT Knapp and LTJG Fuller on their wing and heading for the Hon Gay Railroad yards at the head of a 32-plane strike group. The Hon Gay complex included barracks, railroad yards, transshipment facilities, supply warehouses, and a carbide processing plant. Prestrike photographs handed out in IOIC showed railroad tracks, trains, and intact buildings. But attacking the site would not be easy. Numerous AAA sites surrounded the complex, and it rested well inside the envelope of several SAM batteries. Intelligence officers warned that the strike group might see MiGs coming from no less than three active airfields.

"I was scared to death," recalled LT Knapp. After they launched, the length of time it took for all the planes to rendezvous over the carrier amazed him. He had never envisioned this manner of approaching the enemy. "What a target," he recalled. With all those aircraft flying in rather close formation into enemy territory, "it looked like a flock of ducks." Unlike the previous day's missions into RP VI-B, this alpha strike drew a heavy response. As they approached the target, they all the heard the unmistakable loud "DEEDLE" indicating a SAM launch. Fuller wrote home, "The sound in my earphones scared me in a way I've never been scared before." Unlike the Air Force, the Navy did not prepare the way for its large-scale strikes by laying down extensive chaff corridors, and with little to confuse the missiles, the first two of at least six SAMs now flew through the formation. Knapp felt more threatened by the other planes than by the missiles. As he recalled, "All I could see was aircraft in every direction; above, below, right and left. It took about 5–7 minutes to regroup." Then CAG Bordone came on the radio, requesting aid to reacquire the target. Knapp and Fuller still saw it, behind them to the left. Bordone now stunned them, telling them to take the lead and roll in. Thinking back on it, Knapp admitted that "I missed the target with our bombs by a mile."[36] In the end, despite his initial feelings, Fuller concluded that his first alpha strike was no worse than any new and unexpected experience in the air—"it was just different." Five seconds later, when they pulled off their target and flew for the water, "it was all right."[37]

The official summary of the Hon Gay alpha strike claimed that "the strike group maintained strict formation discipline" and made no mention of confusion at the roll-in point. Nonetheless, if Knapp's bombs missed, others did not. Poststrike photography suggested that they had partially destroyed three barracks, severely damaged the carbide plant and associated warehouses, hit many storage areas and at least three rail spurs, and caused fires.[38] Or had they? The long-outdated prestrike photo they received showed a thriving industrial scene. Those who flew over the target, however, thought it more closely resembled a series of moon craters. Alpha strikes had targeted the complex repeatedly since 1966; indeed, XO Greene had flown an A-4 in that very first attack to hit the area. Some of the smoke clouds alleged to be fires set by bombs in June 1972 may have been little more than dust clouds from hitting scattered heaps of coal.[39]

Over these past few days, the Sunday Punchers had begun to use their A-6Bs to support alpha strikes. Even after LT Wharton and LTJG Petersen's misadventure on 4 June, junior crews had stepped forward to fly the A-6B. LTJG Fuller, who had qualified during the 1971 Med cruise, saw it as one way to avoid unending tanker hops while positively supporting strikes. "It's a good mission," he noted.[40] LTs Fischer and Wagner already had qualified on the A-6B, too, and on 7 June they flew off the coast near Cac Ba Island in support of the Hon Gay alpha strike. As on most of VA-75's A-6B missions, they carried two AGM-78 standard antiradiation missiles—often called STARMS—and two AGM-45 "Shrike" missiles. They also provided cover for one of the airwing's RA-5Cs. After making a successful photo run, however, the reconnaissance plane got hit by a SAM on its way out of the target area. LT Fischer reported two good parachutes, watched the two crew members land in the water, and picked up the pilot's voice on the radio. AAA and SAMs came up at the A-7s flying rescue combat air patrol (RESCAP) over the crew's position. Fischer and Wagner tried to fire a Shrike at one SAM site, but the missile hung up. Then they fired both a Shrike and a STARM as a helicopter picked up the downed crew. In addition to his relief at the crew's safe return, Fischer expressed a bit of pride about what he and Wagner accomplished that day: "I'm the first one in VA-75 to fire a STARM."[41]

The Fischer-Wagner team demonstrated a growing tendency among Intruder squadrons to use their A-6Bs more aggressively. During VA-196's deployment during the protective reactions strikes of 1971, their A-6Bs fired only four missiles; the "missile birds" assigned to VA-165 the previous year had fired none at all. With the expanded air effort in 1972, however, A-6Bs began to take a more aggressive role rather than merely to continue to provide standoff support. Fischer fired the first of twenty-four AGM-78s that the Sunday Punchers' A-6Bs would launch before the cruise ended.[42] The sense of satisfaction did not compensate them for witnessing the loss of CVW-3's first aircraft, however.

On 8 June, for the third consecutive day, CVW-3 flew three alpha strikes. The largest of the day called for thirty-three planes to make a two-pronged strike in RP VI-B against the Haiphong Petroleum Products Storage area and the Loi Dong Army Barracks and its transshipment point. Most of the oil that entered North Vietnam from tanker ships was processed and stored at the storage area; the facility included tank farms, pumping stations, and facilities to transfer petroleum products to trucks for shipment inland and to the south. Near Loi Dong, in addition to the barracks complex itself, a railroad spur carried coal cars that supplied fuel to North Vietnamese industry. Naturally, the area enjoyed a significant air defense, resting within range of at least ten active SAM sites. Aircraft flying against this target also flew through those SAM envelopes most of the way in and out of the target area. CAG Bordone served as strike leader, while CDR Earnest of VA-75 and CDR C. E. Armstrong of VA-37 devised a plan to divide the force into two coordinated elements and hit both closely situated targets without interfering with each other's run.[43]

CDR Earnest and LCDR Jackson served as navigation lead for the alpha strike. Weather conditions forced them to abandon their initial approach, but they used a secondary ingress route to reposition the strike group for the attack. The cloud deck at 3,500 feet made target acquisition difficult, but the care that had been taken to point out significant landmarks during the briefings paid off. CAG Bordone, with VA-75's planes in his element, headed for the petroleum storage facility; CDR Armstrong split off with most of his A-7s for Loi Dong.

As they rolled in on the petroleum storage area, LCDR Jackson saw evidence of heavy AAA of all calibers and heard repeated calls warning of SAMs in the air in the vicinity of Haiphong. CDR Earnest then spotted two SA-2s coming directly at them and started a split-S maneuver to evade them. The effect was remarkable. As LCDR Jackson later explained, while "pulling G's first one way and then the next, it seems as if time stands still, or it is the 'longest minute' you can ever remember." Again and again over the next few minutes, CDR Armstrong broke in to report SAMs and their direction; they learned later that his ECM gear had failed, so he had developed a genuine need to acquire the missiles visually as early as possible. But Jackson saw none of them. He tried to keep his eyes on the route they had planned. Finally, the skipper turned to Jackson and asked, "Where the hell is the target?" Jackson pointed over Earnest's left shoulder, and they found themselves perfectly positioned to roll in on it. The importance of the crew concept now made an indelible impression on Jackson. For him, it inspired "a deep personal respect and admiration for the individual abilities and strengths that we each brought" to the team.[44]

As Earnest's A-6As broke off target and headed low and fast out to sea, something caught LT John Miller's eye as they flew over the outskirts of Haiphong: children peacefully playing soccer just below them.[45] The official count of SAMs fired against the alpha strike totaled nine. LTs Fischer and Wagner, again flying in an A-6B, counted at least five SAMs and evaded one tracking them specifically; they again fired one AGM-45 and one AGM-78.[46]

The official narrative of the day's action noted that "although most of the missiles appeared to guide on the strike group, correct evasive maneuvering and the presence of extremely aggressive Iron Hand sections severely limited their effectiveness." (In this case and in many such summaries, "Iron Hand" denotes both the A-7s and the A-6s that participated in the SAM suppression effort.) A poststrike photo mission flown by one of the airwing's RA-5Cs showed evidence of several large and sustained fires at the petroleum storage area and numerous storage tanks and related buildings destroyed; at Loi Dong, at least fourteen military structures were destroyed and seven more severely damaged.[47] Total cost to the attackers: no losses.

Not included in the official report was a complaint by the Soviets that one of their ships in Haiphong harbor had been hit by shrapnel during the strike on the petroleum storage facility. Very quickly, questions from CTF-77 came down to *Saratoga*'s airwing and then to the individual crews in the strike. LT John Miller remembered that LCDR Lindland came to each participating pilot and B/N to ask where his bombs went. Miller recalled replying, "Don, my pipper was right on the target." The heavies' sensitivity about the issue underscored for Miller that each of his missions was "a very political exercise."[48]

Individual lesson-learning found no place in official reports either. During this mission, LT Miller had flown as CDR Earnest's wingman. As they exited the target area, in answer to Earnest's radio call, Miller had to admit that in the confusion caused by the SAMs he had lost sight of the skipper. When they got back to the ship, the CO sat down with both members of his young crew—B/N Sanford as well as pilot Miller—and reminded them, as Miller recalled it, that "as a wingman your only job in life is to keep the lead in sight." They would not forget again.[49]

By comparison, the squadron's other two alpha strikes on 8 June proved far less exciting. Down in RP IV, LCDR Lindland and LTJG Lerseth led a two-plane section of A-6As in a larger strike that cratered the approaches to bridges near Ninh Binh. But rapidly changing weather conditions over a target near Vinh forced the strike leader of the day's third alpha strike to break up the formation and divert to targets farther south. Still, the least productive alpha strike provided more excitement than a tanker hop, even those on the fringes of this high threat environment. On 8 June, LTJG Hvidding flew two tankers with LT Pyle.

"This is getting old," he wrote, especially when those who went on the strikes counted 9 SAMs and took heavy AAA. "Everyone came back telling war stories," and "someone said it means a Silver Star for CAG and a DFC [Distinguished Flying Cross] for the element leaders," he complained, adding that "I feel a little like the world (and war) is passing me by while I drone around in the tanker reeling the hose in and out."[50]

After three days of alpha strikes, VA-75 and CVW-3—and, indeed, all the carriers working off the coast of North Vietnam—pulled back a bit. Soviet President Nikolay Podgorny planned to visit Hanoi. Since the Soviet leader was fresh from the Moscow Summit, understood Nixon's intent to negotiate from a position of strength, and could impress the American leader's sincerity on the North Vietnamese, Soviet ambassador to the United States Anatoly Dobrynin had asked for a cessation of bombing during Podgorny's visit. Nixon agreed to reinstate temporarily the restrictions that placed off-limits many potential targets.

Despite the hold put on most alpha strikes, the interdiction effort against the transport of military supplies heading south in RPs II, III, and IV still continued. To that end, the Sunday Punchers now flew missions in the southern route packs and additional seeding operations in the coastal waters and rivers of southern North Vietnam. CTF-77 switched *Saratoga* to the midnight-to-noon schedule for air operations, while other carriers flew the noon-to-midnight or— when the restrictions were lifted—the alpha strike schedule. Except for one alpha strike when the weather cleared on 13 June, *Saratoga*'s airwing flew this schedule through 18 June. For the first time in the combat cruise, its crews flew many of its missions at night.[51]

A crew assigned a night mission generally received one of two kinds of targeting guidance. An order for a night strike identified a hard target but kept open the option to use any remaining ordnance on a predetermined secondary site or unanticipated target of opportunity. The alternative, the armed reconnaissance mission, commonly called a "recce," sent a pilot and B/N looking for truck lights or WBLCs or some other "movers" on a road, bridge, canal, or other target appropriate to the interdiction campaign. On any given night, they might also hit boxcars, railroad sidings, active river crossings, AAA sites, or suspected truck parks or supply dumps. Since they often hit targets of opportunity, crews generally carried a mixed ordnance load, usually a combination of Mk82s and Mk20 Rockeye. The latter—a cluster bomb composed of an outer shell that opened when dropped to scatter hundreds of smaller explosive "bomblets" on the target—quickly became a Sunday Puncher favorite that proved especially effective against vulnerable targets such as a manned AAA site or a supply cache of thin-metal oil drums. It also possessed a substantial kill radius that did not require pinpoint accuracy to cause significant damage.

Low-altitude flight made these night missions especially challenging to the pilots and B/Ns. They flew at 500 feet or below, keeping them under most SAM radars. AAA and ground fire still presented a threat, but unless the gunners had some kind of radar-controlled system, they generally fired at the sound of the aircraft engines. By the time they reacted, they generally fired behind the plane. But low-altitude flight at night required total concentration and high situational awareness. Karst ridges, high hills, even flocks of birds might pop up quickly, and the B/N had to navigate by radar-significant terrain features while the pilot watched his altitude. A sneeze or an inadvertent twitch could send a plane nosing toward the ground.

These night missions gave the B/N his first real opportunity to apply his training. In the absence of visual cues and checkpoints, his ability to select an ingress route, find radar-significant points that took them to the target, and then plot an egress route became essential to the successful completion of the mission. No other carrier-borne aircraft could do this, and the A-6A pilot could not do this while flying the aircraft. Night missions belonged to the B/N.

Each crew had to consider its technical expertise level and flight experience to work out for itself the cockpit procedures that worked best. But a smart pilot with experience quickly learned to use a light hand to teach a young B/N what he needed to know and then show confidence in his ability to do the job and stay alive. Unfortunately, VA-75's few combat veterans could spread their experience only so far.

Just the same, three night missions during a single week in June illustrate the way in which LCDR Lindland taught LTJG Lerseth to become a competent and confident B/N on dangerous night single-aircraft, low-level strikes. For their 9 June night mission against a target near Hon Gay, Lindland let Lerseth plot the primary and alternate ingress and egress routes, plan the delivery mode, and make other key decisions. Lindland did not grill his B/N about his decisions, but just asked a few questions for clarification. When they crossed the beach, they did not have a full system. Night, low-level flight, heavy opposition, difficult mountainous terrain in the target area, minimal system, and a B/N untested in these conditions might have concerned even the most experienced pilot, but Lindland demanded a constant information flow back and forth. They usually kept chatter to a minimum, so Lerseth noticed the change and appreciated it. Despite AAA and a SAM warning—but no launch—they hit their target. In Lerseth's view, this mission "defined our relationship as a crew in all environments." In retrospect, he believed "that mission was the final watershed in our becoming a complete crew."[52]

A few nights later, on 12 June, they flew a night strike beginning near Hon Gay, passing through rugged terrain and ending at a new railroad bridge and transshipment complex eight miles southeast of Kep airfield. Again, Lindland let Lerseth plan the ingress, accepting a route that fell within the envelopes of five active SAM sites and numerous AAA sites. Intelligence reports also warned of nighttime MiG activity in the area. They coasted in near Hon Gay and made their first turn toward the target at the Waterloo Red line, the southern edge of the Chinese buffer zone. Flying under 500 feet, they pressed their attack. On their first run, they dropped six Mk82s that triggered several secondary explosions. On a second run—not usually advisable against such heavily defended targets—they dropped four Mk20s that started a sustained fire. As they egressed, contested by AAA gunners and painted by SAM radars, they saw—and avoided— MiGs launching and landing at Kep airfield. But they still had work to do. They headed feet wet along a preassigned road segment and obtained radarscope photography for the task force's intelligence database. But Lerseth did not recall turning on the automatic camera in the B/N's scope hood. "Frankly," he recalled later, "I was too busy keeping us from becoming part of one of the mountains."[53]

Two nights later, on 14 June, Lindland took Lerseth on yet another single-plane strike, this one against the Nam Dinh petroleum storage facility. Again, Lerseth planned the mission. As soon as they dipped down to 400 feet a few miles from the target, the dark sky lit up with AAA fire. Lerseth remembered "tracers arcing over the wings and being surprised at just how much light there was out there in a night that had been perfectly black a second before." Fortunately, Lerseth had a full system and already had locked on target. After the bombs caused a huge explosion, Lindland began high-G low-level evasive maneuvers to avoid the intensifying AAA fire. At that point, Lerseth made the mistake of taking his head out of the scope and looking up. Above him, he saw Nam Dinh and many bright tracers and realized that Lindland now flew nearly inverted. He quickly put his head back in the scope as Lindland went down to 300 feet and continued maneuvering until they went feet wet. As Lerseth recalled, during the debrief, an E-2B crew "ooozzzed about what a neat light show we had created for them and thanked us for it." He rose to retort, but in that moment he remembered perhaps the most important lesson of the past few days: Lindland always had remained perfectly calm in every phase of the planning, flying, and debriefing process. Lerseth knew he had found his role model.[54]

Not all of the Sunday Punchers' night missions into RP VI-B brought similar success. CDR Earnest and LCDR Jackson brought back no significant BDA from a strike on a storage area along Route 13B that led northeast from Hanoi to China. But they did report seeing aircraft lights in airspace where no American planes flew that night. Intelligence officers concluded that the two men had shared the night skies with a MiG, and mission briefs began to pay greater attention to the airborne threat.[55] LCDR Dick Schram had no problem finding his targets. In June 1972, he flew night strikes against at least three wooden bridges he had bombed on his previous combat tour. The targets were not radar significant and could be hard to find, but he and his pilot succeeded. Unfortunately, the structures also could be repaired easily, and the North Vietnamese continued to rebuild bridges he had already destroyed. He expressed his concerns to the CO, but CDR Earnest could offer him no explanation for the target selection. One mid-June evening, entirely dejected, Schram dropped in on LTJG Lerseth, bottle of scotch in hand. The two men drained it, the junior officer listening as the senior B/N vented his dismay and broke down in tears of frustration and anger.[56]

During this first line period, only the squadron heavies—and the few junior B/Ns who paired with them—flew night strikes in RP VI-B. The same held true for reconnaissance missions in that region. When LTJG Warren heard that the squadron had orders to "road recce the road between Haiphong and Hanoi" and another segment "from Nam Dinh to Hanoi, and from Hanoi up to 25 miles of the Chinese border," he made sure that he "didn't do any volunteering for that kind of stuff." Recent complaints by Chinese leaders condemning the intensified American air offensive in northern North Vietnam underscored the danger of working close to the border of a major Communist power on alert against "frenzied acts of aggression."[57] Although he usually joined in with other JOs who wanted a chance to take on more challenging missions before the heavies cleared them to do so, this time he admitted, "I'm not complaining."[58]

During mid-June, junior Sunday Puncher crews gained experience in night strikes by flying missions in the lower route packs. LT Pyle and LTJG Hvidding flew their first night recce into Happy Valley in RP II with high expectations of success. They stayed at about 6,000 feet at first. But almost immediately their airborne moving target indicator (AMTI) malfunctioned. Still, they spotted a moving speck of light, perhaps a truck on a road. Because he had descended from his original altitude to look for vehicles, Pyle started his roll-in much lower than he usually did. When he checked the radar altimeter, Hvidding suddenly discovered they had descended way too low. "Pull Up! Pull Up!" he yelled to Pyle, who responded immediately. In retrospect, Hvidding felt a bit sheepish about his reaction. As he explained, "I think every B/N at one time or another is reluctant to take control of a situation," assuming his pilot had sufficient information. But he appreciated that Pyle trusted him enough to react immediately without question. Pyle learned to value his B/N's alertness; even years later, the pilot believed he had gone below 200 feet before he pulled up out of his dive. Later, they attempted to drop their Mk82s on a bridge, but Hvidding could not find it with the search radar. Thus, he recalled, "on our first [night] mission where I was responsible for the solution, I came up empty." They did not tell the heavies what they had done, fearing that they might be grounded. As Pyle later reflected, "I've learned that it's better to be lucky than good . . . and that night luck was on our side."[59]

If the whole episode left them unsettled, at least they survived to learn from it. CVW-3's night operations to interdict the flow of North Vietnamese military supplies fit perfectly with the capabilities of the A-6, but not all participating aircraft possessed the same technology. This led to hard lessons of a different sort.

On the night of 14 June, the Sunday Puncher pilots and B/Ns and the A-7 pilots from VA-37 suited up for the night's work in the shared locker area near their adjoining ready rooms. The easy relationship between the two squadrons permitted even VA-75's JOs to trade jokes with LCDR John Davis of the A-7 squadron. VA-37's aircraft were not designed for night missions. The A-7 community had developed the flare drop as the only feasible way of helping their pilots identify targets and drop their ordnance at night. In a typical two-plane mission, one pilot would drop a flare and then loiter overhead while the other made his run; when he pulled off the target, the two pilots simply reversed their roles. On this night, while flying an A-6B hop in support of strikes near Vinh, LTs Fischer and Wagner heard Davis call for a flare drop to illuminate WBLCs transporting cargo from Chinese merchant ships near Hon Nieu and Hon Mat islands. Davis rolled in on his target. A few seconds later, Fischer saw a flash denoting an explosion. He first thought one of Davis's bombs had hit something big. Then he heard Davis's wingman, LTJG Edward A. Lyons, trying unsuccessfully to make radio contact with his flight lead. Lyons reported the situation about 0700. Search and rescue (SAR) activity began immediately. But those efforts ended about two hours later with negative results.[60] Except for an oil slick on the water, they found no trace of the plane.

The Navy listed LCDR Davis, who left behind a wife and four children, as missing in action. His loss left LTJG John L. "Hondo" Johnson, one of his squadronmates, to lament, "No one expected it to be John."[61] Even though Davis had not belonged to VA-75, the incident gave the Punchers pause. LT Fischer recorded the officer's loss in his diary that night and added, "Bit by bit, I'm losing my sense of humor."[62]

Just two nights later, LTJG Lerseth joined LT John Cabral of VA-105 for an early meal before the airwing made its night launches. Later, at approximately 0430, he set off with LCDR Lindland on an armed recce to RP III. Cabral, in his A-7, launched a minute or so behind them. After he did so, LT Knapp and LTJG Fuller taxied forward and sat on Catapult 1 at full power, checking their instruments to prepare for launch. Suddenly, ahead of the carrier, a bright flash illuminated the night. Lindland and Lerseth noticed the light down low, as if in the water behind them. Knapp looked up abruptly, distracted by the same flash.

Cabral's aircraft had flown into the water about two nautical miles ahead of *Saratoga* and exploded into flames.

The spectacular crash caused many enlisted personnel on the flight deck to leave their duty stations and rush to places where they could see it more clearly. As they neared the wreckage, many threw emergency lights over the side to mark the site for rescuers. But, in the excitement, they simply forgot about the ongoing air operations. Sitting on the catapult ready to launch, Knapp and Fuller saw senior yellowshirts pounding sailors on the back and shoving them back to work, their efforts reinforced by calls from the Air Boss. Knapp then got signals to throttle back and abort his launch. But if, in all the confusion, the catapult fired after he reduced power, Knapp knew he and Fuller would end up in the sea themselves. Thus, he refused to cut power until the catapult officer stood in front of the plane to demonstrate that the catapult was no longer armed.[63]

Shortly thereafter, crewmen from USS *Glennon* recovered Cabral's body. Knapp took the pilot's death personally. As the VA-75 Landing Signals Officer (LSO) who worked in concert with his counterparts in the other squadrons, Knapp had taken part in several discussions concerning Cabral's flying skills; the A-7 pilot had never erased all doubts about his airmanship. In the end, the accident review attributed Cabral's death to pilot error.[64] Many of those who did not witness the crash when it occurred watched replays on the pilot landing-aid television (PLAT) in their ready rooms. The "spectacular mushroom fireball" only added to a sentiment among some less experienced aviators in the airwing: "Nobody is real hot on night flying now."[65]

Nonetheless, the loss of this A-7, and the likelihood that the pilot flew into the water, reinforced among VA-75 aviators their belief in the superiority of their own aircraft and the value of the crew concept in reducing the possibility of similar accidents. As one wrote home after describing Cabral's death, "The fantastic thing about the A-6 is that there are 2 people to double check each other. We've got two engines and we can conceivably lose one on the cat stroke and still fly. I get off the cat at night with the red flashlight trained on the important instruments just in case of electrical problems. I double check rate of climb or descent, airspeed, altitude etc. Very few A-6s fly into the water for no apparent reason. We make it that way."[66]

After Cabral's death, LT Larry Kilpatrick of VA-105 told LT Fischer, a close friend, about his growing anxiety. Kilpatrick had shared his concerns earlier with one of his own squadron heavies, who suggested that the junior pilot take himself off the flight schedule for a few days. The pilot refused. "I can't fight something by running away," Kilpatrick told Fischer. A successful mission on 16 June seemed to restore his confidence.

About 0255 on 18 June, however, *Saratoga* got word that LT Kilpatrick had been shot down in Happy Valley.[67] Fischer heard him call over the radio that he was going to illuminate a bridge with a flare. When Kilpatrick began his roll in, he said—either to himself or his wingman—"watch your altitude."[68] Then he disappeared. Potential rescuers spotted a parachute in the trees but made no voice contact and saw no one moving on the ground. Kilpatrick had been LT Knapp's roommate in pilot training. Their paths diverged as they entered different communities, but they had stayed friends and enjoyed serving on the same carrier. When word came in of Kilpatrick's loss, Knapp considered it, even after the passage of many years, to be "probably my lowest point of the cruise."[69]

Even though none of these losses belonged to VA-75, the Punchers faced up to the reality of death. Indeed, they understood more than ever that they lived and worked in one of the most dangerous environments in the world, and they never could let down their guard. The recent chaos on the flight deck during LT Cabral's crash underscored to all aboard—not merely the flight crews—that the possibility of death or injury surrounded them. A few days after these incidents, as an element of A-7s moved onto the bow catapults, Gunner Walden completed his ordnance inspection on some A-6s preparing to launch immediately after them. As he crossed the flight deck to find a safe position to watch, a jet blast deflector dropped early, catching him in the exhaust of one of the A-7s, knocking him down, and rolling him backward. When he stood up, another A-7 taxiing forward to the catapults turned, and its exhaust pushed him toward the intakes of other nearby Corsairs. The slender Walden felt himself being sucked toward the nearest one. Suddenly a yellowshirt—Walden never knew who—ran up behind him, grabbed the collar of his flight jacket, and jerked him down flat. The zipper of his jacket cut a nasty gouge into his neck that bled profusely, and he bloodied his hands, knees, and elbows as well. But he lived to tell about it. From their deck spot farther back on the flight deck, LT Wharton and LTJG Petersen had noted the commotion, and they saw someone being led off the flight deck with so much blood flowing from the side of his head that they thought the injured man had lost an ear. Neither man recognized the victim as their own Gunner.[70]

Under such circumstances, the Punchers welcomed any source of diversion or comic relief. After returning from one of his hops, LTJG Warren opened a package from home. Inside he found a doll in the likeness of "Poppin' Fresh," the Pillsbury Doughboy. Some in the squadron had already begun to tag the chunky newcomer with that nickname, but the arrival of the doll sealed it.[71] About the same time, another squadron newcomer, LTJG Sanford, received an even more unlikely gift from home: a stuffed toy rat. At first, as a joke, Sanford stuck it in a pocket of his survival vest. Very soon, Sanford began taking the rat into the cockpit with him. Before long, both the stuffed rodent and his owner alike became "the Combat Rat." Sanford himself soon answered to "Rat."[72]

On 19 June, *Saratoga* went off the midnight-to-noon schedule.[73] With Podgorny gone from Hanoi and a resolution of the Chinese border problem nearing, planning for alpha strikes already had resumed. "I guess the admiral decided we were killing ourselves flying into the ground at night, so he'd give the N. Vietnamese a chance to get us with a few SAMs and AAA" instead, LTJG Warren groused.[74]

Already, CDR Greene had become fully integrated into squadron operations, leading the A-6A elements assigned to alpha strikes and accepting the challenging assignment to plan and lead these large-scale missions. In the late morning of 18 June, he successfully led three A-6As as part of an alpha strike against supply storage areas in RP IV. The next day, he planned an alpha strike against some bridges west of Ninh Binh. His aircraft went down on deck, but LT Lankford and LTJG Warren took LTJGs Tolhurst and Ahrens on their wing and led the strike group to the target themselves. "Everything went well except I think we missed the bridges," Warren reported.[75]

But at least they had located their target. An incident on another alpha strike on 19 June, this one against a storage area on a prominent peninsula in RP III, revealed that the planning process still could not cover all contingencies. During these early alpha strikes, the task of providing navigation lead occasionally fell to F-4s that did not have the A-6s' more sophisticated navigation technology, and one such plane pulled the assignment for this mission. Four A-6As, two carrying eight Mk83 1,000-pound bombs designed to inflict heavy damage on the storage structures, flew well back in the formation. CAG Bordone and LCDR Pieno, leading the A-6A element that day, looked for the strike's very prominent coast-in point and could not see it. Bordone radioed the lead F-4 to ask if they knew where they were. Assuring him that they did, the F-4s began their roll in. But they did not find the target below them. The navigation lead had taken the strike to the wrong peninsula. Worse, the F-4s now ran low on fuel. The entire strike group had to break up and hit secondary targets. The VA-75 master log recorded it as a "weather divert," but after this incident, CAG Bordone never again gave the navigation lead for an alpha strike to the F-4s.[76]

On 20 June, CVW-3 sent twenty-one aircraft on a major coordinated strike against four separate targets: the Nam Dinh Thermal Power Plant, the Trinh Xuyen Highway bridge, the Trinh Xuyen railroad bridge, and a SAM site. The four targets, five miles apart and twenty-four miles inland, rested well within range of two other active SAM sites that had fired on previous strikes and much AAA of all calibers. The value of the transportation targets seemed obvious enough and the thermal power plant provided the only possible energy-generation source for four textile plants at Nam Dinh, while the missile site was one of the key defenses in the area. CDR Earnest and LCDR Jackson planned the mission, designing simultaneous attacks to confuse and split the attention of the defenders. They divided the strike force into two parts: a northern cell, including A-6s and A-7s carrying Mark 84 (Mk84) 2,000-pound bombs, to attack the Nam Dinh power plant, and a southern cell to attack the bridges. The mission came off without a hitch. CDR Earnest and LCDR Jackson served as strike lead to the power plant, and their bombs blew off the roof of the boiler house and destroyed a cooling tower and a 125-foot storage building. At the railroad bridge, the tracks were cut in three places, and the approaches to both the railroad and highway bridges were heavily cratered. No planes were lost.[77]

That same day, LT Ruland with LTJG McFarland led the two-plane A-6A element in an alpha strike on the Thanh Hoa petroleum storage area that included barracks, bunkers, and storage and support buildings. The target itself lay in range of active SAM sites and numerous AAA guns, and the strike force had to deal with the stout defenses of the Thanh Hoa bridge, just one and one-half miles away. The strike lead, CDR W. R. Zipperer of VA-105, planned to use F-4 flak suppressors and A-7s in their Iron Hand role to launch preemptive strikes against the formidable North Vietnamese air defenses.

Until now, junior Sunday Puncher crews who served as section leads in alpha strikes did so because a senior officer's plane went down on deck or air aborted. In this case, Ruland had the lead from the start. As the next most senior pilot after LTs Cook and Lankford—measured both by rank and experience in the cockpit—he merited the next opportunity for increased leadership responsibilities. His assignment as A-6A lead demonstrated the continuing maturation of the squadron as reflected in a leveling of duties. Senior officers flew close by to evaluate his performance; in an unusual occurrence, two heavies—CDR Greene and LCDR Pieno—flew on Ruland's wing.

A summary of the mission complimented all the section leaders for maintaining formation integrity throughout roll in, delivery, and egress from the target zone. But the official write-up did not portray the event entirely accurately. The two A-6As rolled in last, with Greene and Pieno bringing up the rear. AAA filled the skies and, although the strike force had orders to break off the target to the left, or east, Greene and Pieno broke right to avoid the AAA drawn by the twenty-one aircraft ahead of them. They also made a promise afterward that they would never again be the last to roll in on a target once the North Vietnamese gunners located the strike group. In the end, BDA proved difficult to assess since dense smoke blanketed the target area up to 3,000 feet, but the A-6As claimed one sustained fire and one large explosion.[78] At some point over the course of this busy day, VA-75 dropped its two-millionth pound of ordnance.[79]

On 21 June—the last day of *Saratoga*'s first line period, finally—CVW-3 launched two more alpha strikes. A major, twenty-nine-plane coordinated alpha strike hit a pair of highway bridges near Phu Ly in RP IV where the road network linked up with two major waterways crowded with heavily loaded WBLCs and a major petroleum products storage area near Ninh Binh. LCDR Lindland led a three-plane element of A-6As, and, since these targets lay in range of five active SAM sites, CDR Earnest and LCDR Jackson flew one of VA-75's A-6Bs as part of the missile suppression effort. With CDR James Flatley of VF-31 as flight lead, the strike force made several direct hits on one bridge and caused severe damage to its abutments. Lindland's flight set a number of secondary fires on the WBLCs that stalled river traffic. Ninh Binh storage sites also suffered damage, but BDA remained incomplete, noted a mission summary, "because of the holoca[u]st that was raging and the large secondary explosions at the target."[80]

The airwing's final alpha strike in RP VI-B before it left the line targeted a SAM assembly and petroleum storage area in the hills northwest of Haiphong. CAG Bordone, flying in one of VA-75's A-6As with LCDR Pieno, served as strike lead. Their element included two additional A-6As—LT Knapp and LTJG Fuller, along with CDR Greene and LTJG Bob Miller. Bordone's and Knapp's aircraft both carried eight Mk83s to hammer the bunkers that stored the missiles. BDA reported 100 percent bombs on target, with some visually spectacular results. "They had missiles blowing up, scooting along the ground, fizzling, and a little bit of everything, including a dozen or so shot at them," one report noted. Not surprisingly, a major attack on a key supply area triggered significant resistance. North Vietnamese MiGs took to the skies. But the MiGCAP did its job. CDR Sam Flynn, the XO of VF-31, and his RIO, LT William John, engaged three MiG-21s and shot down one of them.[81]

For CDR Greene, the recovery aboard *Saratoga* proved exciting, too. When his aircraft caught the arresting wire, the jolt jarred loose his NATOPS pilot flight booklet from its place on the console behind him. It lodged under the valve cover of his G-suit and blew it up to its maximum capacity. By his own description, he felt like "a blown up blowfish." LTJG Miller noticed his pilot's distress and started stabbing Greene's leg with a ballpoint pen, trying to deflate the suit. Unfortunately, the fabric resealed after each puncture. Finally they fixed the valve and bled off the pressure. A bit later, Greene's leg started to throb. He looked down and realized he was bleeding. Miller had punctured the G-suit so hard that his pen went all the way through Greene's flight suit underneath. The XO carried the scars for years.[82]

By the end of their first line period, the pilots and B/Ns of VA-75 had experienced much and learned more. Some lessons linked directly to operational procedures. Early in the cruise, VA-75's senior leaders adopted a "low and fast" tactic for night armed recces, speeding along at as much as 500 knots and sometimes more. It simply made sense to them that they improved their chances of surviving if they blew by enemy resistance. They soon realized, however, that at such high speeds, the pilot's slightest touch on the stick affected his control. Moreover, flying so fast without a fully operational navigation system asked for trouble, especially if flying through North Vietnam's karst ridges at night. Thus, they recommended a change in their armed recce tactics to "low and slow"—flying at either 360 or 420 knots, because of their easy divisibility by six, which indicated they flew either six or seven miles per minute. An individual crew always could choose to alter its altitude and speed if the mission, the men's experience, and their aircraft's capabilities supported a change.[83]

Down in the squadron's shops, technicians and maintenance personnel continued to learn just how much effort it took to keep an A-6 squadron's planes in the air. The problems first evident in late May increased as the line period continued. By mid-June, several VA-75 aircraft had begun to fail so regularly that they had to be ferried to the better-equipped shops of CVW-3's beach detachment at Cubi. Before the end of the line period, LT Anderson and LTJG Mullins took a tanker that required more corrosion repair than even the beach detachment could handle to the Air Asia rework facility at Taiwan.[84] The impending departure of LCDR Jim Kennedy at the end of the line period forced Chief Warrant Officer Smith and the chiefs in the various shops to consider ways to overcome maintenance concerns until his replacement arrived.

Finally, many discoveries came on the personal level. Many of the junior pilots and B/Ns found a measure of self-confidence they had hoped to find but that was only now tested and proved. Right after his first alpha strike on 6 June, LTJG Swigart had written to his wife, "I think both [LT] Bruce [Cook] and I have gotten that initial fear or apprehension out of our systems [and] we can concentrate more on flying professionally rather than flailing around like a bunch of chickens with our heads cut off."[85]

After *Saratoga*'s combat losses, they also understood the high price their profession could exact. But loss can take many forms, and one Puncher now confronted the death of a dream. Back on 18 June, LT Tom Wharton quietly had asked LCDR Lindland to remove him from the flight schedule. He had overcome the accuracy problems he had struggled with in South Vietnam, but ever since his near miss with the SAM on 4 June, Wharton had become increasingly uncertain of himself in the cockpit. He kept recalling LTJG Petersen's words after they landed: "I'm glad I was flying with *you*." He could not reconcile his B/N's confidence in him with his own self-doubt.

He did not have a course of action in mind when he talked to Lindland initially, but Wharton finally made an important decision: he turned in his wings.[86] Pure and simple, most naval aviators choose their specialty because they love to fly. Wharton had not lost that love. But he could no longer hold himself responsible for the life—and perhaps death—of a brother aviator. He believed that his B/N, married with one son and a child on the way, deserved a better chance to survive than he could promise. Wharton did not talk to his roommate, LTJG Bob Miller, or any of his other friends in the squadron. He did not even inform Petersen about his decision to leave. "It looks like I'll have to find myself another pilot," his surprised B/N wrote home a few days later, adding, "I can't really hold it against him either. I respect anyone who stands up for what he believes in."[87] Other Punchers agreed with Petersen. "At least Tom came over, flew for a whole line period almost, and decided it wasn't his thing. He had the guts to give it a chance anyway," LTJG Warren decided.[88] Indeed, wrote LTJG Fuller, "He's probably the smartest one amongst us."[89]

The first line period ended as *Saratoga* steamed into Subic Bay on the morning of 23 June and moored on the starboard side of Alava wharf. Since 18 May, CVW-3 had dropped 3,416 tons of ordnance. The Sunday Punchers had delivered over 1,000 tons of the total amount.[90]

The men of *Saratoga* and CVW-3 welcomed the break. The aircrews turned in their personal weapons, and all hands anticipated liberty call with eagerness. But first, they had to await the completion of formalities. After morning colors, RADM John S. Christiansen, commander of Carrier Division Seven—all the carriers in Westpac operating against targets in North and South Vietnam, Laos, and Cambodia—broke his colors aboard *Saratoga* to begin a three-month stay. The condition of the carrier's flag quarters did not impress the admiral or his staff. The chief of staff started to list the deficiencies, expecting CAPT Sanderson to fix them immediately. But Christiansen waved him off. He already appreciated that his presence aboard *Saratoga* would inconvenience the captain and crew, and he did not want to be the source of problems. He also understood that *Saratoga* desperately needed a stand-down after its long transit and initial line period. Thus, he accepted conditions as satisfactory if he could just get some fans. But he also made it clear that if he did not get them soon, he would buy them himself and charge them to Sanderson.[91]

Release and relaxation took many forms. Some found it in sleep. Others found it in shopping. Others flocked to Olongapo. Some did it all. Loretta Lankford had gotten a ride from Manila to Cubi, so she was there to meet her husband. Two other Puncher wives who had made the trek to the Philippines intending to stay for an extended period now waited for their officer husbands, too: Diane Miller, wife of LT John Miller, and Barbara Miller, wife of LTJG Bob Miller. Pan Am flight attendant Stephanie Knapp arranged for a schedule that put her in the Philippines when LT Ken Knapp arrived.

Very quietly, LT Wharton left for home. He had a quiet dinner with LTJGs Bob Miller and Fuller at the Subic Bay Officers' Club. He already regretted his decision, but he considered it irrevocable and made no effort to reverse it. He met with CDR Earnest only once, oddly enough not in the formal confines of the CO's stateroom, but in the parking lot of the Cubi Officers' Club. Wharton explained his reasons for leaving yet again, and Earnest acknowledged that he understood. The exchange ended quickly. After the passage of over thirty years, Wharton's clearest memory of that conversation remained the CO's last words: "I don't think you're a coward."[92]

Even as Wharton departed, the Punchers' first augmentation crew arrived. When the squadron left Oceana, they had taken seven A-6A attack planes and four KA-6D tankers with them. Since their arrival in Westpac, two A-6Bs had flown aboard, and departing A-6 squadrons turned over an additional A-6A and one more KA-6D. Anticipating the increase in aircraft, CDR Earnest already had requested from MATWING ONE two additional pilots and B/Ns to man them. The first two men now reported for duty.

The pilot, LT Robert M. Chisholm, had served as an instructor in VA-42. He volunteered to accept orders to VA-75 because he genuinely wanted to test himself in combat. On the flight over, he noticed at the airport that all those "coming back were Army—all going over were Navy. It's our war now." The new B/N, the eager LTJG Thomas Vance who already had volunteered to go to Westpac with the Sunday Punchers, had gotten his wish. They barely reported in when CDR Earnest, XO Greene, and several others insisted on taking them to Olongapo. After a long journey, the two men desperately needed sleep, but their new squadronmates bought them dinner and many drinks and introduced them to some bar girls. "The one that sat with me was pretty loud and obnoxious," wrote Chisholm, who asked her to leave. She refused and grabbed his shirt, creating a big commotion. Finally, he reported, one of the women who ran the place "came over and beat the livin' crap out of her as they pulled her off." She still stood outside issuing threats when they left a while later.[93]

Chisholm's and Vance's adventures had just begun. On 29 June, *Saratoga* steamed out of Cubi for its second line period.

"A Very Real Life Indeed"

The transition from Cubi to active operations happened so quickly that the Sunday Punchers found it difficult to remember that they had had any break at all. At least this time they knew—if current schedules held—that their second line period would be a short one, only nineteen days long. As things stood on 29 June, *Saratoga* expected to operate from Yankee Station until the close of air operations on 17 July. After a quick stop at Cubi for aircraft maintenance and resupply, the carrier then would steam to Hong Kong for a weeklong port call. The entire crew looked forward to the prospects of exploring that exotic city, and many of the married men anticipated a welcome reunion with their wives. At the same time, they knew full well that the needs of the Navy always came first. Any unexpected emergency could cancel the port call. As they left Cubi on 29 June, the Punchers heard that USS *Oriskany* had suffered damage in a collision while rearming, and they immediately began to worry that the accident might force changes in schedules that could alter their plans for Hong Kong.[1]

But all such pleasant musings and worries about future plans had to be put out of mind to focus on the business at hand. As CVW-3 prepared for its second line period, it did so against an increasingly contentious public discourse about the conduct of the air war in which they participated. During the summer of 1972, two related issues became the focal points for discussion, debate, and protest.

First, pointed accusations that American bombers purposefully targeted the North Vietnamese dike system had increased in both number and intensity in May and June 1972. Critics of the war had leveled this charge against the Johnson administration as far back as the start of Operation ROLLING THUNDER in 1965, but by late June 1972, the issue took on a new urgency. *New York Times* editorialist Anthony Lewis now accused Nixon of escalating this kind of bombing. "Over the last month North Vietnamese officials and diplomats have said repeatedly that American planes are bombing dikes," he asserted, adding that "the charges have been extremely specific and detailed." Acknowledging that recent announcements could be part of a North Vietnamese propaganda campaign, he cited two pieces of "hard evidence" that made it difficult for him to dismiss the charges.

Lewis first cited French journalist Jean Thoraval's eyewitness reports of damage to North Vietnamese dikes attributed to American bombs. On 24 June, Thoraval filed an account of his visit to Nam Dinh—a recent target of several VA-75 missions—where he viewed several gaps in the local dike system caused by bombs and described a landscape that reminded him of "almost what one might have expected to find on the moon." Second, Lewis cited an unnamed "highly reliable non-Communist diplomatic source of information on North Vietnam," most likely Swedish ambassador to North Vietnam Jean-Christophe Oberg, who had asserted that "without doubt there is now systematic bombing of the dikes." Accepting these reports as credible, Lewis warned that a continued American air offensive during the rainy season could establish the preconditions for "that much abused word genocide." If the dikes did not hold, at least fifteen million civilians could drown or starve or lose their homes. In late April, Nixon had described the dikes as "a strategic target, and indirectly a military target," but he also made clear that he viewed their destruction as a step he deemed "not needed." Lewis saw in Nixon's words a hint that, under changed circumstances, such bombing could become "needed." Based on the recent reports, Lewis wondered if U.S. Air Force and U.S. Navy planes already had initiated such systematic destruction, and he suggested that "those American officials or members of Congress who care about the possibility of causing mass civilian deaths in North Vietnam might want to ask."[2]

Antiwar journalists and political leaders did just that. In the public press and officially in the *Congressional Record,* correspondents and members of Congress not only raised Lewis's question but also introduced additional evidence, including Thoraval's report on his 30 June visit to Phu Ly to see a dike damaged by three separate American air attacks, on 2, 12, and 21 June. The journalist described in detail women filling bomb craters by hand, houses near the dikes destroyed by bombs, the inoperative sluice gates that could no longer control the water flow, and foot-wide cracks in the dike itself.[3]

The second heated issue—an extension of the first—centered on complaints about American bombs hitting, and perhaps even purposely targeting, genuinely nonmilitary targets, to include North Vietnamese civilians. American newspapers published extensive extracts from Ambassador Oberg's reports and speeches accusing the United States of pursuing a "policy of annihilation" by destroying the entire North Vietnamese economic infrastructure, including "small workshops, small bridges, small railway stations, everything." He considered the "deliberate and precise" attacks on nonmilitary targets by American jets to be "the ultimate atrocity."[4] As *Saratoga* steamed out of Cubi to take up its position on Yankee Station, the *New York Times* took up Oberg's concerns and raised doubts about the validity of official reports about recent air strikes on Hanoi and Haiphong: "The Americans said they had destroyed a military supply depot and repair shops for military vehicles. The North Vietnamese charged that the raiders had hit a tuberculosis hospital and a two-story residential block. And so it went for the rest of the week."[5] Much of this reporting did reflect a well-orchestrated propaganda campaign on the part of the North Vietnamese and their allies. But doubts cast on the credibility of their accusations seldom attracted much attention. Instead, critics took on official MACV statements claiming that American bombers had destroyed North Vietnam's entire steel-making capability and three-fourths of its capacity for generating electricity. Indeed, one reporter reminded readers of General Curtis LeMay's 1965 call to bomb the North Vietnamese "back to the Stone Age," and noted that "something very like that is happening right now."[6]

But when VA-75 began its second line period on 1 July, it did so with a type of mission that somehow escaped the current outburst of criticism. "It looks as if we're (the Saratoga) getting more involved with the mining blockade in addition to our normal attack commitments," LT Lerseth wrote home. *Saratoga,* now on a noon-to-midnight schedule of air operations, prepared to participate in the ongoing effort to refresh the minefields that had closed major North Vietnamese harbors in May. Lerseth's attendance at a short course at the Mine Warfare School in January 1972—and the absence of senior airwing planners with such recent training—made him one of *Saratoga's* subject-matter experts. Indeed, RADM Christiansen asked him to "volunteer" to serve as airwing mining officer. Very soon thereafter, intelligence officers and mission planners began to pepper him with questions. After they interrupted yet another effort to catch a nap, he reached a conclusion familiar to many veterans: "One of these days I'll learn not to volunteer for anything."[7]

Lerseth spent much of 1 July helping LCDR Lindland plan a major mining alpha strike for the next day. The mission required meticulous attention to detail and precise coordination to lay the mines in the preapproved location and most effective pattern. Their plan called for a 34-plane coordinated effort to refresh the minefield at the main channel entrance to the Haiphong harbor. Seven A-6As accompanied by A-7s from both VA-37 and VA-105 would drop the mines, while F-4s and at least one of VA-75's A-6Bs protected them. Lindland and Lerseth served as strike lead, of course, and each of VA-75's A-6As carried sixteen Mk36s. Inclement weather complicated matters significantly, forcing the various elements of the strike group to ingress the target area at very low levels, and the entire strike group flew well within range of numerous AAA batteries and several SAM sites in the Haiphong area. Despite moderate AAA fire and as many as four SAMs fired at the aircraft, they completed the mining effort flawlessly. Indeed, poststrike analysis deemed the minefield that CVW-3 laid on

2 July to be more complete and more accurately placed than the initial drop made in May.[8]

Despite the significance of CVW-3's first major mining effort, most members of VA-75 remembered far more clearly the dramatic results of another alpha strike that same day. CDR Earnest and LCDR Jackson planned to hit military targets clustered thirteen miles southwest of Hanoi. They manned up and launched, but the same bad weather that affected the mining mission soon convinced Earnest to abort the alpha, break up the strike force, and divert to secondary targets well south of their original one.[9]

CDR Earnest took his four A-6As against a warehouse area near Vinh Son in RP III. He located the alternate target easily enough, but when the four aircraft began to roll in, the skies filled with AAA of all calibers. LTJG Swigart, who decided to film some of the action with his new movie camera, observed through his lens a variety of different colored flashes bursting around them, and, as LT Cook made his bombing run, his B/N continued to capture all the action around them.[10]

Assuming that the North Vietnamese gunners expected planes coming in from the north to pull out to the left—eastward—to go feet wet, LT Fischer pickled off his bombs and broke right instead. Then, as he recorded, "boom! a big 85 mm (orange fireball that turns black)—goes off right in front—so I go left— same thing—then straight—same—really thought this was it." After he cleared the area, Fischer looked for his "barf bag," feeling "so terrified that I thought I was going to throw up." The experience did not faze his unflappable B/N; LT Wagner had fallen asleep.[11]

No such calm came over LTs Pyle and Hvidding, however. After they had started their roll-in and approached their release point in the flak-filled skies over Vinh Son, they heard a loud explosion and felt their plane jolt. Nonetheless, they continued their dive and pickled their fourteen Mk20 Rockeye at about 8,000 feet. At about 6,000 feet, as Pyle pulled up, the aircraft responded stiffly. The right flight hydraulic pressure gauge indicated no pressure. Then a radio call alerted the crew to a fire. Pyle asked CDR Earnest to look over his aircraft to see if he could spot the flames. The skipper flew closer and had LCDR Jackson photograph some visible damage just below the intake on the right side of the fuselage, just below Hvidding's boarding ladder. But Earnest saw no fire. As Pyle and Hvidding prepared to land aboard *Saratoga,* they lost the left flight hydraulic pressure as well. Concerned that the damaged plane might have lost its brakes, the carrier cleared the flight deck. The aircraft recovered safely.

The hit on Pyle and Hvidding's plane represented the first substantial battle damage to any VA-75 aircraft during this cruise. The boarding ladder on the B/N's side showed charring, with the paint underneath it discolored. A one-foot narrow hole stretched just aft of the refueling assembly. Maintenance personnel also found a ragged hole in the fin of the centerline drop tank. Shrapnel fragments stopped within six to ten inches of entering the cockpit. Hvidding knew they had been lucky, noting that "a few feet difference in the hit in any direction could have yielded different consequences." Still, despite appearances, only the tank that carried the ethyl alcohol used to clear the windscreen suffered much damage.

All aboard *Saratoga* celebrated the near miss. An officer from RADM Christiansen's staff extended to Pyle and Hvidding his boss's congratulations. The enlisted men in the squadron's maintenance shops asked many questions, and they kidded with the crew to a degree they had never done before. To Hvidding, "it started seeming like a bigger accomplishment than before," but the feeling wore off quickly. Still, as he admitted that night, "really, today was one of those experiences I wanted—to be hit but be able to bring it back with no problem."[12]

Word of the incident reached home quickly. Sandy Pyle, now working as a coronary care nurse at a Baltimore hospital, got a phone call from her mother telling her to contact a friend, the wife of another Sunday Puncher. "I think this must be an emergency," Sandy's mother told her. She dialed her friend immediately, and when the other Puncher spouse asked her how she was bearing up, Sandy felt stunned. While she had not heard a single word about the incident, other squadron wives in Virginia Beach already knew that LT Pyle's plane had been damaged. Stories often improve with the telling, of course, and by the time Sandy heard about it, "their plane had almost burnt up out of the sky" like they had "been hit by a meteor."[13] A few pointed queries in letters from home caused some junior pilots and B/Ns reassure their wives yet again that they had no reason to worry. Since LT Tolhurst knew that his wife frequently talked to Sandy Pyle, he assured her that her friend's husband felt fine. The hit did not even worry Pyle "until he landed and had time to think about it." Then Tolhurst reminded his wife once again, "There is nothing to worry about, this just proves how well A-6's are built."[14]

With everybody safely back aboard, Fischer asked LTJG Bill Wardlaw the name of their target, since he had not seen it on their initial planning charts. "Oh, they call that the Vinh Son gunnery school," the intelligence officer replied tongue-in-cheek, noting that guns near this location reputedly shot down more American aircraft than any other site in North Vietnam.[15]

Air operations returned to the noon-to-midnight schedule on 3 July, with no break planned for the Fourth of July holiday. On the nation's birthday, VA-75's aircraft took part in another major mining mission off the Do Son approaches to the Haiphong harbor and participated in another alpha strike against targets near Nam Dinh.[16] Along with the airwings from USS *Midway,* USS *Oriskany,* and USS *Hancock*—as CAPT Sanderson wrote to the families of the ship's company and

On 2 July 1972, the A-6A flown by LTs Kenneth L. Pyle and Paul C. Hvidding sustained VA-75's first hits from enemy fire for this combat cruise. While returning from their strike on targets near Vinh Son, CDR Earnest and LCDR Grady L. Jackson checked over the aircraft, and Jackson snapped this photograph of damage caused by a small fire. (U.S. Navy photograph, Paul C. Hvidding Collection)

squadrons—the men of *Saratoga* "spent Independence Day backing up the American peacekeeping efforts that guarantee Independence Days in the future."[17] Even if they could not stand down to celebrate the nation's birthday with a picnic as so many other Americans did, the officers at least chowed down on steaks that night. Some enlisted men must have gotten carried away in an effort to enjoy the holiday; four of the ship's company ended the Fourth of July in the brig.[18]

If air operations did not stop for the national holiday, an AOM on the morning of 5 July made up for it, at least for five squadron members. VA-75 celebrated the promotion of LTJGs Hvidding, Bob Miller, Mullins, Tolhurst, and Lerseth to lieutenant. Their new rank officially dated back to 1 July, but the mission schedule had forced CDR Earnest to delay the formal ceremony a few days. The skipper planned to pin on their new insignia himself, but the ship's store had run out of the double-tracked bars. He had to borrow some from the squadron's more senior lieutenants. Only LT Tolhurst left the ceremony wearing his own shiny new bars. Anticipating the event, Pixie had sent him a set.[19]

This particular set of promotions also reminded the lieutenants junior grade a few months junior to those just advanced in rank that they would have to wait longer than expected until they could pin on lieutenant's bars themselves. Following Navy personnel policies then in effect, the five officers promoted on 1 July became lieutenants after three years of service as commissioned officers. With American troop withdrawals from Southeast Asia well under way—and continuing despite the North Vietnamese invasion in March—personnel specialists began to reshape the nation's military establishment for peacetime service. Budgetary pressures also forced the services to delay promotions and save the pay raises that accompanied them. All lieutenants junior grade with three years of service who expected their promotions to lieutenant between 2 July 1972 and 31 December 1973 now had to serve three and one-half years—an additional six months—before they could pin on their new ranks. That change immediately pushed back the promotion dates of LTJGs Sanford, Petersen, Wardlaw, Fuller, Ahrens, McFarland, Warren, and Vance. Even worse for LTJG Swigart, since he had not been eligible for promotion until after 1 January 1974, he now had to serve four years before he became a lieutenant.

The change in promotion schedules became one of two personnel issues that provided distraction for some Sunday Puncher officers during July 1972. Just as the Navy delayed promotions to save money in the transition to peacetime budgets, its manpower planners scheduled a reduction in force designed to strike supernumerary officers from active duty billets. Announcements that "cut lists" would begin to appear during the fall of 1972 put on notice thousands of officers, mostly Reservists, that their days in uniform might come to an unexpectedly quick end. Many welcomed a chance for an early return to civilian life. But for those Reservists who found Navy life to their liking and wanted to make a career of it, prospects now seemed to dim. To improve their chances of keeping their names off cut lists, some officers attempted to change their commissions from the Naval Reserves to the Regular Navy through a highly selective process called augmentation. The deadline to submit formal requests for consideration came during the summer, and some affected personnel worried nearly to the point of distraction about the issue.

LTJG Petersen, for one, represented the Reservists who very much wanted to augment into the Regular Navy. Despite working hard with LCDR Lindland on the wording of his letter of application, he doubted if his quest would end in success. Skipper Earnest already had expressed concerns about losing pilots and B/Ns to the impending cuts, and even if that did not occur, he had told Petersen to expect most of the Reservists to be released from active duty when *Saratoga* returned home. Earnest did not hold out much hope for positive decisions on augmentation, but Petersen decided to try anyway, despite his fear that "on the subject of the Navy as a career, I don't think I'm going to be given the opportunity to choose."[20]

Aggravating the personnel problem, every skipper wanted to retain top performers. Even as CDR Earnest told some devoted and career-minded Reservists about their slim chances for augmentation, he had to try to convince other skilled and reliable Reservists planning to leave the service to file augmentation papers and stay in uniform. To Earnest, newly arrived LT Bob Chisholm represented the kind of experienced, solid performer he should try hard to retain. But Chisholm already had decided to leave the Navy when his obligation ended in the summer of 1973. "The push started tonight to get me to become regular Navy," Chisholm wrote to his girlfriend, Bobbie. But, he assured her, "have told them definitely no."[21] CDR Earnest lost Round One, but he did not accept this as Chisholm's final word.

The poor weather conditions that complicated CVW-3's alpha strikes and mining missions during its first few days back on the line continued through much of the first ten days of July. A number of alpha strikes had to be canceled entirely, diverted to alternate targets, or reduced to single-plane armed recces or one- and two-plane seeding hops. The abbreviated schedule of cyclic operations came at a fortuitous time for VA-75. The Sunday Punchers now faced several significant organizational tasks.

First, now that they had gained a more comprehensive appreciation of the SAM threat in North Vietnam, the squadron heavies encouraged more junior pilots and B/Ns to qualify in the A-6B. While the heavies did not want to put them on strike missions they could not handle, the squadron still had to meet the airwing's operational needs. To this point, only the senior officers and three junior crews—those of LTs Fischer and Wagner, LT Knapp and LTJG Fuller, and the departed LT Wharton and LTJG Petersen—had flown A-6B hops fairly regularly. Now, additional qualified crews needed to enter the rotation. Thus, LT Hvidding flew his first A-6B mission with LCDR Graustein on 7 July. He picked up no emissions from SAM sites and fired no missiles, but, he noted, "it was good training again, and I'm glad I didn't have to shoot one because I don't know enough about the system yet." By 13 July, after several more training hops, however, Hvidding admitted to "getting itchy to 'hose' one of those big $100,000 missiles," but only if he had a good target. While some squadronmates had already fired two or three, he considered them "pretty trigger happy."[22]

Just as essential during July's line period, and for the first time on the combat cruise, the Sunday Punchers' heavies had to integrate new pilots and B/Ns into the regular schedule of air operations by considering the reshuffling of crews. Since LT Chisholm and LTJG Vance reported in when *Saratoga* reached Cubi, their indoctrination began as soon as the carrier left port. After briefings on rules of engagement, the squadron's standard operating procedures, and other key information, both new men appeared on the flight schedule as early as 3 July. Consistent with squadron practice, each flew his first few missions with a pilot or B/N who already had gained some combat experience. First came tanker hops, of course. But on 3 July, LT Cook took Vance on a seeding mission. Chisholm and LCDR Pieno flew on their wing. As they seeded some coastal waters in RP I near the DMZ, Vance admitted that the experience initially terrified him. "It was just a case of nerves after hearing of all the sea stories about combat and people getting shot down" that got to him. Soon enough, however, he adopted the philosophy already shared by most of his squadronmates: "The bad stuff always happened to the other guy."[23]

Chisholm and Vance performed solidly during their first few hops. Additionally, as an experienced pilot fresh from instructor duty, LT Chisholm had accumulated more hours in the A-6 than anyone else in the squadron except LCDR Lindland. By 6 July, Vance and Chisholm obtained CDR Earnest's permission to fly together. They launched on their first strike mission the next day, and on 8 July they participated in their first alpha strike. The Chisholm-Vance pairing worked well. After hitting the port facilities at Hon Gay on that 8 July strike, Chisholm wrote with enthusiasm, "It was really neat[,] about 25 planes all rolling in at the same time[,] big fire balls, little AAA. Just flat wiped out the port."[24] By 9 July, they had qualified for A-6B missions, well ahead of many crews that had deployed with the squadron in April. As Chisholm described the "missile birds," it seemed like a "really exciting game like cat & mouse. . . . Not yet sure who the mouse is though." Fortunately, he added, "I like games."[25] Still, like other crews new to the combat environment, they continued to fly on the wing of a senior crew for much of their first line period. By late July, however, the heavies cleared Chisholm and Vance to fly all of the squadron's different missions.

Other new personnel arrived, too. On 6 July, two new pilots reported in to VA-75. LT George A. Hiduk, a 1967 graduate of the Naval Academy, had flown previously in A-4s and had put in a tour as an instructor pilot in Texas. New to A-6s, he received orders to Westpac while still assigned to the East Coast RAG. From the day he came aboard *Saratoga*, he expressed qualms about his new assignment. He had sufficient reason to do so. He had not completed his entire training syllabus at the RAG, he was not NATOPS qualified, and he genuinely believed himself unprepared to fly in combat. Indeed, he told his new squadronmates that his superiors at Oceana had informed him that he would fly only tanker hops.

The second new pilot arrived in response to CDR Earnest's emergency call to MATWING ONE in late June for a replacement for LT Wharton. LTJG Stephen C. Bryan learned quite suddenly that his impending orders to another A-6 squadron had been pulled for new orders to VA-75. He left for Westpac even more quickly than had the Punchers the past April. Within twenty-four hours, he said good-bye to his wife, Chris, and left Oceana for San Francisco and a charter flight to the Philippines. From Clark Air Force Base, he caught a plane to Danang and then flew out to *Saratoga*. When he arrived, he saw a familiar face waiting to welcome him aboard—CDR Greene, a recent VA-42 graduate himself and the only man in his new squadron whom Bryan knew.

Bryan, who had played linebacker at the University of Virginia, had suffered knee injuries so severe that he probably should not have been accepted into pilot training at all. His desire to fly, however, inspired him to reverse the course taken by so many young men of his generation: He obtained letters from physicians supporting his effort to get *into* the Navy. He considered his quick trip from the East Coast to Southeast Asia to be a blessing; it gave him no time to reflect upon his anxiety about going to war. He arrived ready to go.[26] Indeed, the quick separation proved to be much tougher on Chris, a schoolteacher whose first letter to her husband began with her straightforward admission: "This morning I got up & worked a little thinking everything was ok. Then all of a sudden everything was not ok!!" But she did not want him to worry, assuring him that "there are just a few really bad moments." Then she added, in a moment of wishful thinking, "I know all that eases with time."[27]

Even more help arrived for VA-75 in early July. Perhaps to give him a break after his harrowing experience over Vinh Son, CDR Earnest sent LT Pyle to Cubi on 5 July to pick up an additional KA-6D left for the Sunday Punchers by the Marine A-6 squadron that just had completed a combat cruise aboard *Coral Sea*. The same day Hiduk and Bryan arrived aboard *Saratoga*, Pyle returned with the plane and a new B/N. LT George L. Hart—familiarly known as Roy—came from a Navy family. His father had commanded an A-4 squadron in Vietnam earlier in the war, and Hart, who had completed a Med cruise with VA-65, also aspired to a naval career. On 27 June, he had volunteered for this combat assignment and departed for the Philippines only three days later. As it happened, since he and Pyle passed fuel to some F-4s on their flight from Cubi to the carrier, Hart logged his first combat support sortie before he formally checked into the squadron. The routine tanking made a huge impression on the newly arrived B/N, but Hart learned quickly that even spectacular events quickly became old news. Even though it had happened just a few days earlier, "Ken didn't mention he had taken a hit when we met in Cubi," Hart recalled, and for a long time, he did not hear a single word about it.[28]

Unlike the more experienced Chisholm and Vance, who already had developed a rapport with each other in the cockpit, Bryan, Hiduk, and Hart had to be integrated into flight operations far more deliberately. Since success in the air depended heavily on reliable crew pairings, the heavies decided to team each new man with a more experienced Puncher. As a consequence, some of the proven crews that had deployed in April had to be broken up to find new combinations that worked. For now, that meant that Hiduk and Bryan flew tanker hops with a series of experienced B/Ns, while Hart did the same thing with experienced pilots. When the heavies deemed him ready, each man would ease into appropriate strike missions.

One final addition completed the Punchers' officer roster for July. To replace LCDR Kennedy, LT James "E" Hudson arrived to serve as the squadron's new LDO maintenance officer. A mustang—a former enlisted man—with many years of service, Hudson now became the oldest officer in the squadron. But he knew maintenance. He reviewed squadron procedures with Chief Warrant Officer Smith, and he haunted VA-75's workspaces day and night to evaluate the strengths and weaknesses of the maintenance effort. He identified two interrelated problems early on: maintaining an acceptable number of mission-ready aircraft and resolving ongoing logistical problems related to the supply of spare parts. He had met CDR Greene on a previous tour, and Hudson and the XO soon established a close day-to-day working relationship that, in time, paid dividends as they tried to resolve these thorny issues.

LT Hudson had no illusions about the difficulties of keeping an A-6 squadron in the air. With the exception of 2 July's alpha strikes, CVW-3 continued to fly as much of their noon-to-midnight schedule as weather permitted without a scheduled stand-down day until 10 July. Even during abbreviated operations, at least one KA-6D had to launch to support each cycle. Although VA-75 had just received a sixth tanker, maintenance personnel still found it tough to keep enough of them in the air to meet the airwing's needs. Indeed, the pressure to keep tankers in the air put the KA-6Ds at the top of maintenance priorities, even surpassing the push to keep A-6A strike aircraft at top readiness. On 7 July, LT Lankford and LTJG Warren discovered just how suddenly a tanker could develop a major problem.

Shortly after 1400, Lankford and Warren took off in a fully loaded KA-6D, the first plane to launch at the start of a cycle. As soon as they cleared the bow, Lankford's right engine fire warning light flashed on. The normal course of action called for an immediate shutdown of the engine, but Lankford could not do that. He had just taken off and needed more airspeed to keep the loaded tanker in the air. As soon as he could, however, he jettisoned all five of his full drop tanks, reducing weight by 10,000 pounds. At the same time, other cockpit lights began to flash. As an experienced crew, Lankford and Warren recognized the key symptoms denoting a bleed air failure. They had to return to the carrier immediately.

Bleed air is superheated air from the engine's combustion chambers that can be redirected to power other aircraft systems. It is drawn off (or "bled off") from the chambers through ducts to those points where it is needed. Metal clamps called "V-bands" connected duct segments, and the A-6 community already had experienced problems with faulty clamps. When one of these connectors failed, the hot air escaped into the engine compartment and could burn through hydraulic lines, rendering the plane uncontrollable. Worse, it could happen in only five to eight minutes. The situation called for quick diagnosis and equally quick response.

Warren immediately contacted *Saratoga,* reported that Lankford had already shut down the right engine and jettisoned the drop tanks, and informed them that the strong likelihood of a bleed air failure would require their immediate return to the ship. Because they launched first, they knew it would take ten to fifteen minutes to respot the planes lined up behind them to prepare a ready deck.

About then, the tanker's radio malfunctioned. Warren used one of his handheld emergency radios to reestablish contact with the carrier. LTs Pyle and Hvidding, just returning from the previous cycle, joined on Lankford and Warren's wing to look them over. They spotted some smoke but saw no charred metal or other indications of catastrophic damage. Then CDR C. E. Armstrong, XO of VA-37, joined up on the tanker to look for flames. He saw none. By now, Warren could no longer reach *Saratoga* with his own radio, so, for a while, Armstrong relayed messages between the KA-6D and the carrier. Then another VA-75 plane flew alongside. The pilot reassured the tanker crew that they saw no fire and told them to dump their fuel to minimum landing weight. After Lankford did so, he reduced his speed at 5,000 feet and put the flaps and gear down to make sure that he could continue to control the plane even with one engine.

Now a new problem arose. Lankford got an unsafe nose-gear indicator light. Even after attempting to blow the gear down, the light remained on. According to NATOPS procedures, if the plane is flying on a single engine and with unsafe gear indications, recovery required the use of the crash barricade, a long reinforced nylon net stretched across the flight deck to trap damaged aircraft. The Air Boss, CDR H. A. French, had to make a decision. The aircraft returning from the previous cycle had to be recovered before they ran out of fuel. But Lankford and Warren already had dumped most of their JP-5. Nonetheless, CDR French decided to recover the returning planes first and then rig the barricade. Lankford and Warren had been in the air for about twenty minutes. Safety procedures called for their recovery ten minutes earlier.

As the other planes landed, Lankford and Warren contemplated the very real possibility that they might lose hydraulics and have to eject. They had lost all radio contact now, and Warren had to use hand signals just to communicate with the other aircraft. Finally, they saw the greenshirts who had just launched the last plane of Lankford's cycle running aft down the flight deck to rig the barricade. The other Puncher crew gave Lankford and Warren a signal to land, even though the men in the stricken aircraft did not see a deck ready to recover them. Later on, they learned that their squadronmates gave them the go-ahead to land without authorization, figuring that if Lankford and Warren entered the landing pattern and started down the glide slope, the men on the flight deck would work that much faster.

Lankford set up for a long straight-in approach as called for in the NATOPS manual. A half-mile from the ship on final approach, they received a green light to land. As Lankford eased the plane down toward the deck, the greenshirts completed the rigging of the barricade and ran for the safety of the catwalks. Finally, Lankford caught both a wire and the barricade. The tanker stopped.

When Lankford shut down the remaining engine and cracked the canopy, both pilot and B/N breathed a sign of relief, and, as Warren explained, "both of us, in the back of our minds, were thinking 'maybe we didn't have such a big problem after all.'" When the plane captain lowered the B/N's boarding ladder, however, Warren spotted the charring and burned paint. That was all he needed to see. "I about killed the plane captain getting out of the plane—one step out onto the top of the intake, one step onto the plane captain's back, and I was on the deck—never touched the boarding ladder!!"

The maintenance people performed a thorough examination of the tanker. The nose gear did not come all the way down; the action of the barricade had forced it forward and locked it into place. And they confirmed that the aircraft had suffered a bleed air failure. Fortunately for Lankford and Warren, however, their KA-6D did not suffer a typical V-band malfunction, and that had made a great difference. The problem came from a hole at an elbow joint in one of the bleed-air ducts. From that location, the bleed-air stream simply required more time than usual to burn through the hydraulic lines. The maintenance crew determined that the tanker could only have lasted a minute or two more before losing its hydraulics. "In other words," Warren later concluded, "if our wingie had not taken it upon himself to tell us to land it, we would have waited for the ship to tell us that, and it would have been too late!" In any case, neither Lankford or Warren protested when the airwing medical officer, LT Robert P. Randolph, the "Combat Quack," showed up on deck to proffer some "medicinal samples" to calm their nerves.[29]

After Lankford and Warren's adventure, if the Punchers needed more lessons to impress upon them just how centrally their tanking capability affected airwing operations, they only had to know what LTs Pyle and Hvidding experienced later on the night of 7 July. During their routine stop at IOIC before their tanker hop, they heard reports of MiGs in the air near the BARCAP and of F-4s being vectored to investigate what appeared to be an A-6B without an IFF (identification friend or foe) that would not answer calls to identify itself. Rumors of skies full of unfriendlies or potential unfriendlies gave them pause when they

LT Ron Lankford and LTJG Dave Warren still sit in the cockpit, immediately following the successful emergency recovery of their damaged KA-6D. The barricade—the reinforced nylon netting—remains draped over the aircraft, and the extended tailhook also caught an arresting wire. The crew walked away unharmed. (U.S. Navy photograph, Ronny D. Lankford Collection)

got into their tanker and found that its ECM gear would not work. When troubleshooters could not fix it, the crew downed the plane. After the flight deck crew pulled the aircraft off to the side, Pyle and Hvidding went down to the ready room to await reassignment. Skipper Earnest met them at the door and told them to get back in the tanker—since they did not go over the beach, he reminded them that they did not need ECM gear. The mission continued uneventfully, but when they returned, Earnest firmly but quietly voiced his displeasure. "We had really caused a mess," Hvidding wrote that night, because "the BAR-CAP had reached minimum combat gas and the admiral had begun to send all the ships out of the Gulf of Tonkin because of the MiG activity." If they had appreciated the vital nature of their mission, they would not have made the decision to abort. Indeed, upon quick reflection, the B/N decided that refusing to launch "was a dumb move, really." Since Earnest had been chewed out by CAG Bordone, CAPT Sanderson, and RADM Christiansen in turn, Hvidding felt he owed him something for his comparative restraint and admitted that the skipper "earned a little more of my respect."[30]

MiGs did not attack the carrier task force that night, but the report of an A-6B without an IFF indeed proved to be true. It also demonstrated that some of the more junior crews still continued to experiment, testing the fine line that separated aggressive airmanship from boneheaded mistakes. LT Knapp and LTJG Fuller flew that A-6B. They had decided to turn off the IFF in a misguided attempt to encourage the North Vietnamese to lock their radars onto the unidentified aircraft "so we could kill them all," as Fuller later explained. They did not appreciate that, on a night when reports of MiGs aloft filled the airways, the presence of an unidentified aircraft over the water generated serious concerns on the carriers. On the guard frequency, Knapp and Fuller heard a call for the unidentified aircraft to turn on its IFF. They figured that the call was meant for a different aircraft because they continued to fly exactly where they had briefed they would; even without IFF, *Saratoga*'s intel shop should have known their identity. A second call for the unidentified plane to turn on its IFF gave them pause, but they still did not comply. When the third call came, they turned on the IFF. The calls ended.

When Knapp and Fuller recovered and headed to their debrief, LCDR Lindland intercepted them. He asked if they had had trouble with the IFF. When they admitted that they had shut it off to fool the North Vietnamese, "he looked at us like you'd look at a couple of little kids who admitted to running into a wall to see if it would hurt," Fuller recalled. Lindland did not raise his voice. He asked if they realized that the E-2B had vectored the BARCAP F-4s toward them, and if they had not turned on their IFF on the third call, the Phantoms would have been cleared to shoot at them. "I would hope we made some smart ass response to this," Fuller noted in retrospect, but in any case, he recalled Lindland walking away, shaking his head, "as if he couldn't believe what he had to deal with."[31]

But not all experimentation turned out poorly. On 8 July, CDR Earnest and LCDR Jackson took up an A-6B with an unfamiliar ordnance load. In addition to the usual two AGM-78 missiles, they also carried eight ASQ-41 sonobuoys. The Sunday Punchers had successfully dropped them during their 1971 Med cruise as part of the test of the CV concept. Now, Earnest and Jackson would attempt to lay them in the waters of coastal North Vietnam. They dropped four in the anchorage of Hon La island and then placed four more in the anchorage off Hon Nieu. All eight activated and sent back useful information. They successfully completed *Saratoga*'s first attempt to execute this mission in a combat zone.[32]

During those hectic early July days of *Saratoga*'s second line period, all aboard realized that serving as RADM Christiansen's flagship complicated the ship's operations. The carrier's message traffic jumped fourfold. Worse, CAPT Sanderson became a "hotel keeper," responsible for housing the admiral and his staff in appropriate quarters and supporting the visits of dozens of dignitaries who came to see him. One visitor established a special—if somewhat controversial—connection to VA-75.

John F. Lehman, Jr., a member of Henry Kissinger's staff, came aboard to learn more about RADM Christiansen's interest in expanding the mining effort outside the port of Haiphong. The admiral wanted to stop the large Communist-bloc freighters that anchored in protected and unseeded waters from offloading their cargos onto WBLCs. His plan to lay mines outside recognized shipping channels and without warning placed civilians at a much higher risk, however, and that represented only one objection to Christiansen's plan. A naval reservist who on occasion had fulfilled his two-week active duty obligation in Westpac, Lehman had been sent to learn more about the admiral's intentions.

Christiansen knew he had to meet this man he viewed as "one of Kissinger's bagmen" with a "forty-dollar hairdo." Over dinner, he blistered Lehman about Washington's restrictions on fighting the war. Lehman began, "Admiral, I want to tell you something. You don't understand Washington." Christiansen replied, equally heatedly, "John, you're full of shit! I was in Washington before you got out of high school." He told Lehman that, despite his Reserve time, he did not understand war and then offered him a chance to learn about it in the hostile skies over North Vietnam. Christiansen then asked CDR Earnest to teach Lehman a lesson to remember.[33]

In his autobiographical *Command of the Seas,* Lehman wrote of participating fully in an alpha strike near Haiphong on 8 July as his "first (and only) over North Vietnam." As he explained, "I was flying as a lieutenant (JG) bombardier with Attack Squadron 75," describing how he unfolded the wings and completed the B/N's preflight checklist while CDR Earnest did his final checks from the pilot's seat of an A-6B. They launched and flew over Cat Ba Island in Haiphong harbor. When North Vietnamese gunners fired toward them—but well out of range since VA-75's A-6Bs did not yet go over the beach—Earnest assured his guest that they had not been targeted by a SAM. Just the same, he put the aircraft through some evasive maneuvers.[34]

Lehman made much of his flight, mostly because—over time—he came to view CDR Earnest as the kind of talented professional the U.S. Navy desperately needed. But Lehman made little impression on the Sunday Punchers in July 1972. Indeed, in later years when he wrote about this mission, squadron members and authors raised questions about his story's veracity, especially since he had made it appear that he flew that mission as an active participant and not as a passive observer. As author Gregory L. Vistica asserted, Lehman "perpetuated the yarn that he had been a naval aviator during the war, which was not true." The experience aboard *Saratoga* only inspired what later developed into a real "romance with naval aviation." Lehman decided only after that flight with CDR Earnest to get his wings, and he did not become a qualified B/N until at least five years later.[35] Indeed, VA-75's master log bears this out. VA-75 aircraft did participate in an alpha strike in RP VI-B on 8 July, but CDR Greene and LCDR Pieno flew the A-6B assigned to that mission. In the entire master log, the only mention of Lehman's presence comes in a brief entry on 6 July in which CDR Earnest ferried him to Danang.[36]

On 10 July, *Saratoga* enjoyed a stand-down day with no flight operations. The crew enjoyed the break and the cookout on deck. LT Hvidding had just received some slides of his 6-month old daughter, Jennifer, so he borrowed a slide projector from LTJG Wardlaw for "a little matinee."[37] Usually after a stand-down day, the carrier began a different flight schedule. When flight operations began on 11 July, however, *Saratoga* found itself still flying alpha strikes.

CVW-3 had orders for three major multiplane missions for 11 July. Three VA-75 aircraft, led by LCDR Dick Engel, took part in an alpha strike against a petroleum storage area north of Hai Duong. CDR Earnest and LCDR Jackson flew an A-6B in support of the mission. Located about halfway between Hanoi and Haiphong and close to the northeast railway to China, the target rested in some of the most heavily defended airspace in North Vietnam. Earnest and Jackson fired one AGM-78 at what they believed to be SAM site VN-142, just east of Hanoi, which threatened the strike group. In addition to the missile threat, several major airfields surrounded the target area, and intelligence briefers suggested that the strike group might face a higher-than-usual threat from MiGs. As the strike group neared the target, two F-4s from VF-103 flying MiGCAP engaged two MiG-17s. During the ensuing engagement, a MiG shot down the F-4 piloted by LT Robert I. Randall with RIO LT Frederick J. Masterson. They ejected and became prisoners of war; since the North Vietnamese did not make public their capture, however, the airwing listed the two simply as MIA. The strike group made its bombing run unhindered.[38] The other two major strikes that day called upon elements of A-6As to lead a pair of seeding missions into specific sections of "the Hourglass"—a coastal region in RP IV—where two river channels bent close to each other before breaking away again to flow into the Gulf of Tonkin. LCDR Lindland and LT Lerseth led a two-plane element in one strike, while CDR Earnest, with LTJG Swigart serving as his B/N, led three other VA-75 aircraft in the other. Each plane successfully dropped its sixteen Mk36s on target.[39]

Saratoga did not remain on the alpha strike schedule for long. The very next day, 12 July, the carrier went to the midnight-to-noon schedule. Most Sunday Punchers did not like this schedule. It forced the pilots and B/Ns to reverse entirely their basic biorhythms. The midnight-to-noon schedule turned day into night, dinner into breakfast, and sleep time into prime time for flight operations. LT Tolhurst understood that "night flying, of course, demands the utmost in concentration," but the change in eating and sleeping times played so much havoc with their normal routines that "everybody feels tired and has an upset stomach for most of the time."[40] As LT Chisholm remarked, "Every time I go to get something to eat, it's breakfast time. Had poached eggs for b[reakfast], fried for l[unch] and omelet for dinner."[41]

Not surprisingly, little annoyances far too trivial for grown men to care about in other circumstances now blossomed into major aggravations. When the flight crews showed up at 2300 for the preflight meal LT Chisholm described, they asked for orange juice to go with their eggs. The galley workers informed them that they only served this beverage during traditional breakfast hours, a time when aviators on the midnight-to-noon cycle would be briefing, flying, debriefing, or sleeping. Their requests for juice at night ignored, some of the Puncher crews took matters into their own hands. When they manned their aircraft and confirmed their flight-ready status, a pilot announced, "501 ready, no juice." The next Puncher pilot might add, "504 ready, no juice." The Air Boss, CAG Bordone, and even CAPT Sanderson inquired about the unorthodox protest. Soon afterward, the galleys served orange juice around the clock.[42]

When *Saratoga* made the mid-July switch to the midnight-to-noon schedule, all the carriers in the Gulf of Tonkin temporarily labored under newly placed and unwelcome operating restrictions. As LTJG Petersen wrote home, "When I first got here, the bombing was fairly unlimited as far as targets, but now we are starting to get the 'forbidden target' lists again."[43] Three interrelated factors explained the temporary shifts in targeting: the continuing controversy about bombing dikes, Jane Fonda's arrival in Hanoi, and the start of yet another round of peace talks in Paris on 13 July.

On 11 July, French journalist Thoraval published yet another descriptive narrative about an American bombing run against a dike system outside the village of Nam Sach in the Red River delta. He had witnessed it himself. The North Vietnamese had allowed him and other journalists to inspect damage from an earlier raid, and perhaps a dozen American aircraft rolled in on nearby targets shortly after the reporters arrived. "The jets went into a dive and released several bombs and rockets against the dikes on which we were standing," Thoraval wrote. He and the other journalists present "unanimously agreed" that the aircraft had targeted the dike specifically.[44] Jane Fonda—who arrived in North Vietnam on 8 July—also visited Nam Sach, and in a statement attributed to her by the North Vietnamese news agency, she saw "no military targets" around the hamlet. "There is no important highway, there is no communication network, there is no heavy industry." She compared the North Vietnamese peasants to "the farmers in the midwest many years ago in the U.S.," describing them as "happy people, peace-loving people," and she described attacks upon such people as "the type of terrorist tactic that is unworthy of American people and of American flags."[45]

Assistant Secretary of Defense for Public Affairs Daniel Z. Henkin tried to douse the fires of controversy right away. He confirmed that Navy jets had hit the Nam Sach area. (These aircraft did not launch from *Saratoga*.) But he also denied yet again that the planes targeted the dikes. He stated for the record that the attack aircraft aimed for a SAM site, an oil and petroleum storage site, and an above-ground oil pipeline. He used Thoraval's own words—that "only two or three SAM missiles were fired at the attackers"—to validate that, indeed, legitimate military targets existed near Nam Sach. Challenging the writer's claim that "the pilots dropped their bombs at random" during the raid, Henkin repeated what many Pentagon and White House spokesmen had asserted before—that the North Vietnamese frequently placed SAM sites, supply storage areas, and oil pipelines near roads built on top of dikes. The attack aircraft accused of hitting the dikes actually had targeted the military supplies on and around them. Henkin also doubted that the North Vietnamese admitted to Thoraval that "there was a pipeline or a SAM site there."[46] As public protest rose, the State Department distributed copies of the North Vietnamese government's call for citizens to help build and repair dikes before the onset of the rainy season. Hanoi did not blame American bombs for the poor condition of the dikes, the State Department took pains to point out. Instead, they blamed the very severe floods caused by 1971's monsoons.[47] The Pentagon took a different approach, presenting at press conferences a naval aviator recently returned from Southeast Asia who verified for any journalist who would listen that "it has been emphasized and reemphasized to the pilots that dikes are not authorized targets."[48]

The resumption of peace talks in Paris on 13 July also made the Punchers wonder how the negotiations might affect air operations. Nixon had ordered bombing pauses as recently as the previous month for political reasons, but they hoped he would not put restrictions on targets again so soon simply to encourage Le Duc Tho and other North Vietnamese diplomats to talk seriously about ending the war. If the bombing slowed now, the pilots and B/Ns expected to face even more intense opposition from North Vietnamese air defenses if the talks failed and they returned to those hostile skies. The switch to the midnight-to-noon schedule on 12 July—and the change from alpha strikes to single-plane missions—raised suspicions among some Sunday Puncher pilots and B/Ns that air operations once again bowed to political concerns. During the late morning daylight hours, they knew, CVW-3 could continue to fly alpha strikes to keep up the pressure of June and early July. But between 12 and 16 July, VA-75 took part in only two "mini-alphas"—ten to fifteen aircraft instead of the twenty-five or more on a typical alpha strike. One went into RP IV against a transshipment point near Nam Dinh on 12 July and one flew in RP IV-B against the Ho Doi military complex on 13 July.[49]

A contemporary description of the conduct of the 12 July mini–alpha strike deserves notice. That day, eleven aircraft—including four A-6As from VA-75—launched against a target along the Nam Dinh Giang River that included at least seventy-five warehouses, over 1,000 feet of wharf space, a significant open storage area, and a rail line encircled by batteries of 37, 57, and 85 mm AAA and resting in the envelope of two active SAM sites. As the strike leads—CDR Earnest and LCDR Jackson—examined the prestrike photography, intelligence officers pointed out clusters of civilian housing near the military targets. Therefore, during the briefing phase, Jackson provided the crew of each strike aircraft with a photograph of its assigned military target, including an exact aim point designed to maximize its destruction while limiting the threat of danger to nearby civilians.

After they launched, they flew into bad weather. Isolated thundershowers and a solid overcast layer reduced visibility around Nam Dinh, giving SAM sites an advantage if the North Vietnamese utilized their recent tactic of firing blindly without turning on their radars for any length of time. If they did try to track the strike group, however, both of VA-75's A-6Bs had been assigned to the mission, giving the small force at least twice the SAM suppression support usually devoted to a strike of this size. CDR Earnest decided not to divert, and the careful preplanning allowed for a successful ordnance drop. Poststrike photography by one of *Saratoga*'s RA-5Cs revealed fourteen large storage buildings and at least twenty medium storage buildings damaged or destroyed, along with four double-bay warehouses and one of medium size. The photographs showed hits on many small military structures and several cuts in the rail line, but no damage to civilian housing.[50] Along with specific targeting in the planning phase, the diminution of the SAM threat also helped to explain the accuracy of the ordnance drop. Early on in the action, LCDR Lindland and LT Lerseth fired an AGM-45 at an enemy radar tracking the strike group. As a result of their strike, the radar shut down, stayed silent, and did not guide any SAMs at all.[51]

The care they took to avoid damage to civilian targets made their reaction to Jane Fonda's commentaries all the more angry. Her first broadcasts over Voice of Vietnam Radio, delivered shortly after her visit to Nam Sach, appealed to "all the U.S. servicemen involved in the bombing of North Vietnam." She asked them to think about the millions who could die by drowning or starvation if they continued to destroy the dikes. Once again, she compared North Vietnamese peasants to midwestern American farmers and suggested that "perhaps your grandmothers and grandfathers would not be so different from these peasants." She concluded, "All of you in the cockpits of your planes, on the aircraft carriers, those who are loading the bombs, those who are repairing the planes, those who are working on the 7th Fleet, please think what you are doing. Are these people your enemy? What will you say to your children years from now who may ask you why you fought the war? What words will you be able to say to them?"[52]

At least for now, the Punchers' reactions to Fonda remained far more visceral than reflective. The ordnancemen, already accomplished graffiti artists adept at chalking their own sentiments onto the bombs they loaded, now wrote in bold letters, "Open wide, Jane!" on some of the Mk82s hung on VA-75 aircraft.[53] Several of the JOs poured over the latest reports of her whereabouts, and even though the Navy had put restrictions on bombing there, LT Anderson, for one, hoped he would get a target close enough to drop just one Mk82.[54] Others hoped they did not get assigned such a target, lest they give in to the temptation. The real impact of Jane Fonda's activities in July did not affect many of the pilots and B/Ns until August, after they had a chance to get off the line and reflect upon the implications of her activities. The seed of genuine anger and resentment had been planted, but not yet harvested.

If the Punchers read too much into the change in targets, they expressed a perverse sense of pleasure that they experienced no reduction in operational tempo. Noting that he was scheduled for two hops on 14 July, LT Chisholm guessed rightly that "there will be no slow up in the bombing with the peace talks going on" this time.[55]

At the same time, many of the squadron's pilots and B/Ns now discovered a genuine attraction to the excitement and challenge of the single-aircraft night strike mission. Senior crews continued to take most of the missions headed for RP VI-B, but LT John Miller and LTJG Sanford got the chance to try it on 13 and 15 July.[56] On 14 July, LT Pyle found himself scheduled for his first single-plane night mission into RP VI-B, the only Puncher pilot on his first-ever cruise to get that opportunity so far.

Pyle had a hard target—supply buildings near Thai Binh—and he and LT Hvidding planned a simple route that allowed them to hit their target and go feet wet quickly. Once airborne, however, they received orders diverting them southward to hit trucks moving near Vinh Son. Just then, they developed a problem with their ECM gear and "declined to stick our nose too far into the SAM environment." Instead, they looked for trucks along a fifteen-mile coastal stretch of Route 1A north of Brandon Bay. They spotted some lights, but the truck drivers quickly shut them off. They flew feet wet for a while and then reentered North Vietnamese airspace near the Hourglass. They dropped their Mk20s on some trucks and their Mk82s on a segment of road near a river, but observed no results. "It was disappointing not to be able to go as planned," LT Hvidding admitted that night, "but I think it's a good policy not to start pushing into targets without all the ECM gear." He believed that CDR Earnest and some more experienced crews might take that chance, but he felt equally sure that the skipper did not expect them to do so on their first night mission in such a hostile environment. Still, he remained "slightly sensitive" about it because of their decision the previous week to down a tanker for lack of ECM.[57]

Both senior and junior crews flew many road recces during *Saratoga*'s last five days on the line. On 14 July, LT Lankford and LTJG Warren also went out looking for trucks near Vinh Son. They shared the airspace with some of CVW-3's A-7s. When a pair of A-7s spotted moving vehicles and initiated their standard practice of dropping flares to illuminate a target, they uncovered a concentration of trucks far exceeding the number their own bombs could destroy. Lankford and Warren decided to complete the destruction. The A-7s had drawn heavy AAA fire, but the crew of the A-6A nonetheless flew into the area lit up by the A-7s' flares, persevered in a visual dive attack, and dropped on the trucks. As they pulled off, they witnessed at least one major secondary explosion and four medium secondaries as well. Their aggressiveness eliminated a lucrative target of opportunity.[58]

Along with the never-ending tanker hops, seeding runs—most executed in the morning in at least partial daylight but a few by night—provided variety during VA-75's last six days on the line. On 12 July, LCDR Dick Engel took LT Hart on his first A-6A strike mission, to seed a river mouth in RP IV. "I was extremely nervous," Hart remembered, "especially the closer to the coast we got." The weather, already bad, worsened as they neared the target area, and Hart found it difficult to update his system. The briefers had reinforced the importance of precision in the delivery of mines, so, to make absolutely certain of things, Engel made three passes over the target before he pickled their load of twelve Mk36 DSTs. Below them, Hart saw men in "fishing sampans" who were "firing their AK47s at ME." But they dropped their ordnance successfully, just the same.[59] The next night, two A-6As, each loaded with sixteen Mk36s, made a particularly exciting run to drop their ordnance off Haiphong. LT Lankford and LTJG Warren took the lead, with LT Ruland and LTJG McFarland on their wing. "We came in screaming," McFarland recalled, and they flew not one hundred feet off the water. The master log listed in its "delivery type" column this simple abbreviation: "Min alt." After the mines released, the absence of any appreciable drag on the aircraft allowed them to egress at extremely high speed. McFarland had never flown that fast in an A-6 before.[60]

The operational tempo maintained such a fast pace that even good news had to wait. On 16 July, LT Fischer, the squadron duty officer for the day, accepted an emergency message for LTJG Petersen. Fischer suspected that he knew the news the telegram contained, but he also realized that Petersen had a mission to fly. Thus, he waited until Petersen trapped aboard to deliver the long-awaited good

This A-6A belonging to VA-75 recovers aboard Saratoga *after completing a mission. Its multiple ejector racks under the wings are empty. The pilot has deployed the speed brakes at the wingtips, and the extended tailhook is about to snag the "3-wire" of the arresting gear. (John R. Fuller Collection)*

news. Jeane Petersen had given birth to Laurie Jeane on 13 July, and both mother and daughter were happy and healthy. Petersen, who already had purchased a box of cigars earlier in the line period to celebrate the promotions of five of his fellow lieutenants junior grade, now set up the box in the ready room, complete with a sign that read, "I didn't get promoted but I got a baby ——." He filled the blank with "daughter!"[61] It provided a bit of good news on which to end the second line period.

As *Saratoga* left Yankee Station, VA-75 prepared its end-of-line-period report as required. They had flown 116 A-6A strike missions of various sorts, 34 of them at night. The A-6Bs had flown 57 missions, 24 at night. The squadron's KA-6Ds proved their value yet again, launching 226 tanker hops, including 49 at night. They had dropped just under 500 tons of ordnance.[62] In all, CVW-3 had flown a total of 708 combat strike sorties and delivered 1,198 tons of ordnance, underscoring VA-75's sizable contribution to the tonnage dropped on North Vietnamese targets.[63]

During the line period, the squadron's Operations and Maintenance departments worked together to develop a new system for keeping the maximum number of squadron aircraft in the air, a genuine difficulty during cyclic ops when a single plane could be scheduled for three hops in one day. The maintenance people worked up a list of "sierra report codes," assigning to each common airframe and system gripe a special numerical designator. For instance, if the screen on an aircraft's Pilot's Horizontal Display (PHD) went blank or got too dark or too light, the crew could report a "9-U" even before recovery. ECM gear malfunctions required a "12" call, followed by a specific set of letters to identify the equipment that would require attention upon landing. This information was relayed to Maintenance Control, where Chief Warrant Officer Smith could alert appropriate personnel to a specific incoming problem. The notification system gave troubleshooters the time they needed to get the tools for quick adjustments with the aircraft still on the flight deck. To fix planes with reported gripes beginning with a "3—aircraft hard down," however, Smith worked with flight deck personnel to establish a system of "hot drops." In those cases, the aircraft handlers simply learned to direct a damaged A-6 straight to Elevator #1 and drop it to the hangar bay, allowing the pilot to taxi close to the appropriate work area before shutting down his engines. During this sixteen-day tryout, the sierra code system became standard operating procedure, and all VA-75 pilots and B/Ns carried the gripe designators on a kneeboard card along with the rest of their essential information.[64]

Also during this brief second line period, VA-75's senior leaders made significant headway in integrating the squadron's newest pilots and B/Ns into air operations. The fully qualified crew of LT Chisholm and LTJG Vance provided the best illustration of a successful pairing. Decisions about other crews took longer. During his brief time aboard, LT Hart flew as a B/N on nine tanker hops. LCDR Lindland, who proofed the daily schedule, assigned him to fly those tankers with nine different pilots. "This was the Ops Officer's way of letting me and the pilot get to know each other," Hart understood. He also picked up two strike missions. Finally, the heavies paired him with the experienced LT Anderson.[65]

Since LT Wharton's departure, LTJG Petersen had flown with all three recently arrived pilots. He deemed LT Chisholm the best of the three, his decision reflecting his bias in favor of experience. As he wrote to his wife, "This just isn't the place to learn to fly the airplane." Still, since he no longer flew as part of an established crew pair, he complained, "I'm the duty floater B/N. I'll fly with anybody." When CDR Earnest permitted Chisholm and Vance to pair up, Petersen then asked to fly with LTJG Bryan, convinced that the young pilot "is a good stick who just needs some experience to be able to handle anything over here."[66] The heavies approved this arrangement.

LT Hiduk's case proved more difficult to resolve. As if to validate his belief— or maybe fulfill his wish—he flew tankers only during his entire first line period. He alone among all the new pilots and B/Ns had not gone feet dry to drop ordnance during the second line period. Since no B/N wanted to fly tanker hops only, no one stepped forward immediately to volunteer to crew permanently with Hiduk. As *Saratoga* came off the line, the squadron heavies still had not decided how to settle this issue.

They, like everyone in the squadron, needed time to unwind, reflect, and relax. The airwing celebrated the end of the line period with a pizza party. Referring to CAG Bordone, LT Chisholm explained, "We have an Italian commander of the Air Group," and thus "it's a big occasion." They enjoyed movies in the ready room and then went "off to pizza—what a big nite." Complaints flew when the pizza ran out early.[67]

Now they had time to catch up on the news, and the publication of the now-famous photograph featuring Jane Fonda seated behind a North Vietnamese antiaircraft gun aimed at the skies where VA-75 had just flown triggered an emotional outburst from some Puncher pilots and B/Ns. She also struck a nerve with her description of her visit to Nam Dinh, a place nearly all Puncher crews knew well. Planes from every carrier in the Gulf of Tonkin had hit targets near there at some point during the war, but after VA-75's detailed and purposeful planning to avoid civilian casualties in that area just a few days before, Fonda's words stung. She asserted, "I was taken to all parts of the city. I saw with my own eyes that in this city which is the textile capital of Vietnam, there are no military targets." She accused naval aviators of bombing residential streets, destroying the main hospital's pediatric department, and, of course, repeatedly hitting local dikes.[68] LT Fischer simply could not understand why the American people would accept her commentary as a credible source of war news. "Everyone would laugh at the Secretary of State or the president if they tried their hand at making a movie or cutting a record," he wrote in his diary on 19 July, so it made no sense to him that they could "listen to Jane Fonda and other 'stars' when they make pronouncements about the politics of the war."[69]

For now, however, many of the squadron's married men could not remain distressed for long. In a few more days they would enjoy long-anticipated reunions with their wives in Hong Kong. Some spouses, including Nini Lerseth and Linda Ahrens, had made their own travel plans to get there early. Most, however, took the special charter flight that Lilliane Greene and the wives of the senior officers of CVW-3's Oceana-based F-4 squadrons had arranged. Back in Virginia Beach early in the month, many of them had discussed travel plans at a buffet dinner that Duddie Graustein had hosted. CDR Foote, newly arrived home after the change of command, warned them that last-minute changes in *Saratoga*'s schedule might leave them stranded in Hong Kong without any chance to meet their husbands, but they had pressed on with their plans anyway.[70] This meeting initiated Chris Bryan into the VA-75 officers' wives group, and she listened to the animated conversation about the trip with interest and wistfulness. "I wish I could be there with you so you won't be lonesome," she wrote. Perhaps to soften the blow, she also told a small white lie: "There are many wives who aren't going."[71]

But most married Puncher pilots and B/Ns did expect to meet their spouses. They vied for seats in the first aircraft flying off *Saratoga* to Cubi, intending to catch a commercial flight from Manila to Hong Kong rather than lose two days steaming over on the carrier. When bad weather caused them to miss their plane in the Philippines, the Navy arranged for a C-130 to take them to Hong Kong instead. LT Ruland took that flight to meet Brigid, now several months pregnant with their first child, for their only visit during her pregnancy.[72] Less fortunate officers had to wait at Cubi until *Saratoga* steamed for Hong Kong two days later.

While *Saratoga* offloaded damaged aircraft and refueled at Cubi, many of VA-75's sailors gave in once more to the lures of Olongapo. When the ship left for Hong Kong, however, one Puncher missed movement. The squadron leadership did not take it lightly when junior enlisted men committed such offenses, but this time the offender was a senior chief aviation mechanic. XO Greene understood that he faced a touchy situation here. He could not let the matter slide; indeed, some of the other chiefs and warrants who worked with the man openly debated whether or not he would lose his rank over the incident. But he also had a solid reputation as one of the squadron's hard workers and it would not serve to come down too hard on him, either. Thus, the chief found himself simply placed in hack, restricted on future in-port periods.[73]

Saratoga reached the Green Island anchorage at Hong Kong on 20 July, and liberty for most hands began soon thereafter.[74] Unmarried officers generally felt they received unfair treatment during such in-port periods. The same held true for married men whose wives did not make the trip. Invariably, these men pulled the preponderance of duty assignments during their stay. Indeed, even one so new to military life as Chris Bryan could chide her husband that, since she could not make the trip, "you can be on watch."[75] LT Chisholm had to remain aboard *Saratoga* the entire first day in Hong Kong to serve as SDO. LT Fischer drew shore patrol duty, linking up with British, Australian, and Gurkha soldiers who served in the permanent garrison. They guaranteed Fischer a quiet tour with a simple "don't worry, sir, we'll take care of the blokes." He asked to see the kukri knife one of the Gurkhas carried and, not realizing that it could not be resheathed until the soldier drew blood, stood aghast when the soldier nicked his thumb to shed the required drops.[76]

Once ashore, the squadron members did not make a clean break from the Navy and the war. The squadron set up its admin ashore at the Hong Kong Hilton. Serving as communications center, rendezvous spot, bar, and spare bedroom, the admin generally saw an active flow of traffic in and out. But most of the pilots and B/Ns reserved their own rooms at that hotel. After he finished his shore patrol duty, LT Fischer went back to his hotel room and found LT Knapp out cold on the bathroom floor and LT Hart ordering more scotch and charging it to Knapp. Next morning, Knapp and Fischer slept through all efforts by house-keeping to wake them, until Fischer felt a presence in the room. He opened an eye and saw the hotel manager looking down at him. "Hellooooo, friend," said the manager. "We would like to make up the room." Fischer and Knapp dragged themselves downstairs so the maid could make the beds and then dropped right back into them.[77] A few days later, Fischer, Knapp, LTJG Bob Dunne from *Saratoga*'s helicopter detachment, and several more officers took a boat ride out into the harbor. They drank, they swam, or—as in Knapp's case—did both. He won respectful applause when he dove into the murky water with an open beer bottle and resurfaced drinking from it.[78]

Most Punchers who had no one meeting them—and plenty of couples, too—checked out the nightlife. Some of the more adventurous went to Polaris, a nightclub on the sixteenth floor of the Hong Kong Hyatt that featured a stain-less steel dance floor for "the 'with it' people of the '70s." Those who arrived during "Aquarian Hours"—1800 until 2000—could enjoy free oysters.[79] LTs Wagner and Mullins and LTJG Petersen were sitting in another bar sipping their drinks when someone grabbed Petersen out of the crowd to participate in a limbo contest; he made it under the bar twice. The crowd applauded loudly, and when the lights went up, Petersen understood why. "We were a foot taller than anyone in the place," the 6-foot-2 officer noted, explaining that "it was an all Chinese bar."[80] LT Anderson noted that "many of the routines that were de-veloped with repeated trips to the Philippine ports of call were not available" in Hong Kong, but it was just as well. He added, "Many wives were there which also meant limited frivolity."[81]

That sentiment likely was not shared by the men whose wives made the trip, though. For those reunited couples, Hong Kong proved to be a joyous respite from the war. This proved especially true for two fathers-to-be who saw their wives for the first time since learning the news of their impending parenthood. LTJG Sanford's wife, Brenda, joined him for several days of touring, shopping, and eating, and a photograph of the two found a place in *Saratoga*'s 1972 cruise book. LT Ruland also enjoyed himself immensely, even as Brigid fought contin-uing bouts of morning sickness; he took over her care from Pixie Tolhurst and Sandy Pyle, who had fed her saltine crackers to control the nausea all during the trip to Hong Kong.[82] Even a plaintive letter from home from their son—written on specially purchased stationery emblazoned with an F-4 Phantom—could not distract Chief Warrant Officer Howard Smith and Myrna from enjoying their time together, though they admitted they found it a bit disconcerting to learn that young Ronnie lost all his pennies "playing poker" and that he desperately wanted "someone to tuck me in and kiss me."[83]

For five days, the Sunday Punchers traveled up to Victoria Peak at sixty cents (approximately eleven cents in U.S. currency) per tram ride, watched the English play cricket, looked through binoculars at Communist Chinese soldiers at a border checkpoint, and rode the Star Ferry. A number of the pilots and B/Ns took their wives on a boat ride to a nearby island rarely frequented by tourists and walked through the streets of a small town. The Lankfords spotted an old woman sitting on the steps of her porch breaking apart strips of molded plastic human figures. As they watched, she patiently trimmed the excess plastic from the edges of each one, and they suddenly realized that the woman earned her pay that day finishing toy U.S. Army soldiers for the American market.[84]

An attractive exchange rate made it possible for the Sunday Punchers to enjoy themselves in high style. Since one U.S. dollar equaled in value 5.70 Hong Kong dollars and VA-75's personnel had amassed their regular pay, hazardous duty pay, and—for the pilots and B/Ns—flight pay, the options for entertainment multiplied.[85]

Freed from the limited selection of shipboard food, they indulged in a culinary tour of the city. It seemed like every sailor aboard the carrier had heard of the San Francisco Steak House, and the lines stretched out the door and around the block to wait for a table there. When LTJG Vance and several other officers arrived by taxi and saw the line, they considered their options and decided to check out the Hyatt House Hotel instead. When they told their driver to take them there, he simply did a big U-turn and announced "Hyatt House." Although the destination proved to be just across the street from the Steak House, he charged them for the extra ride.[86] At the Hongkong Hotel, the hot dishes on the menu included everything from hot dogs and potato salad to lamb curry to "emince of beef Mexicaine" to fried eggs served with ham or bacon and a side of French fries. They ate at French restaurants in Kowloon. They dined on pizza at Joe's Restaurant. They indulged in deep-fried ice cream at Jimmy's Kitchen, advertised as "one of the Colony's oldest, most popular restaurants." Some visited the Tai Pak Floating Restaurant and enjoyed their crabmeat with sweet corn soup, fried fresh prawns, baked lobster and onion sauce, and crabmeat fu yung.[87]

Advance planning helped to make some of these culinary experiences quite memorable. CDRs Earnest and Greene, who had visited Hong Kong on previous deployments, knew to go to the Parisian for the best Kobe beef. Since Minna Earnest did not make the trip, the Greenes took the skipper there to make certain he took time to relax. In turn, CDR Earnest forced Gunner Walden—whose "good Navy wife" stayed home with their children—to set aside his paperwork for a while to share some Peking duck at the skipper's favorite Chinese restaurant.[88] LTJG Swigart and Penny planned to visit a restaurant his parents had greatly enjoyed. Along with several other couples, they set out to find the place, but quickly had second thoughts when they discovered its back-alley location and its lighting: naked light bulbs on slender wires. But they stayed, ordered the special food Swigart's parents had recommended—a dish featuring a large black mushroom—enjoyed perhaps too much of the local wines, and ended the evening by renting rickshaws and racing them through the streets.[89]

Everybody shopped. Hong Kong's many tailors made it simple to be measured for civilian attire that could be picked up or delivered the next day, at prices too low to be believed. Deliveries generally arrived when promised, but Chief Wright Cade, who had visited Hong Kong on previous cruises, discovered the weakness in the arrangement: The tailors used cheap thread, causing even some expensive purchases to rip at the seams the first time the sailors wore them.[90] Nonetheless, many of the Sunday Punchers ordered custom-tailored shirts, suits, and sport coats. LTJGs Petersen and McFarland had a friend take photographs of their "fashion show" for Jeane and Shari, who had stayed home.[91]

For a week, Hong Kong's economy flourished from the buying activities of the free-spending Americans from *Saratoga*. Sailors patronized Hong Kong's custom shoemakers—including the Lee Kee Boot and Shoe Maker. Pixie Tolhurst found the experience exhilarating because she finally located a place willing to make her hard-to-find size 4½ shoes. Local tobacco shops profited; CDR Earnest bought at least one new pipe. Loretta Lankford bought a Singer sewing machine. LT Chisholm located his prize purchase at a jewelry shop, a 1.58-carat emerald with small diamonds set in a 14K silver gold band. He bought it for Bobbie, hoping that it might serve as their engagement ring.[92]

On the morning of 27 July, *Saratoga* prepared to leave Hong Kong to steam back to the Gulf of Tonkin. The carrier departed a few days earlier than planned; USS *America* had experienced engineering problems and had to return to the Philippines for repairs after only four days on the line.[93] The farewells proved to be just as painful as they had been at Oceana in April. As LT Chisholm observed, "Many wives were kind of shakey like last goodbyes."[94] Nini Lerseth, Linda Ahrens, and Penny Swigart, however, came to Hong Kong already planning to join the other Puncher wives in the Philippines. They now met up with Loretta Lankford, Barbara Miller, and Diane Miller and headed to Manila.

LT Fischer summed up the Hong Kong stop: "Really had a ball. A new, good outlook on life. Haven't had as much fun in the past 5 years—never have laughed so long." But he also appreciated a special irony that went with it. On 28 July, as *Saratoga* headed directly for the Gulf of Tonkin, he mused, "One minute having a ball—next in combat—what an artificial life—or maybe perhaps [a] very real life indeed."[95]

CHAPTER SEVEN

"On a Treadmill"

When the Sunday Punchers left Hong Kong for Yankee Station, they returned to a seemingly familiar routine. As LT Lerseth wrote home, "We're doing pretty much what we've been doing for the last two line periods," flying "alpha strikes during the day and low level single aircraft missions at night."[1] LT Hvidding now found his day-to-day activities of briefing, flying, debriefing, and preparing for the next launch so stultifying that he stopped keeping his diary because he had nothing new to say.[2] Senior officers worried about complacency. Even before active operations began, CVW-3 issued to all squadrons a mimeographed five-page "policy and procedures" sheet to review the myriad of details concerning mission planning and execution. In special "preventative" lectures and mandatory AOMs, each squadron's heavies reiterated warnings against carelessness on the flight deck and in the air.[3]

This illusion of "sameness" coexisted with ongoing changes in the war and the Sunday Punchers' perception of their role in it. The substantial political support for the mining and bombing campaigns in May and June disappeared, and Congress once again seemed hostile to the war effort. In mid-July, the Democratic National Convention nominated antiwar candidate George McGovern to run for president in the November elections. "I think we've reached the point in the war again where it's just a war of attrition—who's going to outlast the other guy," LT Lerseth wrote his mother, after learning about the Senate's passage of the Cooper-Brooke Amendment, which called for the withdrawal of all U.S. troops within four months of the return of all American POWs. Even though the Senate ultimately defeated the entire bill, he believed the public debate about the amendment "nullified a lot of what we've managed to accomplish." He concluded, "You know, it's damned frustrating and maddening to be sent out here and then watch the politicians in D.C. pull the rug out from under us right along. Let's go in and do it right or get the hell out, no ifs, ands, or buts."[4]

They now knew, as well, about growing international protests against the air war. While the Punchers enjoyed Hong Kong, the Reverend Dr. Eugene Carson Blake, Secretary General of the World Council of Churches headquartered in Geneva, refused to ignore any longer allegations that the U.S. military planned to destroy dikes "both by bombing and artificially induced rainfall."[5] UN Secretary General Kurt Waldheim appealed to the United States "to stop this kind of bombing which could lead to enormous human suffering, enormous disaster." Hanoi claimed that American bombers had caused massive destruction to dikes at least sixty times, and the State Department refuted the charges with photographic evidence.[6] On 27 July, President Nixon held a press conference to reiterate that the United States had shown "greater restraint than any great power has ever shown in handling this war," and, citing the destruction North Vietnamese troops had caused in South Vietnam during the spring, he condemned critics of the air war who accepted Hanoi's propaganda as true and judged U.S. efforts by "a hypocritical double standard."

Two days after Nixon spoke, former Attorney General Ramsey Clark arrived in North Vietnam. Against advice from the State Department, Clark went to witness the alleged destruction of the dikes for himself. As he later explained, "I felt the strong moral compulsion to go as an American to make a statement, primarily to the Vietnamese."[7] Clark's actions, even more than those of Jane Fonda, infuriated LT Fischer. In 1968, at Villanova's spring commencement, the attorney general had handed the future Sunday Puncher his diploma. Fischer often thought of that day with pride, but now the disillusioned pilot only wanted Clark to visit South Vietnamese towns destroyed during the Easter offensive and see "the churches where the VC rolled in with tanks and killed the people." [8]

But, probably most striking for all aboard *Saratoga,* they discovered that during their absence, the air war had intensified right along with global protests. Henry Kissinger's meeting with Le Duc Tho in Paris in mid-July concluded yet again without a resolution, and Nixon became increasingly impatient with North Vietnamese intransigence. Although most political pundits at the time believed that Nixon wanted to end the war before the November elections, Henry Kissinger later suggested that by late summer the president "saw no possibility of progress until *after* the election and probably did not even desire it." Seemingly confident that the Communist Chinese and the Soviets would not intervene, Nixon "preferred another escalation before sitting down to negotiate."[9]

Thus, by late July when *Saratoga* neared Yankee Station, the air war against North Vietnam had become more heated than the conflict they had left just ten days earlier. In June, sortie rates against North Vietnamese targets had jumped 11 percent over those in May; July witnessed another 6 percent increase, and now planners called for another 6 percent increase in August. The approach of the rainy season called for a heavy push now, before monsoons grounded planes lacking all-weather combat capabilities. The timely arrival of additional air assets provided more punch; by mid-July Marine Corps tactical aircraft and helicopter hunter-killer teams had begun to strike North Vietnamese targets in RPs I and II, and new or enlarged air bases in Thailand accommodated newly arrived Air Force units from the United States and redeployed Marine Corps A-6 and F-4 squadrons from South Vietnam. The improving military situation in South Vietnam also permitted the reallocation of aircraft for strikes against North Vietnamese targets, a move considered essential when intelligence reports noted a recent jump in discoveries of stockpiled supplies that might support a fall offensive. Finally, in late July, the Joint Chiefs of Staff also expanded the approved target list to permit strikes on a number of previously banned military sites near Hanoi and Haiphong.[10]

To refresh their skills, CVW-3's squadrons started their third line period with FAC-controlled missions against targets in northern South Vietnam to support the ARVN counteroffensive in that area. In retrospect, a close-support mission in MR I on 29 July on the way back to Yankee Station became a harbinger of things to come for VA-75 during this third line period. LTs Pyle and Hvidding's radio did not work well in inclement weather. They never connected with their FAC. They jettisoned their bomb load at sea—including the squadron's three-millionth pound of ordnance.[11]

Maintenance issues of all sorts continually cut into the number of mission-capable aircraft VA-75 could launch during *Saratoga*'s third line period. As the airwing's sortie requirement increased, the number of A-6s ready to fly those missions declined sharply. Several of the squadron's planes remained with the beach detachment at Cubi, and even the accession of several additional aircraft to augment the squadron's strength did little to alleviate growing concerns about A-6 availability.

On 30 July, *Saratoga* followed the alpha strike schedule. One event called for CVW-3 to hit a petroleum products supply point one-half mile west of Haiphong. CDR Earnest, the strike lead, planned to take four A-6As from VA-75 on this mission, but his own aircraft went down on deck.[12] LCDR Graustein, alternate strike lead, launched successfully, but his plane developed ECM problems, and he had to return to the carrier. LT Lankford and LTJG Warren became the strike lead, and neither they nor the only other A-6A still with them possessed a working computer to run their weapons system. Still, since they flew in daylight, they could acquire their target visually and drop their ordnance in ways that did not rely on a systems release. They had no reason to turn back.

The effects of the brief layoff evinced themselves early; the formation strung out badly. About twenty miles from the target, the crews picked up the distinctive loud "DEEDLE" signifying a SAM launch. Lankford's ECM gear indicated they had become the target of a missile launched from a site dead ahead. Lankford began to turn left, when Warren yelled to break hard right immediately. A green SAM with orange stripes zipped under the right wing but did not explode.

They flew on through heavy black flak, reminding both men of World War II movies they had seen. Even though the cloud deck lowered, the strike group hit its targets, starting a number of fires in storage areas, shipbuilding facilities, and rework shops that burned for some time. All aircraft returned to *Saratoga* safely. To Warren, that alone made it "a good strike."[13]

The alpha strikes of 30 July served as a warm-up for a so-called "super alpha" scheduled for 31 July. The target, Haiphong Shipyard Number 3, now appeared on the target list for the first time since the Joint Chiefs of Staff had declared it off limits in 1967. The reasons for the boatworks' previously protected status seemed clear enough. Even though a legitimate military target, the shipyard lay near the population center of the city of Haiphong close to civilian hospitals, a temple, and, possibly, a POW camp. Thus, even in mid-1972, planners viewed this as a "point target" only, one that demanded great skill and precision to hit. They evaluated many possible targets within the shipyard that might be attacked by individual aircraft or a section of three or four planes, but they focused on a sawmill, three graving docks, a marine railway with cradle, four slipways, a building way, three large petroleum storage tanks, four floating piers, and a floating dry dock.

CDR Robert R. Cowles of VF-103 led the planning group for this strike. Ultimately, the final design called for forty aircraft, including five A-6As and both of VA-75's A-6Bs. Three A-6As led by CDR Earnest and LCDR Pieno headed up one of the two elements that composed the main strike force. Redshirts hung five Mark 84s—2,000-pound bombs—on each of these three A-6As.

VA-75's other two A-6As received a special tasking. Since the Haiphong shipyard enjoyed strong protection by North Vietnamese air defenses, the planners decided to use the two aircraft to surprise the enemy and increase chances for success. About thirty nautical miles from the target, CAG Bordone and LCDR Jackson in one plane, along with LCDR Graustein and LT Mullins in the other, planned to ingress at very low altitude—fifty feet or lower. A few minutes before the rest of the strike force rolled in on their targets, the plan called for these two aircraft to press their low-level attack, each dropping eighteen specially fused Mk82 retarded bombs. If all went as designed, these two aircraft would fly a south-to-north path, release their bombs over the target, and egress quickly. Then, in the chaos caused by the initial run, the two main attack elements would begin their runs from 15,000 feet, one from east-to-west and the other from west-northwest to the east. The planners hoped that the three-pronged, high-low, multiple roll-in, coordinated attack would so completely confuse the air defenders that all the crews could drop their ordnance on target and egress safely. The plan required precision in both targeting and timing.[14]

On 31 July, the strike group—reduced from forty planes to only twenty-six, partly due to aircraft availability problems—launched and rendezvoused as planned. The two A-6As assigned to make the low-level run on the target detached from the main group as scheduled, going feet dry at fifty feet and 420 knots. Then, Murphy's Law took over. As LCDR Jackson navigated to the target, he discovered that his planning map and the visual clues from the ground did not match up. He was unable to get a navigational update from his computer. Then, Jackson recalled, he "foolishly abandoned" the B/Ns' standard practice of using heading and time and distance to navigate. He gave CAG Bordone a heading change based on "where I thought we were." Jackson's course change took them away from their target.

By the time Bordone and Jackson discovered the error and got back to the correct heading, the two high-altitude strike groups had arrived over the target. Indeed, as Jackson recalled, "they could see us quite clearly down there on the ground and saw that we were well left of the target." The high flyers could not continue to orbit at 12,000 to 14,000 feet in the SAM envelope until the two low-altitude planes arrived and made their bombing run. Radar-guided AAA fire already probed the airspace around them, and LTJG Swigart, flying with LT Cook, watched a series of black puffs rapidly closing in on their aircraft. A few SAMs now streaked through the sky, too, one cutting through the narrow airspace separating CDR Earnest's aircraft from LT John Miller and LTJG Sanford on his wing. The missile did not detonate. The two attack elements waited no longer. The sudden release from the pylons of five 2,000-pound bombs, and the absence of MERs to provide drag, created three "slick" A-6As, and Swigart recalled the egress over Haiphong Harbor as "near supersonic."[15]

Once the high-altitude elements began their bombing runs, CAG Bordone's low element had no choice but to stay out of the way. They made a wide turn west of town and circled back toward the target, watching the action. When Bordone and Graustein finally began their own runs, dust, smoke, and fire so completely obscured the area that the two A-6As abandoned their original plan to drop their ordnance at fifty feet and pickled instead at a more reasonable two hundred feet. As they pulled off the target, Bordone and Jackson discovered that five of their eighteen Mk82s had not released.[16]

Officially, of course, the strike was declared a major success. The airwing's annual command history noted that the strike on Haiphong Shipyard Number 3 "marked the first attempt at a strike tactic that was to prove highly effective during the remainder of combat operations. CDR BORDONE led a two plane A6A section at extreme low level (50 feet) to deliver the final coup de grace on Shipyard #3. This tactic of surprise attack against point targets encountered very slight enemy reaction and was to prove itself as a highly effective tactic in A6A combat operations."[17] On one level that assessment certainly seemed to ring true. All planes hit their targets and returned to the carrier safely. The E-2B had spotted MiG activity during the egress and successfully vectored the strike's F-4s to an intercept course, and the MiGs turned away. The presence of the A-7 Iron Hands and VA-75's two A-6Bs rendered the SAM threat far less troublesome than expected. An RA-5C snapped poststrike photographs that revealed immense destruction. As a consequence, the production of Haiphong's barge and light-ship construction fell by 25 percent and tugboat production declined by 33 percent.[18]

But those who participated in the strike knew that this mission did not proceed quite as smoothly or prove to be quite as successful as described in the command history. LT Knapp and LTJG Fuller, in one of the two Sunday Puncher A-6Bs, fired an AGM-78 that proceeded on course toward its target for approximately one nautical mile. But it suddenly reversed course and headed out into the Gulf of Tonkin. As Fuller reached for the radio to send a warning, the runaway missile stood on its tail, spun on its axis very fast, and then blew up. In the other A-6B, LT Fischer fired an AGM-78 that started to tumble after traveling only two and one-half nautical miles.[19] Of course, the low-level attack had not come off as planned, either. LCDR Jackson accepted responsibility for that. As he later advised, "Plan your flight, especially those down at 50 feet using a strict heading and time/distance, which is Navigation 101!" Years later, when Jackson relived the strike with one of the participating A-7 pilots, they shared "a good laugh about me taking CAG on a tour of the countryside outside of Haiphong at 50 feet."[20] CDR Earnest pulled LT Miller aside to remind him of a point made repeatedly during the transit: A wingman must not get directly behind the lead because, as he had just observed nearly to his detriment, "that's where most of the flak went."[21] LT Mullins accorded this alpha strike a pucker factor of 100 percent, one of only four missions to win that designation.[22]

The Haiphong Boatyard strike received national press coverage. As Joseph Treaster of the *New York Times* reported, MACV spokesmen explained that the strike hit a shipyard that "builds and repairs the kind of shallow-draft boats [WBLCs] used to shuttle supplies ashore from the freighters standing off the coast of North Vietnam." While spokesmen could offer no specific information to explain why carrier aircraft hit this target now, Treaster cited the views of unnamed "military analysts" who suggested that the attack might be interpreted as "an indication that too many supply boats were slipping through the American barrier and that senior officers felt it was necessary to go after the craft at their source."[23]

The consequences of failing to stop the boats at their source could be dramatic, and that lesson was reinforced for at least two Sunday Punchers on 4 August. The airwing staff assigned VA-75 a two-plane mining mission near Hon La Island. As part of the effort to stop the offloading of Communist-bloc vessels that anchored in that area, the two crews had to drop their Mk36s in a precise

Photo reconnaissance missions generally did not fall to the Sunday Punchers, but in early August, LCDRs Graustein and Jackson took this photograph of the coastal defenses at Hon Nieu Island, a frequent target of VA-75 airstrikes. (U.S. Navy photograph, Grady L. Jackson Collection)

pattern off the beaches of the island to stop WBLCs from delivering their cargoes ashore. The flight lead determined that the usual straight-and-level system delivery used to drop mines carried excessive risk in that extremely well-defended area and called for a visual dive instead. Then his aircraft went down on the catapult, leaving LT Chisholm and LTJG Vance to continue the mission alone. The weather in the target area deteriorated, however, and the crew knew that the strong winds would catch the deployed fins on their Mk36s and take them in directions they could not control. Chisholm and Vance reconsidered the use of a systems drop, but then made the visual dive as planned. The Mk36s landed off target. Worse, they landed in an unauthorized location. When they returned to the ship, Chisholm debriefed as usual, accurately reporting where their ordnance fell. Then, as he wrote home, "All hell broke lo[o]se," because, as he learned, "we can't have mines there." As soon as Chisholm arrived in the ready room, CDR Earnest immediately escorted him to CAPT Sanderson to explain what happened. The pilot very nearly had to do the same with RADM Christiansen. He anticipated that he and Vance might be pulled off the strike schedule as punishment.[24]

For someone less aggressive than Chisholm, accruing such a penalty on 4 August might have been welcome. The next day, CVW-3 would launch its first alpha strike to the Hanoi area. Some already had begun to call it "the big one." In anticipation of the event, LT Lerseth guessed that it "will undoubtedly be one of the highlights of this tour (so to speak)—sort of like going on a strike to Berlin in WWII." Learning that he and his pilot, LCDR Lindland, would participate, he considered the prospects daunting, but decided that "if I make it through this one, I'll make it through anything." Considering his mother's likely reaction to that comment, he added in parentheses, "That wasn't intended to make you worry—but just to make sure, I'll mail this *after* the strike."[25]

The "big one" called for a 35-plane alpha strike against the Van Dien vehicle depot and supply complex located two miles southeast of Hanoi and generally referred to simply as the "Hanoi truck park." Although media coverage of the strike claimed that this mission constituted the first time since 1967 that the truck park appeared on the approved target list, Air Force strikes already had hit it hard on 3 and 7 July.[26] Still, the target area included a large vehicle repair area, numerous large military storage buildings, and several cranes for lifting and loading trucks and other heavy vehicles. Planners hoped that if they could knock out this facility, they might degrade the ability of the North Vietnamese Army to continue supplying its forces in the south. An official account also asserted that "a strike of this size deep into the enemy's heartland and at the very doorstep of her capital city, could not help but reemphasize the determination and ability to strike any target at will, regardless of location." But attacking that site carried high risk, since it sat in range of four major MiG bases, multiple SAM sites, and heavy concentrations of all calibers of AAA. Moreover, to get to their target, the strike group had to fly more deeply into North Vietnamese airspace than CVW-3 ever had before.[27]

CAG Bordone with LCDR Pieno served as strike leader. LT Knapp and LTJG Fuller flew on his wing. LCDR Don Lindland and LT Lerseth became the alternate strike lead, with LTs Anderson and Hart on their wing. The basic plan called for an ingress south of Nam Dinh and then a northwest turn up through the first mountain valley to the west of the alluvial plain around Hanoi. This unusual step took the strike group briefly outside the boundaries of the Navy-controlled RP VI-B and into the Air Force's RP VI-A. Then, after making a final eastward turn toward the target, hopefully injecting an element of surprise, Bordone called for three coordinated attacks against separate targets in the depot. Bordone and LCDR Pieno took five A-6As and A-7s against the northern end of the vehicle complex. LCDR Lindland and LT Lerseth led seven additional attack aircraft against the vehicle repair facilities at its southern end. LCDR R. L. Earnest of VF-31 (not to be confused with CDR Charles Earnest, the Punchers' skipper) led six more aircraft against the central target area. To protect the strike groups, Bordone called for an aggressive use of the airwing's MiGCAP and SAM suppression capabilities, including A-7 Iron Hands and both of VA-75's A-6Bs.

Once again, the weather proved troublesome. A low cloud deck required complicated rendezvous procedures after launch. Thunderstorms forced the strike to deviate from its initial flight plan. Finally, only twenty miles from the target, the weather cleared sufficiently to resume the planned approach and roll-in on the target. But where was it? In making their course changes, CAG Bordone and LCDR Pieno took the entire strike group up the second mountain valley, not the first, as planned.

In the formal language of official reports, the strike group then "acquired the target visually." LT Lerseth looked to the east, spotted Hanoi, and continued to give LCDR Lindland constant updates. Finally, he said, "Don, the target is now at two o'clock." Lindland nodded toward CAG's aircraft and said, "Damn it! Tell him that!" About the same time, several A-7 pilots informed Bordone of the same discovery, and the CAG reacted immediately. The entire strike group began a sweeping S-curve to the east. For a short time, "it was special because it was incredibly quiet," Lerseth recalled. They heard no reports of airborne MiGs or tracking radars from the SAM sites, and saw no AAA. Lerseth concluded later that, for a few minutes, the North Vietnamese "were completely baffled by our Alpha profile" that took them into RP VI-A.[28] LT Hart also believed that their unorthodox approach had confused the North Vietnamese air defenders "and led them to believe that we were going to a target to the west or northwest of Hanoi until it was too late."[29]

But the quiet soon broke. Fan Song radars from SAM sites finally began to paint the strike group. CDR Earnest with LCDR Jackson in one of VA-75's A-6Bs and LTs Fischer and Wagner in the other looked for targets. Up to now, A-6Bs usually remained feet wet, well away from the airspace where SAMs might hit them. For this mission, however, they took up positions about ten nautical miles in trail and to either side of the strike group itself, much farther over the beach than they ever had gone before. Now, each A-6B had a good missile lock-on and fired an AGM-78, just as the strike group began its roll-in.[30] Fischer then heard his friend LT E. L. Bishop of VA-105's Iron Hand element announce a SAM launch. Fischer looked around but saw no missile. Only later did he learn that Bishop and at least one other A-7 had taken up positions much closer to the strike group—over downtown Hanoi. As Fischer listened, he heard Bishop announce, first, that he fired an AGM-45, and, then, that his engine flamed out. A voice over the radio tersely suggested, "Well, relight it." Still concentrating on the missile threat, Bishop responded, "Wait, I'll fire another Shrike first." Then he restarted his engine.[31] The unusually aggressive work by the A-6Bs and the A-7

On 5 August 1972, B/N LTJG John Fuller snapped this photograph just before his pilot, LT Ken Knapp, began their roll-in on their target at the Van Dien Vehicle Depot. CAG Bordone and LCDR Pieno, in the A-6A pictured here, served as flight lead for this mission and are ready to begin their attack run. In the background below them are the city of Hanoi, the Red River, the famous Paul Doumer bridge, and the Gia Lam airfield. (John R. Fuller Collection)

Iron Hands so completely shut down the SAM sites that the North Vietnamese launched only eight missiles—far below their capability in this dense concentration of defenses—and hit no American aircraft. The strike group also began to receive reports of MiG-21s in the air, but the F-4s assigned to the MiGCAP set off to counter that threat. The MiGs turned back.

When the strike group rolled in, however, all the AAA batteries surrounding the target area opened up. The skies filled with accurate 37- and 57-mm AAA, and possibly some radar-controlled 85-mm AAA as well. Each of the A-6As in the strike group carried five Mk84s, the 2,000-pound bombs. As they had for the 31 July Haiphong Boatworks mission, ordnancemen hung the Mk84s directly on the pylons, so that after release, the A-6As once again became "slick." The crews felt the heavy jolt that accompanied the release of each bomb, and as they rolled off target, the A-6As departed at high speed, making fun of the slower Corsairs that tried to keep up. "I think the A-7s completed egress the next day," Lerseth joked, adding, "We left them in our dust."[32]

But one A-6A also found it difficult to keep up. After LTs Anderson and Hart dropped their ordnance, the B/N noticed that his weapons control panel did not reflect a bomb release on station #1 on the left wing. Anderson checked, and, as Hart recalled, "sure enough there was 2,000 pounds of asymmetric loading there." Anderson hit the emergency jettison and dumped it. Then, as they tried to catch up with the other A-6As, their ECM gear broke down. They heard calls about SAMs in the air, but they did not know one was heading toward them. A missile detonated about 1,000 feet above them, but they did not realize it until after they landed, when Lerseth rushed back to see if their aircraft had suffered any damage.[33]

In the end, the strike caused serious damage to the Van Dien vehicle repair facility. Crews reported at least two large explosions, but heavy smoke covered much of the target area. Poststrike photography showed that CAG Bordone's northern element destroyed three large and eleven medium storage or support buildings and heavily damaged one large L-shaped drive-in garage. LCDR Lindland's southern element destroyed eleven large, fifteen medium, and eight small support and storage buildings. LCDR Earnest's central element destroyed two large vehicle maintenance buildings and damaged seven medium support buildings.[34] After he landed, LT Lerseth finished his letter to his mother: "We made it, so I'm mailing it—what a hop! Whew."[35]

CVW-3 had little time to celebrate. The very next day they prepared to fly a second alpha strike against targets near Hanoi. Air intelligence officers studying reconnaissance photographs spotted an open area outside the city with a regular pattern of dots they interpreted as vent pipes for underground fuel storage tanks. CDR J. F. Watson of VA-37 led the planning team and served as strike lead. VA-75 contributed three A-6As and its two A-6Bs. LCDR Graustein and LT Mullins led the A-6A strike element.[36]

Perhaps on higher alert after the alpha strike of the previous day, North Vietnamese air defenders did not hold their fire this time. Estimates of the number of SAMs fired at the strike group ranged from eighteen to thirty-three. All the aircraft safely reached the target area, but by that time a huge thunderstorm hung over Hanoi. Given the weather and the level of opposition, CDR Watson ordered the strike group to break up, hit prebriefed alternate targets, and return to the ship. The A-6As quickly found targets nearby and rolled in. While Graustein and Mullins made their dive, their aircraft took two AAA rounds in the radome just below the windscreen. Still, all three A-6As dropped their ordnance, and for a second time in one week—the Haiphong Boatyard strike and now—LT Mullins marked a 100 percent pucker factor in his personal log.[37] The two A-6Bs joined up on them as they headed feet wet. As they popped over a ridge and zipped down a valley, they flew so low over a farmer in a coolie hat holding the reins of a water buffalo that the man ducked.[38]

All of the Punchers' aircraft made it back to the ship safely. Even LCDR Graustein's plane proved to be so lightly damaged that it flew again that night. But at least one SAM found a mark. A missile exploded right under LT Jim Kiffer's RA-5C. As news of the incident made the rounds of the ready rooms, the story got better in the retelling. LT Tolhurst, who had competed on the Naval Academy track team with Kiffer, reported that the Vigilante came back with sixteen holes in it. LT Fischer's log recorded that the RA-5C had taken thirty hits. LTJG Warren claimed the aircraft returned with sixty-seven holes. In any case, that night Fischer and Kiffer went to Mass together, even though Kiffer was not Catholic. The chaplain told him he was glad to see him, and Kiffer could only reply, "I'm glad to be anyplace, Padre."[39] The memory of so many SAMs flying through the air left its mark on those who took part in the strike, at least one of whom later began to call it "Watson's World Famous Sunday SAM Suck."[40]

Not all the excitement came from the big alpha strikes. Later that night, well after the planes from the Hanoi mission had returned to ship, several Puncher crews became part of another developing drama.

On the evening of 6 August, VA-105 sent out two A-7s to interrupt Communist-bloc freighters unloading cargo along the North Vietnamese coast near Vinh. LCDR Art Bell and LT Jim Lloyd found nothing to sink that night and answered a call from another section of A-7s operating further inland to hit some trucks not far from Vinh Son. As Lloyd pulled off his target amid a barrage of AAA, he tried—and failed—to evade a SAM. Its explosion so severely damaged his aircraft that Lloyd had to eject. The first reports of Lloyd's downing reached *Saratoga* at about 2130.[41] LCDR Bell became on-scene commander for a potential rescue effort.

All CVW-3 planes in the air that night diverted toward Lloyd's last reported position after completing their own missions. LCDR George Duskin of VA-37—on Iron Hand duty near the coast—determined to stay in the area in case the SAM site turned its radar back on. He refused to leave until more SAM suppression aircraft showed up, and finally he began to run desperately low on fuel. LT Lankford and LTJG Warren, flying a KA-6D well out over the water, had just given two F-4s most of the fuel they carried. When they received an emergency message from Red Crown to tank an A-7 involved in a SAR operation, they responded that they had little gas to give. Then Duskin broke in, asked them to come up on a different frequency, and explained his low fuel state. Lankford and Warren immediately headed toward him.

LCDR Duskin had not yet gone feet wet, and tankers seldom went feet dry because they possessed little ECM gear. But Lankford and Warren shut off all external lights and asked the E-2B to vector them toward Duskin's plane. Informed that two more A-7s with Shrikes were on their way, Duskin turned toward the coast, only a few hundred pounds of fuel in his tanks. When Lankford and Warren turned on their lights. Duskin flew to them and plugged in. When they connected, both planes were feet dry.

The tanker gave Duskin all it could give. The fuel transfer stopped automatically at 1,500 pounds so the tanker could not drain itself dry. Both aircraft flew back to the carrier. The A-7 landed first. The KA-6D recovered next, carrying only 500 pounds of fuel, well below the 3,500 to 4,000 pounds a tanker usually brought back aboard. It seemed as though no one other than Duskin truly appreciated what they had done. When Lankford and Warren debriefed, the airwing's assistant operations officer screamed at them for landing so low on fuel.[42] CAG Bordone called Lankford to his stateroom. "I thought maybe I'm going to get an immediate medal," the pilot later recalled, but instead Bordone just "chewed my ass for screwing up the recovery and I never told him the story."[43]

Overhead near Lloyd's last known location, LCDR Bell ran low on fuel, and LCDR Bernie Smith of VA-105 replaced him as on-scene commander. Aboard *Saratoga*, CAPT Robert Rasmussen, RADM Christiansen's chief of staff, woke his boss. They initially considered sending in a SAR helicopter, but Christiansen decided against it as too dangerous.[44] Only after CDR David McCracken, an experienced SAR commander, convinced the admiral that the mission remained within the capabilities of the Big Mother SH-3 helicopters of HC-7, did Christiansen reconsider. LTs Harry J. Zinser and William D. Young, then posted as the North SAR helicopter aboard USS *England* and about one and one-half to two hours from Lloyd's position, got the call to go. The crew considered themselves to be "day VFR kinds of folks," and they had not trained much for nighttime rescue operations, but they headed out immediately.

No final decision to insert the helicopter would be approved until someone made voice contact with Lloyd on the ground. When Zinser and Young lifted off, no one knew Lloyd's position. LCDR Smith finally found him by flying back and forth over the general area and communicating with Lloyd through microphone clicks to turn left or right to get a fix on his position. Smith stayed in the air for 4.3 hours that night, refueling twice.

Back aboard *Saratoga*, CDR Earnest and LCDR Jackson prepared to launch to take Smith's place as on-scene commander. They carried eight Mk20 Rockeye and only two Mk82s; the redshirts actually removed several Mk82s so the aircraft would not use up quite so much fuel. After they launched, they took on between 6,000 and 8,000 more pounds of gas. As LCDR Jackson wrote, "All I remember is that it was the most gas we had ever taken on while flying a mission over North Vietnam." Smith gave the VA-75 aircrew Lloyd's position, using a bearing and distance from a prominent bend in a river. They found the landmark easily, flew toward Lloyd's last reported location, and tried to make radio contact.

By now, many North Vietnamese soldiers and civilians had begun a sweep through an area very close to Lloyd's position. He begged the A-6A to fly off so it would not give him away. For nearly two hours, Earnest and Jackson orbited farther inland. They could do so with some degree of safety, since LT Knapp and LTJG Fuller—still in the air after their own mission—moved their A-6B into position along the coast and even a bit feet dry to suppress any further SAM activity. "We refueled 2–3 times that night and stayed out for . . . 3 separate launch cycles to remain on station," Knapp later recalled. They stayed in the air 3.6 hours that night.[45]

Since Earnest and Jackson managed to maintain voice contact with Lloyd, Zinser and Young were cleared to attempt a rescue. As the helicopter neared the location, the crew in the A-6A turned on their lights to guide them. Then, as Earnest and Jackson neared what they believed Lloyd's position to be, they realized they had lost radio contact with him. If they could not talk to him, the rescue effort could not continue. Jackson prayed, "God help!" They returned to the river bend, the landmark coordinates that allowed them to find Lloyd the first time, and soon picked up his voice again. His radio signal had begun to weaken, so they stayed overhead at about five hundred feet to maintain contact. They still kept their lights on to guide the helicopter.

Since Lloyd could not talk directly to the helicopter, Jackson passed on the crew's request that he send up a flare. When he did so, pencil flares popped up all over the area. Jackson then relayed Lloyd's pleas to ignore the bogus signals. The chopper pulled off, temporarily, but with guidance from the A-6A crew, it soon returned to Lloyd's immediate position and turned on its landing lights. Lloyd waved to the helicopter, but the crew did not see him on the first pass. Jackson did, however, and told Zinser and Young to turn around and try again. This time, they requested that Lloyd shine a light. He only had his strobe, however, and feared it would look too much like ground fire. He relayed this concern to the chopper crew through Jackson, but then he turned on his light. A few seconds after he did so, several other strobes also winked on. A 57-mm AAA gun also opened up on the chopper then, but Aviation Metalsmith Airman Matthew Syzmanski had spotted Lloyd's strobe. While Szymanski provided cover fire, the helicopter landed in a nearby rice paddy, and Aviation Electronics Technician Third Class Douglas Ankney pulled Lloyd to safety. Then they turned off their lights and headed for home. Earnest and Jackson dumped their eight Rockeye on that 57-mm AAA position. As the helicopter crew approached feet wet and finally began to relax, three fireballs passed the ship at high speed only yards away. Zinser saw flying "telephone poles," suggesting that the North Vietnamese had launched SAMs at them. Indeed, as they too headed feet wet, Knapp and Fuller briefly picked up signals from a Fan Song radar, but it shut down very quickly when the A-6B reversed course. Thus, the missiles did not track, and they missed the helicopter.

LCDR Lindland and LT Lerseth had been ordered to replace Earnest and Jackson as on-scene commander, but their aircraft's constant speed drive generator malfunctioned and the engines would not start. "It was the only night mission up north when I *really* wanted to launch," Lerseth later recalled.[46] Thus, as the skipper and his B/N finally went feet wet, they only had 2,000 pounds of fuel, well below the expected level for a carrier landing. If their fuel situation had gotten more desperate, however, LTs Anderson and Hart and LT Cook and LTJG Swigart had taken up two additional RESCAP tankers to replace Lankford and Warren. In the end, though, CDR Earnest and LCDR Jackson safely trapped aboard.

Knapp and Fuller recovered safely, too. Knapp admitted later that he gave Lloyd only "1 in 4 chances of getting out. It was unbelievable that it was successful and I am thrilled that we were part of it."[47] After they trapped back aboard *Saratoga*, Fuller recalled, they walked across the flight deck with CDR Earnest and LCDR Jackson, all agreeing on the spot that "nothing we had done to date compared with this." Indeed, the entire crew celebrated the successful recovery of one of their own. Lloyd's inland rescue, the first by a Navy helicopter since 1967, had required support from *Saratoga*'s entire airwing, with additional assistance from *Midway* and several surface vessels.[48]

But LT Lloyd's rescue did not interest correspondent Joseph B. Treaster of the *New York Times* when he came aboard *Saratoga* on 8 August. He planned to interview naval aviators about the charges concerning the bombing of dikes and nonmilitary targets that put civilian lives at risk. CAG Bordone assigned LCDR Jackson to represent VA-75.

Jackson decided to relate the details of a recent mission he thought might enlighten the reporter. He described a low-level night strike that he and CDR Earnest had flown against a transshipment point on an island near Haiphong. Photo reconnaissance showed a huge storage area, but at night, flying below 500 feet, acquiring the target proved difficult. Apparently even the North Vietnamese understood that. As the A-6A neared a fishing village close by the target, Jackson noticed that all the civilian boats were illuminated, because, as he explained, "they know that Americans . . . won't bomb the lights." Skipper Earnest asked his B/N if they could drop their ordnance without hitting noncombatants. Jackson expressed doubt: "I wasn't real sure, and I saw the lights, and I felt sorry for them, so I told him, 'Well, no, let's go around again.'" As they circled around to get a more precise fix on their target, AAA sites opened up on them. They decided not to go after the original target, dropped their bombs on the guns firing at them instead, and returned to the carrier. "There is a point to be made that people out here"—in North Vietnam—"realize that we don't bomb indiscriminately," Jackson noted.[49]

When the correspondent published his report, he explained, "The pilots aboard this aircraft carrier swear that they have never tried to bomb the dikes of North Vietnam and they say they are hurt and irritated that so many Americans at home do not seem to believe them." As CAG Bordone himself explained, "'The thing that hurts us . . . is that we make every effort to avoid the dikes. We do not, absolutely not, go after dikes.'" *Saratoga's* aircrews explained their briefing process, which included the review of standing rules of engagement, a requirement to consider the possibility of civilian casualties as part of the planning, and the viewing of reconnaissance photos of the target area to avoid or minimize noncombatant deaths. The only part of LCDR Jackson's experience Treaster used came in a single sentence acknowledging that the B/N and his unnamed pilot—CDR Earnest—had "turned back from a target in the vicinity of Haiphong a few weeks ago because they felt it was too close to civilians."

The reporter tried—albeit with some condescension—to explain the aviators' feelings about the accusations lodged against them. "It seems important to the pilots that they be believed," he wrote, adding, "They put their lives on the line every day and they stand together under an old-fashioned code of military honor. They see themselves as patriots in the service of their country and their President. They would like to have been respected and appreciated. Now they will settle for being believed."[50] The officers had good reason to make their case. Just as Treaster received assurance from Jackson and other naval aviators that they did not purposefully target dikes, ten senators urged the Congress to demand that they stop such practices anyway. Speaking for the group, Senator Edward M. Kennedy (D-MA) asserted that "if the dikes are in close proximity to a potential bombing target, the policy of the Administration is to bomb the dikes anyway, regardless of the consequences." He added, "It does not take a Philadelphia lawyer to label this policy for what it is—a policy of deliberately bombing dikes."[51]

Bordone and Jackson had not merely parroted official policy. Their comments complied fully with the rules of engagement put in place at the start of LINEBACKER, airwing practice, and, in VA-75's case, personal experience. All pilots and B/Ns clearly understood that they would be held accountable if they broke those rules. As LT Chisholm noted, "Despite what Jane Fonda sez, we are not bombing dikes—strictly forbote (German I think) and will be put in hack if you do such tricks."[52] LT Tolhurst assured his wife, too, that "we are not hitting any dikes. In fact we brief carefully so as to not bomb dikes."[53]

The Punchers deeply resented all such accusations. LT Wagner composed a poem, which he read over the radio during a tanker hop, to express his feelings about two of their most strident critics:

Jane, Jane, with thoughts of sin.
Left the States for old Nam Dinh.
When she got there it was dark
So out she went to look for Clark.
Who said after a prolonged kiss
We can't go on meeting like this.
But that's the last thing that was said
'Cause A-6 Rockeye killed them dead.[54]

In his probing questions about civilian deaths, Treaster entirely missed a story about lifesaving that happened right under his nose. That same day, VA-75's Chief Aviation Structural Mechanic Frank J. Pittman came into the Aviation Intermediate Maintenance Department (AIMD) office to use the photocopier. Trying to give the chief a hand, LT Hugh F. Holden went to connect the copier to an extension cord already plugged into the wall. Immediately after picking up the two cords, Holden began to shake violently. Pittman grabbed the officer around the waist and pulled him loose, breaking him away from a potentially lethal ungrounded 115-volt AC current. If Pittman had touched anything metallic in that small space, both men might have died. For saving LT Holden's life at the risk of his own, Chief Pittman received the highly respected Navy and Marine Corps Medal.[55]

About the time Treaster left *Saratoga,* LT Lankford took a plane into Cubi for maintenance and went to check on Loretta.[56] He spent almost a week in Manila, learning firsthand of the spouses' unanticipated problems. Their hotel rooms hosted gigantic cockroaches. The monsoon rains poured through leaks in the roof, creating the effect of a waterfall cascading down a wall of the closet in Diane and Barbara Miller's room. The hotel manager who answered their complaint saw the torrent, threw up his hands, and proclaimed, "It's a miracle!" They faced harassment from local men who hissed at them to express their displeasure at the miniskirts and other immodest clothing the women wore. Linda Ahrens suffered sunburn so severe that they sought help from the USO to find a dermatologist to treat her. They finally moved to the Manila Hilton in a better neighborhood, where they enjoyed much better accommodations, each paying about $9 per night.[57] As their stories got back to the squadron, LT Tolhurst wrote Pixie, "Some of the guys are wishing that their wives had decided to go home."[58]

During Lankford's absence, President Nixon officially ordered his enhanced air assets in Westpac to increase their interdiction efforts. The Pentagon now required the U.S. Air Force to launch forty-eight strikes each day at targets north of the 20th parallel, a significant upward jump. Similar orders tasked CTF-77 to send all sorties from at least three carriers each day against LINEBACKER targets. On 9 August, ADM John S. McCain, Jr., commander-in-chief of the Pacific

Command, forwarded the order, making clear that he expected his carrier airwings to redouble their energies. "There is growing concern here and in Washington that insufficient effort is being applied against the North Vietnamese heartland," he wrote, adding, "To signal Hanoi in the strongest way possible that our air presence over their country will not diminish, I wish to intensify the air campaign in Northern NVN."[59]

CVW-3 had worked to do just that, flying either the alpha strike schedule or the noon-to-midnight schedule since its return to the line in late July. The increased activity from Yankee Station triggered a more aggressive response from North Vietnamese MiGs. Thus, CVW-3 began to support even one- and two-plane armed recces with MiGCAP protection, putting at least one F-4 in the air during each cycle and keeping a manned spare on deck. Whenever an F-4 MiG-CAP launched, a dedicated VA-75 KA-6D also took off to refuel it. During the last few cycles of 10 August, while several VA-75 crews flew single-plane night strikes, MiG activity between Thanh Hoa and Vinh caused LCDR Gene Tucker and LTJG Bruce Edens of VF-103 to launch, top off their fuel tanks from a KA-6D flown by LTs Ruland and Wagner, and then seek a target. After a ninety-mile high-speed chase after a MiG-21, they fired two AIM-7E-2 Sparrow missiles to achieve the first night MiG kill by naval aviators during the Vietnam conflict.[60] Improvements in F-4 combat air patrol coverage during this line period rested on the reliability of the support they received from the KA-6Ds.[61]

Despite increasingly bad weather, CDR Earnest and LCDR Jackson, along with LCDR Lindland and LT Lerseth, planned an important replenishment of two minefields near Haiphong for 11 August. An intense solar storm over 3–8 August had caused strong geomagnetic fluctuations, and on 4 August, several aircraft reported the spontaneous explosion of underwater ordnance. Observers reported between twenty and twenty-five explosions in one DST field alone.[62] VA-75 would drop the larger Mark 52 (Mk52) 1,000-pound mines, rather than the Mk36 500-pound destructors to which they had become accustomed. In addition to the damage done by the solar storm, the Mk52s laid in three minefields in the main ship channel to Haiphong in May neared their preset deactivation time of one hundred days.[63] The strike plan called for thirteen aircraft from *Saratoga*. Four A-6As from VA-75—each carrying four Mk52s—and five A-7s would split into two elements to replenish the minefields. In addition, one A-6B and one A-7 Iron Hand provided SAM suppression capability, while two F-4s flew as TARCAP. To provide a diversion, a second strike group prepared to hit an airfield thirteen miles inland. Bad weather quickly cancelled the diversionary attack, but the mining mission could not be delayed.

Flying under VFR conditions even in bad weather, the strike group descended to 1,000 feet to maintain group integrity. As the aircraft approached the target, the rain fell so hard that the pilots descended to 500 feet. As they prepared to make their runs, the two mining elements split off and descended to 400 feet, Earnest and Jackson leading one element and Lindland and Lerseth the other. The heavy rain interfered with the search radar on both lead planes. Nonetheless, even with significant AAA in the immediate target area, the aircraft began dropping their Mk52s.[64] Most of the ordnance dropped as designed. But LT Hart, flying on Lindland's wing with LT Anderson, realized that only the first of their four mines released properly. Then, as they approached the far side of the harbor and turned south, two more mines spontaneously dropped. Those two fell, as Hart recalled, "definitely not on target." They still had one more mine, so they returned to the initial point and made a second run. It still did not release, and they jettisoned it.[65]

Still, the airwing declared the replenishment exercise a success. The bad weather protected the strike group far more than it complicated their mission. The MiGs stayed on the ground. LT Knapp and LTJG Fuller fired an AGM-78 from their A-6B, the A-7 Iron Hand fired two AGM-45s, and the strike group saw no SAMs fired in their direction. The F-4s dropped Rockeye on several AAA sites, reducing the only threat that caused the strike any real concern.[66] Ironically, that same day, the Central Intelligence Agency presented in a White House briefing an assessment of the impact of the bombing and mining program. Despite considerable optimistic official endorsement from political and military leaders of the operation's effectiveness since its start in May, the report ultimately concluded that "the bombing and mining program probably will not, of itself, pose unmanageable difficulties to the North Vietnamese regime—either now or through early 1973."[67]

The weather on 12 August forced a stand-down day, and 13 August remained so inclement that CVW-3 flew only limited numbers of sorties. Still, the last few launches on the noon-to-midnight schedule—along with the increasing demand for strike sorties that only A-6s could fly in bad weather—provided opportunities for VA-75's heavies to introduce more junior aircrews to single-plane night missions. On 13 August, LT Tolhurst and LTJG Ahrens went on their first solo night mission over the beach, a seeding hop southwest of Vinh in RP II. In that comparatively benign environment, they dropped their twelve Mk36s on target. LT Tolhurst noted that they ran in high and comparatively fast: "We ran in at 1000 ft. and 450 kts. We only got shot at once and that was well behind us." Still, he noted that "it was really a different experience and one I'll remember even after we have many more night hops over the beach. You really have to be alert and use everything you have learned to do well."[68]

The squadron got an unanticipated break on 14 August, when the entire carrier task force received word to batten down for an unexpected attack by Mother

Nature. About 1845, reconnaissance aircraft had reported a tsunami, a tidal wave forty-five feet high, ninety miles east of Danang and heading west. Since its impact could be expected to affect carriers deployed in Yankee Station, *Saratoga* executed the heavy weather bill.[69] For a few hours, air operations shut down and brownshirts chained down all aircraft until the danger had passed. VA-75 took advantage of the time to hold a qualifying board for five new plane captains.[70]

The break in the middle of the third line period also marked the appearance of a few cracks in squadron morale and effectiveness. After the end of air operations on 11 August, LTJG Ron McFarland went to CDR Earnest's stateroom to turn in his wings. He had joined the Navy to become a pilot, but his eyesight had landed him in the NFO pipeline. Promised a chance to recycle through pilot training after a cruise as a B/N, he now heard that the Navy had cancelled the program. Far worse, McFarland had come to feel like a noncontributor. In a telling commentary about the fragility of the A-6A's navigation and weapons system, in all his strike hops to date, his full system had worked only one time. He had come to feel that "I was trying to do a mission and operate some equipment that didn't work, was never used, and I was useless in the airplane." In short, "I wasn't helping." Most of all, McFarland had grown disillusioned with a war "we weren't trying to win." He could not shake the feeling that "one of us, very likely, would be the last to die." And he added, "I did not want to be the last to die."

CDR Earnest did not want McFarland to act rashly. He refused to accept his wings immediately. Instead, he ordered the junior B/N to explain his intentions, in turn, to XO Greene and each of the squadron's lieutenant commanders. Over the next several days, McFarland spoke in turn to each of the heavies about his intentions. He found CDR Greene seemingly sympathetic but dismissive. In contrast, LCDR Graustein worked hard to convince him to change his mind and avoid making a big mistake. But LCDR Lindland's words struck particularly hard. The VA-75 operations officer felt that he himself had committed to a naval career and that he should meet his obligations. But McFarland felt Lindland respected his views, too. Finally, yet again acknowledging the importance of the crew concept, McFarland talked to his pilot, LT Ruland. No one could change his mind. In the end, on 15 August, Earnest accepted the B/N's wings.[71]

"No one really looks down on him for making that decision," LTJG Warren wrote home about McFarland's actions, adding that, after all, he "stuck with it for quite a while."[72] But not everyone shared Warren's sentiments. To meet his sortie requirements, CDR Earnest made McFarland the squadron duty officer for the next few days, freeing up a pilot or B/N to fly. For at least four days, McFarland answered the phones. LT Mullins, for one, resented his continuing presence after he had rejected the unit's core mission, and they exchanged sharp words several times. McFarland left *Saratoga* a few days later.[73]

No other Puncher pilot or B/N turned in his wings in August. But a few already had developed reputations for downing aircraft. All carrier aviators could refuse a plane they considered to be unsafe for the kind of mission they planned to fly. Some gripes—engine or hydraulics system malfunctions or inoperative radios, for example—made the decision an easy one. According to squadron practice, anything less than the minimum requirements for systems availability—a stable table for the INS, search radar, and VDI, plus radar altimeter and ECM gear—did not satisfy standards for a "mission ready" aircraft for a night sortie into RP VI-B. But pilots and B/Ns also understood that the decision to down a plane might be shaped by situational factors. A crew that rejected an aircraft considered unacceptable for a night mission near Haiphong might well fly that same plane on a daylight strike into RP II or for close air support under FAC control in South Vietnam when they did not need systems to drop their ordnance. In practice, some aggressive pilots and B/Ns pushed the limits of safety by flying aircraft in less-than-acceptable shape on nearly any mission that came their way. Most others followed basic squadron and airwing safety standards but made their decisions on a case-by-case basis. A few, however, seemed to prefer a very literal interpretation of the standard operating procedures and downed any aircraft that did not meet 100 percent of established performance requirements. In every case, maintenance logs recorded each gripe, and by August, the enlisted men who tried hard to keep the planes in the air noticed when certain names appeared with increasing frequency. While strapping LTJG Fuller into his ejection seat, one of VA-75's troubleshooters—Aviation Electronics Technician Third Class A. Whitcomb, who had worked in the B/N's branch shop—surprised him by asking bluntly if there was any truth to rumors questioning the courage of one Puncher crew.[74]

Unfortunately for any man tarred with this perception, the line period's heavy sortie load genuinely had begun to wear on the squadron's airplanes. Indeed, the Sunday Punchers launched their entire assigned mission schedule on only two days during the whole line period. On 30 July alone, a rash of deck and air aborts limited the squadron to flying only eight of its thirteen scheduled A-6A sorties. On 15 August, the squadron flew only five of its scheduled eight A-6A hops, and three days later, only seven of ten. A-6B performance became spottier, too. On eleven of the twenty-six flying days during this line period, the squadron failed to meet the small number of A-6B missions assigned to it; indeed, on 10 August, only two of the six scheduled A-6B missions launched, and the next day only one of three. Each aircraft possesses unique quirks, but A-6Bs had more than their share. Wiring diagrams in technical manuals rarely resembled the reality a technician faced. Worse, the squadron had only two enlisted men with specific experience working on A-6Bs, and one rotated home mid-cruise, leaving only Aviation Electronics Technician Second Class Tim Simpson to carry the bulk of the responsibility for the rest of the cruise.[75] Only tanker availability remained reasonably consistent. The squadron met—or missed by only one—its KA-6D requirements on every flying day but one.[76]

The concerns that first surfaced in 1965 about the A-6's lack of durability had never entirely disappeared. Over the years, in annual command histories, Intruder squadrons invariably saved their strongest language or most colorful prose to address their maintenance concerns. In summary comments following its 1969 combat cruise aboard *Coral Sea,* for instance, VA-35's command history noted of its aircraft, "Built into [them] were maintenance problems, which, if one did not retain a sense of humor, could cause the most dedicated and professional maintenance expert to become disenchanted."[77]

Over time, raw numbers and statistics revealed a pattern. VA-35 reported that during its first line period in 1969, the average number of "full up" aircraft at the start of daily flight operations numbered five; by the end of the day, the total dipped to two.[78] In 1970, VA-85 reported launching 41.9 percent of its sorties during one line period with full-up systems with a decline to 39 percent upon recovery. The squadron history officer noted, "These figures are a considerable improvement over previous line periods." Just two line periods later, however, the percentage of full-up systems had dipped to 35.8 percent; for the entire cruise, the systems reliability of the squadron's aircraft hit 39.2 percent.[79] In VA-165 that same year, at one point in their combat cruise they could count only 31.5 percent of its systems as "full up" on launch, and only 25.6 percent remained "up" on return.[80]

Even as he tried to increase the pressure on North Vietnam, RADM Christiansen understood the problems all his A-6 squadrons faced. As he reflected years later, "Jesus Christ himself couldn't keep a squadron of A-6As up."[81] While VA-75 did not preserve extensive maintenance data in its 1972 command history as required, extant records of VA-196 that also served in Westpac that year at least can suggest the dimensions of the continuing problem. At the start of its 1971–72 combat cruise, VA-196 began with "a full up systems concept, i.e., only full up systems aircraft left the ship." But by the end of its December 1971 and January 1972 line period, the squadron relaxed its systems requirements to a "mission-capable concept" that allowed more planes to fly, but also—as a consequence of their increased use—resulted in an overall decrease of systems availability. Late in the cruise, only 21.3 percent of A-6As landed with full systems; a modified full system parameter, requiring only search radar, INS, computer, and VDI, increased the percentage to only 35.2 percent. By contrast, systems statistics for the KA-6D showed a full systems rate of 81.0 percent, probably because it lacked the ECM gear and the sophisticated technology of the A-6A and A-6B.

On its subsequent redeployment in late 1972, the squadron's full systems rates showed significant improvement at first. In October 1972, 51.6 percent of VA-196's A-6As landed with an operative full system. It dipped to 46 percent at the end of the second line period. By the end of December, however, it returned to 50 percent. The report remains suspiciously silent, however, on whether the maintenance officers used the "full up" concept or resorted to the "mission-capable concept" to reach these numbers.[82] Still, if the navigation and weapons system at the core of the A-6 mission could only be counted on 50 percent of the time after seven years of experience in a combat environment—and anecdotal evidence from VA-75 suggests that the Sunday Punchers did not enjoy this high a rate—A-6 pilots and B/Ns had legitimate reason to raise concerns about it.

Additionally, much of the longstanding problem related not merely to durability of the aircraft but to the supply chain required to support it. As late as 1970, VA-165 summarized the continuing issue, reporting that it had "experienced the same maintenance difficulties as reported by other A-6 squadrons deployed to WESTPAC. Supply support remains the major problem that must be solved. . . . From a maintenance standpoint, a successful deployment requires timely action at all supporting levels on squadron-supplied usage data."[83] Cannibalization rates—using parts from hard-down aircraft to fill short-term needs—remained unacceptably high.

Finally, in August, CDR Earnest made an official report to CAG Bordone about his squadron's need for better supply and technical support to keep his airplanes flying. He, XO Greene, and LT Hudson all had briefed the airwing staff on the supply and maintenance issues most troubling VA-75, but the problems continued. Bordone appreciated Earnest's "aggressive pursuit and tenacity to provide full-up system aircraft," and he knew it troubled VA-75's skipper to inform him that, without drastic changes in the resupply of critical spare parts and increased technical support for the A-6's navigation and weapons system, he could not guarantee his squadron's continued readiness.[84]

VA-75 did not stand alone in this concern. All squadrons aboard *Saratoga* shared the Sunday Punchers' maintenance crisis. The VAW-123 command historian described the August line period as a "maintenance horror show." Indeed, "the supply support monster was enraged by our continual demands and responded by devouring our meager assets into his system." Only an exchange of key parts with the two other VAW squadrons on the line and 167 separate cannibalization actions kept that squadron's aircraft flying. If they had not been able to find short-term solutions, the critically important E-2Bs "could have gone a few days without flying."[85] VF-31, too, for the first time during the cruise, not only had to keep a "grossly cannibalized 'parts bird'" to get parts for fixable aircraft, but also, by the end of the line period, forced its mechanics to remove critical parts from any planes they could not fix quickly to repair those that could be kept in the air.[86]

CDR Earnest's message at this time sent a ripple of concern up and down the chain of command.[87] He made his point clearly enough, however, and the JOs who linked high systems-availability rates to their ability to do their best work respected him for taking a stand. LT Pyle, years later after he had commanded his own squadron, looked back at CDR Earnest's action as one of the times he felt most proud of the skipper.[88] While Earnest dealt with his superiors, CDR Greene and LT Hudson devoted hours to finding solutions.

The maintenance problem could not be resolved overnight, and VA-75 still had missions to fly. Increased sortie rates against a stiffening resistance presented the hard-pressed maintenance crews with battle damage to repair, in addition to routine gripes. A flyable aircraft hit too badly to be repaired aboard *Saratoga* had to go to Cubi. On 14 August, LT Bruce Cook and LTJG Swigart flew an armed recce against a target in RP III. As Cook pulled off the target, Swigart saw fuel streaming from the right wing and asked his pilot if he had turned on the fuel dumps. When Cook replied that he had not, Swigart informed him that they had been hit. Indeed, when they returned to the carrier, they found a two-inch hole in their wing. That hole could be patched, but another round had cracked a wing spar that could only be repaired by the beach detachment.[89]

Not all of the squadron's increased operational tempo could be blamed on command decisions from Washington, the North Vietnamese, the pressure of weather, or problems in keeping aircraft ready to launch. USS *America*, *Saratoga*'s fellow East Coast carrier, had reentered the Gulf of Tonkin on 10 August for its second period on the line, and a series of mistakes quickly convinced RADM Christiansen to send it off the line for a few days to review procedures and correct problems. During *America*'s brief absence, *Saratoga* and the other carriers on the line picked up much of its mission load.

On 15 and 16 August, *Saratoga* switched briefly to the midnight-to-noon schedule. Bad weather and heavy winds hampered recovery on 16 August, and LT Lankford and LCDR Schram took up an extra tanker to refuel planes waiting to trap. They dispensed all they had to give and more—they had only 2,500 pounds left—and lined up for fuel from the KA-6D sent to relieve them. Then, the RA-5C in front of them damaged the relief tanker's refueling basket. Lankford simply could not plug into the once-round opening that now looked like a half moon. Lankford and Schram prepared to eject, but a final attempt to plug into the damaged basket succeeded. During the refueling process, however, JP-5 first went into the wing tanks, not into the nearly empty main tank, and, once again, Lankford and Schram prepared to swim. Fortunately LCDR Lindland, monitoring the situation from the ship, radioed Lankford to turn on his wing dump

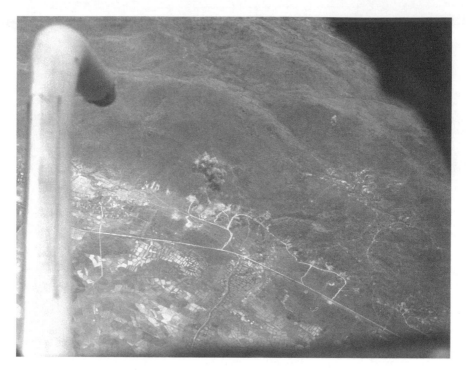

LTJG John Fuller took this photo from his bombardier-navigator's seat at the start of his pilot's ordnance drop. The target of this two-plane daytime recce in mid-August was a suspected truck park hidden in trees. The puff of gray smoke in the center of the frame denotes the detonation of the bombs dropped by the flight lead on the mission. The distinctive bent refueling probe of the A-6 is visible on the left edge of the photo. (John R. Fuller Collection)

switch. He did, and the needle on the fuel gauge showed his main tank beginning to fill. Even the experienced Lankford admitted, "I didn't know that trick."[90]

CVW-3 needed all its aircraft as it prepared to launch three alpha strikes for 17 August. Inclement weather diverted two of them scheduled to hit targets in RP III to alternate targets in RP II. Only the third alpha, against targets near Phu Ly in RP IV, came off as planned. LTs Anderson and Hart delivered the squadron's four-millionth pound of ordnance, as part of the Phu Ly strike.[91]

The talk of the ready room that day, however, centered not on ordnance but on a SAR effort near Nam Dinh. VA-37's LCDR Dale V. Raebel and LT Edward A. Lyons, assigned initially as Iron Hands for one of the cancelled alphas, diverted to protect one of *Saratoga*'s RA-5Cs overflying the Hourglass region. About fifteen miles inland, Raebel and Lyons both heard SAM launch and guidance signals, but the overcast skies hid two missiles from them. Both SAMs exploded near the belly of Raebel's aircraft. The pilot tried to maintain control, but eight miles from the water—less than two minutes from feet wet—his plane pitched nose down and spun toward the ground. Raebel ejected, and Lyons spotted his parachute and made contact with him on the ground. SAR efforts began immediately. LT Chisholm and LTJG Petersen flew their A-6B toward the coastline, occasionally probing feet dry to convince the SAM sites to remain silent. Indeed, they fired an AGM-45 at a SAM site near Nam Dinh and stayed on station for 2.7 hours to protect the rescue effort. Lyons ran low on fuel and never found tanking easy, but LT Ruland and LCDR Jackson kept the RESCAP KA-6D steady and helped him plug into the basket.[92] Unlike the rescue of LT Lloyd in early August, however, the SAR effort for LCDR Raebel did not end in success. The search ended at 1845, Saratoga's deck log noting, "Pilot assumed captured by hostile forces."[93] Raebel remained a prisoner of the North Vietnamese until March 1973.

Bad weather continued to limit the airwing's effort to increase pressure on North Vietnam. On 19 August, CAG Bordone, with LCDR Schram as his B/N, led an alpha strike against targets near Hai Duong in RP VI-B. LT Ruland paired with LTJG Fuller to fly on Bordone's wing on the mission. Their ECM gear warned of approaching SAMs, but the heavy cloud deck made them impossible to spot. The A-6As made good hits, though, and all aircraft returned safely.[94]

Inclement weather cancelled a major alpha strike planned against targets near Hanoi later that day, but rather than jettison their ordnance loads and return to the carrier, the strike group turned to the secondary target, the Thai Binh Army Barracks and storage area in RP IV. VA-75 contributed four A-6As to the strike, with CDR Earnest in the lead. The barracks complex contained numerous administrative and training facilities, and the storage area included a number of long warehouses never before hit by American aircraft.

The weather in the target area included a scattered cloud layer at about 8,000 feet with a heavy haze that reduced visibility to about five miles. Mission planners had decided in advance that if the strike force diverted to Thai Binh, it would split into two elements, with LCDR Frederick W. Wright III, the CVW-3 operations officer, leading one against the storage area and CDR Earnest taking all four A-6As against the barracks. Despite heavy AAA fire, all planes delivered their ordnance on target. Sustained fires in the storage area testified to the hits made by LCDR Wright's element. CDR Earnest's element devastated the barracks. Two strings of fourteen Mk20 Rockeye—one dropped by the skipper and the other by LTJG Bryan—ran the full length of the complex and inflicted especially heavy damage.[95]

The next day, 20 August, bad weather actually worked to CVW-3's advantage during a major alpha strike on three targets located close to each other: the Haiphong Military Storage area, the Haiphong Transformer Station, and the Haiphong Bridge over the Ha Ly Canal. VA-75's CDR Bill Greene, his B/N, LCDR

Pieno, and LCDR Bernie Smith of VA-105 planned the mission. In addition to the usual concerns about hitting military targets near densely populated civilian areas, they faced an unusually high MiG threat. Kien An airfield, about five miles from the targets, could support jet aircraft, and recent reconnaissance photos showed the presence of as many as fifteen MiGs.

The weather on the day of the strike featured a thick and layered cloud deck and frequent thunderstorms. A hard rain pelted the flight deck. They considered canceling or diverting to a secondary target but decided to go as planned. The clouds extended up to 20,000 feet—the usual rendezvous altitude over the carrier—so CDR Greene shifted the rendezvous point to a location twenty-five miles away. Thunderstorms over the planned ingress route to the coast-in point near the Do Son peninsula required an in-flight change in the inland navigation route to afford a clear run to the target. Fortunately, to this point, they had met no resistance from the North Vietnamese.[96]

Low scattered clouds partially obscured the target, but the aircraft began to roll in on their release points as planned. Now, desultory AAA fire opened up and a few Fan Song radars painted them, but little more happened. "There was so little reaction that nobody can believe it even now," LT Tolhurst wrote home afterwards. "We really hit the target hard," he added, explaining that "there were five A-6s with 14 five-hundred pound bombs apiece. . . . It was unbelievable, the whole area was just about leveled."[97] Poststrike BDA confirmed that they destroyed 70 percent of the open supplies and numerous small warehouses at the storage area and hit five other large warehouses, among other damage. The single SAM fired at the group missed. The MiG threat proved empty.[98]

From 21 August until the end of air operations on 23 August—the end of the line period—Saratoga's flight deck continued to hum with activity. Even though worsening weather ended alpha strikes after 20 August, the carrier returned to an active noon-to-midnight schedule of one- and two-plane armed recces for 21 and 22 August. Over the last week, VA-75 had begun to fly some of the toughest missions naval aviators in Westpac ever faced: night armed recces to the northeast railway linking Hanoi and China. The North Vietnamese concentrated their air defenses along those tracks. As LCDR Jackson told his wife, "We haven't scheduled the young guys very much for these." Following squadron practice, "the experienced crews, only the experienced crews are doing it."[99]

CDR Earnest and LCDR Jackson flew a harrowing single-plane night mission into that area on 21 August. For a while the skies cleared. Jackson recalled it as "an unusually very bright moonlit night with no clouds." They flew low-level up Route 51 to Bac Ninh, northeast of Hanoi, and along the northeast railway, carrying eight Mk82 Snakeye retarded bombs that could be dropped from 300 to 500 feet and four Mk20 Rockeye. CDR Earnest coasted in at 400 feet and 360 knots. At that speed, their engine noises did not project far ahead of the aircraft, leaving little time for AAA gun crews to react to their presence. At 360 knots, the A-6 also had maximum energy available to ensure maneuverability if they faced a SAM, and that decision paid off when they spotted an SA-2 heading straight for them. They heard no warnings. Only after they spotted it did their missile launch light flash red and the very loud and distinctive "DEEDLE" fill their headsets. Jackson concluded that the optical tracker on the Fan Song F, new technology that could track aircraft down to 300 feet, had found them. CDR Earnest simply took the plane down to 200 feet, and they watched the missile pass 500 to 1,000 feet behind them and fly into the ground. For best effectiveness, the optical tracker required clear skies, and after that mission, as Jackson noted, "we were glad that cloudless bright moonlit nights were few and far between."[100]

LCDR Lindland and LT Lerseth experienced a similar situation on their armed recce against a segment of the northeast railway that same night. Carrying the identical ordnance load as Earnest and Jackson, they charted a course through the envelopes of thirteen active SAM sites, in an area well known for concentrated AAA fire and a significant chance of meeting MiGs in the air. They planned to fly no higher than 400 feet, but to break numerous Fan Song radar lockups, Lindland took his plane to even lower levels than CDR Earnest had, perhaps as low as 150 feet. Poststrike photography verified that they cut the rail line in three places just ten miles from downtown Hanoi.[101]

By the last few days of the line period, many pilots and B/Ns felt physically and emotionally drained. The pace of operations altered their sense of time. "I never know what day of the week it is," LCDR Jackson complained to his family. Dirty laundry piled up outside stateroom doors signified that "tomorrow is Thursday, but that's about the only way we have of knowing what day it is. . . . Every day is like another day out here."[102] In the continuing absence of definitive information about the end of their deployment, some gave in to temporary disillusionment. "We're all going through a pretty rough period now," noted LT Fischer, admitting that "we feel as if we've been gone forever (haven't we?) and have a long way to go yet (and we do!)."[103] Inspired by frequent showings of the movie *Little Big Man,* LT Chisholm admitted to feeling occasionally like a "misplaced Custer" at the Little Big Horn.[104] For LTJG Bill Wardlaw, stress came from two sources—his nonstop duties in the intel shop and his growing worries about the health of his wife, now in her eighth month of a difficult pregnancy. Skipper Earnest finally sent him into Cubi on 19 August, just to give him a chance to call home. When he learned that Jean had been confined to the hospital on total bed rest and that the Red Cross recommended he come home, he returned to *Saratoga* with an even heavier heart.[105]

In bull sessions in staterooms and along Buff Boulevard, the Sunday Punchers continued to fortify themselves with bridge or popcorn or scotch or gin and tried not to make much of a grim reality: Since the start of the deployment, over 10 percent of *Saratoga*'s airwing already had been shot down or failed to return from missions. Some now openly wondered if the high cost produced any worthwhile results. LT John Miller now welcomed the slumber that freed him from thinking too hard about the fruitlessness of his recent efforts. "It was like you were on a treadmill," he later explained, adding that "it seemed as if there was really no end in sight because they weren't giving you the targets that would make a difference."[106] "I wish I could say I understand the situation over here, but I don't," LTJG Petersen wrote home, adding, "We seem to be trying to kill an ant with a sledge hammer, but we're not hitting the ant, we're beating the hell out of the mound."[107] Even squadron heavies harbored doubts. As Kissinger and Le Duc Tho continued to talk, LCDR Jackson declared his readiness to leave "any day they make the decision. It won't break my heart at all."[108] Even CDR Greene admitted, "We are hitting some targets not previously struck [in] downtown Haiphong—but I don't see any value in it all—it's not proving too much and the politics of it all are as sickening as ever."[109]

Still, through it all, they responded to CDR Earnest's reminders that as naval aviators they represented an instrument of diplomacy, one that delivered ordnance over the beach. As professionals, they had an obligation to perform consistently to their best ability. Regardless of their personal views, he reminded them, "it's most important that there be airplanes over the beach dropping bombs every night. That's what we're trying to do."[110] Thus, when their names appeared on the flight schedule, they manned up and they launched.

At the end of air operations against targets in MR I on 23 August, a unique entry in *Saratoga*'s deck log for that day spoke volumes with the addition of one exclamation point: "Commenced transit for Subic Bay, R.P.!"[111] During this line period, VA-75's pilots and B/Ns who made the 1971 Med cruise became *Saratoga* "double centurions"—they had made two hundred traps on the carrier—and many of the more recent arrivals had crossed the one-hundred-trap threshold to become "centurions." LT Wagner reached "triple centurion" status "for fearlessly riding through more than 300 carrier landings including over 100 at night." They enjoyed a candlelight dinner on the transit to Cubi, complete with music from the stewards. CAG Bordone handed out the awards and congratulated them on their efforts.[112] Photographs taken that night, however, show faces more exhausted than exuberant.

Although the timeframe does not parallel *Saratoga*'s line period perfectly, CTF-77's attack sortie count against North Vietnamese targets in August

Exhaustion rather than exuberance marks the faces of these new Saratoga *centurions during ceremonies coming off the line in late August 1972. From left to right: LT Robert M. Chisholm, LT Kenneth L. Pyle, LT Robert A. Tolhurst, Jr., LTJG John J. Swigart, Jr., LTJG David F. Warren, LCDR Richard W. Schram, CDR Charles "M" Earnest, LT Kenneth K. Knapp, LTJG Leslie M. "Sandy" Sanford, Jr., and LTJG Douglas W. Ahrens. (U.S. Navy photograph, Robert M. Chisholm Collection)*

reached 4,746, the highest monthly figure for all of 1972.[113] During their third line period, which included a few days in July, CVW-3 flew a total of 1,373 sorties. VA-75's A-6As flew 222 strike hops, including 46 at night. The A-6Bs flew 94 missions, 28 at night. The KA-6Ds continued to prove their value, flying 271 hops, 99 of them at night. VA-75 launched a total of 559 missions. The airwing delivered 2,439 tons of ordnance, VA-75 alone dropping nearly 1,000 tons. In time, both CVW-3 and VA-75 looked back on this line period as the most active of the entire combat cruise.[114]

Fortunately, they dodged a rough ending. When RADM Christiansen wanted to go to the Philippines before *Saratoga* docked, LCDR Graustein put him in his B/N's seat, with LTs Lankford and Bob Miller flying as escort. Shortly after launch, Graustein handed over the lead to Lankford, who expected the air controllers at Cubi to guide them in on the approach. But the weather once again deteriorated and Cubi's radar went down. When Lankford dipped under the goo to get a fix on his location, he discovered he was nowhere near his destination. Fortunately, he recognized Corregidor below him and led Graustein and the admiral on a low-level route around the coast to the Cubi airstrip. As Lankford later reflected, "I think the Admiral was glad to climb out of the right seat."[115]

Saratoga moored at the starboard side of the Leyte pier at Subic Bay at 1755 on 24 August.[116] The sailors welcomed their break, but recent monsoons limited entertainment options. "Nothing like leaving a combat zone for a little R&R in a disaster area," LT Chisholm wrote home.[117] Many went to Olongapo, of course, but LT Jim Hudson lured a number of the junior officers to a firing range to try their hand at skeet shooting.[118] With little fanfare, LTJG Wardlaw said quick farewells and left for home; CDR Earnest approved his early departure when Wardlaw's replacement—LTJG David H. Radcliff—arrived early.[119] Happiest of all, LTJG Petersen got leave to go home to Utah for three days to meet his six-week-old daughter.

The six Puncher pilots and B/Ns whose wives waited for them in the Philippines got little rest. The spouses had taken advantage of all kinds of bargains, and they had decided to store their purchases on *Saratoga* for transport home. As Nini Lerseth described it, successful shoppers greeted their husbands with, "Hello, I love you. Here!" as they handed over bags and boxes. Some couples went to Baguio, a mountain resort area. Golfers found the course there to be so steep that the players had to use vine ropes—sometimes motorized—to pull them up from one hole to the next. Filipino caddies, always well tipped, earned their pay with generous spots of the sailors' slices and hooks. Others spent time in Manila, enjoying nights on the town that contrasted sharply with the war and life on a carrier on station.[120]

Most of the pilots and B/Ns found their way to the Cubi officers' club, for music and gambling and drinking. The more they imbibed, the darker their moods became. After spending an evening with LCDR Schram, LTJG Fuller entirely lived up to his squadron nickname—"Warmth"—in agreeing with him "that this war is screwed up. Why should we hang our asses out when no one at home really seems to want us to? It seems like they all wish the hell we were somewhere else." The two determined to find something positive in the professional appeal of "experiencing things that no one else but the few that had been through it would be able to comprehend."[121] LCDR Jackson had reached the same conclusion. "I've seen enough and I've done enough out here to last me for a lifetime, and I really don't care if I have to do it again," he admitted. But he quickly added, "I don't think I would give anything for the experiences I've learned out here," noting that "there's no substitute for actually being there and actually doing it."[122]

ADM Zumwalt arrived in the Philippines in late August, visiting *Saratoga* briefly. A flight deck parade—never before held during this combat cruise—took place on 27 August.[123] VA-75's Aviation Maintenance Administrationman Second Class Joe Raubar presented the CNO with a model of an A-6.[124] As LT Fischer reported, the admiral "said he and Pres[ident Nixon] are proud of us."[125] That was all fine and good, but as LTJG Fuller noted, the admiral hedged when they asked him their most pressing question: "Unfortunately, he could not say when we would be going home."[126]

CHAPTER EIGHT

"Got an Ace Hit"

ADM Zumwalt had more on his mind during his eight-day visit to Westpac than simply gladhanding with his sailors. A hands-on CNO, he had decided he needed to see for himself the state of morale and readiness in the Seventh Fleet. He visited not just *Saratoga,* but *Kitty Hawk, America,* and *Midway,* as well as eleven escort ships, three amphibious ships, three auxiliaries, and the facilities at Cubi Point and Subic Bay. He even made a brief stop in Olongapo. He returned from Westpac profoundly disturbed.

Operation LINEBACKER had required the deployment of a substantial percentage of the U.S. Navy's assets. Nearly one-quarter of the entire service now participated in the military effort in Southeast Asia, including six of the Navy's sixteen carriers, 30 percent of its cruisers and destroyers, and 41 percent of all its fighter and attack squadrons. As the planned reduction-in-force took effect, the percentage of deployed squadrons would increase even as the overall size of the Navy shrank. Longer overseas tours increased the strain on ships, equipment, and sailors. Nearly 16 percent of the enlisted men had served at sea almost continuously for more than four years, and retention rates reflected their discontent. Indeed, he noted, "the manning level in PacFlt is marginal and the trend is down," and many vacancies in key skills remained unfilled. VA-75 felt the effects in their own enlisted ranks. As sailors routinely rotated home or cross-decked to other ships at the end of their assignment aboard *Saratoga,* their replacements—if their slots were filled—often lacked necessary technical know-how. Ironically, many rated sailors arriving from stateside A-6 squadrons now knew more about maintaining the new A-6E than the specific skills required to keep the older A-6As and A-6Bs flying.

Zumwalt also noted, "Almost 50 percent of our pilots are on their second or third combat deployments; 10 percent of the pilots in four squadrons aboard USS *Midway* are on their fourth such deployment." VA-75's situation did not reflect Zumwalt's gloomy description. Only the XO, CDR Greene, now served on his fourth tour in Westpac. But within a month, the Sunday Punchers, too, greeted far more veterans than nugget pilots and B/Ns into its ranks.[1]

Indeed, just before *Saratoga* steamed out of the Philippines on 1 September, the squadron welcomed aboard its second four-tour combat veteran. LCDR

Harold W. King, who had enlisted near the end of the Korean War, first saw the Gulf of Tonkin in 1965 when he served in A-3s on *Coral Sea* as a member of VAH-2. He had returned in 1967 to fly A-6s with VA-165 for two consecutive combat cruises on USS *Ranger*. His detailer had told King at that time that the Navy considered him "combat limited" and would not assign him for yet another Westpac tour. He then served for several years as an instructor with the East Coast RAG, training many of the Sunday Punchers' junior pilots and B/Ns. If he called them "King-trained men," he meant it as high praise indeed.

King received orders to join VA-75 soon after the squadron's emergency recall. When he delivered one of the A-6Bs to Westpac in late May, he asked CDR Earnest to respect his "combat limited" status and send him back to Oceana to oversee squadron affairs there. Earnest agreed—he needed no more senior officers then—but added two qualifiers: If the war heated up or the squadron lost personnel, he would have to call upon King. Now VA-75 needed a B/N to fill LTJG McFarland's slot, and in mid-August, King received orders to depart for Southeast Asia within forty-eight hours.

King quickly learned to his dismay that the "combat limited" rule no longer applied. He griped, of course, but he accepted the orders, asking only for a brief delay before reporting so he might attend the graduation of his oldest son from Navy recruit training. His request approved, he put on his rarely worn choker whites to accept a special invitation to watch the ceremonies from the reviewing stand. King's arrival in Westpac in late August, while welcome, seemed to validate the truth of a rumor the Sunday Punchers had heard—that back at Oceana, junior pilots and B/Ns in the A-6 RAG who received orders to Westpac had begun to refuse them. Even worse, they did so at no apparent detriment to their careers. Thus, veterans such as King had to take up the slack.[2]

The brief respite in the Philippines ended on 1 September when *Saratoga* left Subic Bay at 0600. The Sunday Punchers now headed out for their fourth line period. LT Tolhurst hoped "it will be as good for us as the others have been with no lost aircraft or crews. With the experience we have all gained this should be an attainable goal."[3]

For a few days, at least, the release on 2 September of three downed American aviators by the North Vietnamese ignited a small spark of optimism that this action presaged more serious peace talks. At the very least, it triggered a very brief cessation of bombing north of the 20th parallel, keeping dangerous sites around Hanoi and Haiphong off the target list. LTJG Warren welcomed the restrictions to some degree, jesting that "they should release a couple every few days and then we wouldn't have [to go] north of 20 again."[4]

No additional POW releases followed, however, and *Saratoga* headed for the Gulf of Tonkin. Once again, complications slowed the airwing's return to active air operations. A virus picked up in the Philippines swept through the crew. According to LT Fischer, "1/2 of ships company and 1/2 of Air Wing are down with the flu."[5] The illness hit the VA-75's pilots and B/Ns particularly hard while ashore, and CDR Earnest, LTs Knapp, Anderson, and Hart, and LTJG Sanford, among others, still suffered from at least a minor touch of the ailment. Some flew anyway, but the persistence of the illness over the next three weeks compromised scheduling and made more work for those who stayed healthy.

Deteriorating weather also slowed airwing operations. September marked the start of the rainy season, and the Sunday Punchers already expected to fly fewer alpha strikes and far more one- or two-aircraft missions, especially at night or in bad weather. The prospect of flying the latter missions excited those who appreciated the capabilities of the A-6 navigation and weapons systems. "It would be kind of neat" to have a few days of heavy rains "so we could have the value of the A-6 recognized by everyone on board," LT Tolhurst wrote home. "Most of the guys feel this way," he noted, and they really wanted "to show the full system concept to everyone and how well we can make it work. It really makes us feel proud of our airplane, our ability in it, and our professionalism." He hoped that his wife did not consider him "a nut," but he remained certain that "deep down I know you understand how we feel, and why we think we are the best squadron over here."[6]

If RADM Christiansen had his way, VA-75 would get that opportunity. As *Saratoga* approached Yankee Station, Typhoon Elsie also took aim on the region. Christiansen hoped to use the storm to his advantage. Knowing that the North Vietnamese used typhoons to cover the southward movement of troops and truck convoys, the admiral decided to try a quick end run around the storm to launch strikes in the southernmost route packs at a time when the North Vietnamese did not expect them. The element of surprise might result in the destruction of significant amounts of military materiel. Understanding that he needed to find new ways to hit the enemy when the wet season reduced his capability to launch large-scale alpha strikes, he decided to try to catch the North Vietnamese with a full spread of one- and two-plane low-level strikes against key targets.[7]

Christiansen's idea had merit, but at first the squadron did not receive it well. On 2 September, LT Fischer complained that CAG Bordone "tried to launch us in the middle of typhoon ALMOST." Conditions deteriorated so quickly, however, that he finally cancelled the strikes.[8] Typhoon Elsie grounded the entire airwing for two days. The weather finally broke on 4 September.

By the time the skies cleared, the brief bombing halt against targets around Hanoi and Haiphong also had ended. The prisoner release had produced no additional positive results, and it had even stirred up resentment—not gratefulness—at home. Jeane Petersen, increasingly less supportive of the war effort, expressed deep dismay that the North Vietnamese had released only three POWs. Initial reports in the Salt Lake City newspaper suggested that perhaps fifty or one hundred might come home. "I should have known better," she wrote. "Those dirty bastards make me sick." While happy for the families of the three released men, she still found it sad that two of them had been recent captures. Thinking of the first Navy POW shot down in August 1964, she wondered, "What about [LTJG Everett] Alvarez? Is he still alive?"[9]

On 5 September, *Saratoga* worked on an abbreviated schedule of single-aircraft armed recces in RPs III, IV, and VI-B. Finally, RADM Christiansen's attempt to surprise the North Vietnamese bore fruit. Two of VA-75's A-6As embarked on a daylight low-level mission against the Thai Binh army barracks in RP IV, with CAG Bordone and LCDR Jackson in one aircraft and LCDR Graustein and LT Mullins in the other. They selected an ingress route based on good visual checkpoints that they could spot easily even in marginal weather, crossed the beach at fifty feet, maneuvered independently to acquire their individual targets, and dropped on them. Most interesting, they achieved tactical surprise. Coming in under the weather, they met no opposition on either their ingress or egress.[10] LT Mullins described the enemy response as "light" in his personal log, and he gave this mission a 20 percent pucker factor, due more to weather and low-level flying than to enemy resistance.[11] Other VA-75 crews met with similar results on their own missions.

Improving weather reports for 6 September convinced CTF-77 to resume alpha strikes. *Saratoga* launched a 34-plane coordinated strike, split into two components, against two closely situated targets outside Haiphong. CAG Bordone, as strike lead, planned to take four A-6As and two sections of A-7s to hit the Kien An airfield and crater its runways. The plan called for the second strike component, consisting of A-7s and F-4s, to roll in against specified targets nearer to Haiphong. Since the entire area rested well within multiple SAM envelopes, planners added an A-6B and A-7 Iron Hands to support the strike force.

On the morning of 6 September, the rain stopped, the seas calmed, and much of the cloud deck broke up. Still, layers of scattered overcast remained at 5,000 and 8,000 feet. Intelligence briefers reminded all crews that North Vietnamese air defenders liked to use cloud cover as a shield to obscure the launch of SAMs, giving those in the cockpits limited warning and reaction time.[12]

Despite this warning, when compared with many other strikes they had flown in RP VI-B, this mission seemed relatively straightforward. The targets lay only ten miles inland, and the planned approach from the southeast minimized the time the strike force would remain exposed to North Vietnamese air defenses. By now, VA-75's pilots and B/Ns knew ingress and egress routes, the most recent location of mobile SAM sites and AAA batteries, and various navigation points in the area. Indeed, for the first time, LT Lerseth chose not to prepare a specific mission chart. During the crew brief, tradition more than fear inspired him to emit his usual loud whimper upon the naming of the target. Sometimes, that whine genuinely represented heartfelt feelings, but on 6 September, he noted, "it *was* just a performance. I had good vibes about this mission."[13]

This was a big day for LT George Hiduk—"The Duck"—who had continued to fly mostly tanker hops during the August line period, just as he had done since joining VA-75 in July. The mission against Kien An airfield marked his first alpha strike. As the briefing broke up, Lerseth slung an arm around Hiduk's shoulder and warned him that it was duck season in North Vietnam. The pilot's own laughs convinced Lerseth that this "Duck" was ready to fly. As they manned up, no one could have guessed that the squadron's collective memory of the rest of the fourth line period would be overshadowed by 6 September's events.

As strike lead, CAG Bordone, flying with LCDR Pieno, flew in "Ace One." On Bordone's wing as "Ace Two" flew LT Tolhurst, paired as usual with LTJG Ahrens. In "Ace Three," LCDR Lindland served as alternate strike lead, with LT Lerseth in the right seat of his aircraft. On Lindland's wing in "Ace Four" flew LT Hiduk, with LT Bob Miller. Each of these four aircraft carried eight Mk83s—1,000-pound bombs—to crater runways. LT Chisholm and LTJG Vance flew the A-6B in support of the strike.

Beginning at about 1300, the launch and rendezvous went smoothly, and the entire strike group proceeded at about 13,000 to 15,000 feet to its familiar coast-in point near the Do Son Peninsula. Various North Vietnamese radars picked them up, standard practice by now. Chisholm and Vance tried to get a good lock on one of the signals, but they took care not to fire in haste. LCDR Lindland, informing them during the mission brief that the carrier had begun to run low on AGM-78s, had encouraged them to bring back any STARMs for which they could not find a good target.

When the strike group went feet dry, the planes picked up speed as they descended to roll-in altitude. Due to the nearness of their targets to the coast, they only needed about one minute to reach the roll-in point after they crossed the beach. In the A-6As, each B/N flicked on his master arm switch and informed his pilot that he had a hot pickle. Signals from Fan Song radars from the area's SAM batteries grew louder now. LCDR Pieno felt certain they painted his lead aircraft, and CAG Bordone began mild evasive maneuvers. The other A-6As, each in its proper place in the formation, followed his lead. The Iron Hand A-7s attached to the strike group launched AGM-45s to shut down SAM sites as the attack aircraft began their run.

While the portion of the strike force hitting targets near Haiphong rolled in as planned, a lingering cloud layer obscured the airfield at Kien An, and CAG

Bordone held his element at roll-in altitude. They swung out in an arc so that he could acquire the target visually. This delay in hostile air space violated accepted practice. LT Tolhurst, among others, later admitted "we probably were pushing our own safety rules" by continuing the mission under those circumstances.[14] Very soon they heard the distinctive loud "DEEDLE" of a Fan Song radar controlling a SAM's flight.

Finally, CAG Bordone located the target, began his attack, and called, "Ace One is in." LT Tolhurst, in Ace Two, followed. At that moment, as he later explained, an excited voice on the radio interjected, "break hard left, SAMs below you." LCDR Pieno spotted two, but Tolhurst and Ahrens did not see them. LT Lerseth in Ace Three could not find them either, but he popped off a couple of bundles of chaff, just in case.

Indeed, two SAMs now headed for the A-6As rolling in on Kien An, both tracking well. They missed Ace One. Tolhurst and Ahrens in Ace Two had just started to pull up after dropping their bombs when the SAMs flew right under their plane. One detonated nearby. Tolhurst wrote his wife the next day, "We felt the concussion . . . very lightly," but, in truth, the blast caused Ace Two to bank sharply.[15] That first SAM exploded just under the tail of Ace Three as LCDR Lindland and LT Lerseth began their roll-in. The plane jolted hard, and Lerseth heard someone on the radio yelling, "Got an Ace hit." After the thump and the radio call, he looked to the right and saw a hole about two feet wide at midwing, spewing jet fuel. He informed Lindland of the damage immediately, then suggested they turn toward the coast. Lindland pickled off his bombs, then turned toward feet wet. Only a few seconds had elapsed.

Now they felt a second big thump. The second SAM also detonated nearby, and their A-6A nosed over into a steep dive. It shook so violently that Lerseth could not read his instruments. Ace Three had caught on fire. CDR C. E. Armstrong of VA-37 radioed to them to eject, but they never heard his call. Ace Three lost all hydraulics, too, and the aircraft's flight controls failed. Lindland fought to control the plane, even as it continued its steep dive. Then he ejected.

"It is a real wake-up call when you find yourself all alone in an A-6 aimed directly at the earth," Lerseth noted, "particularly if you are in the B/N seat." Lindland probably had made an ejection call to his B/N, but the intercom no longer worked so Lerseth never heard it. Rejecting the possibility that he could regain control of the plane himself, he too activated his Martin-Baker ejection seat. It seemed to take forever to fire. "They say time flies when you are having fun," he later wrote, but "I can confirm that the opposite is true when things are going to hell."

In the A-6B, LT Chisholm entertained a horrible thought. He and Vance had held their fire as LCDR Lindland had ordered. Finally, they had launched an

AGM-78 at the site apparently responsible for firing the two SAMs at the A-6As. He had seen explosions near the aircraft, but, as he later explained, he did not recognize the bursts as detonating SA-2s. He thought instead about the unique flight path his AGM-78 followed and the amount of time it took to cover a given distance. He concluded, "In my mind, it was our missile. We had just impacted our own aircraft with our own missile."[16] If Chisholm had voiced his concern, Vance could have relieved his anxiety; the B/N had seen the SAM contrails heading toward the strike group.[17]

Shrapnel from the first SAM to hit Ace Three also hit Ace Four. It shattered LT Hiduk's windscreen and tore at least twenty holes in the aircraft. From the B/N's seat, LT Bob Miller saw a bright flash and then watched Hiduk slump over against the left side of the canopy. Miller thought Hiduk had been hit and might even be dead. The Duck merely had leaned to the left to look around the damage to his windscreen, but before he realized that, Miller put out a frantic Mayday call. In the air, confusion reigned.

When CDR Armstrong first called out that an Ace had been hit, Lerseth in Ace Three and Miller in Ace Four each believed the message referred to his own aircraft. Even if they had understood the reality of the situation, neither had time to make clear to others in the air that shrapnel from one SAM had damaged two planes. At this point, many in the air and aboard Saratoga listening to the radio traffic believed that only one A-6A had been hit, that it was still flying, and that it had headed for the coast. CAG Bordone and LCDR Pieno in Ace One, also believing this to be the case, checked the damage to Ace Four.

At this point, LCDR Gene Tucker of VF-103, the F-4 lead, broke in with "OK, 211's got two good chutes." At that moment, Bordone, Armstrong, and others realized something was not quite right. Bordone asked the damaged A-6A still flying to identify itself. Miller in Ace Four replied with side number 506. The identity of one aircraft now confirmed, Bordone demanded more information about the report of two good chutes. When the F-4 repeated the location as two miles due east of the airfield, it became clear to all concerned that two A-6As—not one—had been hit. And, worse, one of them had gone down.

Bordone immediately sent LT Tolhurst and LTJG Ahrens in Ace Two to the aid of Ace Four. Its severely damaged windscreen prohibited a carrier landing. Thus, Ace Two accompanied Hiduk and Miller to Danang, where they safely landed their damaged aircraft.[18] But Ace Three's crew came to ground much more roughly. Lindland and Lerseth, their parachutes now deployed, did not land in sight of each other. Each man found himself on his own.

Before he landed, Lerseth looked east toward the coast to orient himself and to assess his chances for rescue. But he quickly realized he had more immediate concerns. The force of the ejection shattered his left femur, fractured both his left tibia and fibula, and hyperextended ligaments in his left knee. He also suffered a compression fracture of the right tibial plateau, point fractures of both elbows, and a dislocated left elbow. Both hands bled from cuts suffered as he ejected through the aircraft's canopy. In addition, he had lost his helmet, oxygen mask, glasses, gloves, boots, sidearm, kneeboard, radios, and survival vest. The force of the ejection also may have deafened him temporarily. He floated down toward a river until a last-minute gust of wind carried him into a rice paddy.

He saw an F-4 make a pass overhead, heading west, and he rightly assumed that the pilot had begun to consider attempting a rescue. He also understood that in this highly populated and heavily defended area, a SAR effort carried significant risk. Still, he tried to get the RESCAP's attention; positive knowledge of a live aviator on the ground in a specific location shaped decisions to press or call off a rescue effort. He tried to make sure the beeper in his seat pan had activated. In so doing, he tugged on a lanyard, which produced a quickly inflating one-man life raft. "Getting a life raft instead of an operating beeper was the final insult," Lerseth recalled, adding, "I don't know why, but I laughed." The F-4 made a second pass, so low that Lerseth could see the details on the crewmen's helmets. Tucker flew at such a low altitude that he had to relay messages to LT Art Pitman and LTJG Paul Pencikowski, who sent on the information to *Saratoga* from a second F-4 flying overhead.[19]

Lerseth could take heart from knowing that his comrades would try their best. Already, the Office of Naval Research had begun to collect data on aircrew rescues. The evidence supported two factors that dictated "that every aircrewman downed in combat be given an optimum chance for survival and rescue. The first is moral; the second is economic." No one doubted the moral obligation of attempting to rescue a downed comrade. But the economic reasons strongly reinforced the responsibility to do all possible to retrieve them. "The replacement costs are very high," the final report noted, adding that the sum "for a Lieutenant Commander flying in Vietnam operations exceeds one million dollars." The report did not include the specific dollar figure for a lieutenant.[20]

Just the same, LT Lerseth feared that "they would try too hard to make something happen that couldn't."[21] Angry Vietnamese voices came nearer and nearer. Rifle bullets whizzing through the rice paddy were trying to kill him or force him to reveal his hiding place. Fortunately most of the shots hit his collapsed parachute about twenty yards away. He plunged his holster into the sticky mud and finally decided to draw their attention rather than die from a random AK-47 round. Very quickly a cluster of North Vietnamese armed with a great variety of weapons surrounded him. A young boy slashed his face with a broken bottle, then began to kick his mangled left leg. Older men in khaki pulled the boy away, stripped Lerseth of his flight suit, and carried him out of the rice paddy. His left leg dangled in constant movement, every jolt inflicting excruciating pain. "The procession out of that rice paddy was the worst experience of my life," Lerseth later explained, admitting, "I would gladly have blown myself away if I could have put a hand on a weapon. I really wanted to die."

But he did not die. He could not even make himself pass out. His captors first took him to a hut. There, an older woman seemed empathetic and, when Lerseth made drinking motions to convey thirst, she brought him some very hot tea. Later that day, a small truck picked him up and took him to a Haiphong hospital.

The same F-4 crew that had made the initial call confirming two good chutes also reported that they saw both men alive on the ground and running. This could not be true, of course—Lerseth could not stand, let alone walk. If they had spotted a running man in a flight suit, they saw LCDR Lindland, whose actions after ejection on 6 September remain shrouded in mystery. While Lerseth had his injuries tended to at the hospital in Haiphong, he endured his first interrogation. They asked him about his pilot. When he said he knew nothing about Lindland's whereabouts, one showed him a kneeboard card, partly stained with blood. One young guard whispered to him that the man who carried the card had died. Lerseth considered the possibility that the guard had been told to lie. He simply did not want to believe that LCDR Lindland could be dead.[22]

The first reports to reach *Saratoga* confused VA-75's pilots and B/Ns who had not taken part on that mission. The first message that LT Ruland heard suggested that only Ace Four—Hiduk and Miller's aircraft—had been hit but remained flyable, with no reference to Lindland and Lerseth's plane at all.[23] LT Hart heard first that both Ace Three and Ace Four were down, then only Ace Four flown by Hiduk and Miller, and then finally the clarification that the downed plane really was Ace Three.[24] The report of two aviators running on the ground provided the only glimmer of good news.

Word of a downed aircraft swept through the squadron quickly. LT Jerry Mullins passed the word to LTJG Petersen, Lerseth's roommate. LT Ruland told his own roommate LTJG Fuller, "We lost a plane." Fuller asked, "What do you mean?" Ruland repeated his statement, and Fuller asked again, "What do you mean?" Then Ruland clarified, "We lost a crew." As Fuller later recalled, "I think I knew what he meant from the start but didn't want to accept it."[25] Most of the Puncher pilots and B/Ns went to their ready room for the latest news. Others wandered to IOIC in search of information.

The news quickly filtered down into the squadron's work spaces as well. Everyone—from Lindland and Lerseth's plane captain to the sailors who worked in the shop where Lerseth served as branch officer—sought all the news they could get. After initial garbled reports of a plane down, hope soared with the news of chutes sighted and beepers heard. But just as quickly, their

LCDR Donald F. Lindland, VA-75's operations officer, ejected from his SAM-damaged A-6A on 6 September 1972. The U.S. Navy declared him "missing in action." (Everett W. Foote Collection)

spirits sank as word spread that the crew had landed in an area inaccessible to SAR helicopters. CDR Earnest called no meeting and issued no formal statements immediately. That left individual chiefs to decide whether or not to talk to their men about the reality of loss in wartime. A few did, while others did not. Most simply controlled their emotions and continued to do their jobs. But when it became clear that they had lost a crew—as Chief Pittman recalled—"tears were shed."[26]

As each crew on that strike recovered aboard the carrier, CDR Earnest followed them to IOIC to hear the debriefs. When LT Tolhurst and LTJG Ahrens trapped aboard after escorting Ace Four to Danang, CDR Earnest immediately pulled them aside to get their report. LT Chisholm also talked to them after visiting IOIC for any information he could get about the damage to Ace Three and Ace Four. When he learned from Tolhurst and Ahrens that Hiduk's aircraft sustained most of its damage on its underside, he felt great relief. Given the AGM-78's unique up-then-down trajectory, if Chisholm's missile had impacted on the aircraft, the crew of Ace Two should have seen significant damage to the canopy and upper half of the plane.[27]

The Sunday Punchers faced a situation they happily had avoided until now. There was much to do, and most of it had to happen quickly. Skipper Earnest finally held an emergency AOM to update everybody about the knowns and unknowns. He repeated the RESCAP report of two deployed parachutes and two runners on the ground and surmised that Lindland and Lerseth most likely had become prisoners. But he warned the men against speculating further about what had happened in the air or about the fate of their friends on the ground when writing home about the incident. "Just the names of people and where they were hit is all the CO wants us to say, and even then he wants us to wait until the next of kin are notified before writing names," LT Tolhurst wrote home, despite the warnings. He also admitted, however, that the skipper's admonition "makes sense so please don't tell anyone about my last letter or this one except that Don & Rog were hit south of Haiphong."[28]

Earnest's responsibilities had just begun. The flight schedule had to be revised to fill the gaps made by the loss of Ace Three and the diversion to Danang of Ace Four. Ironically, this duty usually fell to LCDR Lindland, who, as operations officer, made required schedule adjustments. CDR Earnest immediately named LCDR Graustein to take over Lindland's duties. The new ops officer had to assign crews to the 15-minute tanker alert originally given to Hiduk and Miller from 1630 until 1815 and to take their tanker at 1815. He reassigned the armed recce initially given to Lindland and Lerseth, scheduled to launch at 2000, to LT John Miller and LTJG Sanford. That mission ultimately had to be scrubbed when Miller became so ill with the flu that he had to take himself off the flight schedule for a week.[29] A lieutenant commander had to take Lindland's watch in the Carrier Air Traffic Control Center (CATCC) at 0115 the next morning.[30]

The contents of the two downed aviators' safes and staterooms had to be inventoried and packed up. LCDR Jackson did this for Lindland, his roommate. LTJG Petersen, with LCDR King's help, cataloged Lerseth's property. Then they forwarded the lists to LCDR Pieno, the Administrative Department head and B/N in Ace One when Ace Three went down. He acknowledged that they "did a good job . . . considering it was something very new to us."[31]

Most important, CDR Earnest had to make sure that Bobbe Lindland and Nini Lerseth knew what had happened to their husbands. He did so through official channels and with personal communications, beginning both processes immediately. He sent official word to MATWING ONE at Oceana so that the Navy could officially notify the aviators' families. Then CDR Earnest took the time to write a personal letter to each wife. He detailed the circumstances of the shootdown, as best he could. He explained that the RESCAP had seen two good chutes and spotted both men alive on the ground. He reported incorrectly in Lerseth's case that he "was mobile." "All indications are that they were captured shortly after ejection," he wrote, and that "their official status is now missing in action."[32]

It would take a few days for those letters to arrive, of course. Official notifications would be made first. In his official casualty report, CDR Earnest included a personal message to CDR Richard A. Zick, commander of MATWING ONE, with a request that CDR Don Boecker—as a personal friend of the Lindlands and an old VA-75 hand—be part of the notification team to deliver the news to Bobbe in Virginia Beach. The skipper related the sighting of two good chutes and reports of both men alive on the ground. "I am listing them as MIA until we get further confirmation but am confident that they were in good health after reaching the ground," he added.[33] Zick, Boecker, and close family friends LCDR Ted and Janet Been went to break the news to the pilot's wife. The Reverend Robert Newland, the local Episcopal priest, arrived soon after. When she saw the assemblage at the door, Bobbe intuitively understood the reason for their visit. She heard them out and then asked two questions: What personal weapons did her husband carry that day? Did anyone make a tape of the mission that caught the radio traffic during the shootdown? She knew that her husband did not want to be captured, and she needed some reassurance that he carried with him the means to resist.[34]

CDR Earnest had included in his message to Zick a few words for his own wife. "These are trying times," he told Minna. It was tough to lose Lindland, "both a professionally outstanding naval officer and a close personal friend," and Lerseth, "his equal in all but experience." He urged her to give Bobbe all assistance she could, thus maintaining "the highest traditions of the cohesive naval family we all belong to."[35] The Lindlands had requested in advance that, in the event of bad news, the squadron wives break with usual practice and call before coming over to the house. Minna Earnest respected that wish, and Lilliane Greene, the XO's wife, called the spouses of the other department heads to activate their telephone trees just to get out the word to the junior officers' wives. Still, when Duddie Graustein and Linda Jackson drove over to the Lindland residence, just to check on their friend, they found the house full of people. Someone had made coffee, while others cleaned up around the house. Bobbe's house "always looked good," Linda recalled, adding, "I don't remember why they were cleaning." Because the pilot and B/N had been listed as "missing in action" and not "killed in action," the mood remained cautiously optimistic, and Bobbe seemed to be "holding it all together."[36] Duddie Graustein admitted that she worried a bit, though, suspecting that her own husband would step into Lindland's job as operations officer and, as a consequence, take even more high-risk missions himself.[37] She did not know that he already had received the assignment.

The wives in Virginia Beach, including Bobbe Lindland, sought every fragment of additional information they could find, and they did not hesitate to talk to friends at Oceana to get the latest news trickling out from the naval air station. But, in those first days, rumors blended with substantiated fact, and confusion reigned. Some had heard from friends in VA-42, for instance, that LT John Miller and LTJG Sanford had flown in Ace Four on LCDR Lindland's wing. The local papers provided little news. On 7 September, the *Virginian-Pilot* carried a North Vietnamese report that its air defenders had "scored glorious victories by downing five U.S. aircraft" on 6 September, including a notice that the self-defense force of Haiphong "downed one A-6 and one F-4 at 1220 and captured the aggressor pilots." But, except for a line about raids on targets "southwest of Haiphong carried out by *Saratoga* pilots," the paper included no specifics about the loss of any VA-75 aircraft.[38] (*Nhan Dan*, another North Vietnamese paper, reported on 7 September the downing of seven American planes the previous day, including one A-6 near Haiphong.[39]) Some of the wives began to bicker about the reliability of the information they received from various friends. When Carol Warren asked her husband for clarification, he verified that Miller and Sanford had not been involved, then added a warning against listening to rumors. "Everybody has their 'sources,'" he wrote, "and 99% of them are *wrong*."[40]

Delivering official notification to Nini Lerseth in Manila proved far more difficult. About noon on 7 September, she, Penny Swigart, and Loretta Lankford went up to the rooftop swimming pool of the Manila Hilton for a swim and lunch, when she received a phone call. As soon as she heard her mother-in-law's quavering voice, she quickly asked, "Are you alright? Is everyone okay at home?" In that moment, Lillian Lerseth realized that Nini did not know what had happened. The Navy had tried to notify her, but LT Lerseth's personnel file did not contain contact information reflecting Nini's decision to go to Manila. Thus, his mother had received the bad news first, and now she dropped the receiver rather than try to talk to her daughter-in-law. Another relative finally picked it up and told her what had happened. With each additional tidbit of news, Nini asked in louder tones, "What?!" Penny and Loretta suspected the worst, and all doubts seemed to disappear when Nini collapsed to the ground in a dead faint.

Penny and Loretta carried her back down to her room. The hotel physician put her under sedation. Deeply shaken as well, Loretta and Penny were still sitting with her when a Navy chaplain finally arrived. His conduct outraged the women. Offering little consolation, he seemed entirely uninterested in helping them. Indeed, he called his office—from Nini's room, and in her presence—to get permission to leave, mumbling, "I'm sorry, good-bye." Nini's roommate, Linda Ahrens, along with Barbara and Diane Miller, returned from a shopping trip about then, learned the news about Lerseth—but not about the damage to the aircraft in which Barbara's own husband had flown—and rallied to Nini's support, as well.

A bit later, a Navy captain posted to the U.S. embassy at Manila arrived to serve as her temporary casualty assistance officer. When it became evident that Nini already knew about her husband's shootdown, he added what little additional information he had gleaned from the message traffic and apologized for the delay in notifying her. Nini held her emotions in check—no hysterical crying, her voice a monotone. In reality, she felt so numb she simply had difficulty expressing herself. As she later related, "I was afraid that if I got really upset that I'd be so gone that I'd never come back."

The officer made it clear that the Navy expected Nini to go back home. At first, she balked. She decided that her departure equated to betraying her husband, abandoning him when he needed her most. She adamantly held to her commitment to stay in Manila. That night, she had a dream that included a representation of a map of Vietnam with her husband's naked body superimposed on it. She interpreted that vision to mean that he was alive, but hurt and vulnerable. Manila "was the closest spot to where he was." If she went home, it would be like "there was nobody to take care of him." But she soon had a change of heart. During those few short days between the time of the emergency recall and the squadron's departure in April, they had discussed this possibility and decided that if he were killed or captured, Nini would take care of his mother and sisters. Since his father had just died in March, Lerseth had worried about the potential impact on his mother of the loss of both a husband and a son.

When she announced her decision to go home, the captain offered to arrange for an official escort. Her first thought centered on her father, a retired Marine

Corps colonel. When that option did not work, she then requested the services of LCDR Grady Jackson, for whom her husband had worked. The captain sent Nini's request to CDR Earnest. After LCDR Lindland's loss, however, Earnest did not feel he could afford to detach another senior officer. He reluctantly turned down the request. Jackson wrote Nini a letter instead, thanking her for thinking of him, and assuring her that her husband had the "strength, wit, and determination" to get through all the challenges he might face.[41]

When informed of the skipper's decision two days later, rather than complain she simply chose a more junior officer to take her home. LTJG Fuller and her husband were good friends, and since Sally Fuller's initial plans to come to Manila to join the other wives had not worked out, Nini decided to give her a few days free from worrying about her husband. Fuller did not know that Nini had asked for him. When CDR Earnest and LCDR Jackson asked him if he would go, he objected at first. He did not consider it fair to ask other B/Ns to pick up his hops, nor did he think it right to force LT Knapp to fly with unfamiliar B/Ns for an extended period of time.[42] Fuller reconsidered when Jackson himself agreed to take all his missions.

On 9 September, Fuller flew to Danang and proceeded to Clark Air Force Base. Nini and Linda Ahrens met him there. Linda had become Nini's stalwart protector, and Fuller found her "alot stronger than one, or at least I, would have thought." Linda, however, just felt overwhelmingly glad to see him, because, as she recalled, they had "all been in a pressure cooker situation" over the last few days. He shared the women's outrage about Nini's shabby treatment from the chaplain. The two women wanted all the most recent news, of course, and although he had not participated in the strike, Fuller told them what he knew and reported the prevailing view that both men were probably POWs. As he recalled later, "Nini just said as far as she was concerned Roger was alive until proven otherwise." Initially Fuller had agreed simply to go to the Philippines to offer any help he could provide Nini there. Now he agreed to escort her back to California. As he finally wrote home to Sally, "After what you said you'd like and the fact I know what I'd like done for you in a similar situation and what Grady said, I decided to go."[43]

The next morning, Nini and Fuller boarded a flight to Japan and then picked up a connection to San Francisco. Fuller bought magazines, but Nini could not focus on them. She also could not sleep, so they talked for much of the trip home. Every now and then, Fuller wrote, "she'd get a faraway look and that's when the questions about Rog would come." She worried that if she talked about her husband too much, she would start to cry, but she found the strength to hold together. After they landed, he delivered Nini to her parents. CDR Earnest had told Fuller he could take a couple of days' leave and go home, but, remembering the skipper's need for crews, he returned immediately, staying only long enough

LT Roger Lerseth and Nini joined LTJG Doug Ahrens and Linda for dinner at one of Manila's fine restaurants during their late-August in-port period. Approximately one week after this photograph was taken, on 6 September 1972, Lerseth and his pilot were shot down. Nini relied on Linda and the four other Sunday Puncher wives staying in the Philippines for emotional support until she returned to the United States. (Roger G. Lerseth Collection)

to call his wife and parents. He reached *Saratoga* on 16 September and went back on the flight schedule the next day. He also confided to Sally, "I'm glad I went but I don't think I could do it again."[44]

During Fuller's absence, the men of VA-75 had come to grips with the loss of their squadronmates. The senior officers, most of whom had experienced the loss of friends before, followed the lead of CDR Earnest and wrote to the wives of the missing pilot and B/N. LCDR Engel explained that he had flown a tanker during the alpha strike and had heard the whole thing on his radio. He offered his prayers and reinforced CDR Earnest's offer of all possible squadron support.[45] CAPT Sanderson also shared the information he had and, to Nini Lerseth, wrote, "At a time when our national character seems to be self-centered, Roger's outlook is not. He is a brave and courageous Naval Officer. He believes in what he was doing and is firmly convinced that the right of our beloved nation to do its own bidding and choosing is inalienable. The war has become a very personal event as Roger and his fellow aviators carry out their duties in hopes of an early release of our prisoners-of-war." He committed every man aboard *Saratoga* to "make any sacrifice necessary" to ensure Lerseth's release.[46]

But VA-75 lost more than one plane and one crew in the 6 September alpha strike. Some of the JOs speculated about the future of the crew of Ace Four, due back from Danang on 7 September. Some felt certain that "The Duck," sure to be shaken by the experience of his first alpha strike, would turn in his wings. When Ace Four's crew arrived, however, Hiduk surprised his squadronmates. He seemed ebullient at taking such a hit and surviving. In a more reflective moment shared in the quiet of their stateroom a bit later, though, LTJG Bryan thought his roommate still seemed to be considering all of his options.[47] LT Hiduk made no immediate decision about his future. Ultimately, however, he decided to stay.

More surprising to many, however, LT Bob Miller had made up his mind to go. Never strong in support of the war, he nonetheless had flown many tough missions, including a number of high-risk strikes as a senior officer's B/N. He came to hate alpha strikes and—always the engineer—even worked out a calculus "formula" to derive "G-Man's Combat Fear Factor," based on SAM sites, AAA batteries, and MiG bases.[48] He had promised himself and his wife that if he ever brought back a plane so badly damaged that it could not land aboard the carrier, he would stop. When he arrived back aboard *Saratoga* on 7 September, Miller went to CDR Earnest and turned in his wings.

Only those who realized that Miller had served as SDO for two consecutive days picked up on his imminent departure.[49] He did not talk much about his decision. He said little to his roommate, LT Hart.[50] He stopped by to say good-bye to LTJG Fuller—a close friend—gave him his bright pink reflective cloth panel for his survival kit, and wished him luck.[51] CDR Earnest asked LTJG Sanford, another of Miller's close friends, to see if he could talk him out of leaving. But the B/N had made his decision. He departed the ship quickly, asking Sanford to check him out of the officer's mess and ship home his cruise box. Miller also granted "the Combat Rat" an "exclusive right" to the small refrigerator that he and LT Wharton had brought aboard back in April. He ended with a personal request: "Take care of yourself and the Duck."[52] Barbara Miller left Manila soon afterward, reducing the number of Puncher wives there from six to four.

Some VA-75 pilots and B/Ns tried hard not to dwell on absent comrades. To give in to sentimentality seemed counterproductive, even potentially dangerous. The recent events provided a true test of the utility of the advice they had received from flight surgeons and Navy psychiatrists to hone the ability to compartmentalize the various parts of their lives, to keep personal distractions out of the cockpit. Even in the stark aftermath of 6 September when he explained the day's awful events, LT Chisholm told Bobbie that she should not think him "cold hearted about these incidents. Tis just something you have to accept and continue on. Can't let it get to you."[53]

Still, they genuinely regretted the loss of LCDR Lindland's leadership. "If I had to pick one officer the squadron couldn't do without it would be Don Lindland," LTJG Warren wrote home the night of the incident, adding, "He was a good steadying influence on everyone and he ran the flight schedule pretty damn well, regardless of all the bitching."[54] With the passage of nearly thirty years and the added perspective of command experience of his own, LT Anderson explained that Lindland "had a lot of positive qualities, including airmanship. The loss of a pilot and officer of this stature tested the validity of our own individual vulnerabilities. Everything became a little more real, a little more ugly, and a little more senseless."[55] The events of 6 September also taught LT Tolhurst a lesson he remembered throughout his career: "It could be anyone at any time. You could be aggressive, careful, and good all at the same time, but sometimes there would just be bad luck."[56]

Some translated their emotional reactions into a consideration of professional concerns. LTJG Fuller wondered what the crew in Ace Three had experienced: "What warnings did they have—or not have. Was the ECM gear working like it should?" Fuller served as branch officer for the technicians who serviced that equipment, so, as he noted, "the gear was mine." He wondered, too, "If everything worked, were the NVN doing something new? If so, was the gear still effective?"[57] This kind of analytical approach created a buffer against dwelling on lost friends.

On two points all seemed to agree. First, to a man, the Sunday Punchers hoped that, when hostilities ended, they would see both men walk out of the prison camps alive and well. Second, many developed a stronger personal commitment to work toward the release of the POWs by doing the job they were sent to do. Most of the pilots and B/Ns viewed this as a natural evolution. Even those who occasionally considered the possibility of turning in their wings and going home discovered that their feelings generally remained short-lived. In the end, their strong sense of duty guided their actions.

And for one man, the loss of Lindland and Lerseth steeled a weakening spirit. In the immediate aftermath of the shootdown, the squadron's senior leaders made certain that LTJG Petersen—Lerseth's roommate—did not isolate himself. Many of his friends stopped by to check on him over the first few days, and he and LCDR Dick Schram split a bottle of scotch two nights after the incident during a long talk. A Grumman technical representative, a civilian named John Miller—not to be confused with VA-75's LT John Miller—became Petersen's roommate by 13 September.[58]

In this specific case, the precautions made good sense. After his recent trip home to see his new daughter, he had returned to duty with some reluctance.

When Lindland and Lerseth got shot down, he wrote Jeane, "At first I wanted to just run away from this whole damn mess." But the incident also helped him decide his immediate future. He would not leave. More to the point, "I don't think I can. I have a *personal* interest in ending this thing now," he wrote. "Sure, I'd like to be home for Christmas but I'd like Rog and Don to be home too." Shortly after *Saratoga* deployed, he had sent Jeane an aluminum POW bracelet to wear. He wore one too, as did others in the squadron. Now, "suddenly the POW bracelet says R.G. Lerseth or D. F. Lindland and the thought of it is like a knife in my back. I don't think there is much any of us wouldn't do to get them back."[59] Jeane pleaded with him to change his mind and come home, insisting, "You can't get those guys out all by yourself. In fact I don't think anything can get them out, but the end of the war. All we are doing is just creating more POWs. That war is such a useless mess."[60] But she also understood that it had to be Petersen's decision, and, for now, he decided to stay.

Over the next few weeks, real aluminum POW bracelets engraved with the names of Donald F. Lindland or Roger G. Lerseth, marked with the date 9-6-72, began to appear on the wrists of Sunday Puncher pilots and B/Ns when they were not flying. Sunday Puncher chiefs and enlisted men wore them, too. The reinvigorated Voices in Vital America (VIVA), the purveyors of the bracelets—along with the local "They Are Not Forgotten Committee"—made it possible for many Puncher families back in Virginia Beach to obtain them and send them to their sailors aboard *Saratoga*.[61]

The pilots and B/Ns realized that no matter how badly they felt personally, they had to put the loss and departure of friends behind them and get on with business, now with even fewer hands to do it all. Some of the pilots and B/Ns who fell ill at the start of the line period still felt the effects of the flu and had not returned to full-time flying. Now the absence of LCDR Lindland and LTs Lerseth and Bob Miller had left more gaps in the flight schedule. A few days previously, MATWING ONE notified CDR Earnest to expect an augmentation crew, but the new pilot and B/N had not arrived yet. And now, in addition, the squadron needed a full replacement crew and an additional B/N. Many in the squadron doubted that MATWING ONE would ever send all the help they needed.[62]

Regardless, *Saratoga* expected to be on the line until 18 September. From 7 September through 9 September, the carrier remained on the noon-to-midnight schedule, launching alpha strikes during daylight hours when weather permitted and one- and two-plane armed recces after dark and when the clouds rolled in and the rains began.

On 7 September, LT Chisholm and LTJG Vance made their first low-level, night armed reconnaissance into RP VI-B, carrying the standard ordnance load for such a mission: four Mk20s and eight Mk82s. They worked out a route that would take them westward along a road segment south of Hanoi to drop their Rockeye on moving trucks or other targets of opportunity. They would then turn northeast toward a hard target on which to drop their Mk82s as they egressed. Launch and coast-in went as planned.

They did not find any good targets on the first leg, so when they turned to the northeast, they still carried their Rockeye. At this point they spotted some WBLCs on a river and dropped the Mk20s on them before continuing to fly a straight course to the hard target. When Rockeye dropped, a short lanyard on each weapon detonated a charge that opened the outer shell casing and released the small armor-piercing bomblets within. To an observer—or gunner—below, the detonations from each sequentially dropped round appeared like a dotted line that traced the track of the aircraft. Since they had not changed course after they dropped their Mk20s, Chisholm and Vance gave every AAA gunner in the area a chance to enjoy a lucky night.

All of a sudden the skies lit up. Vance saw tracer rounds coming up at his side of the cockpit and yelled to Chisholm to break left. The pilot looked out his side of the aircraft and spotted AAA coming up from that direction, too. As quickly as it started, the firing stopped. For a few minutes after they egressed, the pilot and B/N said little to each other. Then Vance used his flashlight to look for battle damage. He spotted a jagged six–inch hole in the leading edge of the right wing. As soon as they recovered, a hydraulics and airframes troubleshooter examined the damage, turned to the B/N, and said, "Mr. Vance, looks like you got yourself a bird." The sudden burst of AAA had flushed the unfortunate creature out of its nest and it collided with the low-flying A-6A.[63]

"Always break hard after weapons release" had been one of the squadron's rules to live by. Chisholm and Vance learned from the experience and never violated that rule again. But they did continue to thin the North Vietnamese bird population. Four days later, they hit another one at tree-top level; this one did no damage to the plane, but left feathers and blood everywhere.[64] Thus, for the second time in a few days, they created more reports for the Administrative Department. The Audubon Society had gotten the U.S. Navy to agree to send the remains of all birds killed by its planes to a laboratory for examination and identification to track the impact of the war on avian populations.[65]

On 8 September, LCDR King flew his first strike hop over the beach. CDR Earnest had insisted that even his most experienced new personnel be checked out on tanker hops before clearing them for strikes. LT Cook took him on a mining run on 5 September, but now King wanted to try a few strike sorties. He quickly learned how much the air war had intensified since his last deployment to Yankee Station. A strike with Cook against a target southwest of Thanh Hoa in RP IV met with such heavy AAA that, after landing, he collared CDR Earnest to "thank" him, saying, "Gee, Skipper, I am sure glad you gave me a milkrun."[66]

From 10 September until departing Yankee Station after the close of air operations on 17 September, CVW-3 switched to the midnight-to-noon schedule. During the hours of darkness, VA-75 flew armed recces into RPs IV and VI-B; after dawn, they continued one- and two-plane strikes and seeded rivers and harbors in RPs II, III, IV, and VI-B. On the few days when weather permitted, the airwing launched an alpha strike. But when the rains fell, single-plane missions prevailed.

Senior crews flying into RP VI-B continued to pay special attention to the northeast railway. CDR Greene and LCDR Pieno flew three night missions into that area on 5, 7, and 10 September.[67] Pieno later described the area as having "more guns per inch than anything I had experienced or [ever] would experience."[68] The circumstances of one of those early September night missions remain clear in the crew's memory, even if the precise date does not. They had crossed the beach heading for the railway so often that they regularly used a favored coast-in point where, even flying at 200 feet, they rarely met resistance. But one night, they took heavy AAA from the moment they crossed the beach. At first, the unexpected response startled them. Then CDR Greene reached over and said, "Maybe we better turn the lights off." The XO inadvertently had left the cockpit lights on, and as Pieno described it, "we looked like a pretty flying Christmas tree."[69] Even senior crews could make potentially fatal errors.

After recovery from his 10 September mission, however, Pieno could not get out of the cockpit. He had hurt his back years earlier, but now, for reasons he could not understand, it had locked up on him. Ordnancemen and purpleshirts stood by to ready the plane for the next mission, but Pieno simply could not move. The aircraft had to be moved to the hangar deck, where the flight surgeon gave the B/N some muscle relaxants and called for the assistance of some of the enlisted men to help Pieno out of the plane. Then the doctor grounded him for the next two days.[70]

The injury to Pieno set the stage for LCDR King's first visit to RP VI-B since 1969. Still, he thought himself ready to go, and when he looked at the flight schedule for 11 September, he saw his name listed for a night hop on the northeast railway as CDR Greene's B/N. As King later recalled the mission, "I had been there before when I was in VA-165, and figured that everybody in the Navy goes to the Northeast Railway from east to west." Thus, he planned to go in from west to east. To do that, as he explained to Greene, they would fly over the southern part of Hanoi. Greene reminded him about bombing restrictions around the North Vietnamese capital, and King replied, "We're not going to bomb them. We're just going to sightsee." Greene expressed grave doubts, but they flew the path King chose, meeting little initial resistance. Turning to approach their target from the west, King all of a sudden doubted the wisdom of his decision, re-membering just then that the Air Force flew from west to east from their bases in Thailand. They flew into a solid wall of AAA. King thrust his head into the B/N's radar hood and kept it there while Greene dropped their bombs. They may or may not have hit their target and rolled out right, breaking right around a ridge, and finally went feet wet. King then told Greene, "You know, I know guys who got the Navy Cross for that mission" on his previous cruises. Greene suggested that he just shut up and take his two points toward an Air Medal.[71]

Very quickly, then, King fully qualified to participate in all aspects of the squadron's operations. The heavies had not paired him with anyone yet, await-ing the arrival of the expected augmentation pilot and B/N before making final decisions. On 10 September, LT Thomas H. Connelly arrived. He brought some-thing special from Oceana: a home movie taken at the recent squadron picnic for the families of the officers and enlisted men.[72] Although VA-75 usually drew its pilots and B/Ns from VA-42 or accepted volunteers from East Coast squad-rons, Connelly had followed a different path to join the Sunday Punchers. A vet-eran of a previous combat cruise in A-6s in 1970, he now neared completion of his service obligation, most recently flying with VA-43, a West Coast squadron.[73] Despite the pilot's previous combat experience, however, CDR Earnest did not expect the new arrival to step in with just a dose of refresher training as King had done. Connelly's combat tour had occurred when American planes did not go after targets in RP VI-B. Connelly had never flown a strike hop north of Vinh.

Two days after Connelly's arrival, the new B/N arrived. LT Rudolf P. Wiegand had just completed a three-year assignment teaching Naval ROTC at Yale Uni-versity. He, too, had flown a combat tour in 1969 with VA-35, but he had not been in a cockpit since he returned to the United States. Thus, he had reported to VA-42 expecting the usual six-month stay to relearn his aircraft before assign-ment to a fleet squadron. Only three days after he arrived, however, he received orders to fill VA-75's need for an additional B/N. The VA-42 instructors gave him five training hops for navigation and bombing practice and sent him off to Westpac. On his way over he had called home and learned about the downing of Lindland and Lerseth's aircraft. The news saddened him. He had served with Lindland in VA-35 and had looked forward to flying with him again.[74]

Connelly and Wiegand went through a more intensive integration process than LCDR King had just completed. As Wiegand explained in retrospect, "I was not ready for combat and had sense to know it. I didn't recall the aircraft systems enough to react in the event of an emergency and was still fumbling for switches in the cockpit—not what one would like to be doing in combat." Thus, he expressed his entire satisfaction when CDR Earnest eased him in, starting with tanker hops. Their comparative rustiness suggested that—unlike

Chisholm and Vance who had come to VA-75 directly from a VA-42 instructional billet or an operational squadron—Connelly and Wiegand should not fly as a crew.

Ordinarily, no A-6 squadron would choose to make changes in crew pairings in the middle of a line period unless absolutely necessary. But VA-75 needed to establish additional effective crews immediately, and the arrival of King, Connelly, and Wiegand allowed the heavies to reconfigure several existing crews that, for various reasons, no longer worked well.

LT Ruland had lost his regular B/N when LT McFarland left. Now the heavies assigned LTJG Jay Swigart to fly with him. Since the start of the combat cruise, Swigart—the squadron's most junior B/N—had flown with the seasoned LT Cook. Then it had made sense to pair experience with greenness. But conflicts in personality and judgment in the cockpit had emerged over time. Swigart requested a switch. Cook, too, asked for a change. Pairing Swigart with Ruland seemed to the heavies to be a good fit.[75]

Swigart's specific concerns about flying with LT Cook suggested that the pilot might do his best work with a more experienced B/N. Originally, CDR Earnest planned to pair him with newly arrived LCDR King. But that changed with the arrival of LT Wiegand, who knocked Cook from his position as the squadron's senior lieutenant and became his new B/N. This pairing worked satisfactorily for the remainder of the cruise.

Earnest and Greene decided that LT Connelly's previous combat experience might best be exploited by pairing him with a veteran B/N. Thus, they decided to pair him with LCDR Dick Schram. Connelly's solid airmanship, combined with Schram's steadiness, proved to be a good match also, especially after the senior B/N made clear that they would do things his way. In fairly short order, the pairing provided squadron schedulers with another seasoned crew.

Since the beginning of the combat cruise, LCDR Schram had flown as LCDR Engel's B/N. Before the start of air operations in May and then during Schram's temporary detachment during the second line period, Engel flew with a number of different B/Ns. In A-6 squadrons, where the centrality of the crew concept held sway, a pilot or B/N could refuse to fly with a squadronmate with whom he did not "fit," and a number of junior B/Ns informed CDR Earnest or LCDR Lindland that they did not want to fly combat hops with the Maintenance Department head. To his credit, Engel realized that some B/Ns did not feel comfortable flying with him, but he did not understand why. Clearly concerned by all this, the squadron heavies realized that Engel either needed to be paired with an experienced B/N who could deal with his quirks or relieve him of duty with the squadron. Thus, CDR Earnest asked King to fly with Engel. King agreed, if permitted to do so on his own terms.

Junior by time in grade but far more seasoned in the cockpit, King explained to Engel that he expected his pilot to do as he said without question and flew a few tanker hops to see if they could work with each other in the cockpit. King learned for himself why junior B/Ns did not always feel comfortable in Engel's aircraft, but he also believed the junior officers had made too much of their concerns and felt disappointed that they had let the situation devolve into a potentially thorny personnel issue. The Engel-King crew worked well together for the rest of the cruise.[76]

As all of VA-75—newly paired pilots and B/Ns and the veteran crews who now worked with them—became more comfortable flying with each other, they nonetheless began to feel the effects of their recent efforts. The flu claimed more new victims. Some who remained healthy took extra hops for sick squadronmates, and they became physically worn down, too. LT Tolhurst apologized for a break in his letter writing, explaining, "I had 3 hops two days in a row because we have several people sick. I've been so tired that I came close to falling asleep in the air a few times. . . . I was up 36 hours straight with 4 hops in that period on the 12th–13th."[77]

Despite constant emphasis on the need to fight complacency, as September continued, exhaustion contributed to a steep jump in the number of safety violations observed on the flight deck.[78] Just before 0500 on 14 September, Airman David J. Newcomer unchained an A-6B in preparation for taxi to the catapult. As LTJG Bryan began to move forward, he and his B/N felt a bump. The plane handler motioning them forward had taxied them right over the young sailor's leg. Medical personnel on the flight deck hurried Newcomer down to the surgical suite. The sailor lost part of his limb, but, as the deck log noted, he survived with an overall prognosis of "good."[79] On another occasion, the rudder of one of the airwing's E-2Bs suffered significant damage when the pilot of one of VA-75's A-6s—again following the signals of the flight deck plane handler—accidentally hit it. In the ensuing investigation, examiners attributed the damage to complacency on the part of the flight deck crew, the result of exhaustion and overfamiliarity with a particular repetitive task that bred inattention to detail.[80]

Still, during the hours of darkness on the midnight-to-noon schedule, single-plane, low-level night strikes into RPs IV and VI-B had to launch. Several airwing crews noticed about the same time that the North Vietnamese had begun to use a new "light signal system" to track aircraft. As best they could explain it, when a spotter on the ground heard an airplane overhead, he fired a flare up into the air. Then, if they passed over a second spotter, a second flare shot into the sky. North Vietnamese gunners simply connected the two points to estimate the plane's course and sent up a heavy barrage of AAA fire along its projected path. Several VA-75 pilots and B/Ns saw the flares in their rearview mirrors, and LCDR King reported it to IOIC. LTJG Vance observed a similar system, in which spotters in towers used strobe lights to signal locations of aircraft. From that point on, intelligence briefings to all air crews contained a warning to look for the lights and to break immediately after flying past a second one.[81] Indeed, the crews had observed the results of a recent North Vietnamese effort to improve their air defenses against low-flying aircraft like the A-6 with "observation and alarm systems in the localities" that would "combine closely the use of observation tricks and equipment and information means in each locality" to detect American aircraft "from afar . . . and in time."[82]

When weather permitted, alpha strikes launched during the daylight hours of the midnight-to-noon schedule. On 11 September, the clouds broke sufficiently for the airwing's first alpha strike into RP VI-B since the downing of Lindland and Lerseth's aircraft five days previously. The Ninh Duong army barracks, a major North Vietnamese Army training and staging center, never had been targeted before. The barracks area rested in the envelopes of at least eight active SAM sites, and five nearby airfields based an estimated seventy MiGs. Heavy air defenses lined the entire sixty miles of the ingress and egress routes. Strike leads CDR Earnest and LCDR Jackson and alternate lead LCDR W. T. Inderlied of VF-31 divided the aircraft into two cells for maximum flexibility in bad weather and greater evasive maneuvering capability if the North Vietnamese launched a barrage of SAMs at them.

Earnest and Jackson led the first cell, taking LT Chisholm with LTJG Vance and LTJG Bryan with LTJG Petersen on their wing, each of the three A-6As carrying twelve Mk82s. LCDR Inderlied led the second cell. After a smooth coast-in and about twenty-five miles from the target, they heard a "MiG airborne" call. The MiGCAP turned them away. The strike group evaded at least three SAMs, but an aggressive Iron Hand operation essentially shut down any further threat. "All bombs on target and escape at tree top level," LT Chisholm wrote that night, adding it had been an "untouched target until we hit it and now no more target[—]leveled."[83] Poststrike photography verified the destruction of an ammunition storage building, an administration building, nine double warehouses, six single-bay warehouses, twenty-one barracks buildings, and twelve support structures, with additional buildings damaged. American aircraft suffered no losses and no damage.[84]

But not all alpha strikes achieved such verifiable results. On 12 September, LCDR Graustein and LCDR Jackson served as the alternate lead on an alpha strike against the Kep railroad yard about two miles northeast of Kep airfield near Hanoi. LT Ruland with LTJG Swigart and LT Pyle with LT Hvidding flew on their wing, all three A-6As carrying eight Mk83 1,000-pound bombs. Any strike on the Kep rail sidings, part of the northeast railway system, met heavy resistance. The North Vietnamese launched at least four SAMs at the formation, and radar-guided AAA fire filled the skies. LT Ruland felt certain that they hit their target, but heavy clouds over the target area prevented the airwing's RA-5Cs from getting good poststrike photos to verify initial BDA.[85] Another alpha strike three days later on 15 September aimed at both the northeast railway and the Bac Giang Petroleum Products storage area and transshipment point. CAG Bordone and LCDR Jackson served as both strike and navigation lead, taking two more A-6As on their wing. The RA-5Cs documented only moderate damage. The most noteworthy accomplishment the squadron noted from that hop belonged to the new crew of LTs Cook and Wiegand, who achieved another VA-75 milestone when they dropped its five millionth pound of ordnance.[86]

The airwing got a brief break later on 15 September, when VADM Frederick H. Michaelis, COMNAVAIRLANT, visited *Saratoga* as part of his tour of Atlantic Fleet carriers deployed in the Gulf of Tonkin. When RADM Christiansen introduced the admiral, he complimented *Saratoga* and the men who served on it. "Vice Admiral Michaelis, you sent a whole bunch of tigers out here. This ship is good," he said.[87] Preparing to shift his flag to *America,* he added, "I have watched SARA overcome unnumbered obstacles from the day of your very abrupt departure from Mayport to your position today among the front runners of the SEVENTH Fleet. You can be very proud of your record in WESTPAC. I assure you, SARA takes a back seat to no one, and those who don't already know it soon will." Ironically, the day after a flight deck accident, Michaelis presented *Saratoga* with the Admiral Flatley Memorial Award for aviation safety, a trophy sponsored by North American Rockwell Corporation and named for the grandfather of CDR James H. Flatley III, the CO of VF-31. He then presented individual awards to 116 members of the ship's company and airwing, including Silver Stars to CAG Bordone for the 21 June alpha strike against the SAM storage area near Haiphong and to CDR Flynn and LT John who had downed a MiG-21 that same day. CDR Earnest and LCDR Jackson from VA-75 received Silver Stars for their efforts in the rescue of LT Lloyd in August.[88] In a separate ceremony, LTs Zinser and Young—the pilots of the Big Mother helicopter that picked up Lloyd—each received the Navy Cross.[89]

At the same event, many VA-75 pilots and B/Ns now officially received their first Air Medals. Most who had deployed in April already had accumulated points for a fourth or fifth such award, but this ceremony still inspired LT Fischer to drag himself from his sick bed to get his first one from the admiral.[90] But few of the others felt much like the tigers to which they had just been compared. One JO described the ceremony as "two hours of hot standing for not much."[91] Another concurred about the long period of "sweaty standing," deciding that he would "pass on medals from now on."[92]

LTJG Sandy Sanford—aka "the Combat Rat"—receives an Air Medal and the congratulations of VADM Frederick H. Michaelis during an awards ceremony aboard Saratoga *on 15 September 1972. (U.S. Navy photograph, Leslie M. Sanford, Jr., Collection)*

The grumbling by the JOs reflected a perception among some of them that the squadron's heavies chose their missions with an eye to the medals that might be attached to them. While all concurred that CDR Earnest and LCDR Jackson deserved their Silver Stars for their role in LT Lloyd's rescue, a few JOs already had grown jaded by an awards process they perceived to be tightly controlled by only a few individuals in the squadron. Those who felt this way now made distinctions between two kinds of officers: those who accepted any assignments that came their way and did their duty to the best of their ability and glory seekers intent on self-promotion who improved their chances for Distinguished Flying Crosses or Silver Stars by choosing their missions with an eye to the likely awards that success might bring. To try to keep the playing field level—and to provide visual evidence that each member of the squadron had an equal shot at any mission for which experience and capabilities qualified him—VA-75's operations shop already kept a board in the ready room intended to show all crews that they shared equally the different types of A-6 missions. LT John Miller's mission assignment chart became known as the "ECMF Board"—the Equilibrium Combat Medal Factor board.[93]

After the brief break late on 15 September, the weather continued to worsen. The only alpha strike planned for RP VI-B on 16 September had to be diverted to alternate targets, but four VA-75 aircraft participated in the airwing's only major strike to hit there the next day. All three of the alpha strikes planned for RPs III and IV for 17 September ended as weather diverts to alternate targets. Other strikes were canceled entirely.

After the end of air operations on 17 September, *Saratoga* steamed south once more. On 18 September, during the transit to Cubi, the Sunday Punchers flew a few missions against targets in RP I in North Vietnam. The squadron seldom hit targets here, but they now linked up with "fast FACs"—forward air controllers in Air Force F-4s rather than the "slow FACs" in low-flying propeller-driven aircraft they worked with in South Vietnam—to hit targets near Dong Hoi. LCDR Engel and King led one three-plane strike against a supply depot. LTJG Fuller, who flew with LT Knapp on Engel's wing, recalled the FAC's high praise for their effective drop. BDA reports gave the three aircraft credit for destroying seven warehouses and igniting at least two secondaries.[94]

But mostly, on both 18 and 19 September, they launched on their usual "slow FAC"-controlled sorties in MR 1 just south of the DMZ.[95] To Punchers rolling in on their targets, the region looked otherworldly. "Quang Tri looks like the moon that used to be a city but not any more," one B/N wrote home.[96]

During the eighteen days of their fourth line period, CVW-3 flew 800 combat sorties and delivered 1,340 tons of ordnance. VA-75's aircraft flew 344 missions of all kinds. The A-6As completed 128 strike missions, 90 during the day and only 38 at night, not nearly enough to satisfy LT Tolhurst's desire to show what the aircraft could do. The A-6Bs flew 42 missions, 24 during daylight hours and 18 at night. The KA-6Ds flew a total of 164 refueling missions, 109 of them at night.[97]

Overall, the most notable evidence of improvement during the fourth line period revealed itself in the consistently higher number of mission-ready aircraft, alleviating some of the problems that had plagued VA-75 during the August line period. On only two days—4 and 16 September—had the squadron failed to meet its sortie obligations. CDR Earnest's report had caught the attention of RADM Christiansen, who forwarded it up the chain of command. After raising concern levels throughout the Seventh Fleet, VA-75 quickly followed with a potential solution. LT Hudson, the maintenance LDO, deserved much of the credit for the positive change. Many of the most nagging problems centered on components in the inertial navigation system (INS) and the weapons computers. INS failures upon start up, or "dumps" after or during launch, made automated system ordnance drops impossible. The weapons computer also contained internal magnetic memory components that suffered a high malfunction rate. Unfortunately, many of these components could not be repaired by squadron or carrier technicians or by the beach detachment. Two possible solutions suggested themselves. Navy logisticians had to figure out how to get additional spare and replacement parts into the carrier-level supply system, or the Navy needed a better and faster means for repairing key electronic components on a high priority basis. The closest repair facility staffed and authorized to work on the A-6s electronic components was at Whidbey Island Naval Air Station in Washington. With the encouragement and approval of the airwing and carrier division staff, Hudson took the lead in developing a special repair/resupply process, dubbed "Red Label Service," that allowed him to ship VA-75's malfunctioning components to Whidbey for top-priority repair and quick return.

Hudson's plan succeeded. VA-75 experienced a 28.9 percent increase in A-6A systems reliability almost immediately, and that translated into an increased sortie rate. Indeed, the program proved so effective in improving VA-75's readiness that CTF-77 renamed LT Hudson's process "Project Leapfrog" and extended its operation to other A-6 squadrons on Yankee Station.[98]

When ADM Michaelis addressed *Saratoga*'s sailors during the recent awards ceremony, he had offered hope that they might be home for Christmas. Indeed, he admitted that he already had told the wives' club in Virginia Beach that the carrier would be home in October.[99] As they steamed toward the Philippines, ADM Bernard A. Clarey—commanding officer of the Pacific Fleet—came aboard and reiterated that *Saratoga* might indeed arrive home by the holidays. A tentative schedule circulated on 21 September sent the carrier to Yokusuka, Japan, after their October line period. Then, after a seven- or eight-day stay, and a short November line period, they would head home.[100] That plan did not survive even one day, however. An amended schedule put *Saratoga* back on Yankee Station until 15 October, followed by a two-week in-port period in Japan, and then a return to the line, to rotate in and out of Cubi until at least 9 December.[101]

The late-September in-port period proved to be far from restful. Political dissension had erupted in riots, and on 22 September Philippine President Ferdinand Marcos had declared martial law. The phone exchange closed down temporarily, leaving many in the squadron unable to call home to family and friends. The political situation had become so volatile that *Saratoga*'s crew and airwing now faced a midnight curfew, and daily crew musters for accountability became the norm for the first time during the cruise.[102]

To encourage their enlisted men to stay off the increasingly dangerous streets of Olongapo during such a volatile time, the squadron organized alternative entertainment. At a unit picnic on Dungaree Beach at Cubi, "the cry of more food, more beer, could be heard throughout the land," noted a write-up in the squadron's fall familygram.[103] The sailors drank, soaked up the sun, played softball and other sports, and tossed the officers into the water, one by one. Skipper

LT James "E" Hudson, the Sunday Punchers' Maintenance LDO, earned high accolades for his development of a solution to nagging supply and repair problems affecting A-6 mission readiness. VA-75's "Red Label Service" became better known as "Project Leapfrog" when it extended to include all A-6 squadrons serving in Westpac. Hudson, seen here on the right, congratulates Chief Frank Pittman at his reenlistment ceremony. (U.S. Navy photograph, Frank J. Pittman Collection)

Earnest went in first, with XO Greene not far behind.[104] The squadron's line division had its own party, during which Airman Roland Gardner, dubbed "VA-75's own Bobby Fischer," soundly whipped LTJG Vance, his branch officer, in several intense chess games.[105]

The Punchers prepared to leave Cubi on 28 September to go back to Yankee Station once more. LT Chisholm reminded his parents that this combat cruise was "what my Navy experience was all about—all the training, lectures, flights. I wanted to complete my Navy time with a taste of what all that had gone before was really about. It would have been an incomplete exposure otherwise. Please try to understand this and realize that this is where all the previous training and understanding is all applied."[106] LTJG Petersen wrote: "I think the only reason any of us is over here is for the POWs and because we believe in an organized military organization and [that] military organizations do what they are told." More to the point, he wrote, "I don't know that I could live with myself if I walked out now."[107]

On their last night in port, some of the pilots and B/Ns went to the Chuck Wagon, a hamburger grill at Cubi. A Filipino country and western band provided musical entertainment. The favored song of the evening proved to be John Denver's "Country Roads." Repeated nearly a dozen times, when they reached the refrain, the Punchers belted out a new lyric that suited their mood: "Take me home, to the place I belong, Oceana, mountain mama, take me home."[108]

But they could not go home. During the in-port period, scheduling ambiguities continued. Of course, in the Navy, nothing could be guaranteed. As they steamed out of Subic early on 28 September, CAPT Sanderson announced his most recent update. They would head to Yankee Station and operate against North Vietnamese targets until 22 October and return to Cubi on 23 October. Then *Saratoga* would steam—not for home—but for an in-port stay in exotic Singapore.

CHAPTER NINE

"Peace Is at Hand"

When the Sunday Punchers left the Philippines on 28 September, news of various sorts ignited a spark of hope for an end to the war and dreams of a safe and speedy return home. For once, word of progress in the peace talks seemed genuinely encouraging. Henry Kissinger had returned to Paris yet again for meetings with Le Duc Tho on 15 and 27 September. An improving military situation in South Vietnam, including recent ARVN victories in Quang Tri province, complicated North Vietnamese efforts to portray the Thieu government as ineffectual. In the United States, mid-September polls showing a substantial upward tick in public support for Nixon's conduct of the war solidified the already-strong likelihood of his reelection. Kissinger now noticed in Le Duc Tho an unprecedented eagerness to continue discussions, and he suspected that the North Vietnamese wanted to reach a resolution before November. The 27 September meeting, in particular, revealed a dramatic change in the usual North Vietnamese reluctance to make concessions. "We were, in fact, in the strongest bargaining position of the war," Kissinger later noted, and he agreed to additional talks on 8 October.[1]

The news from Paris cheered LTJG Warren, who wrote home, "It sounds like a lot of things have changed since we were on the line last." He suspected that recent progress on the diplomatic front explained why "they aren't pushing the night low levels into 6B anymore."[2] But if the United States still had to keep up the pressure by hitting targets near Hanoi and Haiphong, some of VA-75's pilots and B/Ns hoped they now might have some additional help from the return to active operations of the F-111, the U.S. Air Force's all-weather, day-night, low-level aircraft. After a rough introduction to combat in 1968, a series of structural defects led to the grounding of the entire fleet soon thereafter. The first F-111s to return to Westpac arrived at Takhli Air Force Base in Thailand on 27 September, scheduled to begin flying missions the next night.[3]

But the high expectations of one day seemed to disappear the next. If the Sunday Punchers hoped the F-111s might carry out some of the night strikes around Hanoi and on the railroads to China, reality quickly quashed their optimism. The very first one sent out on a night mission did not return, and old questions about its reliability surfaced yet again. And as October's events played out, the promise of a successful diplomatic resolution in Paris continued to resist fulfillment. During *Saratoga*'s fifth line period, the Sunday Punchers tried hard to avoid distractions derived either from rising expectations or dashed hopes.

In one unquestionably positive development, one-half of the replacement crew for LCDR Lindland and LT Lerseth arrived. LCDR Barton S. Wade, a veteran B/N, had just concluded a combat tour aboard *Midway* with the Arabs of VA-115. On 12 August 1971, he had won the dubious distinction of becoming one of the few members of the A-6 community to eject from a KA-6D.[4] Wade usually answered to "Black Bart," a nickname that caused LT Fischer to muse, "I don't know whether to go on a mission or rob a bank" with him.[5] Despite his experience in the cockpit, however, Wade—like Connelly and Wiegand—had flown his combat hops before the start of LINEBACKER, in a period of limited air activity north of the 20th parallel. During much of his combat cruise with VA-115, he hit targets in Laos.

Nonetheless, Wade became part of a crew almost immediately. On 3 October, LT Mullins complained of a stomachache and went to sickbay. The doctor started the B/N on antibiotics. Mullins had developed acute appendicitis. If he took medication to control the inflammation, the doctor predicted he could return to the cockpit within a week, and Mullins initially decided to follow that course of treatment. Then the surgeon explained to him that if he got shot down and the appendicitis flared up in a POW camp, "it might go very badly." Since the schedule called for a short line period, Mullins chose the operation. Realizing that his recuperation would ground him for several weeks but still wanting to contribute, he willingly took a job unpopular with most pilots and B/Ns—he became officer-in-charge of the airwing's beach detachment at Cubi.[6] As a consequence of Mullins's operation, LCDR Wade immediately became LCDR Graustein's new B/N.

Operationally, the fifth line period began as the fourth had ended. Between 28 September and 1 October, the squadron flew one- to three-plane FAC-directed strikes against targets in MR I. The ARVN counterattack in the region continued to make good progress, and the veteran aircrews enjoyed contributing to the success. On 29 September, LTs Anderson and Hart dropped fourteen Mk82s against a triangular ARVN firebase that had been overrun by North Vietnamese troops the previous night. "Terry (and I) couldn't miss," Hart later wrote. After their first two bombs fell just outside the base, they made six more uncontested runs and put the remaining twelve bombs right on target, the FAC crediting them with the destruction of four bunkers, four structures, and fifteen "KBA"— North Vietnamese "killed by air."[7] LT Tolhurst bragged to his wife about the success he and LTJG Ahrens enjoyed on a 1 October hop: "We got eight bunkers destroyed, two small secondary explosions and one machine gun post wiped out." Why could such missions accomplish such excellent results? As he explained it, "There was nobody shooting at us at all which is always good to see."[8] The lack of serious opposition likely explained why planes stacked up at altitudes from 15,000 to 23,000 feet, each waiting to drop its bombs. It reminded one pilot of "a holding pattern over JFK."[9]

In a repetition of early September, yet another typhoon in the Gulf of Tonkin limited launches on 2 October and cancelled flight operations entirely on 3 October. The unexpected break in the action complicated taskings to all the carriers on Yankee Station for the next few days. Because all the FAC missions in MR I had been daytime hops and few planes launched during the two days of bad weather, most of CVW-3's pilots had to requalify to launch at night.[10] Most completed the requalification process—with a few touch-and-goes and an arrested landing—during some point on 4 October, but at a cost to mission execution. Of the twenty-five missions tasked to VA-75, only sixteen launched; weather conditions did not account for the cancellation of the rest.[11]

From 4 October until 9 October, Saratoga followed the noon-to-midnight schedule for flight operations. Two new crews successfully led a mining strike on 4 October. LCDRs Engel and King in one A-6A armed with twelve Mk36s and LTs Cook and Wiegand in another armed with twelve Mk82s each led four A-7s into the harbor at Ile de Cac Ba and dropped their ordnance on target. The following day, CDR Greene and LCDR Pieno led a major mining alpha strike into the waters off Haiphong itself. Five A-6As—including two flown by the newly paired crews of LT Ruland with LTJG Swigart and LT Connelly with LCDR Schram—each dropped fourteen Mk36s to refresh a key minefield.[12]

The satisfaction of successful mission completion faded quickly, however. On 5 October, CAPT Sanderson dealt all hopes of celebrating the holidays at home a crushing blow. He finally received credible information about Saratoga's projected timeline in Westpac and delivered the bad news during his nightly announcements. "Our schedule right now is: 28 Oct–7 Nov in Singapore, 8 Nov–6 Dec on the line, 7 Dec–13 Dec, Subic, 15–28 Dec on line," LT Tolhurst wrote Pixie. If that schedule held, the carrier would not outchop from the Pacific Fleet and head back to the United States until about 13 January 1973. VA-75 would not arrive at Oceana any earlier than the end of January and probably not until mid-February.

The news hit hard. LTJG Fuller wrote Sally that the news of their delayed departure made him long for home so much that he could finally admit he even missed "the cat running around like a herd of buffaloes."[13] The thought of missing the holidays proved especially disappointing to men with small children. "That will be real fun, huh, Christmas Day on the line," wrote LT Tolhurst, complaining that "it really makes me mad and I'm sorry to have this happen to you & Kim." But his concerns ran deeper. He worried that the delay in going home "may cause some guys to turn in their wings."[14] That did not happen, though. Instead, someone decorated the palm tree in the squadron's ready room with holiday ornaments.[15] They understood that only the diplomats could reverse this most undesirable situation. "I guess I could kill a Commie for Christ on his birthday," LTJG Warren opined, but he still hoped for a cease-fire that might permit them to leave for home before that.[16]

The certainty of missing Christmas at home gave rise to a flurry of efforts to make the most of the upcoming in-port period in Singapore. Unfortunately, the schedule had solidified so recently that few of the Punchers' wives could make or adjust plans to join their husbands there; indeed, most of the junior officers' wives—especially those who had just returned from Hong Kong—doubted they could afford the expense. Still, many Punchers immediately began to alternate briefing and flying with hurried planning for the next time they left the line. Some simply focused on finding ways to get their wives to Singapore. Others tried to make plans to meet loved ones in Guam, Japan, or Hawaii, until CAPT Sanderson announced that he would permit no personnel to take leave out of the operational area. That news crushed LT Chisholm, who had just asked Bobbie to meet him in Hawaii. He pleaded his case to CDR Earnest, but, as he groused to Bobbie, "Skipper said to bring you to Singapore so he could meet you—sure skipper." He refused even to consider it, especially since Earnest's suggestion "was intermingled with statements like—'you're getting out of [the] Navy so why should I do anything for you.'"[17]

Still, the pilots and B/Ns did not permit such distractions and disappointments to keep them from the job they had trained to do. Even though most of them disliked the confusion of large alpha strikes, some really wanted to fly them now. To convince the North Vietnamese to talk seriously about ending hostilities, one pilot wrote, the air effort had "to start really hurting them to get this damn thing over."[18] But deteriorating weather throughout October forced the cancellation or diversion of most alpha strikes. The A-6 had been built for bad weather, of course, so the Punchers still kept busy with one- and two-plane night missions in RP VI-B, daylight runs into RPs II and III, the occasional A-6B sortie, and—as always—tankers.

At this point in the combat cruise, even the most junior crews that deployed with the squadron in April drew assignments to night strikes and road recces in RP VI-B. After searching for trucks there on 6 October, LT Tolhurst—VA-75's most junior pilot in April—pulled a road recce near Hai Duong on 7 October. Writing to Pixie before he manned up, he admitted that he and LTJG Ahrens expected to "get some reaction, AAA and maybe some SAM strobes," but he also explained that he planned to fly below 500 feet to stay below most North Vietnamese radars. He closed with a cheery "I'll let you know how it turns out when I get back." The entire mission took less than two hours, and, as promised, he preserved the details while they remained fresh in his memory: "The hop was all right but a little scary. We went in at 300'–400' and 360 KTS. We were really shot at quite a bit, but only about four of the AAA sites came real close to us. It is really dark over the beach there at night. We were over the beach for about 15 minutes but it seemed like about an hour. We cover about 90 miles in 15 minutes when we go 360 KTS. We hit a storage area and also 4 AAA sites with our bombs. It is sort of frightening and yet gives you a feeling of satisfaction to make the aircraft perform low and at night over strange territory."[19] The heavies also gave RP VI-B night missions to the more experienced crews among the more recent arrivals—Chisholm and Vance, along with Connelly and Schram. Only the squadron's two least experienced junior pilots—LT Hiduk and LTJG Bryan—remained off the strike and recce schedule for targets around Hanoi and Haiphong.[20]

As the diplomats continued to talk, North Vietnamese air defenders continued to keep even the most seasoned crews' adrenaline flowing during those night strikes. On 8 October, at least two VA-75 crews ran up against a new kind of enemy response, quite different from SAMs or the usual AAA. CDR Earnest and LCDR Jackson launched to drop twelve Mk36s at a ferry crossing well inland, west of the city of Thanh Hoa, upstream from its famous bridge. They planned to coast in north of the bridge, drop their ordnance from an altitude of about 500 feet, then roll out toward the south. A few seconds after rolling off the target, Jackson realized that the azimuth ring on his radar scope had frozen and they had begun to fly north, directly into the airspace over the heavily defended bridge. They then tried to head east toward the coast, letting the intensity of the AAA tell them if they flew too near the span. They knew they came too close when, all of a sudden, they came in range of a highly lethal Russian-built ZSU-23-4. The weapon "sent out a steady stream of 23mm tracers that looked like something was shooting a high pressure stream of water at you, but you know it was hot lead!" CDR Earnest "did the fastest jinking turn away from that ZSU-23-4 that I had ever seen him do at night and while low level."[21] LT Anderson, flying with LCDR King against a railroad siding southeast of Hanoi in RP VI-B, destroyed several vehicles and cut the rail line, before they, too, ran into the fire of a ZSU-23-4.[22]

The most productive night while *Saratoga* ran the noon-to-midnight schedule came on 9 October. CDR Earnest and LCDR Jackson, while flying a road recce in RP VI-B along a section of Route 5 between Hai Duong and Hanoi, spotted a convoy of perhaps two hundred trucks running with their lights on, a tempting target for any A-6 pilot or B/N. They dropped their eight Mk82s on the roadway at one point and then dropped their four Mk20 Rockeye on trucks nearby, destroying six to eight vehicles and leaving even more burning.[23] Just a bit farther south, LCDRs Engel and King, carrying only eight Mk82s, made four separate runs on various truck convoys, starting nine medium secondaries, one large secondary, and one large fire in their wake. LT Knapp and LTJG Fuller got credit for destroying a gun at an AAA site.[24]

But, despite such colorful results, could one- and two-plane strikes like these really make a difference? In the United States, antiwar journalists renewed their efforts to portray the interdiction effort as both ineffective and costly in civilian lives. James McCartney of the *Miami Herald* announced that the American air war had entered a new phase. "Carrier based Navy pilots are running out of fixed targets," he wrote, adding, "They say they've hit them all. Now they just 'go hunting.'" Citing the Cornell University studies on the effectiveness of bombing offensives, McCartney quoted Professor Norman Uphoff as arguing, "Armed reconnaissance is just another way of saying hunting expedition. They are looking for 'targets of opportunity.' A flier gets maybe two seconds to decide whether he's looking at a 'military target' or not, and no one is around to say that his decision was wrong." Thus, more civilians died and the bombing brought the war no closer to ending. In such a situation, Uphoff and others concluded that the United States had turned to "a terror campaign through bombing."[25] Journalist Peter Arnett, who traveled near Nam Dinh with the three recently released American POWs, wrote about the energy of the "ant power" that repaired bomb damage and kept supplies and men moving southward. He wrote of women "carrying mud in their bare hands to fill in the craters, and they seemed to be enjoying it." The three aviators showed him AAA sites disguised to look like grave mounds that could not be spotted on reconnaissance flights as well as seemingly casually parked vehicles that became convoys at night. As Navy LT Markham Gartley told Arnett, "I used to fly over this place and it seem uninhabited. But look, it is teeming with life." The activity spoke volumes to U.S. Air Force Major Edward Elias, who commented, "It is technology against ideology." The former POW wondered "how far technology can go, because the Vietnamese habitually beat it."[26]

Still, CTF-77 planners continued to believe the effort worthwhile, and they did not hesitate to go after specific targets that had to be neutralized or eliminated. Intelligence reports placed at least two MiG-21s on the ground at the Bai Thuong airfield in RP IV, west of Thanh Hoa and not far from the Laotian border, flown there by top-notch North Vietnamese pilots. MiGs flying from this airfield might threaten B-52s pounding targets in the southern route packs and alpha strikes headed for targets farther north. Although the airfield lay in a route

Each of these ordnancemen—the "redshirts" or simply "the ordies"—lifted and hung thousands of pounds of bombs, mines, and other ordnance onto VA-75 aircraft during the combat cruise. LCDR Dick Engel and LCDR Hal King, the two bareheaded crewmen in this photo, and all Sunday Puncher pilots and B/Ns appreciated the hard work of the squadron's "BB stackers." (U.S. Navy photograph, Jerry L. Walden Collection)

pack traditionally controlled by the Navy, the Air Force decided to destroy the aircraft before they took off again and to crater the two runways that ran north-south and northeast-southwest. The Air Force decision reflected a recent change in the planning of air operations in Westpac. ADM Noel A. M. Gayler, ADM McCain's successor as commander-in-chief in the Pacific theater, authorized an alteration to the longstanding route package system in northern North Vietnam. To encourage more effective interservice cooperation for "mass application of force" on targets around Hanoi and its railroad network, he described the area as an "integrated strike zone" that gave both the U.S. Air Force and U.S. Navy the option to plan and execute missions there.[27] But the foul weather that grounded the North Vietnamese aircraft at Bai Thuong also stopped the Air Force strike force in Thailand from flying over the Annamese mountains to hit the airfield. Thus, the Navy picked up the mission. About mid-afternoon on 10 September, when CVW-3 received orders to hit the Bai Thuong airfield, CAG Bordone realized that only a strike by the all-weather A-6As of VA-75 offered any promise of success.

Since CDR Earnest was not available when Bordone called the VA-75 ready room, CDR Greene went to IOIC to discuss the special mission. With input from airwing operations and intelligence personnel, they decided upon a two-plane A-6A strike. Since the mission clearly carried extremely high risk, Bordone decided that he would pilot one A-6A, taking LCDR Pieno as his B/N as he had done several times before. CDR Greene agreed to fly the second strike aircraft.

That decision greatly disappointed two junior crews. Before Bordone and Greene discussed the tasking, LTs Pyle and Hvidding and LT Tolhurst and LTJG Ahrens, as the next A-6 crews on the flight schedule, already had worked their way through much of the mission-planning process for a strike on the airfield. When Greene informed them that they had been dropped from the hop, both Pyle and Tolhurst grew angry. They regarded the heavies' decision as arbitrary and unfair. The two pilots felt sufficiently confident in their ability to do the job. Then, when they learned that admirals at the task force level and perhaps even higher attached great importance to the destruction of the target, they also realized that success likely meant significant awards to the crews that executed the mission. Rightly or wrongly, they immediately concluded that their ouster from the strike represented yet another example of senior officers' selecting specific missions based on medal potential.[28]

If Bordone and Greene knew of their JOs' anger, they dismissed it. More critical now, since Pieno usually flew with Greene, the XO needed a B/N to fly in his right seat. Both Pieno and LCDR Graustein went to find one. Several junior B/Ns who heard about the mission being taken away from Pyle and Tolhurst refused the opportunity. Then Graustein spotted LTJG Fuller, just returned from an aborted alpha strike. The ops officer explained the mission and made clear that he sought a volunteer. Fuller agreed to go, if he could talk to his pilot first.

The refusal of several junior B/Ns to take the mission, along with Fuller's request to speak with LT Knapp before making a decision, again demonstrated the strength of the crew concept among those whose aviation experience rested exclusively in A-6s. The Knapp-Fuller crew had become committed believers in the concept. Just as he checked with Knapp before he escorted Nini Lerseth back to California in September, Fuller now cleared it with him again. Only when Knapp raised no strenuous objection did he agree to fly as Greene's B/N on this special mission.

Since the strike had such a high priority, and inclement weather precluded the execution of a full schedule of flight operations anyway, all other airwing operations essentially stopped. After an analysis of the target area and a consideration of tactics, Bordone, Greene, and Pieno came up with a plan. They decided to hit their target at dusk's last light. They drew up a timeline. From launch to feet dry would take about ten minutes. To fly from feet dry to the target area would take about fifteen minutes more. Thus, to hit their target as planned, they had to launch approximately twenty-five minutes before last light. Then the two planes planned to rendezvous and fly at approximately 360 knots at extremely low level the entire route. This low-level departure broke from the norm, and, as LCDR Jackson had learned during the strike on Haiphong Boat Yard Number 3 on 31 July, it made the mission more difficult. As Fuller later explained, "Altitude helps here because you can 'see' further if you are higher (either visually or on radar) and thus find a point or two to update your position and help solve the nav[igation] problem. Low all the way is more of a gamble."

The two crews then discussed the coordination of their attack on the Bai Thuong airfield itself. About five miles—or one minute—from the target area, Bordone and Greene planned to split and maneuver independently, each preparing to crater a specific runway with his load of fourteen Mk82s equipped with retarding fins for low-level release. Bordone and Pieno took the north-south strip while Greene and Fuller hit the one angling northeast-southwest. To make this work, one aircraft—Bordone and Pieno's plane—had to slow down a bit to allow Greene and Fuller to move into position for their bombing run. "I remember this," Fuller wrote later, "only because the idea of slowing down in the target area struck me as an act of great foolishness."

As they approached the airfield, each plane had to gain altitude briefly to make positive identification of its target. If the MiGs happened to be present, they would try to destroy the aircraft. If not, the runways got their full attention. In either case, each aircraft would execute its run on its individual target at 200 feet and at 360 knots, laying its bombs at interval settings designed to maximize the damage. They chose the specific timing and tactics, combined with marginal weather, to surprise the enemy and minimize their exposure to the AAA batteries known to surround the base. An especially tricky part of the plan called for the planes to cross each other's path, but the split before the attack built in a sufficient time differential to prevent damage to the second plane from the shrapnel of the first plane's exploding ordnance.

As the planning process ended, CDR Earnest and LCDR Jackson arrived and tried to oust Greene and Fuller from the mission. "However, with [Bordone's] help and my persuasion," Greene recalled, Earnest "reluctantly decided to let it stand as planned." Before they left the planning room, CAG Bordone made a bet with the XO: he would buy martinis for life if Greene lived.

During the preflight check of the planes assigned to the mission, Fuller spotted a fuel leak on the starboard side of the aircraft readied for him and CDR Greene. JP-5 dripped on the catapult track in a nearly steady stream. The aircraft had to be downed. Greene and Fuller now had no plane, but they spotted LCDRs Graustein and Wade in the ready spare. Usually, when an aircraft went down on deck after manning, the crew in the spare aircraft—who went through the briefing, too—took its place. In this case, however, CDR Greene claimed ownership of the spare. Graustein protested that it went against squadron practice, but Greene countered that since he and Fuller had not gotten into the leaking plane yet, the rule did not apply. A heated discussion ensued, but rank finally won out. Graustein and Wade exited the spare. Fuller truly enjoyed the incident. "I felt like a little kid dancing around behind his older brother going 'nyah, nyah' at the other kids while big brother did all the dirty work. JGs aren't often on the winning side."

Finally, both crews ran their preflight checklist and prepared to launch. The atmosphere at that moment struck CDR Greene as "surrealistic." Most of the time, flight deck operations suggested a wide variety of purposeful activities, but as Greene recalled, "This mission had little of these. It was almost eerily quiet with limited flight deck activity. Two aircraft and their requirements are almost miniscule in comparison with cyclic operations we normally encountered." They launched and flew "low—really low." CAG Bordone, as Fuller noted, "was a great believer in the lower the better and he practiced that on this flight." Indeed, on an earlier road recce when Bordone and Pieno had gone trolling for moving vehicles, they had flown so low that the B/N had announced a potential target on a hillside road with "CAG, trucks—twelve o'clock high!" Now, they flew low again, perhaps ten feet off the deck. As they coasted in, Fuller could look through the door of a hut on the beach and see the family's cooking fire inside. CDR Greene decided to fly a little higher than Bordone, and to do so he rose to fifty feet. As Fuller looked down into CAG's cockpit, he could see the chart on Pieno's knee. A low overcast hung at about 1,000 feet and rain sporadically splattered on their windscreens.

They made their way to the target area unopposed. Then Fuller discovered a glitch. When he went to check his timing, he realized that he had failed to start his elapsed time clock. He felt little concern since everything seemed to be progressing as planned, and he figured he would just start it at the next checkpoint. Right then, CDR Greene asked him how they were doing on time. Fuller admitted that he did not know, but he assured the XO that all was well. "I'm not sure if he bought that or not," Fuller recalled.

CAG Bordone planned to make about a 90-degree left turn to the south to align with his target. CDR Greene intended to proceed further west and use a bend in the river and a specific distance from the end of a shallow ridgeline as the turning point to the southeast that would align him with his target. As the two planes separated, however, Fuller realized that he still had not started his clock. Thus, he would have to decide from visual cues when Greene should make his turn. At first, Fuller felt no qualms about this since river bends had provided good navigational marks in the past. Then he looked down and discovered that his chart did not show what actually existed, a winding river that made a major bend every twenty feet or so from their current position out to the western horizon. When they arrived at a point that looked right to Fuller, he told Greene to make the turn. Greene looked down to locate the mark and, seeing the same serpentine river, asked, "Where?" The XO used a tone Fuller recalled as "one of incredulousness," but, feeling confident, the B/N replied, "Right there! Turn now!" Greene turned, earning his B/N's eternal respect, and when they did so, the runway was only a few degrees off the nose of the aircraft.

Bordone made his run first. As Greene noted, "I observed CAG in his run on the other runway passing left to right and his ordnance detonating up the runway at intervals as planned." He and Fuller also noticed that the strike had begun to receive a smattering of AAA fire, "which was easy to see, as there were tracers and the low light level made them bright and highly visible." Most of it traced the path of Bordone and Pieno's plane.

Greene then began his run. Just before he pickled his bombs, he saw an indistinct object in the runway near the halfway point. He could not identify it. He just knew it seemed quite bulky. As his bombs began to release at their preselected intervals, he and Fuller noticed that their plane, too, now drew the attention of the AAA gunners. Fuller did not consider the fire to be particularly intense, mostly a startled reaction to their presence. When the two men looked behind them to see where their bombs hit, Greene saw "a very large explosion near the area of the object that had been observed half way down the runway." It rested near the center of their string of bombs.

Their run completed, Greene and Fuller broke off target to link up with Bordone and Pieno. Now, to Greene, at least, the AAA fire seemed to grow stronger and more accurate. He could not figure out why; they had no indications of radar-controlled fire, and the growing darkness should have prevented gunners from acquiring them visually. Then Bordone and Pieno saw what appeared to be an explosion under Greene and Fuller's aircraft. During their run, Fuller had hit the chaff/flare dispenser to confuse any radars that might be tracking them. All the chaff emptied out while overflying the runway. Then, since the system was set on automatic—at Greene's direction and against Fuller's advice—the first of the flares popped out and ignited. The light from the flares likely aided the AAA gunners as Greene and Fuller egressed, but the plane went unscathed.

Bordone and Greene trapped back aboard *Saratoga* within thirty seconds of each other. After all that effort, little in the way of official BDA followed. Still, the four men believed they had accomplished their mission and rendered the runways unusable for the immediate future. No one ever verified the identity of the "large object" Greene's bombs hit, although speculation centered on either a fuel truck or perhaps even a camouflaged MiG. For CDR Greene, a veteran of over 420 combat missions, the Bai Thuong strike stood out in his memory as "one of those missions you do not forget" because it was "interesting and had all of the elements of being a worthwhile mission with real targets that meant something."[29]

Despite the successful results, the Bai Thuong mission continued to bother some of the Punchers' junior pilots and B/Ns still wrestling with perceived inequities in mission assignments. "These 'squadron leaders' over here really make me angry sometimes," a still furious LT Tolhurst wrote home that night. "They tell you how they plan to even up all the hops so the junior guys won't get stuck with all the tankers. Then the next minute they take a strike hop away from you for themselves because the admiral called and wants the target hit if the weather is bad, which they expect it to be. That way they stand a good chance of getting more medals for a hard hop." In this case, he asserted, "of course Doug [LTJG Ahrens, his B/N] and I could fly it just as well but why let a junior crew get a good hop like this? The real final straw . . . is that they want you to go to the brief and take the hop if the weather is good; because it will be fairly routine with no case for a medal. [T]hey don't want it if that happens. It really gets old with this 'stuff' all the time."[30] Not all the JOs felt that way, of course. When the four men who flew the Bai Thuong strike were recommended for Silver Star medals, LTJG Warren admitted that "they deserved it."[31]

The airwing enjoyed a welcome stand-down day on 11 October. When air operations began on 12 October, *Saratoga* took the midnight-to-noon schedule through the last recovery on 16 October. Inclement weather and the reappearance of nagging maintenance issues now worked together to limit the number of hops the squadron flew each day. As early as 4 October, a pilot complained that the squadron's strike aircraft were "falling apart," and he was "on the verge of taking anything as long as both engines will start."[32] That day had not been one of the Maintenance Department's most shining moments, but it also had been an exception. Still, as the month progressed, long-term downing gripes seriously degraded the number of mission-ready squadron aircraft. All four of VA-75's A-6B missions for 5 October had to be scrubbed for lack of working planes.[33] One developed a cracked wing that could not be repaired on the ship; it spent the entire October line period on the hangar deck. The other one came back from its last hop on 4 October with a damaged engine, torn up so badly that the mechanics had to replace it.[34] The "missile bird" only stayed down for two days, but the squadron flew most of the October line period with half its usual A-6B support capability. With the increased emphasis on full-systems hops to support night missions, the Fire Control Branch assigned recently arrived Chief Aviation Firecontrolman Joachim Yakovleff "to bear the brunt of the B/Ns wrath at a 'down' system," relieving a second-class petty officer who gladly gave up the duty. One of the night check crew joked that in October they increasingly began to use "a lot of technical language this period, like 'It's broke,' and 'It don't work.'"[35]

To help the squadron meet sortie requirements, CDR Earnest sent LT Chisholm and LTJG Vance to Cubi to pick up a repaired A-6A. They waited five days for their plane to clear maintenance, and not even LT Mullins could expedite the work. In an end-of-cruise evaluation, the airwing's beach detachment fared poorly. It had no officer-in-charge for most of the cruise, as Mullins's temporary posting to that slot demonstrated, and thus it lacked a single accountable head to encourage timely, high-quality work and to secure necessary equipment. "Supervision was minimal and thus the detachment was not very efficient," one squadron's report concluded.[36] CDR Earnest ultimately gained an aircraft, but he lost a pilot and B/N from 9 through 13 October.

Chisholm and Vance arrived in the Philippines just after Penny Swigart left for home. After watching Nini Lerseth and Barbara Miller depart, Penny decided to leave, too. As she considered why their little group of Puncher wives so quickly shrank from six to four, she remembered how, as a child, she had sung about "ten little, nine little, eight little Indians." The attrition rate of pilots and B/Ns—and their wives in Manila—increasingly bothered her. She worried about her own husband and asked herself, "What if he's the next little Indian?" She decided that if bad news came, she wanted to be in the familiar environment of home. One small hitch: her visa expired on 7 October and she could not get a flight out until 9 October. All efforts to get a two-day extension failed, so she fell back on the expedient of using a pen to change the expiration date herself. She tried hard to disguise her nervousness as she checked in for her flight, but a great wave of relief washed over her when the Filipino immigration agents failed to scrutinize her credentials closely. She returned to Virginia Beach.[37]

Despite detached crews and departing wives, the missions continued. Even for those without a superstitious bent, 13 October—a Friday—fully lived up to its unlucky image. LT Lankford and LTJG Warren flew an armed recce into the "golden triangle," the area bounded by Ninh Binh, Phu Ly, and Nam Dinh in RP IV, its nickname denoting the accuracy of its concentrated AAA batteries. They found some trucks to drop on before heading toward the nearby ferry slip they planned to hit. As they neared their target, however, the AAA grew so hot that they broke off their attack. They dropped on a nearby ferry instead and returned safely to the ship. The whole experience spooked Warren. "I've never seen AAA so accurate as last night," he wrote, noting that the "amazing thing was it was all *in front* of us shooting *at us* instead of behind us like it normally is. It's almost as if they could see us."[38]

That same night, CDR Earnest and LCDR Jackson flew a seeding mission to a bridge near Bac Giang in RP VI-B, near the northeast railway. They planned their ordnance drop to create a chokepoint in the busy waterway, setting up the area for a potential large-scale alpha strike on a mass of WBLCs. Along their entire route, they faced such extremely heavy and accurate fire that Jackson, too, recorded it as the "worst AAA ever seen at night."[39] In 1973, after the squadron returned to Oceana, Jackson spoke to reporters about this mission, and one journalist reacted as if he had found a big story. The next day, he revealed what every Sunday Puncher pilot and B/N already knew—that along with the mining of North Vietnam's harbors, "there was also a continuing effort to mine waterways [far] inland."[40]

Both of these night strikes likely saw the impact of ongoing North Vietnamese efforts to form "fighting clusters" or "firenets" to shoot down American aircraft. During the autumn of 1972, provinces and towns began organizing "one hand on the plow, the other on a gun" and "one hand holding the fishing net, the other on a gun" militias. Some communities built more fortifications along flight paths frequented by American planes. In some areas, efforts had begun to "assure the providing of many more soldiers with fighting experience to do the observing, aiming, and firing" at the aircraft.[41]

Probably the worst experience of Friday the Thirteenth happened to LTJGs Bryan and Petersen in the squadron's only flyable A-6B. On 13 October, they provided cover for night strikes headed against targets in RPs IV and VI-B. When they got a lock on a Fan Song radar, they fired off an AGM-78. Usually the missile dropped and ignited and then flew straight and level while accelerating ahead of the aircraft for a few seconds, before pitching up high in the air and then descending toward the target. Two seconds after Bryan and Petersen fired, however, the missile exploded prematurely and broke up right under the aircraft. All Bryan saw was "a big orange ball." Fortunately no shrapnel from the missile damaged the plane, and the crew recovered safely.[42]

Even though that A-6B remained airworthy, the incident added to the doubts about the aircraft harbored by some in the A-6 community, especially XO Greene. Every time an A-6B fired a missile, the crew had to fill out a report for the Naval Weapons Station at Corona, California. The weapons analysis center there evaluated them, and when they detected a pattern of incidents revealing a problem such as this one, they often sent a technical representative to investigate. It happened frequently enough that Greene, for one, began to wonder if it was worthwhile to continue to risk squadron assets for questionable gain. It became standard practice for many A-6B crews to fire a missile, move off, and "get out of the way of that thing."[43]

Although the A-6 possessed the technology to fly in bad weather, missions launched into leaden skies still surprised crews with unexpected twists. A night seeding hop near a bridge complex fifteen miles north of Thanh Hoa on 16 October should have offered few challenges that LT Lankford had not experienced before. But this mission, flown at about 300 feet, kept the aircraft in the clouds most of the time. Pulling off the target after dropping his twelve specially fused Mk82s, Lankford suffered a severe case of vertigo. He so completely lost his sense of direction that he thought he was flying upside down. His B/N talked to him constantly and updated him on altitude and direction, and all the while both of them ignored distracting reflections from exploding AAA bursts eerily illuminating the clouds surrounding them. LTJG Warren stretched the truth when he concluded that the hop was "fairly simple and reasonably safe, if you can call it that."[44]

Back in the United States, neither Bobbe Lindland nor Nini Lerseth could apply "reasonably safe" to the reality of flying combat. LCDR Lindland's wife remained in Virginia Beach, where at least she could tap into a substantial support base of very active local POW/MIA support groups that, especially since 1970, had raised awareness of the fate of captured American servicemen. The Norfolk and Virginia Beach members of the "They're Not Forgotten Committee" continued to sell POW/MIA bracelets. The National League of Families of American Prisoners and Missing in Southeast Asia set up a local office, opened a speakers' bureau, and held petition drives, publicity campaigns, and fundraising events. Jane Denton, the wife of CDR Jeremiah Denton of VA-75—a POW since July 1965—served as one of its more active members.[45] Phyllis Galanti, wife of LT Paul Galanti—a POW since 1966—visited Bobbe the day after LCDR Lindland and LT Lerseth's plane went down, to offer support and to tell her about League activities.[46]

Nini Lerseth enjoyed none of this kind of interest-group support. True to her agreement with her husband, she left San Francisco for Spokane to be with her mother-in-law. LT Lerseth's mother continued to go to work each day, and his sisters remained busy with school. But Nini had no such distraction. Thus, when Bobbe Lindland called her and asked her to come to Washington for a meeting of the National League of Families on 16 October, she readily agreed. She relied upon the pilot's wife for guidance. After all, she later explained, "I didn't know what to say or what to do."[47]

The meeting of the League of Families came at a most interesting point in POW affairs. Just a month previously, when Hanoi had released the three aviators, North Vietnam handed them over to Cora Weiss and David Dellinger, cochairs of the Committee of Liaison with Families of Servicemen Detained in North Vietnam, an avowed antiwar and pro-McGovern group. Pro-administration media scrutiny suggested that these three men obtained their freedom because two of them publicly condemned the Vietnam War and expressed support for McGovern while the third man's mother vehemently and publicly denounced the Nixon administration.[48] By 1972, POW/MIA families, once stalwart supporters of the war effort, no longer marched in lockstep behind the president, and the Weiss-Dellinger organization represented only one faction claiming to speak for the families of missing American servicemen. Senator Edward M. Kennedy maintained communication with this group, however, and Bobbe Lindland contacted his office, hoping to work through his connections to get Hanoi leaders to acknowledge publicly that they held LCDR Lindland as a POW. If they did so, she believed, North Vietnam then would have to keep him alive to avoid potential embarrassment during repatriation at war's end. But Senator Kennedy brushed her off rudely, bluntly accusing her husband of killing innocent North Vietnamese civilians, and she sought no further assistance from the Weiss-Dellinger group.[49] Nor did she turn to the POW/MIA Families for Immediate Release, a group that split from the League of Families and, at the same time, withdrew their support for the war effort.[50]

The League of Families generally stuck with the administration, and Bobbe Lindland and Nini Lerseth sat in the crowd when President Nixon himself came to the Statler-Hilton Hotel to address the group on 16 October. He had usurped Henry Kissinger's place on the program to thank the group for their support and inspiration. As one of the League's spokespersons attested, "Most of us feel that whatever happens is going to rest on his shoulders and we had better give him our support." In return, he promised not to abandon the POWs and MIAs, and, as he noted, he used the word "abandon" deliberately. "We cannot leave their fate to the goodwill of the enemy. We must have some strength in ourselves," he said. To stave off defeat after the March 1972 invasion of the South, he had mined North Vietnam's harbors and reinstituted the bombing of its military targets. That decision, which led to the downing of LCDR Lindland and LT Lerseth among others, he declared to be "the right decision militarily." Moreover, Nixon argued, "it has been effective." He thanked the families of the POWs and MIAs for their encouragement. "I would not have made that decision unless I thought it would contribute to our goal of achieving an honorable peace in Vietnam," he told them.[51] He desired peace, but not peace at any price. Any acceptable solution required the release of or a full accounting for the POWs and MIAs, and he asked for patience during the ongoing talks in Paris to end the war on those terms.

Nixon's and Kissinger's diplomatic efforts to end the war also continued to shape the air war in which the Sunday Punchers flew. Indeed, in mid-October, as diplomatic affairs continued to unfold in Paris, Henry Kissinger met yet again with Le Duc Tho. As part of the give-and-take and as a sign of good faith, the Nixon administration on 17 October once again restricted the bombing of

North Vietnam to only that portion of the country south of the 20th parallel. Strikes against military targets in the immediate vicinity of Hanoi and Haiphong ended. Moreover, on that same day, the Joint Chiefs of Staff severely cut back the number of daily strikes against North Vietnamese targets to a mere seventy-six strike missions. Those same restrictions capped at seventy-four the number of missions the carriers could fly against targets in South Vietnam.

The slowdown in air operations did not go unnoticed by VA-75. "We've been flying 60 a day, the Saratoga alone," LTJG Warren noted, "and that's *bomb dropping* ops. It doesn't include tankers, BARCAP, etc. Saratoga flies about 120 total missions a day. Now we'll average 25 *strike sorties* (bombers) a day."[52] Before the announcement of the bombing restrictions, CVW-3's planning staff prepared for three major alpha strikes for 17 October. Weather and policy changes cancelled them. Pilots and B/Ns with fewer missions to plan made more frequent appearances to check up on their enlisted men. LCDR Pieno and the branch officers of the Administrative Department came in so often that, as the family-gram reported, "in the background can be heard the lament, sure as H ___ wish *they* would start flying again so we can get some work done!"[53] The final flight schedule for 17 October assigned VA-75 only six strike hops and a reduced tanker obligation. Still, the day ended with news of a possible cease-fire that inspired a thirteen-hour party in LTJG Petersen's stateroom before they learned the sad truth that nothing had changed.[54] On 23 October, the Pentagon reinforced the new limitations on airstrikes by announcing the termination of Operation LINEBACKER.

Even though they no longer could hit targets in RP VI-B, *Saratoga* repositioned itself farther south, and the Sunday Punchers found plenty of work in MR I and II in northern South Vietnam. President Thieu, under pressure to show additional positive evidence of the success of Vietnamization, now pressed harder for ARVN counterattacks to retake territory lost to the North Vietnamese army during the Easter Offensive. Senior ARVN ground commanders asked MACV for additional American air support.

On 18 October, and for the next three days, *Saratoga* answered that call. Air operations picked up in tempo as VA-75 and the rest of CVW-3 flew a significant proportion of the Navy's authorized strikes against targets in South Vietnam. A familiar face joined them for these last few days on the line. LT Michael A. Schuster, the replacement pilot CDR Earnest had requested, had flown with VA-75 during the 1971 Med cruise. He already knew many of the squadron's pilots and B/Ns, and he volunteered to go to Westpac to fill the place of one of those friends, LCDR Lindland. Schuster had known LT Lerseth well, too; indeed, back in the Med, the two had flown together. As a first-cruise B/N, Lerseth had learned many lessons from his experienced pilot, often reinforced by a sharp rap on the helmet. When he left his instructor billet in VA-42, Schuster flew from Oceana to Cubi in a new A-6A to replace Lindland and Lerseth's plane. As it went through final checks at the CVW-3 beach detachment, an eager Schuster pumped LT Mullins for information about recent air operations.[55] Then, as soon as he arrived aboard *Saratoga,* he pulled aside a few of the squadron pilots and B/Ns to ask, "How many Sidewinders are you carrying?" When he learned that the A-6As dropped only general-purpose iron bombs and mines, the A-6B fired only air-to-ground missiles, and only F-4s carried the air-to-air MiG-killing ordnance, disappointment showed all over his face.[56] Still, he went to work immediately. Probably because the squadron heavies believed they knew his skill level, Schuster did not begin with the tankers and milkruns that had initiated King, Connelly, Wiegand, and Wade; he flew strike hops against targets in MR I and II within two days of arrival, paired up with any B/N assigned to him.

Perhaps it was fortuitous that CVW-3 flew a less challenging operational schedule on 18 October. In the early hours of the morning, starting down on the mess deck, *Saratoga* joined the lengthening list of U.S. Navy vessels experiencing racial violence.

The Navy, like the other services since the integration of the American armed forces in 1948, had opened many doors for its minority personnel. Indeed, the first African American admiral, Samuel L. Gravely, pinned on his stars in June 1971. But many African American sailors believed the Navy treated them unfairly. Part of their resentment stemmed from strong opposition in the African American community to the war, which had diverted funding from important domestic programs. Mistrust also grew from unfulfilled ambitions, sustained by a belief that white sailors received preference in promotions and job training. Much of this perception stemmed from a lack of understanding about the assignment of duties aboard carriers. Many nonrated airmen and airmen apprentices expected to begin immediately the technical training promised when they enlisted. When instead they found themselves temporarily detached from their squadrons to work in the laundry or the galley—duties routinely performed by the carrier's most junior sailors regardless of permanent assignment—they felt cheated. Race further complicated their resentment.

To deal with issues of race, CNO Zumwalt had ordered the assignment of a "human relations" officer in all Navy units. In practice, this duty often fell to an already overworked junior officer or senior chief. The Sunday Punchers had no African American officers and only one chief, Wright Cade of the Power Plants branch. Still, the previous year, the recuperating LT Mullins had volunteered for the job. Although he still languished at Cubi, he had seen no imminent signs of racial unrest among the Sunday Punchers' enlisted men and harbored no doubts about the morale and professionalism in the squadron's shops. Back in July he had invited the sailors from the Power Plants Branch to choose their favorite club in Olongapo for an informal "wetting down" party to celebrate his promotion. He gave the club manager some money and announced the beer was on him, but the black sailors from his shop stayed for only a couple of drinks, paid their respects, and left for other bars that drew a largely African American clientele. He did not take their departure as a sign of hostility, noting that "it was just how they did it." But these men all held technical ratings. He felt less certain about the mood of the squadron's junior sailors who worked hard at menial tasks, waited their turn to step into technical billets, and associated with "people who . . . could not qualify for anything else."[57]

Race-based violence peaked in the Seventh Fleet in October 1972. *Saratoga* already had experienced a taste of growing interracial tension during its most recent visit to the Philippines, when two white petty officers from VAW-123 got mugged by a group of black sailors at the Subic Bay Naval Base.[58] Shortly after the captain of *Kitty Hawk* informed his crew about the extension of their already long deployment, anger boiled over on 11 October and a fight broke out between the carrier's white and black sailors at a club in Olongapo. Two days later, back at sea, when a black sailor called in for questioning about the fight brought friends to support him, a riot broke out on *Kitty Hawk*'s mess deck, spread to the hangar deck, and Marines—with weapons drawn—had to break it up. At least thirty-three sailors suffered injuries during the fight, two hurt so badly that they had to be evacuated to shore-based hospitals. A few days later, on 17 October, a similar—but smaller—outbreak of race-based unrest occurred on the fleet oiler *Hassayampa*.[59]

The two incidents drew home-front attention immediately, both from civil rights activists and from reactionaries on race relations. In a radical African American paper, headlines blared, "You Can't Be Black and Navy Too," criticizing CNO Zumwalt's recent changes in race relations as "meaningless" and concluding that "racism cannot be eradicated by issuing a directive."[60] On the other hand, to encourage an end to "forced intermixing of the races, equal employment interference, and racial percentage allocations," Representative John R. Rarick (D-LA) pointed out that the fifty injuries produced in these two incidents nearly equaled the number of combat casualties suffered in the same time period. He decried the exploitation of naval vessels as "sociological experimental training laboratories" to satisfy "a handful of ideologists and egalitarians" and warned that a commanding officer might use the recent unrest to demand a segregated crew.[61]

While Congress and the media deliberated at home, the contagion of racial discord spread to *Saratoga* on 18 October. Rumors of potential trouble circulated throughout the ship. African American sailors called for a meeting with the ship's senior leadership to discuss their grievances. Chief Cade did not attend. It interfered with his work, and he simply did not have time for such activities; other black chiefs in the airwing also stayed away. VA-75 counted a significant number of African-American men among its first- and second-class petty officers; a few of them attended the meeting, mostly from curiosity, but then returned to their shops.[62]

As the atmosphere became increasingly hostile, some of VA-75's African American personnel took steps to separate themselves from trouble that might occur. Some of the sailors working in the line division approached LTJG Vance to request permission to come to his stateroom so they would not be drawn into any race-based group action against their will.[63] When CDR Greene learned of their concerns, he agreed to a temporary arrangement permitting the squadron's African American sailors to move out of their assigned berthing compartments and into their shops and work spaces where their safety could be guaranteed. "They lived right there for a few days. And we brought the food to them," recalled Greene, noting that "they just stayed right there. And that's what they wanted."[64]

Still, despite these precautions, a fight started early in the morning of 18 October, just after the end of air operations. With no known provocation, a black sailor walking down a passageway near the galley punched a white sailor. Friends of both parties gathered, and the growing mass of angry men swept across the mess deck. CAPT Sanderson took quick steps to end it before it got out of control. At 0202, he ordered the ship to General Quarters. Each sailor aboard *Saratoga* now had a choice to make: He could be a sailor, respond to orders, and report to his duty station immediately; or he could be thrown into the brig. All but a small handful of black sailors immediately reported to their duty stations. The ship stood down from General Quarters an hour later.[65]

The officers of VA-75 praised Sanderson's handling of the situation. Looking back on it, many blamed the African American sailors in the ship's company for starting the fight. However, the day after the flare-up, LTJG Warren, the squadron's legal officer, faced an unhappy duty. The man who threw the first punch belonged to VA-75—a very junior sailor, temporarily assigned to the ship's laundry, and thus not influenced by the camaraderie that usually marked the squadron's day-to-day operations. He had not been identified as a troublemaker before, but now Warren had to escort him to Captain's Mast for disciplinary action.[66]

The next day, CDR Earnest called an all-hands meeting on the forecastle. He usually held such a gathering just before the start of each in-port stay to congratulate the men on their recent performance, to remind them to behave themselves on liberty, and to answer their questions. He invariably called upon LT Martin, the squadron's senior air intelligence officer, to summarize where squadron aircraft had flown and what they had hit. He called his meeting earlier than usual this line period, however, to clear the air and to attempt to forestall a repeat of the previous day's events. Another brief outbreak of violence involving VA-75 sailors occurred a few nights later, but no one could determine if race played a role in it.[67]

The men of the squadron and airwing had to put the incident behind them quickly. Air strikes against North Vietnamese troop concentrations in South Vietnam spiked upward on 20 and 21 October. On 20 October, accurately reported one B/N, "We flew more sorties and dropped more ordnance than we ever have in a single day over here." He put his flight gear on at 0715 that morning and did not take it off until 1715 in the afternoon; he spent six and one-half hours in the air that day.[68] Even CAPT Sanderson considered the accomplishment sufficiently noteworthy to mention it in his periodic letters to *Saratoga* families back home, noting that CVW-3 aircrews hammered the Pleiku area: "We were asked to surge in response to an attack by North Vietnamese troops in the Central Highlands. Surge we did."[69] Their efforts did not go unnoticed. The U.S. Army advisers on the ground sent a letter of commendation to *Saratoga* to thank its airwing for its effective work.[70]

The hectic pace maintained by some pilots and B/Ns reflected in part the early departure for Singapore of a number of other Sunday Punchers who received permission to leave the ship to meet their wives. In addition, when *Saratoga* stopped flying strike missions in North Vietnam, two more crews departed to take the squadron's damaged A-6Bs to Cubi. As a result, during the hard push of 20 October, 13 Puncher pilots flew 34 missions in a single day.[71]

The same high tempo continued on 21 October, but at the end of flight operations, *Saratoga* turned toward Subic Bay. CVW-3 had flown 991 combat strike sorties and had delivered 1,659 tons of ordnance.[72] VA-75's A-6As had flown 207 of those strike missions, 83 of them at night. Problems with the A-6B aircraft had reduced their flying time during this line period, with only 32 missions flown. The KA-6Ds continued to be the squadron workhorses, launching for 209 tanker hops, 93 at night. The most revealing statistic, however, showed the impact of the inclement weather in the Gulf of Tonkin; exclusive of days when monsoon rains cancelled all air operations, the airwing scrubbed an additional 67 missions from VA-75's flight schedule.[73]

Unfamiliar and unique stressors of this line period clearly wore on the entire crew. On 22 October, as the carrier steamed toward Cubi, *Saratoga* went to General Quarters three separate times. The first call proved to be a drill, and the second came in response to a fire on the hangar deck. But the third sounded when yet another fight between black and white sailors broke out on the mess deck.[74] No Sunday Puncher personnel were involved in this latest incident of racial discord.

A Sunday Puncher KA-6D tanker. The need to refuel the entire airwing often gave tankers priority over A-6A strike aircraft in Sunday Puncher maintenance shops. (U.S. Navy photograph, Everett W. Foote Collection)

The strain carried over to the pilots and B/Ns too. Questions and concerns voiced in letters from home now forced some Punchers to consider more deeply their reasons for staying the course. In the end, each man in his own way decided he had a professional commitment to meet. Some pilots and B/Ns tried to put in words their appreciation for those at home who could do little but pray for their safe return and wait while they did their job. "Whether you realize it or not, a serviceman's wife, and I'd like to say especially one whose husband's halfway around the world, daily risking his life, serves her country just as much as the serviceman does," LTJG Warren wrote Carol. "Out here," he noted, "everyone is literally in the 'same boat.' Misery loves company, and out here we have plenty of it. . . . All I can say is you're really helping the cause whatever the cause is."[75] LT Tolhurst thanked Pixie for understanding his need to do his job: "I know this cruise and the war, etc. are really a strain on you, but you haven't let it turn you against my flying. I really enjoy flying and I thank you for putting up with it, even though there are much safer jobs possible."[76] As LTJG Petersen saw it, most Sunday Punchers wanted only three things: "an end to the war; release of American POWs, and to be home for Christmas." But he wanted one thing more: "Maybe this war will teach us a lesson that will keep Danny out of a Vietnam."[77]

Even within the tight-knit squadron, the trust that bound them together weakened a bit. Some continued to speculate quietly about the willingness of individual pilots and B/Ns to see out the combat cruise.[78] At the same time, junior officers continued to complain about mission assignments. Finally, LT John Miller, the squadron schedules officer, received orders to prepare a summary of flight statistics, current through the end of the line period just concluding.

If the senior officers hoped it would quash any further complaints about unfair allocation of missions, the JOs believed that numerical evidence would support their views. Miller broke down each pilot and B/N's missions into three columns: A-6A, A-6B, and KA-6D hops. Most of those who deployed with the squadron in mid-May now had accumulated at least 130 missions of all sorts. Among the pilots, CDR Earnest and LCDR Engel each had flown 140 hops; among the B/Ns, LT Hvidding had logged 143, LT Wagner and LTJG Petersen each had accumulated 142, and LTJGs Sanford and Swigart each had taken 140.

But that single number did not tell the whole story. Looking only at the A-6A hops—the strike missions—the JOs discovered evidence of the disparity in mission assignments they resented. Among the pilots, CDR Earnest had flown 86 such missions, with LCDR Graustein in second place with 77 and LCDR Engel in the third spot with 70; even CDR Greene, who had joined the squadron well into their first line period, had logged 67 strike missions. By contrast, the four most senior pilots among the lieutenants lagged well behind—Cook with 57, Lankford with 55, Pyle with 51, and Ruland with 42. Among the B/Ns, the disparity seemed even more marked. LCDRs Jackson and Pieno had served through the entire combat cruise so far, and they had logged 89 and 88 strike missions, respectively; LCDR Schram, detached for part of the first line period and most of the second, still had accumulated 61. The next highest tallies, representing B/Ns from the JO ranks who had served through the entire deployment to date, were LTJG Sanford at 61, LTJG Warren at 59, and LTs Hvidding and Mullins at 56.

The statistics also seemed to validate the JOs' complaints that they carried the bulk of the less challenging tanker hops. While CDRs Earnest and Greene and LCDR Graustein had flown only 27, 23, and 44 tankers to date, respectively, LTs Cook, Lankford, Pyle, and Ruland had flown 65, 66, 69, and 82, respectively. Among the B/Ns, LCDR Jackson had flown only 27 tankers, and LCDR Pieno had flown only 25; but LT Wagner had accumulated 59, LT Hvidding had 67, LTJG Sanford had 72, and LTJGs Warren and Ahrens each had 78.[79]

Since the start of the cruise when they had first sensed they might lose strike missions to their senior officers, some junior crews had qualified in the A-6B. Up to now, the highly technical nature of its systems had discouraged some from attempting to master it. Others, such as LCDR King, simply disliked the A-6B mission. But now more crews began to study the technology in the "missile bird." LT Tolhurst and LTJG Ahrens spent much of their time during October's bad weather learning the A-6B systems. They explained it to their wives as a safer option than regular strike hops. As Tolhurst wrote to Pixie, "It is safe because we don't send it over the beach due to the fact that we only have two of them on the ship."[80] He no doubt meant the offhand comment to assure his wife he was not putting himself in additional danger, but junior crews increasingly looked at an A-6B mission as a "good hop" that received the same two points toward an Air Medal that a strike mission carried and as an opportunity to fly something more exciting than a KA-6D. While CDR Earnest had piloted 27 such missions, CDR Greene had limited himself to 12, LCDR Graustein to 16, and LCDR Engel to only 9. In contrast, among those more junior pilots who qualified on the A-6B system, LT Fischer accumulated 35 such missions, LT Knapp counted 34, LT Anderson had 22, and even the more recently arrived LT Chisholm had 21. Among the B/Ns, while LCDR Jackson—an ECM specialist—had flown 22 A-6B missions, LCDR Pieno only logged 18 and LCDR Schram only 1. But among the junior B/Ns, LT Wagner led with 41, followed by LTJG Fuller with 36 and LTJG Petersen with 30, with LT Hvidding and LTJG Vance only a bit behind with 20 each.[81] Miller's statistics, while enlightening, did not lead to any changes in mission assignments.

Recent contentiousness of all sorts made the upcoming in-port period a welcome break. The exodus began even before air operations concluded. LT Lankford convinced XO Greene to let him and LTJGs Bryan and Ahrens make their way to Singapore by way of Danang and Saigon, so they could meet their wives a few days earlier than if they remained aboard *Saratoga*. When they got to Danang, they found the few Americans still there in the process of handing over the post to ARVN troops. They also found no transportation to Saigon. As they wondered what to do next, Lankford learned that some classified materials had to be taken to MACV headquarters and only an officer of O-3 rank with an appropriate security clearance could serve as courier. As VA-75's nuclear weapons officer, he qualified. Lankford quickly struck a bargain with U.S. Army advisers. He agreed to deliver the materials, but only if the Army provided transportation for all three Navy officers. They haggled a while, but finally, with a briefcase handcuffed to his wrist and a pistol in his belt, Lankford and the two other officers got their ride to Saigon.

Too late for a commercial flight to Singapore after he delivered his briefcase, Lankford spent the night at the quarters of some FACs with whom he had previously worked. The next morning when he stepped into the communal shower, several Vietnamese women came in and began their own morning ablutions—with considerably less embarrassment than that Lankford endured.[82] Somehow, all three men made it to Singapore before their wives arrived. When Loretta got there, Lankford surprised her with a bouquet of daisies, her favorite flower. But LTJG Ahrens became the day's big winner. To find enough daisies to make a respectable bouquet, Lankford had to buy several arrangements of mixed blossoms. He gave to Ahrens all those flowers he did not want. Lankford's "leftovers" allowed Ahrens to present Linda with a gorgeous spray of showy orchids.[83]

The Sunday Punchers who took the carrier to Singapore met with adventures of their own. The party at the bar at the Cubi Officers' Club during a brief stop in the Philippines to offload damaged aircraft exceeded all previous squadron events. An unusually high number of VA-75's pilots and B/Ns had October birthdays. At XO Greene's direction, LCDR Wade organized a Sunday Puncher birthday party. To fuel the festivities, they liquidated their "penalty fund," into which an officer deemed guilty of some gross misbehavior paid a fine. For this party, the accumulated sum paid for at least sixty or—depending on which version of a squadron legend one believes—perhaps more than one hundred bottles of wine. The party quickly got out of hand. Someone emptied a bottle over Wade's bald head, a particular sore spot with him. They broke many glasses and did much damage to the club. XO Greene paid the tab. But the officers did not get off unpunished. Many Punchers nursed serious hangovers the next day. "I just can't drink that much of that stuff," LTJG Warren admitted, adding, "A bottle or so is okay, but after that it really gets to me."[84]

That day, as they nursed their headaches, a rumor almost too good to be true swept through *Saratoga*. The Hanoi government announced that Henry Kissinger and Le Duc Tho finally had reached agreement on the conditions for an end to the hostilities. The main points of the concord included a plan for a cease-fire, with the withdrawal of all American and allied forces (but no mention of a concomitant departure of North Vietnamese troops from South Vietnam) within sixty days, the release of all captured military and civilian prisoners in that same sixty-day period, a promise that the Vietnamese people would decide their own future through internationally supervised elections, a guarantee of respect for the independence and neutrality of Laos and Cambodia, a nod toward the reunification of the two Vietnams by peaceful means, and a substantial commitment of U.S. funds to help with reconstruction of all of Indochina. The Hanoi government had announced the agreement before Kissinger intended for it to be released. Many fine points still needed to be clarified. The United States, he said, "will not be stampeded into an agreement until its provisions are right." He also warned the recalcitrant Thieu government, "We will not be deflected from an agreement when its provisions are right." Despite Kissinger's qualifiers, however, only one phrase swept the nation—and *Saratoga*: "Peace is at hand."[85]

As the carrier steamed for Singapore early on 24 October, the Punchers hoped—but did not quite believe—that they might have completed their last line period. The promise of peace made the lure of sunny days in Singapore all the more exciting. Those whose wives met them there enjoyed their time immensely. LTJG Fuller threw a surprise birthday party for Sally, unexpected chiefly because she was born in December. LCDR Schram, LTs Ruland and Lankford, and LTJGs Ahrens and Bryan, and their spouses—except for Ruland's wife, now far too pregnant to make the trip—all joined in the festivities. It began with drinks at the hotel. Then they headed out for dinner at one of Singapore's fine restaurants. Some of the group suspected that the management made special arrangements for any large gatherings of sailors who came to their establishment: They set up tables on the front lawn, not in the building itself. Too much alcohol and not enough rest caught up with LT Ruland, who quickly fell asleep at the dinner table and landed face-first in his entrée.[86] Sally Fuller decided to celebrate by trying the escargot in garlic butter. Later that night and well into the next morning, she deeply regretted it.[87]

VA-75 set up its admin ashore at the Hyatt Hotel. The suite had a sitting room and a bedroom, and each of the officers had kicked in twenty dollars to stock up on beer and stronger spirits. Many shopped for Christmas, finding especially good bargains on jewelry and pewter. CDRs Earnest and Greene found an interesting store that specialized in model airplanes and trains, the latter of special interest to the skipper. As they poked around, they discovered a display of new digital calculators, the first of their kind on the market. They had no memory capability and only limited functions, but Greene found himself so intrigued that he bought one for $120. Greene and LCDR Pieno found a music store that offered all manner of bootleg tapes; the XO picked up some cassettes to send home to his daughter, Dawn. In the evenings, of course, they enjoyed the city's finest eating and drinking establishments. At one restaurant that featured regional cuisine, LT Cook imbibed so freely of the local beers that he did not notice CDR Greene quietly stirring spoonfuls of various spicy condiments into his entrée. When Cook finally put down his drink and took a bite, Greene later recalled, "his head almost came off." The XO never admitted his guilt.[88]

But not all of the Puncher pilots and B/Ns went to Singapore. Several stayed behind in the Philippines to visit friends, and at least two left on longer journeys, one that the heavies had authorized and one they had not approved.

Toward the end of the line period, LT Ken Knapp received an emergency message that his wife, Stephanie, a Pan Am flight attendant, had fallen ill during a stopover in Barcelona. Indeed, stress and worry about her husband's safety brought on a severe outbreak of the hives. She had to be put on a commercial flight as a passenger to return to Virginia Beach. Fortunately, when Stephanie arrived back home, Sharon Schram—also a flight attendant—took care of her. Sharon also got word to the squadron, reporting what had happened. LT Knapp immediately checked into the possibility of taking leave to return to the United States during *Saratoga*'s in-port period in Singapore.[89]

The squadron's senior leaders gave him permission to go home. CDR Greene felt a bit uneasy about the decision, knowing that Knapp's support for the war had never been strong. Now, with the declining number of sorties and the possibility of a cease-fire, he wondered if the pilot would decide to return. But he also understood that until Knapp knew his wife's health had improved, he might carry his concerns into his cockpit and become distracted when he could least afford it.[90] So, while most of his squadronmates went to Singapore, Knapp went home to Virginia Beach. He and Stephanie enjoyed a few days together. Her health steadily improved. For a few days they avoided it, but they knew that before long they would have to talk about a difficult subject. Would LT Knapp return to the war?

While the Knapps contemplated their immediate future, LT Chisholm thought more about the rest of his life. For much of October, he researched marriage laws in Hawaii. He still had the emerald and diamond ring he had bought for Bobbie in Hong Kong. After CAPT Sanderson banned *Saratoga* personnel from taking leave outside the theater, Chisholm obtained permission to stay in Cubi when the carrier headed for Singapore, reserved a seat on a commercial flight to Honolulu, somehow arranged for leave papers, and decided that no one—not CDR Earnest, not CAPT Sanderson, not even the U.S. Navy—would keep him from Bobbie. He told LTJG Vance where to find him in an emergency, then he headed for Hawaii.

On 29 October, while the Punchers—wherever they were—enjoyed their break from active operations, they all received an unwelcome reminder that they worked in a dangerous world. Shortly after noon, a fire broke out in *Saratoga*'s Main Machinery Room 2. A sailor performing routine maintenance on a fuel line had replaced some filters, reconnected the line, and prepared to repressurize it. The connection did not hold, and fuel spewed out, hit steam lines, and ignited. Two minutes after the first report of the fire reached the bridge and the in-port fire party investigated, *Saratoga* went to General Quarters. The ventilation system spread thick black smoke throughout the middle one-third of the carrier. The fire spread so quickly that sailors scrambled for fresh air. Even the ship's chaplain had to crawl on hands and knees down a darkened passageway through the smoke to reach safety.[91]

The VA-75 ready room lay not far from the source of the fire, and several officers still remained aboard. When wisps of smoke began to seep through the ventilation system, one yelled, "Fire!" Sailors knew the hazards of any blaze aboard ship. Since the conflagrations on *Oriskany* in 1966 and *Forrestal* in 1967, each sailor had to complete a firefighting program as a requirement for serving on a carrier. The special dangers of fire and smoke aboard a naval vessel even inspired a specific vocabulary. Officers on ships do not command gun crews or missile crews to "fire" their weapons. The proper command is "shoot." If a sailor heard "fire," it meant one thing only.

LT Wiegand, closest to the ready room's rear door—the usual way in and out—opened it to investigate the noise in the passageway and saw thick black smoke billowing toward him. He slammed the door shut and ran to the front of the room. By the time he reached it, smoke began to seep under the back door. He and the other Punchers exited through the front door and down seventy-five feet of passageway toward a ladder to the hanger bay. By the time they reached the ladder, the smoke thickened so much that they could see only a few inches ahead. Nonetheless, all the Puncher officers made it to the safety of the hanger deck before ascending to the flight deck to stay out of the way of the sailors fighting the fire.[92] Some VA-75 enlisted men still aboard joined firefighting parties to help extinguish the blaze. Others prepared to hold an accountability muster to make certain they could locate all personnel.

Saratoga's liberty boat had just cast off for shore when the fire started. Several Sunday Punchers saw black smoke issuing from the carrier and wanted to return. But LCDR King, senior officer aboard, did not want to complicate an already chaotic scene, and decided to push on to Singapore.[93] King's instincts proved to be correct. Later that day, when some sailors and junior officers tried to return to the carrier, the shore patrol stopped them at the pier.[94]

It took nearly ninety minutes to contain the fire in Main Machinery Room 2. As soon as it was contained, a second, smaller fire flared up in Main Machinery Room 3. Thirty more minutes elapsed before fire teams extinguished it. The carrier did not secure from General Quarters until 1724, almost four and one-half hours after the first alarm had sounded. Three men died, two enlisted sailors from the ship's company and Harry J. Schanz, a civilian Naval Investigative Service agent assigned to the carrier.[95]

When the Punchers finally returned to the carrier, they discovered that the smoke and fire had severely damaged the VA-75 ready room. The heat had melted the grease pencil on its plexiglass board.[96] Soot covered everything. Initial press accounts listed *Saratoga*'s fire as the third in a string of serious accidents to occur aboard U.S. Navy vessels in Southeast Asia during October alone. On 1 October, nineteen sailors on the cruiser USS *Newport News* had died in an explosion and fire in a gun turret. Although the incident took place while shelling North Vietnamese positions on-shore in MR I, official spokesmen described the explosion as accidental. The 13 October racial clash aboard *Kitty Hawk* made news all over the United States at mid-month. Following these incidents, the fire aboard *Saratoga,* complete with rumors of possible sabotage, seemed to hint at

From the deck of the liberty boat taking him and other Sunday Punchers into Singapore, LTJG Dave Warren took this photograph of thick smoke billowing from Saratoga *during the major fire in Main Machinery Room No. 2. Some of his fellow pilots and B/Ns evacuated VA-75's ready room just before the smoke filled it. (David F. Warren Collection)*

deeper problems.[97] It did not help that two more fires—much smaller than that of 29 October—broke out aboard the carrier over the next few days.[98]

On the morning of 3 November, four days ahead of schedule, *Saratoga* once more left for Yankee Station. Rumors continued to circulate through the ship suggesting that, since "peace is at hand," they definitely would head home after the November line period. "The main and only topic of conversation is when are we going home," wrote one VA-75 enlisted man in the admin shop, who added, "Presently there are bets on dates ranging from 1792 [*sic*] to 1984," but "anything in between will be alright too."[99] Confident that the war would end very soon, Loretta Lankford and Diane Miller decided at the end of their stay in Singapore to return to the United States rather than go back to Manila.

But CDR Earnest refused to encourage such optimism. In his message for the fall familygram about to go to press, he wrote, "The decisions that would bring us home early rest in the highest hands of three countries. These are very complex matters and it would be foolish for us to build our hopes too high." Reminding one and all that "our hopes for a successful end to the conflict are more importantly directed" not toward going home but "toward the release of all POWs," he asked the family and friends of Sunday Punchers to support POW organizations working for the return of LCDR Lindland, LT Lerseth, and all those imprisoned with them. As *Saratoga* headed back to the Gulf of Tonkin, he thanked the families for their sacrifices, assuring them that "it is your love, support, and understanding that has kept us going. For that we are most grateful. I hope that we can reward you with a safe and speedy return."[100]

CHAPTER TEN

"Lord, Guard and Guide the Men Who Fly"

USS *Oriskany* lost a screw, as if trying to outdo the "Sorry Sara" for bad luck at sea.[1] "The Oriskany is going to Japan for repairs," LTJG Fuller noted. "That's the second time since we got out here," he complained, adding, "What does the Sara get? A note from the CNO congratulating her on the rapidity with which she got herself operational again" after the fire.[2] Like Fuller, few Sunday Punchers appreciated the kudos. The curtailed in-port period in Singapore and the profound disappointment that followed the collapse of the peace process stung. As the author of the 1972 command history of one of CVW-3's F-4 squadrons wrote, "The premature optimism of peace talks, and the realization that *SARATOGA* would not arrive home for Christmas certainly did not enhance morale." Although he noted that the "good old Navy 'can do'" spirit made up for the "emotional setbacks," reality did not always match the boast.[3]

As *Saratoga* steamed toward the Gulf of Tonkin and into yet one more typhoon, Skipper Earnest and XO Greene checked the status of their aircrews. LT Mullins, now recovered from his emergency appendectomy, had returned. Since LCDR Graustein had paired up with newcomer LCDR Wade, Mullins now became LT Schuster's B/N.

When the carrier had made its brief stop at Cubi before proceeding to Singapore, LTJG Charles Kaiser, a B/N sent to replace the departed LT Bob Miller, had reported for duty. The final replacement or augmentee of officer rank to join VA-75 during the combat cruise, Kaiser came to Westpac straight from VA-42. Of six B/Ns going through the RAG in his class, only Kaiser had significant experience with the A-6A and A-6B; the others had spent far more time learning the new A-6E system. But Kaiser also volunteered to join VA-75. His father had trained to fly B-25s during World War II, but the conflict had ended before he saw combat. Kaiser wanted to experience what his father missed. Another personal factor drove him, too. He and four fraternity brothers at the University of New Mexico had enlisted for military service after graduation. By November 1972, only Kaiser remained alive.[4]

But even with Kaiser's arrival, the squadron still remained shorthanded when air operations began on 5 November. The change in schedule caught by surprise those Punchers not yet aboard the carrier, and the approaching typhoon threatened to strand four of them in the Philippines. LCDR Jackson had spent the last week with the airwing's Beach Detachment at Cubi. Three squadron officers were supposed to return to *Saratoga* with him, but only LTJG Vance had arrived early enough to fly back to the carrier before the rains came. Jackson delayed his own return until the other two officers reported back for duty. His worries dissipated significantly when LT Ken Knapp arrived from emergency leave. Stephanie had recovered from her stress-induced hives, and, once again, as in April, after considering all options, Knapp decided to return to Westpac.[5] LT Chisholm, still single, also slipped back into the Philippines from Hawaii, changed back into uniform, and received more than a few curious looks from Jackson when he reported back for duty.[6] By 9 November, all of VA-75's pilots and B/Ns had flown back aboard *Saratoga*, where air operations had begun four days previously.

"Many restrictions on us now," LT Fischer wrote in his diary. "No mine or DST (we were to lay corridor across country) no offshore Wiblic—no alphas . . . no north of 20th N."[7] Thus, VA-75 began its sixth line period with a full week of daytime strike missions to support ARVN forces operating in MR I and II in South Vietnam. To a lesser degree, the Sunday Punchers also continued to launch day and night strikes, road recces, and seeding hops into RPs I, II, and III in an effort to stop the North Vietnamese from stockpiling military supplies close to the DMZ before any cease-fire took effect.

Such actions assumed the diplomats finally would reach an agreement. When the anticipation of late October evaporated, however, at least one Sunday Puncher refused to believe the war would end anytime soon. When LT Schuster and LTJG Warren aborted a tanker hop because of a gripe in the fuel transfer system, the B/N took the newly arrived pilot down to 400 feet, ran him through some turns and breaks, and made him fly only by instruments "to help him to get prepared in case we ever go back into 6B at night." While others remained hopeful of a quick resolution to the current impasse, Warren now believed that if Kissinger and Le Duc Tho did not hammer out a cease-fire soon, "the restriction on flying north of 20'00" will be lifted. Maybe not, but I feel that it will."[8]

The squadron's return to flight operations after the "peace is at hand" announcement triggered even deeper reflection among some Puncher families at home. One morning in early November—not long after midnight—Lilliane Greene heard a knock at the front door. Despite the late hour, she and her daughter Dawn opened it, fully expecting to see an official notification team standing there. But, to their relief, they found only a worker from the water company passing through the neighborhood to spread word about a brief interruption in service. Relieved, both Lilliane and Dawn broke down and cried. Early on, the XO's wife decided that if they received the worst possible news, "we are not going to cry, we are not going to wail, and we are going to be very stoic about all this." Her reaction to the false alarm reconfirmed her earlier decision that the Greene family would face their loss with dignity.[9]

In early November, as the rest of the nation watched the presidential election, few of VA-75's pilots and B/Ns followed the campaign rhetoric very closely. They did not lack interest but, simply put, most already knew how they planned to vote. Many sent in an absentee ballot—although not all could recall if they cast a vote or not—and, with few individual exceptions, they backed President Nixon's reelection.

Still, few seemed to take much satisfaction in the president's new mandate. As LT Mullins later recalled, "I held my nose and voted for Nixon. So did my shop, even the black guys. We talked about it once. We all knew then that Nixon was a crook, but McGovern came across to us as a naïve fool, and for president, better a crook than a fool."[10] The "peace is at hand" announcement that so quickly proved wrong left some feeling a bit betrayed by the man for whom they cast their vote. LTJG Petersen, reflecting cynically on the election returns, wrote, "I must realize that I am but an instrument of foreign policy. The only problem is that the instrument I feel like is an enema syringe." He concluded that Kissinger's announcement had been nothing more than a political ploy timed to influence the election, almost convincing the B/N that "the American public may have witnessed the greatest 'wool over the eyes' trick in modern political history. Peace my ASS."[11]

From 5 November until 12 November—with the exception of 7 November, when weather forced the cancellation of all air operations—*Saratoga* flew mostly FAC-controlled sorties against targets in MR I and II during daylight hours, with first launch between 0600 and 0800 and the last recovery completed by 2000.[12] On 5 November LTJG Kaiser prepared to fly his very first combat hop with LT Bruce Cook. When CDR Earnest checked on the new B/N after the mission brief, Kaiser admitted that he felt "wound up like a twenty-six hour clock." Earnest advised him to remember the little things. Aviators die, he told Kaiser, because of inattention to details like setting their switches correctly. Cook and Kaiser, with three other A-6As, then launched in support of ARVN troops fighting just south of Danang. When they rolled in on their target and Cook pickled his bombs, nothing happened. Kaiser had forgotten to throw the master arm switch to the "on" position. "I just cringed," Kaiser recalled, "because Skipper Earnest had already told me, it's the little things, the damn switches that kill people." But Cook made no comment, made a second run, and dropped the ordnance as planned.[13]

A few days later, the squadron heavies officially paired Kaiser with an experienced pilot, LT John Miller. The assignment took LTJG Sanford out of Miller's right seat, but the heavies had plans for him, too. Given the "Combat Rat's" aggressive reputation, it seemed logical to match him with a pilot who might need a bit of a push in the cockpit. The senior officers now gave Sanford an opportunity to fulfill LT Bob Miller's request that he "take care of the Duck." They paired him with LT Hiduk. VA-75 now had its "animal crew"—"Duck" and "Rat."[14]

For all the crews—new and old—the primary operational novelty during this first week of their sixth line period came in the form of missions called "buddy bombing." To hit targets in the southernmost route packs and in MR I and II, ordnance-laden aircraft from *Saratoga* now worked with Air Force "Fast FACs" flying F-4s equipped with Long Range Navigation (LORAN) technology. LORAN permitted these special F-4s—called "Pave Phantoms"—to guide aircraft carrying bombs to prebriefed coordinates, where the pilots released their ordnance at 14,000 feet or higher, even through thick cloud decks. Now, a flight leader from the carrier contacted the Defense Air Support Center (DASC) in Danang, which hooked him up to an Air Force Fast FAC with a mission. The strike force then joined up on him and followed him to the target zone. Any kind of carrier-borne aircraft capable of dropping ordnance could take part in buddy bombing. Thus, when weather permitted, CVW-3's A-6As, A-7s, and F-4s all participated in the effort. Indeed, on days when the clouds broke, a formation of twenty or more *Saratoga* aircraft followed the lead of an Air Force Pave Phantom. In bad weather, however, VA-75's A-6As flew the bulk of the hops.

Planners referred to these hops as "Combat Sky Spot" missions. But as LTJG Warren described it, "We used to refer to that mission as a 'Combat Sky Puke'— go out and puke your bombs off on somebody's signal, and go back to the ship."[15] The pilot carried most of the responsibility for successful execution, relegating the B/N to serving as little more than an extra set of eyes to make sure his aircraft did not run into any others in the tight formations.

Few of the Punchers took much satisfaction from buddy bombing missions. "I just didn't like the idea of dropping [bombs] into the clouds, not knowing what's underneath there," LT Hvidding recalled years later.[16] They seldom received BDA reports, and they put little faith in those they got. As LT Schuster noted, the strike groups usually "had enough aircraft in them to appear to be a mini arc-light" that could devastate an enemy troop concentration.[17] Far more typically, however, as LT Tolhurst concluded, "the hops are fairly boring and repetitious and I doubt if they accomplish much, but at least we get to fly some."[18] But the missions added to the sortie count, and Puncher air crews continued to respond to the FAC's "stand by, stand by, pickle, pickle, pickle."

LTJG Dave Warren took this photo of an Air Force F-4 "Pave Phantom" escorting at least three A-6As from VA-75 on a "buddy bombing" mission in November 1972. (David F. Warren Collection)

Buddy bombing required all elements of a strike group to fly in a tight formation and maintain visual contact with the FAC. Recent arrival and second-tour pilot LT Tom Connelly prided himself on his airmanship and did not want to develop a reputation for unreliability in the air. Thus, on one such hop, after linking up with his FAC, he seemed stunned when, after a quick glance down at his instruments, he looked up and could no longer see him. Over the radio, the FAC began his standard procedure: "Standby—standby." At "pickle," Connelly had to be prepared to drop his bombs. At the first "standby," Connelly spotted his FAC far ahead. He threw his engines to full power, catching up with the FAC just in time to deliver his ordnance on target. But the mere fact that he temporarily lost sight of his lead deeply embarrassed him.

LCDR Schram, Connelly's B/N, no doubt enjoyed the moment. Every crew worked out its own cockpit procedures, but from the start, these two combat veterans had engaged in a battle of wills that spilled over into the ready room. After this mission, however, everyone noticed a change. Connelly took off his flight gear and tossed it into the corner, as usual. Without raising his voice, Schram told him to pick it up. To the amazement of all, Connelly complied without argument. Indeed, from that day on, he seemed to acquiesce to Schram's every whim. The B/N later explained that Connelly felt so mortified by his failure to keep his lead in sight that he asked Schram what it would take to keep him silent. Schram uttered just two words: "Obey me." It worked.[19]

Since the A-6A's superior ordnance load made it a good fit for buddy bombing missions, from 5 through 9 October VA-75 flew no strikes at all in North Vietnamese airspace. They continued the effort on 10 and 11 November as well, with the exception of only five single- or two-plane armed recces that hit interdiction targets in RP I.[20] A modicum of variety and excitement still could be found in A-6B sorties, however. Since they did not need to cover the buddy bombing missions in South Vietnam, the A-6Bs launched to cover strike hops and reconnaissance missions flown by the airwing's other squadrons into the lower route packs of North Vietnam.[21]

As the diplomatic impasse continued, the Sunday Punchers understood all too well the consequences of the new bombing restrictions under which they operated. Since American planes no longer threatened targets in the northern half of the country, the North Vietnamese high command moved a significant number of SAMs and AAA batteries south of the 20th parallel. Over the first ten days of November, the Navy lost five aircraft in the increasingly dangerous skies over the southern half of North Vietnam.[22] On 10 November, an A-7 from VA-37 piloted by LCDR Frederick W. Wright III—the airwing operations officer and a veteran of the Cuban missile crisis—went down just after noon in RP I. No one reported a deployed parachute or a beeper. Thus, no SAR effort began.[23] The Navy listed Wright as "missing in action."

The geographical limitations imposed on the bombing campaign did not translate into a slower operational tempo. When the North Vietnamese began to delay and obfuscate after the premature announcement of imminent peace, October's restrictions on the daily number of authorized strike sorties disappeared. Even if they still could not hit targets north of the 20th parallel, CTF-77 planners took advantage of the concentrated airpower of several carriers to hammer the target-rich environment just north and south of the DMZ. Very quickly, VA-75's pilots and B/Ns lost the benefits of their relaxation in Singapore. In the first two and one-half days after he returned to *Saratoga*, LT Chisholm—like other VA-75 pilots—flew six hops. "No stand down days. No limited number of strike sorties. We're back to balls to the wall," he wrote.[24]

The combination of frustrated hopes for peace and the fast pace of air operations magnified each day's little aggravations. LT Schuster complained frequently, each time the "autodog"—the soft ice-cream machine—broke down. When the carrier ran out of new movies, the officers in VA-75's ready room occasionally took the films they already had screened and ran them backwards just for something new to do.[25] The mood suffused the entire squadron, not simply the ready room. Down in the Fire Control shop, the enlisted men posted a new sign: "Five thousand years ago, Moses said, 'Park your camel, pick up your shovel, mount your ass, and I shall lead you to the promised land.' Five thousand years later, FDR said, 'Lay down your shovel, sit on your ass, and light up a camel. This is the promised land.' Today Nixon will tax your shovel, sell your camel, kick you in the ass, and tell you there is no promised land.'"[26]

Through it all, from the squadron's most senior pilots and B/Ns to the most junior sailor, the men kept to their jobs. Indeed, they could find plenty of evidence of positive accomplishment. Since the A-6 remained the airwing's most reliable aircraft in inclement weather, the squadron's redshirts continued to hang bombs on Sunday Puncher planes, and on 9 November, LT Connelly and LCDR Schram delivered VA-75's seven-millionth pound of ordnance. A few days later, on 12 November, Chief Aviation Electronics Technician Joseph Sims and Aviation Electronics Technician First Class Jorge Wilkes received cash bonuses for recent suggestions to improve aircraft performance while reducing the time and cost of maintenance.[27]

Among the Puncher pilots, LT Hiduk now stepped up and flew the types of missions he never had attempted before. On 16 November, he flew his first night road recce into RP II. Even though their cockpit intercom broke and LTJG Sanford's oxygen mask malfunctioned, the team of Duck and Rat hit a road intersection and some trucks. A satisfied Sanford concluded his nightly diary entry with, "Hurt 'em."[28] The Duck's first successful night strike became one of two he and Sanford flew during the period of 13–18 November when *Saratoga* shifted to the midnight-to-noon schedule. Now, as weather permitted, VA-75 stopped daytime buddy bombing in South Vietnam for an intense strike schedule of one- and two-plane night and day sorties and road recces in RPs II and III. On their second night recce mission in RP II, Hiduk and Sanford lost their radar and their ECM but once again dropped their eight Mk82s and two Mk20s on targets of opportunity. Sanford jotted in his diary, "Hurt 'em again."[29]

LT Schuster also prepared to launch on his first night strike north of the DMZ. He and LT Mullins had flown together now for about two weeks, and on 14 November they told LCDR Graustein that they felt ready. Indeed, they appeared on the schedule that night because Graustein specifically ordered LT John Miller to assign them to a strike mission.

The order presented Miller with a bit of a quandary. Earlier in the cruise, he had never challenged LCDR Lindland on issues concerning crew assignments. But he had learned much over the past six months, and he felt that his experience obligated him to express his professional opinion when something in the schedule struck him as ill-considered. He felt some qualms about taking such a step now, however. He had not meshed as well with Graustein as he had with Lindland. The latter had given Miller a freer hand to do his job as his expertise developed. By contrast, Graustein preferred a far more hands-on style, and Miller still found himself adjusting to his new boss's ways. In this specific case, though, Miller questioned Schuster's readiness for the demands of a night mission in the skies over North Vietnam. Graustein disagreed, so Miller assigned Schuster and Mullins to the hop as ordered. But Miller remained convinced that the heavies had made a bad call.[30]

The scheduler's hunch turned out to be correct. As they approached their target, a section of A-7s operating near Schuster and Mullins illuminated a target off their right wing by dropping flares. The bright flashes startled and confused Schuster, who did not know that the A-7s were operating so close by. At first, he thought they were SAMs and began evasive maneuvers. The more experienced Mullins had recognized the flare drop, however, and thus, he neither expected nor appreciated Schuster's abrupt movements. His head popped out from under the B/N's hood, and, as Schuster recalled, he "let me know it!"[31] Despite his experience in the cockpit, Schuster still had much to learn about flying in combat.

And CDR Earnest still had much to teach. Even now, he continued to test the skill and will of some of his more junior pilots and B/Ns. On 18 November, five VA-75 aircraft in two successive cycles launched on seeding missions against a river crossing on the Song Ca River in RP II, about ten miles from the coast. The target area rested between mountain ridges and in the envelope of an active SAM site. If the North Vietnamese fired a missile, strike aircraft had no maneuver room to evade it. CDR Earnest took LTJG Vance as his B/N, launched in darkness, and at first light while still feet wet descended to 500 feet. On their right wing flew LT Miller and his new B/N, LTJG Kaiser. On their left flew the experienced crew of LCDRs Engel and King. Nearing the target, Vance flicked his master arm switch to the "on" position, using hand signals for Miller and Kaiser to do the same.

All of a sudden, the skies around them lit up with AAA. Earnest pickled off his ordnance on target and broke left around a large hill to head feet wet. Engel and King did the same. But when Miller came off the target, he radioed the skipper that their mines did not drop. Kaiser had turned the master arm switch on, but nothing happened.

They joined up on Earnest and Vance, and the skipper asked Miller and Kaiser if they wanted to make a second run. While they considered options, Earnest took advantage of a "teaching moment" to ask Vance whether they should lead the junior crew back in or let them circle around and make the run themselves. Vance considered a third option—refuse to make a second run over a contested target, as airwing practice dictated—but Earnest had not suggested that course of action. Thus, the B/N suggested leading Miller back to the coast-in point and then letting them make the run again. Earnest concurred. Then, Miller and Kaiser informed the skipper that they wanted to give it another try, Earnest's unspoken preference.

LCDR Bob Graustein and LT Mike Schuster discuss an upcoming mission in the VA-75 ready room. (Duddie Graustein Andrews Collection)

Vance continued to mull over the tactical problem, still believing that the skipper should have led Miller to a safe area to jettison the ordnance rather than permit a second run. Years later, after accruing more professional experience, he decided that CDR Earnest likely based his decision on the greater significance CTF-77 planners generally attached to mining missions. But on that day, Vance continued silently to question the skipper's decision. While Miller and Kaiser dropped their ordnance flawlessly on the second run, one large-caliber AAA gun began tracking them as they rolled off target. Then Earnest and Vance lost radio contact with them. But Miller quickly erased all worries, evading the gunfire and popping up into the clouds, going inverted, pulling hard on the stick, and scooting over a mountain, all without taking a single round.[32] The Miller-Kaiser team performed well.

The intense rains and thick cloud cover, broken only occasionally by temporarily clearing skies, made it increasingly difficult to stick to a specific schedule. On 19 November, weather conditions cancelled air operations entirely. On 20 November, under marginal conditions, *Saratoga* returned to the noon-to-midnight schedule. That day, SAMs took down an F-4 from VF-103 flying BAR-CAP for B-52 raids near Thanh Hoa. Weather conditions contributed to faulty navigation that inadvertently sent LCDR Vincent Lesh and LTJG Don Cordes into the SAM envelope, and two missiles exploded near their Phantom. They managed to fly nearly nine miles offshore before ejecting, and a Big Mother SAR helicopter quickly rescued them. Inclement weather also turned both 21 and 23 November into unscheduled stand-down days.[33]

The irregularity of flight operations in mid-November gave LCDR Graustein time to compile a reminder sheet for his pilots and B/Ns. "With the onset of the miserable flying weather over the friendly skies of Vietnam," he wrote, "it would be a good time to review our navigation procedures and methods of avoiding areas where we really don't want to be." He reminded them that "since it is *your* responsibility to keep your young derriere out of trouble, every possible means of checking and rechecking your position must be used." Indeed, he noted, "if in doubt, move to where there is no doubt." He urged them to review navigation procedures thoroughly before each takeoff, including what they would do if their navigation system crashed. His bottom line remained straightforward as always: "If you're feet dry and don't know where you are, it's the dumbest of all dumb ____. The results will probably be both colorful and catastrophic." His use of the word "colorful" led him to a quick review of procedures for evading SAMs at night: "When there's a bright flash, start moving."[34]

From 22 through 26 November, whenever the weather broke, the squadron returned once again to daytime LORAN strikes against targets in MR I and II and single-plane night strikes in RPs II and III. At least for the A-6s, the pace of activity did not slow. At night, VA-75's strikes into the route packages represented "the bulk of the airwing [sortie] load."[35] On 25 November, only sixteen days after LT Connelly and LCDR Schram reached the squadron's seven-million-pound milestone for ordnance dropped, LT Knapp and LTJG Fuller delivered the eight-millionth pound against a target in MR I. Fuel deliveries offered another measure of productive activity, and now LT Ruland and LTJG Swigart delivered the squadron's eight-millionth pound of JP-5.[36]

The work of the men on the flight deck in these trying conditions drew special notice now. The weight of the bomb loads hung on VA-75 aircraft, reported the squadron familygram, "appears even more staggering when computed on the basis of pounds loaded per ordnanceman," an estimated 400,000 pounds per man. That number did not tell the whole story, however. "If you take that number and multiply it by two or three, that's the number of bombs handled, uploaded and downloaded," Gunner Walden later explained of his redshirts' workload in mid-November, when they had to remove ordnance from already-loaded planes grounded by inclement weather.[37]

At least the VA-75 redshirts knew they could count on the support of other airwing ordnancemen on duty. Indeed, cooperative efforts had become such common practice that an end-of-cruise evaluation by the senior leaders of

LTJG John Fuller and LT Ken Knapp, who delivered VA-75's eight-millionth pound of ordnance of the combat cruise in mid-November 1972. (U.S. Navy photograph, John R. Fuller Collection)

VF-103 singled out the "extremely close working relationship between squadron ordnance crews" as especially noteworthy for its ability to "make possible the safe and prompt loading, unloading, arming, dearming, testing and repairing of aircraft when the tempo of operations was at a peak."[38] VA-75's pilots and B/Ns considered it a measure of squadron professionalism that they, too, helped to hang ordnance when the pace of operations demanded it.[39]

Other Punchers working on the flight deck matched the ordies' pace. "Perhaps the most confused bunch of bodies in the Maintenance Department are those belonging to the Plane Captains and Troubleshooters of the Line Division," noted the branch's contributor to the squadron familygram. "The fault does not lie with the bodies themselves[. It] is simply due to the weird and frequently varied schedule it is necessary for them to adjust to." The plane captains assigned to individual aircraft worked whenever the ever-changing flight schedule called for their plane to fly. As the Line Officer, LTJG Vance issued a tentative work plan at the start of each line period, but, as the familygram noted, "of this schedule there is only one thing certain, which is, that it will change." Troubleshooters faced the same problem since their specialties came into play mostly during flight operations. "Some days we fly during the night and some nights we fly during the day and sometimes we just split it half and half, always, of course, subject to immediate change without notice," the line division's chronicler explained, adding with pride that they never failed to meet the challenge.[40]

Some of the officers spent even more time with branch duties now, trying hard to keep their men informed about the war and the efforts to end it and send them home. LT Mullins frequently visited the Power Plants shop to perform card tricks, always leaving without revealing his secrets. "We all still get along great," one of the men wrote of Mullins, "even though he is an officer." LTJG Fuller stopped by the electrical shop more frequently too, ostensibly to learn more about the A-6s from the men who kept them flying. As one of his men observed, "So far, we have been able to teach him how to turn on the lights on his side of the cockpit and which side of the plane is his." Fuller retaliated by "promising we'll be home in time—he just never says in time for what."[41]

A sense of humor—sometimes macabre and other times not—sustained spirits through the daily grind. At some point in November, most Puncher pilots and B/Ns who deployed with the squadron at the beginning of the combat cruise flew their 150th mission. As each man reached this milestone, he was awarded the Vietnamese Cross of Gallantry from the South Vietnamese government. If they appreciated the honor, they did not reflect it in their own name for the award. They called it the "Croix de Gook."[42]

Puncher families at home did what they could to shore up morale. Back in mid-September, at a gathering at Judy Pieno's home in Virginia Beach, the officers' wives had decided to design special t-shirts for their spouses. They could not agree on the shirts' color. The squadron traditionally marked its flight helmets and other gear in green, but CDR Greene—through Lilliane—quickly made clear his dislike of that hue.[43] Nor could they agree on a motto for the shirts. When someone suggested "Fly the Friendly Skies of North Vietnam," Sally Fuller objected, deeming the phrase somewhat inappropriate and disrespectful, especially after the recent downing of LCDR Lindland and LT Lerseth. Remaining silent at first, she finally spoke up; then others voiced similar qualms.[44] Finally, in mid-November, a large box of special t-shirts—deep dark green in color—arrived aboard *Saratoga*. Each bore the phrase "Happiness is the Saratoga in Norfolk for a screw job," a double entendre based on recollections of happier times when so many of the wives "followed the boat" during the 1971 Med cruise and the carrier dropped a screw, keeping it—and their husbands—in port in Athens for a longer time than expected.[45] The squadron's officers posed for a photograph on the flight deck to show off their new finery. Unfortunately, it did not appear in the next familygram as planned—mostly because LT Knapp gave in to an impulse to slip into the shot a very visible middle-finger salute.[46]

While this kind of irreverence thrived, it also masked the personal and professional distress of one small group of Sunday Punchers. The squadron's Reservists seeking augmentation into the Regular Navy awaited each mail delivery eagerly, looking for the decision that would shape their futures. In late October, the board sat in Washington to consider their applications, but it had not announced its findings. What little news got through remained nonspecific and came from unofficial sources such as the *Navy Times*.

More than any other personnel issue of the entire combat cruise, the augmentation process especially bothered CDR Greene. In addition to six of VA-75's Reservists, nearly forty other aviators in the airwing had requested review by the augmentation board. Greene had worked with RADM Christiansen's chief of staff and senior officers on the airwing staff to develop statistics and craft language to support the applications of *Saratoga*'s pilots and NFOs. Hoping to get the results of the board's deliberations a bit more quickly, Greene sent a list of the names of VA-75's potential augmentees—LTs Cook, Martin, Knapp, and Hart, along with LTJGs Petersen and Ahrens—to a well-placed friend in the Navy's Bureau of Personnel. To simplify compliance with his request for news, Greene simply asked him to check either the "selected" or the "non-selected" box next to each man's name as he learned the board's results.[47] Each day that Greene got no answer added to the anxiety of those most eager for news of a positive decision.

As Thanksgiving approached, CAPT Sanderson sent his usual monthly letter home to the families of *Saratoga*'s crew and airwing, noting that the carrier prepared to observe the holiday "with the traditional bountiful feast and our reverent thanks that one can sense the mood of inevitability in the negotiations to reinstate peace in Southeast Asia."[48] But Puncher families back in Virginia Beach saw little to convince them of the "inevitability" of peace. At a recent meeting of the officers' wives club, they talked about what they might do collectively to support the release of the POWs and demand an accounting for MIAs. They all wanted to do something to help LCDR Lindland and LT Lerseth, and most of the senior officers' wives knew even more naval aviators confined in North Vietnamese prisons. But they could not reach consensus about what to do. By now, support for the war among Puncher wives showed signs of a growing split. Where once few had voiced opposition to the bombing effort during the monthly meetings, now more spoke out. Former practices, such as signing and forwarding petitions to political leaders, now seemed to some entirely ineffectual. As she listened to the discussions, a discouraged Stephanie Knapp realized that many of the wives who had spent so much of their adult lives as part of the larger Navy family seemed to assume that "the eyes of the United States were on our guys and appreciating what they were doing." That perception clashed sharply with all she had observed on recent international flights, when she rarely met people who cared about either the war or the prisoners. Too intimidated to speak up lest she be viewed as hostile to the group's efforts to help the POWs, she remained silent, asking herself who really cared about naval aviators held in Hanoi prisons. She found her own answer distressing: "You know what? Maybe [there is support] in the state of Virginia. Maybe in part of the state of Virginia. Maybe in Virginia Beach. Maybe not even in Richmond."[49]

Stephanie's grim assessment seemed appropriate right after the Thanksgiving holiday, when the peace talks stopped yet again, suspended until 4 December. Political observers watched Kissinger and Le Duc Tho carry on animated talks in the garden outside their diplomatic haven on 23 November and interpreted their exchanges as a positive sign of progress. But the very next day the mood reversed entirely, as North Vietnamese spokesmen in Paris ignored the ongoing bombing halt against Hanoi and Haiphong to denounce the "unprecedented" bombing of the area north of the DMZ. They labeled it as evidence of Nixon's "lack of desire to settle the Vietnamese problem peacefully" and a "desire to subjugate the Vietnamese by military force." They pinned the delay in signing peace accords squarely on the American air campaign.[50]

About the only good news—at least for the Sunday Punchers—came in the form of large packages marked "do not open before Christmas." The first of five boxes addressed to CDR Earnest, all filled with Christmas items the officers' wives had made, arrived on 25 November, along with a number of large, tempting packages for various squadron personnel.[51] Some of those unopened boxes belonged to LTJG Petersen. Every time he looked at them, he remembered the letter he had just received from home. Jeane had told him that Danny had curled up in her arms and asked if Daddy would be home for Christmas. She had told him no. When he asked why, she had explained that the Navy had a job for Daddy to do. Then she wrote, "Danny says, 'I could just spank the Navy for not letting Daddy come home.'" After a silence, the little boy announced that he had a job for Daddy, too. "'You do? What?'" she asked. Danny replied, "'Put the balls on the Christmas tree.'"[52]

On 27 November, the airwing enjoyed a stand-down day, with no flight operations scheduled until 1300 on 28 November. CDR Earnest used the break to call together his chiefs to talk about maintenance. They met in the ready room, and the CO reiterated yet again his warnings against complacency. He reminded them to pay attention to detail; this was no time to let down one's guard.[53]

An awards ceremony took place on the hangar deck that day, as well. VADM D. W. Cooper of CTF-77 presented individual awards to fifty-six members of *Saratoga*'s crew and airwing, including nine Sunday Punchers. LT Anderson and LTJG Sanford each won an Individual Action Air Medal for a STARM support mission against targets in Haiphong in October. First Award Strike/Flight Medals went to LTs Hiduk and Hart and to LTJG Bryan. Navy Achievement Medals went to Chief Aviation Electronics Technician Larry Hiott and Aviation Electronics Technician First Class Wilkes.[54] VADM Cooper told the assembled crew: "You gentlemen are heroes. You're heroes to me, to Task Force 77, to the Navy and to the country. The fact that this war is approaching an end—and a successful end as far as the United States is concerned—has been brought about by you gentlemen here. You've done a great job."[55]

The highest awards presented to Sunday Punchers that night went to LCDR Pieno and LTJG Fuller, each man receiving a Silver Star for his efforts on the 10 October mission against the Bai Thuong airfield. Fuller's satisfaction in a job well done competed with the knowledge that his wife did not attach the same value to the accomplishment. A few weeks earlier, after he learned he would receive the medal, he included the news in a letter home. "I realize you figure so what?" he wrote, since recently he had begun to sense that she considered "what I'm doing over here is wrong anyway."[56] Equally disconcerting, Fuller did not understand an incident that took place after the ceremony. He had changed back into his working uniform, wearing on his shirt only his rank, his nametag, and his wings. When he went to the ready room and sat down, he sensed a noticeable tension. LCDR Schram walked by, stopped, and said in a low voice, "You're still one of the boys." Fuller did not understand the comment. When he looked at Schram quizzically, the senior B/N nodded toward Pieno, and said, "He's wearing it, and you're not." Then he moved on. Fuller knew that some of his fellow

JOs despised what they perceived to be the heavies' conscious selection of missions for their medal potential, but he did not understand that some of them tarred him with the same brush for volunteering to go on the mission, especially after several of them had turned it down. Some also viewed his decision to fly the strike as a major violation of the crew concept. Fuller had just returned from a hop and knew nothing of the ouster of the junior crews from the mission, and his accusers apparently did not know—or did not consider it sufficient—that he had talked to LT Knapp before he agreed to go.[57]

After the ceremony, in his nightly review of daily events, CAPT Sanderson reported that aircraft from *America* had spotted a large numbers of trucks on Route 1 running south with their lights on.[58] Other airwings had already launched to hit them, but shortly after midnight on 28 November, the phone in VA-75's ready room rang. LTJG Warren, the SDO that night, handed the receiver to CDR Earnest. The caller was CAG Bordone. Gunner Walden heard Earnest say, "'Yes sir, yes sir, yes, hold on, sir, the Gunner is here right now." Earnest asked how long it would take to load ordnance on three A-6As. Although the skipper did not explain what inspired his question, *Saratoga*'s airwing had gotten orders to launch aircraft immediately—as much as twelve hours earlier than their scheduled 1300 resumption time—to help destroy the trucks that *America*'s crews had spotted. Gunner considered the question and told CDR Earnest that if he had a good deck spot and help with the ordnance, he could do it in thirty minutes.

While the operations officer and flight officer assigned crews, Walden ran for the flight deck and found one of the planes he planned to arm spotted forward near the bow catapult. A second aircraft also had a reasonable deck spot. He found the third aircraft he hoped to arm, however, surrounded by other planes. He went to flight deck control for help, and after a few calls, Walden learned of another A-6A on the hangar deck just clearing maintenance. He received permission to load ordnance on that A-6A while the elevator brought it up from the hangar deck, and he helped his redshirts hang the bombs himself.[59]

CDR Earnest and LCDR Jackson planned to fly one of the three planes in that mission, of course. As he started his standard preflight procedures in Maintenance Control, Jackson discovered that he and the skipper would fly the A-6A coming up from the hangar deck. He also knew that two A-6As were due out of maintenance, so he reviewed the logs of both planes. Nobody could tell him which of the two aircraft would be released first, but he noted no major problem with either of them, and he proceeded to the flight deck. When CDR Earnest joined him there, they prepared to man AC 501 just coming off the elevator, the aircraft on which Gunner Walden already had begun to hang ordnance. LTs Schuster and Mullins and LTs Cook and Wiegand prepared to man the other two A-6As in the first launch.

LCDR Jackson recalled, "I don't remember being in a great hurry to pre-flight and everything seemed in order." They checked the glare shields to ensure nobody had left tools or any loose items that might fly back in their faces during launch. They pulled on handles of various instrument boxes to make sure they were secured. All seemed ready to go. Still, CDR Earnest clearly had felt some pressure to hurry when he manned up. Moving targets rarely remained vulnerable for long. Thus, he turned to Gunner Walden and asked him to preflight his ordnance and tell him when he had completed the process. "I climbed up on the ladder, I personally checked all the ordnance on that aircraft and told him everything was fine. Big ol' smile, 'Thank you very much,'" and then Walden stepped away from the plane.[60]

CDR Earnest taxied to Catapult 1. Jackson held his lighted flashlight against his chest to illuminate the Vertical Gyro Indicator (VGI), which would let him know their attitude if the plane lost electrical power during the launch. LTs Schuster and Mullins sat on Catapult 2, ready to launch, with LTs Cook and Wiegand waiting to follow them. It was 0215 on the morning of 28 November.

Catapult 1 fired. AC 501 with CDR Earnest and LCDR Jackson aboard sped down the flight deck. As the plane cleared the bow, it rose sharply, stalled, rolled to the right, fell off toward the starboard side of the carrier, and crashed into the water. The first thing Gunner Walden noticed was the "silence—most eerie thing in the world," even though the A-6 is "a noisy airplane" and two more remained on deck preparing to launch.[61] Catapult 1 ran right above the stateroom shared by LT Chisholm and LTJG Vance, and the loud noise of the unexpected launch woke Vance with a start. As he recalled it, he heard an immediate excited call on the ship's intercom: "Iron Hand in the water! Iron Hand in the water." Since Iron Hands generally referred to A-7s armed with AGM-45s, he assumed that the stricken aircraft belonged to VA-37 or VA-105.[62] Others heard "aircraft in the water."

Over on Catapult 2, LTs Schuster and Mullins saw CDR Earnest's plane pitch up into a stall and roll right. They also spotted one ejection.[63] Members of the flight deck crew spotted at least one light in the water. Several threw their flotation flashlights overboard to mark the crash scene. Gunner Walden, carrying illuminated wands, threw them into the water, too. Initial reports from the flight deck crew suggested that they spotted two survival vest lights, and the word circulated that both pilot and B/N survived.[64]

Clearly, something had gone very wrong. In the press to launch aircraft, AC 501 had cleared maintenance very quickly, apparently too quickly. In the few hours before the call came to ready the plane for the strike, the technicians in the Fire Control shop had pulled the pilot's horizontal display (PHD) for maintenance. This heavy piece of equipment, about ten inches square and about twenty-four inches long, slid into the instrument panel at about a 40-degree angle on rails that sloped downward. Four bolts held it in place. They had just refitted the PHD into position—without securing those four bolts—when the call came to release the aircraft for the emergency sortie. The plane went to the flight deck before the quality assurance petty officer had an opportunity to look over the work and sign off on it. The plane captain who checked the aircraft on the flight deck noticed several bolts lying loose in the cockpit and removed them, as he would do with any debris. But he did not ask where they belonged. In his haste to launch, CDR Earnest did not pull on the handles of the PHD sufficiently hard to discover that it remained unsecured. An unfortunate series of individual errors led to tragedy.

During a debrief immediately after the accident, LCDR Jackson explained that after the catapult fired and AC 501 moved forward, the unsecured PHD slid out of its fittings and lodged itself against CDR Earnest's control stick, pinning it to his body. Neither man could shove it back into position while the launch's G-forces pressed them back against their seatbacks. Jackson explained what happened next: "As soon as the aircraft cleared the bow of the carrier and the G-forces subsided, I watched as Charlie leaned forward and was trying to push the PHD back in its place. Now both of us had completely lost our instrument scan and we were now both looking at the PHD and nothing else. Neither one of us said anything on the ICS, but we had flown together for months, and we didn't need to communicate to know what to do." Jackson explained that "a voice or thought went through my mind that said if Charlie gets the nose of the aircraft over (we were now climbing to the stars because the stick was full aft), stay with it, BUT if the aircraft rolls left or right, GET OUT!" As soon as he felt the aircraft roll right, Jackson ejected.

The next thing he remembered was being in the water. Only one side of his life preserver inflated, and he became tangled in his parachute. He stripped off his oxygen mask, and he looked around to find out where he was in relation to the carrier. He worried that it might pull him under. Almost immediately, the helicopter plane guard hovered overhead. Due to high seas and the billowing parachute, they did not spot Jackson at first. The light on his flotation vest mixed in with the wands thrown by the flight deck crew, adding to the confusion. As he later recalled, "I remember just like it was last night crying out and saying: 'God, get me out of this, but I am not ready to change my life!' Not like I was telling Him something He didn't already know!" But his prayer was answered. When the helicopter crew finally located him, a rescuer swimmer jumped into the water. The first time, he landed too far away from Jackson. The second time, the swimmer reached Jackson, cut away his parachute, put him in the rescue harness, and gave the signal to lift the B/N into the helicopter.

Jackson's rescue took about thirteen minutes. He suffered a few bumps and bruises and an L-shaped cut just above his left knee, but since Jackson showed no ill effects, the pilot received permission to stay in the area and continue the search for CDR Earnest.

As the rescue effort continued, the other two A-6As launched as planned. LTs Schuster and Mullins on Catapult 2 very briefly considered whether or not they felt mentally prepared to fly after what they had just witnessed. Deciding in the affirmative, Schuster signaled his readiness to launch, and they flew off to hit the trucks. During the hop, they talked briefly about the accident, concluding that neither Earnest nor Jackson could have made a successful ejection and survived. They learned nothing more until they returned to the carrier.[65]

Additional A-6As prepared to follow the first launch almost immediately. Indeed, some had already begun to taxi toward the catapults, and their crews also witnessed the crash. CAG Bordone had planned to fly with LCDR Pieno on that second launch, but he jumped out of the cockpit after CDR Earnest's accident to supervise the rescue effort. LT Lankford, aroused from a deep sleep, took the hop instead. He dressed, ran to the flight deck, and found Pieno already in the cockpit running his preflight checklists. As he strapped in, Lankford knew nothing about his mission, his target, or his routes. He also knew very little about what had happened to CDR Earnest or his plane. He found the confusion most disconcerting.

In the next aircraft, equally concerned, LT Tolhurst and LTJG Ahrens watched a flight deck director motion them toward Catapult 1, from which the skipper's plane had launched. Since both Schuster and Cook had launched from Catapult 2, Tolhurst and Ahrens would be the first to launch from Catapult 1 since the accident. As standard procedure required, the catapult officer immediately had tested the machinery, found no malfunctions, and approved the resumption of operations. Tolhurst and Ahrens did not share that same degree of confidence. Signaled to taxi forward, Tolhurst added some power. But his plane did not move. Finally, the Air Boss broke in, suggesting to the pilot that he might enjoy greater success if he took his feet off the brakes. Subconsciously, he had put just a bit more pressure on the top of the rudder pedal than usual. Now they moved to Catapult 1 and launched normally.[66]

VA-75's crews found those reported trucks—and more. As soon as they went feet dry, Pieno told Lankford to turn to the north, where they flew along Route 1 and spotted lights on the road. They dropped their ordnance and saw several fires to suggest good hits. But then the sky lit up with AAA. Lankford quickly dove to get under it and sped up to get out of its thickest concentration. Suddenly, Pieno shouted to Lankford to pull up. The pilot looked forward and saw, as he recounted, "waves on the beach 'TOO' clearly." In diving to avoid the AAA, he had headed straight for the water. He pulled up the aircraft's nose sharply and later credited Pieno for keeping their names off the squadron's casualty list that night.[67] A bit later in the evening, when LT Chisholm and LTJG Vance reached Route 1, they saw five or six miles of burning vehicles. They lined up on a segment of the road that "didn't seem to be burning as brightly," dropped their Rockeye, and returned to the carrier.[68]

Soon after the "aircraft in the water" call on the 1MC, the Air Boss had called VA-75's ready room and informed SDO Warren that the downed plane belonged to the Sunday Punchers. Since CDR Greene had taken a damaged plane to Cubi, the squadron's senior officers still aboard—LCDRs Wade and Graustein—called an emergency meeting for all officers not participating in flight operations that night. They had little news to share, however. They could only wait.

The SAR effort went on all night. *America* immediately sent a helicopter to assist, and within an hour of the accident, USS *Bainbridge* also joined in the effort. The search continued until 1108 on 28 November, when, in the terse words of the carrier's deck log, it was "terminated with negative results." All they found was a single wing of the plane. The rest of the A-6A and CDR Earnest rested in 276 feet of water in the Gulf of Tonkin.[69]

CDR Greene now commanded VA-75. His first hint of something awry came as a vaguely worded radio message advising him that CAPT Sanderson had sent a plane to Cubi to pick him up. Greene did not know what had happened until LT Connelly landed and broke the bad news. He strapped himself into Connelly's aircraft and returned to the carrier immediately.[70]

Even before CDR Greene arrived, *Saratoga* also sent a confidential telegram to the headquarters of MATWING ONE. After a brief review of the accident and the successful recovery of LCDR Jackson, the message included the B/N's grim report that he had seen no effort by CDR Earnest to attempt ejection. Still, while the rescue effort continued, the official wording of the initial message concluded that "CDR Earnest is being listed in a missing status."[71]

The notification process proceeded as protocol dictated. Once again, it fell to CDR Zick, CDR Boecker, and the base chaplain to deliver the news. But first they stopped at the Greene residence. The CO's wife often accompanied notification teams, but in this case, it fell to Lilliane Greene to do it. The officers knocked on her door about 0700. Certain that they bore the long-awaited bad news about her own husband, she dressed and groomed carefully before answering the door. Dawn came with her. When she opened the door, she simply asked, "Is he alive or is he dead?" Boecker broke the news of CDR Earnest's death. The news surprised Lilliane as much as it shocked her. "I was so sure that Bill was never coming back that I was positive that it was Bill," she recalled. Dawn asked again, "Is Daddy okay?" CDR Boecker confirmed that Greene had been at Cubi when the accident occurred.

CDR William H. Greene, Jr., succeeded to command of VA-75 after the death of CDR Earnest on 28 November 1972. (William H. Greene, Jr., Collection)

Lilliane then left for the Earnest home with the three officers. When Minna answered the knock, Lilliane recalled, she "looked at us and knew right away. Because I was there." Minna did not cry. She simply said, "Something's happened to Charlie." CDR Boecker explained what they knew. Then, together, they told young Brad and Bryan Earnest about their father.

After they left, Lilliane started doing all those things that usually fell to the CO's wife in such situations. She called Judy Pieno to start the telephone tree to inform all the squadron officers' wives about CDR Earnest's death. Then she started to think about how she could help with the memorial service, already being planned for 1 December.[72]

Judy Pieno had a second major task that morning, as well. When the official Navy car pulled up in front of the Jacksons' home, Linda had just finished helping her children get dressed for school. When the doorbell rang, Chris answered it and called for her mother. When Linda got to the door, she found CDR Zick and Judy standing there. This might have been a profoundly disturbing moment, but for one thing—Judy had a big smile on her face. They informed Linda of the accident and reassured her that LCDR Jackson had survived with only minor injuries. Only then did they inform her of CDR Earnest's death. "Of course I was sad for him and Minna," she later recalled, "but I can remember thinking over and over to myself, 'Thank you Lord, you answered my prayers. Thank you Lord, you answered my prayers.'" After she sent Chris and Danny off to school and called both her parents and her husband's to let them know what had happened, she drove over to the Earnest home.[73]

By the time she got there, and despite the Earnest family's request that they not show up right away, many of the other squadron wives had arrived. While a few close friends stayed on as long as they could help, Linda spoke to Minna and left quickly. She realized that her presence created an awkward situation. "The ladies were being happy for me and sad for Minna, and I felt like Minna was the one who needed all their support," she explained.[74] Some of the junior officers' wives, totally distraught, almost could not bring themselves to go to the Earnests' home over the next few days, even when Minna accepted visitors. Sandy Pyle, who greatly admired the skipper's wife, admitted to Duddie Graustein that she did not want to go because she did not know what to do or say. She worried about saying the wrong thing and ruining an important friendship. The senior officer's wife explained that simply being there said enough. Reassured, Sandy went. Later, she asked Duddie how she could thank her for offering her such good advice. Duddie simply said, "You thank me by sometime doing it for someone else."[75]

Skipper Greene sent word of CDR Earnest's death to others who needed to know. LCDRs Engel and King had gone to Japan to pick up a KA-6D, but they quickly completed their business and returned to *Saratoga*. The news of the accident hit Engel hard. "I had lost my older brother in 1962 from a similar catapult accident," he recalled, "so the needless loss of Charlie Earnest hit home at the time. Nobody said that flying off an aircraft carrier was a safe profession," he added.[76]

The new skipper also sent a telegram back to Oceana, with two messages for immediate delivery. The first went to Minna, extending the sincere sympathy of the officers and men of the squadron. CDR Earnest had been "an exceptional officer," he wrote, and "the Skipper's inspiration, devotion and leadership was the foundation of a truly outstanding Sunday Puncher squadron that he was very proud of." Greene's second message went to Lilliane to assure her that "the squadron members will truly miss the Skipper and have shown their professionalism brought by his guidance in continuing as he would want." He hoped that "Minna's bereavement can be eased by the wives' companionship and understanding."[77] On this point, he need not have worried. As Chris Bryan assured her husband, "The girls in the squadron are taking over as far as mail, phone calls, and all the unimportant incidentals of life which Minna need not worry about."[78]

Greene also took time to write a longer personal letter to Minna. "Charlie was exuberant over the mission, as he always was when something different or challenging was put before him," he wrote. Firmly but gently, he made clear that the search had been thorough. Indeed, LCDR Jackson could not confirm that Earnest had ejected. "We are absolutely positive that the area was rigorously searched and had he survived we would have located him," Greene assured her. After explaining the circumstances of the accident, he expressed his admiration—and that of others—for his downed skipper. Then a final thought crossed his mind: "As you well know, he was doing what he loved. Flying was so much a part of his life that hardly a conversation could go by without some reference to it. You don't do some thing for so many years with so much enthusiasm without a true devotion and love for it; all the while knowing full well the inherent dangers involved."[79] He also ordered a formal inventory of CDR Earnest's property. As Administrative Department head, this duty fell to LCDR Pieno. He had to break open Earnest's safe to empty it. The contents included the skipper's standard-issue .38 pistol, which he seldom carried. Pieno separated official from unofficial documents and returned to Minna immediately any personal papers she might find useful. The rest remained stored until VA-75 returned to the United States.[80]

CDR Greene also took steps to keep the squadron operating smoothly. He needed a new XO, but a quick exchange with MATWING ONE informed him that he could not get even a marginally qualified one until January 1973. CDR Morgan France, already slated to become VA-75's prospective XO, could be detached from the staff at Oceana to start RAG training, but he could not deploy anytime soon. MATWING ONE offered to supply a replacement pilot for CDR Earnest by 20 December, but they promised nothing more. Thus, CDR Greene reassigned personnel already serving in the squadron. Until LCDR Engel returned from Japan, LCDR Bart Wade—the senior lieutenant commander in the squadron still aboard—acted as squadron XO. On 3 December, when Engel returned, Greene appointed him to that position.[81] No replacement pilot ever arrived.

Greene also took time to write CDR Foote, describing for the former VA-75 skipper the circumstances of CDR Earnest's loss. Greene expressed regret for relaying such bad news about the death of a mutual friend, but he felt sure that Foote would want to know that "the Navy has lost one of its finest."[82] The next day, he summarized the sad events for Master Chief Jacob Pena, the senior Sunday Puncher serving with the airwing's beach detachment back at Cubi. "Needless to say it was a very tragic loss but the squadron is holding up very well,"

Greene told him, noting that "normal operations are continuing with the usual outstanding results from all the Sunday Punchers."[83] In his reply, Master Chief Pena forwarded a letter of condolence for Minna Earnest on behalf of the squadron's sailors serving at Cubi and added his own heartfelt tribute: "Our Navy lost a brave, hard-driving dedicated man who compacted so much brilliance into a very full but brief life span."[84] Greene even prepared a new opening page for the squadron familygram just going to press. As he announced his assumption of command, he praised CDR Earnest as "a professional—highly respected, and very much admired by all those associated with him. The genuine concern he held for all of us and the dedication he inspired through his leadership will remain in our hearts and minds." He knew that CDR Earnest would want his men to "hold their heads high and continue with our very important jobs in the spirit that he had instilled in us," and he assured those at home that "we will continue."[85]

Greene also knew that he had to talk to his pilots and B/Ns. Although he knew them and they knew him, this would be the first time he faced them as the skipper. Greene did not allow them to dwell on the accident. He admitted with all honesty that he would miss his comrade and friend, but then he looked at his gathered flight crews and said something that hit a few of the men as a jarringly discordant note. He told them he knew all of them were thinking the same thing. Just under their open grief lay a second sentiment, one that might be summarized simply as "better him than me." LTJG Warren, for one, understood what Greene tried to tell them. "This is something that we all live with from day to day," he explained to his wife, adding that "the fact that it happened on Yankee Station had nothing to do with it. It happens in the Med too." Still, he mourned CDR Earnest deeply, admitting, "The skipper will surely be missed very much. He was a good skipper. He was very well liked by the troops too, and they feel his loss dearly."[86]

But they felt anger, too. CDR Earnest had told his crews that if their plane went out of control and they could not save it, eject. "Your life is worth more to you and the Navy than the 28,500# of scrap your aircraft has become," as LTJG Petersen later summarized the skipper's advice. He, among others, believed that Earnest had died while violating one of his own cardinal rules.[87]

Back in Virginia Beach, CDR Greene's family understood that the new skipper bore greater responsibility now. Dawn wrote to him the day after the accident to tell him that "we've (meaning really mom) been on the run ever since Cmdr. E[a]rnest was killed." Even the children had done their part. Brad Earnest had come over to the Greenes' home for a while "and seemed to be taking it very good." Dawn also reminded her father that even though he now had more work to do, he needed to get enough sleep so he could fly safely. But the world of a fourteen-year-old does not always include a deep appreciation of death. So, she very quickly shifted to home-front chitchat, thanked him for the tapes he had sent her from Singapore, and added a plaintive request: "Dad if you have any time could you send me an Alice Cooper tape? Not right away but as soon as you have time!"[88]

CDR Greene did not have much time to fulfill such a request, however. VA-75 still had missions to fly, although new restrictions now reduced CTF-77 to only fifty strike hops on each of the last three days of November and on 1 December. Working under the new limits, *Saratoga* launched sixteen missions per day, only six by VA-75 crews. Flight operations only required a few hours each day.[89] Even so, A-6s could cause significant damage. On 1 December, A-6As from VA-75 and from VA-35 aboard *America* destroyed thirty-three trucks, eliciting congratulations to "all the Task Force 77 truck busting aircrews and to those personnel on the CVA's whose diligent support made it possible to hit the North Vietnamese truckers where it hurts the most."[90]

CDR Earnest's memorial service also took place on 1 December. On the hangar deck at 1300, the Marine color guard posted the colors. Protestant Chaplain P. J. Everts pronounced the invocation, led the Lord's Prayer, and read Psalm 121. Catholic Chaplain G. R. Witt followed with a New Testament reading from Romans. LCDR Jackson performed that sad rite of reading the Navy Flyer's Creed, his voice breaking. The assemblage then sang the aviator's verse of the Navy Hymn:

> Lord, guard and guide the men who fly
> Through the great spaces in the sky,
> Be with them always in the air,
> In darkening storms or sunlight fair.
> O hear us when we lift our prayer
> For those in peril in the air![91]

As CDR Greene tossed the ceremonial wreath into the waves and the Marine honor guard fired a volley in salute, a bird flew through the hangar deck and swooped over the Sunday Punchers' ranks. "It becomes significant when you realize that we haven't (the ship) been within 16 miles of land since we left Singapore on 3 November," LTJG Warren wrote his wife, wondering, "So where did the bird come from?" The unidentified bird seemed to symbolize the soul of a departed aviator, once more taking flight. In the memory of many Punchers, it became a dove.[92] A lone bugler sounded "Taps." LT Lankford felt his knees become unsteady.[93] The color guard retired. Then the somber survivors clustered in small groups, until they wandered away, to mourn alone or simply to return to duty. "One has to attend such a function to know how sad it really is, a very sad moment I shan't easily forget," LT Fischer confided to his diary that night.[94] But not all felt comforted by the chaplains' efforts. LT Hvidding, who thought often about his spiritual well-being, came away from the ceremony impressed by its lack of theological substance.[95]

Back at Oceana the same day, a second memorial service for CDR Earnest took place. A substantial crowd attended, including many of the Puncher wives living in Virginia Beach. Those who wanted to do something special complied with the family's request to send tributes in the form of contributions to the POW-MIA Scholarship Fund of the Red River Valley Fighter Pilots Association, an organization of aviators from all services who had flown combat missions in RP VI-B. It seemed only right; after all, under CDR Earnest's leadership, all of VA-75's current pilots and B/Ns became eligible for membership in this exclusive organization.[96]

For days, tributes to their fallen skipper flowed in, each to be posted on the bulletin board in the ready room. VADM Cooper, who had decorated several Sunday Punchers just a few days earlier, now sent a more somber message: "Those of us who knew Charlie Earnest personally share your great loss. We considered Commander Earnest a stalwart of Navy aviation as well as one of the most promising Naval officers of our time."[97]

CDR Earnest's death bothered every Puncher, but LTJG Petersen had multiple reasons for gloom. Not only did he mourn the loss of his commanding officer, he had also just received the bad news he expected: the Navy had rejected his application for augmentation. Considering CDR Earnest's death and his own treatment by the institution he so badly wanted to serve, Petersen wrote to his wife after the ceremony, "I'll never understand why men are dying out here still." Then he chose to reaffirm life with thoughts of his son and his wishes for the future: "I can't think of a job I'd like better than helping Danny put the Christmas tree decorations on."[98] Most of the other Puncher Reservists had received better news from the selection board. Only LT Knapp professed no interest in the outcome of the deliberations; he had decided to leave the service when he completed his obligation, regardless of the decision.[99]

On 2 December, the weather began to clear, and for the first time in two line periods, CVW-3 flew an alpha strike. That day, CAG Bordone planned to revisit Bai Thuong airfield. Since VA-75's two-plane strike had damaged it on 10 October, North Vietnamese crews had repaired the runways and the adjoining taxiway and ramps. Reconnaissance photos showed new revetments to protect aircraft and, far more important, three MiG-21s based there. If it became operational again, the interceptors flying from that field might threaten American air operations in the region.

Bordone led twenty-three CVW-3 aircraft against the airfield, flying strike lead in one of VA-75's A-6As and taking along LTJG Vance as his B/N. Unlike the

October strike, when the two Puncher aircraft carried the standard Mk82s, Bordone's plane now carried four Mk83 1,000-pound bombs to crater the runways. The other two A-6As each carried five of the even larger 2,000-pound Mk84s. LT Knapp and LTJG Fuller provided STARM support.

Once the aircraft launched and rendezvoused, the strike force split into two cells, each one targeting one runway with its adjacent taxiways. Bordone led one cell and CDR Armstrong of VA-37 led the other. They flew through the envelopes of ten SAM sites, but none seriously contested the ingress of the strike force. Two SAMs launched at Knapp and Fuller in their A-6B, however. They had picked up the Fan Song signals and tried to fire their two AGM-78s at the site, but neither one would lock on target. They finally fired an AGM-45 as the two SAMs headed for them. Knapp evaded them, but one exploded right above their plane. The detonation caused no damage, however.[100] As the strike force neared the Bai Thuong airfield, its formidable AAA batteries opened up. "If [the] war is almost over, you wouldn't know it from this end," one pilot wrote after the strike. Just the same, the two cells executed their mission as planned, and poststrike photography revealed huge craters on both the runways and in the support areas.[101]

The break in the weather on 2 December continued for several more days. Despite limits on sortie numbers and the possible nearness of a cease-fire, aircrews did not play it safe. Indeed, on 4 December, the very day the peace talks restarted, CAG Bordone decided to lead a two-plane low-level daylight raid into RP IV, between Thanh Hoa and the recently bombed Bai Thuong airfield, to hit a SAM site and a nearby missile storage area. Bordone took LCDR Bart Wade as his B/N, while Wade's usual pilot—LCDR Graustein—paired up with LTJG Warren. Each aircraft carried fourteen Mk20 Rockeye. From the start, the lead aircraft headed in the wrong direction, and Graustein and Warren—who knew the CAG's plane had gone off course—had no choice but to follow them. When he located the target, Bordone broke with airwing practice and made three passes over it, each run taking a slightly different course. Graustein followed each time. During that third run, wrote Warren that night, "we came about as close to getting killed as I've ever been." The North Vietnamese fired a SAM at the two aircraft, but it missed. Still, AAA fire cracked all around them. Warren looked over at Graustein and saw his pilot hunched over the stick with his head low and admitted, "I was the same way on the right side. I honestly don't know how they missed us." Warren decided that he had just lived through "the most stupid thing I've ever done over here, flying over a super high threat target *three times*." But they destroyed the missile canisters.[102]

On 4 and 5 December, *Saratoga* continued to fly the midnight-to-noon schedule, launching a limited number of night sorties against targets in RPs II and III and daytime strikes into MR II in South Vietnam. After standing down on 6 December, air operations resumed again the next day. Each night the men listened to the most recent news about the peace talks. During a moment when the news seemed promising, LTJG Fuller confronted an interesting quandary: "I need 5 more traps for 300 and 3 more missions for 100 combat missions," he wrote home. But, he added, "if the war ends on the 12th I guess I won't make either one."[103]

As the line period wound down, LT Chisholm wrestled with a family problem. For much of November, he had quit writing to his parents, furious with them for sending a letter to President Nixon about recent bombing pauses. In early December, he broke his self-imposed silence to send his mother a birthday card and to tell them just how much they had upset him. "Perhaps I have not used good judgement in sharing some of my experiences with you," he began. He had believed that "what I share with you in letters is between you and me and not to be mentioned up the line regardless of how strong your feelings or attachments might be." Repeating to the president his commentary about the southward movement of AAA guns and SAMs "puts me in a very awkward position," he explained, hoping they would try to understand the "possible consequences and unpleasant reflection this could have with my present occupation." Finally, he extended an olive branch: "Please be patient. I will be home."[104]

During this thirty-four-day line period, CVW-3 planes flew 1,088 strike sorties and delivered 2,200 tons of ordnance.[105] VA-75 flew a total of 527 missions of all kinds. The Sunday Punchers' A-6As flew 283 strike hops, including 103 at night. The squadron's A-6Bs launched only 42 times, 10 times at night. Of course, the KA-6Ds continued their flying every day that the weather had not canceled air operations, launching 200 tanker hops, including 69 at night. But the squadron's 143 cancelled missions told the line period's real story. Air aborts remained low, but deck aborts—numbering one or two on each day of air operations between 24 November and 4 December—continued to increase over October's numbers.[106]

As the first week in December passed, the Sunday Punchers made valiant efforts to summon up the Christmas spirit. Sharon Schram sent her husband taped Christmas music by Andy Williams, Nat King Cole, Glen Campbell, and Tammy Wynette. Christmas trees decorated many offices, and by 7 December most of the carrier seemed decked out in seasonal finery. Still, appearances proved misleading. All the red and green decorations reminded hundreds of Punchers that they had to spend the holiday away from their loved ones. About the only good news for some officers came in an unusual form—paperwork. Since *Saratoga*'s deployment in the combat zone was slated to end after the next line period—regardless of the status of the peace talks—some squadron personnel would have a chance to fly home directly from the Philippines rather than spend nearly a month steaming home to Mayport. For once, those who sought a seat on the "Early Bird" did not complain about filling out forms.

On 8 December, many of the Sunday Puncher crews flew the squadron aircraft to Cubi for maintenance. Those who remained aboard partied on Buff Boulevard that night. LTJG Kaiser had fallen asleep in his stateroom, but he awakened to a loud "help me, help me" outside his door. He opened it, looked down, found an officer "swimming" on the deck of the boulevard in a six-inch-deep mixture of various potables, and told him to get up. The drunken man rose to his knees, looked around, muttered his thanks, and left. Now fully awake, Kaiser joined the party and soon got inebriated himself. He returned to his room, soon emerging totally naked except for his cowboy boots and his .38 caliber pistol. An onlooker asked, "Just what in hell are you?" Kaiser slurred out, "I'm a k-boy! Can't you tell?" "Well, where are your guns?" the onlooker asked. The new B/N retorted, "I'm carrying two of them. Are you blind?" From that day forth, everyone addressed LTJG Kaiser as "K-boy"—with the emphasis on the second syllable.[107]

The carrier moored at Alava Pier during the early afternoon of 9 December. On the way, the men continued to read all the news about the peace talks with great interest, only to learn that a few days earlier on 4 December the negotiators once again had hit a stumbling block. They had continued to hope that a quick settlement might spare them from spending Christmas on the line, but the diplomats failed the sailors again. Since the declaration of martial law, opportunities for fun and diversion in the Philippines had become increasingly limited. In recent weeks, Linda Ahrens—the only Puncher wife still in Manila—had become accustomed to the sounds of explosions and gunfire, watched police drag a long-haired motorcyclist off his vehicle and cut his hair in public, and sat stunned in a restaurant during an altercation that ended with a chase through the building, one man waving a handgun wildly in the air.[108] Security around the carrier and the naval air station remained high, and threats of sabotage continued to concern commanders.

Still, the Sunday Punchers tried to make the best of it, assuaging recent hurts and celebrating an early Christmas. Some partied hard. The day after *Saratoga* docked, crews from the entire airwing survived a major drunk at the Cubi Officers' Club. A member of the RA-5C squadron nicknamed "Captain America" streaked through the club, clad only in a mask and cape. Someone tossed a chair through a big plate glass window.[109] As the party wound down and some of the Punchers' junior officers waited for a cab to take them back to the ship, someone cut in line and claimed their taxi. LT Cook challenged the interloper to a fight, then removed his shoes, took up a martial arts stance, and attacked. A donnybrook ensued, and Cook ended up with a bite on his face that required stitches.[110]

A similar incident occurred at the Subic Bay Officers' Club. LTs Anderson and Schuster, LTJG Sanford, and others had begun their own party there, when Marine officers from USS *Inchon* arrived. Anderson, an excellent pianist, began playing the Marine Corps hymn. Had the performance been rendered as a tribute, the crowd would have remained calm. But this rendition only inspired jokes, wisecracks, and insults at the Marines' expense. One began to heckle Sanford, someone threw a punch, and a fight ensued. Another Marine tried to protect his new camera, just purchased earlier that day. Schuster drop-kicked it against the wall. The fight ended for Sanford only when he dove under the piano for cover because, as he later explained, several of the men from *Inchon* "had started playing the Marine Corps Hymn on my nose."[111]

The enlisted men matched their officers for raucous behavior. After yet another hard line period, the Punchers headed for Olongapo. LT Hudson, standing with Gunner Walden up on the flight deck, watched as the redshirts left the carrier as a group. "Well, Gunner," the maintenance LDO said, "I'm going to tell you one thing about your ordnance people. It's not a liberty call for them. It's abandon ship!" No one suggested they had not earned it.[112]

The next day, the squadron threw an all-hands party at a beach on base. The picnic menu featured steaks, hamburgers, and hot dogs. Impromptu football and softball games pitted officers against enlisted men or one shop against another. They swam among the coral reefs. Beer flowed freely, of course, and after a while, the sailors gave vent to everything they found wrong with the Navy and the squadron. The same held true throughout the airwing and the ship's company. Except for the line period that ended in August, the shore patrol or provost marshal broke up more fights or returned more sailors to *Saratoga* for fighting or possible drug possession than at any other time during the cruise.[113]

Perhaps to try yet again to capture the spirit of the season, sixteen Sunday Punchers hosted a Christmas party at the Gordon Heights Elementary School at Olongapo on 15 December. The squadron itself donated the funds to purchase school supplies, candy, and other small gifts for 220 children. But over one thousand greeted them. LTs Ruland, Wiegand, Martin, and Pyle, along with LTJG Kaiser and Gunner Walden, cut and distributed three large layer cakes and poured cup after cup of Kool-Aid. Chief Aviation Structural Mechanic James Yates, Chief Aviation Firecontrolman Carroll L. Stalcup, Aviation Electronics Technicians First Class Edward Wilson and J. Hart, Aviation Maintenance Administrationman Second Class Joe Raubar, Aviation Maintenance Administrationman Third Class Henderson Bailey, Aviation Electronics Technician Third Class Tim O'Sullivan, Aviation Ordnanceman Third Class Keith Galway, and Aviation Structural Mechanic Third Class Jerome Stoklas led the games. Aviation Electronics Technician First Class Rodney Hill played the most memorable role: Santa Claus. Young Rowena Reyes wrote the men a thank-you note, letting them know just how much she appreciated their efforts: "This is the first time that we see Santa Claus here."[114]

As *Saratoga* prepared to leave port, the enlisted men in the Airframes shop expressed the squadron's fondest hope: "There's nothing wrong with a WestPac deployment that being home wouldn't fix."[115] Chief Warrant Officer Smith—CDR Earnest had just pinned on his new Chief Warrant Officer 3 insignia on 16 November—had just received some mail that summed up the squadron's reality even better. His son Bobby had sent a school assignment that included this six-line poem:

> "VA-75"
> Ship, shore
> Flying, repairing, buying
> Fathers, planes, missions, sea
> Bombing, shooting, killing
> Dirty, Bloody
> War[116]

On 17 December, *Saratoga* left the Philippines yet again, and the Sunday Punchers steamed for the Gulf of Tonkin for Christmas on the line.

CHAPTER ELEVEN

"Oh, Christmas Tree, Oh, Christmas Tree"

"Fill up your water bottles—we're going back." So began LCDR Graustein's operations note for 16 December. After a week's lull in the Philippines and with the death of Skipper Earnest still fresh in everyone's mind, Graustein offered a series of warnings designed to snuff out the slightest hint of complacency. He understood that they all wanted to be home—or anywhere else but the Gulf of Tonkin—but, he asserted, "it is imperative that we all recognize this attitude and take whatever steps are necessary to ensure that it doesn't affect flight ops." He appealed to their professionalism: "There is no way that anyone can force you to review your procedures. It's entirely up to you." He reiterated the importance of that fundamental practice, especially after a week's layoff. "There are about 1001 things that can go wrong on a fly aboard," he reminded them, but "if we think about what we're doing and keep ahead of the game, we'll be well on our way to another successful line period."[1]

On that same December day, Henry Kissinger held a press conference to explain the current state of negotiations on a cease-fire. Since the end of October when an agreement had appeared to be imminent, three major obstacles external to the peace process had stymied further progress: overt signs of North Vietnamese preparations for a major offensive into South Vietnam before—or, worse, just after—a cease-fire; misleading public statements by North Vietnamese leaders suggesting that the United States might accept a coalition government in South Vietnam to reach a final settlement; and, finally, specific objections raised by President Thieu to some of the language in the working documents. American negotiators had hoped that the round of talks in early December would clarify interpretive disagreements, set down a plan for international oversight of the cease-fire, and acknowledge the right of both Vietnams to exist without either side imposing its will on the other by force. To date, however, Thieu had not cooperated and the North Vietnamese had failed to make the guarantees most important to the American negotiating team, especially concerning international supervision of any cease-fire. Instead, as Kissinger noted, the North Vietnamese had reopened "a whole list of issues that had been settled—or we thought had been settled" and added new points for consideration. The ever-shifting changes demanded by the North Vietnamese since the 4 December resumption of peace talks clearly frustrated Kissinger. But he reiterated as well the official Washington position to the Thieu government that "we want to leave no doubt about the fact that if an agreement is reached that meets the stated conditions of the President—if an agreement is reached that we consider just . . . no other party will have a veto over our action." He made it clear to both sides that "we will not be blackmailed into an agreement. We will not be stampeded into an agreement." The American goal, he reiterated, was "an end of the war that is something more than an armistice. We want to move from hostilities to normalization and from normalization to cooperation. But we will not make a settlement which is a disguised form of continued warfare and which brings about by indirection what we have always said we would not tolerate." He concluded that, as of 16 December, "we have not yet reached an agreement that the President considers just and fair."[2]

The same day that Kissinger spoke of North Vietnamese intransigence, a *Washington Post* editorialist noted that "President Nixon appeared to be on the verge of a decision yesterday in what one diplomatic source described as 'a war of nerves' between Washington and Saigon over a cease-fire settlement of the Vietnamese war."[3] Political pundits of all sorts watched the stalled negotiations with interest, and they mulled over the military and diplomatic options remaining open to the president to break the stalemate. "Most likely," wrote an editorialist in the *Wall Street Journal,* "some actions will be military." Nixon could opt to halt further troop withdrawals. He could lift the bombing restrictions north of the 20th parallel. The correspondent warned, "If serious talks don't seem likely soon, Mr. Nixon may cancel those self imposed limitations as a means of applying pressure on the Hanoi government."[4]

Saratoga steamed back into the South China Sea on 17 December, its sailors and aircrews not yet aware of the roles they were about to play in the next act of the ongoing diplomatic drama. A week's break had not provided nearly enough time to attend to squadron business. Indeed, two of VA-75's aircraft required so much additional maintenance that two crews—pilots Fischer and Ruland, and B/Ns Ahrens and Swigart—stayed behind to fly them back to the carrier when the beach detachment released them. LT Ruland had an additional reason for staying behind—he expected news at any time that Brigid, due to deliver their first child on 19 December, had made him a father. Aboard *Saratoga,* the Sunday Punchers' mechanics and technicians continued to ready the rest of the squadron's aircraft for the next day's operations, and each JO worked through the mountain of paperwork his branch generated. Some had fallen so far behind that the squadron heavies threatened to keep them off the flight schedule until they caught up. LTJG Fuller, one of those tardy with his reports, commented in a letter home, "I said fine, I bet I can hold out longer than you."[5]

On 18 December, to begin its seventh line period as it had ended its sixth, VA-75 launched six fairly routine FAC-controlled sorties against bunkers and troop concentrations in MR II. But ominous rumors had begun to sweep through the squadron. LT Ken Pyle stuck his head into the stateroom of LTs Mullins and Hvidding to announce, "You're not going to believe this, but there are 300 B-52 sorties tonight going north, and we'll be there tomorrow, heavier than ever." Neither roommate slept well that night.[6]

Indeed, after Kissinger's commentary on 16 December, the North Vietnamese publicly blamed Washington for the latest delays in diplomatic efforts to end the war, now accusing the United States of "asking to change the fundamental content" already agreed upon in earlier negotiations. According to the North Vietnamese press, the alterations represented demands made public by President Thieu in a 12 December political address, arguing, "It is certain that without the permission of the United States, Thieu would not have acted and spoken as he did." Rejecting Kissinger's charges of North Vietnamese foot-dragging, Hanoi pointed to American and South Vietnamese leaders as those most guilty of harboring an "unwilling attitude" to work for peace and orchestrating a "perfidious plot" to continue the war.[7]

For more than a week, Nixon had considered his options if both North and South Vietnam remained unbending in their demands. On 13 December, Secretary of Defense Melvin Laird, with the concurrence of Deputy Defense Secretary Kenneth Rush and Admiral Thomas Moorer, chairman of the Joint Chiefs of Staff, argued that "the dilemma is more apparent than real. We jointly believe that you have only one viable, realistic choice. That choice is to sign the agreement now." They opposed any increase in military action. That same day, Kissinger offered North Vietnam two options: one, the United States could schedule another meeting with Le Duc Tho in early January for one more chance to sign an agreement; or, two, the United States could "turn hard on Hanoi and increase pressure enormously through bombing and other means." He suggested a brief but brutal show of strength, to "include measures like re-seeding the mines, massive two-day strikes against the power plants over this weekend, and a couple of B-52 efforts" to make clear to the North Vietnamese that "they paid something for these past ten days." Nixon decided on the second course, without the limitations in length or scope Kissinger had suggested.

The unprecedented air campaign to which he now committed served two purposes. On 17 December, Nixon informed President Thieu that he meant for this new wave of military action "to convey to the enemy my determination to bring the conflict to a rapid end." But he had a second purpose as well: to show Thieu "what I am prepared to do in case of violation of the agreement." Most important, he put the South Vietnamese leader on notice that he should not mistake the imminent bombing campaign as evidence of "a willingness or intent to continue U.S. military involvement if Hanoi meets the requirements for a settlement which I have set."[8]

Even before *Saratoga* recovered its aircraft from their strikes on 18 December, Nixon's decision set into action Operation LINEBACKER II. The first of three waves of Air Force B-52s from U-Tapao Air Force Base in Thailand and the first of three more waves of B-52s from Andersen Air Force Base in Guam took off for night strikes against selected military targets around Hanoi where no ordnance had fallen since the imposition of bombing restrictions in October. As one pilot summarized the news of 18 December, "It's an all out war once again." The Sunday Punchers once more headed "up North—like way up North."[9]

Although the world media spotlight shone most intensely on the B-52s, the U.S. Navy's carriers on Yankee Station also played an important role in LINE-BACKER II. To deliver their bombs accurately while minimizing civilian casualties—and planners considered both factors—the B-52s had to fly straight and level in the skies in RPs VI-A and VI-B. To pave their way through multiple SAM envelopes, tactical aircraft with night-fighting and all-weather capabilities had to suppress the North Vietnamese air defenses. While Air Force F-111s took most of the missions in support of targets around Hanoi, Navy A-6s carried the bulk of the load against SAM sites and related targets in the Haiphong area. It fell to four A-6 squadrons—VA-196 aboard *Enterprise,* VA-35 aboard *America* (until the carrier departed the Gulf of Tonkin on 26 December), VA-145 aboard *Ranger,* and VA-75 aboard *Saratoga*—to execute most of the Navy's night strike missions in direct support of LINEBACKER II.[10] Unfortunately, even the most detailed studies of this air offensive—most of which adopt the Air Force perspective—accord little attention to naval aviation's contributions to the total effort.[11]

The night of 18 December marked the first of eleven consecutive nights—broken only by a thirty-six-hour pause to include Christmas Day—when Navy and Air Force tactical air assets preceded the B-52s into the skies over Hanoi, Haiphong, or nearby provinces. French journalist Jean Thoraval, whose articles from North Vietnam during the summer of 1972 had inflamed debate about the uses of American airpower, now described the bomb blasts of this new offensive as "immense incandescent mushrooms" that could be seen from the office of the Agence France-Presse in Hanoi. The electricity went out nine times. Reporters worked by candlelight, sometimes from the safety of a bomb shelter. American activist Joan Baez, "in a shelter under several feet of concrete," played her guitar and sang. Hanoi authorities admitted that the B-52s hit some targets for the first time in the war, but they also claimed the downing of six of the big bombers. (In fact, North Vietnamese air defenders downed or crippled only three B-52s, along with one F-111 and a Navy A-7.) In an effort to claim the moral high ground, Hanoi announced that, despite the bombing, they would still honor "unilateral cease-fires of short duration" over Christmas and New Year's Days.[12]

In the United States, journalists and television commentators responded to the start of LINEBACKER II in different ways.[13] Some expressed outrage and incredulity. "The best hope for peace in Indochina since 1954 has been severely shaken by a hail of American bombs on Haiphong and the outskirts of Hanoi in a turn from negotiation once again to confrontation," a *New York Times* editorialist argued.[14] Others approached the events with greater objectivity but expressed confusion about the president's reasons for launching the air campaign. As a *Wall Street Journal* commentator surmised, "Mr. Nixon's newest bombing campaign is more political than military. . . . The goal most likely is to exert military and psychological pressure on the Communist Politburo, forcing it into compromise decisions that might end the war quickly."[15] In any case, stock prices plummeted. Nixon's press secretary, Ronald Ziegler, defended the action, linking it to previously voiced concerns about another North Vietnamese invasion of the south, explaining that "we are not going to allow the peace talks to be used as a cover for another offensive." This argument carried little weight, however, as military analysts responded publicly that they had no knowledge of any such threat.[16]

When asked to think back on it thirty years later, Sunday Puncher pilots and B/Ns expressed neither the media's outrage nor its doubts. Indeed, they recalled cheering the news of the intensification of the air war. Finally, they could unleash the full might of American airpower and hammer North Vietnam as hard as they could. Many can paraphrase the president's comment to Admiral Moorer on the night of 18 December: "I don't want any more of the crap about the fact that we couldn't hit this target or that one. This is your chance to use military power to win this war, and if you don't, I'll consider you responsible."[17] The orders "definitely uplifted" the spirit of the Sunday Punchers, LT Mike Schuster recalled, because they "were being turned loose on targets that may have had some meaningful impact on the outcome of the conflict."[18] CDR Greene described it as "personally very, very satisfying" because "we were going inside of places we were never allowed to go before."[19]

But the consensus the Sunday Punchers revealed thirty years after the fact did not exist in mid-December 1972. Then, they received the news with mixed feelings. On one hand, as LT Mullins recalled, after their briefing and suiting up for their first night of missions in support of LINEBACKER II, when the call came to man their planes, "for the only time on the cruise, there was a little rah rah sort of cheer in the ready room."[20] But the display of enthusiasm obscured genuine concerns, too. As LT Chisholm wrote on 18 December, "Don't like it. . . . Think we are going to have many people bagged. Many a game is lost in the fo[u]rth quarter—this is a pretty big game and the fo[u]rth quarter is upon us."[21] It took LT Pyle only about two weeks to decide that "I believe Nixon did the right thing." But he admitted he had not felt that way when LINEBACKER II first began. Then, alluding to his wife's bitterness about the decision to resume the bombing, he reported, "We were too at first."[22]

Late on 19 December, Day Two of LINEBACKER II, VA-75's pilots and B/Ns took to their cockpits. As one student of the campaign has asserted, "Although unspoken at the time," the purpose of these night strikes by F-111s and A-6s "was not simply to destroy SAM sites but to lure the operators to shoot at them with their precious missiles rather than at the B-52s."[23] But Sunday Puncher crews did not accept the passive role of "bait." They planned their night strikes with an attention to detail that exceeded the degree to which the squadron's crews had become accustomed. As CDR Greene described it, for VA-75, LINEBACKER II "consisted primarily of singular missions, but a lot of them, all at the same time."[24] Their targets, most often SAM and AAA sites, lay clustered fairly close to each other. Typically, two or three aircraft teamed up, either to hit different portions of a single target or to approach one target from different directions. To succeed, each crew had to know where and how the rest of their squadronmates planned to make their runs. Moreover, each of the four airwings in the Gulf of Tonkin had to coordinate its own efforts with those operating in or near the same location and, often enough, with Air Force planners as well. Although VA-75 did not use the phrase, other A-6 squadrons and some airwings gave these tightly coordinated attacks a new name: "delta strikes."[25]

On LINEBACKER II's Day Two, the Sunday Punchers flew eleven night strike sorties, one STARM support flight, and, as always, the usual spread of tankers.[26] Their targets included AAA sites, SAM sites, parts of the Haiphong Navy yard, and the Kien An airfield. As he had so many times, CAG Bordone led one of the first strikes himself, taking up a Sunday Puncher A-6A with experienced LCDR Hal King as his B/N. LTs Pyle and Hvidding launched just after them, both aircraft heading for targets near Kien An. While Bordone attended to airwing business, King planned much of the mission himself. The B/N explained to Bordone very explicitly that he wanted to keep below 500 feet and fly no faster than 360 knots. "Relax, pard," Bordone told him—he called everyone "pard" or "partner"—"no problem." When they went feet dry, however, Bordone still exceeded the agreed-upon speed and—worse—flew at 1,200 feet. They knew that Fan Song radars had painted them—by now, they all expected it—but before Bordone could descend, they heard the loud "DEEDLE" signifying a missile launch.

King spotted the SAM at the one o'clock position, headed right at them. Suddenly, as King explained it, Bordone let out with the "world-famous CAG transmission on UHF for the world, God, and everybody to hear: 'That motherfucker is tracking us!'" Bordone broke hard right, and the SAM exploded exactly where they had been. Then, experience told. They got back on track, rolled in on the runway, and, with Pyle and Hvidding not far behind on a slightly different approach, dropped their loads of Mk82s.[27]

Two other Puncher aircraft found their mission just as memorable. LT Knapp and LTJG Fuller—his ban from the cockpit for tardy paperwork lasted one day—headed for SAM site 661. As they waited to be released for their run, they could see intense AAA fire and SAMs lifting off in the far distance, aimed at a strike heading for Hanoi. To Fuller, it looked like "the finale to the Hudson's Fourth of July show over the Detroit River," back home in Michigan.[28] Their target rested in a non-radar-significant location on the outskirts of Haiphong within the envelopes of at least eight other SAM sites. They planned to fly at 300 feet—knowing they might have to fly lower—to drop their fourteen Mk20 Rockeye for maximum target coverage. They commenced their radar-only run while still thirty miles off the coast. Despite their low altitude, North Vietnamese radars acquired them immediately, and two SAMs lifted off, both aimed at them. Knapp evaded the missiles, and they dropped their ordnance. A huge explosion—indeed, a fireball—boiled up from the site. But they had no time to celebrate. Another SAM site picked them up immediately, and Knapp once again began evasive maneuvers, breaking the lock-on at an altitude below 150 feet. Looking back over their shoulders, they saw a fire so intense that aircraft passing the area much later reported the target still ablaze.[29]

Heading for site 661 about one minute behind Knapp and Fuller flew LTs Anderson and Hart. Since the first aircraft had made such a good hit, Anderson had no trouble finding the target. The flames, however, illuminated his aircraft. North Vietnamese AAA gunners opened up on them, and suddenly several rounds punched huge holes in the plane's horizontal stabilizer. Still, Anderson and Hart quickly dropped their ordnance on target and went feet wet, recovering safely aboard *Saratoga*.[30]

CDR Greene and LCDR Pieno went after a previously untargeted shipyard on the outskirts of downtown Haiphong, complete with storage and loading pens. Pieno's weapons system malfunctioned, but even though their target lacked nearby radar-significant features, the lights of downtown Haiphong eliminated any concern that they might miss it. As soon as they hit their coast-in point, however, they, too, spotted two SAMs heading in their direction. Greene broke hard left, evaded the missiles, then recovered to the right to reacquire the target. Pieno looked out the canopy, spotted the warehouse complex they sought, and simply yelled, "Warehouses! Pickle!" Greene dropped their fourteen Mk82s, and then headed for the harbor. They did not miss their target—the official BDA reported at least one medium fire—and they could not mistake their egress route. All the foreign ships were "dressed," lit up from bow to stern to make themselves visible to American aviators and to warn them off. They flew so low they seemed to be maneuvering between the channel buoys.[31]

Two crews—LCDR Graustein with LCDR Wade and LT Chisholm with LTJG Vance—coordinated their efforts to hit elements of the well-defended Haiphong naval base. The approach to the target took the planes over the city's heart. Worst of all, since they would be the last A-6As to launch that night, they knew the AAA gunners would be ready for them. First Graustein and Wade, and then Chisholm and Vance, buzzed the city at 200 feet and dropped on their targets. The two crews witnessed a tremendous explosion and a large sustained fire in their rearview mirrors. North Vietnamese defenders fired at least two SAMs at them, too.

When he returned from the strike, Chisholm boasted, "All in all [it] was a piece of cake," even adding, "Tomorrow more of the same." The comment sprang neither from bravado nor enthusiasm. Even as he celebrated success that night, he wondered when it would end. "This has to be the biggest air offensive in history," he mused, and "we . . . will pay for it."[32]

On 19 December perhaps only LT Ruland enjoyed a truly good mood. Still at Cubi, he called Bethesda Naval Hospital for an update on his wife. The nurse gave him good news, telling him that mother and child were doing well in the recovery room. When he asked for particulars, however—especially if the child was a boy or a girl—the nurse flatly refused to tell him, explaining that only Brigid could deliver that information. Since the renewal of the bombing offensive suggested that he might have to leave the Philippines before he could talk to his wife, he implored the nurse to fill him in. She finally relented, and LT Ruland learned that he had become the father of a healthy daughter named Jennifer Colleen.[33]

On 20 December, Day Three of LINEBACKER II, VA-75 crews flew eleven more night strikes and two A-6B support missions into the dark skies around Haiphong.[34] LTs Tolhurst and Wagner headed toward a target near now-familiar Kien An airfield. The AAA seemed particularly hot, but LT Wagner calmed Tolhurst with the simple assertion that the North Vietnamese could not possibly hit them. The words barely had left his mouth when the aircraft jolted repeatedly. They had been struck multiple times. Tolhurst looked at his B/N, but before he could say a word, Wagner shrugged and said, "They can't hit us again." And the North Vietnamese gunners did not do so. The crew continued on and dropped their bombs. As they egressed, however, smoke began to fill the cockpit, its pungent smell suggesting an electrical fire. Tolhurst saw that his hook transition light had illuminated, signifying that his tailhook had not locked into either the up or down position. He pulled the hook handle for a manual release and received a strong electrical shock. He tried to get Wagner to pull it, but the B/N refused; he had seen Tolhurst recoil when he tried it. The pilot slowed his aircraft, hoping to reduce the wind stream pressure on the hook, and finally it lowered. When they trapped aboard, they found that a bullet lodged in a wire bundle under the center console—only three or four inches from Tolhurst's foot—had caused the malfunction. Far more dangerous, however, another round had cut seven or eight strands of the seventeen-wire cable that controlled the horizontal stabilizer. Chief Pittman showed Tolhurst the severed wires and surmised that if the pilot had put any more Gs on the plane, he and his B/N likely would have lost control and would have had to eject.[35]

When LCDRs Engel and King and LT Knapp with LTJG Fuller went feet wet after their coordinated strikes against targets near the Haiphong boatyard, LTs Schuster and Mullins still waited to be released for their own run. Schuster heard Knapp warn about the extreme readiness of the North Vietnamese gunners, as he and Mullins reviewed their plan to hit a truck park south of Haiphong. They began their run at an altitude between 200 and 300 feet and took some AAA fire, including a few rounds through the starboard wing. That did not deter the crew, however. Even though Mullins's computer did not work, he still believed he could find the target. In the light of fires caused by earlier strikes, he recognized the road network from reconnaissance photographs. So they pressed on, popping up to about 500 feet to drop their ordnance on target.

As they pulled off, tracer fire cracked close by the right side of their aircraft. "It stayed with us as we turned," Mullins recounted, and that "had never happened to me before." Schuster jinked a bit, which usually took the aircraft out of the flak pattern, but this time it did not work. Mullins, who during night missions normally alternated between looking into the radar hood for two or three seconds and looking outside for two or three more, saw a trail of light and immediately told Schuster that he thought a SAM might be headed for them. Even though they still flew low, intelligence reports warned that North Vietnamese air defenders could fire SAMs without radar guidance and detonate them manually as the missile got close to low-flying targets. The unexpected flash of the suspected SAM kept Mullins's head out of the radar hood a good bit longer than usual. As he later explained, "That second glance was nearly fatal." Neither man paid attention to the terrain avoidance radar, and neither knew that they now flew toward a karst ridge. Mullins could have spotted it on his scope if he had returned his head to the hood.

Just then, a burst of AAA exploded above and to the left of their aircraft's nose. Its force pitched them a bit to the right and downward. At least one 23-mm round hit the refueling probe. The brightness of the explosion, plus the light of the full moon breaking through the overcast, lit up the skies just enough for Schuster to see the ridge ahead.

Mullins never saw the ridge, but he felt the plane shudder as Schuster pulled back on the stick. As the aircraft tried to respond, Mullins also heard and felt a rumble. The aircraft hit something solid. "My first thought was that we had pancaked off flat ground," he explained. But Schuster's quick action had staved off disaster. They had not crashed. As Schuster noted, "We cleared most of the ridge . . . but not everything on it." They had plowed through the tops of a row of pine trees.

Schuster's rapid climb took them up to over 1,500 feet, and Fan Song radars quickly began to paint them. Mullins tried to sound calm as he suggested that they descend below 1,000 feet. Once down to a safer altitude, they took stock. A quick check revealed that they had holes in both wings, they were leaking fuel and hydraulic fluid, the flight controls were getting increasingly balky, and the refueling probe had been damaged. They suspected they had suffered fuselage damage, but they did not know how much. Smoke filled the cockpit. Mullins removed his oxygen mask to sniff the air to determine the nature of the fire. He smelled wood smoke. The engines had ingested tree branches and other vegetation, and, he explained, "the wood, bark, and leaves had caught fire in the later stages of the compressor section, where temperatures reach hundreds of degrees." Some of that compressed air cooled and pressurized the cockpit, and Mullins cleared the smoke away simply by turning off the pressurization.

As Schuster and Mullins went feet wet, an E-2B vectored LCDRs Engel and King to the stricken plane to determine if it could land on the carrier. The senior crew noted at least a dozen instances of damage to the airframe, including the loss of the lower half of Schuster's center-line drop tank, but they still believed he could recover aboard *Saratoga*. King recommended that the pilot try a no-flap/no-slat approach, since some of those moving parts most likely had been damaged and might not work. Schuster concurred, understanding that if he did this, he would exceed normal approach speed. The arresting wire might not hold, and if it snapped, he had to worry about having enough power to climb. If he could not climb, he and Mullins would have to eject. To land without breaking a wire, he knew they had to get down to minimum weight. First, they released the remains of the drop tank and their MERs. They also dumped most of their fuel, realizing that if they did not catch a wire on their first pass, they would not have enough fuel for another.

Aboard *Saratoga*, both the Air Boss and CAPT Sanderson called for a senior member of VA-75 to advise them about all available options. LCDR Pieno, with the carrier's skipper, concluded that the chances of breaking the wire far outstripped the likelihood of a safe landing. The heavies discussed the use of the barricade, but they doubted that the net that had stopped LT Lankford and LTJG Warren in July would stop an aircraft trying to land at Schuster's estimated speed. They did not include Schuster in these discussions; they simply ordered him to fly the plane as best he could. Finally, Sanderson and the Air Boss decided to move all aircraft forward and clear the flight deck of all personnel except the LSOs. That way, they might contain the damage if Schuster snapped an arresting wire. They watched the approach nervously. In the end, however, the pilot's airmanship paid off. Schuster made a great pass and caught the No. 1 wire, and the LSO gave him a landing grade of "OK/ASU," meaning "OK/all shot up."

After they trapped back aboard, Schuster and Mullins finally appreciated the effects of their flight through the trees. Almost immediately, officers and enlisted men pressed around the plane to grab a piece of wood as a souvenir. Schuster and Mullins counted eighteen holes in the aircraft, six of them a foot or more across, most on the leading edge of the wings. In addition to the AAA damage to the fuel probe, LCDR Dick Schram—the VA-75 Safety Officer—discovered twigs lodged in the fuel probe faring. Chunks of wood three inches in diameter stuck out of the wings. They found twigs in the vertical stabilizer. Most remarkable of all, the entire radome was stained pine green. The aircraft became the squadron's "hangar queen," of course, and the smell of pine filled the hangar bay for weeks. It did not sit undisturbed for long, however. Since the front of the plane had taken most of the structural damage, the squadron's airframes teams removed its undamaged horizontal stabilizer and put it on the shot-up A-6A that LTs Anderson and Hart brought back the previous night.

The "flight through the trees" became the stuff of squadron and naval aviation legend. Even after the passage of thirty years, Mullins believed that "I have no business still residing on earth. We were moving around 600 feet per second at impact. I doubt that we would have survived if Mike had pulled 100th of a second later. Epictetus said that fate is character. I hope so."[36]

LT Chisholm and LTJG Vance flew an A-6B in support of the squadron's strikes around Haiphong that night. Across the entire carrier division, a shortage of AGM-78s had caused A-6 squadron commanders to advise their A-6B crews to be stingy in their use. VA-196 had so few of them that they routinely flew their A-6Bs with four AGM-45s for most of their missions.[37] While VA-75 did not find itself in such dire straits, the crews knew they should not fire them without good cause. It had been an exciting evening for Chisholm and Vance so far. Vance spotted a SAM that seemed to be heading for them, and he told Chisholm to break to evade it. The pilot reacted immediately, but the missile tracked far away from their aircraft. A bit later, when Vance spotted a second SAM, the earlier incident

On 21 December, at the height of LINEBACKER II, *LTJG Thomas Vance and LT Bob Chisholm prepare to deliver VA-75's nine millionth pound of ordnance. (U.S. Navy photograph, Robert M. Chisholm Collection)*

caused him to hesitate before he called for the break. This time the SAM exploded about 300 yards away. They recovered aboard *Saratoga* safely, but not before firing two AGM-45s to force the aggressive North Vietnamese SAM sites to shut down.[38]

For one Sunday Puncher, however, the squadron's good luck in the air provided only the second-best news of the day. When LT Hiduk and LTJG Sanford trapped from their mission, the B/N immediately looked for battle damage to their aircraft, too. He had heard a big thud during their hop—even LT Hiduk flew night strikes in RP VI-B during LINEBACKER II—and Sanford wanted to know what hit their plane. A troubleshooter checked out a big hole and soon handed Sanford a souvenir by which to remember that night's mission: a handful of bird feathers. Once again, a low-flying A-6 had cut into the North Vietnamese avian population.[39] When he brought his prize to the squadron ready room, however, Sanford's day improved even more. LTJG Petersen—standing SDO that night—already had posted the good news on the blackboard. Back in Virginia Beach, Brenda Sanford had given birth to a daughter. They named her Sara—for *Saratoga*.[40]

Also back in Virginia Beach, well before LT Schuster could tell his family about his adventure in his own way, Denise Schuster received a copy of an official telegram. The first line of text read simply "Navy Preliminary Message Report of Aircraft Accident." Coming so soon after CDR Earnest's death, the words jolted her. Trying to make sense of the brief text, she read a recitation of the damage to the refueling probe, both wings, and the landing gear door of her husband's aircraft. A few paragraphs later, she read that the plane broke left off target, came under heavy AAA fire, and evaded a SAM before striking the top of trees. By the time she reached the end of the brief account, she found it difficult to accept the veracity of the message's final line of text: "Egress and recovery aboard CVA uneventful." Even more frustrating, the message made no specific comment about the safety of her husband or his B/N.[41]

Other disquieting news reached Virginia Beach that day, too. While all of VA-75's aircraft had survived the night, the North Vietnamese had shot down an A-6A from VA-196. The pilot, CDR Gordon Nakagawa, had flown as LCDR King's pilot on a previous cruise. The two families had become so close that King had named the youngest of his three sons Gordon. On that unseasonably warm December day, Loren King answered the telephone while her younger daughter, Glynnis, played with her Barbie dolls under the Christmas tree. When Loren began to cry and repeat two words—"Oh, no! Oh, no!"—Glynnis immediately feared for her father. Then her mother explained that something bad had happened to "Uncle Gordie."[42] Loren told her middle son, Barry, who knew she was thinking about his father just as much as their family friend. He just hugged her and repeated the phrase that had become the King family mantra: "He'll come back—he always does!"[43] Hal King, Jr., home on leave from the Naval Academy Preparatory School, felt the loss of a close family friend, but his sorrow competed with his thankfulness that his father had rejected Nakagawa's suggestion that he seek a transfer from VA-75 to VA-196 so they could fly together again.[44] Hal had already shared with his sister, Debbie, some of the cockpit tapes his father had sent to him. "It was the first time I ever heard my father cuss, and he was good at it!" she recalled. But those tapes also heightened her concern for his safety, and the loss of CDR Nakagawa brought home her worst fears.[45] Only young Gordie, age 3, had not fully appreciated the gravity of the phone call. A few days later they learned that the North Vietnamese held CDR Nakagawa and his B/N as prisoners of war.

But at least these families heard some substantive news. No one knew what to make of the silence from MACV headquarters in Saigon and other usual information sources. "The United States command was unusually uncommunicative about the new raids," reporter Joseph Treaster noted, adding that "contrary to daily practice for years, the command yesterday refused to disclose even in general terms the number of planes involved in the strikes or the general areas where the strikes took place, or to give any indication of the damage inflicted." With no official news to offer, journalists reported a depressed mood among American officers serving in Saigon, quoting an Army colonel as saying, "People were in the clouds, riding high a few days ago, expecting to be leaving soon. Now everybody is down."[46] Day Three of LINEBACKER II cost the Air Force six B-52s.[47] Optimism prevailed only among leaders of President Thieu's government.[48] Puncher families at home in Virginia Beach read speculation that one of these recent raids "could have been the single largest of this or any other war" and suggestions that the ordnance dropped so far exceeded the famous Allied 1,000-plane missions against Axis targets or Luftwaffe strikes during the London blitz.[49] Worse, if official American spokesmen remained silent, North Vietnamese leaders did not. They described the air offensive as an "insane action" and proclaimed that if Nixon believed it would bring them back to the bargaining table, he indulged in "pure fantasy." They reported high civilian casualties and damaged residential neighborhoods and accused the crews of the B-52s of "committing extremely barbaric crimes."[50]

The Sunday Punchers knew little of the media's outrage at home, however. Indeed, at least from their own limited perspective, the pattern set on their first two nights in the intensified bombing campaign reinforced to all Intruder squadrons on Yankee Station that they carried the Navy's night-strike effort almost single-handedly. Now, as the Punchers suited up for their missions, the A-7 pilots in VA-37's ready room next door yelled loudly, "Roll the movie," and "Where's the popcorn?" While the F-4s continued to fly MiGCAP and BARCAP missions, the A-7s now mostly flew standoff Iron Hand missions and increased surface combat patrols (SURCAP) against the potential threat offered by the discovery of several new Komar-class Soviet-built missile boats.[51] Moreover, since the weather had deteriorated so badly, A-7 missions had to be cancelled or cut back on every one of the twenty-one operating days during the line period. They did not participate on these night bombing strikes.[52] It had become easy to believe, as LT Chisholm expressed, that the "entire carrier war seems to be conducted by A-6's."[53]

The first few days of LINEBACKER II had hit squadron aircraft hard. At least they had not lost any crews, and LT Mullins did not want to tempt fate on that score. After his adventure in the trees, he pulled SDO duty on 21 December. He tried to back out of it, reminding LCDR Graustein that every time he had stood the duty since August, CVW-3 had lost a plane. Graustein credited him with a nice try, but he still had to do it.[54]

The pattern of night missions for the A-6s set on the previous few days continued into 21 December, Day Four of LINEBACKER II.[55] VA-75 launched just seven night strikes against targets in RP VI-B. The reduced number reflected both the availability in undamaged aircraft and the squadron's assignment to two daytime mini-alpha strikes against Hanoi-area targets that weather-diverted to RP IV. One A-6B launched, too.

During their briefing in the ready room, LCDRs Graustein and Wade coordinated with LT Lankford and LTJG Warren, as they prepared to hit Kien An airfield again. They agreed that Graustein would hit the left runway and break off the target to the left to reduce the possibility that Lankford, following a few seconds behind, might fly through the smoke and debris from the first run. Before they left the ready room, Graustein and Wade also talked with LCDRs Engel and King, who planned to fly through the Kien An target area to hit a SAM site defending a petroleum storage area north of Haiphong. Engel and King agreed to wait for a "bombs away" call and an "off target" confirmation of Graustein's turn for the coast before beginning their own run.[56]

As they all suited up, LTJG Warren noticed that Graustein had tucked under his arm a new solid white flight helmet, one so recently unpacked that it had not been painted with the squadron's green colors. The junior B/N expressed surprise that Graustein would start wearing a new helmet at this point in the cruise. As he later explained, "Not that Bob was superstitious, but he refused to change his socks during a line period!"[57]

As the VA-75 A-6As launched, they stacked up in pairs as usual and waited for signals to depart for their individual targets. Graustein and Wade headed out first, with Lankford and Warren following not far behind and to their right as planned. At first, the strike went as briefed. Both aircraft ran in on their targets at 200 feet. Graustein called "bombs away!" Lankford and Warren both noticed large secondaries to their left and concurred that Graustein and Wade must have hit something big. But although they heard the "bombs away" call, neither had heard Graustein's confirmation that he and Wade had begun their break to the left. Going feet wet after dropping their own bombs, they flew to their prearranged rendezvous point over a destroyer sitting just off the coast. But they circled the ship alone. Informing *Saratoga* that they had lost their flight lead, they started back feet dry to find Graustein and Wade. Before they had gone very far, however, they received orders to return to the carrier. They began to wonder about the true nature of the explosions they had seen.[58]

In the meantime, Engel and King had begun their fly-through of the airspace near Kien An airfield. They, too, had heard Graustein and Wade's "bombs away" call and looked north toward their target area. As Engel recalled, he and King witnessed "a large fireball" near that point. They heard no call from Wade or Graustein to confirm their break-off target. After completing their ordnance drop, Engel and King tried to make radio contact. Like Lankford and Warren, they received no response.[59] LT Chisholm and LTJG Vance, flying behind Engel and King, also spotted a fireball as they flew through the Kien An area. They feared from the start that an aircraft had exploded in midair.[60]

Just that fast, the squadron's final line period, once portrayed to them as "a piece of cake," had turned into anything but easy. Back in the VA-75 ready room, SDO Mullins received a call about the overdue status of Graustein and Wade's aircraft and informed CDR Greene. The skipper told LT Knapp and LTJG Fuller, just coming feet wet after a strike, to attempt to radio the missing crew. But they heard nothing to suggest the presence of survivors on the ground. The airwing launched no SAR effort. The Navy listed LCDRs Graustein and Wade as MIA. It seemed irrelevant somehow that Chisholm and Vance had just dropped the squadron's nine-millionth pound of ordnance. Similarly, none of the pilots or B/Ns took note that LTs Tolhurst and Wagner—an unusual crew pairing since their "other halves," LTJG Ahrens and LT Fischer, respectively, still remained in the Philippines—made Saratoga's 175,000th arrested landing that night.[61]

After so many deferred promises of peace, the loss of a crew hit the Punchers especially hard. Down on the hangar deck when he heard the news, LCDR Pieno—Graustein's roommate—vented his anger and frustration on a nearby drop tank, punching and hammering it with clenched fists. LT Hudson had to pull him away, sit him down, and calm him down.[62] Two Punchers now bore personal burdens. "I will forever remember (and regret) kidding him about the white helmet while we were suiting up for this mission," LTJG Warren related years later. "I said something like 'Hell, Graus, you're gonna make a great target, running around on the ground with that helmet after they shoot your ass down!'" LT Mullins faced the reality that when it came to CVW-3 losing aircraft when he was SDO, "I was 5 for 5."[63]

Once more a telegram bearing bad news went back to MATWING ONE at Oceana, where just the previous Sunday the chapel had held an ecumenical service to remember the POWs and MIAs.[64] For the previous few days, however, Puncher wives had enjoyed the happy news about the squadron's two new Christmas babies. Shortly after Judy Pieno, Lilliane Greene, and Duddie Graustein had arrived at the hospital to visit Brenda Sanford and her new daughter, a nurse commander told Lilliane that she had a phone call. At first, she thought one of her children needed a ride, but a sense of foreboding swept over her when she was directed to the chart room rather than to the public area of the nurses' station. She then heard CDR Don Boecker's voice breaking the bad news.

Lilliane immediately had to decide how to tell Duddie, now just down the hall admiring the new addition to the Puncher family. She decided that it would be best to deliver the news in the familiar and comfortable surroundings of the Graustein home and not in the clinical halls of the hospital. Thus, Lilliane asked

Boecker to bring the notification team to her own home. Since she had picked up Duddie for the drive to the hospital, she would take her friend home, meet the officers at her own house, then return with them to the Graustein residence. Without tipping her hand, she made up an excuse to cut short their visit. The drive back to the Graustein home ranked among the toughest things Lilliane Greene ever did. She met the officers and returned to the Grausteins' doorstep. When Duddie saw her, she seemed surprised at first. But when she saw CDR Boecker and CDR Zick, she realized immediately the nature of the visit. And she began to cry.[65]

As the Puncher wives tried to help the Graustein family, at least one had to deal with unexpected obstacles of her own. Sue Engel, wife of the new acting XO, heard her doorbell ring. When she opened the door, she found two uniformed police officers holding a warrant for her arrest. "They declared that I had not paid a fine owed for when our dog Charlie was picked up by the dog catcher for running loose a few weeks earlier," she later explained. She had paid, though, and she had the receipt to prove it. But the policemen persisted, informing her of a second related fee that remained unsettled. Sue would have to go with them to the police station. Coming on the news of the renewed air offensive and the recent loss of two men in her husband's squadron, Sue began to cry. But since that helped nothing, she arranged for a neighbor to watch her two children. The police booked, fingerprinted, and photographed her, then told her she could go if she could pay bail amounting to $150. She sighed in relief, but the Virginia Beach police would not take her check and she did not have that amount in cash. Finally, she made out a check to a neighbor who cashed it and brought back the money so Sue could bail herself out of jail. Only then could she turn her attention to helping the Graustein family.[66]

The other squadron wives gathered, too, of course. Lilliane Greene organized the effort, and Carol Warren—an especially close friend of Duddie's—stayed nearby to provide comfort. All the officers' wives did what they could. Loretta Lankford and Penny Swigart went over to the Graustein home together. Each loss bore down harder and harder now, and Loretta found this one especially difficult to bear. She had learned so much from Duddie, but now she simply did not know what to say or do. She told herself over and over again, "I don't want to do this." But she, too, had asked Duddie's advice about visiting Minna after CDR Earnest's death. So she went.[67]

Back aboard *Saratoga*, CDR Greene once again faced the challenge of keeping the squadron running smoothly. He needed a new operations officer to replace LCDR Graustein and assigned the job to LCDR Jackson, now fully recovered after his November accident. Greene also designated officers to inventory the personal belongings of the two downed aviators. LCDR Pieno took care of his roommate's possessions. LT Chisholm, who collected LCDR Wade's things, found it tough going. They had been good friends, and Wade recently had asked Chisholm to share an apartment with him when the squadron returned to Oceana.[68]

Greene sent a message to Cubi to break the news to the squadron's two crews still awaiting planes coming out of maintenance. LT Fischer reflected on a bitter irony. Early in the cruise when he and LT Wagner had gone to IOIC to plan a strike hop, LCDR Lindland, as operations officer, had looked at their planned route and told them, "You're not going there. You'll get shot down." A few months later, after Lindland was shot down, LCDR Graustein reviewed Fischer and Wagner's planned route for a strike, and he told them the same thing that Lindland had told them. The place the two ops bosses had told the young crew to avoid was Kien An airfield. As Fischer later noted, "They were both lost not too far from the area [where] they didn't let us go!"[69]

On 22 December, Day Five of LINEBACKER II, now down two aircraft—those flown by LT Schuster and LCDR Graustein—and with the A-6A that LT Anderson brought back with a damaged stabilizer not yet repaired, the squadron mustered only enough airworthy planes to fly a total of eight night strikes. To a far greater degree than on the previous nights of the air offensive, the B-52s planned to hit targets near Haiphong.[70] Just as they had done the previous few evenings, Sunday Puncher crews again hit SAM sites, AAA batteries, and airfields that might threaten the big bombers.

After flying a tanker hop, a daytime sortie, and A-6B missions, LCDR Jackson finally scheduled himself for his first night strike since ejecting successfully from CDR Earnest's plane. He crewed with LTJG Bryan to hit SAM site VN-525, a difficult target approximately ten miles northwest of Nam Dinh. They made their run uneventfully and then headed toward Phu Ly and Ninh Binh to look for trucks. Both men were searching intently for lights, when all of a sudden Jackson yelled, "Pull up, pull up!" They had headed for a karst ridge, dead ahead. Bryan pulled back on the stick quickly, and they returned to the carrier safely. The young pilot expected a lecture, but Jackson said nothing about the incident, nor did he consider it sufficiently important to commit the incident to his personal log. Indeed, he noted only that they got "no BDA, but know we got some trucks." But Bryan never forgot the experience. He appreciated Jackson's ability to keep them safe while "giving me confidence."[71]

On 23 December, LT Ruland and LTJG Swigart finally returned from Cubi with one of the squadron's badly needed A-6s. LT Ruland, the proud new father, still walked on air, of course. Swigart, however, brought more distressing news. Just before he left, he had spoken to Penny back in Virginia Beach. The report from home was grim. The wives took the loss of LCDRs Graustein and Wade very hard, and while they provided all the support they could to Duddie and her three boys, the nightly news now made them wonder who might be the next to get a visit from a notification team.[72]

Some families turned off their televisions or stopped reading the newspapers. Reports citing heavy civilian casualties from B-52 carpet bombings and direct hits on Communist-bloc shipping in Haiphong harbor, especially one causing fatalities on the Polish freighter *Jozef Conrad,* aired with increasing frequency. The Communist Chinese denounced the bombing of one of its ships in the harbor, too, and the Cuban and Egyptian governments protested the damage inflicted on their embassies in Hanoi. Traditional allies such as Australia announced their opposition to the bombing, and protesters took to the streets in London, Rome, Copenhagen, Zurich, and Amsterdam. Pope Paul VI openly criticized the effort. A quick poll of seventy-three U.S. senators located by staffers of *Congressional Quarterly* showed that forty-five opposed the new air offensive and only nineteen approved of it. Reports described North Vietnamese SAMs launched in salvos and barrages, and each day brought fresh news of B-52s shot down and photos of captured American airmen. It had not helped morale at home when a Defense Department spokesman suggested that there would be no bombing halt for Christmas—nor did his assertion that "we are early in this engagement."[73]

The strike schedule for 23 December, Day Six of LINEBACKER II, called on VA-75 to launch eight low-level night strikes against SAM and AAA sites and one A-6B flight into RP VI-B, as well as one night strike at a target in RP IV. Kien An airfield continued to draw the squadron's attention, even though no MiGs had used that field over the previous few nights. This time, LCDR Jackson flew with LT John Miller and decided to try a different approach to solve an old problem. They coasted in south of Haiphong as they usually did on such a strike, but then they angled northwest toward Hai Duong and swung toward the east and south, essentially to come in Kien An's back door. Achieving tactical surprise and meeting little opposition, they lined up on the runway and cut it just a little north of its halfway point. They also damaged a revetment protecting a MiG-17. Even on the egress they faced little opposition. One SAM, fired at them about thirty seconds after they pulled off the target, missed them by a considerable distance and disappeared into the overcast.[74]

The SAMs continued to miss, at least in part because the A-6As of VA-75 continued to fly low. Not all Intruder squadrons chose to continue this flight profile. Beginning about 23 December, VA-196, for one, alternated low-slow strikes with high-slow flights, coasting in at approximately 15,000 feet, or 10,000 feet above the cloud deck, at 360 to 400 knots and dropping their ordnance loads with a straight path dive or level release.[75] VA-75 did not turn to this option. However, the same night that Miller and Jackson tried to hit an old target in a new way,

Lankford and Warren went after SAM site VN-539 with new twists of their own. "The standard 400' run we were doing before is now a 200' run. At least for Ron and I it is," Warren explained to his wife. That night they put twelve Rockeye "right down their throats, got 3 large explosions and left a huge fire burning." He did not explain to his wife that he and Lankford had flown through intense AAA and multiple SAM launches to reach their target. When LCDRs Engel and King passed the area on the way back from their own strike against Kien An airfield, they reported the fires still blazing brightly.[76]

By the end of air operations on 23 December, the airwing had completed six days of strikes, five in North Vietnam. Unlike the previous few line periods when bad weather or political restrictions limited the number of hops assigned to each squadron, now the crews launched into the hostile skies nearly every night. Most crews got at least one break from RP VI-B during that time, but LT Chisholm and LTJG Vance found their names on the flight schedule five consecutive nights, including their exciting A-6B hop and one air abort. LT Knapp and LTJG Fuller also launched on five consecutive missions into RP VI-B, one strike hop each night the squadron flew there. Only the last had been an air abort.[77] When his wife asked what he thought about in the cockpit during those December strikes, Fuller explained the complexity of his intellectual and emotional response: "For the first part of the time after launch, I'm sort of busy trying to figure out what works and what doesn't and so I'm not reflecting on anything. Once that's done and I know what I'm going to have then I can contemplate what lies ahead[,] and if the time is sufficiently long before we start our run in[,] then I can get a very hollow feeling in my stomach. Sometimes I'd wonder if the whole thing was worth it, sometimes I worried about hitting the target. There never really seemed to be one recurring worry or fear." He felt sorry for the B-52s that went down, but "I was glad it wasn't me. That's a bit hard, I guess, but it's true."[78]

The pilots and B/Ns took only limited satisfaction from their efforts. Except for the most spectacular fires, no one could make a credible evaluation of their effectiveness. The North Vietnamese had moved away from setting up their SAMs in fixed positions to emphasize mobility and flexibility. A site briefed by intelligence officers one night might be empty ground the next. The A-6 crews of VA-196 also noted that "it is not unusual to find them placed randomly," hoping that the element of surprise would facilitate their ability to circumvent the electronic countermeasures capability of the American planes.[79] Judging the bombing's impact on the morale of the North Vietnamese proved to be no easier. After typically optimistic initial reports from the Joint Chiefs of Staff, editorialist Joseph Kraft prepared an imaginary gift list for Nixon and suggested that he give his senior military men "honorary appointments to Egyptian intelligence."[80] On Christmas Eve, rumors flew that bombs had killed famed North Vietnamese General Vo Nguyen Giap near Haiphong, and just as quickly they disappeared.[81]

Influential columnist Anthony Lewis condemned LINEBACKER II as terror bombing and as "a crime against humanity." He blamed Nixon's personal weaknesses for ordering it, noting that "it was by his sense of inadequacy and frustration that he had to strike out, punish, destroy." What appalled him even more was that nobody in a position of authority or influence seemed to care enough to try to stop it. "Public men always tell themselves that they do more good trying to moderate an evil policy from the inside, but at some point that self-deception has to stop. They also say that one man cannot make a difference," he wrote. Then he added, "In any case, it does not relieve anyone from the responsibility of trying." Lewis's comments, widely disseminated, gave voice, words, and inspiration to many Americans horrified by the bombing offensive.[82]

But still the carriers on Yankee Station continued their work. As LTJG Fuller summarized succinctly in a letter home: "Contrary to what the papers have said, the B-52s are not the only aircraft getting shot at. In the first four days of the renewed bombing there were 15 A-6s battle damaged among the 4 squadrons flying night missions. We had an aircraft get so low it flew through some trees evading a SAM." Still, he wanted his father—an aeronautical engineer—to know that "Grumman Iron Works still builds aircraft—he'll understand."[83] The high tempo of *Saratoga*'s air operations—especially for the Sunday Punchers—inspired an anonymous poet who featured CAPT Sanderson in this "Christmas Sitrep" in the 24 December edition of the carrier's daily newspaper:

> He looked on the flight deck and to his surprise,
> There stood Admiral Zumwalt with big blood shot eyes.
> He looked at the captain and said I want you to know,
> It won't be long and I'll tell the Sara to go.
> But until that time get in there and fight,
> Get them planes out; there will be no sleeping tonight.
> And as "Z" took off without looking back,
> The captain exclaimed, "Damn it, cut us some slack."[84]

As the ode suggested, air operations continued without a break. Late on 24 December, Day Seven of LINEBACKER II, eight Puncher crews received orders for strike missions, again targeting SAM and AAA sites near Haiphong. Even during the planning phase of the missions, before the crews ever manned up, CDR Greene set very strict weather parameters for these missions. He told them that they would not continue if a low cloud deck over the mountains north of Haiphong made it too difficult to execute their drops with reasonable safety. He wanted to protect his men, but, more than that, he did not want a Puncher family to get bad news on Christmas Day.[85]

"We were the sacrificial first plane in and had to make weather recommendation to execute or divert," LT Chisholm wrote, noting that "at 300' and still in the clouds we decided wx [weather] was pretty bad and very disorienting with flashes all around." Trying to lighten his dark mood, he described the AAA as many little reindeer that "all had bright red noses pointed at our aircraft." Then he reconsidered: "Maybe they weren't reindeer."[86]

The other seven VA-75 aircraft launched as planned, while awaiting the weather report. CDR Greene had prearranged a signal to cancel the mission. "Our code word to abort the mission because of the unsatisfactory cloud cover/ weather was 'Happy New Year!'" recalled LCDR Engel. When Chisholm and Vance reported the poor conditions, CDR Greene sent out the "Happy New Year" call. "As much as we were eager to complete our assigned mission," Engel noted, "we were not too unhappy to announce 'Happy New Year' on Christmas eve and return to the ship."[87] All seven of the remaining Puncher crews jettisoned their ordnance at sea.[88] They recovered aboard *Saratoga* shortly after midnight on Christmas Day. The tower told them to watch for unusual FOD on the flight deck: reindeer droppings.[89]

Despite the warnings of a few days earlier, Christmas Day heralded the start of a 36-hour break in LINEBACKER II operations. The Sunday Punchers tried to catch the Christmas spirit, at least for one day. After the last of their eight planes landed safely early on 25 December, the festivities began. In VA-75's Administrative Department offices, the enlisted men invited the officers to join them for their own little party. LCDR Pieno contributed two bottles of scotch to the gathering, and at least one other officer brought along a fifth of rum. The enlisted men decorated the offices and rustled up some cheese and sausages, along with a specially baked cake to mark the occasion.[90]

The Sunday Punchers' officers gathered in the ready room at 0300 on Christmas morning. Back in their staterooms, many of them already had opened their presents from home, and nearly everyone arrived with some seasonal goodies to contribute to the impromptu buffet table. Most of the JOs now faced their first Christmas away from home, but the Officers' Wives club back in Virginia Beach tried to fill a little bit of the emptiness with a special present for each of them. The five boxes that had been delivered to CDR Earnest at Thanksgiving contained a package for each officer. Each married man received a special Christmas stocking prepared by his wife, but the women had included the bachelors in their plans, and everybody had something to open.

The officers and men of the Sunday Punchers' Administrative Department enjoy some Christmas cheer. LCDR Pieno, the department head, stands in his flight suit on the extreme right of the back row. Branch officers in attendance include LTJG Sanford (third from the left, back row); LT Bruce Cook (behind Sanford); LTJG Dave Warren; and LT Rudy Wiegand (over Warren's left shoulder). (U.S. Navy photograph, John A. Pieno, Jr., Collection)

The spouses at home put much thought and effort into the stockings. Every year when LTJG Fuller was growing up in Michigan, his mother had sewn a new small bell on each family member's Christmas stocking. This year, since he could not be home, his wife found a knitted one with a single bell attached to send to him.[91] LT Schuster looked in vain for his Christmas stocking. His wife, Denise, had spent hours embroidering it, gluing on sequins and other decorations to make it as festive as she could, and she had packed it full of little presents, including pictures, a small stapler, and candy. But somewhere along the way, an anonymous thief had enjoyed Christmas at LT Schuster's expense. Much to her dismay, Denise learned well after the fact that her husband got only an empty box from his family at Christmas.[92] CDR Greene returned to Duddie the unopened box containing LCDR Graustein's stocking.[93]

After the officers displayed their gifts, the merriment continued. CAG Bordone put in an appearance. Having so completely enjoyed the hospitality of a number of other ready rooms, he found it difficult just to get through the

Punchers' door and bounced from one side of the doorjamb to the other as he tried to enter. After a bit, CDR Greene announced that it was time for Christmas carols. He had something more than tradition in mind, however. And, indeed, though everyone knew the old melodies, new words for some special carols debuted on Christmas Day 1972.

The author of these new lyrics—LTJG Petersen—had spent hours in his stateroom writing them, and he had compiled mimeographed songbooks for the squadron's festivities. His own personal favorite fit the tune of "I'll Be Home for Christmas":

> Vietnam for Christmas
> What a deal for me.
> There's no snow or mistletoe,
> But just a plastic tree.
> Christmas eve will find me,
> Where the arc lights gleam.
> I'll be here for Christmas,
> Along with the Marines.

Many of the songs made reference to squadron events and personnel. Thus, the familiar carol "Oh, Tannenbaum" now got a new second line:

> Oh, Christmas Tree, Oh, Christmas Tree,
> Mike Schuster bagged a Christmas tree.[94]

Petersen's carols proved to be quite the hit, and not just in the VA-75 ready room. Reproduced several times, the songbook appeared in various parts of the carrier. CAG Bordone enjoyed the carols so much that, later on Christmas Day, he ordered all his senior officers up to IOIC for an impromptu sing-along. In one of his songs, Petersen had made reference to "Charlie," meaning the Vietcong. But because of CDR Earnest's recent death, he had changed the name. The heavies sang the revised words, but Petersen felt himself being fixed by the stare of his own CO, CDR William Greene, who looked at him with a mixture of amusement and confusion and mouthed a single word in question: "Willie?"[95]

After the ready room party, many of the Punchers reconvened in Buff Boulevard. LT Lankford began mixing a batch of Harvey Wallbangers using Galliano liqueur he had purchased during the last stop in Cubi. One of the squadron enlisted men assigned to the galley provided a case of orange juice. Finding vodka presented no problem at all. Friends from the helicopter squadron showed up in unusual party attire: leather flight jackets and ties, long underwear, and flight boots. During the revelry, one of the chopper pilots cut his hand on a piece of broken glass and began to bleed profusely. LT Randolph, the flight surgeon—also an invited guest—looked around for Punchers still capable of walking to carry the injured pilot down to the dispensary for treatment.[96] Nonetheless, the celebration continued until about 0730, when many Punchers decided to sleep through much of Christmas Day to manage both their fatigue and their hangovers.

That evening, *Saratoga*'s galleys produced a veritable feast for officers and enlisted men alike. The menu in the officers' mess even included surf and turf.[97] But except for that single luxury, the enlisted men's Christmas seemed like just another day. Even if aircraft did not launch, maintenance continued. So, they shared the contents of their Christmas packages from home, sang carols, and tried to make the best of it. The most unusual event of their day came when the ship held a man-overboard drill.[98]

Christmas in Hanoi proved even less enjoyable. LT Lerseth, suffering from dysentery for over a month, spent most of the holiday the same place he observed much of LINEBACKER II—on the "honey pot" in his cell.[99] Back at her mother-in-law's home in Spokane, Nini Lerseth knew nothing of her husband's condition. Indeed, she still had no formal confirmation of his status as a POW. She sat down now and wrote to Senator Henry Jackson (D-WA) to request him to press the Department of Defense to demand verification from the North Vietnamese that they held her husband and LCDR Lindland as prisoners. Recalling that North Korea had not released or accounted for all American POWs after the 1953 cease-fire, she explained, "It would be foolish to trust to the good intentions of the North Vietnamese in returning all our men." A public admission that they held the two men increased the chances that North Vietnam might return them alive at the end of the hostilities. "Their lives and freedom depend on all our efforts," Nini added.[100]

Probably the best Christmas present for the entire squadron came in the form of a schedule rotation. As of the morning of 25 December, VA-75 went off the schedule for night strikes into RP VI-B. Other A-6 squadrons on Yankee Station picked up those missions. Indeed, even though the LINEBACKER II bombing offensive recommenced on 26 December for Day Eight of the air offensive, weather conditions did not permit extensive operations for any tactical aircraft around Hanoi and Haiphong. While the B-52s flying above the weather still made their runs—by all accounts LINEBACKER II's most crushing day—VA-75 enjoyed a light schedule; only two tankers launched.[101]

The schedule change came as the men began to receive letters from home, detailing plans for family Christmas celebrations. Pixie Tolhurst in Annapolis and Sandy Pyle in Baltimore, both with young children, arranged to get together to watch the youngsters enjoy the festivities of Christmas Day, all the while wondering about their husbands so far away. Sandy decided to attend services at Our Savior Lutheran Church by herself, and prayed, "Please, Thy will be done, but try not to be too tough on me, okay?"[102] Many more Puncher families celebrated in small gatherings in Virginia Beach. Duddie Graustein, who had made Christmas dinner plans with neighbors long before the news arrived about the downing of her husband's aircraft, followed through with them.[103] Stephanie Knapp chose not to share with her husband one part of her holiday experience. She had worked a flight to London when the news about LINEBACKER II first broke. Before they even left New York, the pilot—who fancied himself a ladies' man—approached her and said, "Well, what do you say we go out in London because you're never going to see your husband again." She froze him with a stare, and when she got home, she bought a Christmas tree and some cheap red ornaments, and celebrated alone.[104]

Many of the same letters that tried to share some holiday cheer also included pleas for hard news about the Punchers' activities, even though family members found it difficult to bring themselves to read it. Chris Bryan, wife of LTJG Steve Bryan, wrote, "It's been so very long since I've heard anything from you. I hope you are okay." Recent newscasts—and the lack of real substance in the reports—frightened her. Indeed, she wrote, "the news is so depressing I don't even watch anymore. I just do not understand what the hell is going on over there or why."[105] Pixie Tolhurst recalled even years later just how difficult it was during the Christmas season of 1972 to help two-year-old Kim "understand why some days Mommy was down or talking back to the TV when the news was on."[106] Linda Ahrens, just arrived back home in Minnesota, watched as her mother became increasingly frightened and distracted during each night's newscast and began to obsess about what she would do if a Navy car pulled up to the house.[107] With so much media focus on the B-52s, anxious wives looking for information about the naval effort found little in the news to answer their questions.

The perception of a news blackout angered some wives, who could not understand why a briefing officer could deny the existence of a "clampdown" and call it only a "protection of information" effort.[108] LTJG Petersen tried to explain to Jeane that the practice helped to deny the North Vietnamese the information they needed to capture downed American airmen.[109] The wives in Virginia Beach could commiserate with a local editorial writer who complained that as long as the information void continued, "we are left to conclude that the President is trying to write with blood an agreement he could not produce with ink."[110]

On 27 December, Day Nine of LINEBACKER II, the squadron did not enter the hostile skies of RP VI-B at all. Bad weather diverted two daytime alpha strikes

In Virginia Beach, Sue Engel, Sharon Schram, and Lilliane Greene attend a Christmas party for the wives of VA-75's officers, providing a small measure of relief from watching the nightly news reports about LINEBACKER II. *(Carol Warren Collection)*

against targets near Haiphong to more accessible targets in RP II.[111] As if they needed to be reminded about the dangers they faced daily, however, many of the squadron's pilots and B/Ns attended the memorial service for LCDR Frederick W. Wright III, the airwing operations officer shot down on 10 November. The Navy had just recently changed his status from MIA to declare him killed in action.[112]

On 28 December, Day Ten of LINEBACKER II, VA-75 prepared once again to launch strikes into RP VI-B. Those on deck just after midnight may well have spotted a battle-damaged B-52 as it flew over the carrier in its attempt to return to its base in Thailand.[113] Three daylight alpha strikes scheduled against targets near Haiphong each called for four Puncher aircraft to participate, but, once again, bad weather prevented the launching of the missions as originally planned. LT Cook and LCDR Jackson, leading an element of four A-6As armed with eight Mk83 1,000-pound bombs, diverted from their original target to a bridge in RP II. A second alpha strike, including a four-plane division headed by LCDRs Engel and King, diverted to the Linh Cam petroleum storage area, also in RP II. The weather did not improve as the day progressed, and a third alpha strike planned for RP VI-B with yet another four-plane contingent from VA-75 ended up following LTs Cook and Wiegand to a railroad bridge in RP II.[114]

Still, despite the recent schedule change assigning *Saratoga* to the daytime schedule, four Puncher crews nonetheless flew into the night skies of RP VI-B on 28 December. Yet again, they aimed at SAM sites in the Haiphong area, hitting their targets shortly before the B-52s arrived on the scene. Beginning on 26 December, the Air Force had stopped sending individual cells of three aircraft over a target on a regular heading and at regular intervals; now they flew in larger waves and made concentrated ordnance drops in a shorter time span.[115] SAMs still came up at the bombers in salvos, though, and as the missiles flew, LT Chisholm and LTJG Vance watched from a safe distance. "Amazing, frightening [sight] in the black of night," LT Chisholm recounted, as he observed "wave after wave of B-52's[,] missiles going off everywhere[,] earth erupting with tons of bombs. Migs attacking—saw one hit and blow up. . . . Totally unreal."[116]

Although they did not yet know it, 28 December marked the last day that the Sunday Punchers would fly combat missions of any sort in RP VI-B. Weather cancelled all air operations on 29 December, and, effective on 30 December, Washington ordered a halt to the bombing effort north of the 20th parallel. While Washington pundits continued to debate the efficacy of the bombing and, now, whether or not it really had forced the North Vietnamese back to the bargaining table, the Punchers really did not care for the niceties of diplomatic discourse. After word of the new bombing restrictions arrived, LTJG Sanford entered the squadron's ready room bellowing at the top of his lungs, "We're gonna live!"[117] On 30 December, VA-75 flew only a few FAC-controlled hops in MR I.

The Sunday Punchers did not fly at all on New Year's Eve, 1972. While confetti and champagne toasts greeted 1973 back in the United States, the Punchers did not share in the gaiety of traditional New Year celebrations. While LT Hiduk and LTJGs Sanford and Bryan offered quiet toasts to a more peaceful twelve months ahead, the squadron's card players dealt hand after hand.[118] Others spent the afternoon watching *The Sterile Cuckoo*. As evening approached, the ship's television showed the previous year's Dean Martin New Year's special. The proud new fathers—LT Ruland and LTJG Sanford—passed around photographs of their new daughters. The fact that Jennifer, daughter of the 6'4" Ruland, arrived with a birth weight of only 2.5 ounces more than Sara, daughter of the 5'7" Sanford, inspired much kidding. As LTJG Fuller explained, "Rules has had to suffer disparaging remarks about his virility relative to the Rat's. But," he added, "I don't think he minds."[119] On New Year's Day, again with no air operations on the schedule, CDR Greene held a special ceremony in the ready room for eight VA-75 enlisted men who had decided to reenlist; eight more men won acknowledgment for their advance in rate.[120] Also on 1 January, LT Fischer and LTJG Ahrens finally returned to *Saratoga*. Just two days earlier, the beach detachment had finally determined it could not fix the KA-6D the two men had planned to fly back to the carrier. During their extended stay in the Philippines, Fischer and Ahrens had enjoyed the Bob Hope Christmas show, but when they flew to Danang on 30 December to catch a helicopter back to *Saratoga,* the base briefly came under attack. The two men spent part of New Year's Eve in a foxhole. Linda Ahrens had worried about her husband every time she watched television coverage of LINEBACKER II, entirely unaware that he had stayed in the Philippines.[121]

The start of a new year often inspires reflection about the past and goal-setting for the future. "The two things I have to be able to walk away with," LTJG Petersen wrote home, "are my life and my self respect." His goal for the future seemed both simple and complex: "If and when I get the chance to welcome Roger Lerseth and Don Lindland back from hell, I want to be able to say, 'I did all I could to get them out.' I'm probably the world's biggest fool, but if Danny ever asks what I did in the war, I don't want to say 'I quit.'" He asked his wife's forgiveness for his selfishness in not turning in his wings and coming home, "But it's something I have to do."[122]

That sense of commitment accompanied each Puncher pilot and B/N during *Saratoga*'s final week of air operations. Current schedules called for them to fly until 8 January 1973. The end of the bombing in RP VI-B and the rapid approach of the end of their last line period generated a real excitement about their outchop for home. Their biggest fears rested on the possibility that the North Vietnamese still might not settle things. "I believe Nixon will go back to Hanoi bombing again if some impasse develops," LT Pyle wrote his parents on New Year's Day. Still, he decided, "you have to respect the man for the courage and ability to make a decision and stick to it, even if he is endangering my own neck!!"[123]

As they watched the progress of the peace talks closely, they embraced every step in the process that would take them home. When the Early Bird list came out on 3 January, those fortunate Puncher officers who found their names on it knew that they might be back in the United States by the end of the month. CDR Greene had to come home with the ship, of course, and LCDRs Engel, Pieno, and Schram would stay behind to help wrap up squadron business; of the squadron heavies, only LCDRs Jackson and King prepared to leave early, the former to prepare the hangar at Oceana. All the augmentation crews who volunteered for detached duty with VA-75—LTs Chisholm, Hart, Schuster, and Connelly and LTJG Vance—got to leave early. The Punchers whose wives came to Manila against the advice of the squadron's senior officers—LTs Lankford, John Miller, and LTJGs Ahrens and Swigart—understood that they would make the transit home on the ship. Pilots and B/Ns with young families usually won seats on the Early Bird, including new fathers LT Ruland and LTJG Sanford, who had not yet seen their children born during LINEBACKER II. LT Mullins, a bachelor, gave up his seat to his married roommate, LT Hvidding. This tangible sign of the impending end of the combat cruise boosted morale immensely. Carly Simon's "Anticipation" quickly became a favorite song.[124]

The professionalism that had driven them for the last eight and one-half months to fly their missions and hit their targets now competed with their desire to get home safely. "Everyone is easing off on the aggressiveness, taking as little chance as possible," LTJG Warren wrote.[125] They still had to contend with the weather and the North Vietnamese. But, as long as they did not fly in RP VI-B, the threat to life seemed lessened somehow.

Thus, novelty now impressed them more than danger. On 3 January, a SAM fired from a site near Vinh hit a B-52 from U-Tapao, setting it ablaze. The pilot steered it south and then east, trying to get over the waters off South Vietnam before ordering a bailout. His tail gunner had not been able to wait that long, however; since flames licked about his turret, he jumped. "That was one of the smartest things that gunner ever did," the pilot later admitted. A rescue helicopter from *Saratoga* picked up the man, and, after the flight surgeon dressed his slight injuries, he ended up in VA-75's ready room where several Punchers enjoyed a chance to hear of his exploits firsthand.[126]

During the early morning hours of 4 January, LT John Miller and LCDR Jackson went looking for trucks on Route 1A near the coast in RP III. At one point, the road ran through a particularly narrow valley bracketed by steep karst ridges. The bottleneck forced the trucks to cluster together, presenting a potentially lucrative target to a crew willing to risk it. Over the years, few had dared to try, however, and the North Vietnamese had come to view that portion of their route as a safe haven. Relying on a confidence borne of experience, Miller and Jackson now descended through the clouds, the two ridges not far off each wingtip. Their reward took the shape of an unending line of trucks, each with its headlights on, unaware of their presence. "It looks like the Massachusetts Turnpike!" Miller exclaimed to Jackson. As soon as the first truck went under his nose, the pilot pickled off the first of his fourteen Mk20 Rockeye. The official BDA report credited them with the destruction of at least fifteen trucks; it may well have been far more. When he reflected back on all his high-risk missions around Hanoi, Haiphong, and Thanh Hoa "to maybe find a truck, maybe kill dirt, get nothing," Miller marveled all the more that "here we did this, and boom!"[127]

That same morning, several VA-75 aircraft planned runs on SAM sites in RP III. LT Ruland and LTJG Swigart flew an A-6B hop in support of their strikes. They soon heard the familiar sound of a Fan Song radar locked on to them. Usually, once a radar operator noted the typical figure-eight flight pattern A-6Bs usually flew, he shut down rather than become a target himself. But this radar operator refused to shut down. As the A-6As began their runs, Ruland and Swigart fired an AGM-78. Swigart had fired an AGM-45 Shrike before, but he and Ruland had never launched an AGM-78 before. It responded to Ruland's pickle so slowly that the pilot pressed again to make sure it fired. Then, all of a sudden, Swigart recalled that "this flying telephone pole ignited under my wing and went tearing off" skyward. The SAM site shut down. The launch impressed Swigart greatly, even at a time in his life when he did not believe that he could be surprised by anything. But he doubted that they had hit their target, considering it a "pretty expensive miss if it didn't [hit] at $500,000 to $1,000,000 a copy!"[128]

Every day between 2 January and 7 January, VA-75 continued to hit targets in RPs II, III, and IV at night. CDR Greene and LCDR Pieno flew the squadron's last hop to RP III to hit a petroleum storage area near Ha Tin. They had not intended to duel with any flak sites, but when AAA filled the skies around them—although, Pieno recalled, "we were ready to say goodbye amicably"—they circled around and dropped their entire bomb load on the guns.[129] That same night, LTs Fischer and Wagner drew a strike hop against a transshipment point in RP II south of Vinh. The weather was overcast and rainy, and Fischer planned to fly feet dry, turn north up a valley, hit the warehouse complex, and continue north until they turned east toward the coast. But Wagner offered an alternative plan. For two days, the B/N tried to talk Fischer into following a missile lockup to the SAM site itself and pickling their bombs right on top of it. Fischer responded, "What? Are you crazy? . . . I don't want to get killed on my last mission." Fischer won the argument, but the flight still became memorable. Just off the coast in an A-6B, LT Lankford and LTJG Warren traced Fischer and Wagner's progress by watching the AAA light their path in the sky. Fischer long remembered Lankford's plaintive sing-song over the radio: "Somebody in there doesn't LIKE you!"[130]

During those last few days, the Punchers also flew FAC-controlled hops in MR II and even a few strikes against targets in Laos. What had once inspired an adrenaline rush now qualified as "milkruns," but they also did not want to grow so complacent that they grew careless. On 8 January—their last day on the line—LT Tolhurst and LTJG Swigart paired up for the only strike mission they flew together. Relying on now-familiar procedures in a comparatively low-threat environment, they flew in at 10,000 to 12,000 feet and made visual contact with their FAC. Then, out of the corner of his eye, Swigart saw AAA bursts. Up to that point, they had felt so safe that Tolhurst had not jinked much, but now the pilot started evasive maneuvers. The rest of the mission progressed as planned, but Swigart could not forget those rounds exploding less than 100 yards away.[131] By comparison, LT Anderson and LTJG Sanford's final mission seemed tame. Down in MR II, they flew in circles around a hill where an AAA gunner opened fire on them. "He was so bad and his lead was so far behind us that we had a good laugh," Sanford recalled, adding, "It was a good way to go out."[132]

When the pilots and B/Ns received VA-75's flight schedule for 8 January, they noticed that Skipper Greene had added his own special comment to the bottom of the form. There, handwritten near his usual signature, he had printed in large block letters, "WHOOP-EE."[133] On this last day of active operations, one Puncher still tried to reach an unfulfilled goal. LT Wagner remained one landing short of the four hundred he needed to qualify as the squadron's only Quadruple Centurion aboard *Saratoga*, and his name did not appear on the flight schedule. When LTJG Sanford saw himself slated for a tanker with LT Connelly, the Combat Rat gave up his seat so that Wagner could get his four-hundredth trap while still in the combat zone.[134]

Some crews made special plans for their final combat hops. When LCDR King landed after his last mission, he reached into his survival vest, pulled something out, and gave it to the startled plane captain at the bottom of his boarding ladder. The crusty King had handed the young sailor a rubber chicken.[135] LT Anderson and LTJG Sanford, after tempting fate with the unskilled AAA gunner, executed an unauthorized low fly-by on their return to the carrier that got them a special invitation to visit CAPT Sanderson for a chewing-out.[136] But LT Hvidding never got to carry out his plan for his last combat hop with LT Pyle. The two men had flown many missions together, and Hvidding had planned to throw his arm around his pilot's shoulders and thank him for bringing them both back safely. But the flight schedule assigned him to fly his last combat hop with LT Cook instead.[137]

Approximately 1400, CDR Greene and LCDR Pieno recovered from VA-75's final strike mission. They had made a routine drop of their fourteen Mark 82s on a target in MR II. After delivering the Sunday Punchers' ten-millionth pound of ordnance, their uneventful flight ended the squadron's air operations.[138] As each crew trapped aboard, the pilot and B/N turned in their blood chits and secured their pistols. Anticipating these routine administrative chores, one pilot looked forward to their completion. "Then," he wrote, "I'll know it's all over."[139]

About 1430 on 8 January 1973, CAPT Sanderson ordered his navigator to take *Saratoga* out of the Gulf of Tonkin for the last time. As the carrier steamed toward the Philippines, leaving the Gulf of Tonkin for the final time, ADM Cooper congratulated the aircrews and all those aboard the carrier who kept them flying. "During the past nine months you have been called upon and responded with alacrity to the most intense air support and interdiction campaigns ever required in the SEAsia war," he wrote, adding that "you have left your professional mark on both air-to-air and air-to-ground combat." He concluded, "You can sail with the satisfaction of having participated in a job well done."[140] The praise was nice but did not come close to describing the most satisfying feeling as the Punchers left the line. As LT Chisholm wrote Bobbie: "Am alive and well and 1973 and forever is ours."[141]

"I'm Part of That Group"

For the men of VA-75, the most difficult part of the combat cruise had ended. But the war itself still continued, the cease-fire not yet in effect. "Glad its over yet very sad over men we left behind," LT Fischer confided to his diary after the close of air operations on 8 January.[1] Indeed, for some, it proved difficult to grasp the reality that they did not have to return to the line. "Almost everybody seems to be in a quiet mood, but I don't think the fact that it's over for us is the let down," LTJG Warren observed. Instead, he explained, "I think it's the fact that we don't have to key ourselves up for war again. We've been strung so high for 9 months now and not to be tensed and ready seems like a depression."[2] Introspective thoughts such as these intruded mostly into private moments, however. In their ready rooms after the last recovery on 8 January, VA-75 and VA-37 threw a party—the only one they ever held jointly—well supplied with champagne. The Sunday Punchers were going home![3]

On 9 January, *Saratoga* steamed back to the Philippines for the last time. As a warm-up for the inevitable party at the Cubi Officers' Club, several Punchers waxed poetic and produced an ode, "From the VA-75 Wardroom to VA-75 wives at the End-of-the-Line Party, 1/9/73":

> Way back in April '72
> The Punchers went to sea.
> We knew we had a job to do,
> But now it's '73.
> We've been away for far too long
> But now our task is done.
> To Cubi Point for wine and song,
> And then we'll head for home. . . .
> Now girls, we'll leave you with this thought:
> Don't forget your pills.
> Lest we should reap a Puncher crop
> To increase next Christmas['s] bills![4]

CVW-3's officers, including many Sunday Puncher pilots and B/Ns, fully lived up to their wild reputation at the "animal bar" in the basement of the Cubi

Officers' Club, breaking up its chairs and stools and repeating the performance upstairs. Escaping just before the shore patrol arrived to eject them from the premises, they headed over to the Subic Bay Officers' Club, only to be kicked out forty-five minutes later.[5] CAPT Sanderson faced an angry admiral the next day, and, in the final accounting, each officer in the airwing paid a portion of the damages.

On 12 January, *Saratoga* left the Philippines for the month-long transit home. VA-75's officers and chiefs made sure no Punchers missed the movement. It simply would not do, as LT Mullins recalled, to "leave behind anyone too enamored of the Olongapo lifestyle."[6] He, among others, redoubled accountability efforts and made certain all the men had returned to the ship. No one got left behind.

Those fortunate enough to get a seat on the Early Bird charter flight had to wait in the Philippines until 19 January. Some of VA-75's officers rented a beach house at Grande Island out in the middle of Subic Bay. They snorkled and went skin diving. LTJG Sanford spotted sharks swimming toward them, pulled LT Anderson in front of him, handed him a speargun, and swam for safety. The Combat Rat finally backed down from a fight! They stayed up well into the night to listen to the Super Bowl. Once in a while, they sent LT Wagner into town to buy supplies, considering him the least likely of the group to "delay all the booze and the steaks."[7]

On the appointed day, they boarded the Early Bird for home. "We were drinking before the plane left the ramp . . . and I don't think anyone quit until they passed out," Sanford recalled, crediting the flight attendants for being "awfully understanding."[8] LT Fischer sat next to LT Jim Lloyd of VA-105, not reminiscing, but trying to figure out how to reset their watches. They left Manila in 94-degree heat, and twenty hours later they arrived in Anchorage to a temperature of 13 degrees below zero.[9] Each man received a card informing him of his status as a health risk, due to exposure to malaria. Although instructed to carry it for six months, most tossed the card into the nearest trash can.[10]

At Anchorage, individual Punchers broke off for flights that reunited them with family and friends. LTJG Petersen headed to Salt Lake City, where Jeane, Danny, and six-month-old Laurie waited for him. LTJG Vance flew to New York City, his mother breaking into tears the minute she spotted him. When LT Pyle walked into his house in the wee hours of the morning, young Mike—barely speaking when his father left for the war—flew down the steps in his pajamas, his eyes wide with excitement, and said, "Oh, mommy, my daddy is home from Bietnam."[11]

Meanwhile, *Saratoga* had set a course for home after a hectic two-day stop in Singapore. Six sailors assigned by LT Mullins made certain that one of his men who had met a girl during their visit to the city in October did not jump ship.[12]

Other officers faced a challenge of a different kind: finding room for final purchases. LT Lankford had to find space to stow new bedroom furniture, two bicycles, and a papa-san chair.[13]

A few days out of Singapore, the shellbacks initiated the pollywogs who had joined the ship's company or the squadrons after the visit of King Neptune and his court in April 1972. The Sunday Punchers' pollywogs included CDR Greene, whose previous combat tours had begun in California and had gone directly to the Philippines, all north of the equator. He finally went through his initiation on 18 January 1973, along with LT Hiduk, LTJGs Bryan, Kaiser, and Radcliff, and VA-75's newest enlisted personnel.[14] Participation in the initiation rites rested on seniority—not in rank but in time served as a shellback. The Punchers who reached that status in April remained too junior to take too active a role. Just the same, LT Mullins snuck into the hose line to get in a few good licks on LTJG Kaiser.[15]

Now, at last, LT Hudson's maintenance crews gave the squadron aircraft the attention they had needed for months. The men continued to work twelve-hour shifts to make sure that none of the squadron aircraft suffered the indignity of being craned off the carrier after it docked. The chiefs oversaw the readying of VA-75's compartments and work spaces for turnover to the ship's company on return to Florida. As Chief Warrant Officer Smith recalled, "There was plenty to keep us busy."[16] The enlisted men in the Power Plants Branch completed one additional task; they threw overboard their bulletin board covered with photographs of Olongapo "girlfriends," practicing yet again the old Navy tradition of "what goes on on the ship, stays on the ship."[17]

CDR Greene ordered the repainting of the trim on all squadron helmets and aircraft to blue, formally breaking from VA-75's traditional use of green. Even before VA-75 left the line for the last time, LTJG Vance won a contest for a new tail design, submitting a sketch that altered the block "AC" on each A-6's tail to one more evocative of Oriental characters to salute their Westpac combat cruise. Now the sailors worked hard to paint the new logo on squadron aircraft for the fly-in at Oceana.

Mountains of paperwork faced every man. Each sailor aboard *Saratoga* completed the United States Armed Forces Customs Declaration form, even if he had made no purchases while deployed. Weapons required an additional permit from the IRS, and the men were reminded that they could claim only one quart of foreign-made alcohol duty free.[18] As awards officer, LT Mullins gathered the remaining officers in the ready room, assigning each man a combat mission for which to prepare justifications for medals. Squadron heavies helped to craft specific language to support the awarding of Silver Stars and Distinguished Flying Crosses. As had become standard practice, they recommended alpha strike leaders—all senior officers—for major awards sometimes disproportionate to results achieved or opposition faced. But they now understood that if they did not do so, they could not "cascade" Navy Commendation medals or other awards to reward junior pilots and B/Ns on the same mission. The A-6's unique capabilities also prevented formal recognition of the success of many Sunday Puncher pilots and B/Ns, because "you just couldn't prove what you did in the dark of night" on single-plane low-level strikes.[19] The profusion of awards write-ups nearly exhausted both the fluid and the paper used in the ship's mimeograph machines, causing one squadron to admit in its command history that this situation "seriously hampered the entire awards procedure."[20]

Diversions of all sorts filled the hours after the completion of routine duties. Enlisted men held talent shows, signed up for karate demonstrations, entered a basketball tournament, and played bingo.[21] They took care of long-delayed dental work and medical problems. Indeed, when LT Lankford went to see about the removal of his wisdom teeth, he found the clinic completely booked and made a special arrangement with a dental officer he had taken up for a flight or two to do the extraction after hours. Flight Surgeon Randolph had received a hair-transplant kit, and he found no shortage of willing subjects who would let him move hair plugs from the backs of their heads to receding hairlines.[22]

Saratoga still remained at sea when CAPT Sanderson announced the death of Lyndon B. Johnson, the president who had "Americanized" the war that they had been sent to end. They remained far from home when the Paris Peace agreements went into effect on 27 January 1973. While others celebrated the cease-fire, LCDR Schram suffered a final hard blow. His close friend, CDR Harley H. Hall, commanding officer of the Blue Angels when Schram had served as their public affairs officer, piloted the last American aircraft shot down before the end of hostilities; the Navy declared him missing in action. His name did not appear on North Vietnam's list of 591 American POWs about to be repatriated in the upcoming prisoner release. The Punchers' spirits soared when they found LT Lerseth listed—along with VA-37's LCDR Raebel and VF-103's LTs Masterson and Randall—but faded when they could not find other names they sought. Most, in their hearts, did not expect to see the names of LCDRs Graustein or Wade. But they did look—in vain—for the name of LCDR Don Lindland.

In early February in Virginia Beach, the wives of the Sunday Punchers' officers gathered for a special dinner. Duddie Graustein hosted, and Minna Earnest and Bobbe Lindland both attended. CDR Earnest's fate had been established, but Duddie still knew nothing firm about her own husband. "For the time being," she told a reporter, "the boys and I will remain here. We have friends here and I try to keep busy." Bobbe Lindland, too, decided to "proceed on day-to-day facts," adding, "Although my husband has never been confirmed as a prisoner, he was seen on the ground, alive and moving, after his plane went down. His navigator has been confirmed as a prisoner and is coming back. I see no reason for [the North Vietnamese] to hold back facts." As the reporter noted, "These women know that life must go on."[23]

And none of them wanted their own situations to take anything away from welcoming home the rest of VA-75's pilots and B/Ns. LCDR Jackson, who came home on the Early Bird, headed an advance team that prepared the hangar and made arrangements for the 12 February fly-in at Oceana. Local billboards proclaimed greetings. The wives made banners and flags. A favorite bumper sticker for the occasion read: "Punchers penetrate deeper, stay longer, & deliver a bigger load[.] Welcome Home VA-75."[24]

Only seven VA-75 aircraft—five A-6As and 2 KA-6Ds—flew off *Saratoga* on 12 February for the flight to Oceana. Others had been left in the Philippines or transferred to other squadrons still on the line. As he left the ready room for the last time, LT Lankford paused to take a photograph of the flight schedule board. CDR Greene and LCDR Pieno led the squadron home in Ace 501. Following them in A-6As were LCDR Engel with LT Wiegand, LT Hiduk with LT Mullins, LT Lankford with LCDR Schram, and LT Knapp with LTJG Fuller. LT John Miller with LTJG Ahrens and LTJG Bryan with LTJG Swigart flew the two tankers. At the bottom of the schedule, someone had chalked in an addition to the list of those coming home: "LT LERSETH arrived Clark AFB, 0330 local time."[25]

A tremendous reception awaited the Sunday Punchers at Oceana. Indeed, the seven aircraft had to orbit until several admirals arrived at the hangar to greet them. The officers' wives waited there, too, of course, including Linda Ahrens, who had spun her mother's eleven-year-old Chevrolet Impala in a complete circle on a snow-covered highway on her way to the base.[26] Sunday Punchers from the Early Bird waited there too, LT Fischer holding his camera and LT Ruland carrying his new daughter in his arms. All eyes scanned the skies, looking for the flight of Intruders.

Going feet dry on the approach to Oceana gave LTJG Swigart an odd feeling; he had to remind himself several times that "no one was going to shoot." Just then, however, a big bird flew close to the plane, greatly startling the B/N when it almost splattered itself on his windscreen.[27] Still, all seven aircraft landed safely on runways cleared of snow. As the crews cracked open their canopies, the freezing air overwhelmed them. "I had been hot for 10 months," LT Mullins recalled, and "the cold took my breath away."[28]

The joy of reunion could not be expressed in words. The celebration that followed was as heartfelt as it was brief. "You're torn by wanting to get away and spend time with wife and family and at the same time reminiscing with your shipmates and friends," explained Swigart.[29] But family generally won out. They eagerly embraced the chance to get reacquainted—especially with their younger children. In ten months, much could change. LCDR Engel got his first big surprise in the parking lot, when he discovered that Sue had bought a brand-new Buick station wagon in his absence.[30] It gave him his first taste of a new reality many Punchers soon experienced. The combat cruise had made their wives more self-sufficient.

Adding to their joy, many of the Puncher pilots and B/Ns turned on their televisions that night to watch the arrival of the first plane of American POWs at Clark Air Force Base. CAPT Jeremiah A. Denton, captured during VA-75's first combat cruise in 1965, announced to the crowd in a steady voice: "We are honored to have had the opportunity to serve our country under difficult circumstances. We are profoundly grateful to our commander in chief and to our nation for this day. God bless America!"[31] LT Lerseth stepped off the plane soon afterward. His injuries proved so severe that the North Vietnamese had released him with the first group to leave. Thus, the first and last members of VA-75 to spend time in the Hanoi Hilton came home together. He called his wife and mother, of course, and then made "the toughest call of his life"—to Bobbe Lindland, to express his belief that her husband would not come home alive. Then he went to the base exchange, got a loaf of bread and big jar of peanut butter, and downed it all.[32] In Spokane with his mother and sisters, Nini watched for him. As she told a reporter, "Seeing him actually move makes him a real person again."[33]

LCDR Grady Jackson and his wife spent that evening with Bobbe Lindland. They watched the telecast closely, scanning each face. They spotted LT Lerseth, too. "That brought out some loud shouts and hollering," Jackson remembered. Sadness tempered that joy. Although they had seen Hanoi's official lists of POWs and had not seen LCDR Lindland's name on it, they still hoped he would step off that plane. Jackson admitted, "That was one long night!"[34]

But better nights followed. The morning after the pilots and B/Ns flew off to Oceana, *Saratoga* docked at Mayport. Military and high school bands played for the crowds, and the USO provided coffee and donuts. Local businesses put up welcome signs in windows and on marquees. Florida governor Reubin Askew and other local dignitaries took a helicopter out to the carrier to greet the sailors, letting them know that their families had begun to gather at dockside at 0630. "They stand there for 46,000 fellow Americans who lost their lives in the war you've helped us bring to an end," the governor told them. And he added, astutely, "They stand there because they know that war is no more appealing to you than to anyone else in America today and they believe this made your sacrifice all the greater."[35] The families of many enlisted Sunday Punchers made the trip south from Virginia to meet the carrier, too. Gunner Walden spotted Joan with one of his oldest friends draping his arm around her. When they came

LT Roger Lerseth in Hanoi on 13 February 1973, upon his release from North Vietnamese control. After a joyful reunion with his family, he endured a lengthy period of hospitalization and physical therapy that ultimately ended successfully with his return to flying status. (Roger G. Lerseth Collection, with special thanks to Christine Picchi)

aboard, they joined Walden and LTJG Kaiser in repeated celebratory toasts with a bottle of champagne and a bigger bottle of Jack Daniels.[36] Myrna Smith told Chief Warrant Officer Smith about watching Lerseth's return.[37] Just as he had seen them off in April, VADM Michaelis now welcomed them home.[38]

Families that had deferred holiday celebrations finally threw impromptu Christmas parties. Loretta Lankford, anticipating her husband's return, decorated a small tree, but needed help from LTJG Warren, who came home on the Early Bird, to fix the lights. She also planned a Christmas party for squadron friends and sent out belated holiday greeting cards. Her sentiments no doubt resonated in all the Puncher families: "At this festive and special time, please join us in wishing for peace and a speedy return of all our POWs and MIAs."[39]

A few days later, LT Lerseth arrived in San Francisco. As Nini and his mother waited, a correspondent noted that, "having held back tears for the tense moments awaiting the plane, both women let them go when Lerseth, looking wan but happy, stepped off the plane."[40] Once he got settled into Oak Knoll Naval Hospital nearby, they sorted through a stack of messages waiting for him. One from the CO of VA-75 read: "The Sunday Punchers are overjoyed, and thank

God for your return. All are anxiously looking forward to seeing you soon, and back in the cockpit." Nini then explained that the message came from CDR Greene, gently breaking the news of CDR Earnest's death. Over the next few days, she sat for brief interviews to discuss her husband's injuries and his upbeat mood.[41] She also acknowledged that his joy remained "incomplete." "He was so impressed by the caliber of the men" he met while imprisoned, she explained, that "his happiness will be complete only when the rest of them are home."[42]

The Sunday Punchers—most of them, at least—had come home. Since they returned to naval bases and traditional military towns, few faced hostile crowds. No one spit on them or heckled them. The war had ended. Most Americans seemed satisfied to forget about it. But these men who had taken such risks and absorbed such losses could not simply turn their backs on the previous year. Still, it took time for most to take stock of their experiences.

Following the cease-fire, some advocates of airpower claimed that LINE-BACKER I, and especially LINEBACKER II, brought the war to an end. Indeed, as General William W. Momyer, one-time commander of the Seventh Air Force in Southeast Asia, asserted: "It was apparent that airpower was the decisive factor leading to the peace agreement of 15 January 1973. The concentrated application of airpower produced the disruption, shock, and disorganization that can be realized only by compressing the attack and striking at the heart with virtually no restraints on military targets which influence the enemy's will to fight."[43]

Even in 1973, however, the link between the 1972 air campaign and the cease-fire seemed ambiguous to leaders well placed to make an informed assessment. As early as January 1973, ADM Moorer made an important distinction: "I would describe the effect of the attacks in military terms as excellent," he commented at a House Appropriations Committee meeting, adding, "The full cooperation and team effort that took place between the Navy, Air Force, and Marine Corps, in the very complicated operation involving many types of aircraft, electronic countermeasures, all kinds of flak suppression, and hundreds of tankings of aircraft, and so on, was a very outstanding professional performance." At the time, however, he also admitted that the North Vietnamese probably could repair the damage in a year's time, a resiliency that led one astonished congressman to retort, "We can't get the area around the Rayburn Building here repaired in 3 years."[44] Time, perspective, successful efforts to declassify the documentary record of the Nixon White House, and increasingly open access to Communist-bloc archives have continued to modify claims for airpower's decisiveness in ending the Vietnam War, making a case instead for successful accomplishment of limited campaign goals rather than grand claims for its conflict-ending capability.

The Sunday Punchers of 1972 intuitively appreciate the ambiguity with which postwar analysts and historians wrestle. Thirty years after their return to the United States, when asked to consider a seemingly straightforward question—"what do you believe you accomplished?"—they formulated their answers from many perspectives.

Some describe a qualified positive gain from their efforts, often within the broader context of Cold War strategy. LT Wiegand wondered if, "by standing firm in Vietnam for the time that we did, we blunted the unrelenting takeover of country after country."[45] LT Tolhurst asserted that the war in Vietnam proved that the United States would not let the Soviet bloc propagate its worldview "without a cost," adding that the American stand against communist aggression in the 1960s and early 1970s ultimately gave direction to the Reagan administration's efforts to win the Cold War.[46] LT Schuster extended the argument a bit further. While the lengthy American involvement in Southeast Asia "put the communist world on alert that we were willing to defend our way of life," the United States had not saved Vietnam. Still, the postwar scrutiny of the performance of the armed forces during that war—and reforms that followed—"set the stage for President Reagan to end the cold war," an accomplishment made possible because the Vietnam experience "slowly galvanized America's resolve" to prevent such a reverse again.[47] LCDR Pieno, focusing more pointedly on the making of national strategy since Vietnam, agreed that the American effort in Southeast Asia forced political and military leaders to rethink when and how the United States should use its armed forces. As Americans continue to debate the credibility of various explanations offered to justify U.S. involvement in Southeast Asia, many appreciate the far greater obligation now imposed upon the nation's leaders—as described in the Weinberger Doctrine and other such policy statements—to delineate a clearly articulated objective, reasoned and reasonable ways and means to achieve it, and an exit strategy to limit or terminate commitment of American blood and treasure.[48] "What we did and the way we did it was not worth the lives it cost," Tolhurst admitted.[49]

LT Mullins reflected philosophically on a more fundamental positive that came from their efforts: "Democracy only works when the institutions given the power of lethal violence follow the orders of the officials properly placed in charge of them. We did that." Even though the United States had not achieved the goal of years of diplomatic and military effort, "our core values survived . . . because the armed services went where they were told and did what they were ordered to do."[50]

Not all Punchers, however, saw positive results flow from their efforts. The war had continued after they left. If they had had a role in ending it, so be it, but few made extravagant claims for this. As LCDR Engel noted, the Sunday Punchers became "part of what brought the end to the war, such as it was."[51] Indeed, some still reflect upon their actions within the context of the war's negative impact upon the nation's credibility around the world. LTJG Kaiser believed "we accomplished nothing more than making lots of holes all over and leaving people behind we promised to help. In the end all we did was delay the inevitable."[52] The "inevitable" came in the spring of 1975 when yet another North Vietnamese military offensive obliterated any remaining shreds of the January 1973 cease-fire agreement. North Vietnamese tanks rumbled into the streets of Saigon on 30 April 1975. "We abandoned the S[outh] Vietnamese and hurt our reputation in the world community," Tolhurst asserted.[53]

A few even look back upon the war as a tragic mistake. As Chief Warrant Officer Smith decided, on the grand scale and "with 20/20 hindsight," the whole war accomplished "not much. We lost 58,000 Americans in a war that we did not win and probably did not have to fight."[54] LTJG Petersen summarized the impact of the entire American effort with "we lost a lot of good men, we all lost our innocence and we made the world safe for strip malls."[55]

Interestingly, other Sunday Punchers saw little reason to wrestle with the question at all. "We accomplished what we were sent to do—we flew the missions that we were trained to fly and were tasked to fly in support of our military and national objectives," LTJG Warren asserted. "I didn't set policy, or formulate strategy, or devise war plans," he rightly noted, and so, beyond a satisfying sense of personal achievement, "I didn't (and don't) try to analyze 'what we accomplished.'"[56] LTJG Sanford summed up his most important accomplishment in a single word: survival.[57]

Beyond those honest admissions, however, few of the Sunday Punchers cared to elaborate. If the war changed them—as LT Hvidding anticipated in his diary in April 1972—the aftereffects remained highly personal ones, mostly locked in the heart and mind of each man. These views are generally not open to public scrutiny. But Warren's comment—"we accomplished what we were sent to do"—speaks to his pride in being part of the Sunday Punchers of 1972. For many of these men, flying through the skies of North Vietnam as part of VA-75 became a high point in their lives. As J. Glenn Gray posited about "the enduring appeals of battle," they shared a commitment to common goals—professional responsibility as officers and personal responsibility to brothers-in-arms—that produces a kind of loyalty hard to define outside the military sphere. Most Punchers would agree with Gray's assertion that "despite the horror, the weariness, the grime, and the hatred, participation with others in the chances of battle had its unforgettable side, which they would not want to have missed."[58]

Thus, the Sunday Punchers seldom turn to metrics to give meaning to what they did, although cumulative statistics speak to the effectiveness of their efforts. During their 309-day deployment—including two long transits—*Saratoga* spent 175 days on the line. It burned nearly 50 million gallons of fuel oil, and each of its four screws turned over 1.1 billion times. CVW-3 flew more than 15,000 missions of all kinds, at least 7,700 of them strike hops that delivered over 28 million pounds of ordnance. Its planes consumed over 32.6 million gallons of jet fuel. As a cruise summary noted, "A fleet of 13,500 Volkswagens (each traveling 12,000 miles/year) could drive nearly five years on that amount of gasoline."[59] The Sunday Punchers flew at least 1,624 of those strike sorties, about 350 of them the night, low-level sorties at which the A-6A excelled. The squadron's KA-6Ds flew at least 1,340 tanker hops and delivered in excess of 12.3 million pounds of aviation fuel. The squadron's two A-6Bs flew over 360 missions to provide the airwing with standoff support against the SAM threat. The Sunday Punchers accounted for over one-third of the total ordnance that CVW-3 delivered—at least ten million pounds. They received credit for the destruction of 295 structures, 17 AAA sites, and 191 vehicles, the damaging of five SAM sites and the cratering of five runways, plus 310 secondary explosions and 148 sustained fires, figures that do not include the BDA from any of the fifty-seven alpha strikes in which VA-75 participated.[60]

But such statistics do not stick in the minds of the 1972 Sunday Punchers. Indeed, the passage of time dims many memories. Some think about their combat deployment every day, while others seldom do. Some remain active in various veterans associations, while others do not. Some make regular visits to "The Wall," especially to panel 1W, where they can find etched in the cold black stone the names of four of their friends. Others have not yet brought themselves to do so. For some, especially those who stayed in the Navy, memories of 1972 blended into subsequent assignments. "It was a cruise—the first for me, so that makes it unique," Warren continued, "but even though it was my only combat cruise, I still think of it as 'one of the five'" in a thirty-year Navy career. As he prepared his personal narrative of 1972, he—and others—went through "a mental 'sorting' procedure" to make sure the event he remembered actually took place during the combat cruise. The trauma of death, in itself, did not provide the demarcation line because, as it turned out, "we still lost planes and people on those peacetime cruises—ALL of them."[61] For others, specific anniversaries always bring them back to 1972. On each 28 November, LCDR Jackson gathers with his family to give special thanks to God for sparing his life; on 28 November 2002—the thirtieth anniversary of his accident—he visited "The Wall" in Washington, DC, to make a rubbing of CDR Earnest's name. Near Christmas, LCDR Engel

On 28 November 2002, the thirtieth anniversary of the accident that cost his skipper his life, RADM Grady L. Jackson, USN, Ret., points to CDR Charles "M" Earnest's name on the Vietnam memorial in Washington, DC. Just to the left of the base of Jackson's thumb can be seen "Robert S."—the first name and middle initial marking LCDR Graustein's place on "The Wall." (Grady L. Jackson Collection)

reflects on LCDR Graustein's death, remembering his own mission that night, seeing the fireball, and sending out radio calls to which responses never came.[62] LTJG Petersen remembers this event regularly, as well; the incident had occurred on 21 December, his birthday.[63]

Thirty years after the Sunday Punchers flew through the December skies over Haiphong during LINEBACKER II, *Boston Globe* columnist James Carroll wrote, "Christmas Eve seems made for memory." Amid the joy of the season, however, he wrote, "another Christmas memory intrudes." He continued, "For people of a certain age, the thought of that unprecedented air assault, lasting from Dec. 18–30, intermittently disturbs the tranquility of the otherwise holy season. How staggered we were," he wondered, "at the reports of the bombs falling day and night on cities across North Vietnam." He wrote of the 4,000 sorties flown that month, including at least 700 missions by B-52s, those "'area bombers,' incapable of precision," that he deemed "a sure sign that this was terror bombing, pure and simple."[64]

Carroll did not mention the A-6s. But then, few accounts of those December nights ever do. Beyond their resignation at being left out of the story yet again, the Sunday Punchers would take issue with Carroll's accusatory tone, as well. They had not felt "staggered." They performed to the best of their professional abilities.

On 8 June 1973, at VA-75's first awards ceremony since returning from Westpac, newly promoted RADM Jeremiah Denton of the Sunday Punchers of 1965 returned to the squadron's hangar at Oceana to decorate the Sunday Punchers of 1972. Many in attendance recall the event as a highlight, a bit of closure that brought them, their war, and their squadron full circle. At that ceremony, Denton presented LTJG Kaiser with the medals he had earned during the last two line periods. Although he had been a Sunday Puncher only a short time and had earned far fewer awards than many others, Kaiser realized that "I was at a point in history that most people will never ever be." As he watched his comrades receive their medals, too, he now understood that "I'm part of that group."[65]

In time, and in addition to individual awards represented by the ribbons on their uniforms, several more Sunday Punchers won special distinctions for their efforts. Quite deservedly, LT Hudson received the 1973 Intruder Maintenance Officer Award, sponsored by the Norden Corporation, maker of the radar sets

One of LTJG Chuck Kaiser's proudest days, 8 June 1973, when he received his Air Medal from RADM Jeremiah Denton during a VA-75 award ceremony. (William H. Greene, Jr., Collection)

used in the A-6.[66] Just as LTJG Vance became Replacement B/N of the Year for 1972, LTJG Kaiser succeeded him in 1973. But all of VA-75 shared in one final accolade. Annually for many years, the Chief of Naval Operations designated one unit as the Navy's most outstanding attack squadron, the winner receiving the Admiral C. Wade McClusky Award. The prize, sponsored by the Vought Aeronautics Company, took its name from a distinguished naval aviator of World War II and hero of the Battle of Midway. The criteria for selection considered "squadron service reputation, aggressiveness and operational performance, including areas of combat and weapons system readiness, combat and/or combat exercises and contribution to weapons system development." The Sunday Punchers who made the combat cruise of 1972–73 take special pride in the best evidence of their professionalism: the CNO named VA-75 the winner of the McClusky Award for 1972.[67]

After a lengthy deployment, a ship's public affairs office often compiles a "cruise book," much like a high school or college yearbook, to preserve images of important events and the people who experienced them. *Saratoga*'s 1972 cruise book devotes several pages of photographs to the Sunday Punchers who went to war.

The composite photograph of VA-75's personnel recalls a very specific point in the cruise, a day in early September. Many of the officers sat for their pictures begrudgingly, Gunner Walden recalled, remembering the veiled threats that forced compliance.[68] CDR Foote had moved on and his photograph does not appear, nor does that of LTJG Bill Wardlaw, who had just left the ship on emergency leave. While the faces of the first replacements and augmentees—LCDR King, LTs Chisholm, Hiduk, and Hart, and LTJGs Vance and Bryan—gaze off the page, later arrivals LCDR Wade, LTs Connelly, Schuster, and Wiegand, and LTJGs Kaiser and Radcliff do not. Pictures of CDR Earnest, LCDR Lindland, and LCDR Graustein—all of whom died after the photo shoot—remind all of war's cost. The faces of the enlisted men—some appearing impossibly young and others presenting proof of the liberality of ADM Zumwalt's views on hair length—represent only those there in September 1972 as well; by the time the carrier returned to Mayport in February 1973, standard rotational policies had changed the squadron significantly from that which had made the hurried deployment in April 1972.

Thus, even before one chapter in its history closed, VA-75 continued to open new ones, each featuring new starring actors. Returning to the routine rotation for East Coast squadrons, a different set of Sunday Punchers flew from the decks of *Saratoga* during unrest in Cyprus and Lebanon in 1975–76. The squadron served aboard USS *John F. Kennedy* in 1982 when Israel invaded Lebanon and stood in readiness to provide air support in the event of an evacuation of American civilians. Six weeks after the bombing of the Marine barracks in Beirut in 1983, VA-75 took part in retaliatory raids. The Sunday Punchers also took an active part in Operations DESERT SHIELD and DESERT STORM.[69]

Indeed, over thirty-three years, VA-75's history and that of the A-6 had become so closely intertwined that it seemed only right that the aircraft and the squadron should retire together. When the U.S. Navy took the A-6 out of its inventory in 1997, VA-75 remained the last East Coast Intruder squadron in service. In the main hangar at Oceana on 28 February 1997, many of the 1972 Sunday Punchers came both to say good-bye to a plane they loved and to witness the disestablishment of the squadron with which they had flown that aircraft in combat. A Sunday Puncher who joined VA-75 well after the 1972 combat cruise aptly explained the great import of the dual event: "One could not hope for a more effective tool to do a more vital mission than all-weather air-to-mud with the A-6 Intruder. Our crews were the 'zen masters' of the attack mission, with innumerable ways to turn valuable enemy assets into fire and twisted scrap metal, and one could not ask to serve with a finer group of warriors than the Sunday Punchers. Their prowess (antics?) on shore and skill in the air will surely be the stuff of Navy legend. It is the kind of thing you remember for the rest of your life."[70] The ceremonies brought both somber moments and light ones. A mock-up of a ready room took the 1972 Punchers back to the day when CDR Earnest slammed his helmet at LT Fischer for announcing his relative location in the air with "I'm over here—by the BIG cloud."

As the Intruder and the squadrons that flew it disappeared from the Navy's table of organization, they joined *Saratoga* in retirement. Gunner Walden became one of the last sailors to go aboard the carrier before its colors were struck for the last time in 1994. He roamed through the entire vessel, a young officer in tow, showing him the site of the October 1972 fire and other places where Sunday Punchers had lived, worked, and made history. After a sailor lowered the Stars and Stripes for the final time, Gunner—the old cumshaw artist—somehow managed to leave the carrier with that banner under his arm.[71] *Saratoga* rested for several years in the Navy yard at Philadelphia to await final disposition. In 2000 the Navy declared it a "museum ship," and it currently is moored at Quonset Point in Rhode Island, where the Saratoga Museum Foundation plans to refurbish it and open it up to the public.[72]

Almost as soon as they returned from Southeast Asia, the Sunday Puncher crews who flew together in combat in 1972 quickly dissolved. By the end of 1973, LTs Fischer, Knapp, Chisholm, Connelly, and LTJG Petersen had returned to civilian life. Punchers who made the 1971 Med cruise before heading to Westpac rotated out of VA-75 for other assignments.

Despite their grousing about military life, many Sunday Puncher pilots and B/Ns enjoyed long active-duty careers. LCDR Jackson rose to the rank of rear

Many Sunday Punchers from 1972 gathered for the February 1997 ceremonies that marked the disestablishment of VA-75 and the retirement of the A-6. Front row, left to right: Paul Hvidding, Dave Warren, Mike Schuster, Jerry Walden. Second row, left to right: Roger Lerseth (with glasses), Jay Swigart, John Fuller. Third row, left to right: Ken Knapp, Howard P. "Smitty" Smith (over Knapp's shoulder), Bob Miller (partly hidden by Lerseth), Alan Fischer, Jerry Mullins, and Steve Bryan. Fourth row, behind Fischer and Mullins: Steve Brierly (a Sunday Puncher of the 1971 Med cruise who did not accompany the squadron to Westpac), Ron Lankford. (Denise Schuster Collection)

admiral and became a leader in the electronic warfare community. CDR Greene rose to captain and commanded USS *Lexington,* while his B/N, LCDR Pieno, rose to the same rank and commanded USS *Forrestal.* CDR Foote became a CAG and commanded a deep-draft vessel before he, too, retired as a captain. LCDRs Kennedy and King retired after serving more than thirty years in uniform. LCDR Engel put in twenty years. In time, many of the junior officers of 1972 became heavies themselves. LTs Wiegand, Schuster, Martin, Anderson, Pyle, Hart, Tolhurst, Lerseth, and Hudson, as well as LTJGs Sanford, Warren, and Vance all served at least twenty years, and some completed a full thirty years on active duty. Chief Warrant Officer Smith retired as a lieutenant commander, and Gunner Walden stayed in for thirty years. But not all stories have happy endings. LCDR Schram died while on active duty at the Pentagon. LT Cook, promoted to lieutenant commander, died in the crash of his C-2 in the early 1980s.

Others remained in the active-duty Navy for only a few more years. LT John Miller won a coveted billet with the Blue Angels before leaving after ten years of service, and LT Wagner and LTJG Swigart also left near the ten-year mark. LT Hvidding ended his naval service after completing an NROTC instructor tour at Purdue University. Still other Sunday Punchers who left active duty soon after the war went into the Naval Reserve and continued their service well over the twenty-year mark. LT Mullins and LTJG Ahrens rose to command Reserve squadrons, as did LT Lankford—who became "Intruder of the Year" in 1977 and retired a captain. Roommates LT Ruland and LTJG Fuller both made captain in the Naval Reserve. When LTJG Kaiser could find no flying billets in the Naval Reserve, he joined the Air Force Reserve and retired as a lieutenant colonel.

Not surprising, several Punchers—LTs Schuster, Chisholm, John Miller, and Fischer—transformed their love of flying naval aircraft into a new career with commercial airlines. Others remained close to aviation by working with the Naval Air Systems Command, commercial airports, and defense contractors. Still other pilots and B/Ns who flew their A-6s through the skies of North Vietnam in 1972 forged successful new careers in fields as diverse as finance, law, education, industry, and business.

Regardless of the path he followed, no Sunday Puncher forgot those who did not come back from Westpac with them. In many ways, the spirit and the memory of those warriors continue to reinforce the strong bonds forged in combat and unite the Sunday Punchers of 1972 long after their return from war.

Bobbe Lindland worked hard for years to remind the public and the government that the fate of LCDR Lindland remained unresolved. Her husband had become a "discrepancy case." As she explained to a journalist in 1973, "They are men who were known to be alive on the ground. We have no further information on them." She worked hard to force the government to release findings to families, asserting, "Out of the 1300 men listed as missing, I say that they are not all dead. They can't be. It is up to each and every one of us to fight and scream and yell, scream bloody murder, to find out where these men are." She continued to wear her husband's POW bracelet.[73] In 1983, the Vietnamese returned an incomplete set of remains identified as those of LCDR Donald F. Lindland. Bobbe herself viewed the remains—57 percent of a full skeleton—to determine that her husband indeed had come home.[74]

The more Duddie Graustein heard about the events of the night of 21 December 1972, the more she became convinced that her husband and his B/N had not survived to be captured. She and her three sons moved back to Fryeburg, Maine, her husband's hometown. In 1975, LCDR Graustein's name appeared on a new list of three naval aviators now officially presumed dead. On 26 March, the family held a memorial service at the First Congregational Church in Fryeburg. A number of Sunday Punchers came to salute their fallen comrade. LT David Warren, who had chided the pilot about his new white helmet that long-ago December night, read the Naval Aviator's Creed.[75] In December 1985, the Vietnamese returned several sets of human remains, among them those of LCDR Robert S. Graustein and LCDR Barton S. Wade. Sunday Punchers also went to New York to mourn with Wade's family.

At a special ceremony on 19 April 1974, RADM John S. Christiansen, now Assistant Chief of Naval Operations for Air Warfare, presented young Brad Earnest with his father's posthumous awards. They numbered thirty-nine in all—a Silver Star with two gold stars to designate a second and third award; a Distinguished Flying Cross with gold stars designating the second through seventh award; a Bronze Star; an Air Medal with numbers to indicate his third through thirty-second award; a Navy Commendation Medal with stars indicating a second through fourth award; and ribbons awarded by the South Vietnamese government.[76] But all those awards could never replace the man. The mortal remains of CDR Charles "M" Earnest rest today where they have lain since 28 November 1972—in the dark waters of the Gulf of Tonkin.

About the time of the retirement of the A-6, a member of the Intruder community helped to dedicate a monument to pilots and B/Ns who died in the line of duty. Much in the same way the history of the air war in Vietnam slights the participation and contribution of the A-6, the speaker intoned, "It has often been our legacy to die alone and unseen. The heart of all-weather attack is two aviators in a single aircraft going to bad places on dark nights. Many families still await a final determination for those who remain missing in action in our hearts. . . . They risked their lives to serve the common good of America." The Sunday Punchers of 1972 shy away from the label of "hero," but they nonetheless fit the speaker's definition: "It has been said that heroes are simply ordinary people placed in extraordinary circumstances."[77] When the dictates of national policy had to be translated into positive action, the Sunday Punchers answered the call to duty.

Notes

PREFACE

1. This saying appears on a VA-75 bumper sticker in the collection of Denise Schuster, wife of pilot LT Michael A. Schuster.
2. Roger G. Lerseth narrative.
3. Richard Holmes, *Acts of War: The Behavior of Men in Battle* (New York: Free Press, 1985), 79.
4. Fred Rochlin, *Old Man in a Baseball Cap: A Memoir of World War II* (New York: Harper Collins, 1999), 146.
5. John Keegan, *The Face of Battle: A Study of Agincourt, Waterloo, and the Somme* (New York: Vintage Books, 1977), 33.
6. Arthur T. Hadley, "Is This Like Your War, Sir?" *Atlantic Monthly* 230 (September 1972): 95.
7. This concept is described in Samuel L. Hynes, *The Soldiers' Tale: Bearing Witness to Modern War* (New York: Penguin Press, 1997), 25.

CHAPTER ONE. "F TROOP"

1. Clarke Van Vleet, "Year of Action . . . 1972," *Naval Aviation News* (February 1973): 13.
2. Unattributed quotation in "Navy" scrapbook, Alan G. Fischer Collection.
3. Roy A. Grossnick, *Dictionary of American Naval Aviation Squadrons: Volume 1, The History of VA, VAH, VAK, VAL, VAP and VFA Squadrons* (Washington, DC: Naval Historical Center, 1995), 132–133; "Disestablished: VA-75 Sunday Punchers," *Naval Aviation News* (September–October 1997): 6.
4. "NAS Oceana: A Wasteland No More," *Naval Aviation News* (October 1971): 36–39.
5. Lawrence M. Mead., Jr., speech, 15 May 1985, in Lou Drendel, *Intruder* (Carrollton, TX: Squadron/Signal Publications, 1991), 3–4.
6. Mark Morgan and Richard J. Morgan, "Pride of the Ironworks: The Grumman A-6 Intruder," *The Hook* (Summer 1997): 23.
7. Drendel, *Intruder*, 5.
8. Morgan and Morgan, "Pride of the Ironworks," 25.
9. VA-75, 1965, command history, Naval Historical Center, Washington, DC (hereafter NHC).
10. Boecker narrative, in Drendel, *Intruder*, 9.
11. Thomas E. Wharton narrative.

12. Jeremiah A. Denton, Jr., with Ed Brandt, *When Hell Was in Session* (reprint ed., Mobile, AL: Traditional Press, 1982), 2–7, and 24.

13. Rene J. Francillon, *Tonkin Gulf Yacht Club: U.S. Carrier Operations Off Vietnam* (Annapolis, MD: Naval Institute Press, 1988), 46, 165; Charles H. Brown, *Dark Sky, Black Sea: Aircraft Carrier Night and All-Weather Operations* (Annapolis, MD: Naval Institute Press, 1999), 165; VA-75, 1965, command history, NHC.

14. Joe Michael, *A-6 Intruder in Action* (Carrollton, TX: Squadron/Signal Publications, 1993), 9.

15. Ibid., 8–9.

16. Kent L. Lee, "The *Enterprise* in Westpac," in E. T. Wooldridge, ed., *Into the Jet Age: Conflict and Change in Naval Aviation, 1945–1975* (Annapolis, MD: Naval Institute Press, 1995), 254.

17. Hal Andrews, "Life of the Intruder," *Naval Aviation News* 79 (September–October 1997): 11.

18. "A Plane for All Seasons," *Time* (25 November 1966): 38.

19. Morgan and Morgan, "Pride of the Ironworks," 28.

20. Peter B. Mersky and Norman Polmar, *The Naval Air War in Vietnam* (New York: Zebra Books, 1981), 85.

21. "All-Weather Plane Stars in Viet War," *Washington Post,* 21 April 1968. The article focused on one A-6 crew, LT Nicholas Carpenter and LTJG Joseph S. Mobley of VA-35, aboard USS *Enterprise.* Carpenter would be killed in action and Mobley would be captured on 24 June 1968. Mobley, released from the Hanoi Hilton in 1973, became the last Vietnam POW to retire from active duty in the Navy in 2001, a vice admiral.

22. Francillon, *Tonkin Gulf Yacht Club,* 146; Chris Hobson, *Vietnam Air Losses: United States Air Force, Navy, and Marine Corps Fixed-Wing Aircraft Losses in Southeast Asia, 1961–1973* (Hinckley, UK: Midland Publishing, 2001), 130, 140; VA-75, 1968, command history, NHC. Both crews were declared missing in action.

23. Paul N. Mullane, "CV: A New, Triple Threat Concept for Carriers," *Naval Aviation News* (March 1972): 49–53; Van Vleet, "Year of Action . . . 1972," 15.

24. Daryl L. Kerr, with Mark Morgan, "The A-6's SIOP Mission," *The Hook* (Summer 1997): 25.

25. Elmo R. Zumwalt, Jr., *On Watch: A Memoir* (New York: Quadrangle Books, 1976), 168–176.

26. Paul T. Gillcrist, *Feet Wet: Reflections of a Carrier Pilot* (New York: Pocket Books, 1990), 365.

27. John M. Miller narrative.

28. Ibid.

29. Wharton narrative.

30. William F. Wardlaw narrative.

31. Paul C. Hvidding narrative.

32. Alan G. Fischer narrative.

33. Wharton narrative.

34. Richard R. Burgess, ed., *The Naval Aviation Guide,* 5th ed. (Annapolis, MD: Naval Institute Press, 1996), 101–102.

35. Interview with Bobbe Lindland, 20 July 2004; Message, USS Saratoga to COM-

SEVENTHFLT, 12 November 1972, concerning recommendation for Bronze Star, copy in Donald F. Lindland Collection.

36. Burgess, ed., *The Naval Aviation Guide,* 103–104.
37. Ibid., 100.
38. Richard L. Engel narrative.
39. James Kennedy narrative.
40. Grady L. Jackson narrative.
41. John A. Pieno, Jr., narrative.
42. Schram biographical sketch, in "Blue Angels, 1971," publicity pamphlet, copy in Leslie M. Sanford, Jr., Collection; Burgess, ed., *The Naval Aviation Guide,* 104–105.
43. Robert A. Tolhurst, Jr., narrative.
44. Kenneth L. Pyle narrative.
45. Terry L. Anderson narrative.
46. Ronald D. McFarland narrative.
47. John J. Swigart, Jr., narrative.
48. Anderson narrative.
49. Pyle narrative.
50. Leslie M. Sanford, Jr., narrative.
51. Douglas W. Ahrens narrative.
52. John R. Fuller narrative.
53. Robert F. Miller narrative.
54. Alden F. Mullins, Jr., narrative.
55. David F. Warren narrative.
56. Anderson narrative.
57. Wharton narrative.
58. Unattributed quotation, in "Navy" binder, Fischer Collection.
59. Thomas C. Ruland narrative.
60. Tolhurst narrative.
61. Ruland narrative.
62. Anderson narrative.
63. Pyle narrative.
64. Anderson narrative.
65. Ruland narrative.
66. Pyle narrative.
67. Robert F. Miller narrative.
68. McFarland narrative.
69. John Darrell Sherwood, *Fast Movers: Jet Pilots and the Vietnam Experience* (New York: Free Press, 1999), 122. The author has seen the notebook in which this was written.
70. Mullins narrative.
71. Hvidding narrative.
72. Ahrens narrative.
73. John J. Swigart, Jr., narrative.
74. Fuller narrative.
75. Mullins narrative.
76. Michael G. McDonnell, "Ragtime," *Naval Aviation News* (October 1971): 11.

77. Sanford narrative.

78. For an excellent summary of RAG training in VA-42 at this time, see McDonnell, "Ragtime," 8–14.

79. VA-85, 1965–1966, command history, NHC.

80. Warren narrative.

81. Lilliane Greene narrative.

82. Unattributed quotation, in "Navy" binder, Fischer Collection.

83. Lilliane Greene narrative.

84. Duddie Graustein narrative.

85. Norfolk, VA, *Virginian-Pilot*, 21 February 1971. See also the response on 27 February 1971.

86. Bobbe Lindland interview, 20 July 2004.

87. Stephanie Knapp narrative.

88. See Barbara Marriott, "The Social Networks of Naval Officers' Wives: Their Composition and Function," in Laurie Weinstein and Christie C. White, eds., *Wives and Warriors: Women and the Military in the United States and Canada* (Westport, CT: Bergin & Garvey, 1997), 19–34.

89. McDonnell, "Ragtime," 11, 13, 16.

90. Message, USS Saratoga to COMSEVENTHFLT, 13 November 1972, copy in Donald F. Lindland Collection.

91. For insights on the introduction of these two versions of the A-6 airframe, see Rick Morgan and Mark L. Morgan, "Pride of the Ironworks, Part 2: The A-6 Intruder, 1969–1973," *The Hook* (Fall 1997): 22–24, 27.

92. Attack Squadron Seventy-Five Familygram, Spring 1972, Roger G. Lerseth Collection; Gillcrist, *Feet Wet*, 374–388.

93. CVW-3, 1971, command history, NHC.

94. Jane Tanner, *The USS Saratoga: Remembering One of America's Great Aircraft Carriers, 1956–1994* (Atlanta: Longstreet Press, 1994), 4; J. R. Tate, "*Saratoga* Revisited," *Naval Aviation News* (September 1972): 44–46.

95. CVW-3, 1971, command history, NHC. See also Gillcrist, *Feet Wet*, 359–364; and Paul T. Gillcrist, *Vulture's Row: Thirty Years in Naval Aviation* (Atglen, PA: Schiffer Publishing, 1996), 218–221.

96. Fischer diary, 23, 24, and 25 February 1972, Fischer Collection.

97. CVW-3, 1972, command history, NHC; "Milestones," Attack Squadron Seventy-Five Familygram, Spring 1972, 2.

98. CVW-3, 1972, command history, NHC; Roger G. Lerseth narrative.

99. Fischer diary, 14 March 1972.

100. Wharton narrative.

101. LTJG Fuller to Sally, 24 March 1972, Sally Fuller Collection.

102. Pieno narrative.

103. Fischer diary, 26 March 1972.

104. Ibid., 28 March 1972. ORI stood for Operational Readiness Inspection, an alternative term for ORE.

105. CVW-3, 1972, command history, NHC.

106. VA-75, 1972, command history, NHC.

107. E. W. Foote to Sunday Puncher Families, 23 March 1972, in Attack Squadron Seventy-Five Familygram, Spring 1972, 5.

CHAPTER TWO. "TEMPORARY ADDITIONAL DUTY"

1. Alan G. Fischer narrative.
2. Dale Andrade, *America's Last Vietnam Battle: Halting Hanoi's 1972 Easter Offensive* (Lawrence: University Press of Kansas, 2001), 2–13. Abrams's quotation can be found on p. 11. See also G. H. Turley, *The Easter Offensive: The Last American Advisors [in] Vietnam, 1972* (Novato, CA: Presidio Press, 1985), 17–32.
3. For a concise examination of the air preparations and the Lavelle affair, see Wayne Thompson, *To Hanoi and Back: The U.S. Air Force and North Vietnam, 1966–1973* (Washington, DC: Smithsonian Institution Press, 2000), 202–210. See also Lewis Sorley, *A Better War: The Unexamined Victories and Final Tragedy of America's Last Years in Vietnam* (New York: Harcourt and Brace, 1999), 316–317. See also Military History Branch, Office of the Secretary, Joint Staff, Military Assistance Command, Vietnam, *1972–1973, Command History Volume 1,* B-2-B-4.
4. Richard Nixon, "Address to the Nation Making Public a Plan for Peace in Vietnam," 25 January 1972, in *Public Papers of the Presidents: Richard Nixon, 1972* (Washington, DC: Government Printing Office, 1974), 101.
5. For the sequence of events in the military buildup before the start of the Easter invasion, see Directorate of Operations Analysis, CHECO/Corona Harvest Division, HQ, PACAF, *Rules of Engagement, November 1969–September 1972,* 31–48.
6. H. R. Haldeman, *The Haldeman Diaries: Inside the Nixon White House* (New York: G. P. Putnam's Sons, 1994), 435.
7. Raphael Littauer and Norman Uphoff, eds., *The Air War in Indochina,* revised ed. (Boston: Beacon Press, 1972), v.
8. Ibid., vi–vii.
9. LCDR Ted Been, VA-42, personal communication to author, 25 June 2002.
10. VA-75, 1972, command history, Naval Historical Center, Washington, DC (hereafter NHC).
11. Robert A. Tolhurst, Jr., narrative; Everett W. Foote narrative.
12. Norfolk, VA, *Virginian-Pilot,* 7 April 1972.
13. Paul C. Hvidding diary, undated April 1972 entry, Paul C. Hvidding Collection.
14. Terry L. Anderson narrative.
15. Kenneth L. Pyle narrative; Sandy Pyle narrative.
16. Everett Foote narrative.
17. VA-75, 1972, command history, NHC.
18. Robert F. Miller narrative.
19. Copy of recall order, in HS-7, 1972, command history, NHC.
20. M. Raymond Demarest, "Sixty Hours and Counting," *Naval Aviation News* (November 1972): 17.
21. Wright Cade, Jr., narrative.
22. John R. Fuller narrative.
23. Hvidding diary, undated April entry.

24. Douglas W. Ahrens narrative.
25. Linda Ahrens narrative.
26. Thomas E. Wharton narrative.
27. Linda Jackson narrative.
28. Penny Swigart narrative.
29. Roger G. Lerseth narrative.
30. Carol Warren narrative.
31. Pixie Tolhurst narrative.
32. Loretta Lankford narrative.
33. Don Petersen narrative.
34. Fischer narrative.
35. Thomas C. Ruland narrative.
36. William F. Wardlaw narrative; Richard DuChateau narrative.
37. Anderson narrative.
38. Alden F. Mullins, Jr., narrative.
39. Fischer narrative.
40. Mullins narrative.
41. John M. Miller narrative.
42. Kenneth Pyle narrative.
43. Jean (Nini) Lerseth Chun narrative.
44. Fischer narrative.
45. Grady L. Jackson narrative.
46. Ronald D. McFarland narrative.
47. Duddie Graustein Andrews narrative.
48. Hvidding diary, undated April 1972 entry.
49. LTJG Bob Tolhurst to Pixie Tolhurst, 17 April 1972, Robert A. Tolhurst, Jr., Collection.
50. Howard P. Smith narrative; Myrna Smith narrative.
51. Judy Pieno Wilkinson, personal correspondence with author, 1 June 2004.
52. Carol Warren narrative.
53. Shari McFarland narrative.
54. Robert F. Miller narrative.
55. Kenneth K. Knapp narrative; Stephanie Knapp narrative.
56. Shari McFarland narrative.
57. Jeane Petersen narrative.
58. Linda Ahrens narrative.
59. Susan Hvidding narrative.
60. Laura Foote narrative; Everett W. Foote narrative. CDR Foote also noted to the author that he never told his wife that he had a choice to stay or go, "but you can tell her now."
61. Lerseth narrative.
62. Judy Pieno Wilkinson correspondence.
63. Ronny D. Lankford narrative; Loretta Lankford narrative.
64. Don Petersen narrative.
65. Mullins narrative.
66. Wharton narrative.
67. Kenneth Pyle narrative.

68. LTJG Fuller to Sally, 11 April 1972. Sally Fuller Collection.

69. Jerry L. Walden narrative.

70. Leslie M. Sanford, Jr., narrative.

71. Everett Foote narrative.

72. Howard P. Smith narrative.

73. Everett Foote narrative.

74. LCDR Been correspondence.

75. Fischer narrative.

76. David F. Warren narrative.

77. Mullins narrative.

78. Lerseth narrative.

79. Mullins narrative.

80. Thomas C. Vance narrative.

81. "U.S.S. Kitty Hawk Leaves for Vietnam Ahead of Schedule: Crewmembers Seek Sanctuary," Jacksonville, FL, *Both Sides Now*, March–April 1972.

82. A photo of the bulletin board can be seen with the article "War End Sought by Officers," Norfolk, VA, *Virginian-Pilot*, 4 January 1971.

83. Ibid., 21 January 1971.

84. Ibid., 8 April 1972.

85. Everett Foote narrative.

86. Lerseth flight log, 10 April 1972, Roger G. Lerseth Collection; Jackson flight log, 11 April 1972, Grady L. Jackson Collection; Jackson narrative.

87. Walden narrative.

88. Sanford narrative.

89. Norfolk, VA, *Virginian-Pilot*, 11 April 1972.

90. Fischer narrative; Norfolk, VA, *Virginian-Pilot*, 10 April 1972.

91. Myrna Smith narrative.

92. Wharton narrative.

93. Walden narrative.

94. HS-7, 1972, command history, NHC.

95. Demarest, "Sixty Hours and Counting," 19; "Readying Sara Seen Logistics Victory," Jacksonville, FL, *Times-Union*, 14 April 1972.

96. Douglas Ahrens narrative.

97. Norfolk, VA, *Virginian-Pilot*, 11 April 1972.

98. Jacksonville, FL, *Journal*, 11 April 1972; David F. Warren narrative.

99. Peter B. Mersky and Norman Polmar, *The Naval Air War in Vietnam* (New York: Zebra Books, 1981), 285.

100. Jacksonville, FL, *Times-Union*, 11 April 1972.

101. Jeane Petersen narrative.

102. Duddie Graustein Andrews narrative.

103. Jackson narrative.

104. Fischer narrative.

105. Robert F. Miller narrative.

106. Everett Foote narrative.

107. Ron Lankford narrative.

108. Ron McFarland narrative.

109. Mullins narrative.
110. Everett Foote narrative.
111. Sally Fuller narrative.
112. Shari McFarland narrative.
113. Laura Foote narrative.
114. Norfolk, VA, *Virginian-Pilot,* 11 April 1972.
115. "Stalemate Through Airpower," ibid., 12 April 1972.
116. Ibid.
117. *Congressional Record,* 92d Cong., 2d Sess., 12199.
118. The full Ad Hoc Committee report can be found in the deliberations of 19 April 1972, in ibid., 13314–13316.
119. Wharton narrative.
120. Kenneth Knapp narrative.
121. Don Petersen narrative.
122. LTJG David Warren to Carol Warren, 11 April 1972, Warren Collection.
123. Lerseth narrative.
124. Richard L. Engel narrative.
125. Bobbe Lindland interview with author, 20 July 2004.
126. Grady Jackson narrative; John A. Pieno, Jr., narrative.
127. Anderson narrative.
128. David Warren narrative.
129. John J. Swigart, Jr., narrative.
130. Anderson narrative.
131. Jackson narrative.
132. Engel narrative.
133. Fischer narrative.
134. Mullins narrative.
135. John J. Swigart, Jr., narrative.
136. Hvidding diary, undated April 1972 entry.
137. Pieno narrative.

CHAPTER THREE. "WOULD YOU BELIEVE?"

1. Alan G. Fischer diary, 11 April 1972, Alan G. Fischer collection.
2. Deck log, USS *Saratoga,* 13, 14, and 15 April 1972, National Archives, College Park, MD; "Only 100 Sailors Missed Sara's Call," Jacksonville, FL, *Times-Union,* 13 April 1972.
3. Paul C. Hvidding diary, undated April 1972 entry, Paul C. Hvidding collection.
4. Fischer diary, 11 April 1972.
5. Wayne Thompson, *To Hanoi and Back: The U.S. Air Force and North Vietnam, 1966–1973* (Washington, DC: Smithsonian Institution Press, 2000), 219–216.
6. Thomas C. Ruland narrative.
7. LTJG Bob Tolhurst to Pixie, 11 April 1972, Robert A. Tolhurst, Jr., Collection.
8. LTJG David Warren to Carol, 12 and 18 April 1972, David F. Warren Collection.
9. *Saratoga* deck log, attachment to 14 April 1972 entry, NA; LTJG John Fuller to Sally, 20 April 1972, Sally Fuller Collection.
10. Richard P. Bordone to author, personal communication, 6 August 2004.

11. John M. Miller narrative.
12. Jerry L. Walden narrative.
13. Don Petersen narrative.
14. VAW-123, 1972, command history, Naval Historical Center, Washington, DC (hereafter NHC).
15. Robert F. Miller narrative.
16. Hvidding diary, undated April 1972 entry.
17. Fischer diary, 17 April 1972.
18. Roger G. Lerseth narrative.
19. A list of topics may be found in addendum to VF-103, 1972, command history, NHC.
20. LTJG Fuller to Sally, 13 April 1972.
21. Alden F. Mullins, Jr., narrative.
22. Paul C. Hvidding narrative.
23. Robert F. Miller narrative.
24. Fischer diary, undated April 1972 entry.
25. Ibid., 20 April 1972.
26. LTJG Warren to Carol, 26 April 1972; John R. Fuller narrative.
27. Hvidding narrative.
28. Terry L. Anderson narrative.
29. John J. Swigart, Jr., narrative.
30. Hvidding narrative.
31. Lerseth narrative.
32. Petersen narrative.
33. Fuller narrative.
34. Ronny D. Lankford narrative.
35. John A. Pieno, Jr., narrative.
36. LTJG Warren to Carol, 26 April 1972.
37. Pieno narrative.
38. Fuller narrative.
39. Hvidding diary, undated April 1972 entry.
40. Douglas W. Ahrens narrative.
41. Fischer diary, 16 April 1972.
42. Ibid., 18 April 1972.
43. Petersen narrative; Lerseth narrative.
44. CAPT Sanderson to Saratoga Family and Friends, 30 May 1972, copy in Leslie M. Sanford, Jr., Collection.
45. Leslie M. Sanford, Jr., narrative.
46. "USS Saratoga & CVW-3, Across the Equator, 18 April 1972, lat. 00–00', log. 30–40'," pp. 4–5, copy in Hvidding Collection.
47. Chief Patrick O'Leary, correspondence with author, 7 January 2004.
48. Pieno narrative.
49. David F. Warren narrative.
50. Walden narrative.
51. Lankford narrative.
52. Fischer diary, 18 April 1972, contains LT Cook's story; a photograph in Loretta Lankford's scrapbook attests to Schram's presence on the hose line.

53. "USS Saratoga & CVW-3, Across the Equator," 16.

54. William F. Wardlaw narrative.

55. LTJG Fuller to Sally, 20 and 21 April 1972.

56. Thomas E. Wharton narrative.

57. John J. Swigart, Jr., narrative.

58. Grady L. Jackson narrative.

59. LTJG Fuller to Sally, 20 April 1972.

60. Hvidding diary, undated April 1972 entry.

61. John M. Miller narrative.

62. Lankford narrative.

63. Fischer diary, [12–15] April 1972; 17 April 1972.

64. Ibid., 22 April 1972; Mullins narrative.

65. LTJG Warren to Carol, 2 May 1972.

66. LTJG Fuller to Sally, 24 April 1972.

67. LTJG Tolhurst to Pixie, 25 April 1972.

68. *Saratoga* deck log, entry for 24 April 1972, NA.

69. Sandy Pyle to Mom and Dad Pyle, 13 April 1972, scrapbook of Sandy Pyle, Kenneth L. Pyle Collection.

70. Jeane Petersen to LTJG Don Petersen, 12 and 14 April 1972, Jeane Petersen Collection.

71. Norfolk, VA, *Virginian-Pilot,* 23 April 1972.

72. Sandy Pyle narrative.

73. Jeane Petersen to LTJG Petersen, 15 April 1972.

74. LTJG Tolhurst to Pixie, 25 April 1972.

75. Carol Warren narrative.

76. LTJG Warren to Carol, 26 April 1972.

77. Fischer log, 25 and 26 April 1972.

78. Kenneth K. Knapp narrative.

79. Fischer narrative.

80. Ibid.

81. Fischer diary, undated April 1972 entry.

82. LTJG Tolhurst to Pixie, 26 April 1972.

83. LTJG Fuller to Sally, 29 April 1972.

84. LTJG Warren to Carol, 2 May 1972.

85. VAW-123, 1972, command history, NHC. The tests came back negative.

86. *Saratoga* deck log, entry for 29 April 1972, NA.

87. LTJG Petersen to Jeane, 25 April 1972, Don Petersen Collection.

88. Wharton narrative.

89. Hvidding diary, undated April 1972 entry.

90. Ahrens narrative.

91. *Saratoga* deck log, entry for 3 May 1972, NA.

92. LTJG Warren to Carol, 2 May 1972.

93. Richard L. Engel narrative.

94. John J. Swigart, Jr., narrative.

95. LTJG Lerseth to "Mom, Jo, and Retta," 7 May 1972, copy in Roger G. Lerseth Collection.

96. This event is reconstructed from Lankford narrative; Pieno narrative; Robert A. Tol-

hurst, Jr., narrative; John J. Swigart, Jr., narrative. The date of the incident is confirmed in LTJG Fuller to Sally, 5 May 1972.

97. LTJG Tolhurst to Pixie, 4 May 1972.
98. "'Sunday Punchers' participate in SARATOGA 'Olympics,'" Attack Squadron Seventy-Five Familygram, Summer 1972, p. 5.
99. Fischer diary, 5 and 6 May 1972.
100. LTJG Tolhurst to Pixie, 5 [6] May 1972.
101. VF-31, 1972, command history, NHC.
102. Fischer narrative.
103. LTJG Fuller to Sally, 5 May 1972.
104. CNO ADM Elmo R. Zumwalt, Jr., to OPNAV, 4 May 1972, copy in Loretta Lankford scrapbook, Lankford Collection.
105. *Saratoga* deck log, entry for 6 May 1972, NA.
106. John M. Miller narrative; Lankford narrative.
107. Howard P. Smith narrative.
108. LTJG Petersen to Jeane, 8 May 1972.
109. Receipt, phone company, May 1972, Douglas W. Ahrens Collection.
110. *Saratoga* deck log, entry for 8 May 1972, NA.
111. LTJG Warren to Carol, 10 May 1972.
112. Wharton narrative.
113. LTJG Lerseth to Mom, 18 May 1972.
114. Fischer diary, 8 May 1972.
115. Mullins narrative.
116. Hvidding narrative.
117. Tolhurst narrative.
118. Howard S. Levie, "Mine Warfare and International Law," *Naval War College Review* 24 (April 1972): 33.
119. Richard M. Nixon, "Address to the Nation on the Situation in Southeast Asia, May 8, 1972," in *Public Papers of the President: Richard Nixon, 1972* (Washington, DC: Government Printing Office, 1974), No. 147.
120. Jackson narrative.
121. *Saratoga* deck log, 10 May 1972, NA.
122. "Squadron Performance during embarked period," 11 April–31 December 1972," [4 January 1973], attached to VF-31, 1972, command history, NHC.
123. Ronald D. McFarland narrative.
124. Ahrens narrative.
125. Hvidding diary, 13 May 1972.
126. LTJG Petersen to Jeane, 14 May 1972.
127. Ibid.
128. Ahrens narrative.
129. Fischer diary, 10 and 11 May 1972.
130. Ibid., 13 May 1972.
131. Ibid., 15 May 1972.
132. Hvidding diary, 15 and 16 May 1972.
133. CAPT Sanderson to Saratoga Family and Friends, 30 May 1972, Sanford Collection.

134. LTJG Petersen to Jeane, 17 May 1972.
135. Military History Branch, Office of the Secretary, Joint Staff Military Assistance Command, Vietnam, *1972–1973, Command History: Volume 1,* B-55. For an account of this process on the *Saratoga,* see, for example, "Transferring Navy Supplies at Sea Still Hazardous," Jacksonville, FL, *Times-Union,* 29 October 1972; Wright Cade, Jr., narrative.
136. LTJG Warren to Carol, 14 May 1972.
137. LTJG Lerseth to "Mom, Jo, & Retta," 7 May 1972.

CHAPTER FOUR. "A PIECE OF CAKE"

1. James H. Willbanks, *Thiet Giap! The Battle of An Loc, April 1972* (Fort Leavenworth, KS: U.S. Army Command and General Staff College, 1993), 21–22, 79–81. Willbanks, a participant in the An Loc fight as a military adviser to ARVN forces, errs in his statement on p. 16 in including USS *Saratoga* among the carriers providing air support in the early April phases of the fighting in Binh Long province. The aircraft off *Saratoga,* including VA-75, will begin to make their presence felt only during the third phase of the fighting in mid-May.
2. For an excellent and concise analysis of the conduct of ground operations in the Mekong Delta during the North Vietnamese 1972 spring offensive, see Dale Andrade, *America's Last Vietnam Battle: Halting Hanoi's 1972 Easter Offensive* (Lawrence: University Press of Kansas, 2001), chap. 32, esp. 461–470. See also Military History Branch, Office of the Secretary, Joint Staff Military Assistance Command, Vietnam, *1972–1973, Command History: Volume 1,* 63–65.
3. Information on a set of kneeboard cards, dated May 1972, in Don Petersen Collection.
4. John M. Miller narrative.
5. Times confirmed by *Saratoga* deck log, entry for 18 May 1972, National Archives, College Park, MD.
6. Details of the launch sequence come from Richard R. Burgess, ed., *The Naval Aviation Guide,* 5th ed. (Annapolis, MD: Naval Institute Press, 1996), 171–175. The number of daily sorties can be found in CVW-3, 1972, command history, Naval Historical Center, Washington DC (hereafter NHC).
7. VF-103, 1972, command history, NHC.
8. VA-75 Master Log, 18 May 1972, MR-4 section, Leslie M. Sanford, Jr., Collection (hereafter VA-75 Master Log, with appropriate date and section); Everett W. Foote narrative.
9. Not all squadrons in the airwing adopted this practice. VF-103, for example, put all its F-4 crews on MiGCAP (MiG combat air patrol) duty from the start. After some mishaps in the air, and the loss of one aircraft, the squadron leaders reassessed their policy and temporarily restricted MiGCAPs to second-cruise crews only. After the junior crews grew in experience, they reassessed in September and restored the original policy. See VF-103, 1972, command history, NHC.
10. Roger G. Lerseth narrative.
11. David F. Warren narrative.
12. Contact procedures outlined on "MR III/MR IV OPERATIONS" kneeboard card, dated 17 May 1972, in Petersen Collection. See also Jan Churchill, *Hit My Smoke! Forward Air Controllers in Southeast Asia* (Manhattan, KS: Sunflower University Press, 1997), 103.

13. VA-75 Master Log, 18 May 1972, MR-4 section; LCDR Grady L. Jackson personal sortie log (hereafter Jackson sortie log), 18 May 1972, Grady L. Jackson Collection.

14. VA-75 Master Log, 18 May 1972, MR-4 section.

15. Alden F. Mullins, Jr., narrative.

16. Mullins log sheets, May 1972, Alden F. Mullins, Jr., Collection.

17. Ronny D. Lankford narrative.

18. LTJG Warren to Carol, 18 May 1972, David F. Warren Collection.

19. John J. Swigart, Jr., narrative.

20. VA-75 Master Log, 18 May 1972, MR-4 section.

21. Lerseth narrative.

22. Sample forms used by CVW-3 for most of these different reports can be found in the appendix to VF-103, 1972, command history, NHC; William H. Greene/John A. Pieno, Jr., joint narrative.

23. LTJG Paul C. Hvidding diary, 18 May 1972, Paul C. Hvidding Collection.

24. VA-75 Master Log, 18 May 1972, tanker section; LT Alan G. Fischer diary, 18 May 1972, Alan G. Fischer Collection.

25. VA-75 Master Log, 19 May 1972, MR-4 section; LTJG Warren to Carol, 19 May 1972.

26. LTJG Petersen to Jeane, 19 May 1972, Don Petersen Collection.

27. VA-75 Master Log, 19 May 1972, MR-4 section.

28. The situation at An Loc in mid-May is described aptly in Andrade, *America's Last Vietnam Battle,* 444–446; Lerseth to his Mother, 18–19 May 1972, Roger G. Lerseth Collection; VA-75 Master Log, 19 May 1972, MR-3 section.

29. Hvidding diary, 18 and 19 May 1972.

30. Fischer diary, 19 and 20 May 1972.

31. Ibid., 18 May 1972.

32. VA-75 Master Log, 20 May 1972, MR-4 section; Fischer diary, 20 May 1972.

33. Terry L. Anderson narrative; for more on South Vietnamese Air Force FACs, see Bernard C. Nalty, *Air War over South Vietnam, 1968–1975* (Washington, DC: Air Force History and Museum Program, 2000), 387.

34. VAW-123, 1972, command history, NHC.

35. VA-75 Master Log, 20, 21, and 22 May 1972, MR-4 section.

36. Hvidding diary, 22 May 1972.

37. Don Petersen narrative.

38. Douglas W. Ahrens narrative.

39. Jackson sortie log, 23 May 1972.

40. LTJG Warren to Carol, 20 May 1972.

41. Hvidding diary, 20 May 1972; the entry for this mission in the VA-75 Master Log, 20 May 1972, MR-4 section, includes no mention of the five duds.

42. VA-75 Master Log, 26, 27, 28, and 29 May 1972, MR-4 section.

43. Jerry L. Walden narrative.

44. Fischer diary, 25 May 1972.

45. LTJG Warren to Carol, 25 May 1972.

46. Hvidding diary, 21 May 1972.

47. Ibid., 20 May 1972.

48. Petersen narrative.

49. Alan G. Fischer narrative.

50. Ronald D. McFarland narrative.

51. VA-75 Master Log, 24 May 1972, MR-4 section; LTJG Petersen tape, May 1972; Thomas E. Wharton narrative.

52. Ahrens narrative.

53. John J. Swigart, Jr., narrative.

54. John M. Miller narrative.

55. Hvidding diary, 26 May 1972.

56. LTJG Warren to Carol, 29 May 1972.

57. John J. Swigart, Jr., narrative.

58. Mullins narrative.

59. Paul C. Hvidding narrative.

60. Thomas C. Ruland narrative.

61. LTJG Petersen to Jeane, 19 May 1972.

62. LTJG Warren to Carol, 29 May 1972.

63. Richard L. Engel narrative.

64. Robert A. Tolhurst, Jr., narrative.

65. Dave Grossman, *On Killing: The Psychological Cost of Learning to Kill in War and Society* (New York: Little, Brown, 1995), 106. See also 107–110.

66. Hvidding diary, 21 May 1972.

67. Ibid., 30 May 1972.

68. Ibid., 23 May 1972.

69. LTJG Tolhurst to Pixie, 21 May 1972.

70. Ibid., 28 May 1972.

71. LTJG Warren to Carol, 27 May 1972.

72. Walden narrative.

73. Hvidding narrative.

74. Leslie M. Sanford, Jr., narrative; Chris Hobson, *Vietnam Air Losses: United States Air Force, Navy, and Marine Corps Fixed-Wing Aircraft Losses in Southeast Asia* (Hinckley, UK: Midland Publishing, 2001), 227; VA-75 Master Log, 27 May 1972, MR-4 section.

75. Fischer diary, 26 May 1972; VA-75 Master Log, 26 May 1972, MR-4 section, verifies target information but not the difference in dive angle.

76. VA-75 Master Log, 25 May 1972, MR-3 section; Jackson sortie log, 25 May 1972.

77. Hvidding diary, 25 May 1972.

78. VA-75 Master Log, 27 May 1972, MR-3 section; Hvidding diary, 27 May 1972.

79. VA-75 Master Log, 28 May 1972, MR-3 section; Petersen narrative.

80. LTJG Warren to Carol, 28 May 1972.

81. Jackson sortie log, 28 May 1972.

82. Hvidding diary, 29 May 1972.

83. Alfred Price, *The History of US Electronic Warfare, Volume III: Rolling Thunder through Allied Force, 1964 to 2000* (N.p.: Port City Press, 2000), 185–186.

84. Penny Swigart narrative.

85. LTJG Warren to Carol, 3 June 1972.

86. Susan Hvidding to Jeane Petersen, 25 May 1972, Jeane Petersen Collection.

87. John M. Miller narrative.

88. Jean (Nini) Lerseth Chun narrative.

89. LTJG Fuller to Sally, 14 May 1972, Sally Fuller Collection; Linda Ahrens narrative.
90. Reported in LTJG Fuller to Sally, 5 June 1972.
91. Copy of affidavit, signed by Douglas W. Ahrens and Donald F. Lindland, Linda Ahrens Collection.
92. Loretta Lankford narrative; Loretta Lankford to LT Ron Lankford, telegram of 31 May 1972, copy in Loretta Lankford scrapbook.
93. LTJG Warren to Carol, 30 May 1972; Andrade, *America's Last Vietnam Battle,* 316–319; Jackson sortie log, 30 May 1972; VA-75 Master Log, 30 May 1972, MR-2 section.
94. VA-75, 1972, command history, NHC.
95. Herman L. Gilster, *The Air War in Southeast Asia: Case Studies of Selected Campaigns* (Maxwell Air Force Base, AL: Air University Press, 1993), 69; John J. Sbrega, "Southeast Asia," in Benjamin F. Cooling, ed., *Case Studies in the Development of Close Air Support* (Washington, DC: Office of Air Force History, 1990), 468; Nalty, *The Air War over South Vietnam,* 398.
96. *Saratoga* deck log, entry for 1 June 1972, NA.
97. Attack Squadron Seventy-Five Familygram, Summer 1972.
98. LTJG Warren to Carol, 29 May 1972.
99. Verification of authorship in Wagner to author, 10 August 2003; LTJG Warren to Carol Warren, 19 May 1972; typescript of the skit, Petersen Collection.
100. LTJG Warren to Carol, 1 June 1972.
101. Virginia Beach, VA, *Beacon,* 6 July 1972.
102. "Navy Takes Viet War Ball and Runs with It," (Pacific) *Stars and Stripes,* 30 May 1972.
103. Jeane Petersen to LTJG Petersen, 31 May 1972.

CHAPTER FIVE. "INTO THE BADLANDS"

1. Roger G. Lerseth narrative.
2. LTJG Fuller to Sally, 1 June 1972, Sally Fuller Collection; John R. Fuller narrative.
3. LTJG Paul C. Hvidding diary, 1 June 1972, Paul C. Hvidding Collection.
4. Military History Branch, Office of the Secretary, Joint Staff Military Assistance Command, Vietnam, *1972–1973, Command History: Volume 1,* B-51, B-53. Figure B-28 on p. B-53 lays out carrier availability on Yankee Station, month by month.
5. The Route Package system, with all its nuances, is spelled out in detail in John B. Nichols and Barrett Tillman, *On Yankee Station: The Naval Air War over Vietnam* (Annapolis, MD: Naval Institute Press, 1987), 21–23.
6. VA-75 Master Log, 2 June 1972, RP-2 section, Leslie M. Sanford, Jr., Collection; LCDR Grady L. Jackson sortie log, 2 June 1972, Grady L. Jackson Collection.
7. VA-75 Master Log, 2 June 1972, RP-3 section.
8. Ibid., RP-2 section; John A. Pieno, Jr., narrative; Thomas C. Ruland narrative; LTJG Warren to Carol, 2 June 1972, David F. Warren Collection.
9. VA-75 Master Log, 2 June 1972, tanker section; Paul C. Hvidding narrative.
10. Hvidding diary, 2 June 1972.
11. VA-75 Master Log, 3 June 1972, RP-2 section; John J. Swigart, Jr., narrative.
12. VA-75 Master Log, 3 June 1972, RP-2 section; Fuller narrative.
13. Thomas E. Wharton narrative; Don Petersen narrative.
14. Robert Hotz, "New Lessons from Vietnam," in *Aviation Week & Space Technology* (22

May 1972), copy in the Douglas Pike Collection, Unit 03: Technology, Vietnam Archives, Texas Tech University.

15. LT Alan G. Fischer diary, 5 June 1972, Alan G. Fischer Collection.
16. LTJG Warren to Carol, 5 June 1972.
17. LTJG Sandy Sanford diary, 31 May 1972, Leslie M. Sanford, Jr., Collection.
18. Richard P. Bordone to author, personal correspondence, 6 August 2004.
19. William H. Greene/John A. Pieno, Jr., joint narrative.
20. John M. Miller narrative.
21. The format of the alpha strike kneeboard card and the standardized alpha strike briefing format can be found in appendix V, tables 3, 4, and 5, VF-103, 1972, command history, Naval Historical Center, Washington, DC.
22. Jackson sortie log, 6 June 1972; Richard L. Engel narrative; VA-75 Master Log, 6 June 1972, section RP-6B.
23. VA-75 Master Log, 6 June 1972, RP-6B section; Alden F. Mullins, Jr., narrative.
24. Mullins logsheet, entry for 6 June 1972, Alden F. Mullins, Jr., Collection.
25. John J. Swigart, Jr., narrative.
26. Lerseth narrative.
27. LTJG Swigart to Penny, 6 June 1972, John J. Swigart, Jr., Collection.
28. Formats for these reports can be found as appendices in VF-103, 1972, command history, NHC.
29. Robert A. Tolhurst, Jr., narrative.
30. William H. Greene narrative.
31. Lilliane Greene narrative.
32. LTJG Warren to Carol, 2 June 1972.
33. VA-75 Master Log, 7 June 1972, RP-2; LTJG Warren to Carol, 7 June 1972.
34. Hvidding diary, 7 June 1972.
35. Mullins narrative.
36. Kenneth K. Knapp narrative; for variations in the ways in which the Navy and Air Force handled this situation, see Marshall L. Michel III, *Clashes: Air Combat over North Vietnam, 1965–1972* (Annapolis, MD: Naval Institute Press, 1997), 223–224; and Wayne Thompson, *To Hanoi and Back: The U.S. Air Force and North Vietnam, 1966–1973* (Washington, DC: Smithsonian Institution Press, 2000), 243.
37. LTJG Fuller to Sally, 13 June 1972.
38. "Summary of Action, Hon Gay," Kenneth K. Knapp Collection.
39. Greene/Pieno narrative.
40. LTJG Fuller to Sally, 13 June 1972.
41. Fischer diary, 7 June 1972.
42. Anthony M. Thornborough and Frank B. Mormillo, *Iron Hand: Smashing the Enemy's Air Defences* (Sparkford, UK: J. H. Haynes, 2002), 112.
43. "Summary of Action *Haiphong PPS/Loi Dong TSP*," Jackson Collection.
44. Jackson personal log, 8 June 1972; Jackson narrative.
45. Leslie M. Sanford, Jr., narrative.
46. Fischer diary, 8 June 1972.
47. "Summary of Action *Haiphong PPS/Loi Dong TSP*," Jackson Collection.
48. John M. Miller narrative.
49. Sanford narrative.

50. VA-75 Master Log, 8 June 1972, tanker section; Hvidding diary, 8 June 1972.

51. *Saratoga* deck log, entries for 9–18 June 1972, National Archives, College Park, MD.

52. Lerseth narrative.

53. Recommendation for Individual Award, LCDR Lindland, 12 November 1972, and Recommendation for Individual Award, LTJG Lerseth, 12 November 1972, both John R. Fuller Collection; Lerseth narrative.

54. Lerseth narrative.

55. Jackson sortie log, 13 June 1972; VA-75 Master Log, 13 June 1972, RP-6B section.

56. Lerseth narrative.

57. *New York Times,* 13 June 1972.

58. LTJG Warren to Carol, 8 June 1972.

59. Hvidding narrative; Kenneth L. Pyle narrative.

60. Timing established by *Saratoga* deck log, entry of 14 June 1972, NA.

61. LTJG John L. Johnson (VA-37) diary, entry of 14 June 1972, John L. Johnson Collection.

62. Fischer diary, 14 June 1972; Alan G. Fischer narrative.

63. Lerseth narrative; Knapp narrative; Fuller narrative.

64. Timing and recovery established by *Saratoga* deck log, entry for 16 June 1972, NA; Knapp narrative.

65. Johnson diary, 16 June 1972.

66. LTJG Warren to Carol, 16 June 1972.

67. *Saratoga* deck log, entry for 18 June 1972, NA.

68. Fischer narrative.

69. Knapp narrative.

70. Walden narrative; Petersen narrative.

71. LTJG Warren to Carol, 11 June 1972.

72. Sanford narrative.

73. *Saratoga* deck log, entry for 19 June 1972, NA.

74. LTJG Warren to Carol, 18 June 1972.

75. Ibid., 19 June 1972.

76. Greene/Pieno narrative; VA-75 Master Log, 19 June 1972, RP-3 section.

77. Jackson sortie log, 20 June 1972.

78. "Summary of Action Thanh Hoa Petroleum Storage, 20 June 1972," Fuller Collection; Greene/Pieno narrative.

79. VA-75, 1972, command history, Report, entry for 20 June 1972, NHC.

80. "Summary of Action Phu Ly Highway Bridges and Ninh Binh PPS, 21 June 1972," Jackson Collection.

81. CVW-3, 1972, command history, NHC; VA-75, 1972, command history, NHC; Jackson sortie log, 21 June 1972.

82. Greene narrative; Robert F. Miller narrative.

83. Engel narrative.

84. Mullins narrative; Anderson narrative.

85. Swigart to Penny, 6 June 1972.

86. Wharton narrative.

87. LTJG Petersen to Jeane, 25 June 1972.

88. LTJG Warren to Carol, 23 June 1972.

89. LTJG Fuller to Sally, 25 June 1972.

90. CVW-3, 1972, command history, NHC; VA-75, 1972, command history, NHC.

91. *Saratoga* deck log, entry for 23 June 1972, NA; John S. Christiansen interview, 21 May 2001.

92. Wharton narrative.

93. LT Chisholm to Bobbie, 29 June and 30 July 1972, Robert M. Chisholm Collection.

CHAPTER SIX. "A VERY REAL LIFE INDEED"

1. LTJG Tolhurst to Pixie, 29 June 1972, Robert A. Tolhurst, Jr., Collection. *Oriskany* had collided with the ammunition ship *Nitro* during an underway replenishment.

2. *New York Times*, 26 June 1972.

3. Ibid., 1 July 1972.

4. Ibid., 29 June 1972; *Congressional Record*, 92d Cong., 2d Sess., 19 July 1972, 24505.

5. *New York Times*, 2 July 1972.

6. Ibid., 3 July 1972.

7. LT Lerseth to Mom and Girls, 2 July 1972, copy in Roger G. Lerseth Collection.

8. Message, USS SARATOGA to CINCPACFLT, 13 November 1972, Recommendation for Individual Award for LCDR Donald F. Lindland, copy in Donald F. Lindland Collection; LTJG Warren to Carol, 1 July 1972, David F. Warren Collection.

9. VA-75 Master Log, 2 July 1972, RP-3 section, Leslie M. Sanford, Jr., Collection; Jackson sortie log, 2 July 1972, Grady L. Jackson Collection.

10. John J. Swigart, Jr., narrative; the author saw the film of this mission, and, despite its deterioration over time, one round passing the cockpit is still quite visible.

11. LT Alan G. Fischer diary, 2 July 1972, Alan G. Fischer Collection.

12. LT Paul C. Hvidding diary, 2 July 1972, Paul C. Hvidding Collection; Kenneth L. Pyle narrative.

13. Sandy Pyle narrative.

14. LT Tolhurst to Pixie, 2 July 1972.

15. Fischer diary, 2 July 1972.

16. VA-75 Master Log, entry for 4 July 1972, RP-4 and RP-6B sections.

17. CAPT Sanderson letter to SARATOGA families, 11 July 1972, Sanford Collection; Clarke Van Vleet, "Year of Action . . . 1972," *Naval Aviation News* (February 1973): 20.

18. *Saratoga* deck log, entry for 4 July 1972, National Archives, College Park, MD.

19. LT Tolhurst to Pixie, 5 July 1972.

20. LTJG Petersen to Jeane, 10 and 11 July 1972, Don Petersen Collection.

21. LT Chisholm to Bobbie, 13 July 1972, Robert M. Chisholm Collection.

22. Hvidding diary, 7 and 13 July 1972.

23. Thomas C. Vance narrative.

24. LT Chisholm to Bobbie, 8 July 1972.

25. Ibid., 9 July 1972.

26. Stephen C. Bryan narrative.

27. Chris Bryan to LTJG Steve Bryan, 1 July 1972, Stephen C. Bryan Collection.

28. George L. Hart narrative.

29. The details of this event have been reconstructed from David F. Warren narrative; Ronny D. Lankford narrative; "Close Call of the Sara," Jacksonville, FL, *Times-Union*, 20 July 1972; and *Navy Times*, 9 August 1972.

30. Hvidding diary, 7 July 1972; Pyle narrative.

31. John R. Fuller narrative.

32. Jackson sortie log, 8 July 1972; Steve Brierly, "Another Intruder First," undated clipping in Jackson sortie log, Jackson Collection. Brierly served as a B/N in VA-75 on the 1971 Med cruise and, flying with LT John M. Miller, dropped four sonobuoys during these tests.

33. The quotations included herein are taken from John S. Christiansen interview, 21 May 2001; in content and wording it follows closely the exchange recorded in Gregory L. Vistica, *Fall from Glory: The Men Who Sank the U.S. Navy* (New York: Simon & Schuster, 1995), 82.

34. John F. Lehman, Jr., *Command of the Seas,* Bluejacket Books edition (Annapolis, MD: Naval Institute Press, 2001 [1988]), 62–63.

35. Vistica, *Fall from Glory,* 80, 86. ADM Holloway admitted that Lehman's presence in the cockpit had everything to do with his status as a VIP from Kissinger's staff, not with his qualification as a naval aviator (ibid., 400, footnotes 21 and 22).

36. VA-75 Master Log, RP-6B section, 8 July 1972, and tanker section, 6 July 1972.

37. Hvidding diary, 10 July 1972.

38. Jackson sortie log, 11 July 1972; VF-103, 1972, command history, Naval Historical Center, Washington, DC; VA-75 Master Log, RP-6B section.

39. VA-75 Master Log, 11 July 1972, RP-4 section.

40. LT Tolhurst to Pixie, 13 July 1972.

41. LT Chisholm to Bobbie, 13 July 1972.

42. John A. Pieno, Jr., narrative.

43. LTJG Petersen to Jeane, 9 July 1972.

44. *New York Times,* 12 July 1972.

45. Hearings before the Committee on Internal Security, House of Representatives, 92d Cong., 2d Sess., 7645. For Fonda's full itinerary, see Henry Mark Holzer and Erika Holzer, *"Aid and Comfort": Jane Fonda in North Vietnam* (Jefferson, NC: McFarland & Company, 2002), 61–62.

46. *Washington Post,* 13 July 1972; *Congressional Record,* 92d Cong., 2d Sess., 19 July 1972, 24504.

47. *Washington Post,* 14 July 1972.

48. *Congressional Record,* 24505.

49. VA-75 Master Log, 12 July 1972, RP-4 section, and 13 July 1972, RP-6B section.

50. "Summary of Action Nam Dinh TSP[,] 12 July 1972," Jackson Collection.

51. Message, USS SARATOGA to COMSEVENTHFLT, 13 November 1972, recommendation for individual award for LCDR Donald F. Lindland, copy in Lindland Collection.

52. Hearings before the Committee on Internal Security, House of Representatives, 92d Cong., 7646.

53. Paul C. Hvidding narrative.

54. Anderson narrative.

55. LT Chisholm to Bobbie, 13 July 1972.

56. VA-75 Master Log, 13 and 15 July 1972, RP-6B section.

57. Hvidding diary, 14 July 1972.

58. VA-75 Master Log, 14 July 1972, RP-2 section; citation, Navy Commendation Medal, LTJG David Warren, for 14 July mission, Warren Collection. As pilot, LT Lankford also received this award.

59. VA-75 Master Log, 12 July 1972, RP-4 section; Hart narrative.

60. VA-75 Master Log, 13 July 1972, RP-6B section; Ronald D. McFarland narrative.

61. Fischer narrative; LTJG Petersen to Jeane, 9 July 1972.

62. VA-75 Master Log, 1–16 July 1972, statistics section.

63. CVW-3, 1972, NHC.

64. Howard P. Smith narrative; "Sierra Report Codes" kneeboard card, undated, in Petersen Collection.

65. Hart narrative.

66. LTJG Petersen to Jeane, 9, 11, and 13 July 1972.

67. LT Chisholm to Bobbie, 16 July 1972.

68. Hearings before the Committee on Internal Security, House of Representatives, 92d Cong., 7650–7651.

69. Fischer diary, 19 July 1972.

70. Myrna Smith narrative.

71. Chris Bryan to LTJG Steve Bryan, 1 July 1972.

72. Ruland narrative.

73. *Saratoga* deck log, entry for 19 July 1972, NA; William H. Greene narrative; Jerry L. Walden narrative.

74. *Saratoga* deck log, entry for 20 July 1972, NA.

75. Chris Bryan to LTJG Steve Bryan, 1 July 1972.

76. Fischer narrative.

77. Ibid.

78. Fischer diary, [20–27] July 1972.

79. Menu from Polaris in the Myrna Smith scrapbook, Howard P. Smith Collection.

80. Don Petersen narrative.

81. Anderson narrative.

82. Pixie Tolhurst narrative.

83. Ronnie Smith to "Mommy and Pop," 18 June [July] 1972, in Myrna Smith scrapbook, Smith Collection.

84. Ronny D. Lankford narrative.

85. Financial information from an exchange table noting rate of exchange in Myrna Smith scrapbook.

86. Vance narrative.

87. All menus from Myrna Smith scrapbook.

88. Lilliane Greene narrative.

89. Lankford narrative.

90. Wright Cade, Jr., narrative.

91. Photographs in Petersen Collection.

92. Lankford narrative; Walden narrative; LT Chisholm to Bobbie, 26 July 1972.

93. VA-35, 1972, command history, NHC.

94. LT Chisholm to Bobbie, 28 July 1972.

95. Fischer diary, [20–27] July 1972.

CHAPTER SEVEN. "ON A TREADMILL"

1. Lerseth to Mother, 4 August 1972, copy in Roger G. Lerseth Collection.

2. Hvidding made his last entry on 4 August 1972; Paul C. Hvidding narrative.

3. The command historian of VF-31 coined the phrase "preventative" lectures. Details

on that squadron's reaction to the airwing memorandum can be found in VF-31, 1972, command history, Naval Historical Center, Washington, DC.

4. Lerseth to Mother, 4 August 1972.

5. *New York Times,* 21 July 1972.

6. Ibid., 25 and 29 July 1972.

7. Ibid., 28 July 1972; James W. Clinton, *The Loyal Opposition: Americans in North Vietnam, 1965–1972* (Niwot, CO: University Press of Colorado, 1995), 252–53.

8. LT Alan G. Fischer diary, 29 July 1972, Alan G. Fischer Collection.

9. Henry Kissinger, *Ending the Vietnam War: A History of America's Involvement in and Extrication from the Vietnam War* (New York: Simon and Schuster, 2003), 299.

10. United States Military Assistance Command, Vietnam, *1972–1973 Command History: Volume 1* (Military History Branch, Office of the Secretary, Joint Staff, MACV, 1973), B-11. See also "Thailand's Role," *U.S. News & World Report* 73 (21 August 1972): 30–32.

11. Hvidding diary, 29 July 1972, Paul C. Hvidding Collection.

12. Jackson sortie log, 30 July 1972, Grady L. Jackson Collection.

13. Ronny D. Lankford narrative; LTJG Warren to Carol, 30 July 1972, David F. Warren Collection.

14. Compiled from "Haiphong Shipyard No. 3 Summary of Action," Jackson Collection.

15. John J. Swigart, Jr., narrative; John M. Miller narrative.

16. Compiled from Jackson sortie log, 31 July 1972; Jackson narrative.

17. CVW-3, 1972, NHC.

18. Compiled from "Haiphong Shipyard No. 3 Summary of Action," Jackson Collection.

19. John R. Fuller narrative.

20. Jackson narrative.

21. John M. Miller narrative.

22. Mullins logsheet, entry for 31 July 1972, Alden F. Mullins, Jr., Collection.

23. *New York Times,* 2 August 1972.

24. LT Chisholm to Bobbie, 4 August 1972, Robert M. Chisholm Collection; Robert M. Chisholm narrative; Thomas C. Vance narrative.

25. Lerseth to Mother, 4 August 1972.

26. *New York Times,* 7 August 1972. See HQ, PACAF, Directorate of Operations Analysis, CHECO/CORONA HARVEST DIVISION, *Linebacker: Overview of the First 120 Days,* 31.

27. "Van Dien Vehicle Depot Summary of Action," Jackson Collection.

28. Roger G. Lerseth narrative.

29. George L. Hart narrative.

30. Jackson sortie log, 5 August 1972.

31. Alan G. Fischer narrative.

32. Lerseth narrative.

33. Ibid.; Hart narrative.

34. "Van Dien Vehicle Depot Summary of Action," Jackson Collection.

35. Lerseth to Mother, 4 August 1972.

36. VA-75 Master Log, 6 August 1972, RP-6B section, Leslie M. Sanford, Jr., Collection.

37. Mullins logsheet, entry for 6 August 1972, Mullins Collection.

38. Don Petersen narrative.

39. Fischer narrative.

40. Fischer diary, 6 August 1972; LT Tolhurst to Pixie, 7 August 1972, Robert A. Tolhurst, Jr., Collection; David F. Warren narrative; Petersen narrative.

41. CVW-3, 1972, command history, NHC; *Saratoga* deck log, entry for 6 August 1972, National Archives, College Park, MD.

42. Warren narrative.

43. Lankford narrative.

44. RADM Christiansen interview, 21 May 2001.

45. Kenneth K. Knapp narrative.

46. Lerseth narrative.

47. Knapp narrative.

48. Basic narrative of the Lloyd rescue reconstructed from PNC (DV) LaMarche, "One Night to Rescue," *SERE Newsletter* (7 May 1973), with details added from Grady Jackson to Jim Lloyd, [early 1998], Jackson Collection; JOC Warren Grass, "Inside Story," *Naval Aviation News* (November 1972): 37–39; the filmed proceedings of "ANA Symposium 1999: Ejection, Evasion, Rescue, August 1972, North Vietnam"; Fuller narrative.

49. LCDR Jackson to family, taped letter, ca. mid-August 1972, Jackson Collection.

50. *New York Times,* 12 August 1972.

51. Ibid., 10 August 1972.

52. LT Chisholm to Bobbie, 6 August 1972.

53. LT Tolhurst to Pixie, 20 August 1972.

54. Fischer narrative.

55. Frank J. Pittman to author, 3 December 2003; statements of LCDR R. W. Repp, LT Hugh F. Holden, Chief Aviation Structural Mechanic Frank J. Pittman, and Aviation Support Equipment Technician Second Class James Vernetti, "Summary of Action," and Pittman's Navy and Marine Corps Medal citation, all in Frank J. Pittman Collection.

56. LTJG Warren to Carol, 10 August 1972.

57. USO information folder for American military dependents in the Philippines, copy in Linda Ahrens collection; Linda Ahrens narrative; Jean (Nini) Lerseth Chun narrative; Loretta Lankford narrative; Penny Swigart narrative.

58. LT Tolhurst to Pixie, 8 August 1972.

59. Quoted in Mark Clodfelter, *The Limits of Air Power: The American Bombing of North Vietnam* (New York: Free Press, 1989), 161. See also Clodfelter, "Nixon and the Air Weapon," in Dennis E. Showalter and John G. Albert, eds., *An American Dilemma: Vietnam, 1964–1973* (Chicago: Imprint Publications, 1993), 172.

60. VA-75 Master Log, RP-3 section, indicates that two crews—CDR Greene with LCDR Pieno, and LCDR Graustein with LT Mullins—were in the air this night; VA-75 Master Log, 10 August 1972, tanker section; VF-103, 1972, command history, NHC.

61. VF-31, 1972, command history, NHC.

62. CNO memorandum, "History of the Mining of North Vietnam, 8 May 1972–14 January 1973," 13 January 1976, Vietnam Archives, Texas Tech University.

63. Ulrik Luckow, "Victory over Ignorance and Fear: The U.S. Minelaying Attack on North Vietnam," *Naval War College Review* 35 (January–February 1982): 24.

64. Jackson sortie log, 11 August 1972; Message, USS SARATOGA to COMSEVENTHFLT, 13 November 1972, recommendation for individual award for LCDR Donald F. Lindland, copy in Donald F. Lindland Collection.

65. Hart narrative.

66. "Haiphong Mining Summary of Action," Jackson Collection.

67. Jeffrey Kimball, *The Vietnam War Files: Uncovering the Secret History of Nixon-Era Strategy* (Lawrence: University Press of Kansas, 2004), 240.

68. LT Tolhurst to Pixie, 14 August 1972; VA-75 Master Log, RP-2 section.

69. *Saratoga* deck log, entry for 14 August 1972, NA.

70. Attack Squadron Seventy-Five Familygram, Fall 1972.

71. Ronald D. McFarland narrative.

72. LTJG Warren to Carol, 14 August 1972.

73. McFarland narrative; Alden F. Mullins, Jr., narrative.

74. Fuller narrative.

75. Ibid.

76. Statistics compiled from VA-75 Master Log, Third Line Period (28 July–23 August 1972), statistics section, Sanford Collection.

77. VA-35, 1969, command history, NHC.

78. Ibid.

79. VA-85, 1970, command history, NHC.

80. VA-165, 1970, command history, NHC.

81. Christiansen interview, 21 May 2001.

82. VA-196, 1972, command history, NHC.

83. VA-165, 1970, command history, NHC.

84. Richard P. Bordone to author, personal correspondence, 6 August 2004.

85. VAW-123, 1972, command history, NHC.

86. VF-31, 1972, command history, NHC.

87. William H. Greene, Jr., narrative.

88. Kenneth L. Pyle narrative.

89. VA-75, Master Log, 14 August 1972, RP-3 section, Sanford Collection; John J. Swigart, Jr., narrative; LTJG Warren to Carol, 15 August 1972.

90. Lankford narrative.

91. News Release 29–72, untitled, ca. late August 1972, by LT G. L. Hart, VA-75, 1972, command history, Addendum, NHC.

92. Edward A. Lyons (VA-37), correspondence with author, 9 February 2004; VA-75 Master Log, 17 August 1972, tanker section, Sanford Collection; and ibid., RP-4 section.

93. *Saratoga* deck log, entry for 17 August 1972, NA.

94. VA-75 Master Log, 19 August 1972, RP-6B section, Sanford Collection; Fuller narrative.

95. "Thai Binh Army Barracks/Storage Area Summary of Action," Jackson Collection.

96. "Haiphong Military Storage Area Summary of Action," Jackson Collection; Jackson sortie log, 20 August 1972.

97. Tolhurst to Pixie, 20 August 1972.

98. "Haiphong Military Storage Area Summary of Action," Jackson Collection.

99. Jackson tape to family, ca. mid-August 1972.

100. Jackson sortie log, 21 August 1972; Grady Jackson, "SA-2 Optical Engagement of A6A on Night Mission over NVN in 1972"; Military History Branch, Office of the Secretary, Joint Staff Military Assistance Command, Vietnam, *1972–1973, Command History: Volume 1,* B-16.

101. Draft, "Recommendation for Individual Award, LT Roger Gene Lerseth," 12 November 1972, John R. Fuller Collection.

102. LCDR Jackson to family, taped letter, ca. 8 August 1972, Jackson Collection.

103. Fischer diary, 16 August 1972.

104. LT Chisholm to Bobbie, 8/9 and 10 August 1972.
105. William F. Wardlaw narrative.
106. John M. Miller narrative.
107. LTJG Petersen to Jeane, 16 August 1972.
108. LCDR Jackson taped letter to family, ca. mid-August 1972.
109. CDR Greene to Lilliane, ca. August 1972, Greene Collection. This note was jotted on a copy of CAPT Sanderson's July letter home to the *Saratoga* families; internal evidence about Lilliane's return travel home supports a post–Hong Kong date of writing.
110. Pyle narrative.
111. *Saratoga* deck log, entry for 23 August 1972, NA.
112. "Saratoga (CV-60)," *Naval Aviation News* (December 1972): 12; Fischer diary, [23 August 1972].
113. Military History Branch, *1972–1973, Command History: Volume 1*, B-19.
114. CVW-3, 1972, command history, NHC; VA-75 figures compiled from VA-75 Master Log, statistics section, Sanford Collection.
115. VA-75 master log, 23 August 1972, tanker section, Sanford Collection; Lankford narrative.
116. *Saratoga* deck log, entry for 24 August 1972, NA.
117. LT Chisholm to Mom and Dad, 23 August 1972.
118. Leslie M. Sanford, Jr., narrative.
119. Wardlaw narrative. Derek was born healthy on 29 September, and LTJG Wardlaw was discharged from the Navy on schedule on 31 October 1972.
120. Jean (Nini) Lerseth Chun narrative; Lankford narrative.
121. LTJG Fuller to Sally, 27 August 1972.
122. LCDR Jackson taped letter home, ca. mid-August 1972.
123. *Saratoga* deck log, entry for 27 August 1972, NA.
124. Attack Squadron Seventy-Five Familygram, Fall 1972.
125. Fischer diary, 26 August 1972.
126. LTJG Fuller to Sally, 27 August 1972, second letter.

CHAPTER EIGHT. "GOT AN ACE HIT"

1. Elmo R. Zumwalt, Jr., *On Watch: A Memoir* (New York: Quadrangle Books, 1976), 215–217.
2. Harold W. King, "Milk Runs Hell!" unpublished manuscript, Harold W. King Collection.
3. LT Tolhurst to Pixie, 1 September 1972, Robert A. Tolhurst, Jr., Collection.
4. LTJG Warren to Carol, 2 September 1972, David F. Warren Collection.
5. LT Alan G. Fischer diary, 3 September 1972, Alan G. Fischer Collection.
6. LT Tolhurst to Pixie, 1 September 1972.
7. RADM Christiansen interview, 21 May 2001.
8. Fischer diary, 2 September 1972.
9. Jeane Petersen to LTJG Petersen, 4 September 1972, Jeane Petersen Collection.
10. "Summary of Action," Grady L. Jackson Collection; VA-75 Master Log, 4 September 1972, RP-4 section, Leslie M. Sanford, Jr., Collection.
11. Mullins logsheet, entry for 5 September 1972, Alden F. Mullins, Jr., Collection.
12. John A. Pieno, Jr., narrative.

13. Roger G. Lerseth, untitled and unpublished manuscript concerning shootdown, 31 January 1998, copy in possession of author, 2–3.
14. Robert A. Tolhurst, Jr., narrative.
15. Ibid.; Tolhurst to Pixie, 7 September 1972.
16. Robert M. Chisholm narrative.
17. Thomas C. Vance narrative.
18. LT Tolhurst to Pixie, 7 September 1972.
19. LTJG Paul S. Pencikowski (VF-103), personal correspondence to author, June 2004.
20. Martin J. Every and James F. Parker, Jr., "A Review of Problems Encountered in the Recovery of Navy Aircrewmen under Combat Conditions," Office of Naval Research Report, June 1973, 148, copy in folder 05, Box 19, Douglas Pike Collection, Unit 03: POW/MIA issues, Vietnam Archives, Texas Tech University.
21. Lerseth manuscript, 11–14.
22. The shootdown of Ace Three described in the previous paragraphs was reconstructed from Roger Lerseth, untitled manuscript, 31 January 1998; Roger G. Lerseth narrative; and John Darrell Sherwood, *Fast Movers: Jet Pilots and the Vietnam Experience* (New York: Free Press, 1999), 124–128.
23. Thomas C. Ruland narrative.
24. George L. Hart narrative.
25. John R. Fuller narrative.
26. Frank J. Pittman narrative.
27. Chisholm narrative.
28. LT Tolhurst to Pixie, 9 September 1972.
29. Leslie M. Sanford, Jr., diary, 6 September 1972, Sanford Collection; John M. Miller narrative.
30. The original flight schedule for the day can be found on "Attack Squadron Seventy-Five Flight Schedule," 6 September 1972, copy in John A. Pieno, Jr., Collection.
31. Pieno narrative.
32. CDR Earnest to Nini Lerseth, 6 September 1972, Lerseth POW Collection.
33. Message, CDR Earnest to COMMATWING ONE and CDR D. V. Boecker, 6 September 1972, copy in Donald F. Lindland Collection.
34. Ted Been narrative; Bobbe Lindland interview, 20 July 2004.
35. Earnest to COMMATWING ONE and CDR D. V. Boecker, 6 September 1972.
36. Linda Jackson narrative.
37. Duddie Graustein narrative.
38. "Allies Engage Reds; Navy Jets Hit Depots," Norfolk, VA, *Virginian-Pilot*, 7 September 1972; full text of North Vietnamese message, picked up by the BBC, in Lerseth POW Collection.
39. *Nhan Dan*, 7 September 1972, copy and translation provided by Bobbe Lindland.
40. LTJG Warren to Carol, 15 September 1972.
41. LCDR Jackson to Nini, 9 September 1972, Lerseth POW Collection.
42. Fuller narrative.
43. LTJG Fuller to Sally, 14 September 1972.
44. The previous five paragraphs are built upon information in LTJG Fuller to Sally, 14 September 1972; Fuller narrative; Linda Ahrens narrative; and Jean (Nini) Lerseth Chun narrative.

45. LCDR Engel to Jean Lerseth, 7 September 1972, Lerseth POW Collection.

46. CAPT J. R. Sanderson to Mrs. Roger G. Lerseth, 7 September 1972, Lerseth POW Collection.

47. Stephen C. Bryan narrative.

48. "G-Man's Combat Fear Factor," copy in Sanford Collection.

49. Vance narrative.

50. Hart narrative.

51. Fuller narrative.

52. Miller to Sanford, undated, but shortly after ca. 8 September 1972, Sanford Collection; Leslie M. Sanford, Jr., narrative.

53. LT Chisholm to Bobbie, 6 September 1972.

54. LTJG Warren to Carol, 6 September 1972.

55. Terry L. Anderson narrative.

56. Tolhurst narrative.

57. Fuller narrative.

58. Don Petersen narrative.

59. LTJG Petersen to Jeane, 9 September 1972, Don Petersen Collection.

60. Jeane to LTJG Petersen, 14 September 1972.

61. "POW Bracelets a Constant Reminder," Norfolk, VA, *Virginian-Pilot,* 14 September 1972; Virginia Beach, VA, *Beacon,* 1 October 1972.

62. LTJG Warren to Carol, 10 September 1972.

63. Vance narrative.

64. Ibid.; Chisholm to Bobbie, 8 and 12 September 1972.

65. Pieno narrative.

66. VA-75 Master Log, 5 September 1972, RP-2 section, Sanford Collection; ibid., 8 September 1972, RP-4 section; Harold W. King narrative.

67. VA-75 Master Log, 5, 7, and 10 September 1972, RP-6B section, Sanford Collection.

68. Pieno narrative.

69. Greene/Pieno joint narrative; Pieno narrative.

70. Pieno narrative.

71. King narrative.

72. LTJG Warren to Carol, 12 September 1972.

73. Ibid., 10 September 1972.

74. Rudolf P. Wiegand narrative.

75. John J. Swigart, Jr., narrative.

76. King narrative; Richard L. Engel narrative.

77. LT Tolhurst to Pixie, 14 September 1972.

78. VF-31's end-of-line-period report for September, for one of the very few times during the cruise, devoted space to listing the worst of the violations, including flight deck directors taxiing aircraft too close to deck edges and catapult holdback bars, unchecked yellow gear, and shortcuts in directing recovering aircraft to deck spots before earlier arrivals completed the tie-down and shutdown processes. See VF-31, 1972, command history, NHC.

79. *Saratoga* deck log, entry for 14 September 1972, NA; LTJG Petersen to Jeane, 14 [September] 1972.

80. VAW-123, 1972, command history, NHC.

81. King narrative; Vance narrative. LT Chisholm and LT Anderson also recalled spotting flares or lights.

82. "Develop the Might of the Firenets to Shoot U.S. Aircraft Flying at Low Altitude," originally published in September 1972 in *Tap Chi Quan Doi Nahn Dan* and read over Hanoi radio on 7 October 1972. Translation in Folder 01, Box 02, Douglas Pike Collection, Unit 03: Technology, Vietnam Archives, Texas Tech University.

83. LT Chisholm to Bobbie, 11 September 1972.

84. VA-75 Master Log, 11 September 1972, RP-6B section, Sanford Collection; "Summary of Action [Ninh Duong Army Barracks]," Jackson Collection.

85. Ruland narrative; Jackson sortie log, 12 September 1972.

86. Jackson sortie log, 15 September 1972; News Release 37–72, untitled, by LT G. L. Hart, in VA-75, 1972, command history, Addendum, NHC.

87. CAPT Sanderson to "Dear Saratoga Family and friends," 25 September 1972, Robert M. Chisholm Collection.

88. Ibid.; "Saratoga Winner of Flatley Award for Achievement," Jacksonville, FL, *Times-Union*, 4 October 1972.

89. Paul Drew Stevens, ed., *The Navy Cross: Vietnam* (Forest Ranch, CA: Sharp & Dunnigan, 1987), 354, 356.

90. Fischer diary, 15 September 1972.

91. LTJG Petersen to Jeane, 15 August 1972. Internal evidence indicates that the letter is misdated and that it was really written on 15 September 1972.

92. LT Chisholm to Bobbie, 15 September 1972.

93. John M. Miller narrative.

94. VA-75 Master Log, 18 September 1972, RP-1 section, Sanford Collection; Fuller narrative.

95. VA-75 Master Log, 18 September 1972, RP-1 section, Sanford Collection; ibid., MR-1 section.

96. LTJG Petersen to Jeane, 19 September 1972.

97. CVW-3, 1972, command history, NHC; VA-75 statistics compiled from VA-75 Master Log, statistics section, Sanford Collection.

98. VA-75, 1972, command history, NHC; William H. Greene, Jr., narrative; Richard P. Bordone narrative; "Norden-Sponsored Trophy won by Lieutenant Hudson," unattributed and undated newspaper article in William H. Greene, Jr., Collection.

99. Fischer diary, postwar addition to entry for 13 August 1972, when recounting other false promises about the carrier's departure for home.

100. LT Tolhurst to Pixie, 21 September 1972.

101. Chisholm letter, Chisholm Collection.

102. *Saratoga* deck log, entries for 23, 24, 25, 26, and 27 September 1972, NA.

103. Attack Squadron Seventy-Five Familygram, Fall 1972.

104. LTJG Petersen to Jeane, 23 September 1972.

105. Attack Squadron Seventy-Five Familygram, Fall 1972.

106. Chisholm to Mom and Dad, 21 September 1972.

107. LTJG Petersen to Jeane, 21 September 1972.

108. Chisholm to Bobbie, 28 September 1972.

CHAPTER NINE. "PEACE IS AT HAND"

1. Henry Kissinger, *Ending the Vietnam War: A History of America's Involvement in and Extrication from the Vietnam War* (New York: Simon and Schuster, 2003), 319–321.

2. LTJG Warren to Carol, 29 September 1972, David F. Warren Collection.

3. Chris Hobson, *Vietnam Air Losses: United States Air Force, Navy, and Marine Corps Fixed-Wing Aircraft Losses in Southeast Asia, 1961–1973* (Hinckley, UK: Midland Publishing, 2001), 237.

4. Ibid., 215.

5. LT Alan G. Fischer diary, 8 October 1972, Alan G. Fischer Collection.

6. Alden F. Mullins, Jr., narrative.

7. VA-75 Master Log, 29 September 1972, MR-1 section, Leslie M. Sanford, Jr., Collection; George L. Hart narrative.

8. LT Tolhurst to Pixie, 1 October 1972, Robert A. Tolhurst, Jr., Collection.

9. LT Chisholm to Bobbie, 1 October 1972, Robert M. Chisholm Collection.

10. Explained in LTJG Warren to Carol, 3 October 1972.

11. VA-75 Master Log, 4 October 1972, statistics section, Sanford Collection.

12. VA-75 Master Log, 4 and 5 October 1972, RP-6B section, Sanford Collection; VA-75, 1972, command history, Naval Historical Center, Washington, DC.

13. LTJG Fuller to Sally, 7 October 1972, Sally Fuller Collection.

14. LT Tolhurst to Pixie, 5 and 6 October 1972.

15. LT Chisholm to Bobbie, 3 October 1972.

16. LTJG Warren to Carol, 5 October 1972.

17. LT Chisholm to Bobbie, 8 October 1972.

18. Ibid., 5 October 1972.

19. LT Tolhurst to Pixie, 8 October 1972.

20. Compiled from VA-75 Master Log, 5–17 October 1972, RP-6B section, Sanford Collection.

21. Ibid., 8 October 1972, RP-4 section; Jackson sortie log, 8 October 1972, Grady L. Jackson Collection; Grady L. Jackson narrative.

22. VA-75 Master Log, 8 October 1972, RP-6B section, Sanford Collection; Harold W. King narrative.

23. Jackson sortie log, 9 October 1972.

24. Compiled from VA–75 Master Log, 9 October 1972, RP-6B section, Sanford Collection.

25. "Indochina Air War Enters a New Phase," *Miami Herald*, 25 September 1972.

26. "Close-Up of North Vietnam at War: Everything Moves by Night," *New York Times*, 3 October 1972; "Focus on Hanoi's 'Ant Power,'" *Christian Science Monitor*, 3 October 1972.

27. Quoted in William W. Momyer, *Air Power in Three Wars (WWII, Korea, Vietnam)* (Washington, DC: Government Printing Office, 1978), 98–99.

28. Robert A. Tolhurst, Jr., narrative.

29. This narrative of the 10 October mission against Bai Thuong is reconstructed from John R. Fuller narrative, John A. Pieno, Jr., narrative, William H. Greene, Jr., narrative, and Richard P. Bordone to author, 6 August 2004.

30. LT Tolhurst to Pixie, 10 October 1972.

31. LTJG Warren to Carol, 31 October 1972.

32. LT Chisholm to Bobbie, 4 October 1972.

33. VA-75 Master Log, 5 October 1972, statistics section, Sanford Collection.

34. LTJG Warren to Carol, 5 October 1972.

35. "Fire Control Branch," Attack Squadron Seventy-Five Familygram, Fall 1972, Chisholm Collection.

36. VF-103, 1972, command history, NHC.

37. Penny Swigart narrative.

38. LTJG Warren to Carol, 13 October 1972.

39. Jackson sortie log, 13 October 1972.

40. "Award Reveals Inland Mine Laying," undated and unattributed newspaper clipping, Jackson Collection. Internal evidence suggests a date of approximately March 1973.

41. Huu Thap, "Thai Binh Builds Many Additional Fighting Clusters and Mobile Fortifications to Waylay United States Aircraft," explains the broader concept that spread beyond that one province. Originally printed in Hanoi, *Quan Doi Nhan Dan,* 10 October 1972. Translated copy in Folder 01, Box 02, Douglas Pike Collection, Unit 03: Technology, The Vietnam Archives, Texas Tech University.

42. VA-75 Master Log, 13 October 1972, RP-6B section, Sanford Collection; Stephen C. Bryan narrative.

43. Greene narrative.

44. VA-75 Master Log, 16 October 1972, RP-4 section, Sanford Collection; LTJG Warren to Carol, 16 October 1972.

45. Jeremiah A. Denton, Jr., with Ed Brandt, *When Hell Was in Session* (reprint ed., Mobile, AL: Traditional Press, 1982), 160–161.

46. Bobbe Lindland interview, 19 July 2004.

47. Jean (Nini) Lerseth Chun narrative.

48. Knoxville, TN, *Journal,* 22 September 1972, reprinted in *Congressional Record,* 92d Cong., 2d Sess., 3 October 1972, 33555.

49. Bobbe Lindland interview, 19 July 2004.

50. Ibid., 28; see also "A Campaign to Get a Husband Home," *Life* 73 (29 September 1972), 32–38, 42.

51. *Public Papers of the Presidents: Richard Nixon, 1972* (Washington, DC: Government Printing Office, 1974), 986–988.

52. LTJG Warren to Carol, 16 October 1972.

53. "Admin/Pers," Attack Squadron Seventy-Five Familygram, Fall 1972, Chisholm Collection.

54. LTJG Petersen to Jeane, 17 October 1972.

55. Roger G. Lerseth narrative; Mullins narrative.

56. Fuller narrative.

57. Mullins narrative.

58. VAW-123, 1972, command history, NHC.

59. A summary of these racially inspired incidents can be found in Leonard F. Guttridge, *Mutiny: A History of Naval Insurrection* (New York: Berkley Publishing Group, 1992), chapter 19. For a fuller treatment of the events and results, see *Hearings Before the Special Subcommittee on Disciplinary Problems in the United States Navy of the House of Representatives,* 92d Cong., 2d Sess.

60. "You Can't Be Black and Navy Too," *Black Panther,* 16 November 1972.

61. *Congressional Record,* 92d Cong., 2d Sess., 18 October 1972, 27402.

62. Wright Cade, Jr., narrative.

63. Thomas C. Vance narrative.

64. Greene narrative.

65. The time of the incident is established by the *Saratoga* deck log, entry for 18 October 1972, NA.

66. LTJG Warren to Carol, 18 October 1972.

67. Ibid., 19 October 1972; Warren narrative.

68. LTJG Warren to Carol, 20 October 1972.
69. CAPT Sanderson to "SARATOGA Family and Friends," 22 October 1972, copy in Sanford Collection.
70. VA-75, 1972, command history, NHC.
71. LT Tolhurst to Pixie, 20 October 1972.
72. CVA-3, 1972, command history, NCH.
73. Statistics compiled from VA-75 Master Log, 28 September–21 October 1972, statistics section.
74. Fischer diary, 22 October 1972; LTJG Warren to Carol, 23 October 1972.
75. LTJG Warren to Carol, 24 October 1972.
76. LT Tolhurst to Pixie, 30 September 1972.
77. LTJG Petersen to Jeane, 12 October 1972.
78. LT Tolhurst to Pixie, 1 October 1972.
79. Memorandum from Flight Officer [LT J. M. Miller], Attack Squadron 75, to Aircrew members, Attack Squadron 75, 4 October 1972, copy in Sanford Collection. Internal evidence noting that the statistics were current as of 22 October 1972 clearly indicates that this document actually was issued on 4 November 1972.
80. LT Tolhurst to Pixie, 3 October 1972.
81. Memorandum from Flight Officer, Attack Squadron 75 to Aircrew members, Attack Squadron 75, 4 October [November] 1972.
82. Ronny D. Lankford narrative.
83. Linda Ahrens narrative.
84. LTJG Warren to Carol, 23 October 1972.
85. For contemporary assessments of the agreement and its benefits and risks for all parties involved, see "'Peace Is at Hand,'"*Newsweek* 80 (6 November 1972), 33–35; and "The Shape of Peace," *Time* 100 (6 November 1972), 14–18.
86. Lankford narrative.
87. Sally Fuller narrative.
88. Greene/Pieno joint narrative.
89. Stephanie Knapp narrative.
90. Greene/Pieno joint narrative; Fischer narrative.
91. Ibid.; Stephanie Knapp narrative; *Saratoga* deck log, 29 October 1972, NA.
92. Rudolf P. Wiegand narrative.
93. King narrative.
94. Tolhurst narrative.
95. *Saratoga* deck log, entry for 29 October 1972, NA; Jacksonville, FL, *Times-Union*, 30 and 31 October 1972.
96. Tolhurst narrative.
97. *New York Times*, 30 October 1972.
98. A JP-5 fuel tank caught fire early on 1 November, and a smaller fire in a compartment broke out on 2 November. *Saratoga* fire parties extinguished the first in forty minutes and the second in less than ten minutes (*Saratoga* deck log, entries for 1 and 2 November 1972, NA).
99. "Admin/Pers," Attack Squadron Seventy-Five Familygram, Fall 1972, Chisholm Collection.
100. "Notes from the Commanding Officer," Attack Squadron Seventy-Five Familygram, Fall 1972.

1. Peter B. Mersky and Norman Polmar, *The Naval Air War in Vietnam* (New York: Zebra Books, 1981), 292.

2. LTJG Fuller to Sally, 4 November 1972, Sally Fuller Collection.

3. VF-31, 1972, command history, Naval Historical Center (NHC), Washington, DC.

4. Charles Kaiser narrative.

5. Stephanie Knapp narrative.

6. LT Chisholm to Bobbie, 8 November 1972, Robert M. Chisholm Collection.

7. LT Alan G. Fischer diary, 6 November 1972, Alan G. Fischer Collection.

8. LTJG Warren to Carol, 5 November 1972, David F. Warren Collection.

9. Lilliane Greene narrative.

10. Alden F. Mullins, Jr., narrative.

11. LTJG Petersen to Jeane, 9 November 1972, Don Petersen Collection.

12. *Saratoga* deck log, 5–12 November 1972, National Archives, College Park, MD.

13. VA-75 Master Log, 5 November 1972, MR-1 section, Leslie M. Sanford, Jr., Collection; Kaiser narrative.

14. LTJG Sanford diary, 5–9 November 1972, Sanford Collection.

15. David F. Warren narrative.

16. Paul C. Hvidding narrative.

17. Michael A. Schuster narrative.

18. LT Tolhurst to Pixie, 26 November 1972, Robert A. Tolhurst, Jr., Collection.

19. Alan G. Fischer narrative.

20. VA-75 Master Log, 10 and 11 November 1972, RP-1 section, Sanford Collection.

21. Ronny D. Lankford narrative; LTJG Warren to Carol, 6 November 1972.

22. Chris Hobson, *Vietnam Air Losses: United States Air Force, Navy, and Marine Corps Fixed-Wing Aircraft Losses in Southeast Asia, 1961–1973* (Hinckley, UK: Midland Publishing, 2001), 239. A sixth Navy aircraft was lost during this time period as well, due to equipment malfunction.

23. *Saratoga* deck log, 10 November 1972, NA; CVW-3, 1972, command history, NHC.

24. LT Chisholm to Bobbie, 11 November 1972.

25. Denise Schuster narrative.

26. LTJG Petersen to Jeane, 1 December 1972.

27. Attack Squadron Seventy-Five Familygram, 1 December 1972, 4, William H. Greene Collection.

28. Sanford diary, 16 November 1972; VA-75 Master Log, 16 November 1972, RP-2 section, Sanford Collection.

29. Sanford diary, 18 November 1972; VA-75 Master Log, 18 November, RP-2 section, Sanford Collection.

30. John M. Miller narrative.

31. Michael A. Schuster narrative.

32. Kaiser narrative; Thomas C. Vance narrative.

33. *Saratoga* deck log, 19, 20, 21, and 23 November 1972, NA.

34. LCDR Graustein, mimeographed "Operations Note," 21 November 1972, Kenneth L. Pyle Collection.

35. VA-75, 1972, command history, report, NHC.

36. "Sunday Punchers Reach New Milestones," Attack Squadron Seventy-Five Family-gram, 1 December 1972, 5, Greene Collection.

37. Jerry L. Walden narrative.

38. VF-103, 1972, command history, NHC.

39. Walden narrative.

40. "Line Division," Attack Squadron Seventy-Five Familygram, 1 December 1972, 17, Greene Collection.

41. "Power Plants" and "Electrical Shop," in ibid., 10–11 and 13.

42. Hvidding narrative.

43. Judy Pieno Wilkinson, correspondence with author, 1 June 2004.

44. Sally Fuller narrative.

45. Pixie Tolhurst narrative.

46. CDR Greene possesses a copy of this photograph.

47. William H. Greene narrative; CDR Greene to LCDR Hamrick, 19 November 1972, copy in Greene Collection.

48. CAPT Sanderson to "Saratoga Family and Friends," 26 November 1972, Chisholm Collection.

49. Stephanie Knapp narrative.

50. New York Times, 24 and 25 November 1972.

51. LTJG Warren to Carol, 25 November 1972.

52. Jeane Petersen to LTJG Petersen, 25 November 1972, Jeane Peterson Collection.

53. Chisholm narrative.

54. "Nine 'Sunday Punchers' Receive Awards," News Release 60–72, copy attached to VA-75, 1972, command history, addendum, NHC; "'Sara' Men Awarded 63 Medals," Jacksonville, FL, Times-Union, 10 December 1972.

55. CAPT Sanderson to "SARATOGA Family and Friends," 13 January 1973, Greene Collection.

56. LTJG Fuller to Sally, 10 and 17 November 1972, Sally Fuller Collection.

57. John R. Fuller narrative.

58. Thomas C. Ruland narrative.

59. Walden narrative.

60. Ibid.; Grady L. Jackson narrative.

61. Walden narrative.

62. Vance narrative.

63. Schuster narrative.

64. Walden narrative.

65. Schuster narrative.

66. Lankford narrative; Tolhurst narrative; VA-75 Master Log, 28 November 1972, RP-3 section, Sanford Collection.

67. Lankford narrative.

68. Vance narrative.

69. Saratoga deck log, entry for 28 November 1972, NA.

70. John M. Miller narrative.

71. Confidential telegram, USS Saratoga to COMMATWING ONE, 28 November 1972, copy in Greene Collection.

72. Lilliane Greene narrative.

73. Linda Jackson narrative; Judy Pieno Wilkinson to author, 1 June 2004.

74. Linda Jackson narrative.

75. Sandy Pyle narrative; Duddie Graustein narrative.

76. Richard L. Engel narrative.

77. CDR Greene to CDR Almberg, 30 November 1972, copy in Greene collection.

78. Chris Bryan to LTJG Bryan, 30 November 1972, Stephen C. Bryan Collection.

79. CDR Greene to Minna Earnest, 29 November 1972, copy in Greene Collection.

80. John A. Pieno, Jr., narrative; CDR Almberg to CDR Greene, 2 December 1972, copy in Greene Collection.

81. COMNAVAIRLANT to CDR Greene, 30 November 1972, copy in Greene Collection; draft of response, including intent to appoint LCDR Engel as acting XO, in ibid.; VA-75, 1972, command history, NHC, entry for 4 December 1972.

82. CDR Greene to CDR Foote, 30 November 1972, copy in Greene Collection.

83. CDR Greene to Master Chief Pena, 1 December 1972, copy in Greene Collection.

84. Master Chief Jacob Pena to CDR Greene, 1 December, copy in Greene Collection.

85. "Notes from the Commanding Officer," Attack Squadron Seventy-Five Familygram, 1 December 1972, 1, Greene Collection.

86. LTJG Warren to Carol, 28 November 1972.

87. Don Petersen narrative.

88. Dawn Greene to Dad [CDR Greene], 29 November 1972, Greene Collection.

89. *Saratoga* deck log, 30 November–1 December 1972, NA.

90. Flashgram, 3 December 1972, copy in VA-35, 1972, command history, NHC.

91. Time established in Sanford Diary, 1 December 1972, Sanford Collection; CDR Charles Earnest Memorial Service program, John R. Fuller Collection.

92. LTJG Warren to Carol, 1 December 1972.

93. Lankford narrative.

94. Fischer diary, 1 December 1972.

95. Hvidding narrative.

96. Chris Bryan to LTJG Steve Bryan, 30 November 1972.

97. CAPT Sanderson to "SARATOGA Family and Friends," 12 January 1973, Greene Collection.

98. LTJG Petersen to Jeane, 1 December 1972.

99. Kenneth K. Knapp narrative.

100. Fuller narrative.

101. "Summary of Action, Bai Thuong Airfield, 02 December 1972," copy in Thomas C. Vance Collection; LT Chisholm to Bobbie, 2 December 1972; LTJG Warren to Carol, 2 December 1972; VA-75 Master Log, 2 December 1972, RP-3 section, Sanford Collection; Chisholm narrative.

102. LTJG Warren to Carol, 4 December 1972; VA-75 Master Log, 4 December 1972, RP-4 section, Sanford Collection.

103. LTJG Fuller to Sally, 7 December 1972, Sally Fuller Collection.

104. Chisholm to Mom and Dad, 4 December 1972; Chisholm to Bobbie, 4 December 1972.

105. CVW-3, 1972, command history, NHC.

106. Statistics compiled from VA-75 Master Log, 5 November–7 December 1972, statistics section, Sanford Collection.

107. Kaiser narrative.

108. Linda Ahrens narrative.

109. Schuster narrative.

110. Lankford narrative.

111. Leslie M. Sanford, Jr., narrative.

112. Walden narrative.

113. Attack Squadron Seventy-Five Familygram, January 1973, Greene Collection; *Saratoga* deck log, entries for 11 and 12 December 1972, NA.

114. News Release 71, 72, 73, 74–72, "'Sunday Punchers' Treat Philippine School Children to a Christmas Party," VA-75, 1972, command history, addendum, NHC; "Sunday Punchers Give Christmas Party for Olongapo School Children," Attack Squadron Seventy-Five Familygram, January 1973, 2, Greene Collection.

115. "Airframes," Attack Squadron Seventy-Five Familygram, 1 December 1972, 10, Greene Collection.

116. Bobby Smith, "VA-75," in Smith Family Scrapbook, Howard P. Smith Collection; Chief Warrant Officer Smith's notation on the paper containing the poem notes: "Received onboard USS Saratoga, 14 December 1972."

CHAPTER ELEVEN. "OH, CHRISTMAS TREE, OH, CHRISTMAS TREE"

1. "Ops Note," 16 December 1972, copy in Kenneth L. Pyle collection.

2. The text of Kissinger's 16 December press conference can be found in *New York Times,* 17 December 1972.

3. *Washington Post,* 16 December 1972.

4. *Wall Street Journal,* 18 December 1972.

5. LTJG Fuller to Sally, ca. 12 January 1973, Sally Fuller Collection.

6. Alden F. Mullins, Jr., narrative.

7. *New York Times,* 18 December 1972.

8. See Jeffrey Kimball, *Nixon's Vietnam War* (Lawrence: University Press of Kansas, 1998) (copy of document reproduced in illustration section between pp. 212–213); Kimball, *The Vietnam War Files: Uncovering the Secret History of Nixon-Era Strategy* (Lawrence: University Press of Kansas, 2004), 268–273.

9. LT Chisholm to Bobbie, 18 December 1972, No. 1, Robert M. Chisholm Collection.

10. Deployments verified in Rene J. Francillon, *Tonkin Gulf Yacht Club: U.S. Carrier Operations off Vietnam* (Annapolis, MD: Naval Institute Press, 1988), 118, 135, 150, 159, 161. VA-115 on *Midway* took part in only the opening phases of this air campaign, the carrier leaving the Gulf of Tonkin on 19 December.

11. Readers interested in LINEBACKER II may choose from several major studies of this campaign, including James R. McCarthy and George B. Allison, *Linebacker II: A View from the Rock* (U.S. Air Force Southeast Asia Monograph Series, Volume 6, Maxwell Air Force Base: Air University Press, 1979; Karl J. Eschmann's *Linebacker: The Untold Story of the Air Raids over North Vietnam* (New York: Ivy Books, 1989); John T. Smith's *The Linebacker Raids: The Bombing of North Vietnam, 1972* (London: Cassell, 2000); and Marshall L. Michel III's *The Eleven Days of Christmas: America's Last Vietnam Battle* (San Francisco: Encounter Books, 2002). All approach the campaign from a strong Air Force perspective.

12. *New York Times,* 19 December 1972. For a detailed account of Day One, see Michel, *The Eleven Days of Christmas,* 85–122. On losses, see Chris Hobson, *Vietnam Air*

Losses: United States Air Force, Navy, and Marine Corps Fixed-Wing Aircraft Losses in Southeast Asia, 1961–1973 (Hinckley, UK: Midland Publishing, 2001), 242.

13. The best analysis of press coverage, one that finds a more moderate and objective tone than historians often attribute to it, can be found in Martin F. Herz, *The Prestige Press and the Christmas Bombing, 1972* (Washington, DC: Ethics and Public Policy Center, 1980).

14. "Bombs Away," *New York Times*, 19 December 1972.

15. *Wall Street Journal*, 19 December 1972.

16. "A New Target List," *New York Times*, 19 December 1972; *Wall Street Journal*, 19 December 1972.

17. Quoted in Kimball, *The Vietnam War Files*, 274.

18. Michael Schuster narrative.

19. William H. Greene, Jr./John A. Pieno, Jr., joint narrative.

20. Mullins narrative.

21. LT Chisholm to Bobbie, 18 December 1972, No. 2.

22. LT Pyle to Mom and Dad, 1 January 1973, Sandy Pyle Collection.

23. John Darrell Sherwood, *Afterburner: Naval Aviators and the Vietnam War* (New York: New York University Press, 2004), 286.

24. Greene/Pieno narrative.

25. While VA-75 did not tend to use this term, its use can be found in the command history of VA-196, 1972, Naval Historical Center (NHC), Washington, DC, and in several other Navy records of this period. See also Anthony M. Thornborough and Frank B. Mormillo, *Iron Hand: Smashing the Enemy's Air Defences* (Sparkford, UK: J. H. Haynes, 2002), 115.

26. VA-75 Master Log, 19 December 1972, RP-6B section, Leslie M. Sanford, Jr., Collection. For a full narrative of the B-52 effort this night, see Michel, *The Eleven Days of Christmas*, 123–138.

27. Harold W. King narrative.

28. LTJG Fuller to Sally, ca. 20 December 1972, Sally Fuller Collection.

29. "Summary of Action," 19 December 1972, copy in Kenneth K. Knapp Collection.

30. George L. Hart narrative.

31. Greene/Pieno narrative.

32. LT Chisholm to Bobbie, 19 December 1972.

33. Thomas C. Ruland narrative.

34. VA-75 Master Log, 20 December 1972, RP-6B section, Sanford Collection.

35. Robert A. Tolhurst, Jr., narrative.

36. The summary of this event draws on "Mike Schuster," in Lou Drendel, *Intruder* (Carrollton, TX: Squadron/Signal Publications, 1991), 31–34; and Mullins narrative. The story is retold—without names—in "The Scent of Pine: Yankee Station, 1972," *Naval Aviation News* 79 (September–October 1997): 2–3. During a familiarization visit to USS *Theodore Roosevelt* in July 2000, the author heard a reasonably accurate version of this story from the XO of the carrier. When asked who had told him about the incident, he replied, "Captain Tolhurst." CAPT Tolhurst, of course, was the same LT Tolhurst who appears on these pages.

37. VA-196, 1972, command history, NHC.

38. Thomas C. Vance narrative.

39. Sanford diary, 20 December 1972. Taped across the page from that entry, under discolored scotch tape, are two of those feathers.

40. Don Petersen narrative; Leslie M. Sanford, Jr., narrative.

41. USS Saratoga to COMMATWING ONE, 20 December 1972, delivered to Denise Schuster that same day; Denise Schuster narrative.

42. Glynnis King Fadok to author, 20 June 2001.

43. Barry King, "A Son's View," a self-described undated "love letter" to his parents, Harold W. King Collection.

44. Harold King, Jr., to author, 8 July 2001.

45. Deborah King-Barnes to author, 28 March 2001.

46. "Hopes for Peace Dashed," *New York Times,* 20 December 1972.

47. See Michel, *Eleven Days of Christmas,* 140–163.

48. "Ships Pound Coast," *New York Times,* 20 December 1972.

49. Norfolk, VA, *Virginian-Pilot,* 20 December 1972.

50. "Nixon Goal Held a 'Fantasy,'" *New York Times,* 20 December 1972.

51. The arrival of these craft and their potential threat was not greatly discussed during LINEBACKER II itself. The topic is chronicled in *New York Times,* 6 January 1973.

52. VA-37 command history, 1972, NHC.

53. LT Chisholm to Bobbie, 21 December 1972.

54. Mullins narrative.

55. For a summary of LINEBACKER's Day Four, see Michel, *The Eleven Days of Christmas,* 167–174.

56. Richard L. Engel narrative.

57. David F. Warren narrative.

58. LTJG Warren to Carol, 21 December 1972, David F. Warren Collection; Warren narrative; Ronny D. Lankford narrative.

59. Engel narrative.

60. Vance narrative; Robert M. Chisholm narrative.

61. "More New Milestones for the Sunday Punchers," in Attack Squadron Seventy-Five Familygram, January 1973, William H. Greene, Jr., Collection.

62. Pieno narrative.

63. LTJG Warren to Carol, 21 December 1972; Warren narrative; Mullins narrative.

64. Virginia Beach, VA, *Beacon,* 21 December 1972.

65. Lilliane Greene narrative.

66. Sue Engel narrative.

67. Loretta Lankford narrative.

68. LT Chisholm to Bobbie, 22 December 1972.

69. Alan G. Fischer narrative.

70. For a comprehensive account of Day Five, see Michel, *The Eleven Days of Christmas,* 178–180.

71. Jackson sortie log, 22 December 1972, Grady L. Jackson Collection; Stephen C. Bryan narrative.

72. John J. Swigart, Jr., narrative.

73. See the press coverage in *New York Times,* 21, 22, 23, and 24 December 1972.

74. Jackson sortie log, 23 December 1972; citation for Distinguished Flying Cross, LCDR Jackson.

75. VA-196, 1972, command history, NHC.
76. VA-75 Master Log, 23 December 1972, RP-6B section, Sanford Collection; LTJG Warren to Carol, 23 December 1972; King narrative.
77. VA-75 Master Log, 19–23 December 1972, RP-6B section, Sanford Collection.
78. LTJG Fuller to Sally, ca. 12 January 1973.
79. VA-196, 1972, command history, NHC.
80. "A Gift List for Mr. Nixon," Norfolk, VA, *Virginian-Pilot,* 22 December 1972.
81. Ibid., 24 December 1972.
82. "Vietnam Delenda Est," *New York Times,* 23 December 1972.
83. LTJG Fuller to Sally, 26 December 1972.
84. "Christmas Sitrep," *Fighting Cock* [*Saratoga* newspaper], 24 December 1972, 8.
85. Greene narrative.
86. LT Chisholm to Bobbie, 25 December 1972.
87. Engel narrative.
88. VA-75 Master Log, 25 December 1972, RP-6B section, Sanford Collection.
89. Tolhurst narrative.
90. LTJG Warren to Carol, 25 December 1972.
91. Sally Fuller narrative.
92. Denise Schuster narrative.
93. Duddie Graustein narrative.
94. All song lyrics from "VA-75 Sunday Puncher S.E.A. Christmas Songbook 1972 by 'Lo Drag' Peterson [*sic*], LT(JG) USN (Ret)," copy in Don Petersen Collection.
95. Petersen narrative.
96. Lankford narrative.
97. LTJG Warren to Carol, 25 December 1972.
98. *Saratoga* deck log, entry for 25 December 1972, NA.
99. John Darrell Sherwood, *Fast Movers: Jet Pilots and the Vietnam Experience* (New York: Free Press, 1999), 132.
100. Jean A. Lerseth to The Honorable Senator Henry Jackson, 27 December 1972, copy in Lerseth POW Collection.
101. VA-75 Master Log, 26 December 1972, tanker section, Sanford Collection; Michel, *Eleven Days of Christmas,* 193–203.
102. Sandy Pyle narrative.
103. Duddie Graustein narrative.
104. Stephanie Knapp narrative.
105. Chris Bryan to LTJG Bryan, 27 December 1972, Stephen C. Bryan Collection.
106. Pixie Tolhurst narrative.
107. Linda Ahrens narrative.
108. Such an exchange can be found in "The Deadly Message of the Bombers," *New York Times,* 24 December 1972.
109. LTJG Petersen to Jeane, 1 January 1973.
110. "And Still No Explanation," Norfolk, VA, *Virginian-Pilot,* 29 December 1972.
111. VA-75 Master Log, 27 December 1972, RP-2 section, Sanford Collection.
112. Program, "Memorial Service for LCDR Frederick W. Wright III," 27 December 1972, in Warren Collection.
113. *Saratoga* deck log, entry for 27 December 1972, NA, reports the aircraft flying over at 0006.

114. VA-75 Master Log, 28 December 1972, RP-6B section, Sanford Collection.
115. See Michel, *The Eleven Days of Christmas*, 193–217.
116. LT Chisholm to Bobbie, 29 December 1972.
117. Mullins narrative.
118. Sanford diary, 1 January 1973; Ruland narrative.
119. LTJG Fuller to Sally, ca. 12 January 1973.
120. "Reenlistment and Advancement Ceremony Held on New Years Day," in Attack Squadron Seventy-Five Familygram, January 1973, Greene Collection.
121. Fischer diary, 17–30 December 1972 and 1 January 1973; Linda Ahrens narrative.
122. LTJG Petersen to Jeane, 31 December 1972.
123. LT Pyle to Mom and Dad, 1 January 1973.
124. Fischer diary, 3 January 1973.
125. LTJG Warren to Carol, 3 January 1973.
126. Gerald F. Wickline, "More Afraid of Being Branded a Coward Than of Dying," *MiG Sweep*, 17–18; Fischer diary, 4 January 1973; Hobson, *Vietnam Air Losses*, 247.
127. Jackson sortie log, 4 January 1973; Grady L. Jackson narrative; John M. Miller narrative; VA-75 Master Log, 7 January 1973, RP-3 section, Sanford Collection.
128. John J. Swigart, Jr., narrative.
129. Pieno narrative.
130. Fischer narrative.
131. John J. Swigart, Jr., narrative.
132. Sanford narrative.
133. Mimeographed flight schedule, 8 January 1973, copy in Thomas C. Vance Collection.
134. "More New Milestones for the Sunday Punchers," in Attack Squadron Seventy-Five Familygram, January 1973; Sanford narrative.
135. King narrative.
136. Sanford narrative.
137. Paul C. Hvidding narrative.
138. VA-75 Master Log, 8 January 1973, MR–2 section, Sanford Collection; Attack Squadron Seventy-Five Familygram, January 1973.
139. LT Chisholm to Bobbie, 7 January 1973.
140. CTF Seven Seven [VADM Cooper] to USS Saratoga, 8 January 1973, copy in Greene Collection.
141. LT Chisholm to Bobbie, 7 January 1973.

EPILOGUE. "I'M PART OF THAT GROUP"

1. LT Alan G. Fischer diary, 8 January 1973, Alan G. Fischer Collection.
2. LTJG Warren to Carol, 11 January 1973, David F. Warren Collection.
3. LTJG John L. Johnson diary (VA–37), 8 January 1973, John L. Johnson Collection.
4. "From VA-75 Wardroom to VA-75 wives at the End-of-the-Line Party, 1/9/73," copy in Denise Schuster Collection.
5. LTJG Warren to Carol, 11 January 1973.
6. Alden F. Mullins, Jr., narrative.
7. Leslie M. Sanford, Jr., narrative.
8. Ibid.
9. LT Fischer diary, 19 January 1973.

10. Sanford narrative.
11. Kenneth L. Pyle narrative.
12. Mullins narrative.
13. Ronny D. Lankford narrative.
14. "The Fighting Cock, USS Saratoga (CV-60), Plan of the Day," 18 January 1973, John A. Pieno, Jr., Collection.
15. Mullins narrative.
16. Jerry L. Walden narrative; Howard P. Smith narrative.
17. Mullins narrative.
18. "The Fighting Cock, USS Saratoga (CV-60), Plan of the Day," 18 January 1973.
19. John A. Pieno, Jr., narrative.
20. VF-103, 1972, command history, Naval Historical Center (NHC), Washington, DC.
21. Mullins narrative.
22. Lankford narrative.
23. "Sadness, Joy Poignant Mix for Wives," Virginia Beach, VA, *Beacon*, 4 February 1973.
24. Copy in Denise Schuster Collection.
25. The flight schedule is the subject of a photograph in Loretta Lankford's scrapbook.
26. Linda Ahrens narrative.
27. John J. Swigart, Jr., narrative.
28. Mullins narrative.
29. John J. Swigart, Jr., narrative.
30. Richard L. Engel narrative.
31. Jeremiah A. Denton, Jr., with Ed Brandt, *When Hell Was in Session*, reprint ed. (Mobile, AL: Traditional Press, 1982), 178–179.
32. Roger G. Lerseth narrative.
33. "State Families Get Long Awaited Telephone Calls," *Seattle Times*, 12 February 1973, copy in Lerseth POW Collection.
34. Grady L. Jackson narrative.
35. "Full-Scale Homecoming Planned for Saratoga, Feb. 13," Jacksonville, FL, *Times-Union*, undated clipping from the *Times-Union* archives; "We're Glad and Thankful to Be Back," ibid., 14 February 1972.
36. Walden narrative.
37. Smith narrative.
38. Tampa, FL, *Tribune*, 14 February 1973; Smith narrative.
39. Lankford Christmas card for 1972, in Loretta Lankford Scrapbook.
40. *San Francisco Examiner*, 18 February 1973.
41. Flashgram, CO ATKRON SEVEN FIVE to NAVHOSP Oakland Ca, personal for LT Roger L. [G.] Lerseth; Mike and Denise [Schuster] to LT Roger G. Lerseth, telegram, 19 February 1973; memorandum, LCDR D. C. Smith to LT Lerseth, 17 February 1973; typescript of press briefing at Oakland Naval Hospital, 18 February 1973, at 1400, all items from Lerseth POW Collection.
42. Spokane, WA, *Spokesman-Review*, 20 February 1973.
43. William W. Momyer, *Air Power in Three Wars (WWII, Korea, Vietnam)* (Washington, DC: Government Printing Office, 1978), 243.
44. Quoted in Jeffrey Kimball, *The Vietnam War Files: Uncovering the Secret History of Nixon-Era Strategy* (Lawrence: University Press of Kansas, 2004), 280–281.
45. Rudolf P. Wiegand narrative.

46. Robert A. Tolhurst, Jr., narrative.

47. Michael Schuster narrative.

48. Pieno narrative.

49. Tolhurst narrative.

50. Mullins narrative.

51. Engel narrative.

52. Charles Kaiser narrative.

53. Tolhurst narrative.

54. Smith narrative.

55. Don Petersen narrative.

56. David F. Warren narrative.

57. Sanford narrative.

58. J. Glenn Gray, *The Warriors: Reflections on Men in Battle* (New York: Harper & Row, 1970), 44.

59. CVW-3, 1972, command history, NHC; "Saratoga/CVW-3 Pride and Professionalism," one-page handout, issued upon return to the United States, Charles Kaiser Collection.

60. VA-75 Master Log, statistics section, Leslie M. Sanford, Jr., Collection; VA-75, 1972, command history, NHC.

61. Warren narrative.

62. Engel narrative.

63. Petersen narrative.

64. *Boston Globe,* 24 December 2002.

65. "Awards," Oceana Naval Air Station, Virginia Beach, VA, *Jet Observer,* 12 July 1973; Kaiser narrative.

66. "Norden-Sponsored Trophy Won by Lieutenant Hudson," unattributed and undated newspaper clipping in William H. Greene, Jr., Collection.

67. *Naval Aviation News* (November 1973): 24; "Change of Command Ceremony, Attack Squadron Seventy-Five, 22 February 1974," program, p. 3, Greene Collection.

68. Walden narrative.

69. Roy A. Grossnick, *Dictionary of American Naval Aviation Squadrons: Volume 1: The History of VA, VAH, VAK, VAL, VAP and VFA Squadrons* (Washington, DC: Naval Historical Center, 1995), 133.

70. Patrick Day, "Good-bye to a Community," *The Hook* (Summer 1997).

71. Walden narrative.

72. For the last years of *Saratoga*'s service, see Steven D. Hill, "Super Sara," *Naval Aviation News* (November–December 1994): 36–41.

73. Quotations from undated 1973 column by journalist Larry Bonko, in Norfolk, VA, *Virginian-Pilot,* copy in Lerseth POW Collection.

74. Photograph of the displayed remains, undated, in Donald F. Lindland Collection.

75. Undated and unattributed newspaper clipping, "Three More MIAs Reclassified as Killed in Action," and program from the memorial service for LCDR Robert Stewart Graustein, 26 March 1975, both in the Warren Collection.

76. "Above and Beyond," *Naval Aviation News* (September 1974): 33.

77. "Navy Bids Good-bye to the A-6," unattributed clipping in Fischer Collection.

Bibliography

PRIMARY DOCUMENTS

National Archives, College Park, MD

Deck log, USS *Saratoga*, 1972

Naval Historical Center, Washington, DC

Command Histories
>   VA-75, 1965
>   VA-85, 1965–1966
>   VA-75, 1967
>   VA-75, 1968
>   VA-35, 1969
>   VA-85, 1970
>   VA-165, 1970
>   CVW-3, 1971
>   CVW-3, 1972
>   HS-7, 1972
>   RVAH-1, 1972
>   VA-35, 1972
>   VA-37, 1972
>   VA-75, 1972, and addendum
>   VA-105, 1972
>   VA-196, 1972
>   VAW-123, 1972
>   VF-31, 1972
>   VF-103, 1972

The Vietnam Archives, Texas Tech University

CNO memorandum. "History of the Mining of North Vietnam, 8 May 1972–14 January 1973." 13 January 1976.

"Develop the Might of the Firenets to Shoot U.S. Aircraft Flying at Low Altitude," translation from Vietnamese. In folder 01, Box 02, Douglas Pike Collection, Unit 03: Technology.

Every, Martin J., and James F. Parker, Jr. "A Review of Problems Encountered in the Recovery of Navy Aircrewmen under Combat Conditions." Office of Naval Research Report, June 1973. Copy in folder 05, Box 19, Douglas Pike Collection, Unit 03: POW/MIA issues.

Huu Thap. "Thai Binh Builds Many Additional Fighting Clusters and Mobile Fortifications to Waylay United States Aircraft." Originally printed in Hanoi, *Quan Doi Nhan Dan,* 10 October 1972. Translated copy in folder 01, Box 02, Douglas Pike Collection, Unit 03: Technology.

1972–1973 DOCUMENT COLLECTIONS OF PARTICIPANTS

Note: "Operational papers" include individual pilots' and B/Ns' official flight logs maintained by the operations yeoman; daily flight schedules; narrative summaries of specific missions prepared as a part of awards recommendations; awards citations; official and unofficial photographs; and copies of Attack Squadron Seventy-Five Familygrams, *Saratoga* newsletters, and similar ephemeral documents. "Personal papers" designate nonmilitary items, including personal letters, diaries, and items of that nature.

Douglas W. Ahrens (LTJG, B/N)
> operational papers, 1972
> personal papers, 1972
> kneeboard card collection, 18 May 1972 through 8 January 1973

Terry L. Anderson (LT, pilot)
> operational papers, 1972

Stephen C. Bryan (LTJG, pilot)
> operational papers, 1972
> personal papers, including letters from wife, Chris, scattered dates, 1972

Robert M. Chisholm (LT, pilot)
> operational papers, 1972
> personal papers, including letters to parents, scattered dates, and to girlfriend Bobbie, 29 June 1972–8 January 1973

Richard L. Engel (LCDR, pilot)
> operational papers, 1972

Alan G. Fischer (LT, pilot)
> operational papers, 1972
> personal diary, February 1972–January 1973
> personal general aviation binders, post-Vietnam

Everett W. Foote (VA-75 CO, 1971–72; CDR, pilot)
> operational papers, 1972
> change-of-command scrapbook, June 1972

John R. Fuller (LTJG, B/N)
> operational papers, March 1972–January 1973
> personal papers, including letters to wife, Sally, March 1972–January 1973, courtesy of Sally Fuller

William H. Greene, Jr. (VA-75 XO and CO, CDR, pilot)
> operational papers, 1972
> personal correspondence, scattered dates, 1972

George L. "Roy" Hart (LT, B/N)
> operational papers, 1972

Paul C. Hvidding (LTJG, LT, B/N)
    operational papers, 1972
    personal diary, April 1972–4 August 1972
Grady L. Jackson (LCDR, B/N)
    operational papers, 1972
    personal sortie log, 18 May 1972–8 January 1973
    cockpit tape of 5 August mission, and taped letter to family, mid-August 1972
    scrapbooks of Linda Jackson
John L. Johnson (LTJG, pilot, VA-37)
    diary
Charles Kaiser (LTJG, B/N)
    operational papers, 1972
Harold W. King (LCDR, B/N)
    operational papers, 1972
    personal papers of King and his family, post-Vietnam
Kenneth K. Knapp (LT, pilot)
    operational papers, 1972
    scrapbooks of Stephanie Knapp
Ronny D. Lankford (LT, pilot)
    operational papers, 1972
    scrapbooks of Loretta Lankford
Roger G. Lerseth (LTJG, LT, B/N)
    operational papers, 1972
    POW scrapbooks
    personal letters to mother and sisters, May 1972–August 1972
Donald F. Lindland (LCDR, pilot) (courtesy of Bobbe Lindland)
    operational papers, 1972
Ronald D. McFarland (LTJG, B/N)
    operational papers, 1972
John M. Miller (LT, pilot)
    operational papers, 1972
Alden F. Mullins, Jr. (LTJG, LT, B/N)
    operational papers, 1972
    personal mission log sheets, 1972
Don Petersen (LTJG, B/N)
    operational papers, 1972
    personal letters to wife, Jeane, April 1972–January 1973
    personal letters from wife, Jeane, April 1972–January 1973
    cockpit tape of May 1972 mission
John A. Pieno, Jr. (LCDR, B/N)
    operational papers, 1972
Frank J. Pittman (Chief Aviation Metalsmith [Hydraulic])
    operational papers, 1972
Kenneth L. Pyle (LT, pilot)
    operational papers, 1972
    personal letters, scattered dates, 1972
    scrapbook of Sandy Pyle

Thomas C. Ruland (LT, pilot)
    operational papers, 1972
Leslie M. Sanford, Jr. (LTJG, B/N)
    operational papers, 1972
    VA-75 Master Log
    personal diary, 1972
    personal mission log sheets
Michael A. Schuster (LT, pilot)
    operational papers, 1972
    personal collection of wife, Denise
Howard P. Smith (Chief Warrant Officer 2 and 3, Maintenance Control)
    scrapbooks of wife, Myrna
John J. Swigart, Jr. (LTJG, B/N)
    operational papers, 1972
    personal letters to wife, Penny, scattered dates in 1972
Robert A. Tolhurst, Jr. (LTJG, LT, pilot)
    operational papers, 1972
    personal letters to wife, Pixie, 11 April 1972–December 1972
Thomas C. Vance (LTJG, B/N)
    operational papers, 1972
Jerry L. Walden (ordnance Warrant Officer)
    operational papers, 1972
David F. Warren (LTJG, B/N)
    operational papers, 1972
    collection of personal letters to wife, Carol, 11 April 1972–8 January 1973
    scrapbook of Carol Warren
Rudolf P. Wiegand (LT, B/N)
    operational papers, 1972

PERSONAL NARRATIVES

During 2001–2003, surviving officers and some senior enlisted men of VA-75 who took part in the combat cruise of 1972–73 reviewed in monthly increments the squadron's 1972 command history and relevant segments of CVW-3's 1972 command history. They then prepared personal narratives to expand upon the histories' commentary or answered questions based upon those histories. In some cases, the author conducted a follow-up interview. Some Sunday Punchers served during only part of the combat cruise or chose to respond only selectively to questions raised by the command histories; thus, not all narratives comment on the entire period of April 1972 through January 1973. All narratives are currently in the possession of the author, with final disposition to be determined at some future date.

Narratives were prepared by Douglas W. Ahrens; Terry L. Anderson; Stephen C. Bryan; Wright Cade, Jr.; Robert M. Chisholm; Richard DuChateau; Richard L. Engel; Alan G. Fischer; Everett W. Foote; John R. Fuller; William H. Greene, Jr.; George L. Hart; Paul C. Hvidding; Grady L. Jackson; Charles Kaiser; James Kennedy; Harold W. King; Kenneth K. Knapp; Ronny D. Lankford; Roger G. Lerseth; William C. Martin; Ronald D. McFarland; John M. Miller; Robert F. Miller; Alden F. Mullins, Jr.; Patrick O'Leary; Don Petersen; John A. Pieno, Jr.; Frank J. Pittman; Kenneth L. Pyle; Thomas C. Ruland; Leslie M. Sanford, Jr.;

Michael A. Schuster; Howard P. Smith; John J. Swigart, Jr.; Robert A. Tolhurst, Jr.; Thomas C. Vance; Jerry L. Walden; William F. Wardlaw; David F. Warren; Thomas E. Wharton; Rudolf P. Wiegand.

Spouses and family members of the men who served VA-75 who also contributed personal narratives or answered specific questions relating to events in the 1972 command history include Linda Ahrens; Duddie Graustein Andrews; Deborah King-Barnes; Chris Bryan; Jean (Nini) Lerseth Chun; Minna Earnest; Sue Engel; Glynnis King Fadok; Laura Foote; Sally Fuller; Lilliane Greene; Susan Hvidding; Linda Jackson; Marion Kennedy; Barry King; Harold W. King, Jr.; Loren King; Stephanie Knapp; Loretta Lankford; Bobbe Lindland; Shari McFarland; Jeane Petersen; Sandy Pyle; Denise Schuster; Myrna Smith; Penny Swigart; Pixie Tolhurst; Joan Walden; Carol Warren; Judy Pieno Wilkinson.

Members of CVW-3, MATWING ONE, and others who answered specific questions relating to events in the 1972 command history include Ted Been (LCDR, VA-42); Richard P. Bordone (CAG, CVW-3); RADM John S. Christiansen (CO, COMCARDIV SEVEN, 1972–73); George Duskin (LCDR, VA-37); John L. "Hondo" Johnson (LTJG, VA-37); Edward A. Lyons (LTJG, VA-37); Paul Pencikowski (LTJG, VF-103); Dale V. Raebel (LCDR, VA-37).

GOVERNMENT DOCUMENTS

Congressional Record, 92d Congress, 2d Session.
HQ, PACAF, Directorate of Operations Analysis, CHECO/CORONA HARVEST DIVISION, *Linebacker: Overview of the First 120 Days.*
———. CHECO/CORONA HARVEST DIVISION, *Rules of Engagement, November 1969– September 1972.*
Military History Branch, Office of the Secretary, Joint Staff Military Assistance Command, Vietnam, *1972–1973, Command History: Volume 1.*

NEWSPAPERS, NEWSLETTERS, AND MAGAZINES

Aviation Week & Space Technology
Black Panther
Boston Globe
Both Sides Now
Christian Science Monitor
The Hook
Jacksonville, FL, *Times-Union*
Life Magazine
Miami Herald
MiG Sweep
Naval Aviation News
Naval War College Review
Navy Times
Newsweek
New York Times
Nhan Dan
Norfolk, VA, *Virginian-Pilot*
Oceana Naval Air Station, Virginia Beach, VA, *Jet Observer*

(Pacific) *Stars and Stripes*
San Francisco Examiner
Seattle *Times*
SERE Newsletter
Spokane, WA, *Spokesman-Review*
Tampa, FL, *Tribune*
U.S. News & World Report
Virginia Beach, VA, *Beacon*
Wall Street Journal
Washington Post

BOOKS AND ARTICLES

"Above and Beyond." *Naval Aviation News* (September 1974): 33.

"All-Weather Plane Stars in Viet War." *Washington Post*, 21 April 1968.

Andrade, Dale. *America's Last Vietnam Battle: Halting Hanoi's 1972 Easter Offensive.* Lawrence: University Press of Kansas, 2001.

Andrews, Hal. "Life of the Intruder." *Naval Aviation News* 79 (September–October 1997): 6–16.

Brown, Charles H. *Dark Sky, Black Sea: Aircraft Carrier Night and All-Weather Operations.* Annapolis, MD: Naval Institute Press, 1999.

Burgess, Richard R., ed. *The Naval Aviation Guide.* 5th ed. Annapolis, MD: Naval Institute Press, 1996.

Churchill, Jan. *Hit My Smoke! Forward Air Controllers in Southeast Asia.* Manhattan, KS: Sunflower University Press, 1997.

Clinton, James W. *The Loyal Opposition: Americans in North Vietnam, 1965–1972.* Niwot: University Press of Colorado, 1995.

Clodfelter, Mark. *The Limits of Air Power: The American Bombing of North Vietnam.* New York: Free Press, 1989.

———. "Nixon and the Air Weapon." In Dennis E. Showalter and John G. Albert, eds., *An American Dilemma: Vietnam, 1964–1973.* Chicago: Imprint Publications, 1993, 167–186.

Cooling, Benjamin F., ed. *Case Studies in the Development of Close Air Support.* Washington, DC: Office of Air Force History, 1990.

Cortright, David. *Soldiers in Revolt: The American Military Today.* Garden City, NY: Anchor/Doubleday, 1975.

Day, Patrick. "Good-bye to a Community." *The Hook* (Summer 1997).

Demarest, M. Raymond. "Sixty Hours and Counting." *Naval Aviation News* (November 1972): 17–19.

Denton, Jeremiah A., Jr., with Ed Brandt. *When Hell Was in Session.* Reprint ed. Mobile, AL: Traditional Press, 1982.

"Disestablished: VA-75 Sunday Punchers." *Naval Aviation News* (September–October 1997): 6.

Drendel, Lou. *Intruder.* Carrollton, TX: Squadron/Signal Publications, 1991.

Eschmann, Karl J. *Linebacker: The Untold Story of the Air Raids over North Vietnam.* New York: Ivy Books, 1989.

Francillon, Rene J. *Tonkin Gulf Yacht Club: U.S. Carrier Operations off Vietnam.* Annapolis, MD: Naval Institute Press, 1988.

Gillcrist, Paul T. *Feet Wet: Reflections of a Carrier Pilot.* New York: Pocket Books, 1990.

———. *Vulture's Row: Thirty Years in Naval Aviation.* Atglen, PA: Schiffer Publishing, 1996.

Gilster, Herman L. *The Air War in Southeast Asia: Case Studies of Selected Campaigns.* Maxwell Air Force Base, AL: Air University Press, 1993.

Gray, J. Glenn. *The Warriors: Reflections on Men in Battle.* New York: Harper & Row, 1970.

Grossman, Dave. *On Killing: The Psychological Cost of Learning to Kill in War and Society.* New York: Little, Brown, 1995.

Grossnick, Roy A. *Dictionary of American Naval Aviation Squadrons: Volume 1: The History of VA, VAH, VAK, VAL, VAP and VFA Squadrons.* Washington, DC: Naval Historical Center, 1995.

Guttridge, Leonard F. *Mutiny: A History of Naval Insurrection.* New York: Berkley Publishing Group, 1992.

Hadley, Arthur T. "Is This Like Your War, Sir?" *Atlantic Monthly* 230 (September 1972): 90–95.

Haldeman, H. R. *The Haldeman Diaries: Inside the Nixon White House.* New York: G. P. Putnam's Sons, 1994.

Herz, Martin F. *The Prestige Press and the Christmas Bombing, 1972.* Washington, DC: Ethics and Public Policy Center, 1980.

Hill, Steven D. "Super Sara." *Naval Aviation News* (November–December 1994): 36–41.

Hobson, Chris. *Vietnam Air Losses: United States Air Force, Navy, and Marine Corps Fixed-Wing Aircraft Losses in Southeast Asia, 1961–1973.* Hinckley, UK: Midland Publishing, 2001.

Holmes, Richard. *Acts of War: The Behavior of Men in Battle.* New York: Free Press, 1985.

Holzer, Henry Mark, and Erika Holzer. *"Aid and Comfort": Jane Fonda in North Vietnam.* Jefferson, NC: McFarland & Company, 2002.

Hynes, Samuel L. *The Soldiers' Tale: Bearing Witness to Modern War.* New York: Penguin Press, 1997.

Keegan, John. *The Face of Battle: A Study of Agincourt, Waterloo, and the Somme.* New York: Vintage Books, 1977.

Kerr, Daryl L., with Mark Morgan. "The A-6's SIOP Mission." *The Hook* (Summer 1997): 25.

Kimball, Jeffrey. *Nixon's Vietnam War.* Lawrence: University Press of Kansas, 1998.

———. *The Vietnam War Files: Uncovering the Secret History of Nixon-Era Strategy.* Lawrence: University Press of Kansas, 2004.

Kissinger, Henry. *Ending the Vietnam War: A History of America's Involvement in and Extrication from the Vietnam War.* New York: Simon and Schuster, 2003.

Lee, Kent L. "The *Enterprise* in Westpac." In E. T. Wooldridge, ed., *Into the Jet Age: Conflict and Change in Naval Aviation, 1945–1975.* Annapolis, MD: Naval Institute Press, 1995, 236–255.

Lehman, John F., Jr. *Command of the Seas.* Bluejacket Books ed. Annapolis, MD: Naval Institute Press, 2001 [1988].

Levie, Howard S. "Mine Warfare and International Law." *Naval War College Review* 24 (April 1972): 27–35.

Littauer, Raphael, and Norman Uphoff, eds. *The Air War in Indochina.* Rev. ed. Boston: Beacon Press, 1972.

Luckow, Ulrik. "Victory over Ignorance and Fear: The U.S. Minelaying Attack on North Vietnam." *Naval War College Review* 35 (January–February 1982): 17–27.

Marriott, Barbara. "The Social Networks of Naval Officers' Wives: Their Composition and Function." In Laurie Weinstein and Christie C. White, eds., *Wives and Warriors: Women and the Military in the United States and Canada*. Westport, CT: Bergin & Garvey, 1997, 19–34.

McCarthy, James R., and George B. Allison. *Linebacker II: A View from the Rock*. Maxwell Air Force Base: Air University Press, 1979.

McDonnell, Michael G. "Ragtime." *Naval Aviation News* (October 1971): 8–16.

Mersky, Peter B., and Norman Polmar. *The Naval Air War in Vietnam*. New York: Zebra Books, 1981.l

Michael, Joe. *A-6 Intruder in Action*. Carrollton, TX: Squadron/Signal Publications, 1993.

Michel, Marshall L., III. *Clashes: Air Combat over North Vietnam, 1965–1972*. Annapolis, MD: Naval Institute Press, 1997.

———. *The Eleven Days of Christmas: America's Last Vietnam Battle*. San Francisco: Encounter Books, 2002.

Momyer, William W. *Air Power in Three Wars (WWII, Korea, Vietnam)*. Washington, DC: Government Printing Office, 1978.

Morgan, Mark, and Richard J. Morgan. "Pride of the Ironworks: The Grumman A-6 Intruder." *The Hook* (Summer 1997): 23–29.

Morgan, Rick, and Mark L. Morgan. "Pride of the Ironworks, Part 2: The A-6 Intruder, 1969–1973." *The Hook* (Fall 1997): 21–32.

Mullane, Paul N. "CV: A New, Triple Threat Concept for Carriers." *Naval Aviation News* (March 1972): 49–53.

Nalty, Bernard C. *Air War over South Vietnam, 1968–1975*. Washington, DC: Air Force History and Museum Program, 2000.

"NAS Oceana: A Wasteland No More." *Naval Aviation News* (October 1971): 36–39.

Nichols, John B., and Barrett Tillman. *On Yankee Station: The Naval Air War over Vietnam*. Annapolis, MD: Naval Institute Press, 1987.

"Plane for All Seasons, A." *Time*, 25 November 1966, 38.

Price, Alfred. *The History of US Electronic Warfare. Volume III: Rolling Thunder through Allied Force, 1964 to 2000*. N.p.: Port City Press, 2000.

Public Papers of the Presidents: Richard Nixon, 1972. Washington, DC: Government Printing Office, 1974.

Rochlin, Fred. *Old Man in a Baseball Cap: A Memoir of World War II*. New York: Harper Collins, 1999.

"Saratoga, CV-60." *Naval Aviation News* (December 1972): 12.

"Scent of Pine, The: Yankee Station, 1972." *Naval Aviation News* 79 (September–October 1997): 2–3.

Sherwood, John Darrell. *Afterburner: Naval Aviators and the Vietnam War*. New York: New York University Press, 2004.

———. *Fast Movers: Jet Pilots and the Vietnam Experience*. New York: Free Press, 1999.

Smith, John T. *The Linebacker Raids: The Bombing of North Vietnam, 1972*. London: Cassell, 2000.

Sorley, Lewis. *A Better War: The Unexamined Victories and Final Tragedy of America's Last Years in Vietnam*. New York: Harcourt and Brace, 1999.

Stevens, Paul Drew, ed. *The Navy Cross: Vietnam*. Forest Ranch, CA: Sharp & Dunnigan, 1987.

Tanner, Jane. *The USS Saratoga: Remembering One of America's Great Aircraft Carriers, 1956–1994.* Atlanta: Longstreet Press, 1994.

Tate, J. R. "Saratoga Revisited." *Naval Aviation News* (September 1972): 44–46.

Thompson, Wayne. *To Hanoi and Back: The U.S. Air Force and North Vietnam, 1966–1973.* Washington, DC: Smithsonian Institution Press, 2000.

Thornborough, Anthony M., and Frank B. Mormillo. *Iron Hand: Smashing the Enemy's Air Defences.* Sparkford, UK: J. H. Haynes, 2002.

Turley, G. H. *The Easter Offensive: The Last American Advisors [in] Vietnam, 1972.* Novato, CA: Presidio Press, 1985.

Van Vleet, Clarke. "A Command History." *Naval Aviation News* (August 1973): 9–15.

———. "Year of Action . . . 1972." *Naval Aviation News* (February 1973): 8–21.

Vistica, Gregory L. *Fall from Glory: The Men Who Sank the U.S. Navy.* New York: Simon & Schuster, 1995.

Wickline, Gerald F. "More Afraid of Being Branded a Coward Than of Dying." *MiG Sweep,* 17–18.

Willbanks, James H. *Thiet Giap! The Battle of An Loc, April 1972.* Fort Leavenworth, KS: U.S. Army Command and General Staff College, 1993.

Wooldridge, E. T., ed. *Into the Jet Age: Conflict and Change in Naval Aviation, 1945–1975.* Annapolis, MD: Naval Institute Press, 1995, 254.

Zumwalt, Elmo R., Jr. *On Watch: A Memoir.* New York: Quadrangle Books, 1976.

Index

Concerned Officers Movement (COM), 51

Congressional Quarterly, 320

Congressional Record, 150

Connelly, LT Thomas H.: background and arrival of, 231, 232; and fifth line period missions, 243, 245; and sixth line period missions, 275; and seventh line period missions, 333; going home, 330; postwar, 349; mentioned, 242, 290, 348

CONSTANT GUARD, Operation, 61

Cook, LT Bruce: and emergency recall, 41, 42, 55; and first line period missions, 97, 100, 105, 107, 120, 122, 124, 128, 146; and second line period missions, 152, 157, 160–161; and third line period missions, 182, 192, 201; and fourth line period missions, 229–230, 235; crewed with Weigand, 232; and fifth line period missions, 243; and sixth line period missions, 273, 286, 287; and seventh line period missions, 328, 333; postwar, 350; mentioned, 144, 266, 183, 300

Coonts, Stephen, xiv

Cooper, VADM D. W., 285, 296, 333–334

Cooper-Brooke Amendment, 178

Cordes, LTJG Don (VF-103), 279–280

Coriolis effect, 68

Cowles, CDR Robert R. (VF-103), 181

"Crew concept," 3, 20, 21–22, 23–24, 30, 109–110; creation of new crews, 156–159, 173–173, 231–233, 274; disruptions of, 120–121, 248, 285; and downing of aircraft, 198; Sunday Punchers' acceptance of, 134, 137–138, 197, 224, 248, 286

Cronkite, Walter, 43

"Crossing the Equator" ceremony, 68–73, 337

CTF-77. *See* Carrier Task Force 77

Cubi Point Naval Air Station, 61, 80–81; airstrip at, 87, 208; base exchange at, 81, 82; CVW-3 beach detachment at, 110, 146, 180, 201, 242, 258, 272, 293–94; Chuck Wagon at, 240; officers' club at, 82, 148, 208, 265, 299–300, 335–336

Cunningham, LT Randy, xiv, 87

CV concept, 8, 14, 29, 30, 86, 163

CVW-3: alpha strike planning process of, 93–94, 126–127; communications procedures of, 92; composition of, 29, 53; end-of-tour statistical summation, 345; flight operation procedures of, 86–88, 92–95, 178, 243; line period summaries, 171, 206–207, 237, 261, 298; and March ORE, 30–32; tactics board of, 61, 62, 64; work with Fast FACs, 274–275; mentioned, 8, 27, 335–336. *See also* alpha strikes; Bordone, CDR Richard P.; *individual squadrons in the airwing*

Danang, 33, 110, 264, 273, 274, 330

Dan Hai, 113

Davis, LCDR John (VA-37), 140

Defense Air Support Center (DASC), 274

Dellinger, David, 255, 256

Delta strikes, 307

Denton, Jane, 255

Denton, CDR/CAPT/RADM Jeremiah A., 6, 255, 340, 347

DESERT SHIELD/DESERT STORM, Operation, 349

DIANE (Digital Integrated Attack Navigation Equipment), 4

Dien Bien Phu, 121–122

Dikes, accusations of U.S. bombing of: criticism from political leaders, 179, 193; press accounts, 149–150, 166, 192–193; Sunday Punchers' views on, 192–194

Dobrynin, Anatoly, 136

Dong Hoi, 237

Do Son Peninsula, 153, 204, 214

Driscoll, LTJG William, xiv, 87

DuChateau, Marie, 40

DuChateau, LTJG Richard, 40

Dunbar, ADRAN Al, 79

Dunne, LTJG Robert (HS-7), 175

Duskin, LCDR George (VA-37), 189, 190

E-2B Hawkeye, 29, 62, 102, 127, 138, 163, 182–183, 190, 200, 233, 311

Early Bird flight, 299, 330–331, 336, 339

Earnest, Bradley, 291, 295, 352

Earnest, Bryan, 291

Earnest, CDR Charles "M": 82, 212, 240, 284, 348, 349, 352; as XO of VA-75, background of, 13–14, 31, 58; and experience in A-4s, 31; and emergency recall, 36, 37, 47, 48, 50, 52–53; as mentor, 65–66, 123, 135, 162, 169–170, 273, 278–279; during transit, 65, 69, 71, 73, 77, 78–79, 82; and first line period missions, 95, 97, 100, 101, 104, 105, 110–111, 116, 122, 124, 128, 134, 138; and change of command, 117, 129; as CO, 148, 162, 164, 184, 197, 206, 211, 216, 285; and personnel issues, 114, 148, 155–156, 232, 244, 260–261; and second line period missions, 152, 163,

319, 320, 321; early target restrictions on, 122; lifting of target restrictions near, 85, 122; mining harbor of, 122, 151–52, 153, 195–196, 243; VA-75 ground targets near, 134, 214

Haiphong Shipyard Number 3: alpha strike on, 181–183, 188; lessons of, 249

Haldeman, H. R., 35

Hall, CDR Harley H., 338

Ha Ly Canal, 203

Hanoi: accusations of hitting civilian targets in, 150–151; during Christmas bombings, 305–306, 308, 326

"Hanoi Hilton," 340; hit during ROLLING THUNDER, 129; target restrictions near, 85, 122, 230; as VA-75 target, 185–188, 203

Hart, LT George L. "Roy": background and arrival of, 158; and integration into squadron, 158–159, 172; and second line period missions, 170; and third line period missions, 185–188, 192, 196, 202; and fifth line period missions, 242; receives Air Medal, 285; and seventh line period missions, 308, 312; going home, 330; postwar, 350; mentioned, 175, 212, 218, 226, 283, 348

Hart, AT1 J., 300

Ha Tin, 332

HC-7 helicopters Big Mother helos, 190, 191, 192, 280

Henkin, Daniel Z., 167

Hiduk, LT George A.: background and arrival of, 157; and integration into squadron, 158–159, 172–173; and fourth line period missions, 214–16, 218, 220, 226; crewed with Sanford, 274; and sixth line period missions, 277; receives Air Medal, 285; and seventh line period missions, 313; going home, 337, 339; mentioned, 245, 329, 348

Hill, AT1 Rodney, 300–301

Hiott, ATC Larry, 285

Ho Chi Minh Trail, 33, 76

Ho Doi, 167

Holden, LT Hugh F., 194

Hollingsworth, MG James F., 91

Hon Gay, 132, 133, 136, 157

Hong Kong, 149, 173–177

Hon La Island, 163, 183–184

Hon Mat Island, 131, 140

Hon Nieu Island, 131, 140, 163

Hope, Bob, 330

"Hourglass, The," 165, 169, 202

HS-7 (helicopter squadron), 29, 53, 67, 175

Hudson, LT James "E": background and arrival of, 159; as Maintenance LDO, 200, 201; encourages skeet shooting, 208; creates "Red Label Service," 238–239; on transit home, 337; named Intruder Maintenance Officer of the Year, 347–348; postwar, 350; mentioned, 300, 317

Hue, 33

Hvidding, Jennifer, 44, 165

Hvidding, LTJG/LT Paul C., background of, 10, 16, 22, 23; and emergency recall, 36, 38–39, 44, 59; during transit, 60, 63, 68, 72, 77, 80, 83, 87; on squadron leaders, 12, 64, 66; and first line period missions, 99, 100, 102, 104, 105, 107–109, 110, 111–112, 113, 114, 121, 123–124, 131–132, 135–136, 139; and second line period missions, 152, 160, 161–62, 169–70; plane hit, 152–153; promotion of, 154; stops keeping his diary, 178; and third line period missions, 180; and fourth line period missions, 234; and fifth line period missions, 248; on "buddy bombing," 274; and seventh line period missions, 304, 307–308, 333; going home, 331; postwar 344, 351; mentioned 165, 296

Hvidding, Susan, 46, 114–115

Ile de Cac Ba, 133, 243

Inderlied, LCDR W. T. (VF-31), 234

Integrated Operational Intelligence Center (IOIC), 64, 77, 126, 132, 161, 218, 220, 248

Iron Hand missions,127; on alpha strikes, 135, 144, 183, 186–187, 202, 214, 234; on mining missions, 195–196

Jackson, Chris, 291, 292

Jackson, Danny, 292

Jackson, LCDR Grady L., background of, 15; and emergency recall, 39, 43, 48, 51, 54, 55, 58, 59; during transit, 65, 69, 71, 79, 85–86; and first line period missions, 95, 97, 100, 101, 103, 111, 113, 116, 122, 128, 134, 138, 144; and second line period missions, 152, 163, 165, 168; and third line period missions, 180, 181–183, 186, 190–192, 192–193, 195–196, 203, 204–205; on Lloyd's rescue, 190–192; talks to reporter, 192–193; on the passage of time, 205; views on the war, 206, 208; and fourth line period missions, 213, 234–235; and loss of Lindland and Lerseth, 221, 224;

Philippine Islands, 61, 87, 88, 208, 238, 299, 336. *See also* Cubi Point Naval Air Station; Manila; Olongapo; Subic Bay Naval Base

Phu Cat, 116

Phu Ly, 145, 150, 202, 253, 319

Pieno, LCDR John A., Jr: background of, 14, 15; and March ORE, 32; and emergency recall, 44, 47, 58, 59; during transit, 65, 67, 69, 79, 83; and first line period missions, 97, 100, 104, 110, 111, 123, 128, 143, 144, 145; and second line period missions, 157, 165, 180; and third line period missions of, 181–183, 185–186, 203–204; and fourth line period missions, 214–216, 230; as Administrative Department head, 221, 257, 293, 318–319, 323; and fifth line period missions, 243, 248–52; in Singapore, 266; receives Silver Star, 285; and sixth line period missions, 289–290; and seventh line period, 308–309, 311–312, 317, 332; on return trip, 330, 339; postwar, 343, 350

Pieno, Judy, 24, 44, 74, 282–283, 291–292, 317

Pitman, LT Art (VF-103), 217

Pittman, Chief Frank J., 72, 194, 220, 310

Plane captains, 93, 161, 197, 218, 282, 288

Pleiku, 33

Podgorny, Nikolai, 136, 143

Positive Identification Radar Advisory Zone (PIRAZ), 121

Presley, Elvis, 52

Prisoners-of-war and missing in action (POW/MIA): 49; belonging to CVW-3, 165, 203; belonging to VA-75, 6, 216–218; bracelets commemorating, 228; during Christmas bombings, 314, 320; as inspiration to VA-75, 228, 269–270; as negotiating point, 85, 178; released by North Vietnam, 211, 212–213, 255–256, 338–339; support activities in U.S., 255–256, 284, 296

"Project Leapfrog," 238

PROUD DEEP, Operation, 34

Pyle, LT Kenneth L.: background of, 16, 17, 18, 21; and emergency recall, 36–37, 43, 47; in the Philippines, 88; and first line period missions, 104, 105, 109, 121, 123–124, 131–132, 135–36, 139–140; and second line period missions, 152, 160, 161–62, 169; aircraft hit, 152–153, 158; on maintenance problems, 201; and fourth line period missions, 234; and fifth line period

missions, 248; on Christmas bombings, 304, 307, 330; and seventh line period missions, 307–308; going home, 336; postwar, 350; mentioned, 300, 333

Pyle, Mike, 336

Pyle, Sandy, 37, 74, 153, 175, 292, 326–327

Quang Tri, 33, 91, 237, 241

RA-5C "Vigilante," 7, 20, 22, 29, 201, 202; and alpha strikes, 127, 135, 168, 183, 235; hit by SAM, 133, 189

Racial issues, U.S. Navy, 10, 258–260

Radar Intercept Officer (RIO), 21, 22, 86, 145

Radcliff, LTJG David H., 208, 337, 348

Raebel, LCDR Dale V. (VA-37), 202–203, 338

Randall, LT Robert I. (VF-103), 165, 338

Randolph, LT Robert P. "Combat Quack," 161, 326, 338

Rarick, John R., 259

Rasmussen, CAPT Robert, 190

Raubar, AZ2 Joe, 209, 300

Reagan, Ronald W., 343

Red Crown, 121, 189

"Red Label Service," 237–238

Red River Valley Fighter Pilots Association, 296

Replacement Air Group (RAG). *See* VA-42; VA (Attack) Squadrons: VA-128

Rescue Combat Air Patrol (RESCAP), 133, 142, 203, 217–218, 220

Reyes, Rowena, 301

Rockeye. *See* Ordnance: Mark 20

ROLLING THUNDER, Operation, 121, 149

Rosenburg, Emily S., xv

Rota, Spain, 29, 118

Route packages, North Vietnam: alterations to system, 247; described, 121–122; operations in I, 125, 157, 179–180, 237, 272, 276, 280; operations in II, 122, 123, 124, 125, 131, 139, 196, 202, 213, 244, 272, 277, 280; operations in III, 122, 124, 140, 143, 153, 201, 202, 213, 237, 244, 272, 277, 297–298, 331–332; operations in IV, 132, 135, 143, 145, 165, 167, 170, 213, 229–230, 237, 246–52, 253, 297, 320, 332 ; operations in VI-A, 185, 186, 305; operations in VI-B, 127, 132–133, 134, 137–139, 145, 167, 169, 213–218, 230, 237, 244, 245, 305, 316, 320, 329. *See also individual North Vietnamese towns and cities*

Ruland, Brigid, 40, 61, 174, 175, 309
Ruland, Jennifer Colleen, 309, 329
Ruland, LT Thomas C. "Kit": background of, 16, 20, 21; and emergency recall, 40, 55; during transit, 61, 77; and first line period missions, 106, 108, 110, 112, 123, 143; and second line period missions, 170; and third line period missions, 195, 203; crewed with Swigart, 232; and fourth line period missions, 234–235; and fifth line period missions, 243; and sixth line period missions, 280; fatherhood of, 303, 309, 319, 329; and seventh line period, 303, 319, 331; going home, 330, 339; postwar, 351; mentioned, 174, 175, 197, 218, 266, 300
Rush, Kenneth, 304

Saigon, 121, 264, 315
SAMs. See Surface-to-air missiles
Sanderson, CAPT James R.: as CO of Saratoga, 29, 30, 162, 166, 240; and emergency recall, 37–38, 53; during transit, 61, 65, 68, 76, 80, 88; and cyclic operations, 94; hosts Christiansen, 147, 163; during second line period, 153–154; during third line period, 184; during fourth line period, 225; and uncertainty of return to U.S., 240, 243; bans leave outside operational area, 244, 267; and racial unrest aboard Saratoga, 260; during fifth line period, 261; during sixth line period, 283–284, 286; and Earnest's death, 290; during Christmas bombings, 311–312, 322, 333; on return home, 336, 338
Sanford, Brenda, 110, 175, 313, 317
Sanford, LTJG Leslie M. "Sandy," Jr.: background of, 17, 23; and emergency recall, 48, 52; during transit, 68–69, 81, 88; and first line period missions, 100, 135; and "Combat Rat," 142–143; promotion delayed, 155; and second line period missions, 169; and third line period missions, 182; and fourth line period missions, 220–221, 222; crewed with Hiduk, 274; and sixth line period missions, 277; receives Air Medal, 285; and seventh line period missions, 313, 329, 332–333; fatherhood of, 313, 110–111, 329; going home, 330, 336; postwar, 344, 350; mentioned, 175, 212, 226, 300
Sanford, Sara, 313, 329
Saratoga, USS: "crossing the equator" cere-monies on, 68–73, 337; description of, 29; and emergency recall, 38, 51–52, 53–54; fires aboard, 267–269, 271; holidays aboard, 153–154, 283–285, 298–300; makes transit, 61–81; mechanical problems of, 29, 283; ORE of spring 1972, 26, 29–32; underway replenishment process aboard, 89; CNO Zumwalt visits, 54, 209, 210; retired, 349. See also CVW-3; Sanderson, CAPT James R.
Saratoga Museum Foundation, 349
Schanz, Harry J., 268
Schram, LCDR Richard W., background of; 15–16; as Safety Officer, 15–16, 312; during transit, 66–67, 69, 70, 77; and first line period, 95, 97, 128, 138–139; and second line period missions, 160–161; and third line period missions, 201–202, 203; views on the war, 138–139, 208; as mentor, 66–67, 227; crewed with Connelly, 232; and fifth line period missions, 243; and sixth line period missions, 275; 245; on return trip, 300, 338, 339; postwar, 350; mentioned, 36, 265, 285
Schram, Sharon, 26, 266–267, 298
Schuster, Denise, 314, 324
Schuster, LT Michael A.: arrival of, 257–258; and fifth line period missions, 258; crewed with Mullins, 271; and sixth line period missions, 272, 277–278, 286, 287, 289; on "buddy bombing," 274; on the Christmas bombings, 306; and seventh line period missions, 310–312, 314, 319; going home, 330; postwar, 343, 351; mentioned, 276, 300, 324, 348
Search and Rescue operations (SAR), 72, 140, 189–192, 288–289, 290; not attempted, 217, 276, 317
SERE (survive, escape, resist and evade) school, 23
Sheehan, Neil, 35
Shrike missile. See AGM-45
Sierra Report Codes, 171–172
Silver Star Medal, 235, 252
Simpson, AT2 Tim, 199
Sims, ATC Joseph, 277
Singapore, 240, 244, 264–266, 336–337
Single Integrated Operational Plan (SIOP), 8
Smith, LCDR Bernie (VA-105), 190, 204
Smith, CWO2/CWO3 Howard P.: background of, 16; and emergency recall, 44–45, 49, 52; during transit, 81; during first